Sunset

RECIPE ANNUAL

1997 Edition

*Peach Cobbler with Grandma Reynolds's
Peach Ice Cream (page 117)*

By the Editors of *Sunset Magazine*
and Sunset Books

Sunset Books, Inc. ■ **Menlo Park, California**

SUNSET BOOKS

President & Publisher
Susan J. Maruyama

Director, Sales & Marketing
Richard A. Smeby

Editorial Director
Bob Doyle

Production Director
Lory Day

Retail Sales Development Manager
Becky Ellis

Art Director
Vasken Guiragossian

STAFF FOR THIS BOOK
Managing Editor
Cornelia Fogle

Indexer
Rebecca La Brum

Production Coordinator
Patricia S. Williams

SUNSET PUBLISHING CORPORATION

President/Chief Executive Officer
Stephen J. Seabolt

VP, Chief Financial Officer
James E. Mitchell

VP, Publisher,
Sunset Magazine
Anthony P. Glaves

VP, Consumer Marketing Director
Robert I. Gursha

Director of Finance
Lawrence J. Diamond

VP, Manufacturing Director
Lorinda Reichert

VP, Editor-in-Chief,
Sunset Magazine
Rosalie Muller Wright

Managing Editor
Carol Hoffman

Executive Editor
Melissa Houtte

Senior Editor,
Food & Entertaining
Jerry Anne Di Vecchio

RICK MARIANI

Grilled Shrimp with Mango Salad (page 134)

A Decade of Great Food

This year marks the publication of our tenth *Sunset Recipe Annual*, each a collection of all the past year's food articles and recipes from the pages of *Sunset Magazine*.

If you've been collecting these volumes for several years, you've seen an evolution in the way *Sunset* readers cook. The spirit of the late 1990s demands quick, lean, and healthy dishes featuring fresh ingredients from around the world. In this book, low-fat recipes (with 30 percent or less calories from fat) make up more than half of the recipes; you'll find them listed on pages 281–282.

You'll find innovative ideas from the West's outstanding chefs and home cooks, ideas for entertaining, and news of the latest food trends and market varieties. Our new recipe format calls out cooking and preparation times clearly, and you'll always find nutritional information listed with each recipe.

Welcome to another year of great cooking and eating!

Cover:
Sunset's Burritos Grandes (page 92).
Cover design: Susan Bryant Caron.
Photographer: Joyce Oudkerk Pool.
Food & photo styling: Susan Massey.

Back cover photographers:
(Top to bottom) Kevin Candland;
Craig Maxwell; Barbara Thompson; Kevin Candland.

First printing November 1996

ISBN 0-376-02701-0 (hardcover)
ISBN 0-376-02700-2 (softcover)
ISSN 0896-2170
Printed in the United States

♻ printed on recycled paper

Material in this book originally appeared in the 1996 issues of *Sunset Magazine*. All of the recipes were developed and tested in the Sunset test kitchens. If you have comments or suggestions, please let us hear from you. Write us at Sunset Books, Cookbook Editorial, 80 Willow Road, Menlo Park, CA 94025

Contents

A Letter from Sunset

At restaurants such as Stars in Palo Alto, our food team keeps up with the trends. From left to right: Eligio Hernandez, Linda Lau Anusasananan, Bernadette Hart, Barbara E. Goldman, Jerry Di Vecchio, Betsy Reynolds Bateson, Christine Weber Hale, and Elaine Johnson.

DEAR READER,

Looking back through the past year's *Sunset Magazine* to assemble this 1997 *Recipe Annual*, I am, as always, surprised at how quickly another year has gone by—and at how many changes and new ideas there are to report.

As in other years, the recipes in this volume combine to fit an overall theme. From start to finish, 1996 can be dubbed the year of speed, health—and great taste. Take a look at the preparation and cooking times we provide right beneath the title of each recipe: you'll see that very few dishes take over an hour to make, and many go together much more quickly. And those that do demand extra time, such as Bûche de Noël (December), definitely merit the effort. It's a spectacular once-a-year production.

We kick off our lean and speedy year with January's "Quick, Light, and Healthy." In just nine pages, you'll find 22 recipes you can prepare in 30 minutes or less—and none derive more than 30 percent of their calories from fat. Your response to this story makes it clear that we hit the mark; typical comments include, "I can't believe it can be so easy, so good, and still so good for me and my family!"

We composed July's "Low-fat Summer Classics" in the same spirit, devising over 20 lean recipes for all-time winners such as potato salad, tacos, and ice cream pies. The focus here is on cutting fat, but many of these dishes, too, can be ready in 30 minutes or less.

Even lasagne, that all-around favorite for family meals and easy entertaining, faces the challenge of the clock. February's chapter brings you One-hour Lasagne—a version you can assemble, bake, and bring to the table in about 60 minutes.

One of this year's most popular desserts (as reader requests for extra copies attest) is another quick fix. February's Warm Chocolate Cake with a Soft Heart takes just 15 minutes to assemble, 15 minutes to bake. True, it tips the scales for richness; but as we've often pointed out, indulgence has its place in lean eating. Good nutrition means balance, not exclusion. When you're serving a luscious dessert, just make sure your entrée is low in fat; you'll find dozens of suitable choices scattered through these pages.

Thinking about the way *Sunset* cooks lean, I've noticed that one key to success lies in taking advantage of low-fat ingredients. At the more exotic end of the lean-by-nature scale is emu, the big bird that tastes like beef; you'll find a report on it in January's chapter. A more everyday choice is the ready-made crêpe (see my June *Food Guide*), a trim, quick start for main dishes or desserts.

The low-fat cooking techniques developed in our test kitchens have become second nature to us when we devise our recipes. They're the backbone of *Everyday Low-fat Cooking*, Elaine Johnson's monthly column; they crop up regularly in the *Food Guide*. And as your *Kitchen Cabinet* submissions prove, you're cooking lean, too. Many of the recipes you send us make very sparing use of fat, and we know this isn't simply by chance. Betsy Reyonolds Bateson and Linda Lau Anusasananan, who put *Kitchen Cabinet* together, now interview the contributors about their cooking strategies.

Linda also continues to solve cooking puzzles in *Why?* This year, she discusses (among other topics) why meat turns dry when cooked (in May) and what to do when you get into trouble making jelly or jam (in June).

As always, Bob Thompson gives practical advice on wines each month. You'll learn what to sip with sausages (January) and Chinese food (July), and find out when you can justifiably send a wine back when dining in restaurants (September).

Cooking with the seasons is as important as ever in this *Recipe Annual*. In March, we enjoy asparagus; in April, we celebrate the artichoke, a Western specialty. In June, we look at that essence of summer, the peach. And though not all peaches are grown in the West, the movement towards bringing you varieties with the flavor a peach ought to have is firmly based here in our backyard.

Some familiar foods are becoming available in ever more variety. Our features on mushrooms (March), bananas (May), and garlic (September) introduce you to the new choices today's markets offer. Of course, we cover the less-familiar too, such as hard cider (February) and passion fruit (March).

In the past, the ethnic foods we've discussed have typically had ties to other lands. But this year, I spotted something new: a focus on foods from our own country. Examples include a green-chili stew from Helen Cordero, the famed creator of storyteller figures at New Mexico's Cochito Pueblo (March); Hawaii's ancient but still timely poke, a fresh seafood salad (September); and winter squash, an American original (October).

So much for the new. What about the traditional? Rest assured, what you've always enjoyed is still here: the recipes you need for the holidays, for family dinners, for easy company menus. With this volume at your fingertips, another year of great cooking and fabulous entertaining is in your hands.

Cheers!

Jerry Di Vecchio

Jerry Di Vecchio
Senior Editor, Food and Entertaining

We like it hot! In Sunset's test kitchens, we conduct our own taste test on hot sauces. From left to right: Linda Lau Anusasananan, Christine Weber Hale, and Elaine Johnson.

TO USE OUR NUTRITIONAL INFORMATION

The most current data from the USDA is used for our recipes: calorie count; fat calories; grams of protein, total and saturated fat, and carbohydrates; and milligrams of sodium and cholesterol.

This analysis is usually given for a single serving, based on the largest number of servings listed. Or it's for a specific amount, such as per tablespoon (for sauces); or by unit, as per cookie.

Optional ingredients are not included, nor are those for which no specific amount is stated (salt added to taste, for example). If an ingredient is listed with an alternative, calculations are based on the first choice listed. Likewise, if a range is given for the amount of an ingredient (such as ½ to 1 cup milk), values are figured on the first, lower amount.

Recipes using broth are calculated on the sodium content of salt-free broth, homemade or canned. If you use canned salted chicken broth, the sodium content will be higher.

FOOD
Guide

BY JERRY ANNE DI VECCHIO

A TASTE OF THE WEST: ## From the earth, a winter pie

The pristine crispness of winter captured in the opening movement of Glazunov's ballet *Les Saisons* always evokes peaceful images for me. I see seeds sleeping beneath frosted soil, gathering strength to burst forth in spring. I think of the root cellar on my family's homestead. There, beneath the thick, insulating ceiling, were baskets of hardy vegetables—potatoes, carrots, turnips, and more. During this barren stretch, they provided serious nourishment for my pioneering kin.

Though seasons no longer have such dramatic impact on the way we eat, they still get their due. Ben Marks, a *Sunset* senior editor, and his wife, Pat, honored those lean times in the restaurateur phase of their lives. At a friend's suggestion, they used root vegetables to make a pie.

Plain-sounding, yes. But like a shy friend who wears well, this pie grows on you. Not only does it qualify as comfort food—satisfying and good-tasting—but it has other virtues, too. It is quite low in fat, helpful as most of us are trying to shed a few holiday pounds. And if you use vegetable broth, the pie is perfect for vegetarian friends.

If you want to give the pie a bit of grandeur, don't change the recipe—just have Glazunov on CD playing softly as you dine.

Ben and Pat's Root Pie

Cooking time: About 45 minutes on top of the stove, 35 to 55 minutes in the oven

Prep time: 30 to 45 minutes

Notes: Three approaches to this pie are a) make and bake, b) make a day ahead and bake to reheat, or c) make filling a day ahead and reheat, then finish in the oven with freshly mashed potatoes.

Makes: 8 servings

  2 onions (about 1 lb. total)

    About 2 pounds carrots

Rutabagas, turnips, and carrots, surrounded by mashed potatoes, make the perfect post-holiday meal.

NOEL BARNHURST

JANUARY

- A root pie, for a hearty change of pace
- New tasks for a coffee grinder
- Coconut milk makes curry low-fat
- The pairing options for sausage, wine

About 2 pounds rutabagas

About 1 pound turnips

1 cup madeira or dry vermouth

2½ teaspoons dried thyme leaves

½ teaspoon ground nutmeg

8 cups chicken or vegetable broth

About 3 pounds russet potatoes

2 tablespoons butter or extra-virgin olive oil

6 tablespoons minced parsley

Salt and pepper

About ¼ cup slivered green onions

1. Peel and cut half the onions, carrots, rutabagas, and turnips into about ¼-inch dice. Cut remaining onion, carrots, rutabagas, and turnips into wedges or slices no more than ½ inch thick.

2. In a 5- to 6-quart pan, combine diced vegetables, madeira, thyme, nutmeg, and 1 cup broth. Boil on high heat, stirring often, until liquid evaporates, browned bits stick to pan (or vegetables), and vegetable edges are tinged dark brown, 15 to 20 minutes.

3. Stir 3 cups broth into pan, releasing browned bits, then add vegetable wedges and slices. Bring to a boil and cover vegetables. Simmer until the firmest vegetable is just tender when pierced, about 30 min-

utes. Uncover and boil on high heat, stirring occasionally, until liquid is reduced to about 1 cup, about 15 minutes.

4. Meanwhile, peel potatoes and cut them into about 2-inch chunks. Put into a 5- to 6-quart pan with 4 cups broth. Bring to a boil over high heat, then cover and simmer until potatoes are tender enough to mash, 15 to 20 minutes. Drain and save the liquid.

5. Mash potatoes with butter and parsley, adding enough of the drained cooking liquid (about ¾ cup) to make the potatoes as soft as you like. Season to taste with salt and pepper. Save extra liquid for other uses, such as soup.

6. Spread potatoes thickly around sides of a shallow 3½- to 4-quart casserole, making an even wall that extends above casserole rim. (If making ahead, put vegetables in casserole, then swirl potatoes evenly over vegetables. Cover and chill pie.)

7. Pour vegetable mixture into the center of the potatoes.

8. Bake, uncovered, in a 375° oven until potatoes are lightly browned, about 35 minutes (bake about 20 minutes longer if pie has been chilled).

9. Garnish pie with green onions. Scoop out portions to serve, adding salt and pepper to taste.

Per serving: 293 cal., 19% (56 cal.) from fat; 9.6 g protein; 6.2 g fat (2.7 g sat.); 56 g carbo.; 247 mg sodium; 7.8 mg chol.

GREAT TOOL

Life after coffee grinds

When the tip of one blade on my electric coffee grinder snapped off, the grinder still functioned, but it made a lot more noise. So I bought a new one. However, unable to part with a tool that still worked, I cleaned the old grinder of its pervasive coffee aroma and put it to excellent use as a spice and herb grinder. It's the fastest way to get a quantity of fresh-ground pepper. And because I like to grind spice seed for maximum flavor, I whirl cumin, cardamom, mustard, and such to fine powders in it. I also combine fresh herbs and dried spices. All grind better and faster here than in a mortar and pestle, a blender, or a food processor (seeds jump too much to grind well). And because electric coffee grinders are easily found for $15 or less (especially in discount stores), I plan to buy a new one just for spices if the rescued machine ever fails.

GREAT INGREDIENT

Coconut milk with less fat

Thai coconut curries sweep me away. I love their complex union of sweet, heat, and spice. But they have a drawback. Most use canned coconut milk, which is pretty rich—about 32 grams (288 calories) of fat per cup.

Jennifer Brennan, a Southeast Asian culinary expert and cookbook author, gave me my first skinnier option—low-fat milk flavored to taste with coconut extract (find it alongside vanilla at the market). But a more authentic choice is now available in most supermarkets—canned low-fat coconut milk. It has 8 grams (72 calories) of fat per cup.

Low-fat coconut milk, although it satisfies, isn't as potently flavored as the full-fat version. And it's even more inclined to separate when cooked, so blend in a little diluted cornstarch before heating. Modest thickening also enhances the sense of richness, as in this soup (recipe next page).

Chicken Curry Soup with Low-fat Coconut Milk

Cooking time: About 45 minutes

Prep time: 15 to 20 minutes

Notes: For a heartier dish, add 1½ cups diced potatoes to soup along with the chicken. If making ahead, don't add peas until mixture is reheated. Chill soup, covered, up to 1 day.

Makes: 4 main-dish servings

- 1 onion (about ½ lb.), chopped
- 2 tablespoons minced fresh ginger
- 2 tablespoons mustard seed
- 1 tablespoon curry powder
- 4 whole chicken legs, about 2½ pounds, skin and fat trimmed
- 3 cups chicken broth
- 1 red bell pepper (about ½ lb.), stemmed, seeded, and chopped
- 1 can (14 oz.) low-fat coconut milk
- 3 tablespoons cornstarch
- 1 package (10 oz.) frozen petite peas
- ¼ cup chopped fresh cilantro
  Salt
  Lime wedges

1. In a 5- to 6-quart pan, combine onion, ginger, mustard seed, and ¼ cup water. Stir often over high heat until onion is tinged with brown, 5 to 7 minutes; pan bottom will be dark brown. Add curry powder and stir about 30 seconds.

2. Add chicken, chicken broth, and bell pepper to pan; stir to release browned bits. Bring to a boil, then cover and simmer until chicken is tender when pierced, about 25 minutes.

3. Blend a little of the coconut milk with cornstarch until smooth, then add the remaining coconut milk. Pour mixture into the chicken, stirring. Add peas and continue to stir until mixture boils, about 10 minutes.

4. Ladle curry into wide bowls, sprinkling each with cilantro. Add salt and lime juice to taste.

Per serving: 455 cal., 28% (126 cal.) from fat; 41 g protein; 14 g fat (5.8 g sat.); 33 g carbo.; 361 mg sodium; 130 mg chol. ■

Curry soup made with low-fat instead of regular coconut milk has 75 percent less fat.

NOEL BARNHURST

BOB THOMPSON ON WINE: What goes with sausages?

Occasionally some quirk of chemical makeup makes perfect mates out of a wine and a food. Mostly, though, personal experience counts for more. Permit me to give you the sausage as an example.

In Alsace, sausages on a bed of sauerkraut—the famous *choucroute garnie*—usually demands Gewürztraminer (Trimbach, Domaines Schlumberger, Gisselbrecht), though some Alsatians would rather have Riesling or Pinot Gris. In the bistros of Paris, even more in the Burgundian countryside, sausages call for Beaujolais (rarely served with a label in Paris, mainly from Georges Duboeuf or Jean-Marc Aujoux here).

And in the Piemonte, when sausages are in or alongside a risotto, a glass of Barbera (Vietti, Domenico, Clerico, Pio Cesare) will be the companion at a majority of tables, though Nebbiolo would have proponents, and so would Dolcetto.

The sausages from any of the three regions differ only slightly. On the other hand, almost nothing of taste or texture joins the three wines together. The intensely spicy flavor and rich feel of Gewürztraminer could not be less like fresh-as-a-berry, lighter-than-air Beaujolais. Neither remotely resembles the mysteriously tart smack of Barbera from Alba or Asti. Yet every one of these wines pairs splendidly with sausages.

Well, it is hard not to be charmed by Gewürztraminer and sausage when you have Guebwiller for a backdrop. Ditto for Beaujolais in a classic Paris bistro, or Barbera at a hideaway off the Via Vittorio Emmanuele in Alba.

It is just as easy to be charmed by them here. However, when we have sausages on our home turf, we usually choose one of the juicy Zinfandels (Nalle, Seghesio, J. Fritz). As wine, Zinfandel fits somewhere between Beaujolais and Barbera. As a companion to sausages, it is an old friend we bring out for old friends, at restaurants or when they come over for a casual dinner plus a Clue tournament, or an audition of Duke Ellington records, or any of the other tastes that make us us and not Parisians, or Piemontese.

DAVID MARTINEZ

Quick,

light,
& healthy

From pasta to paella, *22* good-for-you recipes that are ready in *30* minutes or less

IT'S THE MODERN COOK'S ULTIMATE CHALLENGE: preparing a great-tasting, healthful weeknight meal in record time, using ingredients found in almost any supermarket. For a lot of us, it's a challenge we're facing more and more often.

With that in mind, we've created this special recipe collection. Think of it as your little black book for the kitchen.

Each entrée takes 30 minutes or less to prepare and derives 30 percent or less (often far less) of calories from fat. But when it comes to flavor, we've made no compromises. In fact, we predict you'll serve many of these dishes to company.

You'll find smart tips for the quick cook, suggestions for rounding out each meal, and a list of

staples to have at the ready when there's no time to shop. Staples include quality packaged products that help you get a jump on dinner. Spanish rice mix, for instance, is the base for Presto Paella (page 14).

If you give each recipe a quick read-through before trying it, you'll notice that many preparation and cooking steps should be done simultaneously to make the most efficient use of your time. And speaking of time, we started the clock once ingredients and equipment were assembled.

BY ELAINE JOHNSON • CHRISTINE WEBER HALE • LINDA LAU ANUSASANANAN
FOOD PHOTOGRAPHS BY PHILIP SALAVERRY

flakes in a 2- to 3-quart pan. Cover and bring mixture to a simmer, stirring occasionally, over medium-high heat.

2. Add pasta to water. Cook until tender to bite, 3 to 5 minutes for fresh or 7 to 8 minutes for dried. Drain pasta well.

3. Mix pasta with broth mixture, turkey, cilantro, and lime juice. Transfer to a serving bowl or individual plates. Sprinkle with peanuts.

Per serving: 394 cal., 16% (62 cal.) from fat; 29 g protein; 6.9 g fat (1.5 g sat.); 53 g carbo.; 769 mg sodium; 106 mg chol.

Angel Hair Pasta and Vegetables

Cooking time: About 15 minutes

Prep time: About 15 minutes

Notes: Offer an herbed cheese (such as Rondelé) to spread on chunks of Italian-style bread.

Makes: 4 servings

- ¾ pound broccoli florets
- 1 pound carrots, thinly sliced
- 1 cup frozen pearl onions
- 2 cups vegetable or chicken broth
- ½ cup dried tomatoes (not packed in oil), minced
- ¼ teaspoon hot chili flakes (optional)
- ¾ pound fresh or dried angel hair (capellini) pasta
- 3 tablespoons prepared capers, drained
- ¼ cup shredded parmesan cheese

1. Bring water for pasta to a boil over high heat. To boiling water, add broccoli and cook just until broccoli turns bright green and is slightly tender when pierced, about 1 minute. Remove broccoli with a slotted spoon and immediately transfer to ice water. Drain before using.

2. Add carrots and onions to boiling water. Cook until onions are thawed and carrots are just tender when pierced, about 6 minutes. Meanwhile, bring broth, tomatoes, and chili flakes to a boil in a 1- to 2-quart pan over high heat; reduce heat to keep warm.

3. Without removing carrots or onions, add pasta to boiling water. Cook until pasta is just tender to bite, 2 to 3 minutes. Drain pasta and vegetables well, then mix with broth-tomato mixture, broccoli, capers, and parmesan cheese. Transfer to a serving bowl or individual plates.

Per serving: 371 cal., 9% (35 cal.) from fat; 17 g protein; 3.9 g fat (1.3 g sat.); 69 g carbo.; 408 mg sodium; 66 mg chol.

Peanuts lend crunch to spicy linguine flavored with garlic, ginger, soy sauce, and lime juice.

P A S T A

Thai Pasta with Turkey

Cooking time: About 15 minutes if using fresh pasta, about 20 minutes with dried

Prep time: About 8 minutes

Notes: To complete the meal, prepare a salad with coleslaw mix and your favorite bottled Asian-style dressing.

Makes: 4 servings

- ¾ cup reduced-sodium chicken broth
- ¼ cup seasoned rice vinegar
- 2 tablespoons reduced-sodium soy sauce
- 1 tablespoon *each* minced fresh ginger and garlic
- ¼ teaspoon hot chili flakes
- ¾ pound fresh or dried linguine
- ½ pound cooked turkey, cut into thin strips
- ⅓ cup minced fresh cilantro
- 2 tablespoons lime juice
- 2 tablespoons chopped roasted peanuts

1. Bring water for pasta to a boil over high heat. While water heats, mix together broth, vinegar, soy sauce, ginger, garlic, and chili

SHORTCUTS • Start heating water for pasta before doing anything else (cover for faster heating). • Fresh pasta cooks in about half the time it takes for dried pasta. • You can freeze fresh pasta for future use—no need to thaw before cooking.

Orzo with Shrimp, Feta, and Artichoke Hearts

Cooking time: About 11 minutes

Prep time: About 8 minutes

Notes: Serve with a Greek-style salad of romaine lettuce, cucumbers, sliced tomatoes, and a low-fat dill dressing, and offer a well-chilled Chardonnay or Sauvignon Blanc wine.

Makes: 4 servings

- ¾ cup reduced-sodium chicken broth
- ¼ cup dry white wine
- 1 tablespoon finely shredded lemon peel
- ½ pound orzo pasta
- 1 cup frozen petite peas
- 1 jar (6 oz.) quartered marinated artichoke hearts, drained and thinly sliced
- ½ pound shelled cooked shrimp (36 to 42 per pound)
- ½ cup feta cheese, crumbled

1. Bring water for pasta to a boil over high heat. While water heats, combine chicken broth, wine, and lemon peel in a 2- to 3-quart pan. Cover and bring to a boil over high heat. Keep warm.

2. Add pasta to water and cook pasta until just tender to bite, about 5 minutes. Add peas to pasta, cook 1 minute, then drain pasta and peas well.

3. Mix pasta and peas with broth mixture, artichokes, shrimp, and all but 2 tablespoons feta. Transfer to a serving bowl or individual plates. Sprinkle with remaining feta.

Per serving: 398 cal., 19% (77 cal.) from fat; 25 g protein; 8.5 g fat (3.3 g sat.); 52 g carbo.; 708 mg sodium; 126 mg chol.

Fettuccine & Smoked Salmon

Cooking time: About 10 minutes if using fresh pasta, 15 minutes with dried

Prep time: About 9 minutes

Notes: Serve with crusty Italian bread, butter lettuce dressed with raspberry vinegar, and a Chardonnay.

Makes: 4 servings

- 1 cup reduced-sodium chicken broth
- 1 tablespoon *each* grated lemon and orange peel
- ¾ pound fresh or dried fettuccine
- 1 cup nonfat sour cream
- 2 tablespoons minced fresh dill
- ⅓ pound smoked salmon, cut into bite-size pieces

  Dill sprigs and lemon wedges (optional)

1. Bring water for cooking pasta to a boil over high heat. While water heats, combine broth and lemon and orange peel in a 2- to 3-quart pan. Cover and bring to a boil over high heat, 3 to 4 minutes.

2. Add pasta to water. Cook until just tender to bite, 3 to 5 minutes for fresh or about 7 minutes for dried. While pasta cooks, whisk sour cream into broth mixture until smooth; keep warm over low heat.

3. Drain pasta well. Mix pasta with sour cream mixture, minced dill, and salmon. Transfer to a serving bowl or individual plates. Garnish with dill sprigs and lemon wedges.

Per serving: 338 cal., 9% (32 cal.) from fat; 21 g protein; 3.6 g fat (0.6 g sat.); 51 g carbo.; 497 mg sodium; 71 mg chol.

Penne with Sausage, Roasted Peppers, and Greens

Cooking time: About 16 minutes

Prep time: About 8 minutes

Notes: As an accompaniment, buy a prepared lettuce mix with radicchio and endive. Dress with a vinaigrette made from red wine vinegar, olive oil, and Dijon mustard.

Makes: 4 servings

- ½ pound turkey Italian sausage, casings removed
- 3 cloves garlic, minced
- 1 onion (about ⅓ lb.), chopped
- ¾ pound dried penne pasta
- 1 can (15 oz.) no-salt-added tomato sauce
- ½ cup dry red wine
- 1 jar (7.25 oz.) peeled roasted red peppers, drained and cut into thin strips
- 3 cups (about 3 oz. total) thinly sliced mustard greens
- ¼ cup shredded parmesan cheese

1. Bring water for pasta to a boil over high heat. While water heats, combine sausage, garlic, and onion in a 3- to 4-quart pan over medium-high heat. Stir often until sausage is browned, about 10 minutes.

2. Add pasta to boiling water; cook until tender to bite, about 8 minutes. While pasta cooks, add tomato sauce, wine, and peppers to sausage mixture; simmer over high heat, stirring often. Stir in mustard greens and all but 1 tablespoon cheese.

3. Drain pasta well, then mix it with tomato sauce. Transfer to a serving bowl or individual plates. Sprinkle with remaining cheese.

Per serving: 533 cal., 16% (86 cal.) from fat; 25 g protein; 9.5 g fat (2.8 g sat.); 82 g carbo.; 611 mg sodium; 34 mg chol.

Boldly flavored penne features mustard greens and Italian sausage in a rich tomato sauce.

Polenta cooked with creamed corn soothes frayed nerves after a hectic day.

V E G E T A R I A N

Creamy Corn Polenta

Cooking time: About 22 minutes

Prep time: About 5 minutes

Notes: You can substitute instant polenta, which cooks in about 5 minutes, for regular polenta. Simply cook according to package directions, then stir in corn. Serve with crusty bread, a green salad dressed with marinated artichoke hearts, and red wine.

Makes: 4 servings

1   quart vegetable or chicken broth

1   cup polenta or yellow cornmeal

2   cans (about 15 oz. each) creamed corn

6   ounces teleme or münster cheese, thinly sliced

½   cup thinly sliced green onion

½   cup canned peeled roasted red peppers, rinsed and patted dry

Freshly ground pepper

1. In a 3- to 4-quart pan, mix broth and polenta. Bring to a boil over high heat. Reduce heat to low and stir often over low heat until polenta is creamy and smooth, about 13 minutes.

Stir in creamed corn; cook, stirring often, until hot, about 5 minutes.

2. Spoon polenta into 4 bowls. Lay ¼ of the cheese on each bowl of polenta; sprinkle with sliced green onion. Cut red peppers into strips; arrange decoratively over polenta. Sprinkle with pepper to taste.

Per serving: 466 cal., 27% (126 cal.) from fat; 19 g protein; 14 g fat (8.3 g sat.); 71 g carbo.; 1,162 mg sodium; 41 mg chol.

Moroccan Vegetable Stew

Cooking time: About 20 minutes

Prep time: About 5 minutes

Notes: Serve with wedges of pita bread and a salad of sliced cucumbers and onions dressed with yogurt. Fresh tangerines, dates, and hot mint tea make a refreshing ending.

Makes: 4 servings

S H O R T C U T S • Look for precut vegetables in your supermarket's produce section, salad bar, or freezer. • To quickly thaw frozen vegetables, place in a colander and rinse with hot water. • Spice blends can provide instant flavor. Intensify flavor with extra cayenne or chilies. • Canned peeled roasted red peppers provide a quick, colorful garnish.

1 teaspoon olive oil

1 onion (½ lb.), coarsely chopped

1 teaspoon *each* ground ginger and cumin

½ teaspoon cayenne

¼ teaspoon ground turmeric

2 cans (14½ oz. each) stewed tomatoes, with juice

1 can (15 oz.) reduced-sodium garbanzos, rinsed and drained

2¼ cups vegetable or chicken broth

1 box (10 oz., 1½ cups) couscous

1 package (1 lb.) frozen mixed vegetables (carrots, broccoli and cauliflower florets, green beans) thawed

2 tablespoons chopped fresh mint leaves or parsley

1. In a 3- to 4-quart pan, combine oil and onion; stir over high heat until onion is limp, about 5 minutes. Stir in ginger, cumin, cayenne, and turmeric. Add tomatoes, including juice. Bring to a boil.

2. Add garbanzos to pan. Cover; simmer over medium heat until hot, about 5 minutes.

3. Meanwhile, in a 2- to 3-quart pan, bring broth to a boil over high heat. Stir in couscous. Cover and remove from heat; let stand until liquid is absorbed, about 5 minutes.

4. Stir thawed vegetables into tomato mixture. Cover and simmer over medium heat until hot, about 5 minutes.

5. Spoon couscous into 4 bowls or into a large serving dish. Spoon vegetable mixture over couscous. Sprinkle with mint.

Per serving: 475 cal., 8% (36 cal.) from fat; 19 g protein; 4 g fat (0.4 g sat.); 94 g carbo.; 821 mg sodium; 0 mg chol.

Grilled Onion Quesadillas

Cooking time: About 20 minutes

Prep time: About 10 minutes

Notes: Offer lemonade or beer with the quesadillas. Juicy rounds of fresh pineapple, plain or drizzled with orange-flavor liqueur, make a quick dessert.

Makes: 4 servings

1 red onion (½ lb.)

4 low-fat flour tortillas (10 in. wide)

1 can (1 lb.) nonfat refried beans

¼ pound reduced-fat jarlsberg cheese, thinly sliced

Salsa

4 cups finely shredded cabbage (about 1 lb.) or coleslaw mix (about ½ lb.)

4 green onions, ends trimmed (optional)

1. Place a 10- to 12-inch frying pan over high heat. Cut red onion crosswise into ⅓-inch-thick rounds. Lay slices in pan; cook, turning once, until browned, 10 to 15 minutes total.

2. Lightly brush tortillas on both sides with water. Spread ¼ of the beans over half of each tortilla. Separate onions into rings and lay over beans. Top each with ¼ of the cheese. Fold tortilla over filling. Place filled tortillas slightly apart on 2 pans, each 12 by 15 inches. Bake in a 500° oven until tortillas are crisp and golden, 6 to 8 minutes. Switch positions of baking sheets halfway through.

3. Meanwhile, mix 1 cup salsa with cabbage. Transfer quesadillas to plates. Mound cabbage mixture alongside quesadillas. Offer additional salsa to add to taste. Garnish with green onions.

Per serving: 376 cal., 19% (73 cal.) from fat; 20 g protein; 8.1 g fat (2.6 g sat.); 55 g carbo.; 1,049 mg sodium; 15 mg chol.

Black Bean Chili

Cooking time: About 20 minutes

Prep time: About 15 minutes (part done concurrently with cooking)

Notes: Serve this mildly spiced chili with a green salad and warm tortillas. For dessert, offer ripe Comice pear slices to dip into a warmed chocolate topping.

Makes: 4 servings

1 onion (½ lb.), chopped

1 teaspoon salad oil

3 tablespoons chili powder

1½ teaspoons cumin seed

½ teaspoon cayenne

4 cans (15 oz. each) black beans, rinsed and drained

3 oranges (½ lb. each)

½ cup coarsely chopped radish

2 tablespoons lime juice

4 whole radishes, optional

Reduced-fat sour cream

1. In a 3- to 4-quart pan, cook onion in oil over high heat until onion is soft, about 4 minutes. Reduce heat to low. Stir in chili powder, cumin, and cayenne. Add beans. Squeeze juice from 1 orange to make about ½ cup; add juice to beans. Cover and simmer over low heat, stirring occasionally, for 15 minutes.

2. Meanwhile, cut peel off remaining oranges deep enough to remove white pith and membrane. Cut oranges into ½-inch chunks; mix with chopped radish and lime juice.

3. Spoon beans equally into 4 bowls. Spoon orange-radish mixture over top. Garnish with whole radish. Add sour cream to taste.

Per serving: 345 cal., 13% (45 cal.) from fat; 18 g protein; 5 g fat (0.4 g sat.); 61 g carbo.; 751 mg sodium; 0 mg chol.

Shopper's guide to quick-cooking staples

FOR THE PANTRY

Grains: couscous, polenta or instant polenta, long-grain white rice, instant rice, Spanish rice mix

Dried pastas: capellini, fettuccine, linguine, orzo, penne, spaghettini, and rice noodles

Fresh thin-skinned potatoes

Canned vegetables (look for reduced-sodium versions): black beans and nonfat refried beans, garbanzos, corn, baby corn, marinated artichokes, pimientos, peeled roasted red peppers, tomatoes, dried tomatoes

Other canned and packaged goods: low-fat marinara sauce, no-salt-added tomato sauce; reduced-sodium chicken, beef, and vegetable broths; clam juice; reduced-fat coconut milk; pineapple packed in juice; honey; cherry jam; roasted peanuts; pita breads; instant mashed potatoes

Vinegars: white and red wine, balsamic, seasoned rice, raspberry

Condiments: salsa, Dijon mustard, chutney, capers, horseradish, reduced-sodium soy sauce, hoisin sauce

Seasonings: dried herbs and spices, hot chili flakes, garlic

Wines: dry white, Merlot or other dry red, dry sherry

FOR THE FREEZER

Poultry: ground turkey and chicken, boned, skinned chicken breasts, cooked turkey and chicken

Meat: Pork tenderloin, top sirloin steak, ground lean lamb, smoked pork chops

Sausage: turkey kielbasa, turkey Italian linguisa

Seafood: cleaned squid, shelled cooked crab and shrimp, halibut and snapper, smoked salmon

Other: mixed vegetables, petite peas, pearl onions, sourdough bread

FOR THE REFRIGERATOR

Fruits and vegetables: lemons, limes, oranges; bell peppers, broccoli, carrots, celery, greens (mustard, spinach, and chard), jalapeños, onions (red, white, and green), preshredded cabbage, radishes

Fresh herbs: dill, cilantro, fresh ginger, mint, rosemary, parsley, Italian parsley

Fresh pastas (you can also keep these in the freezer)

Tortillas (low-fat flour)

Dairy: nonfat sour cream; feta, parmesan, teleme, and reduced-fat jarlsberg cheeses

1. In a 10- to 12-inch frying pan over high heat, bring broth and saffron to a boil. Stir in rice and seasoning packet, reduce heat, and simmer, covered, until rice is tender to bite, 16 to 18 minutes.

2. Meanwhile, in an 8- to 10-inch frying pan over medium heat, stir linguisa and bell pepper until well browned, 10 to 12 minutes. Remove from heat (if using frozen shrimp, add to pan and stir often until they're warm to the touch, about 4 minutes).

3. To rice, stir in sausage mixture, shrimp, squid tubes and tentacles, and peas over medium heat. Cover and cook until squid are no longer translucent and peas are hot to touch, about 4 minutes.

Per serving: 361 cal., 27% (99 cal.) from fat; 23 g protein; 11 g fat (3.8 g sat.); 43 g carbo.; 826 mg sodium; 154 mg chol.

Clams in Tomato-Fennel Broth

Cooking time: About 25 minutes

Prep time: About 15 minutes (part done concurrently with cooking)

Notes: Serve the clams with breadsticks and steamed broccoli.

Makes: 4 servings

- 1 pound fennel bulb, tough outer parts removed, tops trimmed, sprigs reserved
- 4 cloves garlic, minced
- 2 bottles (8 oz. each) clam juice
- 2 cups chicken broth
- 1 cup dry white wine
- 1 can (about 1 lb.) reduced-sodium sliced tomatoes
- 4 pounds clams in shells, suitable for steaming, scrubbed

  Freshly ground pepper

1. Thinly slice fennel bulb crosswise. In a 5- to 6-quart pan over high heat, place fennel, garlic, clam juice, broth, and wine; cover and bring to a boil. Reduce heat and simmer, covered, until fennel is tender when pierced, about 10 minutes.

2. Stir in tomatoes and clams. Cover and return to simmering over high heat, then reduce heat and simmer, stirring occasionally, until clams open, 3 to 4 minutes. Ladle into bowls. Mince enough fennel sprigs to make 2 teaspoons; scatter over soup. Garnish with a few whole fennel sprigs and add pepper to taste.

Per serving: 148 cal., 14% (21 cal.) from fat; 13 g protein; 2.3 g fat (0.5 g sat.); 12 g carbo.; 463 mg sodium; 23 mg chol.

For shortcut paella, dress up Spanish rice mix with saffron, seafood, and green peas.

S E A F O O D

Presto Paella

Cooking time: About 28 minutes

Prep time: About 10 minutes (done concurrently with cooking)

Notes: Start pilaf before preparing other ingredients. Serve with an arugula salad.

Makes: 4 servings

- 2 cups unsalted or reduced-sodium chicken broth
- 1/4 teaspoon powdered saffron
- 1 box (about 7 oz.) Spanish rice mix
- 3 ounces linguisa, halved lengthwise, then cut into 1/4-inch slices
- 1 cup chopped green or red bell pepper (or a combination of both)
- 8 (1/3 pound) shelled, cooked fresh or frozen shrimp
- 1/4 pound peeled squid tubes (cut into 1/2-inch rings) and tentacles, or 1/4 pound bay scallops
- 3/4 cup frozen petite peas

SHORTCUTS • Fish and shellfish cook so quickly that in just a minute or two they can be overdone—so keep an eye on them. Frozen cooked shrimp take only a few minutes to warm; for many recipes, you can use them right from the freezer. • If you don't have time to cook onion, tame its raw flavor by chopping it, then soaking it briefly in ice water.

Halibut with Horseradish Mashed Potatoes and Chard

Cooking time: About 12 minutes

Prep time: About 10 minutes

Notes: French or American hard cider is delicious with this dish. For hearty appetites, serve with steamed artichokes and warm sourdough bread.

Makes: 4 servings

> Instant mashed potatoes for 8 servings (to make 4 cups)
>
> 1 to 2 tablespoons prepared horseradish
>
> 1 pound halibut fillets (1 to 1½ in. thick), cut into 4 pieces
>
> 1½ teaspoons olive oil
>
> Salt and freshly ground pepper
>
> 1 pound red Swiss chard (stems removed), coarsely chopped
>
> About ¼ cup balsamic vinegar

1. Prepare potatoes according to package directions, omitting butter. Add horseradish to taste and keep warm.

2. Rub fish with oil and sprinkle with salt and pepper. In a 10- to 12-inch nonstick frying pan over medium-high heat, cook fish, turning occasionally, until no longer translucent in center, about 6 minutes.

3. Meanwhile, in a 5- to 6-quart pan over high heat, bring ¼ cup water to a boil. Add chard, cover, and cook until chard is wilted, about 3 minutes.

4. Place equal portions of potatoes on 4 plates, flattening tops. Spoon chard onto each, then fish. Season to taste with vinegar and additional salt and pepper.

Per serving: 292 cal., 17% (50 cal.) from fat; 30 g protein; 5.5 g fat (1.2 g sat.); 31 g carbo.; 343 mg sodium; 40 mg chol.

Snapper with Fruit Salsa

Cooking time: About 7 minutes

Prep time: About 15 minutes

Notes: Louise Ross of Elk Grove, California, shared this recipe. Try the fish with whole-wheat couscous.

Makes: 4 servings

> ¼ cup chopped red onion
>
> ¾ cup chopped, prepeeled fresh pineapple (or use pineapple canned in juice, drained)
>
> ¾ cup chopped ripe papaya
>
> ¼ cup lime juice, plus lime wedges
>
> 1 tablespoon minced fresh ginger
>
> ¼ teaspoon hot chili flakes
>
> 4 rockfish fillets (each ½ in. thick, 1 pound total), such as snapper
>
> Salt and pepper
>
> 1 teaspoon salad oil

1. Place onion in a bowl and cover with ice water. In another bowl, combine pineapple, papaya, lime juice, ginger, and chili flakes. Set mixture aside.

2. Sprinkle fish with salt and pepper. In a 10- to 12-inch nonstick frying pan over medium-high heat, brown fish in oil, turning occasionally until no longer translucent in center, about 6 minutes. Lift onto plates.

3. Drain onion and stir into fruit mixture. Spoon fruit salsa over fish. Squeeze lime wedges over fish, and add additional salt and pepper to taste.

Per serving: 150 cal., 19% (28 cal.) from fat; 22 g protein; 3.1 g fat (0.6 g sat.); 8.4 g carbo.; 73 mg sodium; 40 mg chol.

Asian Seafood Soup

Cooking time: About 15 minutes

Prep time: About 10 minutes

Notes: This soup is medium-hot. Add another tablespoon of jalapeño if you'd like it very spicy. Follow the soup with a plate of fresh kumquats and apple slices.

Makes: 2 quarts, 4 servings

> 6 cups chicken broth
>
> 2 tablespoons minced fresh jalapeño chili
>
> 2 lemon grass stalks (3 oz. total), split lengthwise and cut into 4-inch pieces
>
> 4 ounces dried thin rice noodles (also called rice sticks), broken into 1- by 3-inch chunks
>
> ⅓ pound mustard greens, stems removed, leaves chopped
>
> 1 can or jar (15 oz.) baby corn, drained
>
> ¾ cup reduced-fat coconut milk
>
> ½ pound shelled cooked tiny shrimp, or larger shelled cooked shrimp
>
> ⅓ pound shelled cooked crab

1. In a covered 5- to 6-quart pan over high heat, bring broth, chili, and lemon grass to a boil. Reduce heat and simmer for 5 minutes.

2. Return to boiling, add noodles, greens, and corn, and simmer, covered, until greens are tender to bite, about 5 minutes. Remove from heat. Stir in coconut milk, shrimp, and crab; let stand until hot to touch, about 1 minute. Discard lemon grass.

Per serving: 314 cal., 21% (66 cal.) from fat; 28 g protein; 7.3 g fat (2.9 g sat.); 34 g carbo.; 447 mg sodium; 148 mg chol.

Few will guess that the horseradish-potato base for the fish and chard has an instant start.

Take 10 minutes to brown the peppered chicken, then quickly cook the corn with capers and wine.

P O U L T R Y

Chicken with Corn Relish

Cooking time: About 22 minutes

Prep time: About 8 minutes

Notes: This recipe was created by Emily Kim of San Mateo, California. Serve with a salad of watercress, butter lettuce, and orange segments, and crusty bread.

Makes: 4 servings

- 4 boned, skinned chicken breast halves (1 lb. total), fat trimmed

  Coarsely ground pepper

- 1 teaspoon olive oil

- 2 cloves garlic, minced

- ¼ cup diced celery

- ¼ cup thinly sliced green onion

- ¾ cup dry white wine

- 1 tablespoon prepared capers, drained, plus 2 tablespoons caper liquid

- 1 can (15 oz.) reduced-sodium corn, drained

- 1 jar (2 oz.) diced pimientos, drained

  Italian parsley leaves

1. Sprinkle chicken with pepper. Place 1 teaspoon oil in a 10- to 12-inch nonstick frying pan over medium-high heat. When hot, add chicken. Turn occasionally until well browned and no longer pink in center, 10 to 12 min-

utes. Lift from pan and keep warm.

2. In pan, frequently stir garlic, celery, and onion until browned, 2 to 3 minutes. Over high heat, stir in wine, capers and liquid, corn, and pimientos; cook until most of the wine has evaporated, 2 to 6 minutes.

3. Spoon corn onto a platter and arrange chicken on top. Garnish with parsley.

Per serving: 236 cal., 12% (28 cal.) from fat; 28 g protein; 3.1 g fat (0.7 g sat.); 17 g carbo.; 357 mg sodium; 66 mg chol.

Chicken Chutney Burgers

Cooking time: About 10 minutes

Prep time: About 10 minutes

Notes: Serve with cups of vegetable soup from the deli or spinach salad made with a low-fat dressing.

Makes: 4 servings

SHORTCUTS •When broiling, start preheating the broiler before you prepare the recipe. •Rice works well for quick meals; regular white rice takes only 20 minutes to cook. Instant white or brown rice takes even less time, just 10 minutes.

- 2/3 cup Major Grey chutney, large pieces chopped
- 1 1/2 tablespoons lemon juice
- 1 tablespoon Dijon mustard
- 3/4 pound ground chicken
- 1/4 cup sliced green onion
- 1/2 teaspoon ground cumin
- 8 slices (each 1/2 in. thick, 3 by 6 in.) sourdough French bread
- 4 thin slices red onion
- 20 prewashed spinach leaves (each about 4 in. long)

1. Combine chutney, lemon juice, and mustard; set 2/3 of mixture aside. Combine remaining chutney mixture with chicken, green onion, and cumin. Shape into 4 patties, each about 4 inches wide, and place on a rack in a 12- by 15-inch broiler pan. Broil 3 inches below heat until well browned on both sides, turning as needed, 6 to 7 minutes.

2. Meanwhile, brown bread in a toaster, then spread 1 side of each slice with reserved chutney mixture.

3. Separate red onion into rings and place between bread with burgers and spinach.

Per serving: 416 cal., 20% (82 cal.) from fat; 20 g protein; 9.1 g fat (2.2 g sat.); 61 g carbo.; 946 mg sodium; 71 mg chol.

Turkey Kielbasa Soup

Cooking time: About 20 minutes

Prep time: About 7 minutes

Notes: Louise Ross of Elk Grove, California, contributed this recipe. Enjoy the soup with rye bread toast or croutons and your favorite microbrewery amber ale.

Makes: 7 cups, 4 servings

- 3 1/2 cups chicken broth
- 1 can (1 lb.) reduced-sodium garbanzos, rinsed and drained
- 3 cups purchased shredded green cabbage (or cabbage with shredded carrots)
- 1 cup chopped thin-skinned potato
- 1/2 cup chopped onion
- 1 clove garlic, minced
- 1/2 pound turkey kielbasa sausage, cut into 1/4-inch slices
- 1 tablespoon white wine vinegar
- 1 1/2 tablespoons minced parsley, plus sprigs

In a 5- to 6-quart pan over high heat, bring broth, garbanzos, cabbage, potato, onion, and garlic to a boil over high heat. Reduce heat and simmer, covered, until potato is tender to bite, about 10 minutes. Add kielbasa and simmer until it's hot, about 5 more minutes. Stir in vinegar and minced parsley. Garnish bowls with parsley sprigs.

Per serving: 254 cal., 27% (69 cal.) from fat; 19 g protein; 7.7 g fat (2.2 g sat.); 32 g carbo.; 834 mg sodium; 38 mg chol.

Spaghettini and Meatballs

Cooking time: About 17 minutes

Prep time: About 10 minutes

Notes: Buy one of the fat-free or low-fat marinaras (0 to 1 g fat per 1/3 cup). This dish calls for classic accompaniments: Caesar salad, perhaps from your market's salad bar, and a gutsy Zinfandel.

Makes: 4 servings

- 3/4 pound ground turkey
- 1/2 cup chopped onion
- 1/4 cup grated parmesan cheese
- 1/4 cup chopped parsley, plus sprigs
- 3/4 teaspoon dried oregano leaves
- 2 1/2 cups (26 oz. jar) purchased fat-free or low-fat marinara sauce with mushrooms
- 3/4 pound dried spaghettini

1. Combine turkey, onion, parmesan, 3 tablespoons parsley, and oregano. Shape into 20 equal balls and place on a rack in a 12- by 15-inch broiler pan. Broil 3 inches from heat until well browned all over, turning as needed, 10 to 12 minutes.

2. Meanwhile, in a 2- to 3-quart pan over medium-high heat, stir marinara until simmering, about 5 minutes. Reduce heat, add meatballs, and simmer, stirring occasionally, for 5 minutes to blend flavors.

3. While meatballs cook, half-fill a 5- to 6-quart pan with water and bring to a boil over high heat. Add spaghettini and cook until barely tender to bite, 6 to 8 minutes.

4. Drain pasta and place on a platter. Spoon sauce on top, sprinkle with remaining parsley, and garnish with parsley sprigs.

Per serving: 553 cal., 20% (108 cal.) from fat; 31 g protein; 12 g fat (3.5 g sat.); 78 g carbo.; 640 mg sodium; 47 mg chol.

Chicken–Bok Choy Stir-Fry

Cooking time: About 28 minutes

Prep time: About 20 minutes (done concurrently with cooking)

Notes: A Gewürztraminer with a hint of sweetness is a refreshing accompaniment.

Makes: 4 servings

- 1 1/4 cups long-grain white rice
- 3/4 cup chicken broth
- 1 1/2 tablespoons cornstarch
- 3 tablespoons lemon juice
- About 2 tablespoons reduced-sodium soy sauce
- 1 tablespoon honey
- 1 teaspoon ground ginger
- 4 boned, skinned chicken breast halves (1 lb. total), fat trimmed
- 2 teaspoons peanut oil or salad oil
- 1 1/4 cups 1-inch squares red bell pepper
- 8 baby bok choy (each 4 to 6 in. long, 1 lb. total), split lengthwise; or 1 pound regular bok choy, cut into 2-inch chunks

1. Place rice and 2 1/2 cups water in a 2- to 3-quart pan; bring to a boil over high heat. Reduce heat and simmer, covered, until liquid is absorbed, about 20 minutes.

2. Meanwhile, stir broth, cornstarch, lemon juice, 2 tablespoons soy sauce, honey, and ginger until smooth; set aside.

3. Cut chicken crosswise into 1/2-inch-wide strips. Place a wok or 12-inch frying pan over high heat. When hot, add oil, then chicken. Stir often until chicken is no longer pink in center, 2 to 3 minutes. Lift out and cover to keep warm.

4. To wok, add bell pepper, bok choy, and 2 tablespoons water. Cover tightly and cook until bell pepper is barely tender-crisp to bite, 1 1/2 to 2 minutes; lift out and set aside.

5. Stir broth mixture, then pour into wok and stir until bubbling, about 1 minute. Gently mix in chicken and vegetables. Spoon rice into center of a platter and arrange chicken mixture alongside, placing baby bok choy around rim of platter. Add additional soy sauce to taste.

Per serving: 420 cal., 10% (43 cal.) from fat; 33 g protein; 4.8 g fat (1 g sat.); 60 g carbo.; 476 mg sodium; 66 mg chol.

One-pan meal: a satisfying soup of vegetables and sausage simmers in just 20 minutes.

Brochettes of lean pork tenderloin stay moist and tender with a garnet-hued cherry glaze.

M E A T

Cherry-glazed Pork

Cooking time: About 20 minutes

Prep time: About 10 minutes

Notes: Accompany this dish with steamed green beans or sautéed spinach and a glass of Merlot.

Makes: 4 servings

- 1 cup cherry jam
- 1 cup Merlot or other dry red wine
- 3 tablespoons raspberry or red wine vinegar
- 2 tablespoons minced fresh or 1 teaspoon crumbled dried rosemary
- 8 green onions, ends trimmed
- 1 pound pork tenderloin, cut into 20 equal pieces
- 2 cups reduced-sodium chicken broth
- 1½ cups couscous

1. In a 10- to 12-inch frying pan, mix together jam, Merlot, vinegar, and rosemary until thoroughly combined. Bring to a boil over high heat. Boil until reduced to 1 cup, about 11 minutes.

2. While cherry mixture boils, cut onions in half crosswise. Thread pork and green onion pieces alternately onto 4 metal skewers (at least 8 inches long), dividing pork and onions equally between skewers. Lay skewers on a broiler pan; brush tops evenly with about ⅓ of the cherry mixture.

3. Broil pork about 4 inches from heat until well browned on top, 5 to 6 minutes. Turn skewers over, brush with half the remaining cherry mixture, and broil until other side is browned, 2 to 4 minutes.

4. While pork cooks, bring broth to a boil in a 2- to 3-quart pan over high heat. Add couscous, cover tightly, remove from heat, and let stand until liquid is absorbed and couscous is tender to bite, about 5 minutes.

5. Spoon couscous onto a platter or individual plates and top with skewers. Spoon remaining cherry mixture over meat and onions.

Per serving: 670 cal., 9% (62 cal.) from fat; 34 g protein; 6.9 g fat (2.3 g sat.); 109 g carbo.; 375 mg sodium; 71 mg chol.

Blackened Steak Salad

Cooking time: About 14 minutes

Prep time: About 7 minutes

Notes: Crusty rolls, warmed in the oven, are all you need to round out the meal.

Makes: 4 servings

- ¾ pound top sirloin steak (about 1 in. thick), fat trimmed
- 1 tablespoon Cajun or blackening spice blend
- ½ cup salsa
- ½ cup nonfat sour cream
- 2 tablespoons lime juice
- ¾ pound prewashed spinach leaves

- 1 can (15 oz.) black beans, rinsed and drained
- 1 jar (7.25 oz.) peeled roasted red peppers, drained and cut into thin strips
- Pepper

1. Pat steak with spice blend to coat both sides evenly. Heat a 10- to 12-inch frying pan over medium-high heat. When pan is very hot, add steak. Cook, turning occasionally, until meat is well browned on the outside and done to your liking, about 14 minutes for medium-rare.

2. Meanwhile, whirl salsa, sour cream, and lime juice in a blender or food processor until smooth. Arrange spinach, beans, and peppers decoratively in a large serving bowl.

3. When meat is done, cut it into thin bite-size slices; add to salad. At the table, mix salad thoroughly with dressing. Add pepper to taste.

Per serving: 247 cal., 17% (42 cal.) from fat; 27 g protein; 4.7 g fat (1.4 g sat.); 22 g carbo.; 1,370 mg sodium; 52 mg chol.

Hoisin Lamb in Pita Pockets

Cooking time: About 13 minutes

Prep time: About 9 minutes

Notes: Look for hoisin sauce in the Asian foods section of your supermarket. Offer carrot sticks, red pepper strips, and thinly sliced jicama, with low-fat ranch dressing for dipping. Serve with Chinese beer.

Makes: 4 servings

- ¾ pound ground lean lamb
- 1 onion (about ⅓ lb.), minced
- 3 cloves garlic, minced
- ¼ cup minced fresh cilantro
- 3 tablespoons hoisin sauce
- ¼ cup *each* dry sherry and chicken broth, smoothly mixed with 1 teaspoon cornstarch
- 4 pita breads (6½ to 7 in.), cut in half crosswise
- 3 cups finely shredded Napa cabbage

1. Combine lamb, onion, and garlic in a 10- to 12-inch frying pan over medium-high heat. Stir often until meat is well browned, 12 to 14 minutes.

2. Add cilantro, hoisin, and broth mixture. Stir until sauce boils; keep warm over low heat.

3. Fill pita pockets with equal amounts of cabbage. Top with equal amounts of lamb mixture. Serve immediately.

Per serving: 371 cal., 16% (61 cal.) from fat; 24 g protein; 6.8 g fat (2.2 g sat.); 47 g carbo.; 633 mg sodium; 56 mg chol.

SHORTCUTS • Use ground meat and small meat pieces, such as pork tenderloin cut into brochette-size chunks, to speed cooking. • To save time, use canned beans rather than cooking dried beans. • Don't overlook couscous when planning meals. Just add to boiling broth and cover tightly, then remove from heat and let stand about 5 minutes.

TO THICKEN THE SYRUP, *let the tart cool before turning it onto the plate.*

Upside-down French apple tart

Bake it in a frying pan with the crust on top, then flip it over to serve

TARTE TATIN IS LIKE APPLE PIE BUT even better. Now restaurants all over the West are bringing back the French classic, which has a rich crust topped with tender apples and a caramelized sugar-butter syrup. Long a French specialty, this tart became famous around the turn of the century when the Tatin sisters served the dessert at their hotel-restaurant in a small town about 80 miles south of Paris. Great flavors account for part of its resurgence in popularity on this side of the Atlantic; the dessert is also easy and fun to make.

In an ovenproof frying pan, cook sugar and butter to caramelize, then spoon sliced apples on top. Roll crust dough into a circle (no fluting needed), lift onto apples, and bake. At serving time, turn the tart upside down so that the caramel flows over the apples.

Tarte Tatin

Cooking time: About 65 minutes

Prep time: About 50 minutes, plus at least 2 hours cooling

Notes: You'll need an ovenproof frying pan to bake the tart. Avoid using a cast-iron pan, which can darken the apples and give them a metallic flavor.

Makes: 10 to 12 servings

- ⅓ cup plus ¼ cup cold butter or margarine
- 1¼ cups sugar
  About 1¼ cups all-purpose flour
- 1 large egg plus 1 large egg yolk (omit yolk if using margarine)
- 3½ pounds Golden Delicious apples
- 3 tablespoons lemon juice
  Vanilla ice cream (optional)

1. Cut ⅓ cup butter into chunks. In a food processor or a bowl, whirl or mix with your fingers the butter chunks, ¼ cup sugar, and 1¼ cups flour until mixture looks like fine meal. Add egg and yolk (if used); whirl or stir vigorously until dough holds together. Pat into a 5-inch disk, wrap in plastic, and chill to firm somewhat, 30 to 40 minutes.

2. Peel and core apples, then slice lengthwise ⅓ inch thick; mix slices with lemon juice and set aside.

3. In a 10-inch ovenproof frying pan over medium heat, melt remaining ¼ cup butter. Add remaining 1 cup sugar, and stir often until sugar melts, turns deep caramel color, and just barely starts to smoke, 6 to 8 minutes. Remove from heat.

4. Quickly (to cool caramel) and carefully (to avoid spattering) spoon apples and juice over caramel, filling pan compactly.

5. On a board, overlap sheets of plastic wrap to make a 16-inch square. Unwrap dough, dust with flour, and place on wrap. Cover with more plastic wrap. With short, gentle strokes, roll dough into an even 11-inch round. Remove top layer of plastic, invert dough over apples, and remove remaining layer of plastic. Tuck edge of dough between apples and pan. Cut 3 vents near center of dough, each about 2 inches long.

6. Bake in a 375° oven until pastry is deep golden and juices start to bubble in center, 55 to 60 minutes. Let cool on a rack until pan is no longer hot to touch, at least 2 hours or until next day (if it stands overnight, apples will absorb most of sauce). Loosen crust from side of pan. If tart is very juicy, tip pan, and spoon or siphon out some of the sauce. Place a rimmed serving plate over crust, and invert. Top wedges with sauce and ice cream.

Per serving: 283 cal., 32% (90 cal.) from fat; 2.4 g protein; 10 g fat (5.9 g sat.); 48 g carbo.; 98 mg sodium; 59 mg chol. ■

By Elaine Johnson

A SPIRITED GIN SAUCE *and a juniper-peppercorn crust season seared emu slices, served here with an oven-roasted potato.*

Emu—the big bird that tastes like beef

But it's leaner than chicken

"Emu *again*?" This just may be the cry in 21st-century homes. Australia's national bird—as impressive in size as the ostrich—has the flavor of lean beef, and it is lower in fat, calories, and cholesterol than skinned chicken.

Australian aborigines have long prized the emu not only for its meat but also for its oil (rendered from the fat), which they use as a skin softener and healing unguent. Emu oil is being used commercially in cosmetics, and the feathers play a role in fashion, feather dusters, and fishing lures. The cured hide makes a soft and supple leather. And the eggshells,

with eight layers of different colors, are carved into cameos.

New interest in emu meat is behind the rapid growth of the Western Emu Association, which now has close to 300 members, and the American Emu Association, which now has 5,000. Though the USDA has not yet approved domestically produced emu meat for sale, emus are being raised in this country, and breeding pairs cost big bucks. The flightless bird has quite a reputation: it is hardy and disease-resistant, adapts well to a range of climates and temperatures, and thrives on grain and insects. Emus have a high survival rate as chicks, and after a year they yield as much as 30 pounds of meat from the drum (upper leg), rump, and saddle (back). Unlike most birds, emus have no breast meat.

Order emu imported from Australia through a meat market, or from Polarica (Game), 105 Quint St., San Francisco 94124; (800) 426-3872. All cuts cost about $12 per pound plus shipping.

Because emu meat is very lean and firm, we find it to be most tender and moist if cut into slices and pounded thin, then cooked quickly at a high temperature.

Emu Medallions with Gin Sauce

Cooking time: About 25 minutes

Prep time: About 20 minutes

Notes: Up to 1 day ahead, prepare juniper-peppercorn paste and pound meat, then cover and chill. Overcooking makes emu tough.

Makes: 4 servings

- 2 tablespoons green peppercorns
- 1 tablespoon dried juniper berries
- 2 cloves garlic
- 1 tablespoon salad oil
  About 1¾ pounds emu
- 1 tablespoon butter or margarine
- ½ cup *each* beef broth and port
- 2 tablespoons minced shallots
- 1 tablespoon gin
- 1½ teaspoons cornstarch mixed smooth with 1 tablespoon water
  Chive spears and salt

1. *Juniper-peppercorn paste.* Combine peppercorns, juniper berries, and ½ cup water in a 1- to 1½-quart pan. Bring to a boil over high heat; simmer 5 minutes. Drain mixture in a fine strainer. Combine seasonings with garlic and oil in a blender or food processor; whirl until a smooth paste.

2. *Emu.* Trim off and discard silvery membrane on emu. Cut meat, across the grain as much as possible, into ½-inch-thick slices; then cut them into 12 to 14 equal portions.

3. Gently pound meat with a flat mallet between sheets of plastic wrap until slices are about ¼ inch thick. Rub slices evenly on both sides with juniper-peppercorn paste.

4. In a 10- to 12-inch nonstick frying pan over high heat, melt ½ the butter until it sizzles. Fill pan with meat; do not overlap slices. Turn slices as they brown; cook just until pink in center (cut to test), about 1½ minutes total. As slices are cooked, keep warm in a rimmed pan in a 300° oven. Melt remaining butter in pan, add meat, and continue until all slices are cooked.

5. When frying pan is empty, leave on high heat and quickly add broth, port, shallots, and gin. Boil until reduced to ½ cup, about 4 minutes. As sauce cooks, drain juices from cooked emu into it. Stir cornstarch mixture into sauce; stir until boiling. Arrange emu on plates, and pour sauce onto meat. Garnish with chives, and season to taste with salt.

Per serving: 347 cal., 25% (88 cal.) from fat; 47 g protein; 9.8 g fat (3.4 g sat.); 8.2 g carbo.; 177 mg sodium; 122 mg chol. ∎

By Christine Weber Hale

Broccoli bouquet makes a budding salad

FLOWERS ARE AN ATTRACTIVE ADDI-TION to salads, but their appeal is more to the eye than to the palate. Flower buds, on the other hand, can be real eatin' food: artichokes, broccoli, and cauliflower bear witness.

Broccoli is the major element in Walter Miller's Broccoli, Onion, and Bacon Salad. He uses not only the buds—or florets—of broccoli, but the stems, too. (He peels the stems so they will be equally tender.) The dressing is a sweet-sour blend of honey, mustard, and vinegar, along with the tiniest remnant of bacon drippings. Raisins accentuate the sweetness of the dressing.

Broccoli, Onion, and Bacon Salad

Cooking time: About 5 minutes
Prep time: 10 to 15 minutes
Notes: The broccoli stays green and fresh-looking for several hours after the salad is dressed.
Makes: 4 to 6 servings

    About 1½ pounds broccoli
1   mild red onion (4 to 5 oz.), thinly sliced
½   cup raisins
6   slices bacon (about 5 oz.)
¼   cup rice vinegar
2   teaspoons prepared mustard
3   tablespoons honey

1. Rinse broccoli. Cut off and thinly slice florets. Peel tender parts of broccoli stems and thinly slice; discard tough ends. Put broccoli, onion, and raisins in a bowl.
2. Brown the bacon in a 10- to 12-inch frying pan over medium heat; discard drippings but don't rinse pan. Drain bacon on paper towels; crumble when cool and

add to the broccoli salad.
3. To the pan in which bacon cooked, add vinegar, mustard, honey, and 2 tablespoons water. Stir to free browned bits, then pour dressing over broccoli. Mix and serve, or let stand up to 2 hours.

Per serving: 147 cal., 29% (43 cal.) from fat; 4.9 g protein; 4.8 g fat (1.6 g sat.); 24 g carbo.; 157 mg sodium; 6.6 mg chol.

Windsor, California

IN A CLASSIC RATATOUILLE, THE vegetables simmer gently over a very low fire or bake in a casserole for an extended period to blend flavors. Neither procedure is difficult, but both are time-consuming. Amber Barger uses modern technology, the microwave oven, to make a rapid ratatouille. Surprisingly, the speed doesn't inhibit traditional flavor bonds. You might, with justice, call the dish rat-a-tat-touille.

Rapid Ratatouille

Cooking time: 23 to 28 minutes, plus 5 minutes standing
Prep time: 20 to 25 minutes
Notes: To make a vegetable dish to go with other meat or fowl, omit the sausage. Instead of Italian herb mix, use ¼ teaspoon *each* dried basil and dried oregano.
Makes: 6 servings

1   red bell pepper (5 to 6 oz.), seeded and diced
1   green bell pepper (5 to 6 oz.), seeded and diced
1   onion (5 to 6 oz.), thinly sliced
1   eggplant (about 1 lb.), stem trimmed, cut into ¾-inch cubes
    About 1 pound zucchini, ends trimmed, thickly sliced
1   can (14½ oz.) Italian-style stewed tomatoes
½   teaspoon Italian herb seasoning mix
1   package (14 oz.) turkey kielbasa (Polish) sausage, thinly sliced

1. In a 4- to 5-quart microwave-safe casserole, combine red pepper, green pepper, onion, eggplant, zucchini, stewed tomatoes and their juices, and Italian seasoning.
2. Cover and cook on 100 percent power 10 minutes. Stir well, cover, and cook until vegetables are very tender when pierced, about 10 to 15 minutes longer.
3. Stir sausage into vegetables and cook, uncovered, about 3 minutes more. Let stand 5 minutes.
4. Spoon into wide soup plates.

Per serving: 167 cal., 30% (50 cal.) from fat; 14 g protein; 5.5 g fat (1.8 g sat.); 18 g carbo.; 840 mg sodium; 44 mg chol.

Carmichael, California
By Joan Griffiths, Richard Dunmire

Sunset's Kitchen Cabinet

Readers' family favorites tested in our kitchens

By Betsy Reynolds Bateson

DICK COLE

Quick Breakfast Braid

Sherry Sauers, Olympia, Washington

Over the last 30 years, Sherry Sauers has developed countless recipes to use her homegrown raspberries, blueberries, and cherries. Her family especially enjoys this jam-filled braid she makes from a simple, biscuitlike dough.

Cooking time: 20 minutes
Prep time: 15 minutes
Makes: 8 servings

  1 small (3 oz.) package cream cheese, cut into pieces
  ¼ cup butter or margarine, cut into pieces
  2 cups all-purpose flour
  1 tablespoon baking powder
  ⅔ cup low-fat milk
  ¾ cup fruit preserves or jam, such as raspberry or blueberry
  1 tablespoon powdered sugar

1. In a food processor or medium bowl, whirl (using pulses) or cut with a pastry blender the cream cheese, butter, all-purpose flour, and baking powder, until mixture resembles fine crumbs. If using a food processor, transfer mixture to a medium bowl. Slowly stir in milk until dough forms a soft ball.

2. Between 2 sheets of plastic wrap, roll dough into a 10- by 15-inch rectangle. Remove 1 layer of plastic, and invert dough onto a lightly greased 10- by 15-inch baking pan; if needed, push dough with fingers to fit pan. Spread preserves lengthwise down center in a 3-inch-wide band, leaving a ½-inch border without preserves at each end. With a sharp knife, about 3 inches apart on each long edge, make 3-inch-long slits from edge toward preserves. Alternating between sides, gently fold strips over preserves, overlapping ends in center to resemble a braid; pinch to secure strips.

3. Bake braid in a 400° oven until lightly browned, about 20 minutes. Cool slightly; dust with powdered sugar.

Per serving: 292 cal., 34% (99 cal.) from fat; 5 g protein; 11 g fat (6.2 g sat.); 46 g carbo.; 296 mg sodium; 28 mg chol.

Fast Fajitas

Charleen Borger, Beaverton, Oregon

After almost a dozen attempts, Charleen Borger came up with a streamlined fajita recipe that fits nicely into her busy schedule. She slices the flank steak first to reduce marinating time and increase flavor. Then, while the meat marinates, she prepares the vegetables and heats the tortillas. Her kids love the meal because they get to choose garnishes beyond the basic shredded lettuce and salsa. Their choices might include avocado, black beans, and sour cream.

Cooking time: About 20 minutes
Prep time: 30 minutes (includes marinating)
Makes: 4 servings

  1 flank steak (about 1 lb.)
  3 tablespoons *each* orange juice and red wine vinegar
  1 teaspoon *each* seasoned salt, dried oregano leaves, and dried cumin seed
  ¼ teaspoon hot chili sauce
  2 cloves garlic, minced
  1 onion, thickly sliced (about ¾ lb.)
  1 green or red bell pepper, halved, cored, and seeded
     About 2 teaspoons olive or salad oil
  6 warm burrito-size flour tortillas
     About 3 cups shredded iceberg lettuce
     Purchased salsa

1. Slice steak across grain ⅛ inch thick. Combine with juice, vinegar, seasoned salt, oregano, cumin, chili sauce, and garlic, coating evenly. Marinate 10 minutes or up to 1 hour.

2. Meanwhile, place onion and bell pepper on a broiler pan; broil 4 to 6 inches from heat, about 10 minutes, turning as needed to brown all sides evenly. Turn broiler off; close oven door. Let vegetables set 5 minutes; remove skin from pepper and slice.

3. In a 10- to 12-inch frying pan, heat 2 teaspoons oil over high heat. Add half of beef; stir-fry until barely pink, 3 to 5 minutes. Repeat with rest of beef; add more oil if needed. Place beef, onion, and pepper on a platter; serve with warm tortillas, lettuce, and salsa.

Per serving: 420 cal., 39% (162 cal.) from fat; 28 g protein; 18 g fat (5.9 g sat.); 36 g carbo.; 612 mg sodium; 59 mg chol.

Grapefruit and Avocado Salad

Christine Pickering, Tacoma, Washington

Her introduction to balsamic vinegar and goat cheese resulted in a refreshing winter salad that Christine Pickering and her husband enjoy with French bread and a glass of wine. She combines juicy pink grapefruit with avocado, mixed salad greens, and the cheese. And for just a touch of garlic, she lightly crushes a garlic clove, lets it sit in the vinaigrette while she's assembling the meal, then removes it before dressing the salad.

Prep time: About 40 minutes

Makes: 2 servings

- 6 cups (about 1/3 lb.) mixed salad greens
- 3 tablespoons balsamic or red wine vinegar
- 2 tablespoons olive oil
- 1 clove garlic, lightly crushed
- 1 teaspoon Dijon mustard
- 1 pink grapefruit (about 1 lb.)
- 1 avocado (about 10 oz.)
- 1/3 cup crumbled goat cheese (about 2 oz.)
- 2 green onions, ends trimmed and thinly sliced
  Crusty French bread

1. Rinse, drain, and chill greens. In a small bowl, whisk together vinegar, oil, garlic, and mustard. Cut off grapefruit peel and white membrane. Then cut between inner membranes and fruit to release segments, saving juice. Cut avocado in half, twist halves apart, and remove pit. Peel; cut each half into 8 slices. Drizzle juice over slices.

2. Distribute greens on 2 plates. Alternately arrange avocado and grapefruit on greens. Crumble cheese over salads; sprinkle with onions. Remove garlic from dressing; drizzle over salads. Serve with bread.

Per serving: 448 cal., 76% (342 cal.) from fat; 10 g protein; 38 g fat (10 g sat.); 22 g carbo.; 227 mg sodium; 22 mg chol.

Saffron Chicken with Rice

Susan Gutierrez, Fresno, California

Susan Gutierrez loves experimenting with foods and cooking techniques. So when a call to her Spanish great-aunt produced an old family recipe for peasant's paella—without seafood, but with plenty of flavor—Gutierrez did some alterations to make the recipe her own.

Cooking time: About 1 hour

Prep time: 25 minutes

Makes: 8 servings

- 2 cups long-grain white rice
- 1 onion, finely chopped
- 3 cloves garlic, minced
- 2 tablespoons olive oil
- 3 cups chicken broth
- 3 pounds skinless chicken thighs, cut into 16 pieces
- 1 red bell pepper, cored, seeded, and diced
- 1 can (8 oz.) tomato sauce
- 1 can (4 oz.) diced green chilies
- 1 teaspoon ground turmeric
- 1/2 teaspoon salt
- 1/2 teaspoon pepper
- 1/4 to 1/2 teaspoon saffron threads

1. In a 6- to 8-quart ovenproof pan over medium-high heat, cook long-grain white rice, finely chopped onion, and minced garlic in oil, stirring, until onion and rice are golden, about 12 minutes.

2. Add chicken broth, chicken pieces, diced bell pepper, tomato sauce, diced green chilies, turmeric, salt, pepper, and saffron threads; stir to blend flavors.

3. Bake, uncovered, in a 400° oven until rice has absorbed all liquid and top is golden brown, about 50 minutes.

Per serving: 436 cal., 23% (99 cal.) from fat; 39 g protein; 11 g fat (2.5 g sat.); 44 g carbo.; 588 mg sodium; 141 mg chol.

Low-fat Garlic Mashed Potatoes

Christopher A. Brickner, Lynnwood, Washington

It was natural for Christopher Brickner, who loves potatoes, to develop a great-tasting, low-fat potato dish. But he never expected stardom. That's what he got after family and friends encouraged him to enter his savory mashed potatoes in a TV station's recipe contest. This lightened potato classic with nonfat yogurt, dill, chives, and garlic made him a winner as well as a celebrity chef.

Cooking time: 1 hour

Prep time: 15 minutes

Makes: 8 servings

- 8 russet potatoes (about 4 lb.)
- 2 to 4 cloves garlic
- 2 quarts chicken broth
- 1 cup nonfat milk
- 1/2 cup unflavored nonfat yogurt
- 2 tablespoons thinly sliced chives
- 1 tablespoon minced fresh dill
- 1 teaspoon salt
  White pepper
- 1/2 cup shredded reduced-fat jack cheese (about 2 oz.)
  Fresh chives or dill sprigs

1. Peel and quarter potatoes. Place with garlic in a 6- to 8-quart pan; cover with broth. Bring to a boil over high heat; reduce heat, cover, and simmer until potatoes are tender when pierced, about 20 minutes.

2. Drain potatoes and garlic; return to pan. Mash with milk until smooth. Stir in yogurt, chives, dill, and salt; add pepper to taste. Spoon mixture into a 2- to 3-quart shallow baking dish; sprinkle top with cheese. If making ahead, cover with plastic wrap and chill up to 1 day.

3. Bake in a 375° oven until warm in center and melted cheese is lightly browned, about 30 minutes (about 1 hour if chilled). Garnish with chives or dill sprigs.

Per serving: 230 cal., 16% (37 cal.) from fat; 11 g protein; 4.1 g fat (1.7 g sat.); 41 g carbo.; 488 mg sodium; 5.9 mg chol.

FOOD

Guide

BY JERRY ANNE DI VECCHIO

A TASTE OF THE WEST: Roast pork loin

The spur-of-the-moment spirit in our house usually surfaces about 10 A.M. on Saturday. We pick up the phone to check in with Sally and Gil, Jackie and John, Josie and Bailey, or other friends. Next thing you know, a dinner party is in the works.

Of course we're unprepared, so we shop quickly and with a strategy. This time of year we like dinners from the oven. You put the foods in, you take them out. No constant jumping up and down. And one of our most dependable oven dinners starts with a boned pork loin roast. You can buy it cut to preferred length, and because it's skinny, it cooks fast—regardless of weight (a center-cut roast may be as long as 24 inches). No carving skill is required, and cold leftovers make the best sandwiches.

Flexibility is another asset of this meal. The pork can go into the oven as the doorbell rings—a plus when we know guests have to deal with unpredictable traffic.

In the hour of cooking, there's time to visit, sip a pleasant wine, and begin with appetizers and a salad.

With the meat, we also roast the vegetables. Years ago, in Rome, I was introduced to pork's affinity for fennel—as well as sage—when both were used to season a memorable suckling pig. So sage goes onto the meat, while thick slices of fresh fennel go into the oven along with onion halves. Both vegetables get sweet, soft, and browned. It's surprising how far beyond potatoes you can go.

Roasted Pork, Fennel, and Onions

Cooking time: About 1 hour
Prep time: 10 to 15 minutes
Notes: Be sure to specify a single pork loin roast; occasionally, butchers roll 2 loins together to make a bigger roast. If

A peppery rub coats roasted pork, which is topped with sage leaves and served with peas and roasted fennel and onions.

DAVID DUNCAN LIVINGSTON

FEBRUARY

- Oven smarts for relaxed entertaining
- Choosing and using California cherimoyas
- Are reserve wines worth the price?

you have a large oven, meat and vegetables can cook at the same time. If you don't have enough space, cook the vegetables first, then reheat for 10 minutes before serving. If fresh sage is not available, add ½ teaspoon rubbed sage to the cumin and pepper mix. Accompany with hot peas.

Makes: 6 to 8 servings

> 2 tablespoons butter or olive oil (optional)
>
> About 1 cup fresh sage leaves (optional)
>
> 1½ tablespoons black peppercorns
>
> 2 teaspoons cumin seed
>
> 1 boned, fat-trimmed, rolled and tied center-cut pork loin roast (2¾ to 3 lb.)
>
> 3 or 4 red onions (about 3 in. wide)
>
> 2 or 3 fennel heads (3 to 4 in. wide) with feathery tops
>
> About 2 tablespoons olive oil
>
> 1½ cups orange juice
>
> ½ cup chicken broth
>
> 1 tablespoon balsamic vinegar
>
> Salt

1. Melt butter in a 6- to 8-inch frying pan over medium-high heat. Add ½ cup sage leaves and stir until leaves are slightly darker green and crisp, about 1 minute. Transfer with a slotted spoon to towels to drain. When leaves are cool, wrap in towels and seal in a plastic bag (they soften unwrapped). Save butter.

2. Finely grind peppercorns and cumin in a blender or spice grinder.

3. Rinse pork and pat dry; rub pepper mixture all over the meat. Tuck remaining sage leaves equally under the strings on the smooth (fattiest) side of roast. Set the

pork, herb side up, on a rack in a 10- by 15-inch pan.

4. Cut onions in half crosswise; don't peel. Trim off feathery fennel tops and reserve. Trim any bruises or dark spots from fennel. Rinse, then slice each vertically to make 3 or 4 equal slices.

5. Pour oil into a 10- to 12- by 15- to 17-inch rimmed pan and tilt to coat. Turn onions cut side down in pan. Turn fennel slices in pan to coat with oil.

6. Put roast on middle rack in a 400° oven. Drizzle fennel with ¾ cup orange juice. Set vegetables on rack beneath pork. Bake until fennel slices are browned lightly on the bottom, about 35 minutes, then turn slices. Continue to cook with onions until both vegetables are browned on the bottom, about 20 minutes longer. If drippings in pan get dark enough to scorch, pour a couple of tablespoons water onto them and tilt pan to distribute moisture. Bake pork until a thermometer inserted in the center reaches 145°, about 45 minutes.

7. Transfer meat to a large platter and keep warm; let stand at least 10 minutes. Add 2 tablespoons water to vegetables and tilt pan to distribute moisture; leave in pan and keep warm.

8. Remove rack and discard fat, then add reserved butter, remaining ¾ cup orange juice, broth, and vinegar to roast pan. Boil on high heat, stirring to release browned drippings, until reduced to about ½ cup, about 10 minutes. Drain juices from pork into pan.

9. Arrange onions and fennel with pork. If desired, add some of the feathery greens from fennel tops. Sprinkle with the fried sage leaves. Slice roast and serve with vegetables and sauce. Add salt to taste.

Per serving: 308 cal., 35% (108 cal.) from fat; 37 g protein; 12 g fat (3.2 g sat.); 13 g carb.; 157 mg sodium; 98 mg chol.

SEASONAL NOTE

Cherimoya, the ice cream fruit

I first ate my fill of cherimoyas in Chile. With each encounter, I found myself trying to pinpoint the elusive flavors—overtly, a blend of banana and pineapple, more subtly, strawberry and vanilla, and more.

In Chile, cherimoyas are as common as apples. And in even the most out-of-the-way spots, we had them for dessert or at breakfast, sliced into bowls of orange juice. The juice goes well with

the fruit, but more important, it keeps the white flesh from darkening.

Cherimoyas are smooth and round or slightly heart-shaped, with a green, almost reptilian-looking skin. The flesh is so creamy and smooth, despite the big shiny seeds in it, that nicknames like custard apple and ice cream fruit make sense.

The Incas grew them, as they did tomatoes and potatoes. But cherimoyas haven't had the same worldwide impact, probably because they are very fragile and fussy about their growing environment. But they have found land to their liking in Southern California,

Cherimoya and orange slices make an easy, refreshing dessert or salad.

and the output increases each year. The season runs from November through late May and sometimes into June. The winter peak is just coming on and lasts into April. However, you'll find cherimoyas year-round at produce stands or supermarkets with a good variety of produce. (Chilean fruit fills in during our off-season.)

When ready to eat, cherimoyas give to gentle pressure, just like a ripe peach. If you buy a firm, unripe cherimoya, it should be an even green color with no soft spots or other signs of bruising. Let it ripen, unwrapped, at room temperature. If you chill the fruit, it stops ripening. But once it's soft, you can chill it three to four days. Here's a curious way to check a cherimoya—cut a tiny slit through the skin. If the fruit isn't ready, the slit usually seals, and ripening continues.

Cherimoyas tend to be expensive, as much as $4 to $5 a pound, and California fruit average ¾ to 1 pound. For value, combine cherimoya slices with orange segments in orange juice. For a flavor fillip, I also like a squeeze of lime juice or a splash of orange liqueur.

Per ⅓ pound peeled cherimoya: 141 cal., 4% (5.4 cal.) from fat; 1.9 g protein; 0.6 g fat (0 g sat.); 40 g carbo.; 0 mg sodium; 0 mg chol.

NEWS NOTE
A bottle worth keeping

Leonard Cohen is an affable fellow from Avila Beach, California, where he and his father own the Olde Port Inn at the end of the pier. Leonard is the chef, but he has also added winemaking to his list of tasks, and he's busy tweaking tradition. Instead of putting wine in a standard bottle, he's using tall, square 750-ml bottles that are imprinted with fish. His rationale for using cornered bottles: this is earthquake country, and round bottles roll. Square bottles also take up less space on shelves. Logically, he's named the winery Four Corners Cellars.

Leonard dropped by with several bottles to sample, and the wine is certainly quaffable. Right now, distribution is only in California, Hawaii, and Texas; call (800) 800-5599 for a source. There's only one problem. It's hard to toss such nice-looking bottles. I want to fill them with vinegars and oils, and I have only so much counter space.

What do you get with reserve?

About private reserve, *riserva, gran' reserva,* reserve whatever: unless you mean to hoard your finest red wines for years, think twice before you shell out the extra money, because the profits—if any—are tied to patience.

Most vintners in Italy's Chianti Classico and Spain's Rioja have long since settled on vineyards that produce slow-starting but long-lived wines for their reserves. On top of that, the winemaking concentrates on durability at the expense of early charm.

Laws require producers to keep Chianti Classico Riserva in the winery one year longer than they hold Chianti Classico. Rioja Reserva and Gran' Reserva must wait even longer compared with quickly ready Crianza. But no winery is required to wait until its reserves have come to full flower.

One instructive set of prices: Marchesi Antinori has friendly-now Santa Cristina for $7, the slightly sterner Villa Antinori Chianti Classico Riserva for $11, and the regal Riserva from Badia a Passignano for $30.

For their part, made-in-America reserves provide a contradictory group of stories. With neither laws to limit them nor tradition in the vineyards to guide them, vintners here let *reserve* mean whatever they want it to mean. The word goes on everything.

Alas, too many home-grown reserves come from the more-is-better school, the one that believes Sophia Loren would be more beautiful if she were 8-foot-6. Most such reserves are better put on the auction circuit to raise money for charity than drunk.

A few wineries do make the sort of slow-starting, long-lasting reserves that live up to their name. Two examples: true-to-type, ready-now Louis M. Martini North Coast Cabernet Sauvignon goes for $8, its richer Napa Valley Reserve for $14. Clos du Val's Stags Leap District Cabernet Sauvignon costs $20, its lustrous Estate Reserve $35 to $45.

Can any reserve be worth such premiums? To a collector, you bet. (Squirrel a truly age-worthy reserve away for 5 to 10 years, and it will repay cost and wait with qualities and character a soon-faded youthful charmer never had.) But to everyone looking for a wine for now, heck no. ∎

Of the Pacific's gifts to our tables, the Dungeness crab is the most improbably delicious. Carapaced and truculent, it scuttles like a refugee from a sci-fi flick. But once resting on a plate, no seafood is more succulent.

Cancer magister, the Dungeness's scientific name, in Latin means *chief* or *master crab,* neatly evoking the regard in which we hold it. The Dungie derives its everyday name from a sand spit on Washington's Olympic Peninsula, but the crab is a far-flung species, at home on shallow ocean bottoms from central California to the Aleutians. Crab populations fluctuate from year to year, but overall, the West Coast harvests about as much crab as it ever has.

Still, it often seems that Dungeness were once more abundant than they are now—or maybe it's just that there were fewer crab fans around to compete for them. In *The*

KEVIN CANDLAND

A CRAB LOVER'S GUIDE

★ HOW TO EAT, COOK, AND CATCH

DUNGENESS AT ITS PEAK ★

♥

Egg and I, her funny account of Olympic Peninsula life in the 1930s, Betty MacDonald recalls buying Dungeness for a dollar a gunnysackful. Today you could put a down payment on a car with that gunnysack, but price is apparently little object when it comes to Dungeness crab. Christopher Plemmons, chef at Seattle's Women's University Club, recalls what happened when cost concerns led him to pull crab from his menu: "I almost got fired."

February is a particularly appropriate time for Dungeness crab. Like a midwinter plunge into the Pacific, crab fulfills a seasonal desire for the clean, cold taste of the sea. In this valentine month, the Dungeness resembles a lover's heart: guarded on the outside, tender within, a fortress willing to surrender to finesse, romance, and a splash of champagne.

By Peter Fish

The Perfect Roasted Crab

I'M ADDICTED to the roasted garlic crab at Tra Vigne, a restaurant in St. Helena, in the heart of California's Napa Valley.

Each year I can barely wait until the glorious Dungeness makes its first appearance on restaurant tables. And I anticipate with almost as much pleasure its perfect companion, Trefethen Napa Valley Dry Riesling.

Tra Vigne's garlic crab has all the essentials. It's fresh. It's delicious. And it's messy—at least half the fun is licking the spicy, garlicky sauce from shells and fingers, or mopping it up with crusty French bread. Sometimes I ask for the sauce to be served on the side, which gives me a little more control and requires fewer napkins.

When there are two of us, we've been known to split a large crab and a Caesar salad—ensuring the enjoyment of a double garlic fix.

BY HAROLYN THOMPSON

Tra Vigne's Roasted Garlic Crab

Cooking time: About 1 ½ hours (includes 40 minutes to bring water to a boil to cook live crabs)

Prep time: About 25 minutes

Notes: For the best results, boil live crabs yourself in a large kettle before roasting. If you're squeamish or short on time, you can roast fresh-cooked, cleaned, cracked crab from the market.

Makes: 4 servings

- 1 cup distilled white vinegar
- ½ cup salt
- 1 lemon, quartered

CRAIG MAXWELL

¼ cup pickling spice

1½ teaspoons hot chili flakes

4 live Dungeness crabs (about 1¾ pounds each) or 4 cooked, cleaned, cracked Dungeness crabs (about 5 lb. total)

½ cup mayonnaise

¼ cup fresh lemon juice

1 teaspoon ground New Mexico chili or regular chili powder

6 tablespoons butter

⅓ cup extra-virgin olive oil

3 tablespoons minced garlic

¼ cup minced Italian parsley

Parsley sprigs (optional)

Lemon wedges (optional)

Crusty French bread

1. If using purchased cooked, cleaned, cracked crab, skip to Step 6 (and omit first 5 ingredients). In a 12- to 16-quart kettle, combine 2 gallons water with vinegar, salt, lemon quarters, pickling spice, and chili flakes. Bring to a boil over high heat, about 40 minutes.

2. Pick up a crab, holding body from rear; plunge headfirst into boiling liquid. Repeat with a second crab. Cover pan, and cook 10 minutes (when boil resumes, reduce heat to maintain a gentle boil). With tongs, lift out crabs; place on backs to drain. Repeat with remaining 2 crabs.

3. When crabs are cool enough to touch, pull off and discard triangular belly tabs. Turn crabs over; lift off shells from rear and break off tiny front paddles on bodies. Scoop creamy mixture (crab butter and juices) from shells and reserve. Rinse back shells; save for garnish.

4. On body section, pull off and discard red membranes. Scoop and save crab butter from bodies; pull off soft gills and discard. Rinse bodies well, and twist off legs; then crack legs along shell edge, using a nutcracker or small wooden mallet. With a knife, cut bodies into quarters.

5. Push reserved crab butter and juices from crabs through a wire sieve; add strained butter to a 2- to 3-quart pan over medium-high heat. Cook until thick and reduced to about ½ cup, about 15 minutes. Cool; mix ¼ to ½ cup cooled crab butter (according to taste) with mayonnaise, 1 tablespoon lemon juice, and ground chili. Chill until ready to serve.

6. In a 12- by 17-inch roasting pan, combine butter, oil, and garlic. In a 500° oven, heat mixture just until hot, about 2 minutes. Add cracked crab pieces; stir to coat all pieces. Roast just until garlic is golden and crab is hot, about 10 minutes. (If you bought cooked crab, stir together mayonnaise, 1 tablespoon lemon juice, and ground chili.)

7. Sprinkle minced parsley and remaining lemon juice over hot crab and pan juices; stir to coat all pieces.

8. Spoon crab pieces and pan juices onto a large platter for family-style dining, or arrange pieces of 1 crab on each of 4 dinner plates. Garnish servings with parsley sprigs, lemon wedges, and back shells. Serve immediately with crab butter–mayonnaise mixture or seasoned mayonnaise, and warm, crusty French bread.

Per serving: 690 cal., 78% (540 cal.) from fat; 34 g protein; 60 g fat (17 g sat.); 6.5 g carbo.; 904 mg sodium; 175 mg chol.

HOW TO EAT A CRAB

PEOPLE TACKLE cracked crab in two ways: pick-and-eat or pile-it-up-then-eat. The method used is telling.

Philosophically, pick-and-eaters are much more inclined to take life as it comes, rolling with the punches. Financially, the old hand-to-mouth routine—existing on cash flow—is your style. And environmental sensitivity is irrefutable if you use your fingers to snap cracked shells apart and then pull sweet white chunks from leg and body sections with the tip of a crab leg. You also savor the soft, creamy crab fat and butter.

This is me.

Across the table is the other approach. His is not lackadaisical. Control, control. All the crab meat he wants is on the plate before he takes a bite—the big payoff. And he's deep into high tech: crab cracker and lobster pick must be at hand before a finger is lifted. Needless to say, I get his share of the "soft stuff"—the fat and butter.

Do we worry what friends think as we so blatantly perform? Do they hesitate to expose their inner selves before us? Hardly. Instead, they puzzle—usually aloud—"How can you bear to eat crab 'that' way?"

Who can decide what's best? Does it matter? In the end, there's just a pile of empty shells.

BY JERRY ANNE DI VECCHIO

WINES FOR CRAB

THE SWEET TASTE of pure crab rises to new powers in the company of a ringingly fruity Riesling. For sweeter alternatives to the dry Trefethen mentioned on the facing page, look for *Smith-Madrone Napa Valley Riesling, Paul Thomas Columbia Valley Johannisberg Riesling,* or *Geyser Peak North Coast Soft Johannisberg Riesling.* If your crab swims in a rich sauce from its own butter or something kindred, seek out *De Loach Russian River Valley Chardonnay, Cuvaison Napa Valley–Carneros Chardonnay,* or any other with no more than a faint hint of oak aging.

BY BOB THOMPSON

Serious crabbers head by boat to the best spots. Novices may prefer trying their luck from a pier or dock.

JOSHUA GREENE

HOW TO CATCH A CRAB

FOR CRABBING, there may not be a better spot in Oregon than Newport. Yaquina Bay supplies the crabs, and the town's waterfront supplies the pier, crab pot rentals, and bait. Show up any-time during store hours, crab as long as you want, and have the crabs cooked on the waterfront before you leave. No mess, no hassle, and plenty of local shops for the noncrabbers in your bunch: sounds easy.

But it helps to get some friendly advice. Mine comes from Randy Hatman of Newport Tradewinds, a char-ter operation next door to the Abbey Street Pier. Randy offers more than bait. When I stopped in for supplies, he wrin-kled his brow. "Crabbing is best on an incoming tide," he said, running his fin-ger down the tide table, "and this one is headed out. We rent crab pots or rings for 24 hours at a time ($5, plus $30 deposit) because tides fluctuate."

Having said this, he took a long look at my wife, Anna, and our four kids—all impatient for different reasons—and pulled out the gear and fish-carcass bait. "Watch out for the sea lions" were his parting words.

Now, if we'd been serious crabbers, we'd have rented a motorboat and three rings ($45 to about $55 for a half-day, with bait) at the Embarcadero Bait Shop (503/265-5435) or at Newport Marina Store and Charters (867-4470) across the bay, had them map out the bay's hot spots, and probably caught the limit in a few hours. We aren't and we didn't.

Instead, we dropped the pot off the pier. In an instant a pair of sea lions pointed their whiskers at the splash and submerged. Five minutes later Randy and I were having another talk. "Wire the bait under the bottom of the trap this time, instead of inside it, and you might succeed."

We baited up again and tossed the pot into the bay. The sea lions were on it in 4 seconds. We checked the trap. Randy was right: the bait was still there.

Soon Anna left to wander among the shops and galleries along Bay Boulevard. And the kids abandoned me and the pot in favor of a kite store.

I pulled up the trap and released a large female Dungeness crab—you can take only males—as the tide continued to fall. Eventually we took the crab pot back to Randy. "Come up empty?" he asked. "Not really," I said. "But the crabs are safe for another day."

We ambled down to the Embarcadero and out onto the dock, where crab cook-ers steamed. Had we caught legal crabs, we'd have paid $3 a dozen to cook them here. Embarcadero Bait Shop will sell you a cube of butter, for dipping, that you soften in their microwave.

That's if you succeed. If you don't, keep walking: Embarcadero Seafood Restaurant, just down the dock, often offers an excellent house specialty that's not on the menu: fresh local Dungeness crab. As I said, this is easy. In a place like Newport, even when you lose, you win.

BY JIM MCCAUSLAND

GOING TO THE SOURCE

THE DUNGENESS SPIT—at 5½ miles—is the largest natural sand spit in the nation; it hooks into the Strait of Juan de Fuca from the northeast coastline of Washington's Olympic Peninsula. The spit has been a national wildlife refuge since 1915 and is a popular hiking area rich with dunlin, sanderlings, and waterfowl at this time of year. Crabbing near the spit may be limited in the future to protect the wildlife. However, you'll find early-morning crab pots boiling—and plenty of crab on the menu—at The 3 Crabs restaurant, a longtime fixture on the beach. One-hundred-year-old Groveland Cottage, a B&B, dominates the tiny village of Dungeness nearby. For brochures to help plan a visit, call (800) 942-4042.

The delicious cooked crab hoisted by server Theresa Rubens at The 3 Crabs restaurant (left) gets its name from the Dungeness spit (right) off the northeast coast of Washington's Olympic Peninsula.

RICH FRISHMAN

ROSS HAMILTON

SPOTS FOR A GOOD CATCH

NOVICE CRABBERS can try their luck from piers or docks, or boats. Along the Oregon coast, marinas often have crabbing packages—small boats, crab rings, and bait—that accommodate four or five people. Plan to reserve in advance if you're going on a busy weekend. Deposits on gear are often required; bait costs $1 to $2.50. California and Washington require a recreational crabbing license, sold at marinas and bait shops. Below are some places to start; or you can check with the chamber of commerce at your coastal destination.

KEVIN CANDLAND

★**ANACORTES AND GUEMES ISLAND, WA.** Crab at the public pier just off the north end of Commercial Street in Anacortes, which is 1½ hours northwest of Seattle. Call the Port of Anacortes (360/293-3134) for a schedule; some days the pier is closed. Bait and traps are available at Cap Sante Marine in the Cap Sante Marina. For a longer getaway, take a 5-minute ride on the Guemes Island Ferry (at the west end of Sixth Street in Anacortes) to Guemes Island Resort (360/293-6643), where guests can crab off the beach. Cabins start at $75 (two-night minimum); crabbing gear rents for $4 a day.

★**WESTPORT, WA.** On Washington's southwestern coast 22 miles

southwest of Aberdeen, there's good crabbing in Westport's inner harbor. You can crab off any of the floats or docks. Rings and bait are available at the Hungry Whale Grocery (360/268-0136) on Montesano Avenue, the town's main street, and at Neptune Charters (268-0124) across from Float 14.

★**GARIBALDI, OR.** There's year-round crabbing on large Tillamook Bay about 75 miles west of Portland. Crab off the public pier at Garibaldi; rent rings ($3 each) and get bait from Pier's End (503/322-0383). At Garibaldi Marina in the public boat basin, you can rent a 16-foot boat ($30) and rings ($3 each) and get bait; call 322-3312. About 6 miles west of Tillamook, at the Bay Shore RV Park and Marina (842-7774) on Netarts Bay, you can rent a 16-foot boat (with two traps and bait) for 3 hours for $31.

★**WALDPORT, OR.** About 15 miles south of Newport on the central Oregon coast, you can crab from the Port of Alsea docks or rent a boat to crab on Alsea Bay. Dock of the Bay Marina rents gear, and offers a 15-foot boat, three rings, and bait for 3 hours for $40. Call (503) 563-2003 for details.

★**CRESCENT CITY, CA.** You can crab off the B Street pier in this city about 20 miles south of the Oregon border. Popeye's Landing, a bait house near the pier's entrance, rents crab traps.

BY JENA MACPHERSON

CRAIG MAXWELL

The Ultimate Crab Cake

MAKING THE PERFECT crab cake is not as difficult as you might think. The secret? Less is more, except for the crab meat. Crab needs only a few seasonings to complement its naturally sweet flavor. So if you break open a crab cake and the crab itself is invisible, you know you're heading for trouble.

With just one bite you can see, and savor, the crab in this cake. A light sauce with a touch of lemon plays up the crab, but does not dominate, and a mixture of greens served alongside makes a refreshing accompaniment.

BY BETSY REYNOLDS BATESON

Great Western Crab Cakes

Cooking time: About 15 minutes

Prep time: About 20 minutes

Notes: Buy cooked crab the day you use it; the fresher it is, the sweeter the flavor.

Makes: 4 servings

3/4 cup *each* dry white wine and chicken broth

1/4 cup fresh lemon juice

2 teaspoons cornstarch

1 teaspoon sugar

About 2 tablespoons butter

1/3 cup mayonnaise

2 large eggs

1/2 cup thinly sliced green onions

1/4 cup *each* minced red bell pepper and thinly sliced celery

2 tablespoons Dijon mustard

1 clove garlic, pressed

1/8 teaspoon cayenne

1 pound shelled cooked crab

8 cups mixed salad greens, rinsed and crisped (about 1/2 lb.)

Lemon wedges (optional)

1. To make lemon sauce, in a 2- to 3-quart pan bring wine and broth to a boil over high heat; reduce mixture to 3/4 cup, about 6 minutes. Mix together juice, cornstarch, and sugar; slowly stir into broth mixture. Continue to stir until sauce boils, about 10 seconds. Stir in 2 teaspoons butter; keep sauce warm until used.

2. To make crab cakes, in a large bowl combine mayonnaise, eggs, green onions, bell pepper, celery, mustard, garlic, and cayenne; stir until well combined. Pat cooked crab dry on paper towels, then gently fold into mayonnaise mixture.

3. Melt 2 teaspoons butter in each of 2 nonstick 10- to 12-inch frying pans over medium-high heat (or use 1 pan and cook two batches). Spoon 6 mounds of crab mixture (about 2 rounded tablespoons each) into each pan; gently spread with back of spoon into 2 1/2-inch-diameter cakes. Cook until bottoms are lightly browned, about 4 minutes. With a wide spatula, carefully turn cakes over; cook to brown other sides, about 4 minutes more. Transfer 3 cakes to each of 4 plates.

4. Mix greens with 1/3 cup lemon sauce, and place a generous serving next to cakes on each plate. Spoon remaining sauce around cakes. Garnish with lemon.

Per serving: 407 cal., 55% (225 cal.) from fat; 28 g protein; 25 g fat (6.9 g sat.); 8.5 g carbo.; 727 mg sodium; 246 mg chol. ∎

KEVIN CANDLAND

A Mushroom Soup Your Mother Never Made

Cooking time: About 35 minutes

Prep time: About 30 minutes

Notes: The combination of puréed mushrooms and potatoes gives the soup its creaminess. For puréeing, a blender is much more effective than a food processor.

Makes: About 10 cups, 5 servings

- ¾ cup (1 oz.) dried porcini mushrooms
- 5 cups hot chicken broth
- 1¼ pounds fresh mushrooms, sliced
- 1 cup chopped onion
- ½ cup dry white wine
- 2 cups peeled, chopped russet potatoes
- ¼ cup chopped parsley, plus sprigs
- ¼ teaspoon ground nutmeg
- 2½ cups low-fat (1% milkfat) or nonfat milk
- 4 ounces seeded or plain slender baguette (2 in. across), sliced ⅓ inch thick
- 4 ounces chive-flavored or plain soft fresh goat cheese

1. In a bowl, soak porcini in broth until pliable, about 15 minutes. Swish porcini to loosen any grit, then lift out.

2. In a 5- to 6-quart pan over high heat, frequently stir soaked porcini, fresh mushrooms, onion, and ¼ cup wine until mushrooms are dry and juices stick to pan and turn deep brown, about 10 minutes. Stir in remaining wine, and repeat browning process, 2 to 3 minutes. Lift out and reserve about 8 mushroom slices.

3. To pan add broth (discard any grit in bottom of bowl), potatoes, 3 tablespoons chopped parsley, and nutmeg. Simmer, covered, until mushrooms are very tender when pierced, about 20 minutes. Add milk; stir until steaming, about 4 minutes.

4. Meanwhile, place bread in a rimmed 10- by 15-inch baking pan; broil 3 inches from heat until golden, 1 to 2 minutes. Turn bread, spread with half of goat cheese, and broil until cheese melts, about 1 minute. Sprinkle with remaining chopped parsley.

5. In a blender, whirl soup and remaining cheese a portion at a time into a smooth purée. Ladle into bowls, and garnish with reserved mushrooms and parsley sprigs. Serve with toast.

Per serving: 306 cal., 29% (90 cal.) from fat; 18 g protein; 10 g fat (5.1 g sat.); 42 g carbo.; 412 mg sodium; 15 mg chol. ∎

A better mushroom soup

MY FRIEND BUNNIE RUSSELL recently served me a beautifully smooth and creamy pumpkin soup. What's the secret to the velvety texture, I wanted to know. "All you do is cook pumpkin with milk and put it in the blender," she said. That's it? "Oh, and you add ½ cup heavy cream at the end. But it's funny, the soup was just as thick before I added the cream."

Aha! Since then my blender's been on high as I explore how the simple technique of puréeing cooked vegetables creates richly satisfying soups without any cream or butter-flour roux for thickening.

Naturally smooth vegetables like squash and potato work well, and if cooked until tender, so do crisper vegetables such as carrots (great whirled with roasted red peppers and a little nonfat sour cream), cauliflower, corn, and mushrooms.

If the canned variety is your only experience with mushroom soup, the intensely "mushroomy" flavor of this soup, with dried porcini to augment the fresh mushrooms, may come as a surprise. A little goat cheese whirled into the soup (and spread on toast for nibbling) rounds out flavors—and boosts protein to make this a complete meal with salad.

WE'D LIKE TO HEAR FROM YOU!

Do you have tips or recipes for low-fat cooking? Write to Everyday Low-fat Cooking, Sunset Magazine, 80 Willow Rd., Menlo Park, CA 94025, or send e-mail (including your full name and street address) to lowfat@sunsetpub.com.

Lasagne, any way you want it

*It doesn't have to take forever, it doesn't have to have meat,
it doesn't even have to have pasta*

NORMAN A. PLATE

WITH TWO BUSY SONS, A STRONG commitment to community activities, and lots of family and friends, Betsy Stafford often needs a fast dinner for a crowd at home in Sausalito, California. Most recently, her older son's opera group was expected right after a concert. Big appetites are the norm in this crowd, which includes a few vegetarians. Stafford's solution? Party-size casseroles of frozen lasagne from the supermarket—one with meat sauce, and one with layers of vegetables and tomato sauce.

Stafford has found that the purchased product is well received, and she's not alone. Market research indicates that spending for frozen lasagne increased 10 percent last year.

But her solution prompts a question: Why can't home-cooked lasagne be fast and easy?

Touring the grocery aisles with a purpose, I gathered a number of ready-to-use ingredients suited to lasagne. Back in the kitchen, it took just 15 minutes from shopping bag to pan for my lasagne to be oven-ready. Within the same hour, it was on the table—less time than the frozen product takes to heat.

So kiss good-bye the myth that lasagne has to take a lot of time—that's history.

Lasagne is undergoing other changes as well. Vegetables have become familiar stand-ins for meat, and fish lasagnes have their followings, too. Even the pasta can be replaced: creamy polenta is an option that fits right into the mix of flavors.

But there's still something to be said for the most classic preparations of this soul-soothing dish. Primo Lasagne, with its elegant marriage of rich tomato and porcini mushroom sauce, Italian sausages, and creamy béchamel, more than merits a few hours' effort for a special occasion.

Green salad, hot bread, and dessert make any lasagne menu a winner.

One-hour Lasagne

Cooking time: 45 to 50 minutes

Prep time: About 15 minutes, plus at least 5 minutes to cool

Notes: To keep prep time tight, put pasta water on to boil, then assemble filling. Use smoked sausages (they don't need cooking), thaw spinach in the microwave oven, and buy shredded and grated cheeses.

To cut time while assembling by 15 minutes, use uncooked pasta and add 1⅓ cups water to the sauce. Bake, tightly covered, in a 375° oven until the noodles are tender when pierced, about 1 hour.

If making ahead, cover unbaked lasagne and chill up to 1 day. Bake, covered, until lasagne is hot (at least 140°) in the center, about 40 minutes for either cooked or uncooked pasta.

Makes: 8 servings

- 1 package (8 oz.) dried lasagne pasta
- ½ pound smoked or cooked Polish (pork or turkey kielbasa) sausages, finely chopped, or 2 cans (5 oz. each) sliced mushrooms, drained
- 1 jar (28 to 32 oz., about 3½ cups) pasta, marinara, or spaghetti sauce
- 1 package (10 oz.) frozen chopped spinach, thawed
- 1 carton (15 oz., about 2 cups) nonfat or low-fat ricotta cheese
- 2 cups (½ lb.) shredded mozzarella cheese
- ½ cup grated parmesan cheese

Lasagne logistics: 10 savvy tips

1. Use instant dried lasagne pasta. These thin sheets soften quickly as they bake with the fillings. Usually, regular sauces are diluted to provide needed liquid; check pasta package directions for recipe adjustments.

2. Don't cook dried pasta. For each ½ pound dried lasagne pasta, add 1⅓ cups additional liquid, such as water or broth,

HOW MUCH LASAGNE *makes a serving?*
Calculate portions of Primo Lasagne
(recipe on page 36)—and any other
lasagne—by the inch. One of the tips
below tells you how.

to the sauce. The lasagne goes together faster, but it takes about twice as long to bake, and it must be tightly covered. When pasta pierces easily and center is hot, the lasagne is ready.

3. Freshen flavor of purchased tomato pasta sauce. Add to taste chopped fresh or dried herbs (basil, oregano, rosemary, thyme), minced garlic, dried chili flakes, or sautéed chopped onion.

4. Start with packaged shredded or grated cheeses.

5. Skip browning. Use cooked meats—

smoked or ready-to-eat sausages, ham, poultry—and canned mushrooms.

6. Think unstructured. Don't layer lasagne. Mix pasta with sauce, dollop with cheese elements, putting the ones that melt on top, then bake.

7. Bake just until hot. Use an instant-read thermometer to check center temperature; at 140°, ingredients are steaming.

8. Avoid slippage. For neater servings, give baked lasagne a few minutes to firm, then cut portions with a sharp knife and lift out with a wide spatula.

9. Plan portions by the inch. About 12 square inches (a 3- by 4-inch section) of a 1½- to 2-inch-thick lasagne makes an adequate serving.

10. Multiply for crowds. To make lasagne for 16, double the pasta lasagnes in this story, and assemble in a 10- by 14-inch pan or casserole that's at least 2¼ inches deep. If lasagne is not refrigerated, add 10 to 15 minutes to baking time. If lasagne is chilled, or pasta is uncooked, add about 30 minutes to cooking time.

POPULAR POLENTA *replaces pasta in this departure from the classic layered lasagne.*

1. In a 5- to 6-quart pan, add pasta to 3 quarts boiling water. Cook until barely tender to bite, 8 to 10 minutes. Drain, and immerse in cold water.

2. As water heats and pasta cooks, mix the sausages with sauce.

3. Squeeze liquid out of spinach. Mix spinach with ricotta cheese.

4. Drain pasta.

5. In a 9- by 13-inch casserole at least 1¾ inches deep, layer ⅓ the sauce, ½ the pasta, ½ the ricotta mixture, ½ the mozzarella, and ⅓ the parmesan. Repeat layers, ending with sauce and parmesan.

6. Bake, uncovered, in a 375° oven until pasta is hot in the center, 30 to 35 minutes.

7. Let cool 5 to 10 minutes. Cut portions, and lift out with a spatula.

Per serving: 419 cal., 41% (171 cal.) from fat; 25 g protein; 19 g fat (8 g sat.); 36 g carbo.; 1,222 mg sodium; 45 mg chol.

Primo Lasagne

Cooking time: About 1 hour and 15 minutes: 45 minutes for sauces, 30 minutes to bake

Prep time: 30 to 40 minutes, plus at least 5 minutes to cool

Notes: Heat water to cook pasta while assembling the porcini tomato sauce. As the sauce simmers, boil pasta and make the béchamel sauce with milk and cheese.

If making ahead, assemble lasagne, cover, and chill up to 1 day. Bake 30 minutes covered, then uncover and bake until hot (at least 140°) in center and lightly browned, about 20 minutes more.

Makes: 8 servings

 1 package (8 oz.) dried lasagne pasta

 3 tablespoons butter or margarine

 1 onion (about 8 oz.), chopped

 ⅓ cup all-purpose flour

 ¼ teaspoon ground nutmeg

 1½ cups beef or vegetable broth

 1 cup milk

 ½ pound fontina cheese, shredded

    Porcini tomato sauce (recipe follows)

 6 tablespoons grated parmesan cheese

1. In a 5- to 6-quart pan, add lasagne noodles to 3 quarts boiling water. Cook until barely tender to bite, about 10 minutes. Drain, immerse in cold water, and drain when cool. Cover airtight.

2. In the same pan, melt butter with onion over medium heat. Stir often until onion is limp, 8 to 10 minutes. Add flour and nutmeg, and stir until bubbly. Whisk in broth and milk. Simmer over medium-high heat, stirring often, until sauce boils, then simmer

5 minutes longer. Stir in about ⅔ of the fontina cheese, and remove from heat.

3. In a 9- by 13- inch pan or casserole at least 1¾ inches deep, layer ⅓ the tomato sauce, ½ the noodles, ½ the cheese sauce mixture, and ⅓ the parmesan. Repeat layers, ending with tomato sauce, then cover with remaining fontina cheese and sprinkle with remaining parmesan.

4. Bake, uncovered, in a 375° oven until hot in center, 30 to 35 minutes.

5. Let cool 5 to 10 minutes. Cut portions, and lift out with a wide spatula.

Per serving: 594 cal., 52% (306 cal.) from fat; 26 g protein; 34 g fat (16 g sat.); 46 g carbo.; 1,190 mg sodium; 95 mg chol.

Porcini Tomato Sauce

Cooking time: About 35 minutes

Prep time: About 20 minutes

Notes: Italian turkey sausage can be used instead of the pork. If making the sauce ahead, cool, cover, and chill up to 2 days.

Makes: 5 to 5½ cups

 ½ cup (½ oz.) dried porcini mushrooms

 1 pound mild Italian sausages, or chopped regular mushrooms and 2 teaspoons salad oil

 1 or 2 cloves garlic, pressed

 1 onion (about 8 oz.), chopped

 1 cup finely chopped carrot

 1 tablespoon dried basil leaves

 ¼ teaspoon crushed dried red chili

 1 can (28 oz.) tomato purée

 ½ cup dry red wine

1. In a small bowl, combine dried porcini and ¾ cup hot water. Let porcini soak until soft, about 20 minutes. Squeeze porcini gently in water to release grit, then squeeze water from them and lift them out. Chop porcini, and reserve soaking liquid.

2. As porcini soak, remove and discard sausage casings. Put sausages in a 5- to 6-quart pan. Over high heat, break meat into small pieces with a spoon, and stir until meat begins to brown, 5 to 10 minutes. (Or add regular mushrooms and oil to pan, and cover. Cook on high heat until mushrooms give off a little juice, then uncover and stir often until they are lightly browned, about 10 minutes.)

3. Add garlic, onion, carrot, basil, and chili. Stir occasionally until onion is tinged with brown, about 5 minutes.

4. Add tomato purée, wine, and porcini. Carefully pour most of the porcini soaking water into pan, discarding remainder with sediment. Simmer sauce, uncovered, over low heat until reduced to 5 to 5 1/2 cups, about 25 minutes. Use hot or cool.

Per 1/2 cup: 197 cal., 59% (117 cal.) from fat; 7.6 g protein; 13 g fat (4.7 g sat.); 12 g carbo.; 595 mg sodium; 31 mg chol.

Polenta Lasagna

Cooking time: About 1 hour and 15 minutes: 45 minutes for tomato sauce and polenta, 30 minutes to bake

Prep time: 30 minutes, plus 10 minutes to cool

Notes: Make tomato sauce ahead if convenient. Or start tomato sauce, then cook polenta.

If making ahead, let lasagne cool, cover, and chill up to 1 day. Reheat, covered, in a 375° oven about 1 hour, then uncover and continue baking until hot in center (about 140°), about 30 minutes longer.

Makes: 8 servings

- 7 cups chicken broth
- 2 cups polenta
- 1 package (10 oz.) frozen chopped spinach, thawed
- 1 carton (15 oz., about 2 cups) nonfat or low-fat ricotta cheese
- Porcini tomato sauce (recipe precedes), heated
- 2 cups (1/2 lb.) shredded mozzarella cheese
- 1/2 cup grated parmesan cheese

1. In a 4- to 5-quart pan, mix broth and polenta. Stir over high heat until mixture starts to bubble, about 5 minutes. Reduce heat and simmer, stirring often, until polenta feels creamy and smooth when tasted, 15 to 20 minutes.

2. Squeeze water out of spinach. Mix spinach with ricotta.

3. In a shallow 3-quart casserole, spread 1/3 of the porcini tomato sauce. Spoon about 1/2 of the hot polenta in dollops over sauce. Spread or dot polenta with 1/2 the ricotta mixture, and sprinkle with 1/2 the mozzarella and 1/3 the parmesan cheese. Repeat to make 1 more layer, then top with remaining sauce and parmesan cheese.

4. Bake, uncovered, in a 375° oven until hot in center, about 30 minutes.

5. Let stand 10 minutes. Spoon or cut out portions.

Per serving: 577 cal., 44% (252 cal.) from fat; 32 g protein; 28 g fat (12 g sat.); 48 g carbo.; 1,210 mg sodium; 69 mg chol. ∎

By Linda Lau Anusasananan

Why?

Why are foods stored in special ways? Why do they change when stored?

As you unpack your groceries, you automatically put some foods in the refrigerator and others in the cupboard. But there's more to these choices than just keeping some foods cold. The environment in which foods are stored, even briefly, affects their quality and how long they maintain their prime condition.

"At what humidity should foods be kept in the refrigerator?"

—MARGARET STEVENSON
San Diego

Humidity levels in a refrigerator vary, and some locations are better than others for certain foods. You may need to package foods to provide more moisture. Most vegetables and fruits that need to be kept cold contain lots of water and don't have thick skins or peels (like those of melons) to keep the moisture in. If set unwrapped on an open refrigerator shelf, these foods wilt or dry out rapidly. In a refrigerator drawer, which blocks out the circulating dry, cold air, humidity is higher. This is the best place to keep produce such as apples, broccoli, carrots, and cauliflower. Some firm produce, like broccoli and carrots, can be left in plastic bags or wrappers from the market. But if these moistureproof wrappers are sealed, the produce sweats, giving off carbon dioxide and water vapor. If these gases are not allowed to escape, the water vapor condenses, forming moisture between the wrapper and the produce.

TOWELS HELP *prevent decay by keeping wet lettuce from touching plastic bags.*

Molds, which require oxygen and water, grow and cause discoloration and rotting, especially in leafy greens. In our test kitchens, we have found that produce, especially greens, keeps best if wrapped in paper (or cloth) towels, then put in a plastic bag. This keeps the produce surfaces dry and the internal water in place. Fold the bag top over to keep in most of the moisture yet allow gases to escape.

Most refrigerators are set at an energy-efficient temperature of 38° to 40°. However, a temperature of 34° to 36° is significantly more effective in slowing microbial growth that causes deterioration of low-acid foods such as vegetables, poultry, meats, and seafood. These lower temperatures won't harm most produce.

"Why does head lettuce turn pinkish orange after a couple of days in the refrigerator?"

—CATHERINE ARDREY
Bandon, Oregon

Once lettuce is picked, it continues to go through metabolic changes that break down cells and tissue, including oxidation (taking in oxygen). Oxidation makes this pink-orange color develop. It is most noticeable in iceberg (head) lettuce because this lettuce has less pigment, including chlorophyll, than other salad greens.

The discoloration shows up first in pale stem ends and where there is any bruising. If you rinse lettuce before storing, treat it kindly. Drain, then wrap and chill. Drying in a salad spinner makes tiny bruises.

More questions? We would like to know what kitchen mysteries you're curious about. Send your questions to Why?, *Sunset Magazine,* 80 Willow Rd., Menlo Park, CA 94025. Or send e-mail (including full name and street address) to why@sunsetpub.com. With the help of George K. York, extension food technologist at UC Davis, *Sunset* food editors will try to find solutions. We'll publish the answers in the magazine. ∎

By Linda Lau Anusasananan

The ABCs of beautiful bread

Understanding kneading and rising

BAKERY BREAD AROUND THE WEST keeps getting better, and sales of home bread machines keep rising—yet making bread by hand remains among the most satisfying of home cooking projects. The transformation of flour, water, yeast, and salt into a fragrant loaf is nothing short of magical.

Whether you're making bread for the first time or the twentieth, a good understanding of kneading and rising is key to success. Yet most recipes don't detail these building blocks of bread making. You can apply the principles to the following recipe or to any bread recipe.

Kneading. You knead dough to form a stretchy structure called gluten, which traps the carbon dioxide given off by yeast during rising and baking and gives the bread good volume and a fine crumb.

Though vigorous kneading may work out frustrations, gentle, rhythmic movements develop gluten best (and minimize the incorporation of excess flour, which toughens dough). The technique is outlined in the recipe at right.

First rise. During this period, let dough stand until carbon dioxide expands it to double in size. Use the "finger poke" test (photo B), or let dough rise in a large measuring cup to eyeball its progress.

At this stage, if the dough rises a little beyond double it's not a big deal. (A lot beyond double, and it will collapse, but simply knead out the air bubbles and repeat the rise.)

Rising time depends on temperature; 75° to 85° is a comfortable range. When cooler, rising occurs more slowly; above 130° yeast dies. Good rising spots are on top of a water heater or in an unheated oven with a pan of steaming water on the bottom rack. (Remove bread and pan before preheating oven for baking.)

Second rise. After kneading briefly to remove large air bubbles (and to divide smaller ones so bread has a fine texture), shape dough, then let it rise a final time.

Dough should be puffy, but not double, when it goes into the oven (photo C) so there's some "give" left for baking. If under-risen, bread is heavy and compact. If over-risen, it will be coarse, and perhaps misshapen. Remember to preheat the oven so it will be ready when you are.

Dried Tomato–Basil Bread

Cooking time: 18 minutes

Prep time: About 30 minutes, plus about 1½ hours rising time

Notes: All-purpose flour makes denser

BAKER'S REWARD: *two herb- and tomato-flecked wheat loaves. Right, **A:** Knead by folding dough over and pushing it away from you. **B:** With the first rise, finger should leave a definite impression. **C:** Shaped loaves have risen enough when fingertip leaves a faint impression.*

bread; if you prefer more springy, puffy loaves, use bread flour. You'll need a single-edge razor blade (sold with art supplies) or a very sharp knife to make neat slashes in the dough.

Makes: 2 loaves, each 12 to 13 ounces

- 1 package active dry yeast
- 1¼ cups warm (110°) water
- 1 tablespoon dried basil leaves
- 2 tablespoons olive oil
- 1½ teaspoons salt
- 1 cup whole-wheat flour (regular or bread flour)
- 2½ to 2¾ cups all-purpose flour or white bread flour
- ⅓ cup chopped or snipped dried tomatoes (not oil-packed)

1. Mixing. In a large bowl, sprinkle yeast over water and let stand until dissolved, 4 to 5 minutes. Stir in basil, oil, salt, and whole-wheat flour, then gradually mix in 1½ cups all-purpose flour. Beat with a spoon until stretchy, about 5 minutes. Add ¾ cup more all-purpose flour and stir until dough pulls away from side of bowl.

2. Kneading. Scrape dough onto a lightly floured board. With fingertips, lift the side of dough farthest from you and fold dough toward you, overlapping itself by three quarters. Push away with heels of hands to seal at fold line (photo A). Turn dough a quarter turn. Repeat process, keeping a light coating of all-purpose flour on board to prevent sticking. With practice, you'll be able to knead in a quick, continuous movement. Stop when dough is no longer sticky, feels smooth and elastic, and has tiny stretch marks beneath surface, about 10 minutes. Knead in tomatoes until evenly distributed.

3. First rise. Lightly oil bowl, place dough inside, and turn dough over to oil top. Cover airtight; let rise in a warm (75° to 85°), draft-free place until dough is doubled (photo B), 1 to 1¼ hours. Knead on unfloured board to expel air, about 15 turns.

4. Shaping. Divide dough in half. For each loaf, gather dough into a smooth ball by pulling dough to underside to stretch surface; pinch a seam on bottom. On an unfloured board, place ball seam-down and roll with hands into a very smooth 2-inch-

A

B

C

wide log; if necessary to smooth, gently stretch it from underside to top along its length, pinching into a long seam. Place loaves seam-down about 4 inches apart on an oiled 12- by 15-inch baking sheet.

5. Second rise. Cover lightly with plastic wrap. Let rise until dough is puffy and holds a faint impression when lightly pressed (test with a fingertip in an inconspicuous spot; photo C), 15 to 20 minutes.

6. Slashing. Holding a razor blade or very sharp knife at a 45° angle, cut into each loaf a ¾-inch-deep slash spaced about ½ inch toward center from 1 long edge, extending to within 2 inches of each end.

7. Baking. Bake in a 425° oven until bread is deep golden, about 18 minutes. Lift loaves to a rack to cool.

Per ounce: 77 cal., 17% (13 cal.) from fat; 2.3 g protein; 1.4 g fat (0.2 g sat.); 14 g carbo.; 128 mg sodium; 0 mg chol. ■

By Elaine Johnson

Discovering hard cider

A lively, refreshing alternative to beer or wine

PERHAPS YOU'VE ENJOYED THE yeasty fruit flavor of fermented apple cider at a sunny cafe in the French countryside, or at a cozy pub in England. But these days you needn't go abroad for a sip. The West is experiencing a hard-cider boom, with several new domestic producers and a bigger selection of imports. Some makers even add pear or berry flavors to the apple base.

Like beer, fermented cider is a versatile drink. Its tiny bubbles and dry to slightly sweet fruit flavor make it a good thirst quencher on its own, as well as a good accompaniment to food.

Like wine, hard cider is made from specially cultivated fruit (different from table varieties) that is juiced and fermented. It takes skill in choosing and blending the apples to create a good mix of tartness, acidity, and body.

Hard cider is sold alongside beer or, occasionally, wine. It may be labeled fermented or draft cider, or simply cider. Ciders can be completely dry to somewhat sweet; most have a light spritz. Alcohol content ranges from 2.5 to about 6 percent (beer averages 4.5 percent, wine 12). Cider is sold in sizes from four-packs up to regular wine bottles; prices are comparable to those of boutique beers.

At its best, cider has a delicate floral flavor. At its worst, when cider is made using shortcuts (such as apple concentrates rather than fresh juice), the flavor can verge on bitter or caramelized.

PUTTING CIDER TO THE TASTE TEST

Ciders vary widely in style, and what you like will depend on your palate. Here's what our taste panel thought of seven of the most widely available kinds; local selection varies.

Ace Apple California Cider. The lively acidity of this newcomer reminded some tasters of green apples. It's dry with a hint of a bitter finish.

NOEL BARNHURST

SERVE MILDLY *effervescent cider on its own or with foods from fish to stew.*

Bulmer's Woodpecker. The dry, winy, slightly cooked flavor of this import was pleasantly musky (and typically British) to some tasters, a little harsh to others.

Dry Blackthorn. This cider from Britain has a mild, dry apple flavor and a winy, pronounced alcohol taste.

Duché de Longueville. This French cider, the panel's favorite, is medium-sweet with fragrant, true apple flavor.

Seven Sisters. The Idaho-based company produces apple, huckleberry, pear, and raspberry ciders in a delicate, well-balanced, and fruity but dry style.

Woodchuck. This cider from Vermont is dry, only faintly apple-flavored, and rather harsh.

Wyder's. This Canadian company produces both apple and pear ciders. The apple is very dry with an unusual winy taste. The pear has outstanding fruit flavor and pleasant sweetness, and was very popular with taste testers. ■

By Elaine Johnson

DAVID DUNCAN LIVINGSTON

A succulent Vietnamese stew

*Next time you entertain, pull out all the stops with
a spectacular dish of tender braised oxtails*

ONCE CONSIDERED A LOWLY CUT OF meat, oxtails have risen to star status on restaurant menus. They'll cook to meltingly tender perfection in your own kitchen in this interpretation by executive chef Octavio Becerra of Studio City's Pinot Bistro and Michael Otsuka, formerly of Pinot Bistro, now executive chef at Patina Restaurant in Los Angeles.

Inspired by the bold flavors of Southern California's Vietnamese cuisine, the highly seasoned broth is laced with chewy rice noodles. At the table, you customize your individual bowl with a variety of fresh garnishes.

Don't let the long cooking time and lengthy ingredient list put you off. The majority of the cooking is unattended simmering, and you can do most of the work a day ahead. Ask your butcher to order oxtails for you if he doesn't normally stock them, or look for them—as well as star anise, fish sauce, and rice noodles—in Asian markets.

Braised Oxtails from Little Saigon

Cooking time: About 2¼ hours
Prep time: About 15 minutes
Notes: You can work through Step 4 a day ahead. Cover; chill. Reheat, then proceed.
Makes: 8 servings

- 3 star anise
- 3 tablespoons paprika
- 1 tablespoon black peppercorns
- 1 tablespoon hot chili flakes
- 1 teaspoon coriander seed
- ½ teaspoon whole cloves
- 6 pounds beef oxtails, disjointed, fat trimmed
- 3 tablespoons salad oil
- 2 onions (about 1⅓ lb.)
- ¼ cup minced garlic
- 1 tablespoon minced fresh ginger
- 3 quarts chicken broth
- ½ cup tomato paste
- ¼ cup firmly packed brown sugar
- ¼ cup Asian fish sauce (nuoc mam or nam pla) or soy sauce
- 6 carrots (about 1⅓ lb.), peeled and cut into ½-inch rounds
   Lime wedges
- ½ pound bean sprouts
   Basil and cilantro sprigs
- 2 jalapeño chilies, seeded if desired, cut into thin slices
- ¾ pound dried rice noodles (about ¼ inch thick) or dried linguine

AN EXOTIC MINGLING of spices seasons oxtail stew with rice noodles. Add fresh basil, cilantro, bean sprouts, lime juice, and jalapeños to taste.

1. Add anise, paprika, peppercorns, chili flakes, coriander, and cloves to an 8- to 10-inch frying pan. Stir over medium-high heat until spices begin to brown and smell toasted, 3 to 5 minutes (watch carefully; paprika scorches easily). Whirl spices in blender to finely grind, then place in bowl; coat oxtails in spices lightly and evenly.

2. In an 8- to 10-quart pan over medium-high heat, combine half the oil and as many oxtails as fit in a single layer. Cook, turning often, until oxtails are browned on all sides, 6 to 8 minutes. Remove oxtails; set aside. Brown remaining oxtails in remaining oil.

3. Mince ½ onion; add to pan with garlic and ginger. Cook, stirring often, until lightly browned, about 5 minutes. Add broth, paste, sugar, and fish sauce; stir to blend.

4. Cut remaining onions into 1-inch-thick wedges. Add to pan along with carrots and oxtails. Bring to a boil; simmer, covered, until meat is very tender when pierced, 1¾ to 2 hours. Discard any fat on broth surface.

5. While oxtails cook, arrange lime, sprouts, basil, cilantro, and jalapeños decoratively on a platter. Cover with plastic wrap; chill until serving time.

6. Twenty minutes before meat is done, place rice noodles in a bowl; cover with warm water. Soak until pliable, about 20 minutes; drain. (If using linguine, cook until just tender to bite, about 8 minutes. Drain; rinse with cold water.)

7. When done, transfer oxtails and vegetables with slotted spoon to baking pan. Cover loosely with foil; keep warm in 300° oven. Add noodles to broth; simmer until tender (or linguine is warm), 2 to 3 minutes.

8. Arrange noodles in 1 large or 8 individual soup bowls. Top with oxtails, vegetables, and broth. Offer lime, sprouts, basil, cilantro, and jalapeños to taste.

Per serving: 512 cal., 28% (144 cal.) from fat; 33 g protein; 16 g fat; 68 g carbo.; 750 mg sodium; sat. fat, cholesterol unavailable. ■

By Christine Weber Hale

Petite chocolate cakes conceal velvety sauce

The secret is in the baking

BY NO MEANS SHOULD YOU RESERVE these one-serving chocolate cakes just for Valentine's Day—even though their symbolism is perfect. They have warm, soft hearts, and better yet, the hearts are deep, dark chocolate.

Marion Tse, pastry chef at San Francisco's Cypress Club, shares her fine rendition of a dessert that's becoming a regular on dessert menus.

The batter—reminiscent of a soufflé, but stiffer and more stable—is quickly mixed and easy to handle. Baked just enough, the batter forms a solid wall around a soft center. If made ahead, the cakes reheat with excellent results.

For a handsome presentation, serve each cake with a petite scoop of coffee or mocha ice cream and a drizzle of melted chocolate.

DAVID DUNCAN LIVINGSTON

CUT TO THE CENTER, *and soft warm chocolate oozes from this moist dessert.*

Warm Chocolate Cake with a Soft Heart

Cooking time: About 15 minutes

Prep time: 15 to 20 minutes

Notes: If making ahead, cool cakes in baking dishes, then cover and chill up to 1 day. To reheat, bake, uncovered, in a 300° oven just until warm to touch, about 10 minutes. Or heat, 1 at a time and covered, in a microwave oven at 50 percent power just until warm to touch, about 30 seconds.

Makes: 8 servings

- ¾ cup (6 oz.) butter or margarine
- 6 ounces bittersweet chocolate, chopped (about 1 cup)
- 4½ tablespoons all-purpose flour
- About 2 tablespoons unsweetened cocoa
- 5 large eggs, separated
- ⅓ cup sugar
- 1½ tablespoons coffee-flavor liqueur
- ½ teaspoon vanilla
- 1 to 1½ cups coffee ice cream
- ½ to ¾ cup warm chocolate sauce (recipe follows, or use your favorite purchased sauce)
- Powdered sugar

1. In a 3- to 4-quart pan, combine butter and chocolate. Stir occasionally over low heat until melted and smooth.

2. Mix flour with 2 tablespoons cocoa.

3. In a large bowl, beat egg whites with a mixer on high speed until foamy. Gradually beat in sugar, then beat until whites hold stiff, shiny peaks.

4. Stir liqueur, vanilla, egg yolks and cocoa mixture into chocolate-butter mixture, then stir in about ¼ of the whites. Fold remaining whites into chocolate mixture; leave no white streaks. Spoon batter equally into 8 buttered ramekins (6-oz. or ¾-cup size). Set ramekins in a 10- by 15-inch pan.

5. Bake cakes in a 375° oven just until edges feel firm but centers are still soft when gently pressed, 11 to 12 minutes. Let cool 5 minutes.

6. Invert each cake onto a separate plate and place a small scoop of ice cream alongside. Drizzle warm chocolate sauce over cake and plate, then sift powdered sugar and cocoa onto dessert. Serve at once.

Per serving: 404 cal., 70% (279 cal.) from fat; 6.9 g protein; 31 g fat (17 g sat.); 29 g carbo.; 238 mg sodium; 189 mg chol.

Chocolate Sauce

Cooking time: 5 minutes

Prep time: 5 minutes

Notes: If made ahead, cover and chill up to 1 month. Warm to serve.

Makes: ¾ cup

- 4 ounces bittersweet or semisweet chocolate, chopped (about ⅔ cup)
- ⅓ cup milk
- 2 tablespoons coffee-flavor liqueur

Melt chocolate in milk in a microwave oven or over low heat, stirring often until smooth. Stir in liqueur. Serve warm.

Per tablespoon: 57 cal., 55% (32 cal.) from fat; 0.9 g protein; 3.5 g fat (1.9 g sat.); 6.3 g carbo.; 3.3 mg sodium; 0.9 mg chol. ■

By Linda Lau Anusasananan

Oranges: biting into history

To help promote the orange, early Southern California growers published cookbooks filled with everything from recipes to health advice. At the Mission Inn, oranges were always on the menu. We've dusted off three historic recipes, updating them a bit for contemporary palates.

SIMPLE PLEASURES *were the rule in the kitchen at the beginning of this century. Clockwise from left: Orange Butter Cookies, Ambrosia, and Roly-Poly.*

ROBERT OLDING

Orange Butter Cookies

Inspired by a 1910 recipe used at the Mission Inn

Cooking time: About 12 minutes for each baking sheet

Prep time: 30 minutes

Notes: Store airtight up to 2 days; separate layers with waxed paper.

Makes: About 5½ dozen

- 1 cup (½ lb.) butter or margarine
- ½ cup sugar
- 1¾ teaspoons grated orange peel
- 1 large egg
- 1 teaspoon vanilla
- 3 cups unsifted all-purpose flour
- 1½ cups powdered sugar
- 3 tablespoons orange juice

1. Beat butter and sugar until creamy and blended. Beat in 1 teaspoon orange peel, egg, and vanilla. Gradually mix flour into butter mixture; beat until blended.

2. On a lightly floured board, roll out dough to ⅛ inch thick. Cut out with floured decorative cutters (about 2 in. wide), and place slightly apart on lightly greased baking sheets. Gather scraps into a ball, reroll dough, and cut out more cookies.

3. Bake in a 350° oven until pale gold with lightly browned edges, 12 to 15 minutes. Transfer to racks to cool.

4. Mix powdered sugar and orange juice until smooth. Stir in remaining orange peel. Spread or brush glaze over cookies; let stand until icing is dry, about 10 minutes.

Orange Roly-Poly

Inspired by a recipe from a 1920s cookbook published by Sunkist

Cooking time: About 30 minutes
Prep time: About 35 minutes
Makes: 8 servings.

- 4 oranges (about 2½ lb. total)
- 2 cups unsifted all-purpose flour
- 4 teaspoons baking powder
- 1 teaspoon salt
- ¼ cup (⅛ lb.) butter or margarine
  About ¾ cup milk
- ½ cup sugar
  Vanilla ice cream

1. Grate enough peel from 1 orange to make 2 teaspoons; set aside. Cut peel off oranges deep enough to remove pith and membrane; discard peel. Cut fruit into ½-inch chunks; discard seeds. Scoop fruit and any juice into a bowl; set aside.

2. Mix flour, baking powder, and salt. With a pastry cutter or your fingertips, cut or rub in 2 tablespoons butter until fine crumbs form. Stir in just enough milk to moisten evenly. Gather dough into a ball; lightly knead 10 times on a lightly floured board.

3. Roll dough into an 8- by 12-inch rectangle about ½ inch thick. Melt remaining butter; brush 1 tablespoon over rectangle. Mix grated peel and sugar; sprinkle ½ of mixture evenly over dough. Drain orange pieces, reserving juice. Evenly scatter about ⅓ of the pieces over dough. Starting with a short end, roll up dough; pinch seam securely to seal in filling. Cut roll into 8 1-inch slices, and arrange slightly apart in a 9- by 13-inch baking dish. Brush remaining butter over tops of rolls. Sprinkle slices with 1 tablespoon sugar mixture.

4. Measure reserved juice. If needed, add water to make 1 cup. Stir in remaining sugar mixture. Pour juice mixture into dish around rolls. Scatter remaining orange pieces into juice.

5. Bake, uncovered, in a 450° oven until top is richly browned, 25 to 30 minutes. Cool on rack; serve hot or warm. Top with ice cream.

Orange Ambrosia

Inspired by a recipe from a 1920s California Fruit Growers Exchange cookbook

Prep time: About 10 minutes
Notes: Drizzle with orange-flavor liqueur.
Makes: 4 servings

- 4 oranges (8 to 10 oz. each)
- 1 firm-ripe banana (about 8 oz.)
- 2 tablespoons sweetened shredded dried coconut
  Fresh mint sprigs (optional)

1. Evenly cut top ½ inch off oranges; reserve tops. Using a knife with a curved serrated blade, cut around flesh and free from peel, leaving shell. Cut removed flesh into ½-inch chunks, discarding seeds.

2. Peel banana; cut into thin slices. Place ⅛ of the slices in bottom of each shell; top with ⅛ of the orange chunks. Repeat banana and orange layers. Garnish with coconut and mint sprigs. Set each filled shell on a dessert plate with top of orange alongside. ■

By Linda Lau Anusasananan

Per cookie: 18 cal., 15% (2.7 cal.) from fat; 0.4 g protein; 0.3 g fat (0.1 g sat.); 3.4 g carbo.; 5.5 mg sodium; 6.3 mg chol.

Burley, Idaho

TENDER BUTTER LETTUCE IS THE most mild-mannered of its clan, and the unctuous avocado has a flavor that's subtle rather than assertive. Combined in a salad they need the tang of a vinaigrette to set them off. To bring a bit of tropical warmth to the dressing, Rodney Garside (a frequent Chefs of the West contributor) adds minced fresh ginger and mango chutney.

Avocado Salad with Chutney Dressing

Prep time: About 10 minutes

Notes: Major Grey's is a mango chutney.

Makes: 6 servings

- 2 tablespoons olive oil
- 1 tablespoon balsamic vinegar
- 1½ teaspoons Dijon mustard
- 1 teaspoon minced fresh ginger
- 1 tablespoon finely chopped Major Grey's chutney
- 1 head butter lettuce (about ½ lb.), rinsed and drained
- 1 firm-ripe avocado (about ½ lb.), peeled, pitted, and diced
- ¼ pound mushrooms, rinsed and thinly sliced
- ½ cup thinly sliced mild red onion
- ½ cup diced red bell pepper

  Salt and pepper

1. In a salad bowl, mix oil, vinegar, mustard, ginger, and chutney.

2. Break lettuce into bite-size pieces and put in a bowl. Add avocado, mushrooms, onion, and bell pepper.

3. Mix salad with dressing, and season to taste with salt and pepper.

Per serving: 112 cal., 72% (81 cal.) from fat; 1.7 g protein; 9 g fat (1.3 g sat.); 7.7 g carbo.; 67 mg sodium; 0 mg chol.

Tuolumne, California

By Joan Griffiths, Richard Dunmire

Timely tactics for an Old World cookie

THE DISTINCTIVE BUT DELICATE licorice flavor of anise is the flavor of hospitality, whether in the glass of pastis or ouzo that your Provençal or Greek host offers you, the biscotti you crunch with caffe latte, or the cookies served in northern Europe.

Of those anise-flavor cookies, the best known are the German springerle, which are decorated with patterns from a carved rolling pin or cookie molds, then dried for a considerable length of time before they're baked.

James Kircher's Anise Cookies give the same flavor with a lot less work. You don't need a special rolling pin or molds, but you do let the unbaked cookies dry so that when they bake, they form a crisp cookie beneath a dry, glossy icing.

Anise Cookies

Cooking time: About 12 minutes per pan

Prep time: About 50 minutes. Allow at least 6 hours for unbaked cookies to dry.

Notes: Anise oil is available in some specialty food stores and drugstores (you may have to ask for it), but it is worth seeking because its flavor is more intense than that of anise extract.

Makes: About 9 dozen

- 3 large eggs
- 1 cup sugar
- 1½ cups all-purpose flour
- ½ teaspoon baking powder
- ¼ teaspoon anise oil or 1 teaspoon anise extract

1. In a deep bowl, beat eggs on high speed until foamy. While beating on high speed, gradually add sugar, allowing about 20 minutes. Then continue to beat until the sugar is thoroughly dissolved (a little of the mixture rubbed between your fingers should feel smooth), about 4 minutes.

2. Mix flour and baking powder. Add to egg mixture along with anise oil. Stir to blend, then beat until dry ingredients are thoroughly incorporated.

3. Drop batter in 1-teaspoon portions, 1 inch apart, onto heavily buttered and floured baking sheets. Frequently stir batter to keep ingredients mixed. Let unbaked cookies stand until tops feel dry and firm when touched, at least 6 hours or until next day.

4. Bake in a 325° oven until tops feel dry and bottoms are pale golden brown, about 12 minutes.

5. Cool cookies on racks, then serve, or store airtight up to 1 week; freeze to store longer.

SUNSET'S KITCHEN CABINET

Readers' family favorites tested in our kitchens

By Betsy Reynolds Bateson

DICK COLE

Lentil and Kale Soup

Jennifer Stein Barker, Canyon City, Oregon

A large garden at 4,800 feet above sea level has provided Jennifer Stein Barker with an abundance of produce, and cooking adventures that have resulted in *The Morning Hill Cookbook,* which she published herself. This vegetable soup is perfect for a cold winter night and features two of her favorite ingredients, lentils and freshly ground chili powder.

Cooking time: About 1 hour
Prep time: About 15 minutes
Makes: 8 hearty servings

2 onions, diced (about 1 lb. total)
3 cloves garlic, minced
1 tablespoon olive oil
1 tablespoon ground New Mexico or California chili
½ teaspoon ground cumin
2 bay leaves
8 cups chicken broth

¾ cup lentils
1 can (14½ oz.) diced tomatoes
1 pound fresh kale
2 potatoes (about 1 lb.), such as Yukon gold or thin-skinned
1 cup frozen corn kernels
2 tablespoons tamari or soy sauce

1. In a 6- to 8-quart pan over medium-high heat, cook onions and garlic in oil, stirring often, until onions are just golden, about 12 minutes. Add chili, cumin, and bay leaves; cook about 1 minute more.

2. Add broth, lentils, and tomatoes with their juice. Bring to a boil, cover, and reduce heat; simmer until lentils are just tender, about 25 minutes.

3. Meanwhile, trim off tough stems of kale; chop remaining leaves and tender mid-ribs. Scrub potatoes and dice into ½-inch cubes. When lentils are just tender, add kale and potatoes; turn heat to high to resume a soft boil. Cover pan and cook until potatoes are tender to bite, about 15 minutes. Add corn and tamari, and cook just until corn is hot, about 1 minute more.

Per serving: 222 cal., 21% (47 cal.) from fat; 13 g protein; 5.2 g fat (1.1 g sat.); 38 g carbo.; 483 mg sodium; 0 mg chol.

Prune Clafouti

Sheila Eaton, Las Vegas, Nevada

Sheila Eaton had trouble getting good berries to make this *clafouti,* a custard-like dessert typically made with fresh fruit. As a result, she came up with a new version using dried fruit, in this case prunes. Because she loves vanilla, she adds a generous amount, and sometimes includes a touch of lemon and nutmeg. If you place the clafouti in the oven before dinner, it'll be ready for dessert.

Cooking time: 35 minutes
Prep time: About 10 minutes

Makes: 6 servings

½ cup sugar
1 cup quartered pitted prunes (about 9 oz.)
2 large eggs
1 tablespoon vanilla
2 tablespoons all-purpose flour
1 cup half-and-half
1 teaspoon grated lemon peel (optional)
⅛ teaspoon ground nutmeg

1. Sprinkle 2 tablespoons of the sugar over the bottom and sides of a buttered 9-inch ceramic or glass pie dish. Scatter prune pieces over sugar.

2. In a blender, combine eggs, vanilla, and remaining sugar; blend until smooth. Add flour and blend, then add half-and-half and lemon peel and continue to blend until smooth. Pour over prunes; dust top with nutmeg.

3. Bake in a 375° oven until puffed and browned, about 35 minutes. Cool 10 minutes before serving.

Per serving: 260 cal., 23% (59 cal.) from fat; 4.6 g protein; 6.5 g fat (3.4 g sat.); 48 g carbo.; 39 mg sodium; 86 mg chol.

Beer Bread

Gail Hinson, San Marcos, California

Gail Hinson keeps self-rising flour in her cupboard just for this recipe. The bread has wonderful texture and flavor and only five ingredients. For flavor variation, try different specialty beers, such as light ale, porter, or stout.

Cooking time: About 50 minutes
Prep time: 10 minutes
Makes: 1 loaf, 8 servings

- 3 cups self-rising flour, or 3 cups all-purpose flour plus 1 1/2 teaspoons salt and 4 1/2 teaspoons baking powder
- 1/4 cup sugar
- 1 teaspoon caraway seed (optional)
- 1 bottle (12 oz.) beer or light ale
- 1/4 cup melted butter or margarine

1. In a large bowl, stir together self-rising flour, sugar, caraway seed, if desired, and beer. Spoon into a lightly buttered 5- by 9-inch loaf pan; pour melted butter over top of batter.

2. Bake in a 350° oven until loaf is golden brown and begins to pull from edge of pan, about 50 minutes. Remove bread and set on a wire rack to cool slightly. Serve warm or at room temperature.

Per serving: 263 cal., 23% (60 cal.) from fat; 4.8 g protein; 6.7 g fat (3.9 g sat.); 43 g carbo.; 661 mg sodium; 17 mg chol.

Ham-stuffed Manicotti

Bob Falconer, Hillsboro, Oregon

Inspired by eager eaters and cleaned plates, Bob Falconer wrote down this recipe and sent it to us. This family favorite was a spur-of-the-moment creation from cupboard staples. He says any type of ham will work, including leftovers. He admits to not using all the cooked manicotti shells because "some break while cooking and filling," and suggests that you vary the amount of sauce to your taste.

Cooking time: About 1 hour
Prep time: About 20 minutes
Makes: 6 servings

- 1 package (8 oz.) manicotti shells
- 2 cups (5 oz.) shredded parmesan cheese
- 15 ounces low-fat ricotta cheese
- 1/2 pound ham, cut into 1/2-inch cubes (about 1 cup)
- 1/2 cup diced red bell pepper
- 1 large egg
- 1/4 cup fine, dried, seasoned bread crumbs
- 2 cups (16 oz.) prepared spaghetti sauce
- 1 cup (4 oz.) shredded mozzarella cheese

1. In a 5- to 6-quart pan, bring about 4 quarts of water to a boil over high heat. Add manicotti shells and cook until just tender, about 12 minutes. Drain and rinse with cold water.

2. Meanwhile, in a bowl combine half the parmesan cheese with ricotta, ham, bell pepper, egg, and bread crumbs.

3. Fill 12 cooled manicotti shells (you will have more, but a couple may break) with 1/3 cup each of the cheese-ham mixture. Lay filled manicotti in a lightly oiled 9- by 13-inch baking dish. Cover stuffed manicotti with sauce, mozzarella, and remaining parmesan.

4. Bake in a 350° oven until sauce is bubbling, about 45 minutes; cool 10 minutes before serving.

Per serving: 573 cal., 39% (225 cal.) from fat; 38 g protein; 25 g fat (12 g sat.); 49 g carbo.; 1,617 mg sodium; 103 mg chol.

Wintry Couscous

Susan S. Sherman, Greenbrae, California

Because of her Indian background, Susan Sherman wanted to design her own curry flavor for her couscous dish. Rather than using purchased curry powder, she chose the curry seasoning components she valued most. Although you can make this dish in less than half an hour, it has great make-ahead potential. The couscous gets added flavor from almonds and golden raisins. Serve it as a side dish with chicken or pork.

Cooking time: About 15 minutes
Prep time: About 10 minutes
Makes: 6 to 8 servings

- 1 onion, finely chopped
- 1 tablespoon olive oil
- 1/2 cup sliced almonds
- 1/2 cup golden raisins
- 1 1/2 teaspoons ground cumin
- 1/2 teaspoon ground turmeric
- 1/4 teaspoon ground cinnamon
  About 3 1/4 cups chicken broth
- 2 tablespoons butter or margarine
- 2 cups couscous

1. In a 10- to 12-inch frying pan over medium-high heat, cook onion in oil, stirring, until onion is tinged golden, about 5 minutes. Add the sliced almonds and golden raisins and cook 1 minute. Add the ground cumin, turmeric, and cinnamon and continue to cook, stirring, until the almonds and spices are just toasted, about 1 minute more. (If making ahead, add about 1/4 cup broth to help remove the seasonings from the pan, then transfer the cooled mixture to an airtight container; chill up to 3 days or freeze up to a month.)

2. Add 3 cups broth and the butter and bring mixture to a boil over high heat. Stir in the couscous, cover the pan, and remove the pan from the heat. Let the couscous stand until all of the liquid has been absorbed, at least 5 minutes, or hold couscous up to an hour. Fluff with a fork before serving.

Per serving: 295 cal., 27% (81 cal.) from fat; 9 g protein; 9 g fat (2.7 g sat.); 47 g carbo.; 83 mg sodium; 7.8 mg chol.

Share a recipe you've created or adapted—a family favorite, travel discovery, or time-saver, including the story behind the recipe. You'll receive a "Great Cook" certificate and $50 for each recipe published. Send to *Sunset Magazine,* 80 Willow Rd., Menlo Park, CA 94025, or send e-mail (including full name and street address) to recipes@ sunsetpub.com.

FOOD
Guide

BY JERRY ANNE DI VECCHIO

A TASTE OF THE WEST: A stew worthy of celebrations

When the Keresan pueblo people of Cochiti, New Mexico, perform their ceremonial Corn Dance, it is feast day. And once I feasted with them as a guest of the great storyteller potter, Helen Cordero.

The hypnotic drumbeat and stamping feet of dancers on the plaza captured the attention of most of the household, but as they watched, I followed Helen out the back door. Behind her one-story adobe-walled home, she had set up an outdoor kitchen to produce enough food for the feast. At one side was the domed beehive adobe oven where bread was baking. And on a large iron grate, standing over a glowing bed of wood embers, were seven soot-smudged pots, the smallest of which was at least 12-quart. Each contained fragrantly simmering food—pozole (lamb with dried corn), chicken and rice, ears of corn, red beans, chili beans, vegetables with beef, and a green-chili stew. This was just the hot part of the meal.

Ladling the food into big bowls, we carried them inside to a long table with bench space that easily seated 20. Already on the table were salads of greens, tomatoes, and potatoes, hunks of watermelon, thin wedges of dried-fruit pie, old-fashioned fruit ambrosia with marshmallows and coconut, raspberry gelatin with bananas and cream, and *bizcochitos* (biscuitlike cookies).

As diners came and went, in waves that seemingly kept pace with the Corn Dance, they passed through the next room, where a row of Helen's magical clay storytellers—each with children nestled along its arms, legs, and shoulders—were waiting for her paintbrush. Nowadays, museum curators stand in line to acquire these pieces.

It was a good, filling meal of simply seasoned dishes, and the green-chili stew was particularly satisfying. The mild chilies had been roasted in coals,

ROBERT OLDING

Earthy flavors mingle in this succulent lamb stew made with green chilies and corn.

MARCH

- Plenty of green chilies make lamb stew even better

- Sprout choices are sprouting

- Grilling in a frying pan

- A fruit to handle passionately

- If only one wine, which one to pick?

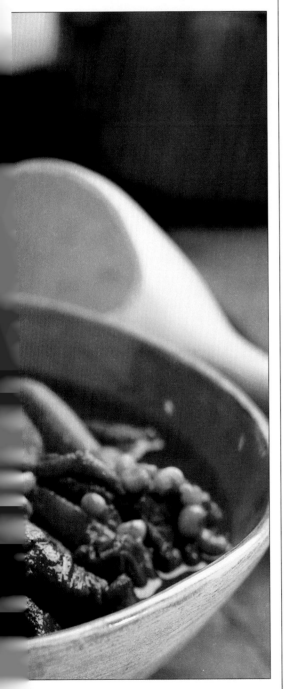

then peeled and seeded. The meat was tender chunks of lamb, and the broth was flavored with chili powder.

As we worked our way on to the sweets, I found myself hesitating as I tasted one of the intricately formed bizcochitos, shaped by Helen's hands. It seemed a sacrilege to bite it.

Green-Chili Stew

Cooking time: About 1 hour and 45 minutes

Prep time: About 30 minutes

Notes: In lieu of tiny carrots, use 1½ pounds of carrots cut into ½-inch-thick sticks. If making ahead, let stew cool, cover, and chill up to 1 day, then reheat.

Makes: 6 to 8 servings

- 3 pounds boned lamb stew meat (shoulder or neck), fat trimmed

- 2 onions (8 oz. each), chopped

- 2 teaspoons cumin seed

- 4 cups beef or chicken broth

- 2 tablespoons chili powder

- 12 thin-skinned potatoes (about 2 in. wide), scrubbed

- 24 carrots (about 4 in. long), peeled

- 2 cups corn kernels, fresh or frozen

- 3 cans (7 oz. each) whole green chilies, torn into wide strips

- Cilantro sprigs

- Salt

1. Cut meat into about 1-inch chunks, rinse, and put in a 6- to 8-quart pan.

2. Add onions, cumin seed, and ¾ cup broth. Cover, and cook over high heat for 20 minutes. Uncover, and stir often until broth evaporates and meat starts to brown, 20 to 25 minutes.

3. When drippings are very dark, stir in chili powder, add ¼ cup broth, and stir to release browned bits. Stirring often, cook until liquid evaporates and browned bits stick to pan, about 1 minute.

4. Pour 3 cups broth into pan, scrape browned bits free, and add potatoes, carrots, corn, and green chilies. Cover, and simmer until meat is very tender when pierced, about 1 hour.

5. Ladle stew into wide bowls, garnish with cilantro sprigs, and season to taste with salt.

Per serving: 532 cal., 22% (117 cal.) from fat; 43 g protein; 13 g fat (4.3 g sat.); 63 g carbo.; 721 mg sodium; 112 mg chol.

SEASONAL NOTE

A guide to young sprouts

Shopping for alfalfa sprouts the other day, I was reminded of the radical statement these green wisps made in the '60s and '70s. If you ate them, you were labeled a health nut (a less positive accusation then than now) or a hippie. But no more.

Many kinds of sprouts are now readily available, and eating them means no more than that you like the way they taste. Each has an interesting personality, and blended sprout mixes take advantage of this. Any of these tender greens fit readily into salads or sandwiches, but that's just for starters.

Peter Henderson grows a lot of sprouts at Sprout House in San Bruno, California, and we gathered a group of them—though not all of the kinds I've spotted—for a tasting.

Clover sprouts. Look a lot like alfalfa sprouts, with a fresh, sweeter, cool flavor; they're just as adaptable.

Onion sprouts. Hair-thin and tipped with black seed, with the look and taste of green onions. Use where a faint touch of onion is desired; I love them rolled into omelets.

Pea sprouts. Sweet, delicate pea flavor. Easier to use than pea tips (or tendrils) from Asian markets because they don't need cleaning. Lovely in salads, chopped and floated in soups of peas or potatoes, or added last to stir-fried dishes.

Radish sprouts. Texture like alfalfa sprouts, with reddish stems and tiny leaves. Have a radish nip. Add to cream cheese on a bagel or to a grilled cheese sandwich.

Sunflower sprouts. Dime-size glossy leaves, white stems. Fleshy, juicy, with mild, slightly grassy flavor. Sprinkle on sushi rice, or mound under grilled salmon steaks seasoned with soy sauce.

Sprouted legumes. Garbanzos, lentils, adzuki beans, and peas are tender enough to chew and to cook fast. They are often suggested for salads, but I find them a bit munchy and prefer them in stir-fried mixtures or stir-steamed on their own (with broth instead of fat and water).

Grill-fry pan

A French friend invited me to her Paris home for a quick bite during a hard day of museum touring, and taught me two useful things. One, if the red wine isn't very good, adding water hides a lot of flaws. Two, a frying pan with a raised grill in the bottom makes grill marks as effectively as a hot barbecue grill, and also keeps melting fat away from the meat as it cooks. These pans work best over medium-high to highest heat. However, fat is inclined to spatter and smoke. To control this, pull the pan off the heat occasionally and mop out the fat with a paper towel. Use the pan to cook meat, firm fish, oiled vegetables, and other small foods suited to the barbecue.

Pans with ridged bottoms come in many metals—typically heavy and often cast iron, which can be plain or enameled. Those with nonstick finishes may not be recommended for highest heats, so you won't get the browning the pan promises. Some pans are shaped like frying pans, some have very low rims, some look like griddles (reversible means you can turn it over and use the flat side for pancakes),

Ridges hold foods just slightly above the frying pan surface so that fat drains away.

NOEL BARNHURST

some are round, some square. The price range I've noticed of late is $25 to about $100. Because cast-iron pans are so durable (though rarely they do crack), they often turn up in secondhand stores and at flea markets. A friend recently found a sound cast-iron grill-fry pan for $10.

Celebrating fresh

I first heard of John Ash about 15 years ago by way of Bob Thompson. Bob and his wife, Harolyn, discovered John after he escaped the corporate world and opened a small shopping-center restaurant in Santa Rosa, California.

Now, John is adviser for another restaurant, which bears his name, in the more serene setting of Santa Rosa's Vintners Inn. But his primary energies are devoted to Fetzer Vineyards' Valley Oaks Food & Wine Center, in Hopland. As culinary director, he has access to wonderful organic gardens cultivated by Jeff Dawson, and to Fetzer wines— obvious inspirations for his newest book, *From the Earth to the Table: John Ash's Wine Country Cuisine* (Dutton, New York, 1995; $29.95). His project partner, Sid Goldstein, is equally devoted to food and wine. (If you know Sid, you know that his enthusiasm is obvious. But it was his mother, my longtime friend Lois, who told me so—long ago.)

By taking advantage of the West's superb produce and multiethnic ingre-

dients in mainstream markets, John has created recipes that burst with fresh ingredients and concepts. Mexican, Asian, and indigenous California influences have led him naturally to lighter dishes. He reserves the cream and butter of his early French training for occasions when they still work best.

I was intrigued by the description of his shift from French basic sauces (brown, white, mayonnaise, hollandaise, and such) to his own lighter mixtures like reduced stocks, salsas, chutneys, pestos, and vinaigrettes. The corn, tomato, and mushroom stocks in the soup chapter sound delicious on their own, and are marvelous as components in other dishes. Vegetarian main courses such as Moroccan Cinnamon Couscous with Sweet Spice Vegetables have no hint of denial. The Marinated and Grilled Flank Steak with Lime-Chipotle Sauce is already a standard at my home.

Lime-Chipotle Sauce

Prep time: About 10 minutes

Notes: John Ash serves this sauce with marinated and grilled flank steak and grilled red onions and red or yellow bell peppers. But it also complements other grilled meats, poultry, and fish. If made ahead, it keeps well, covered and chilled, up to 5 days.

Makes: 1½ cups

- ½ cup honey
- 2 tablespoons minced canned chipotle chilies in adobado
- 3 tablespoons brown or Dijon mustard
- ½ cup lime juice
- 1½ tablespoons minced garlic
- 1 teaspoon ground cumin
- ½ teaspoon ground allspice
- ½ cup chopped fresh cilantro
   Salt and freshly ground pepper

Mix honey with chilies, mustard, lime juice, garlic, cumin, allspice, and cilantro. Season to taste with salt and pepper.

Per tablespoon: 27 cal., 6.7% (1.8 cal.) from fat; 0.2 g protein; 0.2 g fat (0 g sat.); 6.8 g carbo.; 31 mg sodium; 0 mg chol.

A fruit with passion

Passion fruit has followed a convoluted route to our markets, as have many other foods native to Central and South America. It's been grown for some years in Hawaii (its taste gave the punch to a fruit-flavored drink named for the islands), initially for commercial food production. The real move into the fresh produce section was made with fruit from New Zealand. And now, several varieties of passion fruit are grown in California. We mostly see two, one with a dark purple shell, the other with yellow.

The fruit is extremely aromatic, and the pulp is very sweet-tart. Chefs who like dramatic flavor contrasts use it in sweet desserts and with meats.

But home cooks should feel equally comfortable with it, especially now that it's more widely available.

Before the fruit is ready to use, its balsa-weight shell is firm and smooth. To ripen, it needs to stand, unwrapped, at room temperature until the shell shrivels and looks wrinkled. Once ripe, it keeps up to a week in the refrigerator.

Cut open, the shell contains gelatinous pulp surrounding small seeds. You can eat the seeds with the pulp, or rub the pulp through a fine strainer and discard the seeds.

A single fruit doesn't yield much. One that is 2 inches wide contains 3 to 4 teaspoons of pulp—often enough for a single dessert.

Forms other than fresh are making

ROBERT OLDING

Just a little passion fruit pulp, fresh or frozen, is potent enough to turn ice cream on a meringue into an exotic dessert.

passion fruit easier and less expensive to use. Frozen passion fruit concentrate sits alongside orange juice concentrate in some supermarkets and many Latino markets—where you can also find frozen passion fruit pulp, with or without seeds, and plain or sweetened. If I can't use a whole container, I refreeze leftovers with no loss in flavor.

Get to know passion fruit (fresh, frozen, or concentrate) with foods that are low-key foils. Spoon onto vanilla ice cream, baked custard, or rice pud-ding, or mix with whipped cream or vanilla custard sauce. For a refreshing beverage, swirl a few spoonfuls with chilled club soda (add sugar if too tart), ice, and, perhaps, a little rum.

I also like it mixed into sour cream to dress shrimp salad, or used in place of lemon or lime juice in marinades for pork or lamb.

Per tablespoon passion fruit with seeds: 12 cal., 7.5% (0.9 cal.) from fat; 0.3 g protein; 0.1 g fat (0 g sat.); 2.8 g carbo.; 3.4 mg sodium; 0 mg chol.

Adaptable Chiantis for any circumstance

The old question came up at a companionable dinner table the other night: Which red wine would you want if you were a castaway on a desert island? We all gave the same answer: Chianti, especially Chianti Classico.

The pickiest of our would-be castaways specified Chianti Classico *normale* if prospects were good for a rescue within three years, *riserva* if he were going to be abandoned for longer.

Chianti won because it comes closer than any other wine to being a year-round red and because it has indelible flavors, but not such strong ones that

the wine wears you out even when you have it with dinner every night.

In balance, Chianti is a middleweight, gentle enough to go with roast chicken on a muggy September night, yet forceful enough for a platter-size steak on as bleak and cold a rainy November afternoon as ever was. Young, Chianti has an almost floral flavor—the hallmark of its principal grape, Sangiovese. After two to five years in the bottle, the wine develops a spicy note that might remind you of the smell of cedar. Normales make this flavor shift quicker than firmer, richer-flavored riservas.

The region called Chianti covers most of the Italian province of Tuscany. The part called Chianti Classico is the heart, the rolling hill country between Florence and Siena. All of Chianti produces admirable wines, but vigorous

competition among a large number of producers has raised the bar a notch or two higher in Chianti Classico.

In Italy, prices stay within $8 to $12 for well-regarded normales, $12 to $15 for riservas. Here, for mysterious reasons, importers push the top end of the range much higher. Some of the quality producers widely available in the western United States: Castello di Fonterutoli, Badia a Coltibuono, Castello di Ama, Castello di Lilliano, Fattoria di Felsina, and, of course, Marchesi L & P Antinori. Rarer are Castello di Verrazzano and Isole e Olena.

If you are planning to spend your castaway years in wealth and luxury, take along ample supplies of Fonterutoli's Ser Lapo and/or Antinori's Tenute Marchese, top-of-the-line riservas both. ■

meet the mushrooms

1. Chanterelle. Golden-hued and vase-shaped with delicate flavor and texture; harvested wild seasonally except for a cultivated black variety; available dried; very expensive ($15 to $30 per pound fresh); good in risottos, pasta sauces, and salads.

2. Pompon (also known as Pom Pon Blanc, Lion's Mane, Bearded Tooth). Resembles a little white sea sponge, solid in the center with "teeth" on the surface; cultivated; sweet crablike flavor when roasted or sautéed until crisp; expensive (about $16 per pound); good with seafood.

3. Crimini (also known as Italian brown, brown). A hearty, darker-colored relative of the white button, with a more intense, earthier flavor; cultivated; inexpensive ($2 to $3.50 per pound, comparable to the white button); versatile in cooking.

4. Enoki. A fragile, tiny white mushroom with delicate flavor, a long stem, and a tiny cap; grows in small clusters; cultivated; relatively inexpensive (about $2 per 3½-ounce package); best used fresh in salads or as a garnish, or added at the end of cooking.

5. Morel. Brown, cone-shaped, and spongelike, with hearty flavor; harvested wild (a limited supply of commercially grown morels may soon become available); commonly found dried; very expensive ($18 per pound and up fresh); requires careful cleaning; good in sauces.

6. Oyster. Named for its oyster shell–shaped cap, oyster color (although hues range from white to dark, and include blue and golden varieties), and, some say, its slight oyster or fish flavor; cultivated; relatively inexpensive ($5.50 to $7 per pound); firm-textured when cooked; good in sauces or sautéed for salads.

7. Porcini (cèpe). Looks like a fairy-tale toadstool; brown color; harvested wild only; commonly available dried; delicate, rich flavor; very expensive (about $30 per pound fresh); good in sauces, risottos, and many other dishes.

8. Portabella. A giant crimini mushroom with a cap at least 4½ inches wide; cultivated; rich, meaty flavor and chewy texture; relatively inexpensive ($4 to $10 per pound); wonderful grilled or roasted.

9. Shiitake (Black Forest). Resembles a miniature umbrella; tan to dark cap, tough brown stem (discard before cooking); cultivated; readily available dried; rich, woodsy flavor; expensive ($7 to $16 per pound fresh); versatile in cooking.

The mushroom boom

You'll find a whole lot more than the traditional button in Western markets these days. Here's how to choose, store, and cook specialty varieties

Every day, from thousands of trays of soil at Monterey Mushrooms in Watsonville, California, portabella mushrooms begin their journey to restaurant kitchens and grocery store shelves. Not far away, Hazel Dell Mushrooms is packing shiitake and oyster varieties, also in tremendous demand across the country.

It's no accident that farms that produce these specialty mushrooms are proliferating. The West's coastal region provides perfect weather for growing the edible fungi. And, as more varieties become cultivated, demand for them is soaring. Although the white button still accounts for more than 90 percent of mushroom sales, production of relatives such as the crimini (Italian brown) and giant portabella (a mature crimini), and of oyster and shiitake varieties, is expanding rapidly.

Demand is also increasing for wild mushrooms in season, particularly morels, chanterelles, and porcini (cèpes). Of course, you're likely to pay dearly for these scarce, exquisitely flavored beauties. And many cultivated varieties are pricey as well.

Keep in mind that terms such as *specialty* and *exotic* do not indicate wild mushrooms. They simply refer to mushrooms other than the common button variety. Those labeled *wild,* however, have been picked in the wild, even if the variety is usually cultivated.

Because wild mushrooms such as chanterelles, porcini, and morels are available only seasonally, you'll find them dried during much of the year. The cultivated shiitake is also available dried and, like wild mushrooms, lends rich flavor when rehydrated in soups, stocks, and sauces.

Recipes that showcase these mushrooms begin on page 52. Paul Bertolli, chef-owner at Oliveto Cafe and Restaurant in Oakland, created the mélange, vinaigrette, and torte recipes.

SUCCULENT *sautéed mushrooms in a flaky crust make a savory first course (see recipe on page 53).*

ROBERT OLDING

Bertolli's Mushroom Mélange

Cooking time: About 20 minutes

Prep time: About 15 minutes

Notes: This is good spooned over soft polenta or risotto. If you prefer, substitute 4 ounces assorted dried mushrooms (about 5½ cups dried) for the 2 pounds fresh after soaking them for about 1 hour in 4 cups warm water. Add mushrooms with their clear soaking liquid to cooked shallots and prosciutto (step 3), cook 15 minutes over medium heat, and proceed to step 4.

Makes: About 4 cups; 8 servings

- 2 pounds (3 or 4 kinds) assorted mushrooms, such as chanterelle, crimini, morel, oyster, pompon, porcini, portabella, shiitake, and button
- 2 tablespoons olive oil
- ¼ cup finely diced shallots
- 2 ounces (½ cup) prosciutto, finely diced
- ⅛ teaspoon *each* salt and pepper
- ½ cup *each* whipping cream and chicken broth
- ¼ cup fresh white bread crumbs
- 1½ tablespoons freshly chopped herbs, such as parsley, thyme, marjoram, and rosemary

1. Clean and prepare mushrooms (see directions below). Slice large mushrooms lengthwise ¼ to ½ inch thick; leave smaller ones whole.

2. To a 10- to 12-inch frying pan over medium-high heat, add oil, shallots, and prosciutto. Cook, stirring, until shallots are limp and tinged brown, 2 to 3 minutes.

3. Add mushrooms, salt, and pepper. Cook, stirring, over high heat until all liquid released from mushrooms has evaporated, about 15 minutes.

MUSHROOMS VINAIGRETTE *stars in a simple salad with arugula.* *Top with shaved parmesan and ground pepper.*

4. Add cream and broth, and cook until reduced by half, about 5 minutes; mixture will be moist but not runny.

5. Add bread crumbs and herbs; stir just to mix. Serve, or cool to use in Mushroom Torte (recipe on page 126).

Per ½ cup: 127 cal., 68% (86 cal.) from fat; 5.1 g protein; 9.6 g fat (3.7 g sat.); 7.3 g carbo.; 190 mg sodium; 22 mg chol.

Mushrooms Vinaigrette

Cooking time: About 30 minutes

Prep time: About 5 minutes

Notes: These tangy herbed mushrooms are perfect for salads, for topping toasted Italian country bread, or for serving alongside roast meats such as veal or pork.

Makes: About 2 cups

- 1 pound mushrooms, such as oyster, porcini, portabella, or small shiitake
- 1 tablespoon white wine vinegar
- ¼ teaspoon salt
- ⅛ teaspoon ground pepper

- ½ cup extra-virgin olive oil
- 6 sprigs (2 in. each) fresh rosemary
- 3 cloves garlic, thinly sliced

1. Clean mushrooms (directions below). Leave shiitake and oyster mushrooms whole. Cut others lengthwise into ¼-inch slices.

2. Fill a 6- to 8-quart pan with ½ inch water (about 3 cups); add a steamer basket. Over high heat, bring water to a boil. Fill basket with single layer of mushrooms; cover tightly, and steam until soft and tan-colored and reduced to about ¾ of original size, 5 to 8 minutes; remove slices to bowl and keep warm. Repeat until all mushrooms have been steamed, then mix mushrooms with vinegar, salt, and pepper. Turn heat to high; reduce steaming liquid to 2 tablespoons, about 2 minutes, and add to mushrooms.

3. To a 1- to 2-quart pan over medium heat, add oil, rosemary, and garlic; let herbs sizzle 2 minutes (do not brown). Remove from heat; let cool.

4. In a clean 1-pint jar, layer mushroom

making the most of mushrooms

Because mushrooms are fragile and highly perishable, proper handling and care are critical.

To select: Choose blemish-free mushrooms with a fresh, smooth (unwrinkled), dry surface. Mushrooms that have a veil (the thin membrane under the cap) have a more delicate flavor when the veil is closed (if open, the flavor is richer). Mushrooms are usually at peak flavor just as the

veil starts to open.

To store: Always refrigerate fresh mushrooms; never wash until ready to use. To prolong the storage of packaged mushrooms, remove plastic wrap, leave in tray or container, and wrap with paper towels (mushrooms stored in unventilated plastic will spoil). Store bulk (loose) mushrooms in a paper bag.

To clean and prepare: *For cultivated mushrooms,* use a

soft brush or gently wipe with a damp cloth to remove dirt particles. Or place mushrooms in a colander, quickly rinse with cold water, and pat dry with paper towels.

For wild mushrooms (especially those with nooks and crannies, such as morels), fill a plastic bag with water, add mushrooms, and quickly swirl water around them to loosen dirt and any small insects. Let water drain from bag. (Never soak mushrooms; they'll absorb water.)

There's no need to peel fresh mushrooms; just trim off any bruised spots, tough or dirty ends or edges, and the stem end if it looks dry. Remove the tough stem of the shiitake, as well as the dry, fibrous end of the portabella stem.

For dried mushrooms, be sure to rinse or soak before adding to your recipe (they may contain dirt, small pebbles, or dried insects). Let any debris sink to the bottom of the cleaning water, then pour off the clear liquid for cooking.

slices with flavored oil, rosemary, and garlic. Let stand at least 30 minutes, or cover jar with lid and refrigerate up to 1 month. Use at room temperature.

Per 1/4 cup drained mushrooms: 48 cal., 73% (35 cal.) from fat; 1.3 g protein; 3.9 g fat (0.6 g sat.); 3.1 g carbo.; 19 mg sodium; 0 mg chol.

Mushroom Torte

Cooking time: 45 minutes
Prep time: 15 minutes, plus at least 1 1/2 hours for chilling crust
Makes: 12 to 14 first-course servings

  10 tablespoons cold butter
     About 2 cups all-purpose flour
     About 2/3 cup ice water
   2 tablespoons ground walnuts
   1 recipe Bertolli's Mushroom Mélange (see page 124), cooled
   1 large egg
   2 teaspoons milk or whipping cream

1. Cut butter into 1/4-inch cubes. In a mixing bowl, combine butter with 2 cups flour, coating all pieces. Add 1/3 cup water. Using a pastry blender or 2 knives, cut through mixture until butter pieces are reduced to 1/8 inch. Pour 1/3 cup more water over dry portions of dough; continue to cut in until all flour is damp and pastry sticks together. If needed, add more water to dough, 1 tablespoon at a time.

2. Gather dough by hand, and divide in half. Gently press into two 5-inch disks. Wrap each in plastic; chill at least 1 1/2 hours before rolling. If not using within 2 days, freeze airtight up to 1 month (thaw in refrigerator overnight before using).

3. On a lightly floured board, roll out one disk into a 12-inch circle. Arrange on a parchment-lined 12- by 15-inch baking sheet. Combine walnuts with 1 tablespoon flour; sprinkle evenly over pastry, leaving about a 1 1/2-inch border. Spoon cooled mushroom filling evenly over walnuts, then fold pastry edge up and over filling.

4. On floured board, roll out second disk to fit over top of tart (about 11 in.). Beat

A ROASTED PORTABELLA *mushroom rests upon fresh corn polenta; drizzle with balsamic vinegar for a lively finish.*

together egg and milk; brush a little over edge of bottom crust. Lay top crust over filling; press edges to bottom crust to seal. Brush top evenly with remaining egg mixture (you may have a little left over). Cut several slits to release steam. Bake in a 400° oven until golden brown, about 45 minutes. Let cool 10 minutes before serving. Chill leftovers airtight up to 2 days; reheat in a 400° oven for 15 to 20 minutes.

Per serving: 223 cal., 61% (135 cal.) from fat; 5.4 g protein; 15 g fat (7.4 g sat.); 18 g carbo.; 198 mg sodium; 50 mg chol.

Roasted Mushrooms with Fresh Corn Polenta

Cooking time: About 25 minutes
Prep time: About 20 minutes
Notes: Portabellas are striking because of their size, but shiitake, oyster, and even button mushrooms work well.
Makes: 4 servings

   4 portabella mushrooms (each 5 1/2 in. wide) or 8 portabella mushrooms (each 3 in. wide), about 1 1/2 to 2 pounds; or 18 shiitake mushrooms (about 3/4 lb.); or 1 pound oyster or button mushrooms
     Nonstick cooking spray
   3 tablespoons balsamic vinegar
   1 tablespoon olive oil
   4 cups chicken or vegetable broth
   1/2 cup minced onion
   1/4 cup polenta
   4 cups fresh corn kernels (about 4 large ears) or frozen corn kernels
     Parsley sprigs, balsamic vinegar, and salt

1. Rinse mushrooms; trim and discard stems from portabellas or shiitakes. Lay caps on paper towels to drain. Meanwhile, lightly coat a 10- by 15-inch baking pan with nonstick cooking spray.

2. Mix vinegar and oil; evenly brush on all sides of mushrooms. Lay mushrooms in a single layer on baking pan. Bake in a 400° oven until dark brown, 20 to 25 minutes, turning mushrooms after 10 minutes.

3. Meanwhile, in a 10- to 12-inch frying pan over high heat, bring broth, onion, and polenta to a boil; cook, stirring often, until slightly thickened, about 10 minutes.

4. Add corn; continue to cook until sauce is as thick as catsup, about 15 minutes longer.

5. Divide polenta among 4 hot dinner plates; evenly distribute mushrooms over servings. Garnish with parsley sprigs, offer balsamic vinegar to drizzle over as desired, and add salt to taste.

Per serving: 261 cal., 31% (81 cal.) from fat; 12 g protein; 9 g fat (1.6 g sat.); 45 g carbo.; 144 mg sodium; 0 mg chol. ■

By Betsy Reynolds Bateson

ordering specialty mushrooms

Malcolm Clark has been playing with mushrooms for more than a quarter of a century. His company, Gourmet Mushrooms, in Sebastopol, California, was the first to cultivate the shiitake in North America (in 1972). It continues to bring new mushroom breeds to consumers. Although many of Clark's mushrooms have been trademarked and are difficult to find at the retail level, you can order them by mail. For more information, write or call Gourmet Mushrooms, Box 391, Sebastopol, CA 95473; (707) 823-1743, fax (707) 823-1507. The Chef's Gourmet Mushroom Basket (2 pounds) costs about $46, The Connoisseur's Gourmet Mushroom Basket (4 pounds) about $68. You can also order dried mushrooms and kits for growing your own at home.

Three-alarm flavor without the flames

Tone down chipotle's heat to get more of its great taste

RICH NUANCES *of chipotles come through in mellow soup when their heat is tempered.*

NORMAN A. PLATE

WRINKLED CHIPOTLES *are green jalapeños ripened to red, then smoke-dried. Sold dried or canned.*

S MOKE IS THE MAGIC THAT TURNS fresh, ripe jalapeño chilies into chipotles. These fleshy chilies and similar varieties need a little heat to dry their thick walls. As they rest well above a low-burning flame, smoke slips into them so naturally it's hard to believe the resulting complexity didn't develop as the chilies grew.

As the shiny, raw red pods shrink and wither during the smoking process, they turn a dull brown. Their uniquely lusty, almost meaty flavor, however, is anything but dull. Many a timid palate braves potential scorching to savor it, but those in the know temper the chili heat to get more flavor and less fire. Just remove the veins (where the heat is concentrated) and the seeds. Then use the chilies with a freer hand to give a chipotle edge to braised meats, sauces, sandwiches, mayonnaise, dressings, soups, and salsas.

Chipotles come in two forms: canned in adobado (a spicy tomato sauce) or dried. Both are staples in Latino groceries, but they are appearing with increasing frequency in well-stocked supermarkets, too.

Soak dried or rinse canned chipotle chilies. Wear rubber gloves when handling chilies, or wash hands well after touching them. Pour boiling water over dried chipotles and let them soak until soft, about 10 minutes. Pull off and discard stems, veins, and seeds. Or rinse canned chilies and gently pull off and discard stems, veins, and seeds.

Chipotle and Red Pepper Salsa

Cooking time: About 6 minutes
Prep time: About 7 minutes with canned chilies, about 20 minutes with dried
Notes: Serve as a dip or as a sauce for grilled meats.
Makes: About 1½ cups

- 1 onion (about 6 oz.)
- 2 cloves garlic, minced
- 1 cup canned roasted red peppers, rinsed and drained
- 4 or 5 dried or canned chipotle chilies, soaked or rinsed (see preceding)
- 2 tablespoons lime juice
- Salt

1. Slice onion ½ inch thick. In an 8- to 10-inch frying pan, cook onion and garlic over high heat, turning occasionally, until flecked with dark brown, 6 to 8 minutes.

2. In a blender or food processor, whirl till smooth ½ the onion mixture and ½ the red peppers with all the chilies and lime juice.

3. Chop remaining onion and red peppers, and stir into purée. Add salt to taste.

Per tablespoon: 6.2 cal., 15% (0.9 cal.) from fat; 0.1 g protein; 0.1 g fat (0 g sat.); 1.3 g carbo.; 13 mg sodium; 0 mg chol.

Chipotle Corn Soup

Cooking time: About 20 minutes
Prep time: 10 to 20 minutes
Makes: 5 or 6 servings

- 3 or 4 dried or canned chipotle chilies, soaked or rinsed (see preceding)
- 1½ quarts chicken broth
- 1 onion (6 oz.), chopped
- 1 clove garlic, pressed or minced
- ¾ teaspoon cumin seed
- 1 package (10 oz.) frozen corn kernels
- 1 Roma tomato (about ¼ lb.), cored and diced
- ½ pound (about 2 cups) shredded cooked chicken
- 2 tablespoons lime juice
- ¼ cup fresh cilantro leaves
- 1 package (3 oz.) cream cheese, cut into ½-inch cubes

1. In a 3- to 4-quart pan, combine chilies, broth, onion, garlic, cumin, and corn. Bring to a boil, cover, and simmer until flavors are blended, about 15 minutes.

2. Stir in tomato and chicken. Bring to a boil. Add lime juice and cilantro.

3. Ladle into bowls, and add cheese.

Per serving: 208 cal., 48% (99 cal.) from fat; 17 g protein; 11 g fat (4.8 g sat.); 16 g carbo.; 195 mg sodium; 49 mg chol. ∎

By Linda Lau Anusasananan

By Elaine Johnson

ALLAN ROSENBERG

Adding zest to your cookbook library

THERE'S NOTHING LIKE A NEW cookbook to spark my mealtime creativity, especially when its recipes are low-fat as well as delicious. These new titles by Western authors are reminding me how much I love to cook.

Cooking for Heart & Soul (Chronicle Books, San Francisco, 1995; $16.95). Editor Stanley Eichelbaum asked 70 chefs from Northern California how they cut back on fat without sacrificing flavor. Not every one of their 100 recipes passes for lean, but all are inspiring.

Provençal Light (Bantam Books, New York, 1994; $30). Berkeley author Martha Rose Shulman has kept all the vibrant flavors of southern France while judiciously trimming the fat.

The Stanford Life Plan for a Healthy Heart (Chronicle Books, 1996; $25). Even if you're not concerned about heart health per se, this reference cookbook (nearly 600 pages) with enticing recipes will help you implement a low-fat lifestyle and understand nutrition advice.

Low-Fat Vegetarian Cookbook (Sunset Publishing Corporation, Menlo Park, CA, 1995; $9.99). For those who are cooking meatless at least part of the time, this latest low-fat title from Sunset Books gives achievable recipes for healthful dishes. Many of the recipes use eggs and

dairy products; a few include a little meat for seasoning. This pasta recipe from the book has a flavorful sauce that's thickened with puréed cream-style corn.

Southwestern Fettuccine

Cooking time: About 20 minutes
Prep time: About 15 minutes
Makes: 4 servings

12   ounces dried fettuccine
 1   can (15 oz.) cream-style corn
⅔   cup nonfat milk
 1   teaspoon salad oil
½   teaspoon cumin seed
 1   onion (6 oz.), chopped
 1   red or yellow bell pepper (½ lb.), seeded and cut into thin strips
 1   package (10 oz.) frozen corn kernels, thawed and drained
 1   cup (4 oz.) shredded jalapeño jack cheese
¼   cup cilantro leaves, plus sprigs
1½   to 2 cups yellow or red cherry tomatoes, cut into halves
     Lime wedges and salt

1. In a 5- to 6-quart pan, bring 3 quarts water to a boil over high heat; stir in pasta and cook until just tender to bite, 8 to 10 minutes. Drain pasta and return to pan; keep warm. Meanwhile, whirl cream-style corn and milk in a blender or food processor until smoothly puréed; set aside.

2. Heat oil in a 10- to 12-inch nonstick frying pan over medium-high heat. Add cumin, onion, and bell pepper. Stir often until onion is soft, about 5 minutes; add water, 1 tablespoon at a time, if pan appears dry. Stir in milk mixture, corn kernels, cheese. Over medium heat, stir just until cheese melts.

3. Pour corn-cheese sauce over pasta. Add cilantro leaves; mix gently. Divide pasta among 4 shallow individual bowls; sprinkle with tomatoes. Garnish with cilantro sprigs. Season to taste with lime and salt.

Per serving: 627 cal., 22% (135 cal.) from fat; 25 g protein; 15 g fat (6 g sat.); 104 g carbo.; 540 mg sodium; 112 mg chol. ∎

WE'D LIKE TO HEAR FROM YOU!

Do you have tips or recipes for low-fat cooking? Write to Everyday Low-fat Cooking, Sunset Magazine, 80 Willow Rd., Menlo Park, CA 94025, or send e-mail (including your full name and street address) to lowfat@sunsetpub.com.

KEVIN CANDLAND

A rite of spring: Asparagus

Here's how to buy the best, then serve them elegantly

IF ANY FOOD DEFINES SPRING, IT'S asparagus. The very name, related to the Greek word meaning *to swell, burst forth,* describes the season. But in the West, asparagus season has a more practical meaning: feasting. This is asparagus country, and the primary growing areas—California's San Joaquin Delta and eastern Washington—swing into peak production in April and May.

In a single field, the tender shoots of these perennial plants may range from ¼ inch to nearly an inch wide. Size is no indication of tenderness or quality, just a matter of personal preference.

At the store, look for firm spears with compact bracts. At home, rinse and drain asparagus, wrap stems with damp towels to prevent drying, and chill airtight up to a few days.

To prepare asparagus spears, gently squeeze stalks from the stem up, snapping them off at the point where they begin to feel tender. The tough stem ends, sliced thinly to break up their fiber, are a good addition to soups and stir-fries.

Prosciutto-Almond Asparagus

Cooking time: About 10 minutes
Prep time: About 10 minutes
Makes: 6 servings

2 ounces paper-thin slices prosciutto, sliced crosswise ⅓ inch wide

1 tablespoon olive oil

⅓ cup sliced almonds

¾ cup fresh orange juice

⅓ cup red wine vinegar

1 teaspoon cornstarch

1 teaspoon grated orange peel

2 pounds asparagus, tough ends removed

Pepper

1 twist of orange peel

1. In a 10- to 12-inch frying pan over medium heat, stir prosciutto and oil until meat is browned, about 4 minutes. With a slotted spoon, lift prosciutto onto towels.

2. Add almonds to pan. Stir until golden, 2 to 3 minutes. Lift nuts from pan onto towels, and set aside. Discard oil in pan.

3. Stir juice, vinegar, cornstarch, and grated orange peel until smooth. Pour into pan; stir over high heat until bubbling, about 1 minute. Pour into a small bowl; keep hot.

4. Rinse pan. Place asparagus in pan with ½ cup water. Cover tightly, and simmer over medium heat until tender-crisp to bite, 2 to

STRIPS OF CRISP PROSCIUTTO, toasted almonds, and an orange–wine vinegar sauce embellish asparagus.

4 minutes, stirring halfway through cooking. Drain, and arrange on a platter.

5. Pour orange sauce over asparagus, then scatter prosciutto and almonds on top. Season to taste with pepper, and garnish with orange twist.

Per serving: 110 cal., 47% (52 cal.) from fat; 7.6 g protein; 5.8 g fat (0.8 g sat.); 9.7 g carbo.; 178 mg sodium; 7.7 mg chol.

Roasted Asparagus

Cooking time: About 10 minutes
Prep time: About 10 minutes
Makes: 4 servings

1 tablespoon olive oil

1½ pounds very slender (¼ in. wide) asparagus, tough ends removed

3 tablespoons balsamic vinegar

Salt and pepper

¼ cup (½ oz.) parmesan curls

Place a 10-inch ovenproof frying pan in a 500° oven for 5 minutes. Swirl oil in pan. With tongs, roll asparagus in oil. Bake until tender-crisp to bite, 5 to 7 minutes. Drizzle with vinegar; add salt and pepper to taste. Scatter parmesan on top.

Per serving: 77 cal., 55% (42 cal.) from fat; 5.6 g protein; 4.7 g fat (1.2 g sat.); 5.5 g carbo.; 69 mg sodium; 2.8 mg chol.

Asparagus with Tarragon Dunking Sauce

Cooking time: About 5 minutes
Prep time: About 15 minutes
Makes: 6 to 8 servings

1 cup reduced-fat sour cream

¼ cup packed parsley sprigs

2 tablespoons packed fresh or 2 teaspoons dried tarragon leaves

Salt and freshly ground pepper

2 pounds asparagus (tough ends removed), cooked until tender-crisp, iced to chill, and drained

In a blender, whirl until very smooth the sour cream, parsley, and tarragon. Season to taste with salt and pepper. Serve with cooked asparagus for dunking.

Per serving: 72 cal., 53% (38 cal.) from fat; 4.9 g protein; 4.2 g fat (2.0 g sat.); 5.8 g carbo.; 19 mg sodium; 10 mg chol. ∎

By Elaine Johnson

Thai flavors pick up native squash

America's contribution to the world's supply of foodstuffs is immense. Potatoes (white, sweet, and many more), maize, beans, and tomatoes have had their fair share of attention from food historians. Squash is a lesser player, except for the carving pumpkin. We do use squash to stuff ravioli, following the Italian practice, and in soups, as the French do. But Shirley Rush goes further. By employing garlic, curry powder, and cilantro, she creates a Thai-style pumpkin soup.

Thai Pumpkin Soup

Cooking time: About 45 minutes
Prep time: 10 to 15 minutes
Notes: If making soup ahead, cool, cover, and chill up to 2 days, then reheat before serving.
Makes: 4 to 6 servings

- 1 onion (5 or 6 oz.), finely chopped
- ¼ cup diced red bell pepper
- 2 tablespoons curry powder
- 1 teaspoon minced garlic
- 1 can (1 lb.) pumpkin
- 2 chicken bouillon cubes
- 1 teaspoon sugar
- 2 cups unflavored nonfat yogurt
- 1 tablespoon all-purpose flour
- ¼ cup chopped fresh cilantro

1. Place onion, bell pepper, and ½ cup water in a 3- to 4-quart pan over high heat. Stir often until pan is dry and onion browns lightly, 10 to 12 minutes.

2. Add curry powder and garlic; stir 1 minute. Add 2 cups water, stirring well to free browned bits in pan, then add pumpkin, bouillon cubes, and sugar. Cover and simmer gently to blend flavors, 25 to 30 minutes.

3. Meanwhile, mix a little of the yogurt with the flour until smooth, then combine with remaining yogurt. When the soup has simmered, with a whisk, stir yogurt-flour mixture into it. Turn heat to high and stir until boiling, then simmer and stir about 2 minutes. Ladle into bowls or mugs, and top with chopped cilantro.

Per serving: 97 cal., 6.5% (6.3 cal.) from fat; 6.2 g protein; 0.7 g fat (0.2 g sat.); 18 g carbo.; 384 mg sodium; 1.5 mg chol.

Shirley M. Rush

Santa Rosa, California

So linked are roast lamb and mint jelly that some people call the quaking green stuff lamb jelly. But Charlotte McLaughlin uses mint jelly a new way—in place of sugar in cookies.

Grated zucchini is also an ingredient, along with the usual butter and flour. Here's another outstanding play by zucchini, the greatest utility infielder on the vegetable team.

Zucchini Mint Cookies

Cooking time: 12 to 15 minutes per pan
Prep time: 25 to 30 minutes
Notes: Freeze cookies to store more than a few days.
Makes: About 5 dozen

- ½ cup (¼ lb.) butter, margarine, or solid shortening, at room temperature
- 1 cup mint jelly
- 1 cup grated zucchini
- 1 large egg
- 2 cups all-purpose flour
- 1 teaspoon baking soda
- 1 cup chopped walnuts
- 1 cup raisins
- 1 cup unsweetened shredded dried coconut

1. In a bowl, beat butter and jelly until well blended. Add zucchini and egg; mix well. Stir flour with soda, then add to jelly mixture and stir until blended. Add nuts, raisins, and coconut, and mix well.

2. Drop batter in 1-tablespoon mounds 1 inch apart on oiled 12- by 15-inch baking pans. Bake in a 375° oven until cookies are lightly browned and feel firm and dry when touched, 12 to 15 minutes; alternate pan positions after 6 minutes. Transfer to racks to cool. Serve, or when cool, store airtight up to 2 days.

Per cookie: 72 cal., 44% (32 cal.) from fat; 1 g protein; 3.6 g fat (1.7 g sat.); 9.4 g carbo.; 41 mg sodium; 7.7 mg chol.

Charlotte C. McLaughlin

Mesquite, Nevada
By Joan Griffiths, Richard Dunmire

SUNSET'S KITCHEN CABINET

Readers' family favorites tested in our kitchens

By Betsy Reynolds Bateson

DICK COLE

Quick Chicken Mole

Maureen Valentine, SeaTac, Washington

When newspaper editors in SeaTac, just south of Seattle, learned that Maureen Valentine's recipes had been published in *Sunset Magazine,* they wanted her to write a food feature. Instant career? Well, not exactly. Valentine entered her first cooking contest at age 10, then about 10 years ago began submitting recipes to magazines. Her Quick Chicken Mole evolved from watching a travel video about Mexico that featured a woman making mole.

Cooking time: About 30 minutes
Prep time: About 5 minutes
Makes: 4 servings

- 1 teaspoon olive or salad oil
- 1 onion (about 6 oz.), minced
- 2 cloves garlic, minced
- ¾ cup chicken broth
- 1 can (8 oz.) tomato sauce
- 1 ripe banana (about ¼ lb.), mashed
- 1 tablespoon *each* chili powder and unsweetened cocoa powder
- 1 teaspoon *each* ground cinnamon and ground cumin
- ¼ teaspoon *each* black pepper and cayenne
- 4 boneless, skinless chicken breast halves
  Hot cooked rice
- ¼ cup toasted sliced almonds
- 2 tablespoons raisins
  Warm corn tortillas

1. To a 10- to 12-inch frying pan over medium-high heat, add oil, onion, and garlic. Cook, stirring, until onion is tinged brown; deglaze pan with 1 tablespoon of the broth.

2. Add tomato sauce, remaining broth, banana, chili powder, cocoa, cinnamon, cumin, pepper, and cayenne. Bring to a boil; reduce heat, cover, and simmer 10 minutes. Add chicken; continue to simmer until chicken is just firm, and opaque when cut in thickest part, about 15 minutes longer.

3. To serve, place a breast half and sauce atop rice on each of 4 dinner plates; top equally with almonds and raisins. Offer tortillas for scooping and dipping.

Per serving: 258 cal., 24% (63 cal.) from fat; 31 g protein; 7 g fat (1.1 g sat.); 20 g carbo.; 464 mg sodium; 68 mg chol.

St. Paddy's Day Salad

Mickey Strang, McKinleyville, California

The first of many recipes submitted by Mickey Strang was published in *Sunset* almost 50 years ago. She developed this dinner salad as separate components, but soon began mixing them together. Strang cooks her own corned beef with apple juice; however, you can purchase cooked corned beef from a deli.

Prep time: About 30 minutes
Makes: 4 to 5 servings

- 2 cups (about ¾ lb.) shredded or slivered cooked corned beef
- 2 cups thinly sliced cooked potatoes (about 1¼ lb.)
- 2 cups shredded green cabbage (about ⅓ lb.)
- ½ cup *each* thinly sliced radishes and celery
- ½ cup grated carrot
- ½ cup chopped green onion
- ½ cup *each* sour cream and unflavored nonfat yogurt
- 2 tablespoons *each* mayonnaise and cider vinegar
  Salt and pepper
  Parsley sprigs (optional)

1. In a large, shallow bowl, combine corned beef, potatoes, cabbage, radishes, celery, carrot, and onion.

2. Mix together sour cream, yogurt, mayonnaise, and vinegar.

3. Gently fold sour cream mixture into meat and vegetables; add salt and pepper to taste. Garnish with parsley. Serve, or cover and chill up to 2 hours. Stir just before serving.

Per serving: 390 cal., 51% (198 cal.) from fat; 17 g protein; 22 g fat (8 g sat.); 31 g carbo.; 863 mg sodium; 81 mg chol.

Lemon Cheesecake Soufflé

Gemma Sciabica, Modesto, California

A family favorite handed down from Gemma Sciabica's mother, this cheesecake soufflé has all the flavor of traditional cheesecake but a lot less cholesterol and fat. When we tested it, the cake rose out of the cheesecake pan, so we put the mixture into a soufflé dish.

Cooking time: About 45 minutes
Prep time: About 30 minutes
Makes: 10 to 12 servings

About 1 tablespoon butter or margarine
1/2 cup almond biscotti crumbs
1 container (15 oz.) low-fat ricotta cheese
1 cup unflavored nonfat yogurt
3/4 cup sugar
1/4 cup all-purpose flour
1 tablespoon grated lemon peel
1/4 cup fresh lemon juice
1 teaspoon vanilla
1/2 teaspoon salt
2 large eggs, separated, plus 2 large egg whites
1 tablespoon cherry liqueur or maraschino cherry juice
1/8 teaspoon cream of tartar
Sliced strawberries

1. Lightly butter bottom and sides of a 2 1/2- to 3-quart soufflé dish. Coat with biscotti crumbs, leaving any loose crumbs in bottom of dish.
2. To a bowl, add ricotta, yogurt, 1/2 cup sugar, flour, lemon peel and juice, vanilla, salt, 2 yolks, and liqueur. With mixer, blend until smooth.
3. In another bowl, with clean beaters, beat the 4 egg whites and cream of tartar on high speed until soft peaks form; gradually add remaining 1/4 cup sugar, continuing to beat until sugar is thoroughly incorporated. Gently fold whites into ricotta mixture.
4. Pour into prepared dish; bake in a 350° oven until center is firm and top is golden brown, about 45 minutes. Spoon warm soufflé into bowls; top with berries.

Per serving: 150 cal., 27% (41 cal.) from fat; 8.1 g protein; 4.6 g fat (2.1 g sat.); 20 g carbo.; 180 mg sodium; 45 mg chol.

Everybody's Chili

Alan Azulay, Federal Way, Washington

Alan Azulay created this recipe because he wanted a dish that would satisfy everyone at potlucks. It also needed to be easy to make ahead and to reheat in a microwave. His flavor secret is menudo spice mix, which you'll find in the ethnic section at most supermarkets, or in Latino markets.

Cooking time: About 55 minutes
Prep time: About 15 minutes
Makes: 6 to 8 servings

2 teaspoons olive or salad oil
1 onion, chopped
1 red bell pepper, stemmed, seeded, and chopped
1 cup sliced celery
2 cloves garlic, minced
1 can (15 oz.) each pinto beans and kidney beans
1 can (15 oz.) chopped tomatoes with juice
1 can (10 1/2 oz.) red chili sauce or enchilada sauce
1 cup beer or vegetable broth
2 teaspoons menudo spice mix
1/2 teaspoon each ground coriander and ground cinnamon
Lime wedges
1 cup grated cheddar cheese
About 1/2 cup fresh cilantro leaves

1. To a 6- to 8-quart pan over medium-high heat, add oil, onion, pepper, celery, and garlic. Cook, stirring, until tinged brown, 6 minutes.
2. Add beans, tomatoes with juice, chili sauce, beer, menudo spice, coriander, and cinnamon. Reduce heat to medium-low, and cook until flavors are well blended, about 45 minutes. Serve, or cool and refrigerate up to 4 days.
3. Squeeze lime, and sprinkle cheese and cilantro, over individual servings.

Per serving: 221 cal., 26% (58 cal.) from fat; 11 g protein; 6.4 g fat (3.2 g sat.); 32 g carbo.; 1,115 mg sodium; 15 mg chol.

Chinese Five-Spice Oatmeal Cookies

Liz Lauter, Kentfield, California

Liz Lauter gets her kids to do most of the baking of these cookies by baking one sheet before they get home and leaving the bowl of dough nearby. Once the children eat up all the cookies she's baked, they finish making the rest of the cookies.

Cooking time: About 15 minutes per pan
Prep time: About 30 minutes
Makes: About 3 dozen

2 cups quick-cooking rolled oats
1 1/2 cups all-purpose flour
1 cup coarsely ground toasted almonds
1 1/2 teaspoons Chinese five spice
1 teaspoon each baking powder and ground cinnamon
1/2 teaspoon salt
1 cup butter or margarine
1 cup granulated sugar
1 cup firmly packed light brown sugar
2 large eggs
2 teaspoons vanilla

1. Combine oats, flour, ground almonds, Chinese five spice, baking powder, cinnamon, and salt; set aside.
2. In a large bowl, with mixer, beat together butter and sugars until smoothly blended. Add eggs and vanilla, and beat until combined. Add flour mixture; beat until blended.
3. On lightly greased 10- by 15-inch baking pans, drop batter in generously mounded tablespoons about 1 1/2 inches apart; bake in a 350° oven until golden, 12 to 15 minutes. Cool on a rack.

Per cookie: 155 cal., 45% (70 cal.) from fat; 2.4 g protein; 7.8 g fat (3.5 g sat.); 20 g carbo.; 103 mg sodium; 26 mg chol.

Share a recipe you've created or adapted—a family favorite, travel discovery, or time-saver—including the story behind the recipe. Send to *Sunset Magazine,* 80 Willow Rd., Menlo Park, CA 94025, or send e-mail (including full name and street address) to recipes@sunsetpub.com.

FOOD
Guide

BY JERRY ANNE DI VECCHIO

A TASTE OF THE WEST: Mussels to remember

A rule travelers forget, with regret, was violated once when my daughter, then about 10, and I were driving along the coast of Normandy. At first taste, she fell in love with mussels steamed with wine and crème fraîche. She had them for lunch, then she had them for dinner. The next day she did the same thing. On the third day, as we turned inland, I firmly suggested a menu change, promising she could have mussels again later on. Well, they weren't to be found in any town that followed. And like all tourists who anticipate that a regional dish—or an indigenous treasure—will be available on down the road, we failed to enjoy all the mussels we could before passing out of their province. This incident was a sore point for many days. But back home, I was able to redeem myself.

Pacific mussels, whose tender meat is bright orange to ivory, are much like those of Normandy. When I steamed them with homemade crème fraîche and a domestic white wine, all was forgiven. Since then, we've also come to like them steamed with sweet cream as well. It's a pleasing variation.

Not only do native mussels taste like the French ones, but my fish-guru friend in Washington, Jon Rowley, pointed out that some are actually the same. It seems West Coast mussels were joined here by Mediterranean ones so long ago that both were presumed to be native. It's speculated that the Europeans arrived as hitchhikers on the bottoms of the first explorers' sailing ships. With learned inspection, you can see differences between the shell shapes. Another distinction: natives spawn in spring and summer, migrants in winter.

In safer times, before pollution concerns, we often gathered mussels from the seashore—they are all along the coast. When I did, I favored the small mussels, as they do in Normandy,

This very French bowl of mussels is also very easy to prepare.

ROBERT OLDING

60 APRIL

APRIL

- Simple, yet superlative steamed mussels

- No-mess oven-fried meatballs

- Culturing your own crème fraîche

- Baking's best for beets

- Meet the Merlots from Chile

because, to my taste, they are more flavorful and more tender. But prudence makes farmed mussels—the ones you buy—a far wiser choice, even though they are harvested larger than I would like.

Mussels with Wine and Cream

Cooking time: About 10 minutes

Prep time: About 20 minutes

Notes: Buy mussels no longer than 24 hours ahead, and keep them loosely covered in the refrigerator. Scrub just before steaming. Beards, the wiry strands that secure mussel shells to their moorings, are easily pulled free. Scrape off any large barnacles while scrubbing shells.

Makes: 4 main-dish or 8 first-course servings

- ½ cup minced shallots or red onion
- ½ cup minced parsley
- ½ teaspoon dried thyme leaves
- 1 tablespoon butter or margarine
- 1 cup chicken broth
- 1 cup dry white wine
- 1 cup whipping cream or crème fraîche (see page 62)
- 4 pounds (about 3 qt.) black-shell mussels, beards pulled off and shells scrubbed

1. In a 6- to 8-quart pan over medium-high heat, frequently stir shallots, ¼ cup parsley, and thyme in butter until shallots are limp, about 3 minutes.

2. Add broth, wine, cream, and mussels to pan. Cover, and bring to a boil on high heat. Simmer until mussels pop open, 5 to 10 minutes.

3. Sprinkle mussels with remaining parsley, then ladle into wide bowls and add cooking liquid to each bowl.

Per main-dish serving: 377 cal., 60% (225 cal.) from fat; 19 g protein; 25 g fat (14

SEASONAL NOTE

Tender signs of spring

Paul Bertolli is a master at bringing out the best in simple foods. After more than a decade as chef at Alice Waters's renowned Chez Panisse in Berkeley, Bertolli decided to follow his own heritage and moved down the road to Oliveto Restaurant & Cafe, in Oakland. Italian country dishes have captured his imagination. One evening he served a humble-looking but exceptionally fresh-tasting frittata as a first course. It struck just the proper note after a hectic day—enough so that I prepare this easy egg dish at home when in need of a really fast meal for a really tired body.

Spring Green Frittata

Cooking time: 6 to 8 minutes

Prep time: 8 to 10 minutes

Notes: Larger Swiss chard leaves will work, but they aren't as tender. Accompany the frittata with crusty bread and a green salad.

Makes: 1 main-dish serving or 2 first-course servings

- 2 to 3 ounces young Swiss chard leaves (5 to 6 in. long)
- 2 large eggs
- 1 tablespoon milk
- 2 tablespoons freshly grated parmesan cheese
- 2 teaspoons butter or olive oil
- ¼ cup slivered young leeks or green onions (white part only)
  Salt and pepper

1. Trim and discard discolored ends from chard leaves; rinse leaves, and drain.

2. Immerse leaves in rapidly boiling water just until limp, about 30 seconds.

3. At once, drain leaves and immerse in ice water to preserve color. Drain again, and squeeze dry. Chop leaves into about 1-inch pieces.

4. In a bowl, beat eggs to blend with milk and 1 tablespoon cheese.

5. In a 6- to 8-inch nonstick frying pan over medium-high heat, melt butter. Add leeks and 1 tablespoon water. Cover, and cook until leeks are limp but not browned, 2 to 3 minutes.

6. Uncover pan, turn heat to high, and add chard. When liquid has evaporated and butter sizzles, 1 to 2 minutes, pour egg mixture into pan. Cook until eggs barely begin to set at edges, ½ to 1 minute. Center will be runny.

7. Sprinkle frittata with remaining cheese, and broil about 3 inches from heat until top is set and lightly browned, about 1 minute. Slide onto a warm plate, and serve with salt and pepper to taste.

Per frittata: 280 cal., 64% (180 cal.) from fat; 17 g protein; 20 g fat (9.4 g sat.); 7.8 g carbo.; 442 mg sodium; 453 mg chol.

The art of oven-frying meatballs

Once I discovered how to oven-fry meatballs, I never wasted another minute cleaning a grease-spattered stovetop. Oven-frying is not only neater, but also easier and faster, and it requires no added fat.

First, season and shape the ground meat. For moist, tender meatballs, you need to add a little binder and liquid. The basic proportions I like—but often vary slightly—are these: for each 1 pound **ground lean meat** (beef, veal, lamb, pork, chicken, or turkey), mix in ¼ cup all-purpose flour or ½ cup fine dried bread crumbs, ½ cup **chicken broth** (or milk or water), and **seasonings** (salt, pepper, soy sauce, minced fresh ginger, herbs, or spices). If I increase the carbohydrates (such as replacing flour with ¾ cup cooked rice, lentils, or bulgur wheat), I sometimes also add 1 **large egg white** or 1 large egg so the meatballs hold their shape better.

As you shape the soft meat mixture into 1-inch balls, set them about ½ inch apart in a nonstick shallow-rim baking pan. (Meat does not brown well in a deeper pan; if pan isn't nonstick, oil lightly. A 10- by 15-inch pan holds 1 lb. seasoned meatballs.)

Bake in a 475° oven until meatballs are no longer pink in center (cut to test) and are lightly browned, 10 to 15 minutes. If desired, turn with a wide spatula once or twice after balls are browned where they touch the pan. If turned before this skin forms, the balls may stick and tear.

Use meatballs any way you would pan-browned ones: in sauce or soup, or as an appetizer.

For larger meatballs, 1½ to 2 inches wide, bake in a 425° oven until no longer pink in center (cut to test) and lightly browned, 20 to 30 minutes.

Per serving using ¼ lb. of meat: 389 cal., 58% (225 cal.) from fat; 24 g protein; 25 g fat (9.7 g sat.); 16 g carbo.; 223 mg sodium; 85 mg chol.

Keep a flame in your kitchen

Take a torch to crème brûlée.

You can pick up neat cooking tips sitting at the counter in contemporary restaurants with open kitchens. At Chinois on Main, in Santa Monica, I watched a hand-held propane torch used to melt sugar for shiny, crackling caramel glazes on crème brûlée. If you've ever tried to use the broiler to melt sugar for a crackly top on this dessert, you know how hard it is to avoid scorching part of the sugar before it's all melted. The propane torch makes this task much easier to manage because it gives you total control of both the intensity and the placement of the heat. The torch also does a fine job on other caramel-glazed desserts, such as tarte Tatin, and the ubiquitous baked Alaska—any place where quick surface browning or heating is important.

Before you use the torch, be sure to read all directions and safety instructions. You can use it indoors if the room is well ventilated.

To use, set valve to low, light with a match, and practice first at lowest setting, then on medium (the highest flame is too hot for most foods). Hold flame 4 to 6 inches from food surface and move in an even, sweeping motion, slowly enough to brown but fast enough to avoid scorching. Sugar begins to melt in about 30 seconds. Small desserts take about 1 minute to glaze; larger ones, with more space to cover, take longer. Don't turn heat directly onto the container if it isn't ovenproof.

Hand-held propane torches are sold in hardware stores for about $14; the fuel cartridge (usually about 14 oz.) is about $3—and provides about 8 hours of heat at medium setting.

Making crème fraîche

Even though you can buy crème fraîche, it's a bit pricey, considering what it really is—just whipping cream with a culture added. Both whipping cream and crème fraîche have the same cooking advantages: neither curdles when boiled, and each can be whipped.

If you plan a couple of days ahead, you can easily make your own crème fraîche; you can also make it in small quantities.

The culture (starter) that turns whipping cream into crème fraîche can be found in sour cream, plain yogurt, or buttermilk. Just pick a product with a flavor you like, because it will be what you taste in the crème fraîche. The starter should be freshly opened.

To make crème fraîche, heat **whipping cream** to 90° to 100°; remove from heat, and pour into a glass bowl or jar. For each 1 cup whipping cream, stir in 1 tablespoon **sour cream** (regular or low- or nonfat, although some low- or nonfat kinds may not work because of how they are made), buttermilk, or plain yogurt (regular, low-fat, or nonfat). Cover airtight, and let stand at room temperature until cream is as thick as or thicker than softly whipped cream, 24 to 36 hours. Use as is for cooking, or chill to whip or to store up to 4 days.

Per tablespoon: 46 cal., 93% (43 cal.) from fat; 0.4 g protein; 4.8 g fat (3 g sat.); 0.5 g carbo.; 5.6 mg sodium; 17 mg chol.

Beets, greens, and raspberries make up a surprising salad from the Albion River Inn.

GREAT INGREDIENT

Plain old beets

No wonder beets often get by-passed. There's hardly a messier vegetable to cook. Unless...

Yes, there is an easier, better way. Bake them. In Europe, that's the way most beets are sold in the market. Once home, you just slide off the skins and use the beets as you like.

The best reason to bake them, I think, is that they are splendid hot from the oven, split open and seasoned with a little butter and salt. Boiling makes them watery; baking makes them sweet.

To bake beets, scrub them, leave on root ends, and if they have tops, trim down to about an inch. Set beets in single layer in a pan. Bake in a 400° oven just until tender when pierced (they also give very slightly when pressed). Time varies with size; beets take longer than potatoes do. A 3-inch-wide beet may take up to 2½ hours to cook. Serve hot or cool; rub or slip off the skin.

Cold beets make great salads, and a particularly appealing version is served at the romantic Albion River Inn, Albion, California. Chef Stephen Smith shares his recipe.

Roasted Beet Salad

Cooking time: Small beets take 1½ to 2 hours to bake. Bacon and dressing take about 6 minutes.

Prep time: About 10 minutes

Notes: Bake 1½ pounds beets (about 2 in. wide) to get 2 cups, peeled and cut.

Makes: 4 servings

- 2 to 4 slices bacon, chopped
- 1 tablespoon olive oil
- 2 tablespoons minced shallots
- 1 clove garlic, minced
- ¼ cup raspberry vinegar
- ¼ cup chicken broth
- 2 cups julienne strips peeled, baked beets (see preceding)
- 4 to 6 cups (4 to 6 oz.) mixed baby lettuces or salad greens
- ¼ to ½ cup feta cheese, crumbled
  About ½ cup raspberries, rinsed and drained (optional)
- Salt and pepper

1. In an 8- to 10-inch frying pan over medium heat, stir bacon occasionally until brown and crisp, about 5 minutes. Drain off and discard fat; drain bacon on towels.

2. To pan, add olive oil, shallots, garlic, vinegar, and broth, and bring to a boil on high heat. Add beets, and mix. Remove from heat. Use hot or tepid.

3. Mound salad greens equally onto plates. Spoon beet mixture over greens, and sprinkle with bacon, feta, and raspberries. Season to taste with salt and pepper.

Per serving: 110 cal., 57% (63 cal.) from fat; 3.8 g protein; 7.0 g fat (2.3 g sat.); 8.7 g carbo.; 197 mg sodium; 10 mg chol.

BOB THOMPSON ON WINE:

A new Merlot for grill food

Typical Chilean Merlot gives you some of the best parts of Beaujolais and Washington state Merlot rolled into one.

For what seems like forever, Beaujolais has been the model of red wine that charms with frisky youthfulness. Like Beaujolais, fresh, fruity Chilean Merlot spends little or no time in oak. Also like Beaujolais, it goes to bottle and then to market within months of the vintage, designed to be appealing as soon as it is bought.

Its kinship with Washington Merlots comes from much lustier flavors and slightly more drying tannins than Beaujolais offers. If the Chilean editions are not quite as briskly cleansing as the freshest of their cousins from America's Pacific Northwest, they are not far from it.

Those who are already thinking of barbecue, burgers, and pizza are on the right track, especially with Carta Vieja, Concha y Toro, Errazuriz, Santa Alicia, and Santa Rita. Some (Santa Monica) show faint flavors from oak-aging and other winemaking techniques. A few (Carmen, Casa Lapostolle) show definite signs of aging in oak, putting them more in the wait-for-a-steak camp of Chilean Cabernet Sauvignons—or typical oak-aged Washington Merlots.

Merlot from Chile is new in the marketplace, born since varietal Merlot became a hot ticket in the American market. However, growers and winemakers in Chile have had the grape variety in their vineyards for nearly a century and a half, emigrants from Bordeaux having first brought it to the country in the 1850s. As a result, they know exactly how to make the most of their grapes.

There's more good news: the prices of all but a few reserve Chilean Merlots range between $5 and $7 a bottle. Importers market all of the wines noted here throughout this country. Should you travel to Chile, add to your list Torreón de Paredes and Portal del Alto.

Because harvests in the southern hemisphere take place in March and April, most fruit-foremost 1995s can be found on store shelves now. Only the weightiest Reservas await a later day. ∎

aaaaahhhhhhhh
artichokes

Artichokes with
tender peeled stems
soak up a lean dressing spiked
with chili and aromatic coriander and mustard seeds.

If your passion for artichokes was stymied
by last year's prime-season flood damage, relax. The plucky
thorn is never down for long

*L*AST YEAR WE WERE DOWN BUT NOT OUT," REFLECTS DALE HUSS, AN ARTICHOKE GROW-
ER at Sea Mist Farms, describing the impact of the '95 floods that slammed
California's Monterey County just as artichoke production hit full swing. The damage was most dramatic along the Salinas River—which empties into the Pacific just
south of Castroville, the self-proclaimed Artichoke Capital of the World. At least
1,000 acres were underwater, and 40 percent of the crop was lost. And because
California provides virtually 100 percent of the nation's commercial artichokes,
with more than three-quarters of them coming from Monterey County, artichoke
lovers felt the pinch.

But now, rescued plants are revived, new plants are thriving—and though this
year's winter had very wet moments, the spring crop is on track. From March through

By Linda Lau Anusasananan   •   Photographs by Noel Barnhurst

May more than half of the $40-million crop is being harvested.

Artichokes arrived in California in the 1880s; Italian immigrants first planted the edible thistle. Currently, Green Globe is the most widely grown variety. This artichoke, which thrives along the cool, fog-shrouded coast as far north as Half Moon Bay and as far south as Monterey, is planted from cuttings. It's a temperate-weather perennial that produces year-round, with the biggest growth surge from late winter through spring. A second spurt of production occurs in the fall, after the summer slowdown. Most of these plants yield a crop for 10 to 12 years.

Other varieties, grown from seed, can deal with warmer climates. The semithornless Desert Globe is an annual that produces in winter and early spring in the coastal valley of Oxnard and the inland desert valleys. The thornless Big Heart is an annual, and its plantings are staggered for year-round harvest. This variety thrives around Lompoc, north of Santa Barbara, and in the inland Imperial Valley.

Where an artichoke—also called a *choke*—grows on the plant determines its size. The biggest chokes form at the tips of the tall stalks that emerge from the center of the large, arching, serrated, gray-green leaves of the plant. These premium primary buds are the first to mature and be picked. More buds grow on each stalk, with the largest at the top of the stalk and the smallest toward the bottom. Because artichokes mature at different times, they are handpicked. Workers, with packs on their backs, sweep through the fields every seven days, selecting fully formed buds just before they are ready to open. Artichokes are graded for size and boxed for shipping—often right in the fields, in portable packing sheds.

Spring is the best time to buy artichokes. This is when you can get big ones at bargain prices, often as little as $1 each; the tiny, so-called hearts, or baby artichokes (which are also mature), are a good value now, too.

Big chokes, with their sculptural silhouettes, are showy whole or cut, so take advantage of their shape. Even the stem is edible, if trimmed. Enjoy chokes cooked, hot or cold, or try them raw. Regardless of size or presentation, the subtle, nutlike flavor of artichokes shines through.

Thin shavings of raw artichoke bottom, fresh fennel, and parmesan cheese make an intriguing, cool-tasting salad.

artichoke
anatomy

thorns

bracts
(leaves)

stem

immature
florets
(fuzzy
center)

receptacle
(heart or
bottom)

To the uninitiated, an artichoke looks impenetrable. Its thistle thorns prick invaders. Tough leaves hide the fleshy bottom, which is the artichoke's meatiest and most treasured part. But, when you understand an artichoke's anatomy, it's easy to find your way to this succulent heart, packed with silken, immature florets.

What we eat is a flower bud. If the thistle is allowed to bloom, it grows woodier in texture as the leaves fold back and each floret in the center turns a glorious blue-purple, creating a magnificent flower.

On a tiny choke, the fuzzy center and very inner leaves are tender enough to be completely edible. If you want to use the artichoke whole or in pieces, break off the tough outer leaves and trim thorn tips from the tender, pale inner leaves.

To eat a cooked whole artichoke, tackle it leaf by leaf, pulling one at a time between your teeth to scrape off the flesh. Another approach is to cut open the artichoke, scoop out the center, eat what you can using a knife and fork, then tackle the remaining leaves by hand.

Artichoke Fennel Salad

Prep time: About 15 minutes
Notes: Use a vegetable slicer or peeler to thinly slice vegetables. Raw artichokes darken quickly when exposed to air.
Makes: 2 servings

    5 tablespoons lemon juice
    1 artichoke (3 to 4 in. wide)
    2 tablespoons extra-virgin olive oil
    1 to 1½ ounces parmesan cheese
    2 cups paper-thin slices fresh fennel
    2 teaspoons chopped Italian parsley
       Salt and pepper

1. In a bowl, mix 3 tablespoons lemon juice and 3 cups water. Trim artichoke to the bottom (see How to Handle an Artichoke, page 68), and dip into lemon water to preserve its color.

2. Cut bottom into paper-thin slices, dropping them directly into the lemon water.

3. Drain artichoke slices well, and quickly mix with remaining 2 tablespoons lemon juice and the olive oil in a bowl.

4. With a cheese slicer or vegetable peeler, shave about ½ the cheese onto artichoke slices. Add fennel and parsley; mix gently.

5. Mound salad onto 2 plates, and shave remaining cheese onto salads. Add salt and pepper to taste.

Per serving: 243 cal., 70% (171 cal.) from fat; 9.6 g protein; 19 g fat (4.7 g sat.); 13 g carbo.; 444 mg sodium; 11 mg chol.

Artichokes with Seed Dressing

Cooking time: 25 to 30 minutes
Prep time: About 25 minutes
Notes: Select artichokes with 2- to 3-inch stems.
Makes: 6 servings

    6 artichokes (each about 3 in. wide)
 1 1/2 tablespoons mustard seed
 1 1/2 tablespoons coriander seed
  1/4   teaspoon dried hot chili flakes
  1/3   cup white wine vinegar
    1   tablespoon extra-virgin olive oil
    1   clove garlic, pressed
    2   tablespoons chopped cilantro
        Salt and pepper

1. Trim artichokes as directed for artichoke hearts with stems (see adjacent box).

2. Cook artichokes as directed, adding mustard, coriander, and chili to seasoned water (see box), until bottoms are tender when pierced, 25 to 30 minutes.

3. With a slotted spoon, lift out artichokes, and drain. Reserve 1 cup of the cooking liquid. Pour remaining liquid through a fine strainer, and reserve seed mixture.

4. Mix reserved cooking liquid, reserved seed mixture, vinegar, oil, and garlic in a shallow, wide bowl. Add artichokes, turning to coat with dressing. Let stand, turning occasionally, at least 10 minutes, or cover and chill up to 1 day.

5. Stand artichokes, stems up, in a shallow rimmed dish. Or cut in half lengthwise.

6. Pour dressing over artichokes, and sprinkle with chopped cilantro. Add salt and pepper to taste.

Per serving: 104 cal., 31% (32 cal.) from fat; 5.3 g protein; 3.6 g fat (0.4 g sat.); 17 g carbo.; 129 mg sodium; 0 mg chol.

Herb Cheese Artichokes

Cooking time: 40 to 45 minutes
Prep time: About 20 minutes
Notes: Select artichokes with 2- to 3-inch stems. If making ahead, fill artichokes, cover, and chill up to 1 day. Bake as directed for about 20 minutes. If desired, drape each baked artichoke with a thin slice of prosciutto.
Makes: 4 servings

    4 artichokes (each about 3 in. wide)
    1 tablespoon extra-virgin olive oil

how to handle an *artichoke*

An artichoke that is compactly shaped, with leaves tightly cupped, has reached maturity in cool weather. If it is exposed to frost, brown blemishes appear on its leaves, but this discoloration has no flavor effect and disappears as the artichoke cooks.

As days get warmer, the artichoke's leaves are inclined to flare, and thorns are more pronounced because the bud is getting itchy to bloom.

Artichokes that have been cut darken rapidly in the air. To slow discoloration, drop cut artichokes as quickly as possible into acidulated water (3 tablespoons vinegar or lemon juice to each 1 quart water). Leave in water until ready to cook or cut again.

Whole artichokes. Slice about 1/2 inch crosswise off the tops to remove main clusters of thorns, and discard. Pull small leaves off bottoms and stems of artichokes, and discard. With scissors, cut thorny tips from remaining outer leaves. If you want artichokes with stems, peel stems to remove fibrous exteriors, and trim bottoms to make them fairly smooth. If you want artichokes to sit upright when served, trim stems flush with bottoms before cooking.

Artichoke hearts with stems. Break off artichoke leaves (quick-cook, as follows, or discard) down to pale, tender inner ones. Slice off about the top third of the remaining leaves. Peel artichoke bottoms and stems (lengths vary greatly) to remove fibrous exteriors. Trim discolored ends of stems.

Artichoke bottoms. Break off artichoke leaves (quick-cook, as follows, or discard). With a spoon, scrape fuzzy centers from bottoms, and discard. With a small knife, trim stems flush with bottoms. Peel bottoms to make bases smooth.

Cooked artichokes. Choose a pan large enough to hold whole artichokes, artichoke hearts with stems,

or artichoke bottoms—for 4 to 7 whole large artichokes, you'll need an 8- to 12-quart pan. Half-fill pan with **water,** and for each quart, add 1 tablespoon **vinegar,** 1 or 2 drops **olive oil** (optional), and 5 or 6 **black peppercorns.**

Cover pan, and bring mixture to a boil over high heat. Add artichokes, cover, and simmer until bottoms pierce easily, 15 to 20 minutes for artichokes as wide as 2 1/2 inches, 25 to 35 minutes for those 2 3/4 to 3 3/4 inches, and 40 to 50 minutes for those 4 inches or wider.

Drain artichokes, and serve them hot to cool.

Quick-cooked artichoke leaves. After trimming artichokes for their fleshy bottoms, cook leftover leaves just to eat or for their soft pulp to use in dishes made with artichoke pulp or purée. To avoid pricks, trim thorn tips from leaves before breaking off. Immerse **artichoke leaves** in boiling **water** with **vinegar** (for each 1 quart water, add 1 tablespoon vinegar). Cook leaves until pulp at bases is soft enough to scrape off easily, up to 15 minutes for thick leaves. Drain, and let cool briefly. For nibbling, serve with a dipping sauce.

    4 tablespoons coarse dried bread crumbs
    8 ounces reduced-fat or regular garlic-and-herb Boursin or Rondelé cheese

1. Trim artichokes as directed for artichoke hearts with stems (see box above).

2. Cook artichokes as directed (see box) until bottoms pierce easily, 25 to 30 minutes. Drain.

3. Cut artichokes in half lengthwise. Pull out sharp-tipped inner leaves. With a

spoon, scrape out and discard fuzzy centers in bottoms.

4. Rub stems lightly with 1 teaspoon of the oil. Mix remaining oil with crumbs. Lay artichokes, cup sides up, on a baking sheet, and fill cavities equally with cheese. Sprinkle cheese with crumbs.

5. Bake in a 400° oven until cheese is hot and crumbs are lightly browned, about 15 minutes. Transfer to a serving dish.

Per serving: 252 cal., 46% (117 cal.) from fat; 14 g protein; 13 g fat (6.1 g sat.); 24 g carbo.; 601 mg sodium; 22 mg chol. ∎

The right ham for your table

Which kind and size should you buy for dinner? This primer makes it easy to decide

READY FOR CARVING, *juicy baked ham is an easy and impressive Easter entrée.*

HAM FOR EASTER DINNER SOUNDS simple, but shopping brings reality. Getting the ham you want means making choices. Do you want a whole ham or a portion—and how big a portion? Ham with or without bones? Ham that's naturally shaped or re-formed? A cured ham—but cured how? A raw ham or a cooked one? A ham that's smoked or one that's not?

Technically, ham—the hind leg of a hog—can be plain raw pork. But to most of us, including butchers, ham is a cured leg that is pink, sweet, salty, and, usually, smoky. The curing method and the type and amount of smoke used produce very different kinds of hams. The basic cure for ham is a blend of salt, sugar, spices, nitrites, and nitrates (some of both are naturally present in pork). Proportions of these ingredients can vary considerably; each has a specific task. Salt firms and draws moisture out of the meat. Sugar keeps the meat supple and transports spice, smoke flavor, and moisture back into the tissue. Nitrites and nitrates preserve the meat and retain its pink color.

This mixture can be rubbed on as a dry cure, or mixed with water and used as a wet cure.

When smoking is part of the ham-making process, it can be applied several ways. The kind of wood or blend of woods affects the ham's flavor. If the smoking fire is hot, it cooks the meat and colors its surface. If the smoke is cool, it imparts a much more delicate flavor but doesn't cook the ham. Liquid smoke may also be added to the curing mixture.

Dry-curing is the old-fashioned way to make ham. The leg, well coated with the cure mixture, is hung to dry slowly—for a few months to more than a year. As the cure penetrates, the meat dehydrates, becoming firmer and denser, and the flavor grows more complex. As the meat loses liquid, the salt concentration increases until it gets high enough to prevent the growth of bacteria and parasites. The texture of dry-cure hams ranges from smooth to slightly fibrous, creamy to firm, and moist—yet not juicy—to quite dry; the meat is salty. Hams made this way include imported Black Forest (heavily smoked), country (includes Smithfield, usually cool-smoked and also available cooked), prosciutto, and Westphalian (cool-smoked). Most often, these hams are sold thinly sliced from the deli case.

Wet-cure hams are much faster to produce than dry-cure ones. The cure mixture is added to water. This brine is injected evenly and quickly throughout the leg, or the meat is immersed in the brine for a time. Then the ham is cooked and smoked, sometimes simultaneously, to give the juicy meat additional mild flavor. The ham is ready to eat, cold or hot. If you want ham that tastes freshly baked, heat until it is about 140° in center of thickest part. However, if you're short on time, the meat is perfectly safe to eat at any temperature.

Among the most popular cooked hams are those glazed and sliced to the bone for easy serving. And domestically made Black Forest ham is also wet-cured.

Label Lingo

Pay attention to these words on ham labels; they have specific legal definitions.

- **Ham:** no added water; at least 20.5 percent protein.
- **Ham with natural juices:** at least 18.5 percent protein.
- **Ham—added water:** at least 17 percent protein.
- **Ham and water product:** may contain any amount of water; label lists percentage of added ingredients.
- **Bone-in ham:** includes some bone. Available whole (12 to 16 lb.), half (5 to 8 lb., shank or butt end; shank has smaller bone), or in smaller portions.
- **Boneless ham:** bone and fat removed, meat re-formed.
- **Canned ham:** boneless pieces with gelatin, vacuum-sealed, and cooked.
- **Fully cooked ham:** serve cold, or reheat.
- **Cook before eating:** raw or partially cooked ham. Usually needs to be specially ordered. Cook until 150° to 155° in thickest part.

Classic Baked Ham

Select a **fully cooked ham** (wet-cure), bone-in or boneless. If the ham has a rind (skin), trim it off. Also trim fat on the meat to a very thin layer. Diagonally score the surface of the large rounded side of the ham, making cuts about ¼ inch deep and about 1 inch apart. Crisscross the cuts to make diamonds. Insert a **whole clove** in the center of each diamond. Set the ham, cloves up, in a shallow, rimmed pan that's about 2 inches wider than the meat on all four sides.

Bake in a 325° oven until a thermometer inserted in thickest part (not at bone) reaches 140°, about 2½ hours for an 8-pound ham, about 3½ hours for a 16-pound ham. About 30 minutes before ham reaches 140°, brush, if you like, with a glaze such as **brown sugar** mixed with **Dijon mustard,** or apricot jam thinned slightly with balsamic vinegar.

Per ¼-pound serving of fat-trimmed, unglazed ham: 164 cal., 35% (57 cal.) from fat; 24 g protein; 6.3 g fat (2.1 g sat.); 1.7 g carbo.; 1,364 mg sodium; 60 mg chol. ∎

By Linda Lau Anusasananan

An Easter picnic in
Santa Barbara wine country

*Three generations of a vintner's family gather for an egg hunt
and an informal feast of their favorite Greek foods*

W HAT TO SERVE FOR EASTER DINNER IS NEVER A difficult question for Kate and Brooks Firestone, owners of Firestone Vineyards and Carey Cellars in Santa Barbara County. Their family's traditional Greek-themed meal holds strong sentimental value.

The Firestones' interest in the Greek Easter celebration began years ago on their honeymoon when, unknowingly, they arrived in Greece just in time for the Greek Orthodox Easter, which is usually celebrated later than Easter in Western churches. The unexpected experience of this festive religious holiday resulted in an enduring fondness for the country, the people, and the cuisine, and they return to Greece as often as possible.

Now settled in the picturesque Santa Inez Valley near Solvang, the Firestones still favor Greek cooking—and their children and grandchildren have come to love it as well. Kate's Easter menu is, for the most part, traditional, but she has made a few adjustments in flavors and ingredients to take advantage of the local produce and, of course, the Firestones' own wines.

Their feast begins with dolmas—grape leaves wrapped around a mixture of rice, onions, ground beef, and herbs—with an accompanying sauce of yogurt, lemon juice, peel, and a little sugar. Kate makes her own dolmas, but purchased ones are quite good and much less work if you're pressed for time. Look for them (canned or loose) in gourmet stores, Middle Eastern

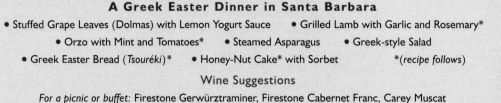

A Greek Easter Dinner in Santa Barbara

- Stuffed Grape Leaves (Dolmas) with Lemon Yogurt Sauce   • Grilled Lamb with Garlic and Rosemary*
- Orzo with Mint and Tomatoes*   • Steamed Asparagus   • Greek-style Salad
- Greek Easter Bread (*Tsouréki*)*   • Honey-Nut Cake* with Sorbet   *(recipe follows)*

Wine Suggestions

For a picnic or buffet: Firestone Gerwürztraminer, Firestone Cabernet Franc, Carey Muscat

For a formal dinner: Carey Chardonnay, Firestone Merlot, Carey Muscat

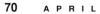

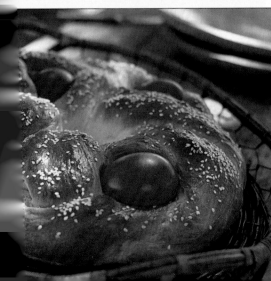

*THE **FIRESTONE FAMILY** dines alfresco under the oaks above their vineyard, but their menu is equally delicious served as a formal dinner indoors. Slightly sweet, orange-spiked Greek Easter bread (at left), studded with red eggs, makes an appealing centerpiece in any location.*

markets, well-stocked supermarkets, and delicatessens.

Barbecued butterflied leg of lamb takes center stage on the Firestones' Easter table. Kate studs the meat with garlic slices and rosemary pieces, then marinates it in a red wine–brown sugar mixture before grilling. To accompany the lamb, she mixes cooked orzo with chopped tomatoes, fresh mint, and lemon

juice. Steamed spring vegetables—often pencil-thin asparagus or young green beans—and a salad of romaine (about 1½ cups per serving), sliced tomatoes and cucumbers, thinly sliced red onions, crumbled feta cheese, and pitted kalamata olives, also grace the table. (Dress the salad with your favorite homemade or purchased vinaigrette dressing.)

Bunches of spring flowers and a Greek

Easter bread (*tsouréki*) often serve as a table centerpiece. Kate shapes this slightly sweet egg bread as they do in Greece, as a braided ring studded with red-dyed hard-cooked eggs (the dyed eggs symbolize Christ's blood).

The Firestones end the meal with a typical Greek dessert—a dense nut cake soaked with a spiked honey syrup. Serve small pieces with scoops of lemon sorbet or vanilla ice cream.

The menu offers great serving versatility. It can be a formal sit-down affair, a buffet, or—the Firestones' favorite—a picnic in the field or in a charming old barn on their property.

Grilled Lamb with Garlic and Rosemary

Cooking time: About 40 minutes
Prep time: About 25 minutes, plus at least 2 hours marinating time

Makes: 14 to 16 servings

1 leg of lamb (about 5 lb.), boned and butterflied

1 to 2 ounces rosemary sprigs, plus additional sprigs for garnish

4 to 5 cloves garlic, thinly sliced

1 ½ cups dry red wine

½ cup firmly packed brown sugar

1 tablespoon soy sauce

1 tablespoon Dijon mustard

1. Trim off and discard any surface fat on meat. Lay lamb boned side up. With a small sharp knife, make small slashes (1 inch long, ½ inch deep) all over meat surface. Cut the rosemary sprigs into 1-inch pieces. Tuck a rosemary piece and garlic slice evenly into each slash.

2. In a deep noncorrodible bowl or 2-gallon heavy-plastic food bag, mix wine, sugar, soy sauce, and mustard. Add lamb, and turn to coat evenly, being careful that garlic and rosemary remain in slashes. Cover or seal, and chill, turning occasionally, at least 2 hours or up to 1 day.

3. To prepare barbecue, ignite 60 charcoal briquets in a barbecue with a lid. When the coals are mostly covered with gray ash (about 30 minutes), push equal portions to opposite sides of the firegrate; place a drip pan in the center. To maintain temperature, add 6 briquets to each side. (Or turn gas barbecue on high, and heat, covered, for 10 minutes, then adjust for indirect cooking.) Place a lightly oiled grill 5 to 6 inches above the coals.

4. Lay lamb on grill; reserve marinade. Brush meat with half the reserved marinade.

5. Cover barbecue (open vents for charcoal). Cook until a thermometer inserted into the thickest part of meat registers 140°, about 40 minutes. Brush halfway through with remaining marinade.

6. Transfer meat to a carving board. Garnish with additional rosemary sprigs. Cut into thin slices to serve.

Per serving: 156 cal., 31% (49 cal.) from fat; 19 g protein; 5.4 g fat (1.9 g sat.); 6.2 g carbo.; 115 mg sodium; 61 mg chol.

Orzo with Mint and Tomatoes

Cooking time: About 15 minutes
Prep time: About 20 minutes
Notes: You can sauté the onions and cook the pasta up to 1 day ahead, but chop the mint, which turns black when it sits, just before serving and add with tomatoes. If pasta mixture seems dry, add more broth, ¼ cup at a time, until mixture is as moist as desired.
Makes: 10 servings

2 onions (about 1 lb. total), chopped

2 tablespoons olive oil

3 cups orzo pasta

About ½ cup chicken broth

⅓ cup lemon juice

¼ cup minced parsley

2 tomatoes (about 1 lb. total), cored, seeded, and chopped

½ cup minced fresh mint leaves, plus mint sprigs for garnish

Salt and pepper

1. Combine onions and oil in a 10- to 12-inch frying pan over medium-high heat. Stir often until onions are browned and taste sweet, about 15 minutes.

2. Meanwhile, cook the orzo in 2 quarts boiling water until tender to bite, 6 to 8 minutes. Drain, rinse with cold water until the pasta is cool, then drain again.

3. In a large bowl, mix together cool cooked orzo, chopped onions, ½ cup broth, lemon juice, and minced parsley. (If making ahead, chill mixture airtight up to 1 day.) Add tomatoes and mint just before serving. Garnish with mint sprigs, and season to taste with salt and pepper.

Per serving: 276 cal., 13% (36 cal.) from fat; 8.8 g protein; 4 g fat (0.6 g sat.); 51 g carbo.; 17 mg sodium; 0 mg chol.

Greek Easter Bread (Tsouréki)

Cooking time: About 30 minutes
Prep time: About 40 minutes, plus 1 ½ hours rising time

Notes: This bread is also delicious for breakfast (you may want to increase the sugar to ½ cup). If you don't want to bother to braid the bread, simply divide the kneaded dough between two greased 5- by 9-inch loaf pans; omit hard-cooked eggs.

Makes: 10 servings

1 cup milk

⅓ cup butter or margarine

¼ cup sugar

1 ½ tablespoons (2 packages) active dry yeast

4 large eggs

¼ cup orange juice

1 tablespoon grated orange peel

½ teaspoon salt

GRANDDAUGHTERS *Madeline Firestone and Fiona Jessup (above) enjoy an egg hunt before sitting down with the family to grilled lamb accompanied by minted orzo and a salad of romaine, tomatoes, onions, feta cheese, and kalamata olives (at right).*

- 4½ cups all-purpose flour
- 4 hard-cooked eggs, dyed red, unpeeled (optional)
- 2 tablespoons sesame seed

1. Heat the milk and butter over low heat or in a microwave until the mixture reaches 110°. In a large bowl, combine the warm milk mixture with 1 teaspoon of the sugar. Sprinkle the yeast over the milk; let stand until yeast softens, about 5 minutes.

2. Add remaining sugar, 3 eggs, orange juice, peel, salt, and 2 cups flour. Beat with a mixer at medium speed until dough is well blended. Stir in remaining flour.

3. To knead with a dough hook, beat at high speed until dough is smooth, shiny, and stretchy, 10 to 15 minutes. To knead by hand, scrape dough onto a well-floured board. Knead until very smooth and elastic, adding just enough flour to keep dough from sticking to the board, at least 10 to 15 minutes. Dough will be sticky. Let dough rise, lightly covered, in the mixing bowl in a warm place until doubled, 1 to 1¼ hours.

4. Transfer dough to a lightly floured board, and knead briefly to expel air. Divide dough into 3 equal portions. Roll each portion into a rope about 20 inches long. Braid the ropes together, then bring ends together to form a ring, pinching ends to join smoothly. Transfer the loaf to a lightly buttered baking sheet. Press dyed hard-cooked eggs into dough, spacing equally around the ring.

5. Lightly cover loaf with plastic wrap. Let rise in a warm place until puffy, about 30 minutes. Beat remaining egg with 1 tablespoon water to blend; brush half over loaf. Bake loaf at 375° for 20 minutes; brush with remaining egg mixture, sprinkle with sesame seed, and bake until golden brown, about 10 minutes longer. Transfer bread to a rack to cool. Serve warm or at room temperature. If making ahead, cool, wrap airtight, and store at room temperature up to 1 day. Reheat, covered with foil, on a baking sheet in a 300° oven until warm to touch. (Hard-cooked eggs are not intended for eating).

Per serving: 351 cal., 28% (99 cal.) from fat; 10 g protein; 11 g fat (5.3 g sat.); 52 g carbo.; 215 mg sodium; 106 mg chol.

Honey-Nut Cake

Cooking time: About 30 minutes
Prep time: About 30 minutes, plus cooling time
Makes: 30 servings

- 2 cups blanched almonds
- 1 cup walnuts
- 2 ounces plain biscotti or zwieback, coarsely broken
- 1 tablespoon grated orange peel
- 6 large eggs, separated
- 1½ cups sugar
- 1 teaspoon vanilla
- ¼ teaspoon cream of tartar
- 2 tablespoons honey
- 1 tablespoon lemon juice
- 1 cinnamon stick (2 to 3 in.)
- ¼ cup Cognac or brandy
  Lemon sorbet or vanilla ice cream (optional)
  Mint sprigs for garnish (optional)

1. In a food processor or blender, combine almonds, walnuts, biscotti, and orange peel. Whirl, in batches if necessary, until finely ground. In a large bowl, beat egg yolks with ¾ cup sugar and vanilla until thick. Stir nut mixture into yolks.

2. In another bowl with clean beaters, beat egg whites with cream of tartar until soft, moist peaks form. Gently fold whites into the nut mixture until just blended. Spoon into a buttered 9- by 13-inch pan; spread top smooth.

3. Bake in a 350° oven until cake is brown and springs back when gently pressed in center, about 30 minutes.

4. While the cake bakes, combine 2 cups water, remaining sugar, honey, lemon juice, and cinnamon stick in a 3- to 4-quart pan. Bring to a boil over high heat. Boil until reduced to 1½ cups, 10 to 15 minutes. Remove from heat and stir in Cognac.

5. Slowly pour the syrup over the cake until all is absorbed. Cool completely. If making ahead, wrap airtight and store at room temperature up to 2 days. To serve, cut into small diamonds or triangles and accompany with sorbet or ice cream. Garnish with mint sprigs.

Per serving: 155 cal., 51% (79 cal.) from fat; 4 g protein; 8.8 g fat (1.2 g sat.); 15 g carbo.; 20 mg sodium; 43 mg chol. ■

By Christine Weber Hale

DOMINIQUE VORILLON

CUSTOMER STAN KOHN *picks up a cooler of fresh-picked vegetables and herbs from grower David Blume at Our Farm, in Woodside, California.*

From the farm to the table

Crave freshly harvested produce? Yearn to connect with the source? Buy in as a farming partner, and reap your benefits in fresh fruits, vegetables, herbs, and flowers

ONE DAY LAST JUNE, A CARDBOARD box filled with lettuce, berries, zucchini, yellow cherry tomatoes, basil, spinach, and bintje yellow potatoes arrived at my front door. It was my first delivery from Farm Fresh To You, of Capay, California. Soft, warm, perfumed, a raspberry beckoned. In my mouth, it melted into a sweet, luscious lump. Dead-ripe. I hadn't tasted one that

A WEEKLY SHARE *from The Root Connection in the fertile Sammamish Valley outside Seattle includes a selection of organically grown vegetables for salads and cooking.*

intense since my camp counselor days on Vashon Island in Washington. Then I moved on to the strawberries. Each was deep red all the way up to its green cap, perfectly shaped, but small by supermarket standards. They tasted the way you imagine strawberries should taste but rarely do. An earwig scampered from the dusty, red-tinged head of lettuce, as if to announce that the produce was organic. I hit the earwig hard and continued with my berry feast.

How do you get produce like this? Invest in a farm's production. Community-supported agriculture (CSA) is a fast-growing way of marketing farm-fresh produce directly to prepaying customers. But there's more to it than just buying vegetables. Participation is a commitment to the survival of a small farm, to the preservation of fertile agricultural land, and to the quality of what you eat.

HOW DOES CSA WORK?

Community-supported agriculture started in Japan about 30 years ago and quickly spread to western Europe. It came to the eastern United States and Canada in the 1980s, then moved west. Today, there are more than 500 CSA farms in North America—at least 125 of them in California, Washington, Oregon, and Colorado.

In CSA's simplest interpretation, a farmer and consumers form a community, or partnership. The consumers agree to support the farm's production. In return, the farmer turns over the harvest to the supporting members. The specific arrangement varies from farm to farm, and at this time, there are no certification regulations.

Generally the farmer sells shares of the harvest for the whole growing season. The membership price is calculated by dividing the cost of crop production by

Getting started

• **Enrollment.** Sign up with a CSA farm before the growing season begins, usually no later than April. Many farms accept a set number of members per season. Some have year-long waiting lists; others add customers anytime.

• **Cost.** Most weekly boxes are valued at $10 to $30, contain 7 to 12 different kinds of food, and are enough for a family of four. Half-shares are often available. Costs may sound high, but they are competitive with those at farmers' markets—sometimes even supermarkets. For the lowest price, sign up in advance for the whole season, and pick up the produce. Short enrollments, home delivery, or delivery at an urban drop-off adds to the cost. Many farms offer monthly, quarterly, or semiannual payment plans, or work shares that make the program affordable to anyone. The Winter Green Farm in Noti, Oregon, has a member-donated fund to provide financial assistance.

• **Options.** Some farms offer tryout periods as short as one month, but getting a feel for the seasons takes six to nine months. Some farms will withhold deliveries during your vacation; others ask you to arrange for pickup—or they may donate your box to a local food bank.

CSA FARMS' FRUIT *and vegetable assortments vary according to season, region, and farmers' choices of crops.*

the number of families the crop can feed. Members pay all or part of the price up front. The farmer uses the money for seed, labor, and equipment. When harvest starts, the members receive weekly paybacks of just-picked produce. Members share the farmer's risks: frost, flood, insects, drought—all may mean less variety or slim pickings for a week or more. On the other hand, optimum weather brings bumper crops and, sometimes, free flowers and new varieties. Consumers may have the option of organizing the produce distribution or helping on the farm in exchange for a lower fee or free produce.

Under another plan, called subscription marketing, the farmer sells produce to a specific group of customers for a prescribed time. Short terms, as brief as one month, may be offered.

PRODUCE AND HANDS-ON EXPERIENCE

As five-year customers of The Root Connection in Redmond, Washington, Maureen Jewitt and her family go to the farm weekly from May through October to pick up their share of organically grown produce. The box might include spinach, bok choy, red radishes the size of Ping-Pong balls, buttercrunch lettuce, sugar snap peas, and beets. Often the family also stops at the U-pick patch of flowers and herbs to gather a bouquet, free to members.

During the growing season, most of the Jewitts' produce is from the farm. Even though they buy items like bananas from the supermarket, generally, Jewitt says, "my children won't eat stuff from the grocery store. It doesn't taste the same as what we get from this valley." The family signs up for the full six-month season. By paying for membership ($546) well in advance, they get the best price, and the farmer gets cash when it's needed.

About 1,300 miles south, Patti Milligan, a member of Be Wise Ranch CSA in San Diego, picks up a basket of produce at her neighborhood drop-off point every other Tuesday. The basket contains 10 to 12 different foods. Milligan's CSA program is similar to the Jewitts', except that her produce mix is suited to sunny Southern California: vine-ripened cantaloupes, tomatoes, avocados, spring salad mix, lettuce, watercress, herbs, green onions, and carrots. This selection changes every two to three weeks. "Everything is so darn healthy. It forces you to eat your vegetables every day." A single allotment is more than Milligan can finish in a week, so she and a friend alternate picking up the weekly baskets. Milligan finds that just-picked produce stays fresh much longer than store equivalents. Carrots are still crisp after a week, and the spring salad mix lasts 10 days in its special bag. In San Diego's temperate microclimate, Be

Choosing a CSA farm

Lists of CSA farms are continually being updated. A likely place to find out about a CSA program is at the local farmers' market—ask for locations of CSA farms, or drum up interest in starting one.

These sources provide CSA information:

Bio-Dynamic Farming and Gardening Association, Box 550, Kimberton, PA 19442; (800) 516-7797. Listings are nationwide.

Community Alliance with Family Farmers, Box 464, Davis, CA 95617; (800) 852-3832. Ask for The California Farm Fresh Directory, which lists 200 CSAs and farmers' markets.

CSA North America, Box 57 Jug End Rd., Great Barrington, MA 01230; (413) 528-4374. Send a self-addressed, stamped envelope, and request a resource list. The organization also offers lists of farms, a detailed CSA directory that includes costs and farm descriptions, and a helpful start-up manual.

CSA West, C/O CASFS, 1156 High St., Santa Cruz, CA 95064; (408) 459-3964. The majority of listings are in California, with a limited list for other Western states. CSA West also lists other CSA resources.

Wise supplies Milligan with fresh produce all year long. She pays about $90 a quarter for her half-share.

Some farms offer specialties, such as mizuna, and uncommon varieties, such as fingerling potatoes and Chinese broccoli. They even work with varieties that are endangered or not otherwise commercially available—to help protect them from extinction. The chile de cera grown on Our Farm, in Woodside, California, is just one example.

CSA guidelines encourage farms to practice organic or biodynamic agriculture: instead of chemicals, these farms use cover crops, compost, and fish emulsion (among other things) to enrich the soil and feed the crops.

On visiting days, families work, harvest, and picnic on the farm. Bailey Stenson of Happy Heart Farm in Fort Collins, Colorado, sees the farm as a haven for adults from their otherwise fast-paced lives.

Some farms have newsletters to keep city folks informed. A report from Fiddler's Green Farm in Brooks, California: "Pelting rain, howling wind, and a late freeze. It's been yet another week of weather extremes. My big gamble on early tomatoes is now an official disaster. First the gale-force wind blew the plastic tunnels off and tattered the vulnerable young plants. Then we had a freeze of 25° last Friday that burned roughly 75 percent of the crops.... Ugh!! Other problems abound, but I'll spare you the details."

Another twist: not all the farms are in rural areas. Urban dwellers are also seeing bare city plots reclaimed for CSA farms.

THE REALITIES

CSA is not a program for everyone.

You get what the farmer grows or what the majority of members decides should be grown. "Our children are at the age where we are constantly on the go, and I don't have the time or energy to focus on how to prepare Chinese cabbage so they'll eat it," says one former customer.

New farm-to-home subscribers, spoiled by the convenience and variety of supermarket shopping, may at first find that cooking with seasonal local produce is confining. You can't pick and choose what looks best. Sometimes you might be stuck with wormy corn or smashed tomatoes.

"People in CSA have to be willing to work at it. It's a commitment. Cooking fresh produce is not convenience oriented, but you can't beat it for freshness and quality," says Ken Kuhns of Peach Valley CSA Farm in Silt, Colorado. Communication is vital, he says. "It's important to tell shareholders up front what we're doing, so people don't think they're getting ripped off." When it works, it's wonderful. "People care enough to understand it's a big risk—any crop can fail at any time—and still be a part of it. The moral support and financial support, and getting together to celebrate and to meet the people involved, are real bonuses." ■

By Linda Lau Anusasananan

MEAT BASTE *starts with tamarind pods.*

Fruit sauce for a tart finish

SWEET-SHARP TAMARIND PULP, WIDELY used for beverages in Mexico and Southeast Asia, also clings well to grilled meat, adding a refreshing tang.

Tamarind Barbecue Sauce

Cooking time: 3 to 4 minutes

Prep time: About 20 minutes

Notes: Tamarind pods are in some supermarkets and widely available in Latino markets. About 10 minutes before meat is done, brush several times with sauce.

Makes: About 1¼ cups, enough for a 4- to 5-pound chicken or 4 to 6 pork chops

1	pound tamarind pods
1¼	cups chicken broth
2	tablespoons firmly packed brown sugar
1	tablespoon minced fresh ginger
1	tablespoon *each* ground cinnamon and ground allspice
¼	teaspoon pepper

1. Pull off and discard pod shells.

2. In a 3- to 4-quart pan over high heat, warm tamarind pulp and seeds in broth until steaming; let cool 10 minutes. Pour mixture into a strainer over a bowl. Rub pulp from seeds; discard residue.

3. Return pulp mixture to pan. Add sugar, ginger, cinnamon, allspice, and pepper; bring to a boil. Use hot or cool.

Total: 521 cal., 5.2% (27 cal.) from fat; 7.4 g protein; 3 g fat (1 g sat.); 128 g carbo.; 120 mg sodium; 0 mg chol. ■

By Christine Weber Hale

NORMAN A. PLATE

By Elaine Johnson

KEVIN CANDLAND

Meat loaf—and two other reader creations

THANK YOU, *SUNSET* READERS. MORE and more of the recipes you're sending us are low-fat as well as creative. I particularly like these three.

Puréed artichokes replace most of the oil in a delicious **Green Goddess Dressing** created by Susan Becker of Tucson. (Note that the number of grams of fat is very low, even though the percentage of calories from fat is high.) Becker likes the dressing with green salads and pasta salads. In a blender, whirl until very smooth (only a few artichoke fibers left) 1 small clove **garlic,** minced; ¼ cup *each* packed **fresh basil leaves** and **white wine vinegar;** 2 tablespoons **lemon juice;** 1 tablespoon **olive oil;** and 1 can (14 oz.) undrained water-packed **artichoke hearts.** Makes 2⅛ cups.

Per tablespoon: 7.3 cal., 49% (3.6 cal.) from fat; 0.2 g protein; 0.4 g fat (0.1 g sat.); 0.8 g carbo.; 0.3 mg sodium; 0 mg chol.

Marilou Robinson of Portland whirls dry-pack dried tomatoes to a coarse powder in a blender (2 to 3 minutes). She adds a spoonful to soups, meat loaf, and sauces for rich flavor with no fat. For Robinson's **Dried Tomato Dip,** whirl 8 ounces **nonfat cottage cheese** in a blender until smooth. Scrape into a bowl, and stir in 1 tablespoon *each* **dried tomato powder,** chopped **fresh basil,**

and chopped **parsley.** Makes ¾ cup.

Per tablespoon: 17 cal., 0% (0 cal.) from fat; 2.5 g protein; 0 g fat; 1.6 g carbo.; 68 mg sodium; 1.7 mg chol.

Karlyn Hochner of Laguna Beach, California, has updated her grandmother's meat loaf by using ground turkey and a lot of fresh vegetables. Ground turkey contains about 7 percent fat, regular ground beef as much as 30 percent fat. Other lean choices include extra-lean ground beef (about 10 percent fat) and ground turkey breast (only 3 percent fat).

Updated Grandma's Meat Loaf

Cooking time: 55 minutes
Prep time: 20 minutes
Makes: 6 or 7 servings

2 cups chopped mushrooms
1½ cups diced broccoli florets
1 cup diced green pepper
1 cup diced carrots
½ cup diced onion
1 teaspoon minced garlic
1 teaspoon salad oil
½ teaspoon celery seed
1 pound ground turkey
⅓ cup catsup
3 tablespoons reduced-sodium soy sauce
2 tablespoons Dijon mustard
3 large egg whites
1 cup dried bread crumbs

1. In a 12-inch frying pan over medium-high heat, frequently stir mushrooms, broccoli, green pepper, carrots, onion, garlic, oil, and celery seed until carrots are tender-crisp to bite, 8 to 10 minutes.

2. In a bowl, combine vegetable mixture, turkey, catsup, soy sauce, mustard, egg whites, and crumbs. Pat into a 4- by 8-inch loaf pan or 6- to 8-cup terrine, gently rounding top. Bake in a 375° oven until firm to touch, 40 to 45 minutes. For a browner crust, broil 3 inches from heat for a few minutes. Let stand 10 minutes before slicing.

Per serving: 216 cal., 27% (59 cal.) from fat; 17 g protein; 6.6 g fat (1.6 g sat.); 21 g carbo.; 725 mg sodium; 47 mg chol. ∎

WE'D LIKE TO HEAR FROM YOU!

Do you have tips or recipes for low-fat cooking? Write to Everyday Low-fat Cooking, Sunset Magazine, 80 Willow Rd., Menlo Park, CA 94025, or send e-mail (including your full name and street address) to lowfat@sunsetpub.com.

¾ cup buttermilk

1 large egg

2 tablespoons salad oil

⅔ cup all-purpose flour

⅔ cup finely ground blue cornmeal

1 tablespoon sugar

2 teaspoons baking powder

¼ teaspoon salt

½ cup blueberries

Maple syrup or applesauce (optional)

1. In a bowl, mix buttermilk, egg, and oil.

2. Stir together flour, cornmeal, sugar, baking powder, and salt. Add to milk mixture, and stir until dry ingredients are evenly moistened.

3. Heat a griddle or 11- or 12-inch frying pan over medium-high heat, then lightly oil. Spoon batter in 2 tablespoon–size portions onto griddle, spread slightly, and drop a few blueberries onto each pancake.

4. Cook until pancake tops look dry and most bubbles have popped, then turn and cook until second side is browned, 5 to 7 minutes total. Serve with maple syrup.

Per pancake: 101 cal., 34% (34 cal.) from fat; 2.4 g protein; 3.8 g fat (0.6 g sat.); 14 g carbo.; 149 mg sodium; 18 mg chol.

Robert G. Stang

Seattle

Pancakes stack up as a work of art

Blue skies, blue seas and lakes, and blue flowers are generally well thought of. Blue food, on the other hand, we are inclined to disdain as being against the natural order of things. It's a visual problem, not a matter of flavor. We simply don't see much true blue food.

Honorable exceptions are blue corn, a Southwest specialty, and blueberries. (The latter are actually purple-black, but they make a lovely blue stain.) Bob Stang uses both of these ingredients in his Blue Cornmeal Blueberry Pancakes.

He prefers small blueberries or wild huckleberries but does not insist on either; the pancakes are delicious plain or with syrup and applesauce.

Bob's Blue Cornmeal Blueberry Pancakes

Cooking time: 5 to 7 minutes per batch
Prep time: 5 to 7 minutes
Notes: Use fresh or partially thawed unsweetened blueberries.
Makes: 10 to 12 pancakes, 5 or 6 servings

Chinese stir-fry cuisine is based on fresh vegetables, a wide variety of seasonings, a modest amount of meat, fish, or poultry, and quick cooking that preserves food color and texture while heightening flavor. American bias toward a high-protein diet often increases the proportion of meat in the dish.

Aaron Stearns, in his Turkey-Spinach Chow, is so inclined. He allows nearly 4 ounces of turkey breast per serving—quite ample, with rice on the side, to make this the whole main course. With a bowl of fruit, the menu is complete.

Turkey-Spinach Chow

Cooking time: 8 to 10 minutes
Prep time: 15 to 20 minutes
Notes: Washing spinach takes the most time. To save about 10 minutes, purchase

this green already washed in ready-to-use packages.

Makes: 4 servings

- ¼ cup chicken broth
- 2 teaspoons cornstarch
- 1 teaspoon hot chili flakes
- About 2 tablespoons reduced-sodium soy sauce
- 1 tablespoon sake or dry sherry
- 1 teaspoon Asian sesame oil
- 1½ pounds spinach, roots and wilted leaves discarded, leaves rinsed and drained
- 2 teaspoons salad oil
- ½ pound mushrooms, sliced
- ¾ to 1 pound boned and skinned turkey breast, cut into ⅛-inch-thick slices
- 4 teaspoons minced fresh ginger
- 3 green onions (ends trimmed), including tops, thinly sliced
- Hot cooked rice

1. In a small bowl, mix chicken broth smoothly with cornstarch, then add hot chili flakes, 2 tablespoons soy sauce, sake, and Asian sesame oil.

2. Place a 12-inch frying pan or a wok over high heat. When pan is hot, add spinach. Cover, and stir often just until leaves wilt, 2 to 3 minutes. If pan is crowded, add ½ the spinach; when it wilts, add remainder and cook until it wilts. Pour spinach into a colander, and let drain.

3. Return pan to heat, and add salad oil. When oil is hot, add sliced mushrooms and stir often until liquid evaporates and mushrooms are lightly browned, 3 to 5 minutes.

4. Add turkey slices and minced ginger. Stir-fry until turkey slices are no longer pink, about 3 minutes.

5. Add broth mixture, and stir until sauce is boiling; stir in green onions and spinach, and stir to heat, about 30 seconds. Spoon onto plates, and accompany with hot rice and soy sauce to taste.

Per serving: 189 cal., 23% (43 cal.) from fat; 27 g protein; 4.8 g fat (0.7 g sat.); 11 g carbo.; 447 mg sodium; 53 mg chol.

Vallejo, California

By Joan Griffiths, Richard Dunmire

Low-fat muffins?
You'd never guess

Natural fat substitutes provide flavor and moistness

DURING THE PAST NINE YEARS, Northern California's muffin lady, Suzanne Epstein, has created more than 80 kinds of muffins for her Suzanne's Muffins retail shops and mail-order business.

When she began developing a low-fat muffin line, she insisted on the same high quality she had set for her other products. "They had to be nutritionally sound, contain all-natural ingredients—lots of fresh fruits and vegetables—and retain the flavor and moistness of our other muffin varieties that are baked with butter and oils," she says.

After a year of testing, Epstein introduced the Very, Very Low Fat Muffin line. Her secret? A prune purée that's blended in the corporate kitchen.

When we tested her low-fat banana walnut muffins in the *Sunset* kitchens, we used puréed prune baby food and another puréed prune product called Just Like Shortenin', and they worked just fine. As Epstein did, we took advantage of nonfat yogurt, mashed bananas, and a soft meringue to give muffins the structure they need to maintain tenderness without fat.

When baking cookies, quick breads, and even cakes, you can usually replace half the fat with puréed fruit, such as prunes, apples, and pears, or with nonfat yogurt. But professional bakers say the secret to low-fat baking is to experiment with the recipe. Take the fat down just a little at a time to see what the recipe will tolerate, and try substituting egg whites for whole eggs, and water for milk.

Suzanne's Very, Very Low Fat Banana Walnut Muffins

Cooking time: 25 minutes
Prep time: About 35 minutes
Notes: Freeze for best storage; reheat in microwave at full power for 45 seconds.
Makes: 24 muffins

- 4 cups all-purpose flour
- 1 tablespoon baking powder

THESE FRUIT-NUT MUFFINS *are tender, moist, and delicious—and they have only 2.5 grams of fat per muffin.*

- 2 teaspoons baking soda
- 1 teaspoon salt
- 2 cups sugar
- ½ cup *each* prune purée and unflavored nonfat yogurt
- 2 tablespoons salad oil
- 1 tablespoon vanilla
- 2 cups (about 4) mashed ripe bananas and ½ cup (about 1) diced banana
- 5 large egg whites
- ⅛ teaspoon cream of tartar
- ⅓ cup finely chopped walnuts

1. Combine flour, baking powder, baking soda, and salt; set aside.

2. With a mixer, blend 1¾ cups of the sugar, prune purée, yogurt, oil, and vanilla. Fold in mashed and diced bananas; set aside.

3. In a clean bowl with clean beaters, beat egg whites and cream of tartar until whites are foamy. Gradually add remaining sugar (about a tablespoon at a time), beating until whites form soft peaks, about 4 minutes.

4. Gently fold whites into banana mixture, then fold in flour mixture until just blended. Don't overmix or muffins will be tough.

5. Line two 12-cup muffin pans with cupcake liners. Fill to top; evenly distribute walnuts over muffins. Bake in a 350° oven until muffins are just firm to touch and edges are golden, about 25 minutes. Cool on racks; serve warm or at room temperature. Store airtight up to a day at room temperature; freeze airtight for longer storage.

Per muffin: 193 cal., 12% (23 cal.) from fat; 3.6 g protein; 2.5 g fat (0.3 g sat.); 40 g carbo.; 274 mg sodium; 0.1 mg chol. ■

By Betsy Reynolds Bateson

SUNSET'S KITCHEN CABINET

Readers' family favorites tested in our kitchens

By Betsy Reynolds Bateson

DICK COLE

Oven-roasted Green Beans with Pasta

Kay Cabrera, Waikoloa, Hawaii

Kay Cabrera and her family really like vegetables. On the island, their choices are somewhat limited, but a surprising d e l i v e r y of *haricots verts,* the small, tender green beans so loved in France, encouraged Cabrera to create this recipe. You can use any fresh slender green beans—or thawed frozen French-cut beans. Cabrera roasts the beans in the oven with garlic and shallots until their edges are brown, which brings out their natural, rich flavors. She uses a vegetable peeler to make the thin parmesan shavings.

Cooking time: About 30 minutes
Prep time: About 25 minutes
Makes: 4 servings

> 2 pounds fresh slender green beans or thawed frozen French-cut green beans

4 cloves garlic, minced
⅔ cup (about 3) thinly sliced shallots
3 tablespoons olive or salad oil
2 teaspoons fresh thyme leaves (optional)
2½ tablespoons grated lemon peel
    Coarse salt (sea salt) and freshly ground pepper
⅓ cup lemon juice
1 pound dried fettuccine, cooked
½ cup (2 oz.) parmesan cheese, thinly shaved

1. If using fresh green beans, trim ends and cut into 2-inch lengths. Place beans, garlic, and shallots in an 11- by 17-inch roasting pan. Drizzle with oil; sprinkle with thyme and lemon peel. Gently fold ingredients to evenly distribute seasonings. Add salt and pepper to taste.

2. Roast beans in a 450° oven until edges are browned and beans are slightly blistered and crisp, about 30 minutes; stir after the first 10 minutes. Pour lemon juice evenly over beans; stir to coat.

3. Add beans to hot pasta, stir well to mix, and top with parmesan. Serve immediately.

Golden California Slaw

Roxanne Chan, Albany, California

An artist in the kitchen, Roxanne Chan enjoys exploring the many flavors and textures of food. This unique slaw combination reaps the benefits of her backyard garden: kumquats, golden beets, carrots, cilantro, ginger, and cabbage. For accent color, she tops the salad with black sesame seed she keeps in her freezer.

Cooking time: About 2 minutes, plus 10 minutes for beets
Prep time: About 30 minutes
Makes: 6 servings

1½ pounds napa cabbage, cored and thinly shredded
1½ cups shredded carrots
½ cup chopped cilantro leaves
½ cup thinly sliced green onions
¾ cup sliced candied or fresh kumquats, seeds removed
½ cup cooked, peeled, and sliced golden or red beets (1 to 1½ in.)
¼ cup slivered crystallized ginger
3 tablespoons *each* seasoned rice vinegar and thawed frozen orange juice concentrate
2 tablespoons *each* salad oil and sesame oil
½ teaspoon ground white pepper

2 teaspoons black sesame seed (optional)

1. In a large bowl, combine cabbage, carrots, cilantro, and green onions. In another bowl, combine kumquats, beets, and ginger.

2. In a 2-quart pan over medium heat, heat vinegar, concentrate, oils, and pepper, stirring, until hot, 2 minutes. Pour half of dressing over each bowl; stir to coat ingredients in each.

3. On six salad plates, evenly distribute cabbage mixture; top equally with kumquat-beet mixture. Garnish with sesame seed.

Per serving: 219 cal., 39% (86 cal.) from fat; 2.4 g protein; 9.6 g fat (1.3 g sat.); 34 g carbo.; 219 mg sodium; 0 mg chol.

Brown Rice and Apple Meat Loaf

Arthur J. Lozier, Spring Valley, California

Arthur Lozier, a self-described meat loaf fan, adds brown rice to his loaf for nutty flavor, apple for sweetness, and herbs and spices for zip.

Cooking time: 1 hour, plus 45 minutes for rice
Prep time: 20 minutes
Makes: 8 servings

1 1/2	pounds lean ground beef
1 1/2	cups cooked brown rice
1	green apple (about 1/2 lb.), diced into 1/4-inch pieces
1	onion (about 1/2 lb.), finely chopped
1	can (8 oz.) tomato sauce
2	large eggs, beaten
3	cloves garlic, minced
1/3	cup Italian seasoned bread crumbs
1	to 2 tablespoons chili powder
1 1/2	teaspoons *each* caraway seed, ground cumin, and dried oregano leaves
1/4	teaspoon *each* ground nutmeg and pepper
1/3	cup (1 1/2 oz.) shredded cheddar cheese

1. In a large bowl, combine beef, cooked rice, apple, onion, tomato sauce, eggs, garlic, crumbs, chili powder, caraway, cumin, oregano, nutmeg, and pepper. Mix until ingredients are well combined.

2. Place in a 5- by 9-inch loaf pan, gently rounding top. Bake in a 350° oven until browned and edges pull from pan sides, about 1 hour. Top evenly with cheese; bake until cheese melts, about 5 minutes longer.

3. Let loaf cool at least 10 minutes before serving. Loosen edges of loaf with knife; using a spatula, gently lift loaf from pan onto a serving platter.

Per serving: 360 cal., 55% (198 cal.) from fat; 21 g protein; 22 g fat (8.7 g sat.); 20 g carbo.; 421 mg sodium; 123 mg chol.

Grilled Lime-Chili Pork

Amy Fairweather, San Francisco

Amy Fairweather surfs the Internet for recipe ideas much the way others search through cookbooks, but this recipe is a result of her love of Mexican foods. She serves the roast with tortillas and a shredded carrot and jicama salad.

Cooking time: 35 to 40 minutes
Prep time: 20 minutes, plus marinating
Makes: 8 servings

2	to 3 (about 1/2 oz. total) dried pasilla chilies, stemmed and seeded
1 2/3	cups chopped onions
4	cloves garlic, chopped
2	teaspoons grated lime peel
2	tablespoons lime juice
1/2	teaspoon *each* ground cinnamon, salt, and pepper
1	boned pork loin roast (about 2 lb.)

1. Rinse chilies; remove stems. Cut chilies open; rinse out seeds. Using scissors, cut chilies into small pieces; add to 1 cup hot water. Let stand at least 15 minutes or up to 1 hour.

2. To a food processor or blender, add soaked chilies with water, onions, garlic, peel, juice, cinnamon, salt, and pepper. Whirl until smooth.

3. Place pork in gallon-size heavy-duty plastic bag. Pour chili mixture over pork; swirl bag to coat meat. Seal; chill at least 4 hours or up until next day. Move meat in bag several times.

4. Ignite 50 briquets on firegrate in barbecue. When spotted with gray ash, about 20 minutes, push equal amounts to opposite sides of firegrate. Or turn gas barbecue on high and heat, covered, 10 minutes, then adjust for indirect cooking; turn heat to medium. Place drained pork (reserving marinade) on center of grill, not over coals or flame. Grill over medium heat (you can hold your hand at grill level only 4 to 5 seconds). Cover barbecue (open vents for charcoal); cook until internal temperature reaches 150°, 35 to 40 minutes; turn about every 10 minutes for even browning.

5. Heat reserved marinade over medium-high heat until boiling, then pour into a serving bowl. Thinly slice loin against the grain, and serve with marinade.

Per serving: 307 cal., 67% (207 cal.) from fat; 20 g protein; 23 g fat (8.3 g sat.); 3.7 g carbo.; 194 mg sodium; 79 mg chol.

Zucchini-Bean Soup

Ginny Hall, Adelanto, California

When a loosened salt shaker lid released the shaker's contents into a pot of zucchini soup, Ginny Hall didn't give up. She combined the soup with a pot of beans and rice on the stove to dissipate the salty flavor. It worked. She also added a favorite seasoning, hot curry powder.

Cooking time: About 35 minutes
Prep time: About 25 minutes
Makes: 17 cups; 10 servings

4	cans (15 1/2 oz. each) pinto beans
2	tablespoons butter or margarine
3	cups finely chopped onions
1	cup chopped celery
1/4	to 1/3 cup hot curry powder
8	cups chicken broth
1	cup long-grain white rice
2	pounds zucchini (about 6), ends trimmed and diced
1/4	cup chopped Italian parsley
3	tablespoons lime juice
	Salt and freshly ground pepper

1. Drain beans, reserving 1/2 cup of the liquid. Rinse beans; set aside.

2. In a 12-quart pan over medium-high heat, cook butter, onions, and celery, stirring occasionally, until lightly browned, 10 minutes. Add curry, and cook, stirring, 3 minutes more. Add broth, reserved bean liquid, and rice; scrape browned bits from pan bottom. Cover; bring to a boil, 2 minutes. Reduce heat; simmer, covered, until rice is just tender, 15 minutes. Stir in zucchini, beans, parsley, and juice. Add salt and pepper. Heat until hot.

Per serving: 258 cal., 20% (51 cal.) from fat; 13 g protein; 5.7 g fat (2.2 g sat.); 44 g carbo.; 529 mg sodium; 6.2 mg chol.

*S*hare a recipe you've created or adapted—a family favorite, travel discovery, or time-saver—including the story behind the recipe. You'll receive a "Great Cook" certificate and $50 for each recipe published. Send to *Sunset Magazine*, 80 Willow Rd., Menlo Park, CA 94025, or send e-mail (including full name and street address) to recipes@sunsetpub.com.

FOOD
Guide

BY JERRY ANNE DI VECCHIO

A TASTE OF THE WEST: Juicy chicken with a bite

The English and the Chinese like it hot. The French just like it, and so do I. The subject is mustard. The French lead in the number of mustard styles they make. The most famous bears the name of a city, Dijon, where the mixture was formulated.

A bit more recently, in the past few decades, there has been a mustard explosion. Overnight, it seemed, market shelves filled with imports. Then domestically made Dijon mustard came along, and now there's a veritable kaleidoscope of flavors, some based on Dijon, coming from all directions—the Napa Valley, Arizona, Santa Barbara, and Hawaii, to name a few places. A logical turn of events, considering that most of the world's commercial crop of mustard seed is grown right next door, in Canada.

I've found merit in most mustard, but smooth, tart Dijon—domestic or imported—is still my number one standby when I want to add zip to foods. This simple recipe evolved from a more complicated dish I once had in France.

Mustard Roast Chicken

Cooking time: About 1 hour

Prep time: About 15 minutes

Notes: Imported coarse-grain Dijon mustard may be labeled à l'ancienne or en grains. If parts of the chicken get very dark before the bird is cooked, drape the area loosely with a piece of foil.

Makes: 4 to 5 servings

  1 chicken, about 4 pounds

  5 tablespoons coarse-grain or regular Dijon mustard

  1 teaspoon dried thyme leaves

  ½ teaspoon ground nutmeg

  6 tablespoons whipping cream

  ¾ pound mushrooms (caps 1 to 1½ in. wide)

KEVIN CANDLAND

Swiss cheese, Dijon mustard, and watercress make for a memorable roast chicken.

1   tablespoon butter or margarine

1   tablespoon lemon juice

1 ½   teaspoons pink or green
     peppercorns, dried or drained
     canned

½   cup finely shredded Swiss cheese

About ¼ pound watercress,
rinsed and crisped

Salt and pepper

1. Pull off and discard lumps of chicken fat, rinse the bird inside and out, and pat dry. Reserve giblets for other uses. Set chicken, breast up, on a V-shaped rack in a 9- by 13-inch pan.

2. Mix 3 tablespoons of the mustard with thyme and nutmeg.

3. Ease your fingers under the chicken breast skin from the front and the back of the chicken to loosen, but leave in place. Smear about half of the mustard mixture evenly over breast meat, under the skin. Add 2 tablespoons of the cream to the remaining mustard mixture.

4. Roast chicken in a 400° oven. After 30 minutes, spoon remaining mustard mixture onto legs and wings, letting it flow into joint crevices. Continue to cook until bird is richly browned, 25 to 30 minutes.

5. Meanwhile, rinse mushrooms, drain, and trim and discard discolored stem ends. Cut mushrooms in half through caps.

6. Put mushrooms in a 10- to 12-inch frying pan with butter, lemon juice, and peppercorns. Stir often over high heat until liquid evaporates and mushrooms are lightly browned, 4 to 5 minutes. Keep warm.

7. Tilt chicken to drain juices into roasting pan. Transfer chicken to a platter, and spoon mushrooms alongside; keep warm.

8. Skim fat from pan drippings. Add remaining 4 tablespoons cream and remaining 2 tablespoons mustard to drippings. Stirring over high heat, bring to a rolling boil.

9. Tilt chicken platter, and spoon juices into the sauce; mix. Pour sauce into a small dish. Sprinkle chicken with cheese, and garnish with watercress. Cut chicken into pieces with poultry shears, or carve. Add salt and pepper to taste.

Per serving: 571 cal., 57% (324 cal.) from fat; 50 g protein; 36 g fat (14 g sat.); 5.2 g carbo.; 389 mg sodium; 179 mg chol.

BACK TO BASICS

Untangling fennel, anise, and licorice

When my daughter was small, she called fresh fennel "licorice celery," which zeros right in on its character—crunchy and moist with a cool, mild licorice taste. Fennel (*Feoniculum vulgare azoricum*) also goes by the names sweet anise, Florentine or Florence fennel, *finocchio* (Italian), and *fenouil* (French). Its feathery leaves have a faint licorice taste. The stems are green and woody, but at the base they are thinner, wider, white, and tender-crisp. These white parts overlap tightly to form swollen heads, which you can eat raw, like celery, or cooked. When fennel is simmered, perhaps in broth, or brushed with olive oil and grilled, its texture shifts from crisp to creamy-tender, and the flavor grows sweeter and less herbal.

Although some people insist on calling the white part a bulb, it doesn't grow underground.

In the Mediterranean and in the West, wild fennel (also called common fennel, *Foeniculum vulgare*) flourishes in the summer. Its feathery green leaves look, smell, and taste like those of cultivated fennel, but its stalks are too woody to eat and it doesn't form a head at the base. The seeds of both kinds of fennel are used for seasoning, often in Italian sausages.

Anise (*Pimpinella anisum*) is an annual herb with distinct licorice-flavor leaves. Its seeds are tinier than fennel seeds, and they have a more intense sweet-licorice taste. Anise seed is used mostly in sweets, especially in traditional biscotti.

Star anise (*Illicium verum*) is the dried ripe fruit of an evergreen tree native to China. True to its name, the complexly fragrant pod looks like a tiny brown wooden star. Each pod spoke contains a shiny brown seed that's less aromatic than the pod. Star anise is widely used in Asian recipes. It's sold whole, in pieces, as seed, and ground.

Licorice comes from the dried root of several related plants (*Glycyrrhiza glabra* is the most common source). The root, sold in pieces or as a powder or an extract, yields a potent sweet-licorice flavor, evident in popular black-licorice candies.

There's also a whole slew of liqueurs flavored with licorice, including pastis and anisette. But that's another story.

Spring onions for all seasons

During thinning-out time in the garden, all onions have tender green tops and white bases (or maybe pink, depending on variety), and you can use them just like green onions from the market. Of course, those market onions are cultivated year-round, so in a sense, spring never ends. European visitors often get quite excited by our green onion availability because back home, their "spring" onions typically have bigger bulbs and aren't always as young or as delicately flavored.

I consider green onions a basic—and a crutch. A few chopped white bottoms and green tops can lift a bland soup, a too-subtle sandwich, a hunk of meat, a static vegetable, even just plain rice into a more appetizing and attractive realm.

Green onions, I am told, are also a bit easier on the digestive system than mature bulb onions. And they grow milder yet when cooked, as they are in this easy but intriguing pan-toasted green onion flatbread. The bread may be Chinese, but, like green onions, it goes with just about everything. It always makes me crave my grandmother's tomato soup.

Chinese Green Onion Cakes

Cooking time: About 15 minutes
Prep time: 45 to 50 minutes, including 30 minutes for the dough to rest.
Notes: For a one-day head start, make

These green onion flatbreads are coated with a light salt-sugar mixture.

the dough and cook the bacon, then cover and chill both.
Makes: 8 pieces

> About 1 cup all-purpose flour
>
> About ½ teaspoon salt
>
> ¼ pound bacon, diced
>
> ½ cup thinly sliced green onions (including tops)
>
> About 1 teaspoon sesame seed
>
> ¼ teaspoon sugar

1. In a bowl, combine 1 cup flour and ¼ teaspoon salt. Stirring with a fork, add ½ cup boiling water and mix until dough is moistened. Pat into a compact ball.

2. On a lightly floured board, knead dough until it feels smooth and satiny, about 3

minutes. Cover dough airtight and let stand at least 30 minutes.

3. In an 8- to 10-inch frying pan over medium-high heat, stir bacon often until brown and crisp, about 5 minutes. Remove with a slotted spoon, and drain on towels. Reserve drippings.

4. On a lightly floured board, roll dough into an 8- by 16-inch rectangle. Brush dough with 2 to 3 teaspoons melted, but not hot, bacon drippings, then sprinkle bacon and green onions evenly almost to edge of rectangle.

5. Starting with a short side of the rectangle, roll up dough to snugly enclose filling and form a compact log. Pinch dough edge to log to seal. Gently press ends against the filled log.

6. Cut log crosswise into 8 equal rounds. Flatten each piece slightly with your palm, then sprinkle each round lightly with sesame seed.

7. Press each round until evenly thick and about 4 inches wide. If filling pops out, press back into dough.

8. Place rounds, without crowding, in a 10- to 12-inch frying pan over medium to medium-low heat. Cook, turning occasionally, until each side is dry looking and well speckled with brown, 6 to 8 minutes total.

9. Mix remaining ¼ teaspoon salt with sugar. As hot, browned cakes come from pan, sprinkle them lightly with salt-sugar mixture. Serve cakes hot, warm, or at room temperature.

Per piece: 100 cal., 29% (29 cal.) from fat; 3.2 g protein; 3.2 g fat (1 g sat.); 14 g carbo.; 207 mg sodium; 4.1 mg chol.

Cooks who really know their roots and greens

Chez Panisse Vegetables, by Alice Waters and the cooks of Chez Panisse, is a particularly significant book. Of the half-dozen titles with the Chez Panisse mantle, this one tells readers the most about the impact that Waters and her Berkeley-based team have had on you and me. Their search for high-quality vegetables, herbs, and fruit has influenced the organic movement, the farming of wonderful varieties that weren't considered commercially viable, and the growth of certified farmers' markets.

The simple treatment of vegetables in

this 320-recipe book (HarperCollins Publishers, New York, May 1996; $32.50) reflects the natural, understated style of Waters's remarkable restaurant and the many talented cooks who have been part of its history. One of these cooks, Patricia Curtan, also designed the book and created its wonderful linocut illustrations.

The chapters are alphabetically organized, from amaranth greens to zucchini, and a short appendix provides a few classic "odds and ends" recipes that could complement many of the vegetable dishes.

The book often puts vegetables in main-dish roles. I, for one, am happy with a dinner of Broccoli Raab Pasta, Chard Stem Gratin, or Grilled Leeks and Stewed Garlic on Toast.

Beyond goat cheese

If you're wondering what kid (baby goat) tastes like, let me share my first impression. It was at a hole-in-the-wall restaurant in Guadalajara, Mexico, that specialized in spit-roasted kid. As we entered, the delectable aromas made my knees weak. Then I tasted the meat. Pale and pink, the kid had a flavor and texture somewhere between chicken thigh and braised pork shoulder. The only seasonings were salt and pepper. A bowl of guacamole with a stack of tortillas came with the order.

Kid has long been available in the spring, on order, through many ethnic markets—Italian (as *capretto*), Latino (as *cabrito* or *cabritilla;* goat is *chivo* or *chivito*), Greek, and Indian. But several springs of late, I've seen fresh kid in a few chain supermarkets, where it is often labeled capretto or cabrito.

According to Sylvia Mavalwalla, who raises goats at S & B Farms in Petaluma, California, there is increasing demand for kid and goat from ethnic population groups. But this availability is also partly because of the growth in goat cheese production. Like cows, goats have to bear young in order to produce milk. But goats are seasonal breeders and deliver late winter through spring. The resulting kid, if it's not female and of dairy potential, frequently meets the same fate as lamb at 5 to 6 months old. Because fresh kid is available for a limited period, some is frozen.

Small kid carcasses look a lot like big dressed rabbits, and they are disjointed about the same way. However, you might ask your meat cutter to do this chore for you. Any opaque membrane and fat should be removed and discarded. Rinse the meat, pat it dry, then rub the pieces lightly with olive oil and sprinkle with dried thyme leaves, salt, and pepper.

Place the meat (without crowding—you may need to cook a few pieces at a time) on a barbecue grill over a solid bed of medium-hot coals or on a medium-hot gas grill (you can hold your hand at grill level 3 to 4 seconds). Cover barbecue, and open vents. Turn pieces occasionally until the outside is well browned and the meat is rosy to faintly pink at the bone. The legs take 30 to 40 minutes; the thin shoulder, back, and loin take a few minutes less. Ribs are best cooked until crisp—no longer pink at the bone.

Prices for a whole kid can be quite dear—$4 to $6 or more a pound (typical dressed weight is 15 to 25 pounds). On the other hand, packaged cuts in the supermarket may cost as little as $1.50 to $2.50 a pound. But one big warning: it may be goat, not kid, even though it is called capretto. And when cooked like kid, goat tends to be very firm, even tough. On one occasion, the kid I ordered at the supermarket turned out to be a mature, red-meat goat (the leg weighed about 6 pounds, just like lamb).

SEASONAL NOTE

Mango prime time

Mangoes are around all year, but they are never in better supply, of better quality, or at better prices than from May through summer. I look forward to my mango indulgence in a mimosa—mango purée, orange juice, and sparkling wine. The combination makes plain mimosas timid by comparison.

The flavor density of mangoes enhances moderately priced sparkling wines that are slightly to noticeably sweet. If domestic, these wines are labeled extra-dry, sec, or demi-sec, but if French, they are sec or demi-sec.

Mango Mimosas

For 6 to 8 servings, peel 1 firm-ripe **mango** (about 1 lb.), and cut fruit from pit into a blender. Add ½ cup **orange juice**. Whirl until fruit is smoothly puréed. Taste, and if the flavor is a little flat, add 1 or 2 tablespoons **lime** or lemon **juice**. If fruit is at room temperature, also whirl in about ½ cup small **ice cubes**.

Make mimosas by the pitcher or by the glass. The fruit purée makes the wine fizz madly, so pour slowly and stir down some of the bubbles. In a large pitcher, combine purée and 1 bottle (750 ml.) **chilled sparkling wine**. Or fill glasses (about 1 cup-

KEVIN CANDLAND

Mango purée, orange juice, and sparkling wine combine for a lively mimosa.

size) about ⅓ with purée, then add wine.

Per serving: 98 cal., 1% (0.9 cal.) from fat; 0.5 g protein; 0.1 g fat (0 g sat.); 9.7 g carbo.; 8.7 mg sodium; 0 mg chol.

BOB THOMPSON ON WINE

Tackling German to find fine Rieslings

German Rieslings always taste better when a considerable body of water lies not too far beyond the farther rim of the glass. Maybe that's because the best of them are born on slopes above the Rhine and Mosel rivers. Anyway, the backdrop is a grace note, not an essential. Any tranquil setting will encourage a proper Riesling to help you smell the spring flowers, before they bloom or after.

All you need to make a *kabinett* or a riper, richer *spätlese* show its finest side are time, a plate of simple butter cookies, and, in season, some berries. Indeed, much more than that and you spoil the effect. Whole meals distract from airy perfumes and tart-sweet equilibriums.

Kabinetts and spätleses—the middle of the German sweetness range—struggle to reach 10 percent alcohol, as against the 13-plus percent typical of dinnertime Rieslings from Alsace or California. Some barely make 9. They do not struggle at all to develop wonderfully pungent flavors somewhere between grapefruit and citrus blossom. True to their grapefruity side, they are so tart that winemakers need to leave an exact shading of sweetness for balance.

Rieslings from the Mosel-Saar-Ruwer teeter between sweet and tart on the highest wire of all. Rheingaus walk a wire a foot or two lower than the rival valley's because the Rheingau sees the summer sun a bit oftener, so the grapes get a bit riper. For that or another reason, they also taste more like citrus blossom and less like grapefruit than typical Mosels.

Newcomers may think German wine names are a trifle daunting. For example, an enticing Rheingau spätlese from Hupfeld goes by the "modest" title of Hochheimer Königin Victoria Berg. But don't worry about town names (which end in *er*) or vineyards (which follow the *er*) until you feel ready. For decades the simple rule has been to focus on the name of the producer-shipper and let the rest take care of itself. In the Mosel-Saar-Ruwer, Rudolf Müller is a reliable shipper, with wines priced from $8 to $14. J. J. Prüm, Selbach-Oster, Schlosskellerei Schubert'schen, and others of the upper crust cost up to twice as much. From the Rheingau, look for Balthasar Ress, Robert Weil, and Schloss Johannisberg. If you prefer to break a rule and buy a community, look first at the Hochheimers. ■

Why we *love* BURRITOS

For fun, flavor, value, atmosphere, and sheer dietary abandon, nothing beats going out for a burrito. Here's where our readers found the best, and how you can make them at home

BY BILL CROSBY
AND ELAINE JOHNSON

CRAIG MAXWELL

AVLOVIAN IS THE ONLY WAY TO DESCRIBE THE RESPONSE we got from readers when we asked where to get the West's best burrito. Hundreds wrote in. More than a few admitted that their mouths were watering as they wrote, or that they were going to have to go out for a burrito fix as soon as they were finished. Be it the flavor, the value, or the sheer gluttonous joy of measuring an entrée in feet or pounds, paragons of this beloved food were praised from Arizona, where they're

Aficionados celebrate a new-wave version of what some call the perfect meal, at San Francisco's Casa Aguila, where the burritos are as wild and robust as the decor. Though our readers' recommendations range from sit-down restaurants like this to hole-in-the-wall take-out spots, they all have one thing in common: burritos worth boasting about.

called *burros*—"There's nothing *ito* about these," writes Kathleen Myers of Tucson—to Wyoming, where "the sauce is divine," according to Zita Izzo of Jackson Hole. Such a response raises the question: is the burrito the culinary glue that holds the West together?

Well, if not glue, gluten. The defining element of any burrito is its wrapper, the humble flour tortilla straight out of northern Mexico. In this corn-deprived region, resourceful cooks created their basic building block with wheat. This soft, glutenous *tor-tilla de harina* could do things its corn-based cousin could not, namely stretch around and seal savory surprises within its glistening skin.

The burritos our readers described in glorious detail inspired us to go on a mission of discovery, field-testing as many recommendations as common sense and the American Heart Association allowed—never more than 15 in a single day—and creating recipes for readers to try at home. Our research identified three burrito styles: traditional, breakfast, and new-wave.

The lively scene at El Tepeyac in Los Angeles is but a prelude to the main event: the classic 5-pound Manuel's special.

The West's best burritos

What makes a great traditional burrito besides a tortilla wrapped around a spicy filling? Size, certainly; comparisons to both Presto Logs and Duraflames were a theme. Messiness seems to be a selling point also. Modest prices are a given. Throw in a tiny bit of uneasiness about the locale and you have the mixture for a sublime burrito experience.

CYLINDRICAL CLASSICS

SOUTHERN CALIFORNIA
El Tepeyac, 812 N. Evergreen Ave., Los Angeles; (213) 267-8668. "I measure all parades by the Rose Parade, all zoos by San Diego, and all other Mexican restaurants by El Tepeyac," writes Nancy Bauer of Wilmington, California. "Unfortunately, everything else falls short." The revered entrée at this top vote-getter, in L.A.'s Boyle Heights neighborhood, is the Manuel's special, a 5-pounder that servers have been known to prohibit solo eaters from ordering, though they can get a smaller version called the Hollenbeck burrito (named after the local police station). Both are wonderfully sloppy concoctions filled with mild red sauce, rice, beans, cheese, tomato, and guacamole (with big chunks of avocado),

and topped with more of the meaty sauce. We concur with reader Francie Hansen of Newport Beach: "They are *huge* and fabulous."

Johnny's, 176 N. Ventura Ave., Ventura; (805) 648-2021. Johnny's was our other top vote-getter, and a "legend in Ventura," according to local Greg Thayer. Both he and Beverly Hills reader Lynne Hiller recommend the chile verde burrito: "lean chunks of pork simmered forever in a green chili sauce, rolled with cheese, and piping hot," according to Hiller.

The chile relleno burrito is also outstanding, cooked just the way it should

---

OUR READERS ON BURRITOS: I DRIVE 2¹/₂ HOURS TO GET THERE... HONKIN' HUGE... ABSOLUTELY ADDICTIVE...

A burrito lover's glossary

● **Al pastor.** "Shepherd-style" marinated pork pieces that are layered, then cooked on an upright rotisserie.

● **Birria.** Slow-cooked goat, kid, or lamb in a savory red chili broth.

● **Burro.** Another name for burrito.

● **Camarones.** Shrimp.

● **Carne adovada** (or adobada). Thinly sliced meat (usually pork) marinated in a red chili sauce, then grilled or griddled.

● **Carne asada.** Butterflied skirt steak or other meat marinated in citrus juices and spices, then grilled or griddled.

● **Carnitas.** Pork simmered with seasonings, then roasted or fried, so chunks are tender inside

and crisp outside.

● **Chicharrónes** (or chicharrón). Crunchy, salted fried pork rind.

● **Chile.** A red or green New Mexican sauce made from chilies.

● **Chile colorado.** Beef or pork simmered in red chili sauce.

● **Chile relleno.** Green chili stuffed with cheese, coated with egg batter, and fried.

● **Chile verde.** Pork or chicken simmered in green chili sauce.

● **Chili.** Any of the peppers that are the key ingredient to the flavor and heat in chili sauces. In New Mexico and in Spanish, these peppers are spelled with an "e" (chile).

● **Chimichanga.** A deep-fried burrito.

● **Chorizo.** Spicy pork or beef sausage.

● **Enchilada-style** (also called wet or smothered). A burrito served with cooked chili sauce on top.

● **Frijoles.** Beans. Typically, refried, or whole pinto, red, or black.

● **Lengua.** Beef tongue.

● **Machaca.** Shredded meat in tomato sauce.

● **Nopales.** Cactus.

● **Picadillo.** Seasoned ground beef.

● **Pollo.** Chicken.

● **Queso.** Cheese.

● **Salsa fresca** (also called pico de gallo). Fresh chunky sauce of chopped tomato, onion, cilantro, and chili.

● **Sesos.** Beef brains.

---

be—not too greasy, perfect batter, tasty chili sauce, and the right amount of cheese. These were among the few structurally sound burritos we sampled. You can reasonably expect to eat one with your hands without having it explode over your shirtfront.

SILICON VALLEY

La Costeña, 2078 Old Middlefield Way, Mountain View; (415) 967-0507. Cross-country isn't too far to travel for a burrito from La Costeña: Joan Donohoe of New Jersey writes, "We fly to California to enjoy them, and have special insulated lunch boxes so we can carry them home with us."

This small take-out spot is also a favorite with the Silicon Valley crowd. Part of the draw is custom-building your own burrito. The most popular filling is whichever one's on special (with a free soda), notes owner Ramon Luna, but "drunken chicken," simmered in Budweiser sauce, has a lot of fans, as does the crisp carnitas (good with extra cilantro and cotija cheese).

Internet cruisers may know La Costeña through *'Rito Rap,* a self-proclaimed "landmark text in burritology," along with *Cylindrical God* on The Burrito Page (http://www.infobahn.com/pages/rito.html). While you're at that page,

don't miss Burrito-Analysis, a personality test based on your selection of burrito fillings and extras. It's more fun than a fortune cookie, and at least as accurate.

SAN FRANCISCO

Taken en masse, San Francisco is the hands-down burrito capital of the West. But the sheer volume of taquerias in the city, especially in the Mission District, means votes were scattered among many deserving locales. We tried most of them and found two standouts.

Taqueria San Jose, 2830 Mission St. at 24th St.; (415) 282-0203 (and two other locations). Hop off BART at the 24th Street station, walk the 100 or so steps to Taqueria San Jose, and immediately order the burrito al pastor: moist, spit-roasted carnitas, sublimely spiced, nestled in a lightly grilled tortilla along with appropriately modest quantities of rice, beans, cheese, guacamole, sour cream, and salsa. This was the model for our make-at-home Burritos Grandes on page 92; a visit to the source will not disappoint.

Taqueria Can-Cun, 1003 Market St. at Sixth St.; (415) 864-6773 (and one other location). "This place is truly a find," writes Brenda Lederman of Santa Rosa, California. Hard to find, too—it can't be more than 12 feet wide and is on a rather seamy stretch of Market Street. Lederman thinks the ultimate burrito is the vegetarian, but she also recommends the *mojado,* a fully loaded bomber topped with ranchera sauce. Add a healthy dollop of Can-Cun's remarkable green salsa and you've got the messy, flavorful means to enter a state of burrito bliss.

COLORADO

Majestic Saloon, 3140 S. Parker Rd., Aurora; (303) 695-4478. Local regular Tonya Sarina had all her friends cosign the letter she sent praising the Majestic and its signature burrito of the same

---

OH, MAN, THIS IS AWESOME... THE JUICE DRIPS DOWN TO MY ELBOWS... EAT 'EM LIKE ICE CREAM CONES...

NEVADA WIER

name. Our field report on the chicken burrito Majestic—all 4 pounds of it—confirms its place in the burrito firmament. Though you have to pass through the billiard area to get to the dining room, it's still a fine place for a family.

WAKE-UP CALLS

Northern New Mexico elevates breakfast burritos to an art form. Scrambled eggs, potatoes, and your choice of breakfast meat are merely the starting point. More than anything, these are an excuse for consuming vast amounts of chile—the intensely flavorful cooked red or green sauce made from local chilies that's ladled on top of burritos (or, at take-out places, slathered inside). Green chile, made from fresh chilies, is the hottest. Red, made from riper dried chilies, is mellower. If you want both, just ask for Christmas.

Santa Fe. *Tecolote Café, 1203 Cerrillos Rd.; (505) 988-1362.* Could any other New Mexican match Bruce Johnson's knowledge of this tubular wake-up meal? "I eat breakfast burritos four times a week," he reports, "and Tecolote makes the best. I've probably eaten there 400 times in the last 14 years." This fixture in the Santa Fe breakfast scene makes arguably the tastiest thick red and green chiles in town. Try the sauces over Tecolote's classic breakfast burrito (with plenty of eggs and a choice of meat—potatoes optional). The carne adovada, made for chiliheads, is lean pork cooked with three kinds of red chilies, lots of garlic, and oregano. Lest you leave hungry, burritos come with a side of beans, pozole, or hash browns.

Tia Sophia's, 210 W. San Francisco St., just off The Plaza; (505) 983-9880. Another excellent choice for the break-

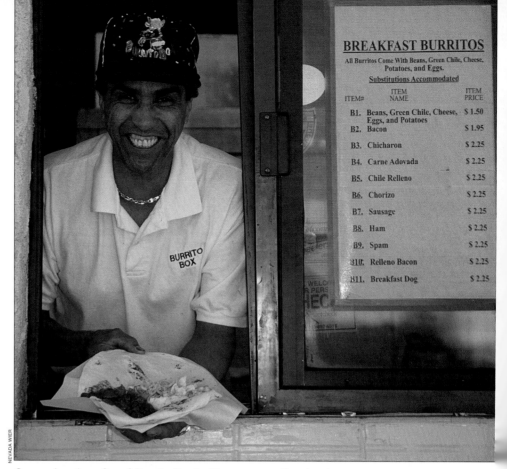

BREAKFAST BURRITOS

All Burritos Come With Beans, Green Chile, Cheese, Potatoes, and Eggs.

Substitutions Accommodated

ITEM#	ITEM NAME	ITEM PRICE
B1.	Beans, Green Chile, Cheese, Eggs, and Potatoes	$ 1.50
B2.	Bacon	$ 1.95
B3.	Chicharon	$ 2.25
B4.	Carne Adovada	$ 2.25
B5.	Chile Relleno	$ 2.25
B6.	Chorizo	$ 2.25
B7.	Sausage	$ 2.25
B8.	Ham	$ 2.25
B9.	Spam	$ 2.25
B10.	Relleno Bacon	$ 2.25
B11.	Breakfast Dog	$ 2.25

NEVADA WIER

Carne adovada or Spam? Burrito Box in Albuquerque tailors burritos to every taste.

fast seeker, this casual sit-down restaurant claims to have started Santa Fe's breakfast burrito craze 20 years ago. Its standard filling of hash browns and bacon (eggs optional) was the inspiration for our breakfast burrito recipe on page 93. The chile that's ladled on top is especially generous. Melted cheddar cheese crowns the works.

Tijeras. *Chuckwagon Cafe, 11805 State Highway 337, at the junction of State 333; (505) 281-9170.* Fifteen miles east of Albuquerque sits a Southwestern-style hole-in-the-wall where regulars wear cowboy hats and discuss the health of their mares. Order the break-

fast burrito and you're set for the day: home fries, onions, eggs, and your choice of meat, all wrapped in a tortilla and topped with chile (the red is excellent, the green a little gluey), colby and jack cheeses, and olives.

THE NEW WAVE

Burritos go healthy. Burritos go weird. Burritos go big business. All these concepts apply to the up-and-coming burrito joints that make up this category.

On the health front, heart-smart menus advertise no lard and offer

SALSAS RANGE FROM MILD TO DEATH PASTE... SETS YOU BACK $3.75 AND ONLY FEEDS TWO PEOPLE... NOT SAFE TO

DEANNE FITZMAURICE

complete nutritional analyses. On the weird front, fillings like Peking duck, grilled vegetables with goat cheese, and smoked tofu are tucked in bright spinach or tomato tortillas. These may only look like burritos, and some, in fact, aren't even called burritos. ("Could we get four burritos to go?" we asked at one place. "Well, only if you call them wraps.")

These new-wave burritos are taking the San Francisco Bay Area by storm. Other regions are catching on. Propelled in some cases by venture capitalists waving market research, these anything-in-a-tortilla meals may just be the next big food craze.

The first listing is in Southern California; the rest are in the Bay Area.

Costa Mesa. *Taco Mesa,* 647 W. 19th St.; (714) 642-0629 (and locations in Mission Viejo and Fullerton). Thank you, Bobbie Bennett of Huntington Beach, for leading us to our personal candidate for the West's best burrito: Taco Mesa's blackened chicken breast. It seems others share our enthusiasm, because this place is packed day and night with 20- and 30-somethings.

Though other fillings are available, they can't top the blackened chicken. The meat is slathered with an outstanding and mysterious dark red, spicy mixture (owner Ivan Calderon will not reveal the ingredients), then grilled and paired with crunchy cabbage relish with cilantro and tomato, beans, sour cream, and cheese, and wrapped in a whole-wheat or white tortilla. Order it plain or covered with warm red chili sauce or green tomatillo sauce.

Alameda. *The Hot Shop Gourmet Burrito,* 853 Marina Village Parkway; (510) 814-9003 (and locations in Concord, Menlo Park, San Francisco, San Ramon, and Walnut Creek). After visiting Gourmet Burrito, we didn't know whether to thank local resident Dottie Duncan for writing, or wish she never

had. It was our third burrito stop of the day. We tried six there. They were so good we could hardly put them down. You get the idea. Choose from 26 fillings, like chicken and artichokes, sweet-hot duck, and prawns and scallops sautéed with lemon and herbs. And loosen your belt. These are hefty.

Danville. *High Tech Burrito,* 202 Sycamore Valley Rd. W.; (510) 838-2333 (plus locations in Alamo, Albany, Berkeley, Mill Valley, Novato, Orinda, San Rafael, Tassajara, and Walnut Creek). Brenda and Stan Rainey of Vancouver, Washington, nominate High Tech's "surf and turf" (with juicy shrimp and marinated steak) as the West's best burrito. They write, "The burrito is large (takes two hands to eat), and it makes more than a meal, but you have to eat every bite." What the Raineys don't mention is that this friendly suburban fast-food stop offers 13 burritos with less than 30 percent of their calories from fat. Maybe they didn't notice. Choices like the California—a gooey combination of guacamole, beans, rice, lettuce, onion, tomato, and salsa—hardly taste like a diet plate (and with 583 to 1,027 calories, many aren't).

San Francisco. *Casa Aguila,* 1240 Noriega St. at 19th Ave.; (415) 661-5593. Colorful, quirky, and just plain fun describes both the ambience and the super-vegetarian burritos readers led us to at this sit-down restaurant on a city side street. Don't be fooled by the streamers into thinking you'll get traditional Mexican fare. Our burritos came filled with rutabaga, turnip, kabocha squash, carrot, lettuce, tomato, onion, bell pepper, apples, raisins, prunes, walnuts, pine nuts, pomegranate seeds, basil leaves, and loads of jack cheese. "Sometimes the cooks get a little carried away," our server confessed. At lunch you can get beans and rice inside or outside the tortilla, at dinner, outside only.

HONORABLE MENTION: READERS' CHOICE

Letters about the following places were simply too mouthwatering not to mention. We tried burritos from about half of these, so there may be some hidden gems… or duds. Many restaurants have several locations.

ARIZONA
TUCSON: *Sanchez Burrito Co., El Rapido*
CALIFORNIA
ARCATA: *¡Hey Juan!*
CARLSBAD: *Jose's Baja Grill*
CHICO: *Speedy Burrito*
COTATI: *Rafa's Mexican Restaurant*
COVINA: *Ray's Tepeyac*
CULVER CITY: *Tito's Tacos*
FREEDOM: *Hector's Bakery*
LA JOLLA: *Fins*
LODI: *Mombo's Mexican Take Out*
LONG BEACH: *Casa Sanchez*
LOS ALTOS: *Estrellita Restaurant*
MOUNTAIN VIEW: *La Bamba Taqueria*
OCEANSIDE: *Jose's Taco Shop*
RANCHO CUCAMONGA: *Felipe's Taqueria*
SACRAMENTO: *Taco Loco Taqueria*
SAN BERNARDINO: *Rosa Maria's*
SAN DIEGO: *Nico's*
SAN FRANCISCO: *Taqueria La Cumbre*
SAN JOSE: *Mucho's Restaurant*
SAN JUAN BAUTISTA: *Jardines De San Juan*
SAN LUIS OBISPO: *Tio Alberto's*
SANTA CRUZ: *Tacos Moreno*
SHELL BEACH: *Shell Beach Cafe*
VACAVILLE: *Favela's Taqueria*
COLORADO
COLORADO SPRINGS: *El Taco Rey*
IDAHO
BOISE: *Atomic Taco at Cristina's Bakery*
NEW MEXICO
ALBUQUERQUE: *Burrito Box*
SANTA FE: *Cafe Pasqual's*
OREGON
BEND: *Rolaine's Cantina*
CORVALLIS: *Nearly Normal's*
EUGENE: *Ritta's Burritos at the Eugene Saturday Market*
MANZANITA: *Left Coast Siesta*
MEDFORD: *Octavio's La Burrita*
PORTLAND: *El Burrito Loco*
WASHINGTON
SEATTLE: *Taco del Mar*
WYOMING
JACKSON HOLE: *Vista Grande*

DRIVE AFTER HAVING THIS MUCH FUN… THE SUBJECT OF BURRITOS MOVES ME!

Three bodacious make-at-home burritos

For those times when a burrito craving hits you hard and the best restaurant is too far away, we've created three magnificent choices to cook at home.

The Grandes hold the works. Forget about calories and go for it.

Scrambled eggs, country-style hash browns, and chorizo fill the breakfast burritos (good for dinner, too). They're smothered in a medium-hot red chile.

When you're in a hurry and want something fairly low-fat, try the chicken– black bean burritos with goat cheese.

Most supermarkets carry "burrito-size" flour tortillas (generally 10 inches wide) in regular white, low-fat, and whole-wheat varieties. For oversize tortillas (13 inches or so), shop at a Mexican market. The fresher the tortilla, the easier it is to wrap around fillings.

Work quickly during assembly to keep burritos hot, and serve on warm plates. If they cool off, you can wrap each pork or chicken burrito in lightly oiled foil and heat in a 350° oven for 10 to 20 minutes.

Ultimate burritos start with pork marinated in chilies and tequila, then grilled. Add salsa, guacamole, cotija cheese, beans, and Spanish

Sunset's Burritos Grandes

Cooking time: About 25 minutes

Prep time: About 40 minutes, plus at least 15 minutes for marinating

Notes: Buy ancho chilies, Mexican sour cream (*crema*), and tangy cotija cheese at a Mexican market or well-stocked supermarket. For less indulgent burritos, omit the guacamole, sour cream, and cheese, and make 6 instead of 4.

Makes: 4 large or 6 regular-size burritos

- 2 ounces (4 to 6) dried ancho, New Mexico, or California chilies
- 1/3 cup tequila
- 1/4 cup lemon juice
- 3 cloves garlic
- 1 tablespoon olive oil
- 1/2 teaspoon dried oregano
- 1 teaspoon salt (optional)
- 1 1/4 pounds pork butt (shoulder), fat trimmed
- 1/2 cup long-grain white rice
- 1/4 cup canned tomato sauce
- 1 can (15 oz.) pinto or red beans
- 4 large (13 in.) or 6 regular-size (10 in.) flour tortillas
- 1 1/4 cups guacamole (recipe follows) or purchased guacamole
- 1/3 cup Mexican sour cream (*crema*) or regular sour cream
- 1 cup crumbled cotija cheese or shredded jack cheese
- 1 2/3 cups Classic Salsa Fresca (recipe follows) or purchased red salsa
- 1/2 cup chopped fresh cilantro

1. Tequila-chili marinade. Stem and seed chilies. Whirl in a blender until finely ground. Add tequila, lemon juice, 1/4 cup water, garlic, oil, oregano, and 3/4 teaspoon salt; whirl until puréed. Cut meat across the grain into slices 1/2 inch thick and 3 to 4 inches long. In a bowl, coat meat with marinade. Chill airtight at least 15 minutes or up to 24 hours.

beans (including most of liquid), rice, cheese, 1 cup of the salsa, and cilantro. Fold over sides and roll up tightly to enclose. Add more salsa to taste.

Per large burrito: 930 cal., 41% (378 cal.) from fat; 45 g protein; 42 g fat (9.9 g sat.); 81 g carbo.; 1,250 mg sodium; 114 mg chol.

Guacamole

Prep time: About 10 minutes

Makes: About 1¼ cups

Pit and peel 2 ripe **avocados** (1 lb. total). In a bowl, coarsely mash avocados with a fork or pastry blender. Stir in 1½ tablespoons **lime juice**, 1 tablespoon chopped fresh **cilantro**, and ½ teaspoon **ground cumin**. Add **garlic salt** to taste.

Per tablespoon: 27 cal., 85% (23 cal.) from fat; 0.3 g protein; 2.6 g fat (0.4 g sat.); 1.3 g carbo.; 1.9 mg sodium; 0 mg chol.

Classic Salsa Fresca

Prep time: About 10 minutes

Makes: 1⅔ cups

In a bowl, combine 1½ cups chopped **ripe tomatoes**, ¼ cup sliced **green onions**, 1½ to 2 tablespoons minced fresh **jalapeño chili**, and 1 teaspoon **lemon juice**. Season to taste with **salt**.

Per tablespoon: 2.7 cal., 0% from fat; 0.1 g protein; 0 g fat; 0.6 g carbo.; 1.1 mg sodium; 0 mg chol.

New Mexican Red Chile Breakfast Burritos

Cooking time: About 45 minutes

Prep time: About 30 minutes

Notes: For especially rich chili flavor, buy ground Dixon or Chimayó chilies (types of New Mexico chilies) from The Chile Shop, 109 E. Water Street, Santa Fe; (505) 983-6080. Per ½ pound, Dixons cost $3.95, Chimayós $6.95; shipping costs extra.

Makes: 6 burritos

1 teaspoon salad oil

1 cup chopped yellow onion

2 cloves garlic, minced

2 tablespoons all-purpose flour

⅔ cup ground New Mexico or California chilies

1½ cups chicken broth
  Salt

1½ pounds thin-skinned potatoes

¾ pound chorizo or 10 slices bacon

6 flour tortillas (10 in. wide)

rice, and enclose in an oversize tortilla. If you like, serve with extra guacamole and salsa.

2. On a large baking sheet, lay parallel about 2 inches apart 2 metal skewers, each about 18 inches long (or use 4 10-inch skewers). Lift meat from marinade and thread each strip onto a pair of skewers. Pat with marinade from bowl.

3. Barbecuing. Place skewered meat on an oiled barbecue grill over a solid bed of medium coals, or medium-high heat on a gas grill (you can hold your hand at grill level only 4 to 5 seconds); close lid on gas grill. Cook, turning often, until meat is well browned and crusty, about 20 minutes.

4. Spanish rice. Meanwhile, in a 1½- to 2-quart pan over high heat, bring ¾ cup water, rice, tomato sauce, and remaining ¼

teaspoon salt to a boil. Reduce heat and simmer, covered, until liquid is absorbed, 15 to 20 minutes.

5. Beans. About 5 minutes before meat is done, place beans and their liquid in a 1-quart pan and cook over medium-high heat until bubbling, about 5 minutes.

6. Tortillas. Lift cooked meat to a platter and cover with foil. Heat 1 or 2 tortillas at a time on grill until lightly browned but still soft, turning once, 30 to 40 seconds. Stack on platter beneath foil to keep warm.

7. Assembly. On a board, remove meat from skewers; cut into ¼-inch-wide strips. Lay tortillas flat. Toward 1 edge of each, fill equally with guacamole, sour cream, pork,

Pepper

8 large eggs

1 cup shredded sharp cheddar cheese

½ cup reduced-fat or regular sour cream (optional)

⅓ cup sliced green onions

1. Red chile. In a 1½- to 2-quart pan over medium heat, frequently stir oil, yellow onion, and garlic until onion is limp, 6 to 8 minutes. Add flour and ground chilies; stir for 1½ minutes to toast. Add broth and 1½ cups water and stir until sauce is smooth and bubbling, about 8 minutes. Reduce heat to low and simmer, stirring occasionally, for 10 minutes. Season to taste with salt. Set aside and keep warm. If making ahead, chill airtight up to 2 days; reheat to use.

2. Fillings and tortillas. Peel potatoes, halve lengthwise, and cut crosswise into ⅓-inch-thick slices. Place in a 2- to 3-quart pan with water to cover and bring to a boil over high heat. Reduce heat and simmer, covered, until tender when pierced, about 6 minutes. Drain.

3. Meanwhile, remove casings from chorizo and crumble into a 10- to 12-inch nonstick frying pan (for bacon, cut into 1½-inch

pieces). Over medium-high heat, stir often until meat is brown and crisp, 8 to 10 minutes. With a slotted spoon, lift meat to towels; drain fat from pan, reserving 3 tablespoons. (If chorizo is very finely crumbled, drain fat through a strainer.) If necessary, add salad oil to equal 3 tablespoons.

4. Seal tortillas in foil and warm in a 350° oven until hot, about 10 minutes.

5. Return 2 tablespoons reserved fat to frying pan. Over medium-high heat, add potatoes and turn occasionally until well browned, about 10 minutes. Season to taste with salt and pepper, remove from pan, and keep warm.

6. In a bowl, beat eggs to blend. Coat pan with remaining 1 tablespoon fat. Add eggs; stir over medium heat until softly set, about 2 minutes. Add salt and pepper to taste.

7. Assembly. Lay tortillas flat. Toward 1 edge of each, fill equally with potatoes, eggs, and chorizo. Fold over sides and roll up tightly to enclose. Place each on a rimmed ovenproof plate or in a ramekin, and ladle chile on top. Sprinkle with cheese and bake in a 350° oven just until cheese melts, 2 to 3 minutes.

8. Meanwhile, put sour cream in a small, unpleated, heavy-duty plastic bag. Seal, then snip off a small corner of bag. Squeeze

squiggles of sour cream over hot burritos. Sprinkle with green onions.

Per burrito: 618 cal., 44% (270 cal.) from fat; 26 g protein; 30 g fat (10 g sat.); 62 g carbo.; 926 mg sodium; 317 mg chol.

Chicken–Goat Cheese Burritos

Cooking time: About 15 minutes

Prep time: About 15 minutes

Notes: To trim about 600 mg of sodium per serving, use a low-sodium salsa.

Makes: 4 burritos

1 pound boned, skinned chicken breast

1 teaspoon ground cumin

½ teaspoon *each* salt (optional) and pepper

4 reduced-fat or other flour tortillas (10 in. wide)

1 can (15 oz.) black beans

1 teaspoon salad oil

½ cup (3 oz.) soft fresh goat cheese, broken into small chunks

1 to 1½ cups purchased fresh green salsa (mild or hot)

1. Cut chicken into ½- by 3-inch strips. In a bowl, coat evenly with cumin, salt, and pepper.

2. Seal tortillas in foil and warm in a 350° oven until hot, about 10 minutes.

3. Place beans and their liquid in a 1-quart pan and cook over medium-high heat until bubbling, about 5 minutes.

4. In a 10- to 12-inch nonstick frying pan over medium-high heat, frequently stir chicken and oil until meat is no longer pink in center, about 6 minutes.

5. Lay tortillas flat. Toward 1 edge of each, fill equally with chicken, beans (including most of liquid), cheese, and ½ cup of the salsa. Fold over sides and roll up tightly to enclose. Add more salsa to taste.

Per burrito: 507 cal., 21% (108 cal.) from fat; 43 g protein; 12 g fat (5.3 g sat.); 57 g carbo.; 1,626 mg sodium; 86 mg chol. ∎

Wake up Southwest-style to hash browns, chorizo, and scrambled eggs, all wrapped up in a tortilla and covered with a dried-chili sauce, cheese, and sour cream.

By Elaine Johnson

Discovering the pleasures of French pizza

AGE 20: MY FIRST TRIP TO FRANCE, my first train ride, and my first encounter with a French pizza. As the train chugged south from Paris to Provence, I wandered into the dining car, hungry. I was hesitant to speak French, lest the "secret" get out that I was American. (Later, I realized my nonpointy shoes gave it away.) But *pizza* was something I could pronounce.

This was entirely different from the cheese-slathered slabs back home. It had a thin, crisp crust; robust flavors of tomatoes, herbs, and anchovies; and nutty-tasting, unpitted olives. The cheese? Just a sprinkling. No wonder the French are so slim, I thought.

It's easy to create this pizza at home using frozen bread dough for the crust, and a very hot oven. For a continental touch, eat with a knife and fork.

Provençal Pizza

Cooking time: About 40 minutes

Prep time: About 10 minutes

Notes: If your store doesn't sell herbes de Provence (a mix of herbs), use ¼ teaspoon *each* dried basil, marjoram, oregano, rosemary, savory, thyme, and crushed fennel seed. For a quicker, *California-style pizza*, omit anchovies; use a purchased thin, baked pizza crust (12 in. wide; 10 oz.) instead of dough; and substitute sliced ripe olives for the niçoise.

Makes: 4 servings

- 1¾ cups thin slivers of onions
- 3 large cloves garlic, thinly sliced
- 1 teaspoon olive oil
- 1 can (6 oz.) unsalted tomato paste
- 1½ teaspoons herbes de Provence
- 1 loaf (1 lb.) frozen bread dough, thawed

  All-purpose flour
- ⅔ cup (1½ oz.) freshly shredded parmesan cheese
- 1 ounce canned anchovies, drained, patted dry, and halved lengthwise
- ¼ cup drained niçoise olives

1. Place a 14- by 16-inch baking stone or 14- by 17-inch baking sheet on bottom rack of a 500° oven. Heat at least 30 minutes.

2. Meanwhile, combine onions, garlic, oil, and ¼ cup water in a 10- to 12-inch nonstick frying pan. Cover and cook over medium-low heat until water evaporates, 10 to 12 minutes. Stir in ¼ cup more water. Cook, covered, stirring occasionally, until water evaporates and onions are very limp and golden, 15 to 20 minutes more.

3. Combine tomato paste, herbes de Provence, and ½ cup water.

4. On a floured board, knead dough briefly to expel air. Gather dough into a smooth ball, then roll out to a 14-inch circle. Drape over rolling pin; transfer to a very well floured baking sheet or piece of cardboard at least as big as dough. Smooth dough circle. Shake pan gently; if dough sticks, lift and dust underneath with more flour.

5. Spread dough with tomato sauce. Scatter with onion mixture, then cheese. Crisscross pairs of anchovy pieces in evenly spaced Xs over pizza. Distribute olives evenly over pizza; press into dough.

6. Slide pizza onto preheated baking stone. Bake until pizza crust is browned and crisp, 9 to 12 minutes. Slide a baking sheet under pizza and lift to a board. Watch for olive pits as you eat.

Per serving: 435 cal., 23% (99 cal.) from fat; 18 g protein; 11 g fat (2.7 g sat.); 68 g carbo.; 1,443 mg sodium; 12 mg chol. ∎

WE'D LIKE TO HEAR FROM YOU!

Do you have tips or recipes for low-fat cooking? Write to Everyday Low-fat Cooking, Sunset Magazine, 80 Willow Rd., Menlo Park, CA 94025, or send e-mail (including your full name and street address) to lowfat@sunsetpub.com.

Exotic bananas to look for in markets include (clockwise from top center) red, manzano, plantain, niño, and burro.

The wild bunch

Stalking the produce shelves reveals a lot more than the plain old banana. And cooking with exotic varieties has a savory payoff

NOT SO LONG AGO, BUYING bananas was a predictable exercise. You simply went to the bananas marked Chiquita or Dole and picked out a bunch. You knew yellow meant ripe, and you could count on them all tasting alike.

But like lettuce, mushrooms, and tomatoes, the humble banana has gone gourmet. Now, tucked among the fruit you've known since childhood are new and exotic-looking varieties, including finger-size niños, plump manzanos, squat and square burros, huge mottled plantains, and dusky reds.

The West's cultural diversity is a driving force behind the new kinds of bananas available in markets. Hundreds of banana varieties are grown worldwide,

and more and more are immigrating to local produce aisles. Some are eaten raw, but others are so starchy that they are cooked and served as a side dish, like potatoes. In many cultures, the degree of ripeness determines how a particular variety is eaten: it may be cooked if green, eaten raw when ripe.

Except for plantains, none of the bananas listed here need to be cooked. To best discern their subtle flavor differences and complexities, first try them raw and unadorned. All lend themselves nicely to cooking, however, and are particularly delicious in the following recipes. You can't always depend on a yellow color to indicate ripeness, so it pays to become familiar with their individual characteristics. Look for these

exotic bananas in well-stocked supermarkets or in Latino or Southeast Asian markets.

Burro. Orinoco, chunky banana, and horse burro are other names for this large, squat banana, which is ripe when its peel is deep yellow with black spots. Its flesh is soft on the outside and slightly crisp in the center, and it has a mildly sweet flavor with subtle lemon overtones. Cooking brings out its starchiness; sautéed slices make a nice vegetable dish.

Manzano. This short, chubby banana also may be called apple, finger, or baby banana. Labels often describe it as ripe when completely black, but it's delicious when still partly yellow, too. The manzano has a creamy texture but slightly grainy seeds. Its flavor is reminiscent of apple and pear. Cooking greatly intensifies the flavor but makes the texture somewhat mushy.

Niño. What the diminutive niño lacks in size—it's only about 3 to 4 inches long—it makes up for in flavor. This banana, also called honey, sucrier, or Dominique, is deep yellow with black spots when ripe. Its golden flesh has a velvety texture and a heady tropical taste with floral overtones. This banana is

BUYING AND RIPENING TIPS

• No matter what banana variety you're buying, avoid fruit with split peels, moldy stems, or soft brown spots (which indicate bruising and should not be confused with the black spots that appear with ripening).

• Proper ripening is essential; these varieties can taste horribly astringent when "green" (even though the skin may not be green). Let them ripen uncovered at room temperature (refrigeration stops ripening); this can take as long as seven days or more.

• Once ripe, the fruit should last at least four days. Refrigerate fully ripe bananas to store longer (the peel will discolor, but the fruit will still taste fine).

A tender, moist cake gets heady tropical flavor from red, niño, or manzano bananas, cinnamon, and fresh and crystallized ginger.

excellent fresh or cooked; cooking develops its creaminess and heightens its flavor and color.

Plantain. Although the plantain has been in Western markets longer than the other varieties, it remains a mystery to many shoppers. The plantain, sometimes known as "the potato of the tropics," has a tough peel that turns from green to black as the fruit ripens; use when brown or black. To peel, cut off both tips, then score peel lengthwise and pull back. The starchy flesh is almost always cooked; plantains are usually used as a vegetable, either sautéed or boiled in stews. They do, indeed, taste somewhat like potatoes, with a faint sweetness. But when extremely ripe, plantains are often sweet enough to eat raw.

Red. This banana's maroon peel does not change color as the fruit ripens, but the banana is ready to use if it feels soft when gently pressed. The flesh is a beautiful pink-orange with a sweet, mildly floral taste. Its texture is similar to, but slightly firmer than, a regular banana's. This banana is good raw or cooked.

The whimsical presentation of the banana cake on page 97 was inspired by a recipe created by California Culinary Academy student Catherine Leland.

Best-ever Banana Ginger Cake

Cooking time: 45 to 50 minutes

Prep time: About 25 minutes

Notes: Bake this versatile cake in a square cake pan and cut into shapes with a cookie cutter, or bake in a loaf pan and slice. To make the gingered whipped cream, fold 2 tablespoons minced crystallized ginger into 2 to 2 1/2 cups slightly sweetened whipped cream.

Makes: 9 servings

>   2 1/4 cups all-purpose flour
>   I teaspoon baking powder
>   3/4 teaspoon baking soda
>   1/2 teaspoon ground cinnamon
>   1/3 cup butter or margarine
>   I cup sugar
>   2 large eggs
>   I cup well-mashed very ripe manzano, niño, or red bananas
>   I tablespoon minced fresh ginger
>   I teaspoon finely grated lemon peel
>   1/2 cup buttermilk
>   Gingered whipped cream (see notes above), ground cinnamon, powdered sugar, crystallized ginger, and fresh mint sprigs (optional)

I. Stir together flour, baking powder, soda, and cinnamon. In another bowl, beat butter and sugar with electric mixer until fluffy. Beat in eggs I at a time, mixing well after each addition. Beat in bananas, ginger, and peel.

2. Stir in flour mixture and buttermilk just until completely blended. Pour into a buttered 9-inch-square cake pan or 9- by 5-inch loaf pan.

3. Bake in a 350° oven until cake is golden brown and center springs back when lightly pressed, about 45 minutes for cake pan, 50 minutes for loaf pan. Cool cake completely. (If making ahead, wrap airtight and store at room temperature up to I day.)

4. If baked in a cake pan, cut into squares or desired shapes with 2 1/2- to 3-inch-diameter cookie cutters (stars and moons are especially attractive). If cake is too thick to get cutter all the way through, cut around cutter

with a small knife. (If you have cake scraps left over, layer them with vanilla low-fat yogurt and sliced bananas for a delicious parfait.) If baked in a loaf pan, slice.

5. If using whipped cream, place dollops on individual plates; top with pieces of cake (standing upright, if possible). Dust lightly with cinnamon and/or powdered sugar pressed through a sieve. Garnish with crystallized ginger (cut into shapes) and mint.

Per serving: 302 cal., 26% (79 cal.) from fat; 5.3 g protein; 8.8 g fat (4.9 g sat.); 51 g carbo.; 262 mg sodium; 67 mg chol.

Caramelized Miniature-Banana Sundaes

Cooking time: About 10 minutes

Prep time: About 15 minutes

Notes: This recipe works well with any kind of banana. With larger varieties, use one banana per person. Before sautéing, cut bananas in half crosswise, then cut each half in half lengthwise.

Makes: 4 to 6 servings

>   8 firm-ripe niño bananas
>   1/4 cup (1/8 lb.) butter
>   1/2 cup orange juice
>   1/4 cup firmly packed brown sugar
>   2 tablespoons orange-flavor liqueur (optional)
>   I quart good-quality vanilla or vanilla bean ice cream

I. Cut bananas in half lengthwise. Melt butter in a 10- to 12-inch frying pan over medium-high heat; add bananas and turn often until golden brown all over, 7 to 8 minutes.

2. Gently remove bananas from pan; keep warm. Add orange juice and sugar to pan. Bring to boiling over high heat, then immediately remove from heat and stir in liqueur.

3. Divide ice cream among 4 to 6 individual bowls. Arrange bananas over ice cream; top with sauce. Serve immediately.

Per serving: 403 cal., 40% (162 cal.) from fat; 4.5 g protein; 18 g fat (11 g sat.); 60 g carbo.; 157 mg sodium; 60 mg chol.

Sautéed Plantains

Cooking time: About 6 minutes

Prep time: About 10 minutes

Notes: As a side dish, these are a refreshing alternative to potatoes.

Makes: 4 servings

>   2 ripe plantains (about 1 1/4 lb. total)
>   About 2 tablespoons salad oil
>   Reduced-fat sour cream and minced chives (optional)
>   Salt

I. Cut off both tips of plantains, then score peel lengthwise and pull back. Cut flesh diagonally into 1/2-inch-thick slices.

2. Heat oil in a 10- to 12-inch nonstick frying pan over medium-high heat. Add plantain slices (in batches, if necessary, adding more oil with each batch) and cook until golden brown on undersides, about 3 minutes. Turn slices; brown other sides. If frying

in batches, keep cooked slices warm.

3. Transfer to a serving dish. Garnish with sour cream and chives. Add salt to taste.

Per serving: 172 cal., 38% (65 cal.) from fat; 1.2 g protein; 7.2 g fat (0.9 g sat.); 29 g carbo.; 3.7 mg sodium; 0 mg chol. ■

By Christine Weber Hale

Crisp chunks of oats, gingersnaps, dried apples, and ginger combine in a lightened-up granola. Top with raspberries and milk for breakfast.

3. Press oat mixture into 2 lightly oiled 10-by 15-inch baking pans. Bake in a 300° oven until mixture is golden brown and sticks together, about 40 minutes.

4. Add apples and ginger equally to pans, and stir until granola breaks into large chunks. Let cool. Use, or store airtight up to 1 month. Serve with milk and berries as desired, or eat plain.

Per ½ cup: 183 cal., 15% (28 cal.) from fat; 5.1 g protein; 3.1 g fat (0.5 g sat.); 34 g carbo.; 78 mg sodium; 0 mg chol.

Postrio Granola

Cooking time: About 30 minutes

Prep time: About 15 minutes

Makes: About 10 cups

- 5 cups (about 1 lb.) regular rolled oats
- 1 cup *each* whole cashews and sliced almonds
- ½ cup firmly packed light brown sugar
- 1 tablespoon grated orange peel
- 1½ teaspoons ground cinnamon
- ½ teaspoon ground nutmeg
- 1 cup (½ lb.) butter or margarine, melted
- ⅓ cup maple syrup
- 1 cup toasted flaked coconut
- ½ cup *each* golden raisins and diced dried apricots

1. In a large bowl, stir together oats, cashews, almonds, brown sugar, orange peel, cinnamon, and nutmeg until well combined.

2. Pour melted butter and syrup over all, and gently mix to distribute evenly. Press mixture into a buttered 10- by 15-inch baking pan.

3. Bake in a 350° oven until mixture is golden brown and sticks together, about 30 minutes.

4. Let cool. When completely cool, break into chunks and stir with coconut, raisins, and apricots. Use, or store airtight in a plastic bag or container up to 1 month.

Per ½ cup: 313 cal., 52% (162 cal.) from fat; 6.1 g protein; 18 g fat (8.5 g sat.); 34 g carbo.; 148 mg sodium; 26 mg chol. ■

Great granolas

Enjoy them for breakfast or a snack—even for dessert

FOR A FAST, FLAVORFUL BREAKFAST, you can't beat granola. These two recipes are particularly wonderful—and the gingersnap granola is really low in fat. A quick egg-white meringue binds ingredients, eliminating the need for butter or margarine.

A marvelous granola made by Anne and David Gingrass, founding chefs of Postrio, now chef-owners of Hawthorne Lane in San Francisco, is packed with dried apricots, golden raisins, toasted coconut, orange peel, and nuts.

Gingersnap Granola

Cooking time: About 40 minutes

Prep time: About 20 minutes

Makes: About 12 cups

- 5 cups (about 1 lb.) regular rolled oats
- 3 cups (½ lb.) gingersnaps, broken into almond-size pieces
- 2 cups spoon-size wheat squares
- ½ cup lightly toasted wheat germ
- 1 teaspoon ground cinnamon
- 3 large egg whites
- ¼ teaspoon cream of tartar
- ⅓ cup sugar
- 2 cups (6 oz.) chopped dried apples
- ⅓ cup chopped crystallized ginger
  Milk and fresh raspberries or strawberries (optional)

1. In a large bowl, stir oats, gingersnap pieces, spoon-size wheat squares, wheat germ, and cinnamon until well combined; set aside.

2. In another large bowl, whip egg whites and cream of tartar until egg whites hold soft peaks. Add sugar 1 tablespoon at a time, whipping after each addition, until sugar is completely dissolved. Stir egg whites into oat mixture, and press ingredients together with hands until all cereal is well coated.

By Betsy Reynolds Bateson

PETER CHRISTIANSEN

PHILIP SALAVERRY

Quick, satisfying salad suppers

Start with ready-to-use greens and eat in 30 minutes or less

SAVING TIME SELLS. NOTE THE SPACE that washed, trimmed, and dried lettuces and other tender ready-to-use salad leaves now command in produce sections. And these greens move out as briskly as they arrive—but not always to play the obvious role of salad.

Embellished with meat, grains, pasta, and extra seasonings, the ready-to-use leaves make wholesome foundations for fast, easy, and filling main dishes.

Each recipe suggests a specific salad green or mix, but if that one is not available, substitute another that is similar. Check the expiration dates on packaged salad greens—these foods are quite perishable. Leaves sold in bulk get handled and misted, so give them a quick rinse and a spin-dry.

Fiesta Beef Salad

Prep time: About 25 minutes
Makes: 3 servings

½ cup orange juice

3 tablespoons wine vinegar

¼ teaspoon cayenne

¼ teaspoon sugar

¼ cup chopped fresh cilantro

1 can (15 oz.) black beans, rinsed and drained

1 can (11 oz.) Mexican-style corn, drained

4 Roma tomatoes (about 4 oz. each), cut into wedges

8 cups (10 to 12 oz.) iceberg lettuce, romaine lettuce, radish salad mix

6 ounces thinly sliced roasted lean beef or turkey, cut into thin strips

Salt and pepper

1. In a large bowl, combine orange juice, vinegar, cayenne, sugar, cilantro, beans, corn, tomatoes, and salad mix. Mix well.

2. With a slotted spoon, distribute salad mix equally on 3 dinner plates. Mix beef

In a hurry? Beef salad gets a fast start with a leafy salad mix, canned black beans, and cooked meat.

with any remaining dressing in bowl, and mound on top of salads. Add salt and pepper to taste.

Per serving: 360 cal., 24% (86 cal.) from fat; 26 g protein; 9.5 g fat (3.1 g sat.); 47 g carbo.; 651 mg sodium; 46 mg chol.

Greek Tabbouleh Salad

Cooking time: About 8 minutes
Prep time: About 20 minutes
Notes: In this country, the French salad mix called mesclun is often labeled as European or spring mix. The salad typically contains small, tender leaves of arugula, various lettuces, watercress, dandelion greens, and chervil.
Makes: 3 servings

⅔ cup bulgur wheat

1 jar (6 oz.) marinated artichoke hearts

¼ cup white wine vinegar

¼ cup chopped fresh mint

2 tablespoons olive oil

1 can (about 15 oz.) garbanzos, rinsed and drained

1 cucumber (6 oz.), ends trimmed and thinly sliced

2 quarts (about 5 oz.) mesclun

⅓ cup crumbled feta cheese

Salt and pepper

1. In a 1- to 2-quart pan, bring 1½ cups water to a boil over high heat. Stir in bulgur; cover and simmer over low heat until tender to bite, about 5 minutes.

2. Meanwhile, drain marinade from artichokes into a small bowl. Add vinegar, mint, oil, and 2 tablespoons water.

3. Pour bulgur into a fine wire strainer to drain, rinse with cold water until cool, and drain well.

4. Mix ⅓ cup vinegar-mint dressing with garbanzos, cucumber, artichoke hearts, and salad greens. Mound salad equally on 3 dinner plates.

5. Mix remaining dressing with bulgur. Mound bulgur equally onto salad greens. Sprinkle with cheese; add salt and pepper to taste.

Per serving: 395 cal., 43% (171 cal.) from fat; 13 g protein; 19 g fat (4.2 g sat.); 47 g carbo.; 625 mg sodium; 13 mg chol.

Chinese Shrimp Salad

Cooking time: About 10 minutes

Prep time: About 5 minutes

Notes: To thaw peas quickly, put them in a colander and rinse with hot water.

Makes: 3 servings

- 1 cup (3 1/2 oz.) dried small pasta shells
- 1/3 cup seasoned rice vinegar
- 1 tablespoon minced fresh ginger
- 1 tablespoon soy sauce
- 1 teaspoon Asian sesame oil
- 2 tablespoons chopped green onion
- 1/4 teaspoon hot chili flakes
- 2 quarts (6 oz.) baby spinach leaves
- 1 cup frozen petite peas, thawed
- 6 ounces tiny shelled cooked shrimp

1. In a 3- to 4-quart pan, bring about 1 1/2 quarts water to a boil over high heat. Add pasta, and cook just until barely tender to bite, 6 to 8 minutes. Drain pasta, immerse in cold water until cool, and drain again.

2. Mix vinegar, ginger, soy sauce, sesame oil, onion, and chili. Measure 3 tablespoons of this dressing into a large bowl, add spinach, and mix. Mound spinach equally on 3 dinner plates.

3. To bowl, add remaining dressing, pasta, peas, and shrimp; mix. Mound equally on spinach. Drizzle salads with leftover dressing.

Per serving: 273 cal., 10% (28 cal.) from fat; 21 g protein; 3.1 g fat (0.5 g sat.); 40 g carbo.; 1,126 mg sodium; 111 mg chol. ■

By Linda Lau Anusasananan

Try the pasta on top. Season it well, mix with shrimp, and serve on tender greens.

An old soup, a light touch

Fresh spinach, asparagus, and peas make this minestrone worthy of spring

IN ITALY IT IS SAID THAT GENOA'S MINESTRONE WAS CREATED to soothe the city's mariners of old. When these seafarers returned from long voyages, they brought a hunger for the glories of a freshening countryside—the taste of succulent young plants, the perfume of aromatic herbs. In this minestrone, laden with tender green vegetables and herbs, they could savor them all.

The soup lives on because it fills modern needs equally well. While tasters continue to appreciate the freshness of the ingredients, they also value this soup because it is low in fat. And cooks like its relatively brief preparation time.

Spring Green Minestrone

Cooking time: About 20 minutes

Prep time: 25 to 30 minutes (including pesto)

Makes: 6 servings

- 2 quarts vegetable or chicken broth
- 2 leeks (about 1 1/4 lb. total)
- 1/2 cup dried orzo (or other tiny pasta)
- 1 pound thin asparagus, tough ends removed
- 1 can (15 oz.) cannellini (white kidney) beans, drained
- 1/2 pound edible-pod peas, ends trimmed
- 1/4 pound baby spinach leaves, rinsed and drained
  Pesto (recipe follows), optional
  Grated parmesan cheese
  Salt and pepper

1. In a 5- to 6-quart covered pan, bring broth to a boil over high heat.

2. Meanwhile, trim and discard tough dark green tops and root ends of leeks. Cut leeks in half lengthwise, and rinse well. Thinly slice crosswise.

This delicate soup is simply vegetables simmered tender in broth.

3. When broth boils, add pasta and boil, covered, 5 minutes.

4. Meanwhile, slice asparagus into 2-inch lengths. After pasta cooks 5 minutes, add asparagus, leeks, beans, and peas.

5. When pasta is tender to bite, 3 to 4 more minutes, add spinach. Cook just until spinach wilts, about 1 minute.

6. Ladle soup into bowls. Add pesto, cheese, and salt and pepper to taste.

Per serving: 203 cal., 19% (39 cal.) from fat; 14 g protein; 4.3 g fat (1.2 g sat.); 34 g carbo.; 268 mg sodium; 0 mg chol.

Pesto

Prep time: 8 to 10 minutes

Notes: If making ahead, cover and chill up to 2 hours.

Makes: About 1/2 cup

- 1 clove garlic, peeled
- 3 tablespoons extra-virgin olive oil
- 3 tablespoons grated parmesan cheese
- 2 tablespoons water
- 1 cup (about 1 oz.) lightly packed fresh basil leaves
- 1/3 cup (about 1/3 oz.) lightly packed fresh mint leaves
  Salt

In a blender, combine garlic, oil, cheese, water, basil, and mint; whirl until smooth. Add salt to taste.

Per tablespoon: 57 cal., 93% (53 cal.) from fat; 0.9 g protein; 5.9 g fat (1.1 g sat.); 0.8 g carbo.; 35 mg sodium; 1.5 mg chol. ■

By Linda Lau Anusasananan

The rewards of patience: it takes several rising steps—but little hands-on time—to create this handsome feta-basil loaf or a plain Italian biga bread. You'll need a heavy-duty mixer or food processor for kneading.

Chewy Italian bread begins with a biga

Creating a yeast-based starter is the first step in making artisan-style bread at home

FULL OF HOLES INSIDE, OFTEN misshapen outside—you have to know these Italian breads to love them. But rip off a chunk, savor the complex wheat flavor and chewy texture, and you know why the West's artisan bakeries have created a huge following for the loaves. Breads of this style may be called *pane pugliese, pane francese, ciabatta,* or other names, but they all have three things in common: a yeast-based starter called a *biga,* a very wet dough, and a slow rise.

A biga is just flour, water, and a tiny amount of yeast stirred together several hours or a day before baking and allowed to ferment. Unlike a sourdough starter, which is replenished and kept going indefinitely, a biga is made fresh each time you bake (you can make enough for a couple of loaves and freeze the extra to use within two weeks).

Though a biga doesn't create a sour taste, it provides other benefits like those from a sourdough starter: well-developed flavor, moist texture, and good keeping quality.

The wet dough used to make this bread is responsible for its large, irregular holes and wonderfully chewy texture. The dough is so sticky you can't knead it on a board—you must use a food processor or a heavy-duty mixer.

Slowing down the rising process helps develop the bread's complex flavor and aroma. Professional bakers put dough in temperature-controlled retarders. At home, you use ice water in the dough to keep it cool, and let the dough rise at room temperature rather than in the warm spot recommended in most bread recipes.

For a classic Italian-style bread, try the basic recipe on the facing page. For a nontraditional (and delicious) variation, add olive oil, a generous amount of basil, and tangy feta cheese.

Glenn Mitchell, owner of Grace Baking in Albany, California, helped us translate the bread-making process from the professional bakery to the home kitchen.

Italian Biga Bread

Cooking time: About 30 minutes

Prep time: 15 to 25 minutes, plus about 8½ hours for rising

Notes: This recipe is best suited for a lazy weekend, but you can gear it to a weekday schedule. The biga can be made ahead and chilled or frozen, and the kneaded dough can rest in the refrigerator up to 24 hours before its first rise.

You can double or triple the biga for later baking (the biga will rise on the shorter end of the noted time). A baking stone (sold with gourmet cookware) makes the thickest, crispest crust, but you can use a large baking sheet.

Makes: 1 loaf: 1 pound, 7 ounces

   ½ cup lukewarm water

   1¼ teaspoons (about ½ package) active dry yeast

   About 3¾ cups all-purpose flour

   1 cup ice-cold water

   2 teaspoons salt

1. Biga. In a bowl, combine ¼ cup lukewarm water and ¼ teaspoon yeast. Let stand until yeast is dissolved, about 5 minutes. With your hands, mix in ¾ cup flour until evenly moistened; dough will be stiff. Gather into a ball, put in a glass measuring cup, wrap airtight, and let stand at room temperature until biga is bubbly and has tripled in volume, 3 to 5 hours. Use as directed below. (If making ahead, stir down biga after it rises, then chill airtight up to 2 days—stirring down once a day—or freeze up to 2 weeks; thaw to use.)

2. Mixing dough. In a small bowl, combine remaining ¼ cup lukewarm water and 1 teaspoon yeast. Let stand until yeast is dissolved, about 5 minutes.

If using a food processor, whirl biga and ¼ cup ice-cold water until smooth. Add yeast mixture, salt, and remaining ¾ cup ice-cold water; pulse until blended. Add 2¾ cups flour; pulse until incorporated, then whirl until dough is very smooth and elastic, about 2 minutes. (If machine stops, wait a few minutes for motor to cool, then resume, or transfer to a bowl and beat by hand.) To test elasticity, stretch apart a 1-inch chunk of dough with your fingers, and hold it up to the light (see photo A); if it forms a thin sheet you can see through and doesn't shred apart, dough is ready. Dough will be very sticky.

If using a mixer with a dough hook, place biga in large bowl with ¼ cup ice-cold water. Using paddle, mix on low speed until fairly smooth. Add yeast mixture, salt, and remaining ¾ cup ice-cold water; mix until blended. Add 2¾ cups flour and beat on medium speed until well blended. Change to dough hook and beat on medium speed until very smooth and elastic, 12 to 14 minutes (see elasticity test above); dough will be very sticky.

3. First rise. Scrape dough into an oiled bowl (a 2-quart measuring cup is ideal). Wrap airtight and let stand at room temperature until tripled, about 3 hours. Or chill up to 24 hours, then let stand at room temperature until tripled, about 5 hours.

4. Shaping and final rise. Sprinkle a board

with 3 tablespoons flour and scrape dough onto it. With floured hands, gently form a smooth log by first folding dough in half, then pinching a seam where halves join (photo B). Turn dough seam side down and gently pat into a 12- to 13-inch-long rectangle (photo C). Lightly sprinkle with flour. Cover loosely with plastic wrap and let stand on board until puffy, about 30 minutes.

5. While dough rises, place a 14- by 16-inch baking stone or 14- by 17-inch baking sheet in oven and set at 425°. Let heat at least 30 minutes.

6. Sprinkle a 14- by 17-inch baking sheet or piece of stiff cardboard with 2 tablespoons flour. Ease hands under dough, pick up, and as you transfer it to floured sheet, gently stretch it to 17 inches long. Shake floured sheet to slide dough diagonally onto hot stone or baking sheet (photo D).

7. Baking. Bake bread until deep golden, 30 to 35 minutes. Let loaf cool on a rack.

Serve, store in a paper bag up to 1 day, or freeze. If a crisper crust is desired, place bread directly on rack of a 425° oven for about 5 minutes.

Per ounce: 75 cal., 2.4% (1.8 cal.) from fat; 2.2 g protein; 0.2 g fat (0 g sat.); 16 g carbo.; 192 mg sodium; 0 mg chol.

Feta and Basil Biga Bread

Follow recipe for **Italian Biga Bread** (at left) through step 2. Once dough meets the elasticity test, mix in until evenly distributed (in a separate mixing bowl if using food processor) 2 tablespoons **extra-virgin olive oil**, ¾ cup coarsely chopped **fresh basil** or ¼ cup dried basil, and ½ cup crumbled **sheep's milk feta cheese**. Continue with steps 3 through 7. Makes 1 loaf: 1 pound, 13 ounces.

Per ounce: 75 cal., 19% (14 cal.) from fat; 2.1 g protein; 1.6 g fat (0.5 g sat.); 13 g carbo.; 178 mg sodium; 2.1 mg chol. ■

By Elaine Johnson

Piping hot ravioli bakes right in the bowl. Soup is ladled in last. Scoop through tender pasta to reach chicken and artichoke filling.

1 large egg white

¼ cup grated parmesan cheese

¼ teaspoon *each* ground nutmeg and white pepper

About 2 tablespoons melted butter or margarine

8 egg roll wrappers (6 in. square)

1 tablespoon *each* chopped fresh basil leaves and fresh mint leaves

Salt and pepper

1. In a 3- to 4-quart pan, combine broth, tomato paste, basil and mint sprigs, and chilies. Bring to a boil, cover, and simmer gently 30 minutes. Lift out and discard basil and mint sprigs and chilies.

2. Meanwhile, in a 10- to 12-inch frying pan, combine oil, onion, and garlic. Stir over medium heat until onion is limp, about 5 minutes. Add chicken to pan; stir until chicken is crumbly, about 3 minutes, then add artichokes. Remove from heat.

3. Mix ricotta, egg white, 3 tablespoons parmesan, nutmeg, and white pepper. Stir cheese and chicken mixtures together.

4. Brush some of the melted butter on rims and interiors of 4 shallow bowls (at least 6 in. wide and suitable for heating in the oven).

5. With a slotted spoon, immerse 4 egg roll wrappers, 1 at a time, in the hot broth, lift out, and center 1 wrapper in each bowl. Place ¼ of the chicken mixture on wrapper in each bowl. Dip remaining wrappers, 1 at a time, in hot broth, and drape 1 over filling in each bowl. Brush edges and tops of egg roll wrappers with remaining melted butter. If making ahead, cover and chill bowls and broth separately up to 1 day. Let chilled bowls stand at room temperature at least 30 minutes to reduce likelihood of breakage caused by extreme temperature changes.

6. Heat remaining broth to simmering. Set bowls in large, shallow, rimmed pans. Ladle about ½ cup broth into each bowl; seal each bowl with foil that's tented so ravioli won't stick to it. Bake in a 350° oven until filling is hot in center, about 25 minutes (40 minutes, if chilled). Heat remaining broth to simmering. Uncover bowls, and ladle remaining broth into them. Sprinkle each ravioli with chopped basil and mint and remaining parmesan cheese. Add salt and pepper to taste.

Per serving: 608 cal., 40% (243 cal.) from fat; 44 g protein; 27 g fat (10 g sat.); 54 g carbo.; 966 mg sodium; 129 mg chol. ■

By Linda Lau Anusasananan

Just one ravioli apiece

It's dramatic and easy, and you bake it

TAKE ONE RAVIOLI AND STRETCH IT out of shape. Make it really big. Then burst the seams that contain the filling. Loosen up the sauce and scent it with fresh herbs. Now you have a super soup ravioli.

These oversize ravioli are akin in flavor to their smaller counterparts but, surprisingly, much easier and quicker to assemble. Purchased egg roll wrappers take the place of homemade pasta. To make each ravioli, lay an egg roll wrapper in an ovenproof soup bowl. Mound the ground chicken and artichoke filling on the wrapper, then cover with another wrapper. Don't worry about sealing the edges; they don't even need to be aligned. Then bake the ravioli in broth. The result is stunning—and the preparation is oh so easy.

Super Chicken Ravioli Soup

Cooking time: About 1 hour
Prep time: About 25 minutes
Notes: Use wide, shallow bowls suited to oven temperatures, such as heavy-duty restaurant china, stoneware, or ovenproof glass. China with gold or silver trim, earthenware with fragile glazes, and regular glass won't work. The ravioli can be completely assembled up to 1 day ahead, then baked to serve.

Makes: 4 servings

5 cups chicken broth

3 tablespoons tomato paste

6 sprigs fresh basil (5 to 8 in. long)

4 sprigs fresh mint (5 to 8 in. long)

2 small dried hot chilies

1 teaspoon olive oil

1 onion (about 6 oz.), chopped

1 clove garlic, minced

1 pound ground lean chicken or turkey

1 package (9 oz.) frozen artichoke hearts, thawed

1 cup low-fat ricotta cheese

For a roast that's succulently rare and deliciously browned, like this slab of beef rib-eye, cooking temperature and time are critical.

Why?

Why does meat get dry?
Can some cuts be safely roasted at low temperatures?
Why does raw meat change color?

MEAT CHANGES IN PUZZLING ways. Identical cuts from the same kind of animal can end up very different. Sometimes cooked meat turns out moist and tender, other times it chews like leather. Raw meat is sometimes bright red, sometimes a darker color. These changes are mostly a result of air and heat, and how the meat is exposed to them.

"Why does meat sometimes cook up tender and juicy and other times dry and hard?"

—GAIL LESLIE
Rockport, Texas

Although each cut of meat has its own characteristic flavor and texture, it's how the cut is cooked that determines its look and taste.

Heat tightens and shrinks the protein in meat, and in doing so it squeezes out moisture; heat also melts intramuscular fat. If cooked by dry heat—pan-browned, roasted, broiled, or grilled—or fried at high enough temperatures, meat retains enough moisture to still be juicy when it's browned and ready to eat.

Searing meat—cooking it quickly over high heat—is said to seal in juices, but this isn't the whole picture. Searing gets the meat hot enough to brown quickly, tightening and firming the surface.

Although the seared surface does help hold in moisture, juice continues to seep, but slowly enough to evaporate quickly and not interfere with browning.

Because high heat also cooks meat faster, juices and melting intramuscular fat don't have much time to ooze out if the meat is cooked to rare.

But if meat is cooked until well done, it loses considerably more moisture and fat. This is why a less tender cut is juicier and seems more tender when rare than when well done. And why meat with more intramuscular fat tastes juicier than lean meat when well done.

Cooking meat longer at lower temperatures allows more time for juices and fat to leak. When you're roasting, grilling, or broiling, this may not be a problem if you want meat cooked well done. Because protein shrinks and tightens less at lower temperatures, a cut cooked more slowly until well done is juicier and more tender than the same cut cooked to the same doneness at higher heat.

However, lower temperatures don't brown meat as well, especially in a pan. Juices take longer to evaporate and the meat can't brown until they do. By the time a lean piece of meat is well done, it's apt to be gray, not browned, very firm, and dry-tasting. Some cooks solve this by browning the meat briefly with high heat—searing it—before or after cooking it at a lower temperature.

But if braising is the final step, gray, cooked meat with more fat and connective tissue (protein that melts) is on its way to succulence. After the juices evaporate, the meat can brown in its own rendered fat to develop exceptionally rich flavor (more than that achieved if meat is floured and browned in fat first), and you can spoon out the rendered fat after the meat browns.

Then, with added liquid in a covered pan—to keep liquid from evaporating rapidly—the meat can simmer until the connective tissue dissolves and adds its own succulence. More time in moist heat also breaks down (softens) the meat protein and the bond between the muscle fibers, contributing tenderness, and lets juices soak back into the meat.

"Is it safe to cook a pork roast all night in the oven at a low temperature?"

—PATRICIA SPIRE
San Diego

If you want the moistness and tenderness slow roasting (225° to 250° oven) can give, you must pay attention to some safety issues.

First, is the interior of the meat bacteria-free? Unless penetrated by a knife or another utensil contaminated by harmful bacteria, whole-muscle roasts such as loins and legs and even whole turkeys and chickens do not have these bacteria below the surface. But if the meat is boned, reshaped, tied, stuffed, or ground, bacteria have an opportunity to get onto interior surfaces. These bacteria grow at warm temperatures. If harmful, they can cause illness when eaten.

You must get the meat surface (or poultry cavity) hot enough to kill harmful bacteria—140°. Even in slow-roasting meats, this is not a problem—it happens long before the interior of the meat reaches a serving temperature.

So it is safe to slow-roast meat, if you choose a whole-muscle roast or unstuffed bird, but it's apt to be very overcooked after a night in the oven.

"Why does ground beef look bright red on the outside and brown inside?"

—FLORENCE KUHLMANN

Raw red meats, especially beef, naturally change color; it's not a sign of spoilage. Freshly slaughtered beef and lamb are a purplish color. Exposed to oxygen in air, iron in the meat turns it bright red on the surface. This is most evident in ground beef. It's often very red on the surface, especially when wrapped in plastic, but inside the oxygen gets used up and the meat turns dark red-purple-brown.

"Why do the bones in chicken legs and thighs turn black when cooked?"

—ALICE BERG
Missoula, Montana

When cooking heat drives off the oxygen contained in blood, the blood turns dark. Blood is produced by marrow in the bones and darkening is usually most noticeable at joints or along leg bones. It's not harmful. The intensity of the darkness varies with the chicken breed.

More questions?
We would like to know what kitchen mysteries you're curious about. Send your food questions to us at Why?, *Sunset Magazine,* 80 Willow Rd., Menlo Park, CA 94025, or send e-mail to why@sunsetpub.com. With the help of George K. York, extension food technologist at UC Davis, *Sunset* food editors will try to find solutions. We'll answer the questions in the magazine. ■

By Linda Lau Anusasananan

This lavish dessert contains 202 calories per wedge—including the meringue cream. A light dusting of cocoa adds to the presentation.

Boldly meeting the chocolate decadence challenge
An expert in sweets has found a healthier solution

ALICE MEDRICH'S REPUTATION, built on chocolate, started with a chocolate truffle in France. Its taste—so rich, so purely chocolate—branded itself in her memory and launched a career. For more than 16 years, customers crammed into her Cocolat shops in California to buy her version of truffles and other desserts, none of which stinted on chocolate, quality, or calories.

In 1989, when Medrich was asked to teach a course on low-fat desserts, she considered the obvious—poached pears, meringues, fruit sorbets. But her husband, Elliott, observed, "What they really want from you is chocolate." Medrich revised her approach, which led to her award-winning book, *Chocolate and the Art of Low-Fat Desserts.* Its mission: chocolate desserts, reduced in fat and calories, that still taste grand.

A major challenge was chocolate decadence. In the '70s, it was the richest, trendiest of desserts—a pound of chocolate "lightened" with butter and eggs. Medrich's updated version trims 11 ounces of chocolate, 5 ounces of butter, and 2½ eggs. Nonfat cocoa in a low-fat milk sauce replaces the omitted ingredients. This streamlined dessert has half the calories and a quarter of the fat. How does it measure up? Medrich says, "When I served my new chocolate decadence at a food conference, they just laughed in my face when I told them it was low-fat."

The New Chocolate Decadence

Cooking time: About 40 minutes

Prep time: About 25 minutes, plus at least 8 hours to chill

Notes: For longer storage, wrap airtight and chill 2 days or freeze up to 2 months.

Makes: 12 servings

  5 ounces bittersweet or semisweet chocolate, finely chopped

  2 large eggs

  1 large egg white

  1 teaspoon vanilla

  ⅛ teaspoon cream of tartar

  ½ cup plus ½ tablespoon unsweetened alkaline-treated (Dutch process) or regular cocoa

  2 tablespoons all-purpose flour

  ⅔ cup plus ¼ cup sugar

  ¾ cup low-fat (1%) milk

     Raspberries

     Meringue cream (optional, recipe follows)

1. Place oven rack in the lower third of the oven, and turn heat to 350°.

2. With a nonstick cooking spray, lightly coat inside rim of an 8-inch-wide, 1½- to 2-inch-deep round cake pan. Line pan bottom with cooking parchment cut to fit.

3. Place chopped chocolate in a large bowl, and set aside.

4. Break 1 egg into a small bowl. Separate remaining egg. Put yolk with whole egg. Put white in a separate, larger bowl, and add the remaining egg white.

5. Add vanilla to the bowl with yolk. Add cream of tartar to egg whites.

6. Combine cocoa, flour, and ⅔ cup sugar in a 1- to 1½-quart pan. Mixing smoothly with a whisk, gradually add milk. Stir over medium heat until mixture simmers, about 6 minutes; don't scorch. Stir and cook 1½ minutes longer, then pour hot mixture over chopped chocolate. Stir until the chocolate is completely melted and smooth. Whisk in whole egg and yolk mixture. Set aside.

7. Beat egg whites with cream of tartar at medium speed until whites hold soft peaks. Beating at high speed, gradually add the remaining ¼ cup sugar, then beat until whites hold stiff but not dry peaks.

8. Stir ¼ of the egg whites into the chocolate mixture, then gently fold in the remaining whites. Scrape batter into prepared cake pan, and smooth the top.

9. Set cake pan in another pan that is at least 2 inches wider and 2 inches deep. Set pans in oven. Fill outer pan with boiling water to ½ the depth of the cake pan. Bake just until center of cake springs back when very gently pressed—it will still be quite gooey inside—about 30 minutes.

10. Lift cake pan from water, and set on a rack to cool. When cake is cool to the touch, cover it with plastic wrap, and chill until thoroughly cold, at least 8 hours or up to 2 days.

11. To release cake, slide a thin knife between rim and cake. Cover pan with a sheet of waxed paper, then invert a flat plate onto paper. Hold pan and plate together and invert; shake gently, if needed, to loosen cake. If cake sticks to pan, place a hot, damp towel on pan bottom for a few minutes; then gently shake pan with plate. Remove pan. Peel off and discard parchment. Invert serving dish onto cake. Supporting with flat plate, turn cake over onto serving dish. Remove flat plate, and discard waxed paper.

12. Cut cake into wedges with a thin, sharp knife, dipping blade in hot water and wiping clean between cuts. Garnish wedges with raspberries and meringue cream.

Per serving decadence: 153 cal., 34% (52 cal.) from fat; 3.4 g protein; 5.8 g fat (2.9 g sat.); 26 g carbo.; 50 mg sodium; 36 mg chol.

Meringue Cream

Cooking time: About 5 minutes

Prep time: 7 to 8 minutes

Notes: If making ahead, cover and chill meringue cream up to 1 day.

Makes: About 1⅔ cups, 12 servings.

  2 large egg whites

  ¼ teaspoon cream of tartar

  2 tablespoons sugar

  ⅔ cup whipping cream

1. In a deep metal bowl, mix the egg whites with cream of tartar, sugar, and 1 teaspoon of water until thoroughly combined.

2. Nest bowl in a pan of simmering water, and stir with a flexible spatula until the mixture registers 160° on an instant-read thermometer, 3 to 5 minutes. Remove bowl from heat.

3. Whip mixture at high speed until it is cool and holds stiff peaks, about 5 minutes. Without washing beaters, beat whipping cream until it holds soft peaks, then fold into whites. Serve, or cover and chill.

Per serving: 49 cal., 76% (37 cal.) from fat; 0.5 g protein; 4.1 g fat (2.6 g sat.); 2.6 g carbo.; 9.2 mg sodium; 15 mg chol. ■

By Linda Lau Anusasananan

Chocoholically Acceptable

Five tips for slimming down chocolate desserts

1.
Replace some but not all of the chocolate with naturally nonfat cocoa.

2.
Don't omit all the ingredients that have fat. Keep those that contribute most to texture and flavor.

3.
Calorie for calorie, egg yolks can often contribute more to a smooth texture than butter or whipping cream.

4.
Replace some whole eggs with whites. Too many whites, however, make baked foods rubbery—substituting 2 whites for 1 of every 4 eggs is reasonably safe.

5.
Use low-fat or naturally lower-fat dairy products instead of nonfat versions containing added ingredients that may alter cooking properties. Try neufchâtel (light cream) cheese instead of nonfat cream cheese, or reduced-fat sour cream instead of nonfat sour cream.

SUNSET'S KITCHEN CABINET

Readers' family favorites tested in our kitchens

By Betsy Reynolds Bateson

DICK COLE

Apricot and Pine Nut Cornish Hens

Ginni Martinez, San Jose

Ginni Martinez has three requirements for her recipes: they need to be easy, exciting, and colorful. Martinez's Cornish hens, with their crunchy, tart-sweet stuffing, meet all three. Martinez knows a whole bird is more than ample for one, but, she says, "they always disappear."

Cooking time: About 1½ hours
Prep time: About 30 minutes
Makes: 4 generous servings

- 1¾ cups *each* chicken broth and water
- 2 packages (about 6 oz. each) rice pilaf mix
- 1 cup (about 6 oz.) thinly sliced dried apricots
- 2 teaspoons dried oregano leaves
- ¾ cup toasted pine nuts
- ⅓ cup thinly sliced chives or green onions
- 4 Cornish hens, about 1½ pounds each
- 1½ cups apricot jam
- 1 tablespoon *each* butter and lemon juice

1. In a 10- to 12-inch frying pan over medium-high heat, bring broth and water to a boil. Add rice pilaf mixes, ½ cup apricots, and oregano. Cook according to pilaf package directions, eliminating last 5 minutes of cooking time (rice should be very moist). When rice mixture is cool, stir in pine nuts and chives.

2. Meanwhile, rinse hens inside and out, and pat dry; remove any extra fat. Fill each hen with rice mixture, packing firmly (reserve remaining rice to serve alongside hens; reheat just before serving). Use poultry pins to secure skin flaps over stuffing.

3. Place hens on a rack in a 10- by 15-inch baking pan. Cover hens in pan with foil, and roast at 400° for 30 minutes.

4. Meanwhile, in a 1- to 2-quart pan over medium heat, combine jam, butter, lemon juice, and remaining apricots; heat until hot.

5. After 30 minutes, uncover hens. Roast 15 minutes longer, then baste with half the apricot sauce. Roast 10 minutes more; baste with remaining sauce. Continue to roast until hens are golden brown, about 10 minutes longer.

6. Let hens rest at least 5 minutes before serving. Pour pan drippings into a bowl; spoon off and discard fat. Serve drippings and reheated reserved rice with hens.

Per serving: 1,577 cal., 34% (540 cal.) from fat; 101 g protein; 60 g fat (16 g sat.); 172 g carbo.; 1,629 mg sodium; 271 mg chol.

Teriyaki Sea Bass

Karol Knox, Sacramento

When Karol Knox wants to impress a guest, she makes this recipe. Knox uses a teriyaki-lime marinade because it provides moisture, flavor, and a delicious basting sauce. With the fish, she serves a blend of long-grain white and wild rice, dried cranberries, and toasted pine nuts.

Cooking time: About 15 minutes
Prep time: About 5 minutes, plus marinating

Makes: 4 servings

- 1½ cups teriyaki sauce
- ¼ cup fresh lime juice
- 1 cup chopped fresh cilantro leaves
- 3 tablespoons minced fresh ginger
- 1 pound Chilean sea bass
- Lime quarters (optional)

1. Combine teriyaki, juice, cilantro, and ginger in a 9- by 13-inch baking dish. Rinse fish; pat dry. Lay in marinade; turn to coat all sides. Cover dish with plastic wrap; chill 15 minutes or up to 4 hours, turning fish occasionally.

2. Remove fish from marinade (reserve marinade); place on a grill over a solid bed of hot coals, or over high heat on a gas grill (you can hold your hand at grill level 2 to 3 seconds); close lid on gas grill. Cook 5 minutes, basting occasionally with marinade; turn fish and continue cooking and basting until fish is opaque when cut in thickest section, 10 to 13 minutes more. Squeeze lime over fish as desired.

Per serving: 162 cal., 13% (21 cal.) from fat; 24 g protein; 2.3 g fat (0.6 g sat.); 10 g carbo.; 2,149 mg sodium; 47 mg chol.

Soft Ginger Cookies

Jani Buckmaster, Beaverton, Oregon

Jani Buckmaster is picky about cookies. And she never buys them, preferring to make all her own. She likes cookies that are big and soft; to keep them soft, she's careful not to overbake them. No newcomer to reader contributions, Buckmaster first published a recipe in *Sunset* when she was 15 years old, and she continues to send in a family favorite every couple of years.

Cooking time: 10 to 12 minutes per batch
Prep time: About 20 minutes
Makes: 30 large cookies

- 2½ cups firmly packed brown sugar
- 1 cup salad oil
- ½ cup applesauce
- 2 large eggs
- 4½ cups all-purpose flour
- 1 tablespoon baking soda
- 2½ tablespoons ground ginger
- 1½ teaspoons *each* ground cinnamon and ground nutmeg
- ½ teaspoon salt

1. In a large bowl, stir together brown sugar, salad oil, applesauce, and eggs until blended.

2. In another bowl, combine flour, baking soda, ginger, cinnamon, nutmeg, and salt. Add sugar mixture and blend well.

3. With your hands, roll dough into 2-inch balls (about ¼ cup each) and place on ungreased 12- by 15-inch baking sheets.

4. Bake in a 350° oven until tops crack and cookies just begin to brown, 10 to 12 minutes. If baking 2 sheets at a time, rotate halfway through baking. Cool on rack; serve warm or at room temperature. Store in airtight container up to 3 days; freeze for longer storage.

Per cookie: 212 cal., 33% (70 cal.) from fat; 2.4 g protein; 7.8 g fat (1.1 g sat.); 33 g carbo.; 174 mg sodium; 14 mg chol.

Spinach and Strawberry Salad

Suzanne Peschelt, Newport Beach, California

Fond memories of eating this salad at her grandmother's home in Minnesota keep this recipe alive for Suzanne Peschelt. It makes a huge bowlful, but this doesn't seem to be a problem for Peschelt's family of five. She makes her own raspberry vinegar by soaking raspberries in seasoned rice vinegar for up to a week at room temperature, then chilling the mixture for about a week before straining out the berries. She keeps the flavored vinegar in the refrigerator for up to a month.

Cooking time: About 6 minutes
Prep time: About 20 minutes
Makes: 8 servings

- 10 ounces washed spinach leaves
- 2 tablespoons sesame seed
- 1 tablespoon poppy seed
- 2 tablespoons olive or salad oil
- ¼ cup raspberry vinegar
- 2 tablespoons sugar
- ¼ teaspoon paprika
- 2 pints strawberries, rinsed, hulled, and sliced
- ⅓ cup thinly sliced green onions

1. Remove any tough stems from spinach; discard. Rinse spinach in colander to crisp, if necessary.

2. In an 8- to 10-inch frying pan over medium heat, cook sesame and poppy seeds in oil, stirring occasionally, until sesame seed is just golden, about 6 minutes; cool.

3. In a large, shallow bowl, stir vinegar, sugar, and paprika until sugar dissolves. Add cooled oil with sesame and poppy seeds, spinach, strawberries, and green onions. Gently mix until all ingredients are well coated; serve.

Per serving: 93 cal., 52% (48 cal.) from fat; 1.9 g protein; 5.3 g fat (0.7 g sat.); 11 g carbo.; 22 mg sodium; 0 mg chol.

Patty's Killer Noodle Salad

Patty McNally, Portland

Patty McNally's friends are going to have to swallow their teasing words about her submitting this recipe to *Sunset*. We love it. Two years ago, McNally threw together a noodle salad for a big barbecue party. It became known as the "killer salad," with its hot chili paste, cilantro, and sesame oil flavoring. McNally likes to serve the tangy salad with chicken and cold Japanese beer.

Cooking time: About 15 minutes
Prep time: About 10 minutes
(done concurrently with cooking)
Makes: 6 servings

- 2 packages (3 oz. each) instant Asian noodle soup mix, such as soba
- ¼ cup distilled white vinegar
- 2 tablespoons *each* lime juice and sugar
- 2 teaspoons Asian sesame oil
- 1 clove garlic, minced
- ½ to 1 teaspoon Asian red chili paste or hot chili flakes
- ¼ teaspoon salt
- ½ cup chopped fresh cilantro leaves, loosely packed
- 1 carrot, grated
- ⅓ to ½ cup chopped dry-roasted peanuts

1. Break up dry noodle bricks (discard seasoning packets). In a 3- to 4-quart pan, bring 2 quarts water to a boil over high heat. Add noodles; cook until tender, about 5 minutes. Drain; rinse under cold water; drain again.

2. To a large salad bowl, add vinegar, lime juice, sugar, oil, garlic, red chili paste, and salt; stir until sugar dissolves. Add cooled noodles, cilantro, carrot, and peanuts. Lightly but thoroughly combine ingredients. Serve, or chill up to 4 hours.

Per serving: 198 cal., 35% (70 cal.) from fat; 4.9 g protein; 7.8 g fat (1 g sat.); 29 g carbo.; 400 mg sodium; 0 mg chol.

FOOD Guide

BY JERRY ANNE DI VECCHIO

A TASTE OF THE WEST: A Northwest baker's vegetable pie

Raw onion rings and tomato slices garnish a thick, savory open-faced pie. It's filled with a mellow mix of cheese and roasted vegetables, and makes fine picnic fare.

The breads of Seattle's Macrina Bakery earned my appreciation when one of them, a sourdough loaf, fared extremely well in a competition at *Sunset* in 1994. And, I've discovered since, there was more to be found. Baker Edward K. Sata turns out a variety of handsome open-faced pies that, borrowing from the French, he calls galettes. If this word means dessert to you, be prepared for a few surprises. He fills them with vegetables, too.

I find this galette, with cheeses and roasted vegetables, especially suited to summer meals, particularly for a garden or picnic menu. It is good at any temperature, although I like it best unchilled. And you can serve it in wedges, which are firm enough to hold in your hand.

Roasting the vegetables for the filling takes a little time but not much attention; they need only an occasional stir. There's also considerable flexibility in what you can do ahead.

Roasted Vegetable Galette

Cooking time: About 45 minutes for filling, about 1 hour for galette

Prep time: 30 to 40 minutes

Notes: You can let the baked pie cool, wrap it airtight, and chill up to 1 day. To reheat, bake uncovered in a 350° oven for 30 minutes, then garnish. For a fast crust, roll 2 purchased refrigerated pie dough rounds together to desired dimension.

Makes: 8 or 9 servings

- 2 eggplant (about 2 lb. total), stems trimmed
- 2 tablespoons olive oil
- 2 red onions (about 1 lb. total)
- 2 tablespoons lemon juice
- 2 zucchini (about ½ lb. total), ends trimmed
- 2 cloves garlic

ROBERT OLDING

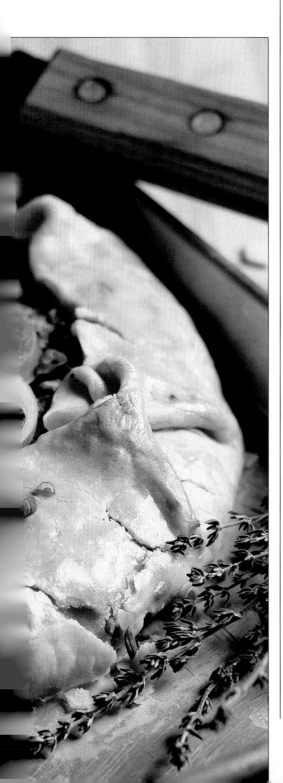

1 tablespoon fresh or dried thyme leaves

2 tablespoons balsamic vinegar

4 large eggs

1 carton (15 oz., about 2 cups) nonfat, low-fat, or regular ricotta cheese

¼ cup shredded parmesan cheese

Salt and pepper

Pastry for a 2-crust, 9-inch pie

3 or 4 firm-ripe Roma tomatoes (2½ to 3 oz. each)

2 tablespoons snipped chives or chopped green onion, including green tops

1. Cut eggplant into ½-inch cubes. Then mix eggplant cubes with olive oil in a 10- by 15-inch pan.

2. Peel onions. Cut 6 thin slices crosswise from the center of 1 onion and mix slices with lemon juice; set aside. Dice remaining onions. Cut zucchini into ½-inch cubes. Mix diced onions, zucchini, garlic, and thyme with eggplant.

3. Bake in a 500° oven, turning pieces occasionally with a wide spatula, until eggplant is very soft when pressed and is slightly browned, 45 to 50 minutes.

Remove from oven and stir balsamic vinegar with vegetables.

4. Beat 3 eggs to blend, and mix in ricotta, parmesan, and cooked vegetables. Add salt and pepper to taste.

5. On a floured board, roll pastry evenly into a 16-inch-wide round. Slide pastry onto a 12- by 17-inch baking sheet.

6. Scoop vegetable-cheese mixture onto center of pastry and shape into a smooth, flat-topped mound, leaving a 3-inch pastry rim around filling.

7. Lift pastry rim up and lay over onto vegetable filling. Neatly overlap pastry as needed to incorporate excess dough. Beat remaining egg with 2 tablespoons water until blended. Brush pastry lightly with egg-water mixture.

8. Core tomatoes and thinly slice crosswise. Cover pie filling with half the onion rings and about half the tomatoes, overlapping (don't place vegetables on pastry).

9. Bake the galette on bottom rack in a 350° oven until pastry is well browned, about 1 hour.

10. Garnish galette with remaining onion and tomato slices and sprinkle with chives. Serve hot or at room temperature.

Per serving: 373 cal., 46% (171 cal.) from fat; 16 g protein; 19 g fat (4.8 g sat.); 35 g carbo.; 335 mg sodium; 100 mg chol.

BOOKS ON FOOD
The fascinating tale of a very special bean

The True History of Chocolate, by Sophie D. and Michael D. Coe (Thames and Hudson, New York, June 1996; $27.50), is not a recipe book. But it's a book cooks can appreciate fully. The intriguing, well-written story follows the complex route that chocolate has traveled, from the ancient Olmec of southern Mexico to Europe with the post-Columbian conquerors, to Pennsylvania with Milton Hershey, and on to the island of Hawaii—where the cocoa plant was first successfully cultivated in 1986 and now produces exceptional chocolate.

The authors' credentials give this book intellectual clout. Sophie, who began the book but died before it was completed, held a doctorate in anthropology. She was particularly interested in the food and drink of the pre-Columbian New World—with a long-time focus on chocolate. Husband Michael, an authority on pre-Columbian civilizations (he wrote *Breaking the Maya Code*) completed her work.

The political upheavals and sociological turmoil that color the history of chocolate may not make your next chocolate bar taste different, but this should add to the savor.

FOOD NEWS
No-fuss crêpes

When I was teaching children's cooking classes at the legendary and long-gone Ma Maison Restaurant in Los Angeles, one of my most ardent students was a 6-year-old named Sunshine. During the crêpe-making lesson, she literally glowed with satisfaction when she mastered the technique. Now I wonder, does she, as a grown-up, still make these simple, thin pancakes? Or does she, like so many others pressed for time, turn to packaged crêpes from the supermarket?

You can use these crêpes (4-oz. packages of 10 crêpes—9-in. diameter—cost $3 to $6) right out of the container, wrapping them around fruit with ice cream, sorbet, sour cream, or softly whipped cream.

I also find the crêpes work very well for a fast dessert like the one offered by street vendors in France. Warm the crêpes (in the oven or microwave oven), brush lightly with melted butter and apricot jam, sprinkle liberally with Cointreau or other orange-flavor liqueur, and fold 2 or 3 onto a plate for a serving. For a fancier dessert, I tuck sliced peaches into the folds.

For a speedy main dish that looks more complex than it is, roll each crêpe around about ⅓ cup of a savory meat mixture (as simple as diced cooked chicken with an equal amount of shredded Swiss cheese and some grated nutmeg—enhanced, perhaps, by sautéed mushrooms or onions). Fit 1 or 2 filled crêpes into a shallow individual baking dish. Cover well with thinly sliced or shredded Swiss cheese, and heat in a 350° oven until cheese melts, about 10 minutes.

Per plain crêpe: 45 cal., 20% (9 cal.) from fat; 1 g protein; 1 g fat; 7 g carbo.; 80 mg sodium; saturated fat and cholesterol information unavailable.

ROBERT OLDING

A Parisian street snack—warm thin crêpes with jam and liqueur—becomes a quick dessert when you use purchased crêpes.

Microwave rice cooker

A good while back, a Seattle friend and I whizzed through Pike Place Market gathering the best of the seasonal offerings for a highly improvised dinner. Among our guests was Tomoko Matsuno, who manages Uwajimaya, the fabulous Asian American supermarket on Sixth Avenue S.

Intrigued by the meal, Tomo asked me to repeat the game, shopping at Uwajimaya instead. I did; we cooked a meal together and haven't stopped talking food since. Last time I was in the store, she presented me with a microwave rice cooker and said, try it, it works. I did, she's right, and for summer I highly recommend it.

Several brands of microwave cookers are available in many Japanese grocery and hardware stores. They cost $10 to $15—and, on sale, are frequently less.

Essentially, the cooker is a plastic bowl with a lid designed to keep moisture from dripping onto the rice as it cooks. You add rice and water, close the cooker, put it in the microwave, and set the timer. It's a little faster than stovetop cooking when you cook up to a cup of rice, about the same if you make more (the cookers hold up to 6 cups of cooked rice).

One bit of advice: check to be sure the directions are in English—or get the Japanese ones interpreted before you leave the store—so you'll know the water-to-rice ratio required by the cooker.

What is skirt steak?

When a butcher volunteers to "tenderize" skirt steak by running it through a machine, or sells the meat rolled into pinwheels, I suspect he (or she) has never cooked this cut. Skirt steak is already tender, and its flavor is exceptional.

The French call it the butcher's choice—because it often goes home with him. For Mexicans, it was the cut used for fajitas—once upon a time. It cooks quickly because it's thin. It also has enough fat to brown well, so you can grill it over hot coals or close to the broiler, or sear it. And it is succulent even when well done.

A pair of these steaks runs parallel, like ribbons, between the front leg and flank on each side of a beef carcass. Their thin shape invites special handling: I often thread a steak on a long skewer, then tuck herbs between the meat and the skewer to add flavor.

You can also cut skirt steak, trimmed of most fat, into serving pieces, sear them in a hot pan, and toss in a few minced shallots when the meat is almost browned. After lifting out the meat, add a spoonful of Dijon mustard and a little red wine to the pan to release the drippings, and you have a fine meat sauce.

Three fresh treats

Big, plump boysenberries make a brief market show in June and, maybe, July. Much of this fragile harvest is IQF (individually quick frozen) for commercial distribution. Though frozen berries are excellent for cooking, nothing compares to the sensual burst of rich, winy flavor of fresh boysenberries.

Another June treasure, which shows up most often in Chinese and Southeast Asian food markets, is the litchi, snugly clad in its thin, brown, leathery jacket. Fresh litchis are known for their perfume and tenderness. Pull off the brown skin to release the translucent white fruit. It's so juicy and sticky, the best way to eat it is to pop the whole thing in your mouth, then spit out the shiny seed.

The third treat I watch for in late June is white nectarines. You can tell which of the varieties is best by smelling the fruit—the ones that are most fragrant taste best. When ready to eat, white nectarines are very fragile and bruise easily, so you may want to select firm (not hard) fruit and let it ripen at room temperature until it gives to gentle pressure, usually two to three days.

When all three of these fruit are available at once, turn them into a simple but most memorable dessert: Combine rinsed boysenberries, peeled litchis, and sliced nectarines in a shallow bowl. Drench them with a chilled Gewürztraminer, late-harvest Gewürztraminer or Johannisberg Riesling, or Muscat dessert wine such as Moscato Canelli or Moscato d'Asti. Any of these aromatic wines brings out the best in the fruit—and the wine slows the rapid darkening of white nectarines. In a pinch, I use canned litchis, and still enjoy.

Basil redux

A few summers back, I explained how I stored herbs in the refrigerator, wrapped in damp towels and tucked into plastic bags, to keep them at their freshest. And I bragged that my basil was usable for up to five days.

But when Bill Wilkinson at Greenleaf Produce in San Francisco remarked that basil doesn't like cold, I listened. And I now offer you a better solution for basil.

Buy a healthy, fresh-looking bunch, preferably with long stems. Then treat it like a bouquet, trimming the ends of the stems so they can draw up water. Put the basil bunch in a container of water, with just the leaves exposed. I use a vase, since the leaves are pretty. For three or four days, you should change the water almost daily. Then change the water when it gets murky or smelly. To use the basil, take it out a stem at a time, making sure the remaining stems stay in the water. If the leaves get droopy, they aren't getting water, so trim the stem ends again.

Even at the end of three weeks, if I haven't used all my basil, the leaves are still green and fresh-looking, and usually the stems are developing roots and the tiny leaves have grown.

I also gave refrigerated basil storage another run. But instead of wrapping the herb in damp towels, I put the stems in water—like the basil on the counter—then capped the leaves with a plastic bag. I had less trouble with wilting than at room temperature, but after a week the leaves had black spots.

While their brief seasons overlap, enjoy fat boysenberries and fresh, translucent litchis with white nectarines in a fruity white wine.

CRAIG MAXWELL

BOB THOMPSON ON WINE: Dog days. Dry rosés. Perfect match

Chilling rosés just short of popsicle-cold on a blazing afternoon does them no serious harm. They still cut through the juices of ground beef, and have enough flavor to match up with a burger and the works. The same goes for grilled sausages. The match with barbecued chicken is as sure as a bet gets. For a bonus, they are at their readiest to drink on the first day they show up in the stores.

The recipe for rosé is simple: (1) Start out to make a red. (2) Change course between 8 and 30 hours into the game and try to make a white instead. In practical terms, this means winemakers begin the fermentation with skins, pulp, and juice in the tank together, then separate juice from solids as soon as the juice colors slightly. If this sounds easy, it is not. With neither sugar nor time available to cover up any rough spots, getting full flavor and agreeable balance in a semi-red tests the skills of any winemaker.

These difficulties explain why there are so few dry rosés, but do not excuse prices that are sometimes far less modest than the wines themselves.

Grenache, the traditional grape variety for rosé in much of France, has been adopted as such in the United States. Two to try: Vin du Mistral California Grenache Rosé from Joseph Phelps ($12, deliciously hearty flavors—almost a red) and Bonny Doon California Vin Gris du Cigare ($8, based on Grenache; as the French words *vin gris*—gray wine—promise, it is paler hued, more delicate in flavor and texture than the Phelps).

The little-planted Grignolino is Grenache's equal as a source of flavorful rosé. The lone example in California: Heitz Wine Cellars Napa Valley Grignolino Rosé ($5.25, surprisingly intense for its medium color, and bone-dry).

Sangiovese, still rare, hints that it soon may perform at the top of the California rosé heap. To try: Iron Horse Alexander Valley Rosato di Sangiovese ($15, permeated by the almost floral perfumes of its grape variety).

Zinfandel has made glorious dry rosés, but I do not know of a fine one in the market now. Maybe that's because sweetish white Zinfandels continue to sell like hotcakes no matter what the weather does. ■

The longer a peach stays on the tree, the sweeter it is. These Gene Elbertas at Ikeda's orchard in Auburn, California, owe their intense flavor to tree-ripening and the fast-draining red-clay soil of the Sierra foothills. The peaches are sold at Ikeda's Fruit and Tasty Burger off Interstate 80 (take the Forest Hill/Auburn Ravine exit).

the taste of summer

How to select, squeeze, store, cream, bake, and generally go crazy over summer's most luscious fruit—the peach

For perfect peaches, try your local farmers' market. Friesen Farms of Dinuba, California, brings its best peaches to as many as 25 markets a week, including this one in Davis, held from 8 until noon every Saturday. Ask for Queencrests through the end of May, Spring Ladys the first week in June.

P ERHAPS IT IS BECAUSE THEY ARE GOLDEN AND ROUND LIKE THE sun, or because they reach their peak of sweetness about the time the thermometer is pushing 90. Perhaps it is even because they are messy, as summer itself can be joyously messy. Whatever the reason, of this there is no doubt: the peach is *the* summer fruit.

Peach season began in April and will continue well into September. But it is in high summer, late June into early August, that the peach reigns supreme. Here come the Flavorcrests, the O'Henrys, the Hales, ripening from Yakima County, Washington, to Box Elder County, Utah, and up and down California's Central Valley. That valley is the peach capital of the world: thanks to it, California grows more peaches than all other states combined (take that, Georgia!). "We get socked in with tule fog in winter," says University of California pomologist Scott Johnson, explaining the region's peach preeminence. "That keeps it just about freezing, which is ideal for peach trees." As for the valley's summer heat: "Peaches love it when it's hot. They grow like crazy."

Like many fruits, peaches have had to adjust to the exigencies of modern harvesting.

By Peter Fish and Betsy Reynolds Bateson

What could be better than peach cobbler or peach ice cream? How about both? Add blueberries to the cobbler if you want to vary color and flavor.

PAUL HAMMOND

To withstand trips to distant supermarkets, peaches are picked firm, as many as seven days from ripeness. But the sweetest, juiciest peaches are the ones that have tree-ripened the longest, and such peaches are too tender to ship well. Peaches pose a classic 20th-century dilemma: individual perfection versus mass convenience.

Even so, an increasing number of growers are producing peaches that taste like, well, the peaches we remember as kids. Tom Dieckmann, who grows 22 varieties of peaches near Yuba City, California, credits farmers' markets for the change. "They have put a whole new light on the peach industry," he says. Selling closer to home means Dieckmann can let his peaches tree-ripen longer. Johnson says that even large commercial growers are tending to "let the fruit stay on the tree a little bit longer, to get a little

more sugar and a little more color."

At the same time, older peach varieties are regaining respect. Just ask David Mas Masumoto. His family has grown peaches near Del Rey, California, for three generations. Last year, he published his first book, *Epitaph for a Peach* (now in paperback). It eloquently tells the story of his struggle to maintain an orchard of Sun Crest peaches. Most modern growers have abandoned Sun Crests because they do not ship well. But listen to Masumoto describe them:

"Sun Crest is one of the last remaining truly juicy peaches. When you wash that treasure under a stream of cooling water …your mouth waters in anticipation. You lean over the sink to make sure you don't drip on yourself. Then you sink your teeth into the flesh, and the juice trickles down your cheeks and dangles on your chin. This is a real bite, a primal act, a magi-

cal sensory celebration announcing that summer has arrived."

A peach like that you don't dismiss lightly. After his book came out, Masumoto recalls, "I got letters—from Pennsylvania, Ohio, Minnesota. All of them said, 'Keep the peaches.' " He did. Because of *Epitaph*'s success, Masumoto is working on another book, but this summer he will again be tending his Sun Crests.

Which is a good thing. Peaches are precious. It isn't simply summer that they recall, but that summer season of life, childhood. Maybe it's the messiness factor again: it is impossible to remain a mature, responsible, worried adult when peach juice is trickling down your chin. Says Masumoto, "When people bite into a peach, they want the childhood memories in that peach." Yes, they do. The taste of a peach is not just a taste of summer, but a passage to a sweeter, more innocent time.

the recipes of summer

It wouldn't be peach season without fresh ice cream and cobbler

ONE OF MY FONDEST CHILDHOOD memories is of helping my grandparents make peach ice cream. Outside on the back porch, grandfather and we kids would carefully fill the ice cream canister with grandmother's concoction of cream and homegrown peaches. As the old electric freezer whirred, we would play in the warm summer-evening air, waiting for the cream to freeze. And then it was done. Even as a small child, I savored each sweet spoonful melting down my throat, the flavor almost floral, like the taste of the best peach ever.

Years later, when I asked my grandmother for her recipe, she responded, "A little of this and a little of that." This recipe gets a bit more specific.

Grandma Reynolds's Peach Ice Cream

Cooking time: About 5 minutes

Prep time: About 20 minutes, plus cooling and freezing time

Notes: Use ripe peaches and one ripe nectarine to add the acid that many peaches lack (and, ironically, to give the ice cream a really peachy color).

Makes: 1 1/2 quarts

- 1 3/4 pounds (about 4) ripe peaches
- 1 tablespoon lemon juice
- 1 ripe nectarine (about 8 oz.)
- 1 cup half-and-half
- 1/2 cup sugar
- 3 large eggs, beaten
- 2 teaspoons vanilla
- 1/4 to 1/2 teaspoon almond flavoring (optional)
- Crushed ice and rock salt

1. Peel, pit, and slice peaches. In a large bowl, mash slices to the texture of salsa; add lemon juice.

2. Peel nectarine and cut flesh from pit. Cut into pieces and place in a blender; whirl into a smooth purée. Add 1/2 cup of the purée to mashed peaches, and set aside.

3. Combine half-and-half and sugar in a 1 1/2- to 2-quart pan. Over medium heat, scald mixture (it should reach 180°; small bubbles will form around the pan's edge). Remove from heat; using a wire whisk,

whisk in beaten eggs, vanilla, and almond flavoring. Add mixture to peaches; chill, covered, for at least an hour, or up to 1 day.

4. Freeze in an ice cream maker (at least 2-qt. capacity) according to manufacturer's directions. Serve when softly frozen, or store airtight in freezer up to 2 weeks; let soften about 15 minutes at room temperature before scooping.

Per 1/2 cup: 110 cal., 30% (33 cal.) from fat; 2.7 g protein; 3.7 g fat (1.8 g sat.); 17 g carbo.; 24 mg sodium; 61 mg chol.

Peach Cobbler

Cooking time: About 45 minutes

Prep time: About 30 minutes

Makes: 8 servings

- 3 pounds (about 7) ripe peaches, peeled, pitted, and thickly sliced
- 1 cup blueberries (optional)
- 3/4 cup sugar
- 3 tablespoons quick-cooking tapioca
- 1 teaspoon grated lemon peel
- 1 tablespoon lemon juice
- 1 teaspoon vanilla
- 1 1/2 cups all-purpose flour
- 1 teaspoon *each* baking powder and ground ginger
- 1/2 cup (1/4 lb.) butter or margarine
- 2 tablespoons minced crystallized ginger (optional)
- 1/2 cup whipping cream

1. In a large bowl, mix together peaches, blueberries (if desired), 1/2 cup sugar, tapioca, lemon peel, lemon juice, and vanilla. Let stand at least 15 minutes or up to 1 hour to soften tapioca, stirring several times.

2. Combine flour with remaining 1/4 cup sugar, baking powder, and ground ginger. With pastry blender or fingers, incorporate butter into flour mixture until very crumbly and no large pieces remain; stir in crystallized ginger (if desired). Add cream and stir just until dough holds together.

3. In a buttered 2- to 2 1/2-quart shallow casserole, spread fruit level. With hands, crumble dough onto fruit.

4. Bake in a 350° oven until fruit mixture bubbles in center and topping is golden brown, 40 to 45 minutes. Serve with peach or vanilla ice cream.

Per serving: 380 cal., 40% (153 cal.) from fat; 3.8 g protein; 17 g fat (10 g sat.); 55 g carbo.; 206 mg sodium; 49 mg chol. ∎

the care and picking of peaches

how to handle

Most peaches arrive at the supermarket hard and need to be ripened at home, usually for several days.

First • Select plump fruit with firm skin. Avoid bruised or cut fruit. Look for a creamy yellow or golden background color; a red blush does not necessarily indicate ripeness; it is a varietal characteristic.

Second • Place peaches in a paper bag, fold it shut, and set on a counter—not in the refrigerator—out of direct sunlight. For faster ripening, add an apple or banana; they give off more ethylene gas, which speeds up the process.

Third • Check peaches daily, squeezing gently. A ripe peach is soft to the touch and has a sweet, fragrant aroma.

Finally • Eat! Refrigerate only after fruit is ripe, and for no more than three days. If your peach fails to ripen, it's been stored improperly in transit and should be returned to the store.

when to buy

This year's peach season began in April and is expected to run through September, with the juiciest, sweetest, and most luscious peaches hitting the market in summer.

Early varieties tend to be clings and are tart and firm (through June, look for Springcrest and June Lady).

Midseason is the best time to run to farmers' markets (late June through July, look for Sun Crest, Whitehaven, Flavorcrest, Babcock, and O'Henry).

Late varieties are freestones, with meaty flesh and little juice; great for pies and canning (August and September, look for Carnival and Fairtime peaches).

Oh, so smooth

Healthful, low-fat, quick, and portable— smoothies are the ultimate '90s fast food

◀ m a n g o - p e a c h

N ext time you crave something cool and refreshing, how about an Egyptian Punch with spirulina and protein powder? Or a little Hawaiian Lust with wheatgrass juice and calcium?

If these sound more like chemistry experiments than beverages, you may need a quick lesson on the coolest drinks around: smoothies.

At shops like Juice Club, a popular California-based chain, customers often arrive long before the stores open, hovering around locked doors in anticipation of a custom-blended fruit smoothie to start the day. Among the waiting crowd are people in exercise clothes on their way to and from workouts, suits-and-ties bound for the office, high school and college students, and parents with infants in strollers.

Juice Club started as a single shop in San Luis Obispo, California, in 1990, when founder Kirk Perron recognized a need for low-fat, healthful food to enjoy after a workout. In just six years, Juice Club has mushroomed into a corporation with 18 stores from San Diego to the San Francisco Bay Area. But it isn't the only flourishing smoothie operation. Hundreds of other smoothie shops are also whirling their way across the West. What's behind this craze for blended fruit drinks?

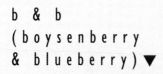

b & b
(boysenberry
& blueberry) ▼

◀ lemony
apple
honey

the main squeeze ▶

An after-work drink gets a healthy new twist at Seattle's sleek Gravity Bar.

you like or feel you need.

And the word *smoothie* isn't necessarily the term of choice anymore. At Gravity Bar, a vegetarian restaurant and juice bar in Seattle, owner Laurrien Gilman is serious about emphasizing smoothies' nutritional benefits. She prefers to call them *juices,* to indicate the freshness of their ingredients and to differentiate them from the bottled smoothies sold at grocery stores. With its sophisticated, modernistic decor, Gravity Bar's downtown store has successfully attracted the business crowd, giving a new definition to the term *after-work drink.*

As Gilman or anyone else who has ever made a smoothie will tell you, there's no big secret to it. You really don't need a recipe, and it's almost impossible to make a bad one.

Simply pick your favorite fruits (a combination of two or three kinds works well) and add a little juice (either the same kind as your fruit or one that you think will blend nicely) and, if desired, some low-fat milk, yogurt, or light ice cream. Whirl it all up in a blender until smooth, and you're done.

A smoothie makes a great breakfast or lunch on the run. You can even make one up the night before, freeze it, and take it with you the next day—by lunch it will be thawed and ready to drink. And smoothies are great to relax with at home, too. We offer the following six delicious smoothie combinations for inspiration, but don't stop there. Let your imagination and summer's bountiful fruit guide you.

THE EXTRAS
Many smoothie shops offer "supplements" or "additions," including tofu, yogurt, wheat germ, calcium, kelp, bee pollen, amino acid powders, and rice, oat, and wheat brans.

The jury is still out on the nutritive value of some of the more exotic supplements. But if you're making smoothies at home and want to give them a boost, you'll find most of these items at well-stocked supermarkets or health food stores. Even without any extras, however, a frosty fruit smoothie is a healthful treat.

BASIC SMOOTHIE INSTRUCTIONS
Simply combine all ingredients in a blender and whirl until smooth. If your smoothie is thick, you may want to stop blending a couple of times and scrape down blender sides with a rubber spatula to ensure an even, smooth texture. Pour into a tall glass and enjoy!

Aaron Souza, co-owner of The Green Planet, a smoothie store in Davis, California, thinks that the smoothie hits all the '90s buzzwords—*low-fat* (though not always low-calorie), *quick,* and *portable*—attracting people on the go who are interested in a healthy lifestyle. And, indeed, The Green Planet is a frequent sponsor of community sport clubs and activities.

Admittedly, smoothies aren't new.

Esther Samuelson, manager at Jungle Juices in Irvine, California, worked at a smoothie-and-sandwich shop 20 years ago. But she notes that today's smoothies are much thicker, and that they're often consumed as a whole meal instead of as a beverage. Another development Samuelson attributes to the smoothie-as-a-meal concept is that more stores offer nutritional "additions": you can customize drinks by adding nutrients

Mango-Peach Smoothie

Prep time: About 6 minutes

Makes: 1 generous serving (about 3 cups)

1 cup peeled mango chunks

1 peach (about 8 oz.), peeled, pitted, and cut into chunks

1 cup peach nectar

2 tablespoons lime juice

Per serving: 322 cal., 2% (6.3 cal.) from fat; 2.8 g protein; 0.7 g fat (0.1 g sat.); 84 g carbo.; 26 mg sodium; 0 mg chol.

Hawaii 5-0

Prep time: About 7 minutes

Notes: This tropical smoothie of blended pineapple, papaya, banana, and milk was inspired by a popular menu item at Seattle's Gravity Bar.

Makes: 2 servings (about 3½ cups total)

1 cup cubed peeled pineapple

1 cup cubed peeled papaya

½ cup pineapple juice or papaya nectar

1 ripe banana (about 6 oz.), peeled and cut into chunks

½ cup nonfat or low-fat milk or vanilla yogurt

⅛ to ¼ teaspoon coconut extract

Per serving: 199 cal., 3.2% (6.3 cal.) from fat; 4.5 g protein; 0.7 g fat (0.2 g sat.); 47 g carbo.; 44 mg sodium; 1.7 mg chol.

Malted Date Deluxe

Prep time: About 6 minutes

Notes: This luscious and unusual smoothie is similar to Juice Club's Date Dazzle. Whirl dates and milk until completely smooth, then blend in malt and frozen yogurt.

Makes: 1 serving (about 2 cups)

½ cup pitted dates

½ cup nonfat or low-fat (1%) milk

3 tablespoons malt powder

1½ cups nonfat or low-fat vanilla frozen yogurt or ice cream

Per serving: 646 cal., 1.3% (8.1 cal.) from fat; 14 g protein; 0.9 g fat (0.1 g sat.); 150 g carbo.; 214 mg sodium; 2.5 mg chol.

The Main Squeeze

Prep time: About 7 minutes, 15 minutes if you squeeze the oranges yourself

Notes: This combination of fruits and juice is a favorite at The Green Planet in Davis, California.

Makes: 2 servings (about 4 cups total)

1½ cups ripe strawberries, hulled and sliced

1 cup raspberries

1 banana (about 6 oz.), peeled and sliced

1 cup orange juice (preferably freshly squeezed)

Per serving: 171 cal., 7% (12 cal.) from fat; 2.7 g protein; 1.3 g fat (0.2 g sat.); 41 g carbo.; 2.9 mg sodium; 0 mg chol.

B & B (Boysenberry & Blueberry) Smoothie

Prep time: About 4 minutes

Makes: 1 generous serving (about 3 cups)

1½ cups boysenberry- or blackberry-flavor juice

1 cup boysenberries or blackberries

1 cup blueberries

Per serving: 327 cal., 2.5% (8.1 cal.) from fat; 2.4 g protein; 0.9 g fat (0 g sat.); 82 g carbo.; 48 mg sodium; 0 mg chol.

Lemony Apple Honey Smoothie

Prep time: 6 minutes

Notes: This refreshing and unique combination was inspired by a popular menu item at Surfside Smoothies (now Jungle Juices) in Irvine, California.

Makes: 2 servings (about 4 cups total)

¼ cup lemon juice

½ cup apple cider

1 apple (about 8 oz.), peeled, cored, and chopped

1 peeled banana (about 6 oz.)

2 to 3 tablespoons honey

1 cup nonfat or low-fat vanilla frozen yogurt

Per serving: 306 cal., 2.1% (6.3 cal.) from fat; 2.9 g protein; 0.7 g fat (0.2 g sat.); 76 g carbo.; 55 mg sodium; 0 mg chol. ■

By Christine Weber Hale

TIPS FOR PERFECT SMOOTHIES

❖ For a thicker texture, blend with frozen fruit. (Wash fruit, dry well, and stem or peel; slice if necessary. Freeze in an airtight container or a ziplock plastic bag until solid, at least 2 hours or up to several days.) If you don't have time to freeze the fruit, simply whirl in some crushed ice (about ½ cup at a time) until smoothie is as thick as you like. You can also try using fruit sorbet instead of juice.

❖ For added creaminess in any of these smoothies, add low-fat or nonfat milk, soy milk, yogurt, frozen yogurt, or ice cream.

❖ To make ahead, blend your smoothie, pour it into a freezerproof glass or cup, cover airtight, and store in the freezer until you want it (up to 3 days). Thaw smoothie until it's ready—a great breakfast or lunch on the run.

❖ If your fruit's not quite ripe, add a small amount of honey or sugar to taste; powdered sugar dissolves faster than granulated, but either one works fine.

❖ You can eliminate milk products in any of these smoothies—except the date shake—by replacing them with more juice.

One-pan meal: tortellini, vegetables, and chicken cook together in an herbed broth with wine.

When time is short, pasta is the answer

These healthful pasta dinners cook in less than 30 minutes

L
OW-FAT, HIGH-CARBOHYDRATE, good-tasting, and ready in no time: it's no wonder pasta is so many people's favorite fast food. And if you've walked through a supermarket lately, you've surely noticed that the options—in new shapes, premium-quality dried pasta, and filled and flavored fresh pasta—just keep getting better.

These whole-meal recipes honor pasta's virtues and versatility. If you're in the mood for traditional noodles with a chunky sauce, try the fusilli with Italian sausage or the vegetarian fettuccine. Orzo stands in for rice in the quick risotto, and you can use your favorite filled fresh pasta in the minestrone.

Except for marinara, many off-the-shelf sauces are high in fat. Our recipes contain a variety of quickly assembled vegetables, broths, and seasonings for robust flavor with little fat. Meats, cheeses, and oil are used sparingly.

Each dish has plenty of vegetables and is so substantial that the only addition you may want is a glass of wine and a little bread.

For fastest preparation, start boiling the water for the pasta before you prepare the other ingredients; cooking times include bringing water to a boil.

Tortellini Minestrone

Cooking time: About 15 minutes
Prep time: About 5 minutes
Makes: 9 cups, 4 servings

1 ½   quarts chicken broth

½   cup dry white wine

½   teaspoon dried oregano

1   cup peeled baby carrots (about 2 in. long), halved lengthwise

1   cup chopped red bell pepper

1   package (9 oz.) filled fresh tortellini or ravioli, such as pesto or mushroom

¾   pound boned, skinned chicken breast halves, cut into 1-inch pieces

2   tablespoons chopped fresh parsley

1. In a covered 5- to 6-quart pan over high heat, bring broth, wine, oregano, and carrots to a boil. Add bell pepper and tortellini; boil, uncovered, for 4 minutes.

2. Stir in chicken and simmer until it's no longer pink in center (cut to test), about 2 minutes. Stir in parsley.

Per serving: 320 cal., 22% (70 cal.) from fat; 30 g protein; 7.8 g fat (2.2 g sat.); 34 g carbo.; 367 mg sodium; 61 mg chol.

Caponata Fettuccine

Cooking time: About 15 minutes
Prep time: About 5 minutes
Notes: Look for caponata (a mixture of eggplant, tomatoes, olives, and seasonings) with canned vegetables.
Makes: 3 servings

1   package (9 oz.) fresh plain or herb-flavor fettuccine or linguine

3   cups broccoli florets (1-in. size)

1 ½   cups (about 16 oz. in jars or cans) caponata

1   can (1 lb.) reduced-sodium garbanzos, drained

¼   cup dry red wine

  Salt and pepper

1. Fill a 5- to 6-quart pan ¾ full of water, cover, and bring to a boil over high heat. Add fettuccine and broccoli and cook, uncovered, until pasta is barely tender to bite, 2 to 3 minutes.

2. Meanwhile, in a 2- to 3-quart pan over medium-high heat, stir caponata, garbanzos, and wine until bubbling, about 5 minutes.

3. Drain pasta and broccoli; toss with caponata. Add salt and pepper to taste.

Per serving: 582 cal., 22% (126 cal.) from fat; 21 g protein; 14 g fat (0.3 g sat.); 88 g carbo.; 992 mg sodium; 62 mg chol.

Asian Soba and Vegetables

Cooking time: About 20 minutes
Prep time: Concurrent with cooking
Makes: 4 servings

- 12 ounces dried soba (thin buckwheat noodles)
- 2 quarts chopped bok choy (1-in. pieces)
- ⅔ pound fresh shiitake (stems removed) or regular mushrooms, cut into ½-inch-wide slices
- ⅓ cup sesame seed
- 1½ cups vegetable broth
- ¼ cup rice vinegar
- 3 tablespoons reduced-sodium soy sauce
- 1½ tablespoons minced fresh ginger
- 1 tablespoon cornstarch

1. Fill a 6- to 8-quart pan ¾ full of water, cover, and bring to a boil over high heat. Add soba and cook, uncovered, until barely tender to bite, about 5 minutes. Stir in bok choy and mushrooms; cook until mushrooms are softened, about 1 minute.

2. Meanwhile, in a 1- to 2-quart pan over medium heat, stir sesame seed until golden, 5 to 6 minutes. Pour from pan; set aside. Mix broth, vinegar, soy, ginger, and cornstarch; add to pan. Stir over high heat until bubbling, about 2 minutes; stir in sesame. Drain soba mixture; return to pan. Toss gently with broth mixture.

Per serving: 417 cal., 16% (68 cal.) from fat; 19 g protein; 7.5 g fat (1 g sat.); 78 g carbo.; 1,678 mg sodium; 0 mg chol.

Italian Fusilli

Cooking time: About 20 minutes
Prep time: Concurrent with cooking
Makes: 4 servings

- 12 ounces dried fusilli pasta
- ½ pound turkey Italian sausage (mild or hot)
- 2 cans (14 oz. each) sliced stewed Italian-style tomatoes
- 2 teaspoons fennel seed, crushed
- 1 cup chopped fresh basil leaves, plus sprigs
  Salt and pepper
  Grated asiago or parmesan cheese (optional)

1. Fill a 5- to 6-quart pan ¾ full of water, cover, and bring to a boil over high heat. Add pasta and cook, uncovered, until barely tender to bite, about 10 minutes.

2. Meanwhile, squeeze sausage meat from casings into a nonstick 10- to 12-inch frying pan; discard casings. Stir sausage over medium-high heat, breaking into chunks, until browned, about 6 minutes. Stir in tomatoes and fennel; simmer, uncovered, for 5 minutes. Stir in chopped basil.

3. Drain pasta and return to pan. Add tomato mixture and toss to coat. Season to taste with salt, pepper, and cheese. Garnish with basil sprigs.

Per serving: 492 cal., 14% (69 cal.) from fat; 23 g protein; 7.7 g fat (1.9 g sat.); 84 g carbo.; 1,075 mg sodium; 30 mg chol.

Asparagus Pasta "Risotto"

Cooking time: About 20 minutes
Prep time: Concurrent with cooking
Makes: 4 or 5 servings

- 2 cups dried orzo pasta
- 6 cups unsalted or reduced-sodium chicken broth
- 4 cups 1- to 2-inch pieces asparagus
- ½ cup grated parmesan cheese
- 2 tablespoons extra-virgin olive oil
- ½ cup fresh sage leaves, plus sprigs
  Pepper

1. Place pasta and broth in a 4- to 5-quart pan over high heat, cover, and bring to a boil. Reduce heat to medium-high; cook, uncovered, for 5 minutes, stirring occasionally. Add asparagus, and cook, stirring occasionally, until pasta is barely tender to bite, 8 to 10 minutes. Stir in cheese; remove pan from heat.

2. Meanwhile, in a 6- to 8-inch frying pan over medium heat, cook oil until ripples form, 3 to 4 minutes. Add sage leaves; stir often until edges begin to curl, 2 to 3 minutes. Remove from heat. With a slotted spoon, lift sage to a towel. Reserve oil.

3. Crumble sage leaves; add sage and reserved oil to pasta, and mix. Garnish with sage sprigs. Add pepper to taste.

Per serving: 444 cal., 26% (117 cal.) from fat; 21 g protein; 13 g fat (3.7 g sat.); 68 g carbo.; 295 mg sodium; 6.3 mg chol. ∎

By Elaine Johnson

Corkscrew-shaped fusilli has a robust tomato-basil-fennel sauce.

Asian seasonings flavor this barbecued beef, which goes well with baby bok choy and rice.

As East meets West on beef

For a dinner party, serve juicy slices of barbecued tenderloin with an Asian marinade

WHEN HUGH CARPENTER, Napa Valley cookbook author and teacher, initially burst upon the California culinary scene in the '70s, his focus was on Asian cooking. But as his enthusiasm for Asian flavors grew beyond cultural limitations, he began to build their subtle complexities into mainstream dishes for everyday cooking. He calls this merging "fusion cuisine." And his pioneering has led to several handsome cookbooks created jointly with his photographer wife, Teri Sandison.

Beef tenderloin is the meat he chooses for this potent wine marinade. In it, hoisin sauce brings an intriguing but not readily defined mellowness. Use part of the mixture as a sauce for the meat.

Chinois Beef

Cooking time: 35 to 50 minutes

Prep time: About 30 minutes, plus at least 30 minutes to marinate meat

Notes: Purchase Asian ingredients at a well-stocked supermarket or a Chinese grocery store. As an alternative to the dark soy sauce, use 4 teaspoons soy sauce and ¾ teaspoon dark molasses.

Makes: 6 to 8 servings

- ⅔ cup prepared hoisin sauce
- ⅓ cup dry red wine
- 2 tablespoons olive oil
- ¼ cup Dijon mustard
- 1½ tablespoons dark soy sauce
- 1½ teaspoons Asian red chili sauce or paste
- 6 cloves garlic, pressed or minced
- 1 tablespoon coarsely chopped fresh or crumbled dried rosemary leaves
- 1 fat-trimmed, center-cut beef tenderloin (3½ to 4 lb.)

  Fresh rosemary or parsley sprigs

1. Mix hoisin sauce, wine, oil, mustard, soy sauce, chili sauce, garlic, and chopped rosemary leaves.

2. Reserve ¾ cup of the hoisin mixture. Place remaining hoisin mixture and beef in a heavy plastic food bag, seal, and turn over to mix well. Let beef stand at least 30 minutes, or chill beef and covered hoisin mixture up to 1 day.

3. *In a charcoal barbecue with a lid,* mound and ignite 40 charcoal briquets on firegrate. When briquets are dotted with gray ash, about 15 minutes, divide in half and push equally to opposite sides of firegrate. Place a drip pan between coals. Add 5 briquets (10 total) to each mound of coals. Set grill 4 to 6 inches above coals. Lift beef from bag and set on grill directly over pan. Cover barbecue and open dampers. Save marinade for basting.

On a gas barbecue, adjust gas for indirect cooking (no heat down center) and set a drip pan in center. Set grill in place. Turn heat to high. Close lid and heat until barbecue is hot, about 10 minutes. Lift beef from bag and set on grill directly over pan. Cover barbecue. Save marinade for basting.

4. Cook beef, basting once or twice with reserved marinade, until a thermometer inserted in the center of the thickest part registers 135° for rare, or 140° for medium, 35 to 50 minutes.

5. Transfer beef to a platter; keep warm and let rest 5 to 10 minutes.

6. Mix reserved hoisin mixture with ¼ cup water and bring to a boil. Pour into a small bowl. Garnish beef with fresh rosemary sprigs. Slice beef and serve with sauce to add to taste.

Per serving meat: 371 cal., 41% (153 cal.) from fat; 42 g protein; 17 g fat (5.8 g sat.); 7 g carbo.; 486 mg sodium; 125 mg chol.

Per 1 tablespoon sauce: 37 cal., 27% (9.9 cal.) from fat; 0.1 g protein; 1.1 g fat (0.2 g sat.); 4.6 g carbo.; 261 mg sodium; 0 mg chol. ∎

By Linda Lau Anusasananan

By Elaine Johnson

RICK MARIANI

For fish, an intense sauce from fresh juices

JIM SHIEBLER IS A CHEF BY VOCATION and a health enthusiast and body-builder by avocation. On the job in The Dining Room at The Ritz-Carlton Marina del Rey in California, he primarily cooks traditional French sauces with butter and cream. On his own time, he experiments with techniques that yield intense flavor with very little fat.

For fish, Shiebler makes a tropical-tasting sauce by reducing carrot and pineapple juices to a syrup. At this concentration, the sauce coats fish beautifully without any thickener or cream. I've added a sweet-hot fruit salsa and an easy rice accompaniment.

Use a juicer if you have one, or buy fresh carrot juice from a juice bar or market, and frozen pineapple juice.

Tropical Fish with Reduced Fresh Juices

Cooking time: About 25 minutes
Prep time: About 8 minutes
Notes: Serve with pressed-rice triangles (recipe follows) or hot cooked rice.
Makes: 4 servings

- ¼ teaspoon cumin seeds
- 2 cups fresh carrot juice
- 1 cup pineapple juice
- 2½ tablespoons fresh lime juice

- 2 teaspoons chopped fresh cilantro, plus 2 tablespoons cilantro leaves
- 1 teaspoon minced fresh jalapeño chili
- ½ cup diced fresh pineapple, or drained canned juice-packed pineapple
- 4 rockfish or mahimahi fillets (½ in. thick, 1 to 1⅓ lb. total)
- 1 teaspoon salad oil
  Salt and pepper

1. In a 3- to 4-quart pan over medium-high heat, shake cumin often until seeds begin to smoke, about 2 minutes. Crush seeds in a mortar or with a rolling pin; set aside.

2. In pan over high heat, boil carrot and pineapple juices, stirring occasionally, until sauce is reduced to ½ cup, 15 to 20 minutes. Stir in cumin and 2 tablespoons lime juice; keep warm.

3. Meanwhile, for salsa, mix remaining ½ tablespoon lime juice, chopped cilantro, chili, and diced pineapple; set aside.

4. Lightly rub fish with oil; sprinkle with salt and pepper. In a 10- to 12-inch nonstick frying pan over medium-high heat, cook fish until no longer translucent in thickest part (cut to test), about 5 minutes, turning once.

5. Dot 4 dinner plate rims with sauce. Spoon remaining sauce in center of plates. Place fish on top, then a band of salsa across fish. Scatter with cilantro leaves.

Per serving: 256 cal., 12% (31 cal.) from fat; 33 g protein; 3.4 g fat (0.6 g sat.); 23 g carbo.; 134 mg sodium; 56 mg chol.

Pressed-Rice Triangles

Cooking time: About 20 minutes
Prep time: About 5 minutes
Makes: 4 servings

1. In a 2- to 3-quart pan, bring 1 cup **long-grain white rice**, 1¾ cups **water**, and ½ teaspoon **salt** (optional) to a boil over high heat. Reduce heat and simmer, covered, until liquid is absorbed, about 20 minutes.

2. With the back of a wet spoon, firmly press rice into an 8-inch square pan to form an even layer. Let cool 5 minutes. Run a knife around pan edge, turn rice onto a board, and cut into 12 triangles, frequently rinsing knife. Serve alongside fish.

Per serving: 169 cal., 1.6% (2.7 cal.) from fat; 3.3 g protein; 0.3 g fat (0.1 g sat.); 37 g carbo.; 2.3 mg sodium; 0 mg chol. ■

WE'D LIKE TO HEAR FROM YOU!
Do you have tips or recipes for low-fat cooking? Write to Everyday Low-fat Cooking, Sunset Magazine, 80 Willow Rd., Menlo Park, CA 94025, or send e-mail (including your full name and street address) to lowfat@sunsetpub.com.

ED CAREY

A twist on strawberry shortcake

*Spoon peak-season berries and zabaglione cream over
a cake with the delicate crunch of cornmeal*

Just as generations of home cooks pass down recipes, generations of *Sunset* staffers let each other in on favorite recipes from past issues. That was how I first came to try *amor polenta,* a recipe for a tender Italian butter cake with a light crunch, last published in 1972. Given the recipe's vintage, I figured it was one of those wonderful old recipes that would gradually fade into obscurity.

But on a recent visit to Zefiro Restaurant & Bar in Portland, I saw a cake similar to the one I knew but with a few twists. Zefiro had gilded the lily. Instead of the plain slices I'd always seen, Zefiro's servings were topped with zabaglione cream and juicy strawberries.

Char Breshgold of the restaurant's pastry department was happy to help with the sauce but confessed that the cake was a bit temperamental. So I went back to *Sunset*'s old recipe, tinkered a little to make it better than ever, and

added Zefiro's almond flavoring.

Because the cake's only leavening is air, be sure to beat the batter as long as specified. Accurate measurements count; sift dry ingredients where noted, then spoon into a dry measuring cup and level off.

Italian Cornmeal Cake

Cooking time: About 1 hour and 15 minutes

Prep time: About 30 minutes

Notes: This cake is best if baked and served the same day.

Makes: 6 to 12 servings

- ⅔ cup soft butter
- 2 cups sifted powdered sugar
- 2 large eggs plus 2 large egg yolks, at room temperature
- 3 tablespoons orgeat (Italian almond syrup) or 1 teaspoon almond extract plus 2½ tablespoons water

Shortcake Italian-style gets its almond flavor from Italian syrup or almond extract.

- 1⅓ cups sifted cake flour
- ½ cup yellow cornmeal
  - Zabaglione cream (recipe follows)
- 3 cups hulled, sliced strawberries
  - Fresh mint sprigs

1. In a large mixer bowl, beat butter on high speed until very creamy, about 2 minutes. (When beating during this and following steps, occasionally stop to scrape side of bowl.) Add a third of sugar at a time, beating on medium speed to blend, then on high speed until very light and fluffy, about 4 minutes total. Add eggs and yolks 1 at a time, beating on high speed until thick, fluffy, and light yellow, about 1 minute per egg or yolk. Beat in orgeat.

2. Combine flour and cornmeal. Add to butter mixture a third at a time, beating after each addition until well combined.

3. Spread batter in a buttered and floured 4- by 8-inch loaf pan. Bake in a 325° oven until a toothpick inserted in center comes out clean, about 1 hour and 10 minutes. Let cool in pan on a rack for 10 minutes, then loosen cake from pan sides and turn out onto rack to cool completely.

4. Cut cake into 12 slices. Place 1 or 2 slices on each plate. Spoon zabaglione cream and sliced strawberries on top. Garnish with mint sprigs.

Per serving cake with cream and strawberries: 374 cal., 51% (189 cal.) from fat; 5 g protein; 21 g fat (12 g sat.); 38 g carbo.; 129 mg sodium; 227 mg chol.

Zabaglione Cream

1. In a large metal bowl, whisk to blend well 6 large **egg yolks,** 3 tablespoons **sugar,** and ¾ cup **sweet marsala.** Fill another bowl, large enough to contain the first bowl, ¼ full of ice water; set aside.

2. Nest yolk bowl in a pan over 1 inch simmering water. Vigorously whisk until zabaglione is thick enough to retain a slight peak when whisk is lifted, 4 to 6 minutes; if overcooked, sauce may curdle. Immediately place zabaglione bowl in bowl of ice water; whisk until sauce is cold.

3. In a bowl, beat 1 cup **whipping cream** until it holds soft peaks; fold into sauce. If making ahead, chill up to 3 hours.

Per serving: 123 cal., 63% (78 cal.) from fat; 1.8 g protein; 8.7 g fat (4.6 g sat.); 5.6 g carbo.; 11.7 mg sodium; 128 mg chol. ∎

By Elaine Johnson

Judge Wes Colley measures a 3-pound-plus onion that won top prize last year. Awards go to so-called colossal onions having the greatest weight and the largest circumference.

Onion Valhalla? Walla Walla!

Head to the onion fields for a sweet celebration

YOU MAY NOT THINK OF ONIONS as "comfort food," but for me nothing's more soothing than to cook up a skillet of onions simmered with some beef consommé and a Polish sausage. So when the first bag of sweet Walla Walla onions came into my life, I almost wore out a skillet. Those big, juicy onions were the most delicious ones I'd ever eaten.

Why do they taste so good? Farmers in the Walla Walla Valley of southeastern Washington say it's the soil and climate. The valley's rich volcanic soil—along with its hot, dry days and cool, moist nights—produces onions that are high in water content, which makes them juicy, but low in sulfur, which is why they're sweet. In recognition of their unique qualities, the U.S. Department of Agriculture in 1995 issued Marketing Order 956, proclaiming that only those onions grown in the Walla Walla area could be sold by the name Walla Walla Sweet.

The only downside is their fleeting availability: because they're so succulent, they don't keep for long—just a month or two. So when these onions are in season, I've learned to strike while the bulb is firm. If you're a real onion lover like me, head to onion Valhalla—the town of Walla Walla—next month and stock up. During harvesttime, in July, a common sight along major Northwest highways is cars with bags of Walla Walla Sweets lashed to luggage racks.

As the onions are pulled from the fields, they're sold at stands along U.S. Highway 12 (the main east-west route into Walla Walla) and other roads. Last year, area farmers produced 15,000 tons of onions worth some $4.5 million.

In celebration of the harvest, this town of nearly 29,000 hosts the Sweet Onion Harvest Fest at Fort Walla Walla Park. The 1996 festival, planned from 9 to 5 on July 14, features 50 booths selling Northwest arts and crafts, and 15 booths selling onion delicacies, including deep-fried onion rings the size of saucers and hamburgers piled high with sautéed onions. Throughout the day on a stage, local chefs show how they prepare their favorite onion dishes. Fort Walla Walla

Park is at the junction of Dalles Military and Myra roads about 4 miles west of downtown.

For a list of growers, including mail-order suppliers, write or call the Walla Walla Sweet Onion Marketing Committee, Box 644, Walla Walla, WA 99362; (509) 525-1031. The committee can also give you tips on how to store the onions so they last as long as possible. Its office, inside the chamber of commerce building at 29 E. Sumach Street, is open 8:30 to 5 Mondays through Fridays. For information about lodging and area attractions, call the chamber at 525-0850. ∎

By Steven R. Lorton

Jelly made with commercial pectin and less sugar than recommended is runny (top). When made exactly as the package directs, jelly is tender, soft, and jiggly, and it holds its shape (center). Overcooked jelly is stiff, hard, and gluey (bottom).

Why?

Why does pectin make fruit juice jell?
Why do jellies and jams need so much sugar?
Why is jelly stiff sometimes, runny others?

AT *SUNSET,* WE KNOW—TO THE minute—when summer jelly and jam making begins. The phone rings, and a panicky voice asks, "What did I do wrong? It's not jelling." Most often, the caller is using a commercial pectin, has almost, but not exactly, followed package instructions, and ends up in trouble.

True, you don't have to use commercial pectin to make jams and jellies, because pectin is present naturally in all fruit, particularly apples. But commercial pectins are popular, and because they are designed to work best with a specific amount of fruit juice (or fruit) and sugar, any deviation in ingredients or method is apt to produce results that generate these questions.

What is commercial pectin? How long does it last? Why won't it work if you double the recipe?

Most pectin you buy at the supermarket is made from apples and imported from Europe. It comes as a powder or liquid (powdered pectin dissolved in water), and its ability to cause jelling does not last forever. Be sure to check expiration dates on packages and discard any pectin that is old.

Commercial pectin tolerates only a certain amount of heat. If you double a recipe using commercial pectin, the mixture takes longer to cook, the pectin breaks down, and the jelling bond fails.

Why does any kind of pectin make fruit juice jell?

Pectin's molecular structure looks like a chain with spikes sticking out. When these chains contact fruit acid in a jelly mixture, the acid charges the spikes, causing the pectin chains to fold in on themselves and trap water to form a gel.

Why do jelly and jam need so much sugar? Can I reduce it?

Because sugar increases pectin's ability to jell, it affects the texture and consistency of jellies and jams as they cool and set. Real jelly is made from fruit juice without any pulp, so the balance of pectin, fruit juice, acid, and sugar is critical to the jelling process. When you are using commercial pectin, if you cut back too much on the sugar, chances are

you'll get syrup instead of jelly.

Jam has fruit solids that add bulk and also contain pectin. These help make jam more tolerant of sugar variation than jelly is, even if you use commercial pectin. In *Sunset*'s test kitchen, we could consistently produce a soft but spreadable gel using commercial pectin and half the recommended sugar with a seeded raspberry purée instead of pure raspberry juice. Jam also has another fail-safe factor—if it's runny, you can cook it longer to reduce the liquid and concentrate the sugar.

If you want to experiment with commercial pectin, be prepared for failures. But if you just want to cut back on sugar, use commercial pectin for low-sugar jams or jellies; it works with about two-thirds the recommended amount of sugar.

If you want jams to have a high ratio of fruit to sugar, or if you want to replace sugar with fruit juice concentrate, see "Fresher, Lighter Jams," on page 112 of the July 1994 *Sunset*.

Why do jelly and jam sometimes get really stiff?

Many culprits make jelly and jam stiff. If you answer the phone as the jelly boils, and conversation distracts you for even a couple of minutes, enough liquid can evaporate to make a mixture that's too stiff to spread well. But more overcooking, say by 10 minutes or longer, can have the opposite effect. The pectin breaks down, and the jelly is juice again. When using commercial pectin, set a timer. Turn it on as soon as the jelly mixture reaches such a vigorous boil that stirring won't make the bubbles settle down.

Too much sugar also makes jelly and jam stiff; the pectin gets too strong. It is important to measure sugar accurately, spooning into a dry measuring cup and scraping the sugar level with the rim. Also, measure all the sugar before you start to cook; it's too easy to lose track of how many cups you've added if you do it 1 cup at a time.

Underripe fruit, which has more pectin than ripe fruit, also makes stiff jellies and jams. Commercial pectin is intended for use with fully ripe fruit.

"Is there any way to save a batch of gluelike jelly?"

—NEVADA LAMBERT
Fernley, Nevada

You can soften stiff jelly by melting it over low heat and stirring in a little fruit juice or water. When the jelly cools, it will be softer, but it won't have a true jelly texture. You can soften jam by reheating it with some additional crushed fruit or a little fruit juice. Store softened jellies and jams airtight in the refrigerator.

"My grandmother's spiced grape jam doesn't seem to set when I use pectin. Why?"

—BETTY SOLLOWAY
Arcadia, California

When you convert a traditional jam or jelly recipe to a quick-cooking one using packaged pectin, compare your recipe with the most similar pectin package recipe and adjust proportions accordingly. It may take a few test runs to get the balance right. If you end up with syrup or a sauce, you can try the following remake steps, check with the pectin manufacturer for additional suggestions, or stop where you are and serve the results on ice cream, pancakes, or waffles.

To remake with dry pectin. For each 4 cups runny jelly or jam: in an 8- to 10-quart pan, mix ¼ cup **sugar** with ½ cup **water,** 2 tablespoons **bottled lemon juice,** and 4 teaspoons **dry pectin.** Stir over high heat until boiling, then add **jelly** or jam. Stir until mixture reaches a full rolling boil, then boil and stir for 30 seconds. Immediately remove from heat, skim off foam, and ladle mixture into hot, sterilized jars, leaving ¼ inch of headspace.

To remake with liquid pectin. For each 4 cups runny jelly or jam: in a bowl, mix ¾ cup **sugar** with 2 tablespoons **bottled lemon juice** and 2 tablespoons **liquid pectin.** In an 8- to 10-quart pan, stir **jelly** or jam over high heat just until boiling. Remove from heat and stir in pectin mixture at once. Return to high heat and stir until mixture reaches a full rolling boil, then boil and stir 1 minute. Immediately remove from heat, skim off foam, and ladle mixture into hot, sterilized jars.

To seal. Wipe jar edges clean and cover with lids and rims.

More questions?

We would like to know what kitchen mysteries you're curious about. Send your cooking questions to Why?, *Sunset Magazine,* 80 Willow Rd., Menlo Park, CA 94025. Or send e-mail, including your full name and street address, to why@sunsetpub.com. With the help of George K. York, extension food technologist at UC Davis, *Sunset* food editors will try to find solutions. We'll answer questions in the magazine. ■

By Linda Lau Anusasananan

A savory tomato starter

In San Francisco, Moose's updates an Italian classic

ONE TASTE OF THE SFORMATO AT Moose's restaurant in San Francisco, and you know you have to have the recipe for the rich-tasting, sweet-tart tomato jelly. Luckily, Mary Etta Moose is willing to share the culinary discovery she made on a recent trip to Italy, where she found sformato (literally, "food cooked in a mold") in a number of restaurants. The delicious baked combination of tomatoes, herbs, cream, and eggs had made its way from Italian home kitchens.

To streamline the sformato, Moose has eliminated the cream and eggs and the need for baking. Instead, she thickens the mixture with gelatin and some olive oil.

Enjoy this herbed tomato appetizer with toasted baguette, arugula, and parmesan.

Mary Etta's Tomato Sformato

Cooking time: About 20 minutes
Prep time: About 15 minutes, plus 4 hours chilling
Notes: Use metal molds or ceramic or glass dishes. For easiest unmolding, fill mold nearly to the top. If unmolding is difficult, simply scoop the sformato from the mold like a dip.
Makes: 3¾ cups, 8 first-course or 16 appetizer servings

   1   can (28 oz.) crushed or ground tomatoes

   1   envelope unflavored gelatin

   ⅓   cup coarsely chopped fresh basil leaves

   ¼   cup coarsely chopped fresh parsley

   1   to 3 teaspoons minced garlic

   1   tablespoon sherry or cider vinegar

   1   teaspoon sugar

   ¼   teaspoon *each* salt and pepper

   About ⅔ cup extra-virgin olive oil

   2   thin baguettes (8 oz. each), cut diagonally into ½-inch slices

   2   to 4 cups (about ⅓ lb.) arugula leaves, rinsed and crisped

   About ½ cup large shavings parmesan cheese

1. Add tomatoes to a 2- to 3-quart pan. Sprinkle gelatin over tomatoes; let stand 1 minute. Bring to a boil over medium-high heat, stirring until gelatin is completely dissolved, about 2 minutes. Remove from heat; let cool until just warm to touch, about 20 minutes. Add basil, parsley, garlic, vinegar, sugar, salt, and pepper.

2. To a food processor or blender, add tomato mixture; while whirling, add ½ cup of the oil in a steady stream. Pour mixture into a 4-cup mold, or into 8 individual 3- to 4-ounce molds or small dishes. Chill filled molds at least 4 hours or until firm to touch; if possible, chill 4-cup mold overnight. Use, or cover and chill up to 2 days.

3. Lightly brush one side of each slice of bread with remaining oil. Place one-third of the slices, oiled side up, on a 10- by 15-inch baking pan. Broil 4 to 6 inches from heat until golden brown. Turn slices; toast other side. Remove from pan and cool; repeat to toast remaining slices. Use, or store airtight up until next day.

4. To serve, fill sink with hot water. Set molds or dishes, 2 at a time, into water for 5 to 10 seconds; be careful not to let water run into molds. Remove; jiggle to see if loosened—if not, repeat. Run a knife around the edge of each mold; turn out small molds onto plates equally covered with arugula leaves. To unmold 4-cup mold, invert a platter over mold, then flip mold and platter together; add arugula around sformato.

5. Top with parmesan shavings and garnish with toasted baguette slices. Serve any extra toasted slices in a basket. Spread with a knife, or use toast for scooping.

Per tablespoon with ¼ oz. bread: 50 cal., 54% (27 cal.) from fat; 1.3 g protein; 3 g fat (0.5 g sat.); 4.7 g carbo.; 93 mg sodium; 0.6 mg chol. ■

By Betsy Reynolds Bateson

Whole-wheat fruit bread made with orange juice, dried cranberries, and oatmeal achieves a tender texture in a bread machine. Use a specially designed serrated knife with an adjustable guide bar to cut even slices of a chosen thickness.

Bread machines are bigger and better

Two recipes to try, and suggestions for easier slicing

THE BREAD MACHINE IS THE leading item on the housewares market. And as bread machine sales have grown, so have the machines. They tend to be bigger (2-lb. machines are becoming a given), bake more consistently, and have more features. Virtually all have a window and a delayed baking cycle.

But there's a problem that still plagues bread machine users: how to cut the soft, peculiarly shaped loaf. A couple of gadgets to solve this problem have hit the market. The best one is a serrated knife that comes with a width-guide bar to help you cut even slices. You can find the knives (about $25) in kitchen shops and most department stores. Another aid is a bread-slicing rack with slots for an elec-

tric knife. It works well but takes up counter space, and slices are always the same width.

One loaf you'll like slicing—and eating—is the Whole-wheat Fruit Bread, which you can flavor with your favorite dried fruits and fruit juices. And making the Savory Herb Pizza Dough is a snap with your bread machine.

Whole-wheat Fruit Bread

Cooking time: Baking cycle times vary among machines.

Prep time: About 10 minutes

Notes: Judith M. Stranathan of Orinda, California, sent this versatile recipe. It should be made in a 1½- or 2-pound machine. Good combinations of dried fruit

and juice are apricots with orange juice, cranberries with cranberry-apple juice, and cherries with apple juice.

Makes: 1 loaf, about 2 pounds 2 ounces

1 cup fruit juice (not thick nectar)

7 tablespoons water

2 tablespoons *each* salad oil and honey

⅔ teaspoon salt

2 cups bread flour

1 cup *each* whole-wheat flour and rolled oats

2 teaspoons active dry yeast

½ cup diced dried fruit

1. Fill machine's bread pan according to

manufacturer's directions with all ingredients *except* dried fruit. Select whole-wheat, fruit-nut, or raisin bread cycle.

2. Observe the dough during first mixing; it should form a soft ball. If the dough won't hold together in a ball and the machine labors, add more water, I tablespoon at a time, until the dough holds together. Or, if too soft to form a ball, add more bread flour, I tablespoon at a time, until a soft ball forms. Add fruit at the "add-in beep" or during the second knead cycle (check instruction book—if added at beginning, fruit may be kneaded into nothing).

3. At the end of the bake cycle, remove the bread promptly; cool bread on a rack before slicing.

Per ounce: 71 cal., 15% (11 cal.) from fat; 2 g protein; 1.2 g fat (0.1 g sat.); 13 g carbo.; 44 mg sodium; 0 mg chol.

Savory Herb Pizza Dough

Prep time: About 10 minutes

Notes: Dough cycle times vary among machines.

Makes: Dough for one 12- to 14-inch pizza crust, about 1 pound 2 ounces

- ¾ cup water
- 2 tablespoons olive oil
- I teaspoon salt
- 2¼ cups bread flour
- 2 tablespoons dried tomato-herb seasoning mix, or 2 tablespoons diced dried tomatoes plus I teaspoon *each* dried basil and oregano leaves
- I teaspoon active dry yeast

1. Fill the machine's bread pan according to the manufacturer's directions. Select the dough cycle.

2. Observe the dough during first mixing; it should form a soft ball. If the dough won't hold together in a ball and machine labors, add more water, I tablespoon at a time, until the dough holds together. Or, if too soft to form a ball, add more bread flour, I tablespoon at a time, until a soft ball forms.

3. At end of dough cycle, remove dough promptly. Roll out dough to fit a 12- to 14-inch pizza pan. Or place dough in a freezer bag, seal, and freeze for later use. Defrost in refrigerator overnight.

4. Top rolled-out dough with pizza ingredients of your choice. Bake at 500° until crust bottom is golden brown, 12 to 15 minutes.

Per ounce dough: 78 cal., 21% (16 cal.) from fat; 2.3 g protein; 1.8 g fat (0.2 g sat.); 13 g carbo.; 123 mg sodium; 0 mg chol. ∎

By Betsy Reynolds Bateson

It takes a knife and fork to do justice to this salad-sandwich.

Bread, beans, and salsa

This hearty main dish puts a cup of garlic to the test

GARLIC BREAD USUALLY PLAYS second fiddle to salad, but here it helps salad reach new heights. The aromatic bread is piled high with beans and salsa, and you tackle the combination with knife and fork. The dish is hearty enough for lunch or a light supper—you might accompany it with a salad of leafy greens.

A whole cup of garlic flavors the bread, but it does so with surprising subtlety because the garlic bite is tamed when the cloves are gently browned in olive oil.

Garlic Bread Salad with Black Beans and Salsa

Cook and prep time: 20 to 25 minutes

Notes: Start with the peeled fresh garlic cloves that are found in the produce section of most supermarkets. Or peel about 2 heads of garlic.

Makes: 4 main-dish or 8 appetizer servings

- I cup peeled garlic cloves
- 3 tablespoons olive oil
- 1½ cups seeded and chopped red tomatoes
- ½ cup yellow cherry tomatoes, stemmed and quartered
- I mild red onion (about ¼ lb.), finely chopped
- 2 green onions, ends trimmed, thinly sliced
- I fresh jalapeño chili, stemmed, seeded, and finely chopped
- I tablespoon finely chopped fresh cilantro
- 2 tablespoons lime juice
- 2 cans (each about 15 oz.) black beans
- I slender (½ lb.) baguette
- Salt

1. Combine garlic and olive oil in a 10- to 12-inch nonstick frying pan. Stir occasionally over medium-low heat until garlic is golden brown and soft when pressed, about 15 minutes. As cloves brown, transfer from pan with a slotted spoon (scorched or burnt garlic is bitter). Discard all but I tablespoon of the cooking oil. Return garlic to pan and mash with a fork or potato masher.

2. In a bowl, mix red and yellow tomatoes, red and green onions, chili, cilantro, and lime juice. Drain beans; put about a quarter of them on a rimmed plate. Drain liquid from tomato salsa mixture onto the plate. Mash the beans on the plate to a smooth paste, then stir in remaining whole beans.

3. Cut baguette in half lengthwise; broil halves 3 to 4 inches from heat until bread is lightly toasted, about I minute. Spread halves equally with garlic; return to broiler about 10 seconds to warm slightly. Cut bread into 8 equal pieces and put I or 2 pieces on each plate. Mound bean mixture on bread, then top with the tomato salsa. Eat with knife and fork, adding salt to taste.

Per main-dish serving: 496 cal., 24% (117 cal.) from fat; 19 g protein; 13 g fat (1.9 g sat.); 78 g carbo.; 946 mg sodium; 0 mg chol. ∎

By Maura Devlin

Sunset's Kitchen Cabinet

Readers' family favorites tested in our kitchens

By Betsy Reynolds Bateson

DICK COLE

Family Hoagie

Robbin McNamara, Klamath Falls, Oregon

A "sandwich night" is one of Robbin McNamara's solutions for hectic weeknight meals. She likes to fix one giant hoagie for her family, which she can have ready for herself and three hungry teenagers in less than half an hour—without destroying the kitchen. McNamara suggests buying what's on sale each week for the filling; we give several options. If her family is really hungry, she's been known to make two hoagies, easily 3 pounds each.

Prep time: About 20 minutes
Makes: 4 to 6 generous servings

- 1 loaf (1 lb.) French bread
- 1 tablespoon mayonnaise
     Lettuce leaves, rinsed and crisped (optional)
- 1 tomato, cored and thinly sliced
- 1 red onion, thinly sliced
- 1 cucumber, peeled and thinly sliced
- 3 tablespoons red wine vinegar or balsamic vinegar
- 1 tablespoon *each* olive oil and Dijon mustard
- ½ pound sliced cheeses, such as cheddar, jack, provolone, havarti, Swiss, or mozzarella
- ½ pound sliced meats, such as ham, roast beef, turkey, salami, or prosciutto
- 1 can (7½ oz.) whole mild green chilies, drained

1. Split bread lengthwise; place cut sides up. Spread bottom half with mayonnaise, then layer evenly with lettuce. Add layers of tomato, onion, and cucumber.

2. Stir together vinegar, oil, and mustard; drizzle a third of vinaigrette mixture over vegetables. Next, layer cheeses and meats. Drizzle with another third of vinaigrette, then top with chilies. Drizzle remaining vinaigrette on cut side of loaf top. Gently press top half over layered bottom. Slice into 4 to 6 pieces.

Per serving: 504 cal., 41% (207 cal.) from fat; 24 g protein; 23 g fat (10 g sat.); 50 g carbo.; 1,492 mg sodium; 63 mg chol.

Plum Dessert Bars

Andrea Lyman, Sandpoint, Idaho

An abundance of ripe, sweet plums accounts for the creation of Andrea Lyman's plum bars. A naturalist, Lyman uses whole-grain products, organic produce, and even wildflower honey. For this recipe, she suggests using fresh prune plums.

Cooking time: About 1 hour
Prep time: About 30 minutes
Makes: 8 dessert servings

- 4 to 6 ripe plums (about 1¼ lb.)
     About ½ cup honey
- 2 tablespoons quick-cooking tapioca
- 1½ cups rolled oats
- 1 cup all-purpose flour
- 1 teaspoon ground cinnamon
- 1 teaspoon grated lemon peel
- ¼ teaspoon *each* baking powder and ground nutmeg
- ¾ cup butter or margarine at room temperature
- 1 teaspoon vanilla

1. Halve plums, and remove and discard pits; finely chop fruit (you should have about 3½ cups). Mix fruit with 3 tablespoons honey and the tapioca; set aside.

2. In a large bowl, combine oats, flour, cinnamon, peel, baking powder, and nutmeg.

3. With a mixer, blend remaining honey, butter, and vanilla. Add flour-oat mixture, and mix until well blended. Pat half of the dough into the bottom of a buttered 8-inch square pan; bake in a 350° oven until golden, 20 to 25 minutes.

4. Spoon honey-coated fruit over crust, then spoon remaining dough in about 2-teaspoon mounds over fruit. Return pan to oven; continue to cook until top is golden brown, 40 to 45 minutes more. Cool, then cut into 2- by 2½-inch bars. Carefully lift bars from pan and serve, or store airtight until next day.

Per serving: 385 cal., 44% (171 cal.) from fat; 4.8 g protein; 19 g fat (11 g sat.); 51 g carbo.; 209 mg sodium; 48 mg chol.

Cilantro Pesto

Barbara H. Shaw, Eugene, Oregon

Barbara H. Shaw created this pesto for special guests when the World Veterans Championships were in town. Instead of the traditional basil and pine nuts, she uses cilantro and sunflower seeds. The seeds add flavor, don't require shelling, and save on cost. Shaw buys raw, hulled seeds in bulk at a natural-food store. The pesto works as a dip for vegetables, crackers, and tortilla chips, and as a topping for pasta.

Prep time: About 20 minutes
Makes: 2 cups

- 1/2 cup salted, roasted, hulled sunflower seeds
- 1/2 cup olive oil
- 2 or 3 cloves garlic, chopped
- 4 cups lightly packed cilantro, tough stems discarded
- 1/2 cup (1 3/4 oz.) coarsely grated parmesan cheese
- 1 tablespoon fresh lemon juice
- 1/4 teaspoon salt
    Assorted vegetables, crackers, and tortilla chips

1. In a blender or food processor, whirl together sunflower seeds, oil, 1/2 cup water, and garlic until smooth.

2. Add cilantro, parmesan, lemon juice, and salt, and continue processing until smooth. If making ahead, cover airtight and refrigerate up to 2 days. If top browns in storage, gently spoon off browned part and discard; remaining pesto will be green. Stir pesto and serve with assorted vegetables, crackers, and tortilla chips.

Per 1/4 cup pesto: 199 cal., 90% (180 cal.) from fat; 3.9 g protein; 20 g fat (3.3 g sat.); 2.6 g carbo.; 221 mg sodium; 4 mg chol.

Green Curry with Chicken

Jennifer Kirkgaard, Burbank, California

The walkway to Jennifer Kirkgaard's home is a dead giveaway that the gardener is a cook. Kirkgaard loves developing recipes that combine herbs from her garden with foods from specialty shops. This recipe uses green curry, coconut milk, and fish sauce from her cupboard, chicken breasts from her freezer, and fresh basil and mint from her garden pots.

Cooking time: About 25 minutes, including cooking rice
Prep time: About 15 minutes
Makes: 4 servings

- 1 tablespoon peanut oil
- 4 boned, skinned chicken breast halves, cut into 1/2-inch pieces
- 1 tablespoon *each* minced garlic and fresh ginger
- 1 red bell pepper, cored, seeded, and cut into 1/2-inch pieces
- 1 can (14 oz.) low-fat coconut milk
- 1 to 2 tablespoons green curry paste
- 1 tablespoon cornstarch
- 2 tablespoons fish sauce or 1 tablespoon soy sauce
- 1/2 cup *each* small, fresh basil leaves and mint leaves, plus sprigs of each
    About 4 cups hot jasmine or long-grain white rice

1. In a wok or a 12-inch frying pan, heat peanut oil over high heat until hot. Add chicken; cook about 2 minutes. Add garlic and ginger; cook 1 minute, then add bell pepper and cook 1 minute more. Remove mixture from pan.

2. To the hot wok, add coconut milk and curry paste; reduce heat to medium and simmer about 4 minutes. Dissolve cornstarch in fish sauce and 2 tablespoons water. Slowly add to coconut milk, stirring to keep mixture smooth.

3. Add chicken back to wok, stir in basil and mint leaves, and bring to a boil. Serve immediately with rice; garnish with herb sprigs.

Per serving: 579 cal., 16% (90 cal.) from fat; 35 g protein; 10 g fat (4.8 g sat.); 72 g carbo.; 417 mg sodium; 68 mg chol.

Ceviche Salad

Tim Finley, Tucson

Tim Finley began perfecting this recipe after tasting conch ceviche in Cancún 10 years ago. He's adapted it to use cooked seafood because of food safety concerns. The combination of shrimp, crab, clams, and drained chopped tomatoes gives this fresh salad great texture and flavor. If the chilies you use are hot (they'll smell hot if they are), it's a good idea to wear gloves while chopping them. The salad is a perfect dish for a hot summer evening.

Prep time: About 1 hour
Makes: 6 salad or 12 appetizer servings

- 1/2 pound (30 to 35 per lb.) shelled cooked shrimp
- 1/2 pound shelled cooked crab
- 1 can (6 1/2 oz.) chopped clams, drained
- 3 lemons (about 1 lb.)
- 3 limes (about 1/2 lb.)
- 2 pounds (about 6) tomatoes
- 1 1/4 cups chopped onion
- 1 poblano or Anaheim chili or green bell pepper, stemmed, seeded, and finely chopped
- 2 jalapeño chilies, stemmed, seeded, and finely chopped
- 2 tablespoons *each* finely chopped parsley and celery tops
- 1 clove garlic, minced
- 1 tablespoon olive oil
- 1/2 teaspoon dried oregano leaves
- 1/2 teaspoon white pepper
    Butter lettuce leaves, rinsed and crisped

1. Chop shrimp into 1/2-inch pieces. Place in a bowl; add crab and clams. Juice lemons and limes; you should have about 1 cup juice. Pour juice over seafood; stir to coat all pieces. Chill at least 15 minutes or up to an hour.

2. Meanwhile, core and seed tomatoes; dice into 3/8-inch pieces. Let drain in a colander. Combine onion, chilies, parsley, celery, garlic, olive oil, oregano, and white pepper.

3. Drain seafood, reserving citrusy liquid. Add seafood and tomatoes to onion-chili mixture, then add reserved liquid to taste, about 1/2 cup. Serve on butter lettuce leaves.

Per salad serving: 177 cal., 21% (38 cal.) from fat; 22 g protein; 4.2 g fat (0.6 g sat.); 14 g carbo.; 224 mg sodium; 122 mg chol.

FOOD
Guide

BY JERRY ANNE DI VECCHIO

A TASTE OF THE WEST: An unexpected shrimp salad

When I visited Thailand about 10 years ago, as more and more Westerners were embracing the cooking style of Southeast Asia, I developed an appetite for the fresh lime mixture that Thai cooks use as a dipping sauce. Christopher Israel, chef of Zefiro Restaurant in Portland, likes this mixture too, but as a dressing for a summertime salad. Like Thai cooks, he also makes use of firm underripe mangoes, because they are less sweet and more vegetable-like.

Tart-sweet, sharp-mild, crisp-tender, cool-hot are the contrasts that play well in this dish. And best of all, as with so many Southeast Asian recipes, the salad is low-fat.

Grilled Shrimp with Mango Salad

Prep and cook time: About 30 minutes
Notes: Up to 1 day ahead, clean the shrimp, watercress, and mint, then cover and chill.
Makes: 4 servings

- 2 firm mangoes (about 2 lb. total)
- 2 tablespoons thinly sliced shallots
- 6 tablespoons lime juice
- 3 tablespoons Asian fish sauce (*nam pla* or *nuoc mam*)
- 1 teaspoon sugar
- ½ teaspoon minced garlic (optional)
- 1 teaspoon minced fresh hot chili such as serrano
- 1 pound shrimp (25 to 30 per lb.)
- 2 cups watercress sprigs, rinsed and drained
- ½ cup fresh mint leaves, rinsed and drained

1. With a sharp knife, cut peel from mangoes. Coarsely shred mangoes by sliding them across a hand shredder.

A surprise role for mangoes: underripe, tart, slightly crunchy shreds of the fruit are served with warm shrimp.

2. In a bowl, mix sliced shallots, lime juice, Asian fish sauce, sugar, minced garlic, and chili. Add shredded mangoes, mix, and set aside.

3. Shell and devein shrimp; rinse well. Divide shrimp into 4 equal portions. Thread 1 portion onto a slender metal skewer. Run a second skewer through shrimp ½ to 1 inch from and parallel to the first to keep shrimp flat. Repeat with remaining shrimp.

4. Place shrimp on a barbecue grill over a solid bed of medium-hot coals or on a gas grill set at medium-hot (you can hold your hand at grill level only 3 to 4 seconds); close lid on gas unit. Cook shrimp, turning once, until opaque but still moist-looking in center of thickest part (cut to test), about 6 minutes.

5. With a slotted spoon, mound mango salad on a platter or 4 plates. Lay shrimp on salad, surround with watercress, and scatter with mint. Then evenly pour remaining dressing in bowl over the shrimp.

Per serving: 244 cal., 13% (31 cal.) from fat; 22 g protein; 3.4 g fat (0.7 g sat.); 34 g carbo.; 597 mg sodium; 140 mg chol.

An easier fish

No bones, no skin, low-fat, and easy to cook. All these appealing characteristics add to the convenience of the ground raw salmon that AquaCuisine, of Campbell, California, has recently introduced in major supermarkets up and down the coast. AquaCuisine starts with Alaska chum salmon, which, unlike king salmon, is a very lean species. And when trimmed of what little fat it contains, the product meets USDA regulations for labeling low-fat.

AquaCuisine is also marketing nonfat salmon sausages, hot dogs (which I find remarkably good), and patties.

I tried the ground salmon several ways. First, the obvious: I shaped it into patties, brushed them lightly with olive oil, and broiled them. I also tried them pan-browned, using a nonstick frying pan with just a little butter for flavor. Because this fish is lean, it gets dry when overcooked, so the center of each patty should be pink and still moist, but not wet and red-looking.

To keep the salmon juicy and make cooking time less critical, I added a few bread crumbs. Shaped into balls and poached in a creamy but nonfat sauce, the salmon made an impressive foundation for this deceptively rich-tasting pasta dish.

Pasta with salmon. With a fork, mix 1 pound **ground salmon** with ¼ teaspoon **salt,** 1 **large egg white,** ¼ cup **chicken broth,** and ¼ cup **fine dried bread crumbs.** Shape into 1-inch balls.

In a 10- to 12-inch frying pan, mix 1 tablespoon **cornstarch** smoothly with 1 cup chicken broth, ½ cup **nonfat sour cream,** and 1 tablespoon chopped **fresh dill.** Stirring over high heat, bring to a boil. Add salmon balls and cook them just until bottoms are firm, then turn them over and continue to simmer until balls are no longer red but still moist-looking in center (cut to test), about 5 minutes total.

Pour hot sauce over 6 cups (1 lb. dried) hot cooked, drained pasta such as **capellini,** spaghetti, or fettuccine. Sprinkle with more chopped fresh dill and **freshly ground pepper.** Makes 4 servings.

Per serving: 628 cal., 3.8% (24 cal.) from fat; 41 g protein; 2.7 g fat (0.4 g sat.); 95 g carbo.; 315 mg sodium; 62 mg chol.

The perfect complement for berries

The cyclic popularity of classic custard desserts makes perfect sense to me: flan, crème brûlée, and floating island are flavor chameleons that adapt to changing fashions.

Another such concoction, a bit less known but equally flexible and certainly less tricky to make, is panna cotta (Italian for *cooked cream*). It is appearing more frequently on restaurant dessert menus.

As a companion for berries, sliced peaches, cherries, and other summer fruits, panna cotta has few peers. Its exceptionally fresh taste comes from blending sour cream into the custard—which I like best speckled with the tiny black seed of a vanilla bean. After cooking the bean with the custard, I rinse it, let it dry, and seal it in a jar of sugar to make vanilla sugar.

Panna Cotta

Prep and cook time: About 15 minutes, plus at least 3 hours to chill

Notes: Use individual molds, or make a single dessert in a 4-cup mold, cutting portions to serve.

Makes: 8 servings

> Pared strip of lemon peel, 3 inches long
>
> ¾ cup sugar
>
> 1 envelope unflavored gelatin
>
> 1 vanilla bean (about 4 in.) or 1 teaspoon vanilla
>
> 1 cup half-and-half
>
> 2 egg yolks
>
> 1½ cups sour cream
>
> Thin strands lemon peel

1. In a 1½- to 2-quart pan, use a heavy spoon to rub the pared strip of lemon peel with sugar to release peel oils (don't mash the peel). Stir in the gelatin, then add ½ cup water.

2. Slit vanilla bean lengthwise but do not cut apart. Add to pan. Heat, stirring, until mixture simmers and is clear.

3. Beat half-and-half with egg yolks to blend, and stir into pan. Stir on low heat for 5 minutes.

4. Remove pan from heat and lift out lemon peel and vanilla bean. Discard peel. Scrape seed from vanilla pod and return seed to pan (or add vanilla).

5. Whisk cooked mixture into sour cream, then return to pan. Nest pan in ice water and stir often until mixture just begins to thicken, 6 to 8 minutes.

6. Pour into straight-sided ½-cup molds (use metal if unmolding). Cover and chill until firm, at least 3 hours.

7. Serve from molds or, to unmold, quickly dip pans, 1 at a time, to the rim in very hot water just until dessert loosens slightly at rim. Dry mold, then invert onto serving plate (you may need to slip a thin knife between dessert and pan to release suction). Garnish portions with thin strands of lemon peel.

Per ½ cup: 224 cal., 56% (126 cal.) from fat; 3.7 g protein; 14 g fat (8.2 g sat.); 22 g carbo.; 39 mg sodium; 83 mg chol.

ROBERT OLDING

An ideal summer dessert, panna cotta is worth making more than once. It changes its character as you change the fruits that go with it.

BOB THOMPSON ON WINE: When the menu is Chinese

Not long ago I got involved in planning the wines for a feast of Chinese foods. Because it was not the same thing as a Chinese banquet, choosing the wines was as easy as falling off a log.

This wine club dinner, organized in courses the way winy meals are with European cuisines, proceeded from fizz with the finger-food starters through a Rhône-style white with the fish to Pinot Noir with the duck.

Taken one dish at a time, wine goes very well indeed with almost all Chinese cookery except the most peppery contributions from Sichuan.

Black cod and Condrieu (a rare, wonderful white Rhône) should make all hands happier than they were when they sat down to dine. Any Cantonese dish that welcomes canned litchis is certainly going to get along with Gewürz-traminer (Navarro Vineyards, Handley Cellars, Husch Vineyards) or, for sweet tooths, Moscato d'Asti ("La Spinetta" by Giuseppe Rivetti, Michele Chiarlo "Nivole"). These same wines benefit Chinese chicken salad, litchis or no.

Mu shu pork and one of the more restrained Zinfandels (Louis M. Martini, Parducci, Frog's Leap) have sent me home satisfied on dozens of evenings.

Any French duck would have a hard time beating the combination of Peking duck and Burgundy (a Beaune or Savigny-les-Beaune from Louis Jadot, Bouchard Père et Fils, Joseph Drouhin, or Jaffelin) or Pinot Noir (Davis Bynum Russian River Valley, Acacia Carneros, Erath Willamette Valley).

Beef in oyster sauce cannot find a much more reliable companion than one of the subtler Cabernet Sauvignons (Clos du Val Napa Valley–Stags Leap, Pine Ridge Napa Valley–Rutherford, Rodney Strong Sonoma County) or Merlots (Columbia Winery Columbia Valley, Chateau Ste. Michelle Columbia Valley, Firestone Santa Ynez Valley). And so on, and so on.

Confusion arises only when the cod, the beef, and the mu shu come to the table together, all in a tumble, the way they do at Chinese banquets.

The solution is easy. As host, give everybody two glasses—one for red, one for white. Put out bottles to cover the two or three main dishes, and let each guest choose the wine that best fits the dish he or she is concentrating on at the moment. As guest, pour a glass to sip when you are working on the dish that fits it best, and give wine a rest in between times. Change the wines when you change focus among the foods. ■

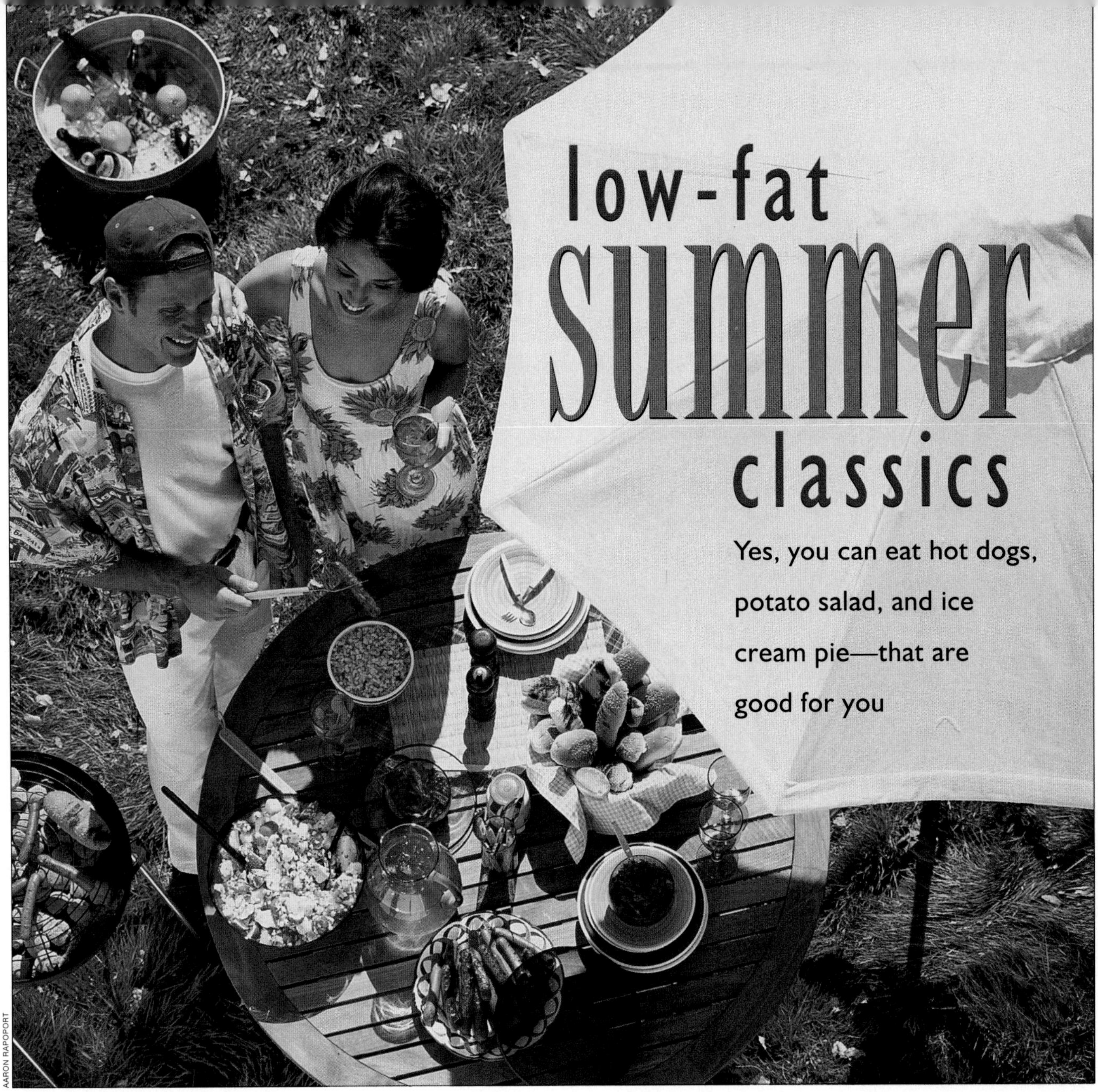

low-fat summer classics

Yes, you can eat hot dogs, potato salad, and ice cream pie—that are good for you

When you think of the summer foods you love best, what comes to mind? Steaks on the grill? Hot dogs and potato salad in the park after a ball game? Cooling, luscious ice cream pies? Of course.

You don't think of food that's good for you, right?

Think again. We've put together 25 summer favorites you can enjoy with a clear conscience. They taste rich, but no more than 30 percent of their calories come from fat. Use these dishes to create whole summer menus, or make just one recipe. Either way, you'll be amazed at how easy these recipes are to put together, and how delicious a summer of healthful eating can be.

BY LINDA LAU ANUSASANANAN ● ANDREW BAKER ● CHRISTINE WEBER HALE ● ELAINE JOHNSON ● KIMBERLY ROTH
FOOD PHOTOGRAPHY BY CHARLES IMSTEPF

Update a classic: pair the best low-fat hot dogs with lively vegetable relishes made with chilies and vinegar.

Hot dogs and relishes A healthy combination, if you shop smart

I F THE PROLIFERATION OF FRANKFURTER styles is any indication, you *can* teach an old dog new tricks. Classic beef and pork dogs are making way for reduced-fat, nonfat, poultry, and even vegetarian hot dogs. (Check out your best bets on the facing page) What else to put in the bun? In honor of the hot dog's lighter profile, we created two fresh vegetable relishes: sweet and sour coleslaw with a mild rice vinegar marinade, and corn with red onion and an exuberant shot of jalapeños.

Sweet & Sour Coleslaw Relish

Prep time: About 15 minutes, plus at least 4 hours for chilling

Makes: 1 ½ cups drained, 8 servings

2 cups finely sliced red or green cabbage, or a combination

⅓ cup shredded carrot

3 tablespoons minced onion

¼ teaspoon hot chili flakes

2 teaspoons mustard seed

⅔ cup seasoned rice vinegar

½ teaspoon salt

In a bowl, combine sliced cabbage, shredded carrot, onion, chili flakes, and mustard seed. Pack into a 4-cup container. Combine vinegar, 1 cup water, and salt. Pour over cabbage mixture. Cover airtight and chill at least 4 hours or up to 1 week. Serve with a slotted spoon.

Per serving: 28 cal., 9.6% (2.7 cal.) from fat; 0.5 g protein; 0.3 g fat (0 g sat.); 6.1 g carbo.; 540 mg sodium; 0 mg chol.

Corn-Jalapeño Relish

Prep and cook time: About 20 minutes
Makes: 1¾ cups, 8 servings

1¾ cups fresh or frozen petite corn kernels

⅔ cup chopped red onion

6 tablespoons distilled white vinegar

¼ cup sugar

2 to 3 tablespoons minced fresh jalapeño chilies

¼ teaspoon salt (optional)

1. In a 2- to 3-quart pan, combine corn, onion, vinegar, sugar, 2 tablespoons chilies, and salt. Bring to a boil over high heat, then reduce heat and simmer, covered, until onion is tender-crisp to bite, about 5 minutes. Uncover and stir until almost all liquid has evaporated, about 5 minutes.

2. Taste relish; if desired, add another tablespoon chilies. Let cool, then serve; or chill airtight up to 2 days.

Per serving: 61 cal., 5.9% (3.6 cal.) from fat; 1.3 g protein; 0.4 g fat (0.1 g sat.); 15 g carbo.; 6.9 mg sodium; 0 mg chol. —E. J.

PUTTING LOW-FAT DOGS TO THE TASTE TEST

First, the facts. Regular hot dogs vary from 14 grams of fat per link to a whopping 32 grams. Their leaner counterparts, on the other hand, range from no fat to 12 grams per link. So the savings in fat range from modest to substantial, depending on the brand.

We tried the gamut of widely available reduced-fat meat dogs, and one veggie dog—11 in all. We evaluated each of them boiled and plain, and then barbecued accompanied by relishes and buns.

Our group reached some general conclusions: One, the vegetarian dog was, well, a dog. Two, a little fat is important for flavor and texture (based on the general unpopularity of the fat-free hot dogs). Three, poultry dogs are very mild-flavored—pleasing to some, bland to others. Four, once you add smoke from the grill, relishes, and a good bun, subtle differences between the better dogs disappear. The final word: many low-fat hot dogs are quite tasty.

Here are our taste panel's five favorite low-fat hot dogs, listed in order of preference:

1. Louis Rich Franks 50% Less Fat (80 cal., 6 g fat per link)
2. Hebrew National Reduced Fat Beef Franks (120 cal., 10 g fat)
3. Ball Park Lite Franks (110 cal., 8 g fat)
4. Oscar Mayer Light Wieners (110 cal., 9 g fat)
5. Foster Farms Chicken Franks (110 cal., 10 g fat)

Potato salads Old-fashioned flavor with lighter, fresher ingredients

Caesar Potato Salad

Prep and cook time: About 1 hour
Notes: If making ahead, add enough chicken broth to moisten to desired texture before serving.
Makes: 6 servings

2½ pounds (about 8) red thin-skinned potatoes, scrubbed

2 cloves garlic, minced

1 teaspoon Worcestershire

2 teaspoons Dijon mustard

3 tablespoons fresh lemon juice

1 tablespoon red wine vinegar

4 anchovy fillets, minced, plus about 5 whole fillets for garnish (about 1 oz. total)

¼ cup grated parmesan cheese

1 tablespoon minced fresh parsley

Salt and pepper

1. In a 5- to 6-quart pan, bring 3 quarts water to a boil. Add potatoes, cover, and cook over medium heat until potatoes are just tender when pierced, 30 to 40 minutes. Remove all but one potato from cooking water; immerse in cold water. When cool, cut potatoes into ½-inch-wide slices. Continue to cook remaining potato over medium heat until very soft when pierced, and skin has begun to peel away, 5 to 10 minutes. Remove potato and cut in half; slice 1 half and add to the other sliced potatoes. Immerse remaining half in cold water until cool to touch, about 3 minutes; peel, cut in half again, and place in a blender with ½ cup of the cooking water. Whirl until smooth. Place in a small bowl; immerse bowl just to the rim in cold water until potato purée is cool.

2. In a medium bowl, combine minced garlic, Worcestershire, Dijon mustard, lemon juice, red wine vinegar, and minced anchovies. Mix in ⅔ cup of the cooled potato purée; pour over sliced potatoes. (Discard remaining purée or reserve for another use.) Add grated parmesan cheese; gently mix to coat potatoes. Garnish with minced parsley and whole anchovy fillets. Add salt and pepper to taste. Serve, or if making ahead, chill up to 1 day.

Per serving: 184 cal., 8.7% (16 cal.) from fat; 6.5 g protein; 1.8 g fat (0.7 g sat.); 35 g carbo.; 300 mg sodium; 5.2 mg chol.

Mediterranean Potato Salad

Prep and cook time: About 1 hour
Notes: If making ahead, add enough chicken broth to moisten to desired texture before serving.
Makes: 6 servings

2½ pounds red thin-skinned potatoes (2¼ to 3 in.), scrubbed

½ cup thinly sliced green onions, including green tops if desired

1½ cups (2¾ oz.) crumbled feta cheese

¼ cup minced fresh basil

6 ounces purchased peeled roasted red peppers (not in oil), drained

½ cup nonfat cottage cheese

½ cup chicken broth

2 tablespoons lemon juice

¼ teaspoon ground pepper

Salt and pepper

A picnic without potato salad? With this great-tasting, healthful new classic, don't even think of passing it up.

1. In a 5- to 6-quart pan, bring 3 quarts water to a boil. Add potatoes, cover, and cook over medium heat until potatoes are just tender when pierced, 30 to 40 minutes. Drain, and immerse potatoes in cold water.

2. When cool, cut potatoes into quarters, or eighths if large (about 1½-in. chunks). In a large bowl, combine potatoes with green onions, feta cheese, and basil.

3. In a blender, whirl red peppers, cottage cheese, chicken broth, lemon juice, and ground pepper until smooth. Mix gently but thoroughly with potato mixture; season to taste with salt and more pepper. Serve, or if making ahead, chill up to 1 day.

Per serving: 220 cal., 14% (31 cal.) from fat; 8.4 g protein; 3.4 g fat (2 g sat.); 39 g carbo.; 299 mg sodium; 13 mg chol.

A New Classic

Prep and cook time: About 1 hour
Notes: If making potato salad ahead, add enough chicken broth to moisten the salad to the desired texture before serving.
Makes: 6 servings

2½	pounds (about 8) red thin-skinned potatoes, scrubbed
1	cup corn kernels
1	cup chopped celery
½	cup chopped red onion
⅔	cup unflavored nonfat yogurt
⅓	cup reduced-fat mayonnaise
½	cup seasoned rice vinegar
3	tablespoons minced fresh parsley

About ½ teaspoon ground pepper

Salt

1. In a 5- to 6-quart pan, bring 3 quarts water to a boil. Add potatoes, cover, and cook over medium heat until potatoes are just tender when pierced, 30 to 40 minutes. Drain, and immerse in cold water. When cool, cut into ¾-inch cubes.

2. In a large bowl, combine potatoes, corn, celery, and red onion.

3. In a small bowl, blend yogurt, mayonnaise, vinegar, parsley, and ½ teaspoon ground pepper; pour over potato mixture. Mix gently but thoroughly; season to taste with salt and more pepper if desired. Serve, or if making ahead, chill up to 1 day.

Per serving: 250 cal., 12% (31 cal.) from fat; 6.3 g protein; 3.4 g fat (0.5 g sat.); 50 g carbo.; 559 mg sodium; 0.5 mg chol. —K. R.

A cooling blend of papaya, berries, and oranges tames the heat of a spicy jalapeño dressing.

Fruit salads Vinegar and citrus dressings make the difference

Papaya, Orange, and Berry Salad with Lime-Chili Dressing

Prep time: About 25 minutes
Makes: 4 servings

¼ cup lime juice

1 tablespoon minced fresh cilantro

1 or 2 red or green jalapeño chilies, stemmed, seeded, and minced

1 teaspoon sugar

1 papaya (about 1¼ lb.), peeled and seeded

2 oranges

1 cup raspberries, rinsed and drained

1 cup blueberries, rinsed and drained

Butter lettuce leaves, rinsed and crisped

1. Mix together lime juice, cilantro, chilies, and sugar.

2. Cut papaya lengthwise into ½-inch-thick slices. Cut peel and white pith from oranges. Cut between membranes to release segments. Discard any seeds.

3. In a bowl, combine orange segments, raspberries, and blueberries. Add lime juice mixture and stir gently until fruit is evenly coated (be careful not to crush raspberries).

4. Line individual plates with lettuce leaves. Arrange papaya wedges in a fan or other attractive pattern. Spoon berries, orange segments, and juice over papaya slices.

Per serving: 116 cal., 4.7% (5.4 cal.) from fat; 1.7 g protein; 0.6 g fat (0.1 g sat.); 29 g carbo.; 7.8 mg sodium; 0 mg chol.

Mango, Pear, and Avocado with Feta Cheese

Prep time: About 20 minutes
Notes: A light sprinkling of lemon juice helps prevent sliced avocados and pears from turning brown.
Makes: 4 to 6 servings

½ cup balsamic vinegar

3 tablespoons honey

½ pound small, tender spinach leaves, rinsed and crisped

2 firm-ripe mangoes (about 2½ lb. total), peeled, pitted, and cut into ½-inch-thick slices

2 firm-ripe pears (about 1 lb. total), peeled, cored, and cut into ½-inch-thick slices

1 avocado (about ½ lb.), peeled, pitted, and cut into ½-inch-thick slices

3 ounces feta cheese, crumbled

Freshly ground pepper

1. Whisk together vinegar and honey until smooth. In a bowl, mix together about ¼ cup vinegar mixture and the spinach. Arrange spinach on a serving platter or on 4 to 6 individual salad plates.

2. Decoratively arrange mangoes, pears, avocado, and feta over spinach, dividing equally if using individual plates. Add pepper and remaining vinegar mixture to taste.

Per serving: 252 cal., 29% (72 cal.) from fat;

4.6 g protein; 8 g fat (2.9 g sat.); 46 g carbo.; 195 mg sodium; 13 mg chol.

Pineapple-Melon Salad with Mint and Basil

Prep time: About 30 minutes
Makes: 4 to 6 servings

1 pineapple, peeled, cored, and cut into 1-inch chunks (about 5 cups)

3 cups 1-inch chunks cantaloupe

3 cups 1-inch chunks honeydew

¾ cup (about ½ oz.) loosely packed fresh mint leaves, plus sprigs

¾ cup (about ½ oz.) loosely packed fresh basil leaves, plus sprigs

¼ cup seasoned rice vinegar

1. Combine pineapple, cantaloupe, and honeydew in a large serving bowl.

2. Stack several mint leaves on top of each other. Cut crosswise into very thin slivers (¹⁄₁₆ to ⅛ inch thick). Repeat to sliver remaining mint and basil leaves.

3. Add slivered mint and basil, and vinegar, to fruit. Stir gently until evenly mixed. Garnish with mint and basil sprigs.

Per serving: 145 cal., 6.2% (9 cal.) from fat; 2 g protein; 1 g fat (0 g sat.); 36 g carbo.; 216 mg sodium; 0 mg chol.   —C. W. H.

Steak Grilling and fat-free marinades add flavor to a sandwich or a meal

Lemon Grass Flank Steak

Prep and cook time: About 45 minutes
Makes: 4 servings

3 stalks (about 2 oz. total) fresh lemon grass

1 cup chicken broth

⅓ cup lemon juice

¼ cup rice vinegar

1 tablespoon soy sauce

1 tablespoon minced garlic

1 teaspoon minced fresh ginger

2 teaspoons sugar

½ teaspoon hot chili flakes

1 fat-trimmed flank steak (about 1 lb.)

1 package (about 7 oz.) rice sticks (*mai fun*)

2 cups bean sprouts, rinsed and drained

½ cup lightly packed fresh cilantro leaves

2 tablespoons chopped mint, plus sprigs

12 butter lettuce leaves

12 thin cucumber slices (optional)

1. Peel off and discard tough outer layers of lemon grass; rinse. Trim off and discard tops and discolored or dry parts of root ends. Thinly slice (you should have about ¼ cup).

2. In a blender, combine lemon grass and ½ cup of the broth. Whirl until lemon grass is finely chopped. Pour mixture into a small pan and bring to a boil over high heat; boil

1 minute. Pour through a fine strainer into a large measuring cup; discard residue.

3. To the strained liquid, add remaining broth, lemon juice, vinegar, soy sauce, garlic, ginger, sugar, and chili flakes; stir until sugar is dissolved. Place steak in a heavy-duty zip-lock plastic bag, pour in ½ cup dressing, seal and shake gently to coat. Let stand at least 15 minutes. Pour remaining dressing into a large bowl.

4. Meanwhile, in a 4- to 5-quart pan, cook rice sticks in 3 quarts boiling water until tender to bite, about 3 minutes. Drain; rinse noodles in cold running water until cool to touch. Drain well, squeezing lightly to extract as much water as possible. Using scissors, cut through noodles a few times to make smaller pieces. Place noodles in bowl with dressing. Add bean sprouts, cilantro, and chopped mint; toss ingredients to coat with dressing. Set aside until serving time.

5. Drain marinade from meat. Heat marinade to boiling in a small pan or in a microwave oven; set aside. Lay steak on a barbecue grill over a solid bed of hot coals or high heat on a gas grill (you can hold your hand at grill level only 2 to 3 seconds); close lid on gas grill. Cook steak to desired doneness, 7 to 8 minutes for rare (cut to test); turn once to brown evenly.

6. Cut meat diagonally across the grain into thin slices. On each of 4 plates, arrange 3 lettuce leaves; equally divide noodle mixture and steak among plates, arranging meat attractively on top. Garnish with cucumber and mint sprigs. Serve with marinade to spoon over meat as desired.

Per serving: 398 cal., 21% (85 cal.) from fat; 28 g protein; 9.4 g fat (3.9 g sat.); 49 g carbo.; 323 mg sodium; 57 mg chol.

Skewered Beef with Toasted Couscous

Prep and cook time: About 35 minutes
Makes: 6 servings

1½ pounds fat-trimmed boneless top loin steak (New York strip)

½ cup dry red wine

1½ teaspoons dried thyme

1¾ cups (12-oz. package) couscous

3 cups beef broth

½ teaspoon ground coriander

2 tablespoons grated lemon peel

About 2 tablespoons lemon juice

About ¼ cup chopped green onions (white and green parts)

18 cherry tomatoes (about 1 lb. total)

2 cans (about 13 oz. each) halved artichoke hearts in water, drained

Salt and pepper

1. Cut meat into 1-inch cubes. In a heavy-duty zip-lock plastic bag, combine wine and 1 teaspoon of the thyme. Add meat, seal, and shake gently to coat evenly. Marinate at least 15 minutes or up to 2 hours.

2. In a deep 12-inch frying pan over high heat, toast couscous, stirring and shaking continuously to prevent burning, until brown and aromatic, about 5 minutes. Stir in beef broth. Bring to a boil, then lower heat to simmer. Simmer, covered, about 1 minute, or until all broth is absorbed; stir to fluff. Remove from heat and let stand,

Grilled steak, onions, and green peppers are sandwiched in a grilled roll, then drizzled with a salsa–sour cream sauce.

uncovered, 5 minutes. Stir in remaining ½ teaspoon thyme, coriander, peel, lemon juice to taste, and ¼ cup green onions.

3. Drain meat. Divide meat, tomatoes, and artichoke hearts evenly among 6 long (at least 14-in.) metal skewers. Lay skewers on a lightly oiled barbecue grill over a solid bed of very hot coals or on a gas grill over high heat (you can hold your hand at grill level only 1 to 2 seconds); close lid on gas grill. Cook, turning to brown all sides evenly, until steak is medium-rare (cut to test), about 5 minutes. Serve over couscous. Garnish with additional green onions, if desired. Add salt and pepper to taste.

Per serving: 456 cal., 17% (78 cal.) from fat; 37 g protein; 8.7 g fat (3.2 g sat.); 54 g carbo.; 108 mg sodium; 65 mg chol.

Fajita Sandwiches

Prep and cook time: About 35 minutes

Notes: Substitute red, yellow, or orange bell peppers if desired.

Makes: 4 sandwiches

½ cup lime juice

2 tablespoons chili powder

2 teaspoons ground cumin

1 teaspoon dried oregano

½ teaspoon ground cinnamon

1 fat-trimmed skirt steak (about 1 lb.)

¼ cup *each* salsa and nonfat or reduced-fat sour cream

1 onion (about ½ lb.), cut crosswise into ½-inch-thick slices

2 green bell peppers (about 1 lb. total), stemmed, seeded, and cut into quarters

4 soft sandwich rolls (6 in. long), cut in half lengthwise

1. In a bowl, combine lime juice, chili powder, cumin, oregano, and cinnamon. Cut steak into 4 pieces; add to marinade, turning to coat evenly. Marinate at least 15 minutes or up to 2 hours.

2. Meanwhile, stir together salsa and sour cream; chill until serving time.

3. Lay onion slices and peppers on a lightly oiled barbecue grill over a solid bed of hot coals or on a gas grill over high heat (you can hold your hand at grill level only 2 to 3 seconds); close lid on gas grill. Cook, turning the vegetables to brown evenly, until vegetables have dark grill marks and are slightly limp, 7 to 12 minutes.

4. Remove steak from marinade and lay on grill. Cook, turning once to brown evenly, until medium-rare, 8 to 10 minutes (cut to test); remove from grill. Cook rolls on grill until crisp and golden on both sides, 1 to 2 minutes.

5. When peppers are cool enough to handle, rub off any loose bits of skin. Separate onions into rings. Slice steak into ½-inch-wide strips.

6. Assemble sandwiches by layering steak, onion, green peppers, and salsa–sour cream mixture on grilled rolls.

Per serving: 428 cal., 27% (117 cal.) from fat; 31 g protein; 13 g fat (5.1 g sat.); 45 g carbo.; 616 mg sodium; 58 mg chol. —A. B.

Warm corn tortillas cradle grilled fish, green tomatillo salsa, and red-cabbage slaw.

Tacos Fish, chili, and chicken fillings plus the perfect tortilla

Grilled-Fish Tacos
with Green Salsa

Prep and cook time: About 25 minutes

Notes: Look for the small green tomatillos with papery husks in some supermarkets and in Latino grocery stores. If unavailable, substitute small Roma tomatoes and add more lime juice to taste.

Makes: 12 tacos, about 4 servings

3½ cups finely shredded red or green cabbage

¼ cup white distilled vinegar

Salt and pepper

¾ pound fresh tomatillos

2 tablespoons salad oil

1 onion (about 6 oz.), cut into ½-inch-thick slices

1½ pounds firm-fleshed skinned fish fillets, such as lingcod or Chilean sea bass

3 or 4 jalapeño chilies (2 to 3 oz. total)

2 teaspoons lime juice

¾ cup lightly packed fresh cilantro leaves

1 clove garlic

1 dozen warm corn or low-fat flour tortillas (6- or 7-in.)

Low-fat sour cream

Lime wedges

1. Mix cabbage with vinegar and 3 tablespoons water. Add salt and pepper to taste. Cover and chill.

2. Remove and discard husks from tomatillos; rinse tomatillos. Thread onto skewers. Brush some of the oil lightly onto onion slices. Rinse fish and pat dry. Brush fish with remaining oil.

3. Place tomatillos, onion, and chilies on a grill 4 to 6 inches above a solid bed of hot coals or over high heat on a gas barbecue (you can hold your hand at grill level only 2 to 3 seconds). Cook, turning as needed, until vegetables are browned, 8 to 10 minutes. Set aside to cool.

4. Place fish on grill over medium-hot coals or gas heat (you can hold your hand at grill level only 3 to 4 seconds). Cook, turning once, until fish is opaque but still moist-looking in thickest part (cut to test), 10 to 14 minutes.

5. Remove stems from chilies; remove seeds (if you want less heat). In a blender or food processor, whirl tomatillos, chilies, lime juice, ¼ cup cilantro, and garlic until smooth. Chop onion. Add the chopped onion to salsa mixture, and salt and pepper to taste. Pour into a small bowl.

6. To assemble each taco, fill a tortilla with a little cabbage relish, a few chunks of fish, salsa, and sour cream. Add a squeeze of lime, and salt and pepper to taste.

Per serving: 432 cal., 23% (99 cal.) from fat; 37 g protein; 11 g fat (1.5 g sat.); 48 g carbo.; 232 mg sodium; 89 mg chol.

Vegetable-Chili Tacos

Prep and cook time: About 30 minutes
Makes: 12 tacos, about 4 servings

1 onion (about ½ lb.), chopped

1 clove garlic, minced

3 zucchini (about ¾ lb. total), cut into ½-inch cubes

3 tablespoons chili powder

1½ tablespoons all-purpose flour

½ teaspoon ground cumin

1 cup vegetable broth

1 can (about 1 lb.) pinto beans, rinsed and drained

1½ cups fresh (about 3 ears) or frozen corn kernels

Salt and cayenne

1 dozen warm corn or low-fat flour tortillas (6- to 7-in.)

3 cups finely shredded iceberg lettuce

1 cup (4 oz.) shredded jalapeño or plain jack cheese

1 cup unflavored nonfat yogurt

1. In a 3- to 4-quart pan, stir onion, garlic, and zucchini in 2 tablespoons water over high heat until onion is limp, and brown film forms on pan bottom, 8 to 10 minutes. Stir in chili powder, flour, and cumin. Add broth. Stir until mixture boils.

2. Add beans and corn kernels to onion mixture. Simmer, covered, until beans are hot, about 5 minutes. Add salt and cayenne to taste. Pour into a bowl.

3. To assemble each taco, fill a corn or low-fat flour tortilla with the bean chili and shredded lettuce; add cheese and nonfat yogurt to taste.

Per serving: 497 cal., 25% (126 cal.) from fat; 24 g protein; 14 g fat (5.5 g sat.); 77 g carbo.; 861 mg sodium; 31 mg chol.

Stir-fried Chicken and Chili Tacos

Prep and cook time: About 30 minutes
Makes: 12 tacos, 4 to 6 servings

2 red bell peppers (about 12 oz. total)

2 fresh Anaheim (California or New Mexico) green chilies or 1 green bell pepper (about 8 oz. total)

4 or 5 fresh jalapeño chilies (3 to 4 oz. total)

1⅓ pounds boneless, skinless chicken breasts

1 tablespoon salad oil

1 onion (about 8 oz.), thinly sliced

3 cloves garlic, minced

1 tablespoon cumin seed

½ cup chopped fresh cilantro

3 tablespoons lime juice

Salt and pepper

1 dozen warm corn or low-fat flour tortillas (6- or 7-in.)

Lime wedges

Salsa

Unflavored nonfat yogurt

1. Stem and seed bell peppers and Anaheim and jalapeño chilies. Cut bell pepper and chilies into thin slivers about 3 inches long. Cut chicken crosswise into thin slices about 3 inches long.

2. Set a 10- to 12-inch frying pan over high heat. Add 2 teaspoons oil. When hot, add chicken, and stir-fry until chicken is opaque throughout, 4 to 5 minutes. Remove chicken from pan.

3. Return pan to high heat. Add remaining 1 teaspoon salad oil, sliced onion, garlic, and cumin; stir-fry for 1 minute. Add the bell pepper and chilies. Stir-fry until they begin to wilt, about 2 minutes. Return cooked chicken to the pan. Add chopped cilantro, lime juice, and salt and pepper to taste. Pour into a bowl.

4. To assemble each taco, fill a tortilla with chicken mixture. Squeeze a lime wedge over the filling. Add salsa and yogurt to the taco to taste.

Per serving: 292 cal., 16% (47 cal.) from fat; 28 g protein; 5.2 g fat (0.8 g sat.); 35 g carbo.; 154 mg sodium; 58 mg chol.
—L. L. A.

SECRETS TO A SOFT WARM TORTILLA

Start with the freshest possible corn tortillas. A trip to a Latino market where they are made fresh daily is worth it. Or use low-fat flour tortillas. Choose one of these ways to warm the tortillas.

On a barbecue grill. Lay tortillas on grill over a solid bed of medium-hot coals or gas heat (you can hold your hand at grill level only 3 to 4 seconds) and turn several times, just until hot and soft, about 30 seconds (they get hard and tough if overheated). As you heat the tortillas, stack them on a thick towel and wrap to keep warm.

In a conventional oven. Wrap a stack of tortillas in foil; bake in a 325° oven until hot and steamy, 15 to 20 minutes.

In a microwave oven. Stack tortillas and wrap in plastic wrap. Place in a microwave oven and cook at full power (100 percent) until hot and steamy, 2 to 3 minutes.

Homemade ginger ale, raspberry lemonade, and iced green tea will revitalize wilting spirits.

Summer sippers Intense flavors refresh vintage coolers and fruity margaritas

Fresh Ginger Ale

Prep and cook time: About 30 minutes, plus chilling time

Notes: Refrigerate leftover cooked ginger, if desired, and stir into softened vanilla ice cream, or sprinkle over vanilla yogurt or sliced bananas.

Makes: About 4 quarts, 12 servings

  2 cups (about 10 oz.) coarsely chopped, peeled fresh ginger

  3 strips lemon peel (about 4 in. each), yellow part only

     About 1 ½ cups sugar

  3 quarts chilled club soda

     Ice cubes

1. Combine ginger, lemon peel, and 4 cups water in a 3- to 4-quart pan. Bring to a boil over high heat; boil gently, uncovered, 10 minutes. Stir in 1 ½ cups sugar and continue boiling until mixture is reduced to 3 cups, about 15 minutes longer. Pour mixture through a fine wire strainer set over a bowl. Discard peel; reserve ginger for another use or discard. Cool syrup, cover, and chill until cold, at least 1 hour or up to 1 week.

2. For each serving, in a 16-ounce glass, mix ¼ cup ginger syrup with 1 cup cold club soda. Add more ginger syrup, ice, and sugar to taste.

Per serving: 100 cal., 0% (0 cal.) from fat; 0.1 g protein; 0 g fat; 26 g carbo.; 51 mg sodium; 0 mg chol.

Berry Pink Lemonade

Prep time: About 15 minutes, plus chilling time

Makes: About 2 quarts, 6 to 8 servings

  ¾ cup sugar

  1 cup fresh lemon juice

  1 cup fresh or frozen raspberries

     Ice cubes

     Thin lemon slices

1. Mix sugar, 6 cups cold water, and lemon juice until sugar is dissolved.

2. Whirl raspberries in a blender until puréed. Press purée through a fine wire strainer over a bowl; discard seeds. Pour purée into the lemonade.

3. Cover and chill lemonade until cold, at least 1 hour or up to 1 day. Stir, and pour into glasses or a pitcher. Add ice to taste.

Garnish with lemon slices if desired.

Per serving: 88 cal., 1% (0.9 cal.) from fat; 0.2 g protein; 0.1 g fat; 23 g carbo.; 0.5 mg sodium; 0 mg chol.

Iced Green Tea

Prep and cook time: About 10 minutes, plus chilling time

Makes: 2 quarts, 6 to 8 servings

  3 tablespoons green tea leaves

  3 tablespoons coarsely chopped fresh mint, plus sprigs

     Ice cubes

  1 to 2 tablespoons sugar

1. In a bowl, combine tea, chopped mint, and 1 quart boiling water; let brew 5 to 7 minutes. Pour through a fine wire strainer over a bowl; discard leaves. Add 1 quart cold water to hot tea. Cool, cover, and chill until cold, at least 2 hours or up to 2 days.

2. Pour tea into glasses or a pitcher. Add ice and sugar to taste. Garnish with mint sprigs.

Per serving: 7.2 cal., 0% (0 cal.) from fat; 0 g protein; 0 g fat; 1.9 g carbo.; 2.7 mg sodium; 0 mg chol.

Watermelon Margaritas

Prep time: About 10 minutes

Notes: These margaritas contain most of the traditional ingredients: lime juice, orange-flavor liqueur, and, of course, tequila. But frozen fruit chunks substitute for ice, adding flavor rather than water.

Makes: About 3½ cups, 4 servings

> ½ cup fresh-squeezed lime juice
>
> 1 tablespoon sugar
>
> ½ cup tequila
>
> 2 tablespoons orange-flavor liqueur
>
> 4 cups frozen seedless watermelon chunks
>
> Coarse salt
>
> Lime wedges

1. In a blender, combine lime juice, sugar, tequila, and orange liqueur. Turn on highest speed; gradually drop watermelon chunks through opening in lid, whirling until slushy.

2. Place coarse salt on a small plate. Rub rims of glasses with lime wedges to moisten. Dip rims in salt and turn to coat evenly. Serve margaritas in salt-rimmed glasses.

Per serving: 166 cal., 3.8% (6.3 cal.) from fat; 1.1 g protein; 0.7 g fat (0 g sat.); 20 g carbo.; 3.5 mg sodium; 0 mg chol.

Cantaloupe-Orange Margaritas

Prep time: About 10 minutes

Makes: About 3½ cups, 4 servings

> ½ cup fresh-squeezed lime juice
>
> 1 cup orange juice
>
> 1 tablespoon sugar
>
> ½ cup tequila
>
> 2 tablespoons orange-flavor liqueur
>
> 3 cups frozen cantaloupe chunks
>
> Coarse salt
>
> Lime wedges

1. In a blender, combine lime juice, orange juice, sugar, tequila, and orange-flavor liqueur. Turn on highest speed; gradually

drop cantaloupe chunks through opening in lid, whirling until slushy.

2. Place coarse salt on a small plate. Rub rims of glasses with lime wedges to moisten. Dip rims in salt and turn to coat evenly. Serve margaritas in salt-rimmed glasses.

Per serving: 185 cal., 1.9% (3.6 cal.) from fat; 1.6 g protein; 0.4 g fat (0 g sat.); 25 g carbo.; 12 mg sodium; 0 mg chol.

Sorbet Margaritas

Prep time: About 5 minutes

Notes: Use your favorite fruit sorbet, such as lemon, raspberry, or mango.

Makes: About 3 cups, 4 servings

> ½ cup tequila
>
> 1 tablespoon orange-flavor liqueur
>
> ½ cup orange juice
>
> 1 pint fruit-flavor sorbet
>
> Lemon or lime juice

In a blender, combine tequila, orange-flavor liqueur, orange juice, and sorbet. Turn on highest speed and whirl until slushy, stirring mixture as necessary to blend evenly. Add lemon juice (1 tablespoon at a time) to adjust sweetness to taste.

Per serving: 208 cal., 0.4% (0.9 cal.) from fat; 0.7 g protein; 0.1 g fat (0 g sat.); 32 g carbo.; 11 mg sodium; 0 mg chol.   —L. L. A., A. B.

A trio of frosty, fresh-flavored fruit margaritas includes, from left, cantaloupe-orange, lemon sorbet, and watermelon.

low-fat summer classics

Chocolate-coffee pie, served from the pan or slipped onto a plate, only looks—and tastes—decadent.

Ice cream pies Eat your sweets in almost any flavor

Chocolate-Coffee Frozen Pie

Prep and cook time: About 20 minutes, plus 1 to 1 1/2 hours for freezing, not including time to prepare crust

Makes: 8 servings

1/3 cup nonfat milk

1/4 teaspoon cornstarch

4 ounces bittersweet or semisweet chocolate, chopped

2 tablespoons coffee-flavor liqueur

1 1/2 quarts nonfat or low-fat coffee ice cream or frozen yogurt, half of it softened

Cookie crust (recipe on facing page), made with chocolate cookies, frozen

1. In a 1- to 2-quart pan, stir milk and cornstarch until smooth. Stir over medium heat until bubbling, about 2 minutes, then remove from heat and stir in chocolate and

liqueur until melted and smooth. Let cool. Spoon 3 tablespoons sauce into a small, unpleated zip-lock plastic bag and seal. Set remaining sauce aside.

2. Meanwhile, spread softened ice cream evenly in crust; smooth top. Freeze, uncovered, until firm to touch, 1 to 1 1/2 hours.

3. Spread reserved sauce from pan over ice cream in crust. Drop 8 equal scoops or spoonfuls of firm ice cream around rim of pie. Snip a small hole in corner of plastic bag; squeeze sauce decoratively onto pie.

4. Serve, or if making ahead, freeze pie, uncovered, until chocolate squiggles are set, about 30 minutes, then wrap pie airtight and freeze up to 1 week. If pie is frozen solid, let stand at room temperature about 15 minutes before cutting.

Per serving: 348 cal., 21% (72 cal.) from fat; 6.6 g protein; 8 g fat (3.4 g sat.); 64 g carbo.; 217 mg sodium; 0.6 mg chol.

Cookie Crust

Prep and cook time: About 30 minutes, plus about 45 minutes for cooling and freezing

Notes: Crumbs should be coarse for best texture. To make coarse crumbs, break cookies into chunks, then pulse in a food processor, or seal in a heavy plastic bag and crush with a rolling pin.

Makes: 8 servings

> 2 large egg whites
>
> 1/4 teaspoon cream of tartar
>
> 3 tablespoons sugar
>
> 1 3/4 cups coarse chocolate wafer cookie, gingersnap, or graham cracker crumbs (about 6 oz.)
>
> 2 tablespoons minced crystallized ginger (for gingersnap crust only)

1. With a mixer, beat egg whites and cream of tartar on high speed until foamy. Add sugar a third at a time, beating about 45 seconds after each addition, until soft peaks form. Gently fold cookies (and ginger, if using) into whites.

2. Drop small spoonfuls of cookie mixture over bottom and sides of a buttered and floured 9-inch pie pan. With a spoon, gently pat crust to evenly cover bottom and sides of pan up to top of rim. Bake in a 350° oven until lightly browned and dry to touch, about 20 minutes.

3. With a metal spatula, loosen cookie crust from sides of pan, then slide spatula under crust a little at a time to completely loosen bottom. On a rack, let cool completely in pan, then place in freezer until cold (at least 10 minutes). Fill crust, or freeze airtight up to 2 weeks.

Per serving chocolate crust: 115 cal., 23% (27 cal.) from fat; 2.3 g protein; 3 g fat (0.8 g sat.); 20 g carbo.; 137 mg sodium; 0.4 mg chol.

Per serving gingersnap crust: 125 cal., 15% (19 cal.) from fat; 2.1 g protein; 2.1 g fat (0.4 g sat.); 25 g carbo.; 155 mg sodium; 0 mg chol.

Per serving graham cracker crust: 113 cal., 12% (14 cal.) from fat; 2.4 g protein; 1.5 g fat (0 g sat.); 21 g carbo.; 149 mg sodium; 0 mg chol.

Blackberry Ripple Alaska Pie

Prep and cook time: About 1 hour, plus 2 hours for freezing, not including time to prepare crust

Makes: 8 servings

> 1 1/2 cups blackberry or boysenberry syrup
>
> 2 tablespoons cornstarch
>
> 2 cups fresh or frozen blackberries
>
> 1 quart nonfat or low-fat vanilla ice cream or frozen yogurt, softened
>
> Cookie crust (recipe at left), made with graham crackers, frozen
>
> 3 large egg whites
>
> 1 cup marshmallow cream
>
> 1 teaspoon vanilla

1. In a 2- to 3-quart pan, whisk syrup and cornstarch until smooth. Add blackberries and stir over medium-high heat until bubbling, 6 to 8 minutes. Place pan in a bowl of ice water and stir occasionally until sauce is cold, about 35 minutes.

2. Drop 1/4-cup spoonfuls of ice cream into crust. Drizzle 1 cup berry sauce on top. Flatten ice cream slightly with back of a large spoon so ice cream is fairly level in pan.

3. Freeze, uncovered, until firm to touch, at least 2 hours. If making ahead, wrap pie airtight and freeze up to 1 week, and chill remaining berry sauce airtight up to 1 week.

4. With a mixer, beat egg whites on high speed until soft peaks form. Thoroughly beat in marshmallow cream, a large spoonful at a time. Blend in vanilla.

5. Swirl meringue over frozen pie all the way to crust edge. Bake in a 450° oven until lightly browned, about 3 minutes. Cut into wedges; spoon reserved sauce on top.

Per serving: 430 cal., 3.5% (15 cal.) from fat; 6.1 g protein; 1.7 g fat (0 g sat.); 98 g carbo.; 224 mg sodium; 0 mg chol.

Vanilla-Brandy Ice Cream Pie

Prep time: About 10 minutes, plus about 2 hours for freezing, not including time to prepare crust

Makes: 8 servings

> 1 1/2 quarts nonfat or low-fat vanilla ice cream or frozen yogurt, softened
>
> 1/4 cup brandy
>
> Cookie crust (recipe at left), made with gingersnaps, frozen
>
> 1/4 cup coarsely ground gingersnaps
>
> 1 1/2 teaspoons minced crystallized ginger

1. Place ice cream in a bowl and stir in brandy. Spoon ice cream evenly into crust and swirl top. Combine gingersnaps and ginger and sprinkle on top of pie. Freeze pie, uncovered, until firm to touch, 2 to 2 1/2 hours. If making ahead, wrap airtight and freeze up to 1 week.

2. If the pie is frozen solid, let it stand at room temperature about 15 minutes before cutting.

Per serving: 309 cal., 7.1% (22 cal.) from fat; 5.2 g protein; 2.4 g fat (0.4 g sat.); 62 g carbo.; 251 mg sodium; 0 mg chol.

Apricot Swirl Ice Cream Pie

Prep and cook time: About 35 minutes, plus about 2 hours for freezing, not including time to prepare crust

Makes: 8 servings

> 3/4 pound (about 6) ripe apricots or peaches, pitted
>
> 3/4 cup sugar
>
> 1 tablespoon cornstarch
>
> 2 teaspoons lemon juice
>
> 3 3/4 cups vanilla nonfat or low-fat frozen yogurt or ice cream, softened
>
> Cookie crust (recipe at left), made with gingersnaps, frozen
>
> 1 tablespoon coarsely crushed gingersnap crumbs

1. Chop half of the apricots. In a blender, whirl remaining apricots and 2 tablespoons water to a smooth purée.

2. In a 1- to 2-quart pan over medium heat, bring sugar and the chopped and puréed apricots to a simmer. Stir apricot mixture often until chopped fruit is tender to bite, 3 to 5 minutes. Stir cornstarch and lemon juice until smooth, add to apricot mixture, and stir until bubbling. Place the pan containing the fruit sauce in a bowl of ice water until the sauce is cold, stirring occasionally, about 10 minutes.

3. In a bowl, stir ice cream to soften. Add cold apricot mixture and give a few broad stirs to swirl. Spoon ice cream mixture into cookie crust. Sprinkle center of pie with gingersnap crumbs. Freeze pie, uncovered, until firm to touch, at least 2 hours. If making ahead, wrap pie airtight and freeze up to 2 weeks.

4. If the pie is frozen solid, let it stand at room temperature about 15 minutes before cutting.

Per serving: 308 cal., 4.5% (14 cal.) from fat; 4.9 g protein; 1.6 g fat (0 g sat.); 68 g carbo.; 200 mg sodium; 0 mg chol. —E. J. ∎

ED CAREY

Grilled chicken
as you like it

**New techniques, great sauces, and fresh marinades
for the whole bird—or easy pieces**

T HE ASSIGNMENT? GRILLED CHICKEN. THE PROCESS? MORE THAN 80
pounds of chicken cooked in pursuit of our goal—*Sunset*'s ultimate
guide to foolproof grilled chicken. If your idea of making this summer classic is basting with bottled sauce, it's time for a wake-up
call. We've put several new spins on this much-loved food.

If you're interested in new grilling methods, try Grilled Whole Chicken
with Plum Sauce Glaze. If you're watching every gram of fat, we can help
with that, too. How about Grilled Chicken Salad with Raspberries?

No matter which recipe you choose—even one of your own—our food
safety tips and grilling chart will help you determine cooking times,
grilling methods, and doneness, for perfect results every time.

BY CHRISTINE WEBER HALE

Low-fat at its best

If your diet demands skinless chicken
breasts, and the adjectives tough, dry, and
tasteless spring to mind, get ready for a
surprise. This lean, versatile cut ranks
with the best when you know the cooking
secrets illustrated by the following two
recipes—quick cooking to seal in moist
juices, and bold seasonings to carry flavor.

Boneless, skinless breasts are pounded thin, rolled in a cornmeal-parmesan coating, and grilled, then topped with tomatoes and arugula. At left, glazed grilled breasts are served with mesclun, goat cheese, and berries.

Cornmeal-crusted Chicken

Prep and cook time: About 35 minutes
Makes: 6 servings

- 6 boneless, skinless chicken breast halves (about 2 lb. total)
- 1 1/4 pounds Roma tomatoes, cored and chopped
- 1 cup (about 1 1/2 oz.) finely slivered arugula
- 3 tablespoons capers
- 2 tablespoons lemon juice
- 1 tablespoon olive oil
- 1 large egg
- 3/4 cup yellow cornmeal
- 1/4 cup grated parmesan cheese
- 1/2 teaspoon black pepper
- 1/4 teaspoon cayenne
- Salt

1. Rinse chicken and pat dry. Place 1 chicken breast half between 2 sheets of waxed paper or plastic wrap on a sturdy cutting board. With a heavy mallet, pound chicken until it is 1/3 to 1/4 inch thick. Repeat with remaining chicken. (If making ahead, cover and chill up to 4 hours.)

2. Combine chopped tomatoes, arugula, capers, lemon juice, and olive oil; set aside at room temperature.

3. In a small bowl, beat the egg with 1 tablespoon water to blend. In another bowl, stir the cornmeal, parmesan cheese, black pepper, and cayenne to blend. Dip each chicken breast half in the egg mixture, turning to coat both sides, then in the

THE SKINNY ON SKINLESS

Skinless, boneless chicken breasts are one of the most popular forms of chicken eaten today. It's easy to see why. A 4-ounce skinless chicken breast has 130 calories and 68 milligrams of cholesterol, compared with 193 calories and 83 milligrams of cholesterol for a breast with the skin on. Besides the savings in calories, when you soak skinless chicken breasts in marinades, seasonings go right into the meat, boosting the flavor.

Because this cut is so lean, it can dry out very quickly on the grill. But with care and the following pointers, you can serve a succulent dish.

- **Don't overcook.** Watch carefully—cooking takes only 10 to 15 minutes. To check for doneness, cut in the thickest part; when meat has just turned from pink to white, it's done. And remember, chicken breasts continue to cook for the first few minutes off the grill.
- **Be sure the fire isn't too hot.** Coals or gas heat should be medium. A flame that's too hot will scorch the outside and draw out juices faster.
- **Baste with a thick sauce.** This can help seal in the juices and keep the chicken meat moist.
- **Oil grill well to prevent sticking.**

cornmeal-parmesan mixture, turning to cover completely.

4. Place the chicken on a well-oiled charcoal grill above a solid bed of medium coals (you can hold your hand at grill level only 4 to 5 seconds), or on a gas grill adjusted to medium heat. Cover gas grill. Cook chicken until undersides are browned, about 5 minutes. With a spatula, turn the chicken over and cook until browned and meat is no longer pink in center (cut to test), 5 to 6 minutes longer.

5. Arrange chicken on a serving platter or on individual plates; top with tomato mixture and add salt to taste.

Per serving: 298 cal., 20% (59 cal.) from fat; 40 g protein; 6.5 g fat (1.7 g sat.); 18 g carbo.; 293 mg sodium; 126 mg chol.

Grilled Chicken Salad with Raspberries

Prep and cook time: About 30 minutes, plus at least 10 minutes (or up to 2 hours) marinating time

Makes: 4 servings

- 1/2 cup raspberry or balsamic vinegar
- 1/4 cup seedless raspberry jam
- 1 1/4 teaspoons finely grated lemon peel
- 1 teaspoon sugar
- 4 boneless, skinless chicken breast halves (about 1 1/4 lb. total)
- 1/2 pound mesclun, rinsed and crisped
- 1 1/4 cups raspberries, rinsed and drained
- 4 ounces log-shaped fresh goat cheese, cut into 8 equal slices
- 8 to 12 chives (optional)
- Salt and pepper

1. Whisk together vinegar, jam, lemon peel, and sugar until jam is completely dissolved and smooth. Reserve half the mixture; pour remaining mixture into a bowl.

2. Rinse chicken and pat dry. Add chicken to vinegar mixture in bowl; turn to coat chicken evenly, then cover and chill at least 10 minutes or up to 2 hours.

3. Place chicken on a well-oiled barbecue grill 4 to 6 inches above a solid bed of medium coals (you can hold your hand at grill level only 4 to 5 seconds), or on a gas grill adjusted to medium heat. Brush chicken with some of the marinade. Cook (cover gas grill) until undersides are browned, about 6 minutes. Turn chicken over, brush with remaining marinade, and cook until other sides are browned and meat is no longer pink in thickest part (cut to test), 5 to 6 minutes longer. Watch chicken carefully during cooking.

4. While the chicken cooks, mix mesclun with reserved raspberry vinegar mixture. Divide lettuce among 4 dinner plates; sprinkle equally with raspberries. Top salads with grilled chicken, and garnish with goat cheese and chives. Season to taste with salt and pepper.

Per serving: 318 cal., 23% (73 cal.) from fat; 39 g protein; 8.1 g fat (4.6 g sat.); 22 g carbo.; 211 mg sodium; 95 mg chol.

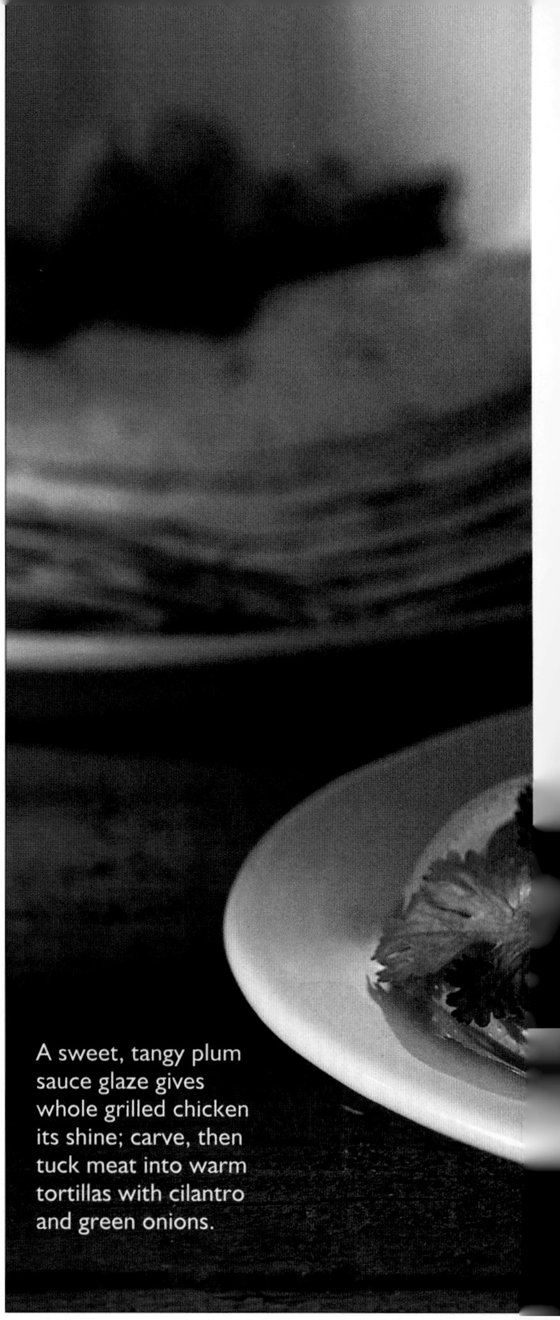

A sweet, tangy plum sauce glaze gives whole grilled chicken its shine; carve, then tuck meat into warm tortillas with cilantro and green onions.

ED CAREY

When the occasion calls for the whole bird

Fans of traditional roast chicken will love this new take on a Sunday-dinner favorite. Cooking the whole bird on the grill adds flavor you can't get from the oven—and eliminates the spattering and smoking that often occurs during roasting.

Grilled Whole Chicken with Plum Sauce Glaze

Prep and cook time: About 1 hour

Notes: For a festive variation on Peking duck, slice grilled chicken and wrap the meat in warm flour tortillas with green

onions, cilantro, and more plum sauce. The glaze works on chicken pieces as well as a whole bird. The sauce's high sugar content makes it burn rapidly, so don't brush it on the meat until the last few minutes of grilling.

Makes: 4 to 6 servings

- ¾ cup prepared Chinese plum sauce
- 3 tablespoons seasoned rice vinegar
- 3 tablespoons orange juice
- 1 tablespoon finely grated orange peel
- 1 chicken (5¾ to 6 lb.)
- 12 warm flour tortillas
- 4 green onions, ends trimmed, thinly slivered

  Cilantro sprigs

1. Mix together plum sauce, vinegar, orange juice, and orange peel; set aside. (If making ahead, cover and chill up to 1 day.)

2. In a charcoal barbecue with a lid, ignite 60 briquets. When coals are covered with gray ash (about 30 minutes), divide in half and bank them along each side of the fire-grate. Add 4 new coals to each side. Place a metal or foil drip pan between coals. Set a lightly oiled grill 4 to 6 inches above coals. (For gas barbecues, adjust heat for indirect cooking and turn heat to high. Cover and let barbecue heat 10 minutes.)

3. While grill is heating, rinse chicken and pat dry. Remove and discard any large lumps of fat. Place chicken on grill over drip pan. Cover barbecue (open vents for charcoal) and cook until chicken is well browned and a thermometer inserted in thickest part of thigh (touching the bone) reads 170°,

about 45 minutes; occasionally brush chicken with juices from inside the cavity.

4. Brush chicken all over with ½ cup of the plum sauce mixture. Cover and continue cooking until thermometer reads 180° and glaze is browned, about 10 minutes longer. Transfer chicken to a serving platter.

5. Lay tortillas on grill; turn several times, just until hot and soft, about 30 seconds (overheated tortillas get tough). Stack heated tortillas on a thick towel; wrap to keep warm. Serve with remaining sauce, green onions, and cilantro.

6. Carve chicken. To eat, cut tortillas in half and spread with a little plum sauce, then fill with chicken, green onion slivers, and cilantro sprigs to taste.

Per serving: 782 cal., 40% (315 cal.) from fat; 61 g protein; 35 g fat (9.2 g sat.); 53 g carbo.; 804 mg sodium; 171 mg chol.

The easiest party fare

Bold New Mexico chilies, shallots, and garlic flavor a delicious thick baste for grilled chicken halves.

Photo credit: JULIE DENNIS

For a cookout, chicken halves are a great cut to manage. Fewer pieces mean less work turning—and the halves cook at the same rate, unlike cut-up pieces, which need to be removed from the grill at different times. Have the butcher split the chickens. Or do it yourself by cutting through the breastbone, then the back, with a heavy knife or poultry shears.

Chicken Halves with New Mexico Chili Sauce

Prep and cook time: About 1 hour

Notes: You can make the sauce a day ahead and use it on any chicken cut.

Makes: 4 to 6 servings

- 2 ounces dried New Mexico chilies, stemmed and seeded
- 2 shallots (about ¼ lb. total), chopped
- 2 cloves garlic, chopped
- 1½ cups chicken broth
- 2 chickens (2¾ to 3 lb. each), split in half

1. Combine chilies, shallots, garlic, and broth in a 2- to 3-quart pan. Bring to a boil over high heat, then cover and simmer until chilies are softened, about 15 minutes. Let stand until slightly cooled, then whirl mixture in a blender until very smooth. (If making ahead, cover and chill up to 1 day.)

2. Rinse chickens; pat dry. Reserve ½ cup of the chili sauce. Brush chickens all over with some of the remaining sauce.

3. Ignite 60 charcoal briquets on firegrate in barbecue. When coals are spotted with gray ash, about 20 minutes, push equal portions to opposite sides of firegrate. Place a metal or foil drip pan between coals. Set a lightly oiled grill above coals. Or turn gas barbecue to high and heat, covered, 10 minutes, then adjust for indirect cooking. Place chickens, skin side down, in center of grill, not over coals or flame. Cover barbecue (open vents for charcoal) and cook, turning often, for 25 minutes; brush both sides of chicken halves with more chili sauce, and continue to cook, basting with remaining sauce, until chickens are well browned and meat at thigh bone is no longer pink (cut to test), 40 to 45 minutes total. Add 4 briquets to each charcoal pile every 30 minutes during cooking if necessary to maintain heat.

4. While chickens cook, warm reserved chili sauce in microwave or on the stove. Cut chicken halves into pieces, if desired; serve with warm chili sauce to add to taste.

Per serving: 467 cal., 50% (234 cal.) from fat; 51 g protein; 26 g fat (7.2 g sat.); 5.3 g carbo.; 172 mg sodium; 161 mg chol.

GREAT GRILLED CHICKEN—ANY TIME, ANY WAY

Use this chart for perfect barbecued chicken, no matter what cut you use. Make sure your fire isn't too hot. If it is, flare-ups will burn the outside of the chicken before the inside is cooked through. Keep a spray bottle of water nearby.

Most cuts are grilled over indirect heat. For indirect heat, divide the ignited coals in half, bank them along each side of the firegrate, then place the chicken on the grill between the piles of coals. The barbecue is always covered for indirect grilling (for the correct technique in setting up the barbecue, see step 3 of the recipe for Chicken Halves with New Mexico Chili Sauce, above). Grill boneless, skinless breasts and skewers of boneless chicken pieces over direct heat—a solid bed of coals (or, on gas barbecues, with all burners on).

TYPE OF CHICKEN	WEIGHT/THICKNESS	GRILL METHOD/TEMPERATURE	DONENESS TEST/COOKING TIME
Whole	4½ to 7 lb.	Indirect; hot, banked	Meat thermometer inserted in thigh reads 180°, 1¼ to 1¾ hours
Whole, butterflied	4 to 4½ lb.	Indirect; hot, banked	Meat thermometer inserted in thigh reads 180°, 40 to 45 min.
Halved or quartered	3 to 4 lb. total	Indirect; hot, banked	Meat near bone is no longer pink (cut to test), 40 to 50 min.
Cut up	3 to 4 lb. total	Indirect; hot, banked	Meat near bone is no longer pink (cut to test); dark meat 35 to 40 min., white meat 15 to 20 min.
Breast halves (bone in)	½ to ¾ lb. each	Indirect; hot, banked	Meat near bone is no longer pink (cut to test), about 20 min.
Breast halves (boneless, skinless)	¼ to ½ lb. each	Direct; medium	Meat is no longer pink (cut to test), 10 to 15 min.
Whole legs, thighs attached	8 to 10 oz. each	Indirect; hot, banked	Meat near bone is no longer pink (cut to test), 35 to 45 min.
Drumsticks or thighs	4 to 6 oz. each	Indirect; hot, banked	Meat near bone is no longer pink (cut to test), about 35 min.
Wings	3 to 4 oz.	Indirect; hot, banked	Meat near bone is no longer pink (cut to test), about 30 min.
Poussins/Cornish hens butterflied	1 to 1½ lb. each	Indirect; hot, banked	Meat near bone is no longer pink (cut to test), 30 to 40 min.
whole (intact)	1 to 1½ lb.	Indirect; hot, banked	Meat near bone is no longer pink (cut to test), 45 to 60 min.
Skewers (boneless pieces)	1-inch-thick pieces	Direct; medium	Meat in center is no longer pink (cut to test), 10 to 15 min.

Tradition with a twist: a homestyle, stick-to-your-fingers sauce flavored with bourbon and molasses cloaks butterflied poussins.

When ordinary chicken won't do

Poussins, basically young chickens weighing about 1 pound each, are prized for their tender meat. Order them from your butcher, or substitute similar-tasting Cornish hens. When they are butterflied (split and flattened), cooking time is decreased and the meat cooks evenly. Parallel skewers inserted along each side help turn the birds easily during cooking.

Butterflied Poussins with Bourbon-Molasses Sauce

Prep and cook time: About 1 hour for poussins or Cornish hens, 1 hour and 15 minutes for a chicken

Notes: If you can't find poussins or Cornish hens, 1 whole broiler-fryer chicken will work just as well. Butterfly and skewer it as directed for poussins, then cut into serving pieces after grilling. You can make the sauce up to 3 days ahead; use it on any chicken cut.

Makes: 4 to 6 servings

2 cloves garlic, minced
1 onion (about 1/2 lb.), minced
1 tablespoon salad oil
1 cup catsup
1/2 cup reduced-sodium chicken broth
1/2 cup bourbon
1/4 cup molasses
1/4 cup firmly packed brown sugar
1 teaspoon dry mustard
1/2 teaspoon ground ginger
1/4 teaspoon cayenne
4 poussins or Cornish hens (about 1 lb. each), or 1 whole chicken (4 to 4 1/2 lb.)

1. In a 4- to 5-quart pan, combine garlic, onion, and oil. Stir often over medium-high heat until lightly browned, about 10 minutes.

2. Add catsup, broth, bourbon, molasses, brown sugar, mustard, ginger, and cayenne; mix well. Bring to a boil; simmer, stirring often, until reduced to 1 1/3 cups, 20 minutes. (If making ahead, cool, cover, and chill up to 3 days.)

3. Rinse poussins and pat dry. With poultry shears or a knife, split each lengthwise through breastbone. Pull birds open. Place skin side up on a flat surface; press firmly, cracking bones slightly until birds lie flat.

4. Thread on sturdy 10- to 12-inch metal skewers (15- to 20-inch skewers for a whole chicken), forcing one skewer through thigh—perpendicular to bone and just above drumstick—into the breast and out through middle joint of wing in extended position. Repeat on other side of bird.

5. Ignite 60 charcoal briquets on firegrate in barbecue. When coals are spotted with gray ash, in about 20 minutes, push equal portions to opposite sides of firegrate. Place a metal or foil drip pan between coals. Or turn gas grill to high and heat, covered, 10 minutes, then adjust for indirect cooking. Place poussins, skin down, in center of lightly oiled grill, not over coals or flame. Cover barbecue (open vents for charcoal); cook, turning occasionally, until both sides are lightly browned, about 15 minutes. Brush birds generously with sauce; continue cooking, turning and basting occasionally with more sauce, until meat near thighbone is no longer pink (cut to test), about 20 minutes longer for poussins, 25 for Cornish hens, 25 to 30 for chicken.

6. Remove from skewers; cut into pieces.

Per serving: 470 cal., 40% (189 cal.) from fat; 38 g protein; 21 g fat (5.4 g sat.); 33 g carbo.; 640 mg sodium; 117 mg chol.

Great marinades

Spicy Thai Marinade

Prep time: About 15 minutes
Notes: Minced green onion and cilantro are the finishing touches; sprinkle them over the chicken just before serving.
Makes: Enough for 4 pounds of chicken, about 6 servings

- ¼ cup reduced-sodium soy sauce
- ¼ cup Asian fish sauce (*nam pla* or *nuoc mam*) or oyster sauce
- 1 tablespoon firmly packed brown sugar
- 1 tablespoon *each* minced garlic and minced fresh ginger
- ½ to 1 teaspoon Asian red chili paste
- 2 tablespoons *each* minced green onion and minced cilantro

1. In a large bowl or 2-gallon zip-lock plastic bag, mix together soy, fish sauce, sugar, garlic, ginger, and chili paste until well blended. Add chicken, cover or close tightly, and chill at least 30 minutes or up to 1 day; stir or turn occasionally to coat chicken evenly with marinade.

2. Drain chicken and discard marinade. Grill over indirect heat as directed in step 3 of recipe for Chicken Halves with New Mexico Chili Sauce on page 154. Sprinkle cooked chicken with minced green onion and cilantro.

Per serving: 44 cal., 25% (11 cal.) from fat; 2.4 g protein; 1.2 g fat (0.3 g sat.); 6.1 g carbo.; 810 mg sodium; 0 mg chol.

White Wine–Herb Marinade with Tomatoes and Feta

Prep time: About 15 minutes
Notes: Sprinkle the chopped tomatoes and crumbled cheese over the cooked chicken just before serving.
Makes: Enough for 4 pounds of chicken, about 6 servings

- 1 cup dry white wine
- ½ cup lemon juice
- 2 cloves garlic, minced
- 2 tablespoons minced fresh oregano
- 1 tablespoon minced fresh thyme
- 3 ounces crumbled feta cheese
- 2 firm-ripe Roma tomatoes (½ lb. total), seeded and finely chopped

CURTIS ANDERSON

1. In a large bowl or 2-gallon zip-lock plastic bag, mix together wine, lemon juice, garlic, oregano, and thyme. Add chicken, cover or close tightly, and chill at least 30 minutes or up to 1 day; stir or turn occasionally to coat chicken evenly with marinade.

2. Drain chicken and discard marinade. Grill chicken over indirect heat as directed in step 3 of recipe for Chicken Halves with New Mexico Chili Sauce on page 154. Sprinkle cooked chicken with feta and tomatoes.

Per serving: 79 cal., 37% (29 cal.) from fat; 2.5 g protein; 3.2 g fat (2.2 g sat.); 4.5 g carbo.; 168 mg sodium; 13 mg chol.

Rosemary, Lemon, and Mustard Marinade

Prep time: About 10 minutes
Notes: Garnish cooked chicken with fresh rosemary sprigs.
Makes: Enough for 4 pounds of chicken, about 6 servings

- ½ cup lemon juice
- 3 tablespoons Dijon mustard
- 2 tablespoons honey
- 1 tablespoon minced fresh rosemary
- Fresh rosemary sprigs (optional)

1. In a deep bowl or 2-gallon zip-lock plastic bag, mix together lemon juice, mustard, honey, and minced rosemary. Add chicken and stir or turn to coat. Cover or close tightly, and chill at least 30 minutes or up to 1 day; stir or turn occasionally to coat chicken evenly with marinade.

2. Drain chicken and discard remaining marinade. Grill chicken over indirect heat as directed in step 3 of recipe for Chicken Halves with New Mexico Chili Sauce on page 154.

Per serving: 34 cal., 2.6% (0.9 cal.) from fat; 0.1 g protein; 0.1 g fat (0 g sat.); 7.2 g carbo.; 185 mg sodium; 0 mg chol. ∎

PLAYING IT SAFE

Poultry, like all low-acid foods, is often a carrier of bacteria, such as the now well-known *Salmonella*. If we're healthy, we can fight off this harmful, widely present microorganism with no problem. However, infants, children, and those with compromised immune systems can't, and are susceptible to the bacteria's ill effects. And, with the right conditions—namely a warm, moist, acid-free environment—and enough time, *Salmonella* can multiply rapidly, increasing the risk that even a healthy person might get sick if he or she consumes a large amount of the bacteria.

Luckily, it's easy to avoid problems from *Salmonella* poisoning with just a few precautions:

- Keep raw chicken from contact with other foods; wash cutting boards and knives used to prepare raw chicken before using them again.
- Cook chicken thoroughly. *Salmonella* begins to die at 140° and is killed rapidly at 160°; the normal cooking temperature for chicken is 180° to 185°.
- Eat cooked chicken right away, and promptly refrigerate leftovers; don't let cooked chicken sit at room temperature for more than 2 hours.
- Never use a marinade as a sauce for the cooked chicken unless you first bring it to a boil. Never baste chicken with an unboiled marinade if the meat will be done in less than 10 minutes.
- Never thaw chicken on the counter at room temperature. Let it thaw overnight in the refrigerator. Or, if you're in a hurry, place the chicken in a plastic bag, then submerge the bag in a bowl of cold water. Change the water often so that it stays cold, and refrigerate chicken as soon as it is thawed.

By Linda Lau Anusasananan

When you serve the perfect berry pie, the juicy filling holds its shape and the bottom crust is browned.

NORMAN A. PLATE

Why do fruit pies get soggy?
What thickener is best?

WARM, FRESH-BAKED FRUIT pie—it's the epitome of a simple, old-fashioned dessert. It's also very easy to make when you start with prepared pastry. But two stumbling blocks crop up regularly: getting the crust, especially the bottom one, brown and crisp instead of doughy or scorched, and getting the filling just thick enough to softly hold its shape when cut.

"Why does the bottom crust of my fruit pie come out soggy?"
—JULIE DUKELOW
Fullerton, California

There are two main reasons: the bottom crust is not baked, and/or the fruit filling hasn't cooked enough. And there's more than one solution.

Check position in oven. Put fruit pies on an oven rack placed at lowest position so bottom crust gets the most heat. Higher in the oven, the top crust browns before the bottom one can cook—in any pie.

Check oven temperature. Crusts on pies baked at a high temperature, such as 425° or 450°, often get sufficiently browned before fillings are hot enough

for the thickener to work. If the thickener hasn't bound the fruit juice, the filling soaks into the crust—even if the crust is baked. If the crust (or other topping, such as streusel) gets brown before the filling bubbles, lightly drape the browned area with foil to prevent scorching. Then, next time, bake the pie at a lower temperature.

Mix thickeners first with sugar and spices (so they can't lump and thicken inefficiently), then mix with fruit.

Cook until thickeners can work. Typical thickeners for fruit pies are all-purpose flour, arrowroot, quick-cooking tapioca, cornstarch, potato starch, and rice starch. The starch in these thickeners doesn't kick into action until heated in liquid to 190° to 195°. Then the starch granules can absorb liquid and begin to swell. When the temperature is held for three to five minutes, the starch granules

begin to leak starch molecules, which form a gel that traps more of the pie liquid, thickening it. At this point, the starch has reached its maximum thickening power—even though the mixture is juicy. You can see the signs: juices in the center of the pie are bubbling, and a quick-read thermometer inserted in this spot registers 190° to 195°. If cooked much more, the gel breaks and the trapped juices break free and thin down the filling.

To reach maximum thickening, the pie has to cool to room temperature. Warm, freshly baked pie may be wonderful, but it's apt to be runny. However, if you rewarm the pie, the filling doesn't thin.

Which thickener and how much?
The amount of thickener needed varies with the kind of fruit (part of the liquid comes from sugar that melts). For 6 cups of moderately juicy cherries or apples, use 2 to 2½ tablespoons quick-cooking tapioca, cornstarch, arrowroot, potato starch, or rice starch. For 6 cups of juicy apricots, peaches, or berries, use 3½ to 4 tablespoons of one of these thickeners. Very juicy plums may need 4½ to 5 tablespoons thickener for 6 cups fruit.

All-purpose flour is less efficient, and you need to use twice as much of it in place of the other thickeners.

Which thickener works best?
Quick-cooking tapioca provides the best and most consistent results. Unlike other thickeners, tapioca soaks up juices upon contact, even when cold, so let filling mixture stand at least 15 minutes before putting into the crust. Also, tapioca contains a high percentage of waxy starch molecules that are able to hold, proportionately, more liquid than the other starches can without getting rigid.

Why is my raspberry pie filling sometimes cloudy and pasty?
It's the thickener. Pure starches—arrowroot, cornstarch, potato starch, rice starch, and quick-cooking tapioca—turn clear when cooked. All-purpose flour doesn't. It contains other components, including protein, that give transparent fruit juices a cloudy, pasty look. ∎

MORE QUESTIONS
We would like to know what kitchen mysteries you're curious about. Send your questions to Why?, Sunset Magazine, 80 Willow Rd., Menlo Park, CA 94025; send e-mail (including full name and street address) to why@sunsetpub.com. With the help of George K. York, extension food technologist at UC Davis, Sunset food editors will try to find solutions, then answer questions in the magazine.

Sunset's Kitchen Cabinet

Readers' family favorites tested in our kitchens

By Betsy Reynolds Bateson

DICK COLE

Fresh Pear Cake

Elsa Kleinman, Topanga, California

Whenever Elsa Kleinman has three ripe pears, she makes her mother's Fresh Pear Cake. Kleinman grew up in Oregon's Rogue River Valley, where she enjoyed plenty of pears, especially in her mother's cake. Her mother always made two cakes at a time, one to eat right away and one for the next day. The cake is perfect for breakfast or dessert.

Prep and cook time: About 1 1/4 hours
Makes: 8 servings

About 2 tablespoons butter
About 1 1/2 cups all-purpose flour
3   firm, ripe (about 1 1/2 lb. total) Bartlett pears
2   large eggs

1   cup granulated sugar
1/2   cup milk
1/8   teaspoon salt
Powdered sugar

1. Lightly butter and flour a 9-inch round pan or baking dish; set aside.

2. Peel, core, and slice pears; set aside.

3. With an electric mixer, blend eggs, granulated sugar, milk, and salt. Add 1 1/2 cups flour; continue to mix until well combined. Gently fold half the pears into batter. Spoon into prepared pan; smooth surface flat. Fan remaining pears over top of batter; dot top with 2 tablespoons butter.

4. Bake in a 350° oven on bottom rack until cake is golden brown, about 55 minutes. Cool. Sprinkle with powdered sugar, if desired, and serve. Or cover airtight and hold until next day.

Per serving: 289 cal., 17% (50 cal.) from fat; 4.9 g protein; 5.6 g fat (2.8 g sat.); 56 g carbo.; 93 mg sodium; 64 mg chol.

Linguine with Chicken Breasts in Orange Sauce

Jack W. Stearns, La Crescenta, California

Jack Stearns has become an expert at boning chicken breasts, which he cooks in many different ways. Stearns finds that a little orange liqueur imparts a wonderful flavor to this dish, which has a rich tomato sauce with Italian seasonings ("marjoram really did the trick") and black olives.

Prep and cook time: About 40 minutes
Makes: 8 servings

1   tablespoon olive or salad oil
About 2 pounds boneless, skinless chicken breasts (about 3 whole), cut into 2-inch chunks
2   teaspoons minced garlic

3   cans (8 oz. each) tomato sauce
1   cup dry white wine
1/3   cup orange-flavor liqueur or 1 tablespoon thawed frozen orange juice concentrate
2   tablespoons grated orange peel (about 2 oranges)
2   teaspoons dried basil leaves
1   teaspoon *each* dried oregano and dried marjoram leaves
1   can (2 1/4 oz.) sliced ripe olives, drained
Salt and pepper
1   pound dried linguine
Orange segments
Freshly grated parmesan cheese

1. Bring 4 to 5 quarts water to a boil for pasta.

2. Meanwhile, heat 1 1/2 teaspoons oil in a 5- to 6-quart pan over high heat. Add half the chicken and half the garlic and stir frequently until meat is lightly browned but still pink in the center (cut to test), about 4 minutes. Spoon chicken into a bowl. Heat remaining oil in pan and cook remaining chicken and garlic. Return cooked chicken and juices to pan.

3. Add tomato sauce, wine, orange-flavor liqueur, orange peel, basil, oregano, marjoram, and sliced olives. Bring to a boil; reduce heat, cover, and cook until chicken is no longer pink in thickest part (cut to test) and flavors have blended, about 12 minutes. Add salt and pepper to taste.

4. At the same time, cook linguine in boiling water just until tender to bite, about 8 minutes. Drain well and pour into a wide bowl. Pour chicken sauce onto pasta, mix to blend, then garnish with orange segments and pass cheese to spoon over individual portions.

Per serving: 437 cal., 10% (45 cal.) from fat; 35 g protein; 5 g fat (0.8 g sat.); 53 g carbo.; 664 mg sodium; 66 mg chol.

Chili Beef Salad

Bonnie Wittekind, Higley, Arizona

With four children—three under age 6—Bonnie Wittekind needs fast weekday meals. A desire for low-calorie dishes has led her to develop many salads, this one with Thai seasonings. Wittekind uses leftover meat for the recipe, or throws a steak on the gas grill for quick cooking. For a spicier rendition, use jalapeño-seasoned beans.

Prep and cook time: About 30 minutes
Makes: 6 servings

- 1 tablespoon salad oil
- 2 to 3 teaspoons chili powder
- 2 cups thinly sliced grilled or broiled beef steak (about ¾ lb. cooked)
- 1 can (15 oz.) black-eyed peas, drained and rinsed
- 2 green onions, ends trimmed and thinly sliced
- 1 red bell pepper (about 8 oz.), stemmed, cored, and cut into thin strips
- 1 can (4 oz.) diced green chilies
- 1 teaspoon grated lime peel
- 2 tablespoons *each* lime juice and chopped fresh cilantro
  Salt and pepper
  About 12 large leaves romaine or iceberg lettuce

1. In an 8- to 10-inch frying pan over medium heat, cook oil and chili powder, stirring, until chili powder is reddish brown, about 1½ minutes.

2. Scrape chili powder and oil into a bowl containing the meat slices; mix to coat. Stir in peas, onions, bell pepper, green chilies, lime peel and juice, cilantro, and salt and pepper to taste.

3. Arrange lettuce leaves on a serving platter. Mound salad in center. To eat, spoon salad into leaves and fold like a burrito.

Per serving: 231 cal., 39% (90 cal.) from fat; 20 g protein; 10 g fat (3.4 g sat.); 15 g carbo.; 389 mg sodium; 39 mg chol.

Edinburgh Eggs Florentine

Graham Lewis, Ashland, Oregon

Graham Lewis was encouraged to submit this recipe by guests who enjoyed it when he owned the Edinburgh Lodge in Ashland. The recipe is easy to expand or reduce. You can use ramekins or any ovenproof dishes about 3 inches wide.

Prep and cook time: About 30 minutes
Makes: 6 servings

- ½ cup reduced-fat mayonnaise
- ⅛ teaspoon pepper
- ⅛ teaspoon dried summer savory or dried oregano leaves
- 1 teaspoon Worcestershire
- ½ cup nonfat milk
- 3 tablespoons thinly sliced green onions, including green tops
- 1¼ cups (5 oz.) shredded sharp cheddar cheese
- 1 package (10 oz.) frozen chopped spinach, thawed and well drained
- 6 large eggs
  Ground nutmeg

1. Lightly oil 6 shallow (about ¾-cup size) ramekins.

2. In a 1½- to 2-quart pan, blend mayonnaise, pepper, savory, Worcestershire, and milk until smooth. Stir in green onions and 1 cup cheese.

Stir over medium heat until cheese melts.

3. Spoon 1 tablespoon sauce into each ramekin; top with an equal portion of the spinach. With the back of a spoon, make an impression large enough to hold 1 egg; break an egg into each spinach cup. Spoon remaining sauce equally over eggs. Sprinkle with remaining cheese; dust lightly with nutmeg.

4. Set ramekins in a large rimmed baking pan. Bake in a 400° oven just until eggs are as firm as you like: allow about 10 minutes for soft yolks, about 15 minutes for firm.

Per serving: 254 cal., 64% (162 cal.) from fat; 14 g protein; 18 g fat (7.4 g sat.); 8.2 g carbo.; 425 mg sodium; 238 mg chol.

Party Polenta

Jan Sousa, Mt. Shasta, California

Jan Sousa created this recipe last summer when she needed a dish that would go well with barbecued salmon for an outdoor party at the base of Mount Shasta. Because corn was plentiful and her garden contained ingredients for fresh salsa, Party Polenta was her solution. It's easy to make and looks great on a large platter, and Sousa says everyone loves it. We suggest using purchased cooked polenta as a shortcut.

Prep and cook time: About 50 minutes
Makes: 6 servings

- 6 to 8 ears (about 3 lb.) white corn on the cob
- 4 strips bacon, chopped
- 1 green bell pepper (about 6 oz.), stemmed, cored, and chopped
- ¼ cup chopped onion
- ¼ to ½ teaspoon hot chili flakes
- ⅓ cup chicken broth or water
- 1 roll (1 lb.) purchased cooked polenta
  About 1 cup shredded cheddar cheese
  Fresh cilantro or parsley sprigs
  About 1 cup purchased fresh salsa

1. Remove corn husks and silk, and discard. Cut kernels from ears into a bowl; set aside.

2. In a 10- to 12-inch frying pan over medium-high heat, cook bacon until golden brown, about 4 minutes. Discard all but 1 tablespoon of fat in pan. Add bell pepper, onion, and hot chili flakes; cook, stirring, until vegetables are limp, about 4 minutes. Add corn with any corn juices, and broth; cook until kernels are just tender, about 5 minutes; set aside.

3. Cut polenta into ½-inch-thick slices (about 12). Place slices in single layer on a platter;

heat in a microwave oven at full power (100 percent) until hot, 2 to 4 minutes.

4. Spoon cooked corn mixture onto a deep, ovenproof platter. Top with hot polenta slices and sprinkle cheese over all. Place dish under broiler to melt cheese, 1 to 2 minutes. Serve hot. Garnish with cilantro sprigs and offer salsa to add as desired.

Per serving: 269 cal., 37% (99 cal.) from fat; 10 g protein; 11 g fat (5.4 g sat.); 34 g carbo.; 895 mg sodium; 25 mg chol.

---

*S*hare a recipe you've created or adapted—a family favorite, travel discovery, or time-saver—including the story behind the recipe. You'll receive a "Great Cook" certificate and $50 for each recipe published. Send to *Sunset Magazine*, 80 Willow Rd., Menlo Park, CA 94025, or send e-mail (including full name, street address, and phone number) to recipes@sunsetpub.com.

FOOD
Guide

BY JERRY ANNE DI VECCHIO

A TASTE OF THE WEST: Tomatillos make the difference

A tomatillo-and-cilantro relish sets this burger apart from the masses.

ROBERT OLDING

At least once a month, our household—including any guests—walks down to the Balboa Cafe for the best burger in San Francisco. The meat, cooked exactly to order, goes onto crusty bread or a soft bun. Although other accoutrements are available, I ask only for mild onions and lettuce. On delivery, I add Dijon mustard and Pickapeppa sauce—it has the tang of tamarinds.

With such perfection only steps away, I've been forced to add special touches to home-cooked hamburgers. And I've borrowed Balboa's straightforward approach to do so. The meat is unseasoned, the bread is crusty, and the extras are lively and fresh. My current favorite burger topping is a raw relish of tart tomatillos and onions in a citrus dressing.

And as a bread fancier, I make use of different kinds. The only trick is to shape the meat to the bread.

The House Burger

Prep and cook time: 20 to 25 minutes

Notes: If the relish stands more than a couple of hours, the tomatillos lose their fresh taste. To nest meat securely in loaf, pull out enough soft bread to make a long hollow that is about 1/2 inch deep.

Makes: 6 servings

> About 1/4 pound tomatillos
>
> 1 mild red onion (8 to 10 oz.), thinly sliced
>
> 3/4 cup orange juice
>
> 2/3 cup lime juice
>
> 1 teaspoon hot chili flakes
>
> 1 cup chopped fresh cilantro leaves
>
> About 1/4 teaspoon salt
>
> 2 pounds ground very lean beef
>
> 1 long loaf (1 lb.) sourdough or French bread, cut in half horizontally
>
> Lettuce leaves
>
> Dijon mustard
>
> Pepper

1. Pull off and discard husks from tomatillos. Rinse and thinly slice tomatillos.

2. In a bowl, mix tomatillo slices, onion slices, orange and lime juices, chili, cilantro, and 1/4 teaspoon salt. Set aside.

3. Shape ground beef into a rectangle as long as the loaf of bread and slightly wider. Cut meat crosswise into 6 equal patties.

4. Cook patties on a grill 4 to 6 inches above a solid bed of hot coals or over high heat on a gas grill (you can hold your hand at grill level only 2 to 3 seconds). Close lid on gas grill. Turn meat once, as it browns. Allow 6 to 8 minutes total for rare, 12 to 14 minutes total for well done.

5. When meat is almost done, toast cut sides of bread on grill, 1 to 2 minutes. Set patties onto the toasted loaf bottom. Press top half of bread gently down onto meat.

6. To divide bread into 6 portions, cut across loaf in between the patties. Drain juice from tomatillo relish and save, then spoon relish onto meat, adding lettuce, mustard, salt and pepper, and reserved tomatillo relish juice to taste.

Per serving: 508 cal., 32% (162 cal.) from fat; 39 g protein; 18 g fat (6.5 g sat.); 49 g carbo.; 669 mg sodium; 94 mg chol.

SEASONAL NOTE

The Midas touch for a bloody Mary

Once hard to find, yellow tomatoes—with hues from rich gold to pale sunlight—now seem to be in the market almost year-round. But they're still best this time of year.

Certainly, one of the easiest ways to serve this pretty tomato is sliced, on a platter. More exciting—combine yellow with red or even green or white tomato slices. Or, for a colorful change, make pasta sauce with yellow tomatoes.

But the most unexpected use of yellow tomatoes may be in cocktails. Serve blond Marys without identifying tomato as their base and note the puzzled expressions that appear as people take their first sip. Palates primed by the golden color are often prepared for orange, not tomato, juice. For a nonalcoholic version, use orange juice instead of the tequila.

Blond Marys for two. In a blender, smoothly purée 1 cored and chopped ripe **yellow tomato** (about 1/2 lb.) with 2 teaspoons chopped **fresh ginger,** 2 tablespoons **lime juice,** and 1 cup small **ice cubes.**

Add 4 tablespoons **tequila** and 2 tablespoons **fresh cilantro,** then whirl just until cilantro is coarsely chopped

For a twist on the bloody Mary, use yellow tomatoes.

(puréed, it turns the mixture green). Pour into two **salt**-rimmed glasses.

Per serving: 73 cal., 4.9% (3.6 cal.) from fat; 1.2 g protein; 0.4 g fat (0.1 g sat.); 7.3 g carbo.; 15 mg sodium; 0 mg chol.

GREAT INGREDIENT

What is hoisin?

Think of salty catsup, and hoisin sauce falls into perspective. Like catsup, hoisin sauce goes with many foods, but soybeans, not tomatoes, form its base. However, hoisin is also tangy-sweet, contains some chilies and garlic, and resonates with star anise. Small dishes of hoisin sauce are often served with mu shu pork, Peking duck, and other full-flavor meat dishes.

You can find hoisin sauce in almost every food market, either with condiments or Asian ingredients. It comes in jars and cans, and once open, it keeps for months in the refrigerator. However, you need to transfer canned sauce to glass or plastic and keep tightly covered.

Among hoisin's many uses:
• Brush on poultry or meat, especially pork, as it grills.
• Use instead of catsup on hamburgers and sausages.
• Put small amounts of hoisin sauce and

chopped green onions into an omelet.
• Substitute hoisin for vinegar in an oil-and-vinegar salad dressing, then taste and add enough vinegar to give the mixture a sharp edge. This dressing clings well to leafy greens.
• Thin hoisin sauce with enough orange juice to make a slightly clingy dressing to pour over sliced oranges, pineapple, ripe peaches, or ripe plums.
• Use hoisin sauce as a dip for cucumber sticks, tiny carrots, green bell pepper strips, even appetizer-size meatballs.
• Blend a little hoisin sauce into stir-fry sauces.

At a Northern Chinese Islamic restaurant in Los Angeles, I came across this exceptionally simple stir-fried lamb served in tortilla-like flour pancakes.

Hoisin-Honey Lamb Tacos

Prep and cook time: 15 to 20 minutes

Notes: To get a head start, cut, cover, and chill the meat up to 1 day.

Makes: 4 servings

1 pound fat-trimmed, boned lamb
from the leg (a chunk or steaks)

6 tablespoons hoisin sauce

2 tablespoons honey

12 green onions, ends trimmed

1 teaspoon salad oil

8 flour tortillas (8 in. wide), heated

2 to 3 tablespoons finely slivered
fresh ginger

1 cup cilantro leaves, rinsed and
drained

1. Cut meat across the grain into ⅛-inch slices. Cut slices lengthwise into ½-inch pieces. Mix with hoisin sauce and honey.

2. Cut onions into 2-inch lengths.

3. Place a wok (about 14 in.) or 12-inch frying pan over high heat. When hot, add oil, then onions. Stir-fry just until onions are tinged with brown, about 2 minutes. With a slotted spoon, transfer onions to a bowl.

4. Pour meat mixture into hot pan and stir-fry until lamb is no longer pink, about 2 minutes; scrape off a little sauce to check. With a slotted spoon, lift out meat, shaking to release sauce. Put meat with onions.

5. Boil sauce, stirring often, until reduced to about ⅓ cup, about 1 minute. Return meat and onion mixture to pan, stir to heat, and pour into a serving bowl.

6. Spoon meat onto tortillas, add ginger and cilantro, and roll up to eat.

Per serving: 475 cal., 21% (99 cal.) from fat; 30 g protein; 11 g fat (2.7 g sat.); 60 g carbo.; 728 mg sodium; 73 mg chol.

BACK TO BASICS

Keeping greens green for salad

Summer salads that contain attractive cooked green vegetables demand attention at two stages. First, when the green vegetables are cooked, and second, when the salad is dressed.

Blanching and chilling are the first important steps. Just dump green vegetables into a generous amount of rapidly boiling water. It's important that they cook fast, so keep the heat on high. As soon as the texture is perfect (I go for tender-crisp, and take a bite or make a cut to test), the color is at its best. Quickly drain the vegetables and immerse in ice water to stop cooking and halt color change. When the vegetables are cold, drain and use, or chill airtight for as long as one day. However, I find vegetables more flavorful at room temperature, so I set them out for a while before serving.

After I've trapped the green color, I refuse to lose it by letting the vegetables stand in dressings that contain acid (lemon and other citrus juices, vinegar, or wine) for more than a few minutes. Acid affects green vegetables so quickly that you can often see their color fade to yellow or khaki.

Some food experts feel that cooked vegetables benefit from more time in dressing. I find that green vegetables don't soak up much seasoning, but less color-sensitive vegetables do, so my compromise is to marinate nongreens (such as the potatoes in the salad below) and add the greens last.

Green Bean and Curried Potato Salad

Prep and cook time: 45 to 50 minutes
Makes: 6 servings

1. Scrub 18 **thin-skinned potatoes** (about 1 in. wide). Cook in simmering water until tender when pierced, about 20 minutes. Drain potatoes, cut them in half, and place in a bowl.

2. Meanwhile, in a pan or microwave oven, heat 1 tablespoon **curry powder** and 1 teaspoon **cumin seed** in 1 tablespoon **salad oil** just until curry smells slightly toasted. Add ½ cup **chicken broth** and ⅓ cup **rice vinegar**.

3. Mix seasonings with potatoes, add **salt** and **pepper** to taste, and let stand at least 10 minutes or up to 4 hours, mixing occasionally.

4. Pinch stem ends from ¾ pound thin **green beans.** Cook until tender-crisp when pierced, drain, chill in ice water, and drain again. Use, or cover and chill up to 1 day.

5. Finely sliver ¼ cup **fresh mint** and 2 tablespoons **fresh dill.** Mix with potatoes and spoon mixture onto beans.

Per serving: 105 cal., 24% (25 cal.) from fat; 2.7 g protein; 2.8 g fat (0.3 g sat.); 19 g carbo.; 15 mg sodium; 0 mg chol.

BOB THOMPSON ON WINE:

Easygoing reds from the Rhône

Drinking one of the lighthearted red wines of Europe right where it is made always adds an extra bit of magic. Often enough, travelers find out that being there is the whole charm—the wine is one of the kind that "doesn't travel well." Fact is, only a few liltingly light red wines can carry a large part of their magic with them when they leave home.

One such is Côtes du Rhône. To be sure, it is at its best when you have a Roman amphitheater within walking distance, or a long view from your hill to a bigger hill on the other side of the Rhône, and you can smell rosemary and olive in the cooling evening air. But it does travel.

A wine called Côtes du Rhône can come from grapes grown in or around any—or all—of 40 villages surrounding the far more prestigious Châteauneuf-du-Pape. Côtes du Rhône-Villages is a slightly more specific appellation of origin. Only the best 17 of those 40 villages qualify to grow it. In both cases, the dominant grape will be Grenache, plus snippets and bits of other, mostly obscure, grape varieties.

Don't worry about the wobbly pedigree. A proper Côtes du Rhône tastes so good with olives, peppers, and all the other Mediterranean flavors that it makes you believe Galileo's line about wine being sunlight held together by water. That's the magic part.

Two general bits of guidance: First, Côtes du Rhône-Villages is likely to be slightly firmer with tannins, slightly winier in flavor, than plain Côtes du Rhône. Second, huge amounts of Côtes du Rhône are bottled by shippers in Burgundy. Smaller lots come from winemakers in the Rhône. Typically, the Burgundian shippers take a lighter approach than the locals do.

So, if lightsome is what you are after, look for a Côtes du Rhône from an address in Burgundy. If you want some oomph, stick with a Côtes du Rhône-Villages from a winery in the Rhône itself. A few candidates, mostly priced in the $7 to $10 range:

From Burgundy shippers: Bouchard Père et Fils, especially its Côtes du Rhône-Villages; Antonin Rodet's Domaine Notre-Dame des Paillères; A. Bichot's Château d'Orsan; and Vaucher (owned by Laboure-Roi).

From export-minded Rhône Valley wineries: E. Guigal, "La Vieille Ferme" from Château de Beaucastel, and, a personal favorite, "Parallèle 45" by Paul Jaboulet. Hard to find but possible: Domaine Fabre by Beaudet, Cellier de Jolibois, and Domaine des Audrans. The really tiny producers require a trip to the source, which is not a bad idea at all. ∎

By Elaine Johnson

DEBORAH DENKER

Yes, you can have your pie and eat it too

I WASN'T SURE IT WAS A GOOD IDEA. A low-fat fruit pie? Could it possibly be as much of a treat as regular pie? The filling wouldn't be a problem, because it doesn't usually contain fat anyway. But how would the crust work out when I reduced a key component? Despite these reservations, I started experimenting.

It turned out that the crust could take only a modest trim (losing 2 tablespoons of fat) and still be tender and flaky; to keep it light I added a little sugar and baking powder.

The real fat savings came from replacing the top crust with an unorthodox streusel. A typical streusel contains a good ½ cup of butter, but the substitution of marshmallow creme for most of the butter worked beautifully—and added a subtle toasted-marshmallow flavor.

The final test was at the table. The pie disappeared in moments.

Apple-Blackberry Pie

Prep and cook time: About 2 hours, plus about 1 hour for cooling

Makes: 8 servings

1½ cups all-purpose flour

½ cup plus 1½ tablespoons granulated sugar

½ teaspoon baking powder

¼ teaspoon salt

2 tablespoons *each* cold butter and vegetable shortening

3 tablespoons quick-cooking tapioca

1 teaspoon grated lemon peel

1 teaspoon ground cinnamon

4 cups peeled, thinly sliced Granny Smith apples (about 1½ lb.)

3 cups blackberries

⅓ cup marshmallow creme

2 tablespoons melted butter

¼ cup firmly packed brown sugar

½ cup regular rolled oats

1. In a bowl, combine 1 cup flour, 1½ tablespoons granulated sugar, baking powder, and salt. With a pastry blender or your fingers, cut in or rub in cold butter until pea-size, then cut in shortening until pea-size. Add 4½ tablespoons ice-cold water, 1 tablespoon at a time, tossing mixture gently with a fork. Gather dough into a ball, pat into a 4-inch disk, and chill airtight 30 minutes.

2. Meanwhile, in a bowl, combine remaining ½ cup granulated sugar, tapioca, lemon peel, and ½ teaspoon cinnamon; mix in apples and blackberries. Let mixture stand about 15 minutes for tapioca to soften, stirring occasionally.

3. In a bowl, stir marshmallow creme and melted butter until smooth. Add remaining ½ cup flour, remaining ½ teaspoon cinnamon, brown sugar, and oats. Mix with fingers to blend, then break streusel into small clumps.

4. On a lightly floured board, gently roll out crust to an even 12-inch circle, lifting dough and reflouring board if necessary to prevent sticking. Ease into a 9-inch pie pan. Roll under edge of dough so it is flush with rim; flute. Evenly fill crust with fruit. Pat streusel on top to within 1 inch of rim.

5. Bake in a 375° oven until pie is bubbling, 60 to 70 minutes; check after 45 minutes and cover lightly with foil if pie is getting dark. Let cool on a rack about 1 hour before serving.

Per serving: 372 cal., 24% (89 cal.) from fat; 4 g protein; 9.9 g fat (4.5 g sat.); 70 g carbo.; 179 mg sodium; 16 mg chol. ■

WE'D LIKE TO HEAR FROM YOU!
Do you have tips or recipes for low-fat cooking? Write to Everyday Low-fat Cooking, Sunset Magazine, 80 Willow Rd., Menlo Park, CA 94025, or send e-mail (including your full name and street address) to lowfat@sunsetpub.com.

Prize Salmon

By Linda Lau Anusasananan • Food photographs by Ed Carey

A bike ride on a berry-enshrouded Northwest trail inspired Roger McDorman's second-place salmon and blackberry combination.

The first-place winner, Richard Kronick (below), steams his Salmon Rising Sun, a savory custard surrounded by salmon "rays."

Sunset's Salmon Cook-off produced six winners who understand the flavors of the West. Get ready to eat well.

T'S 2 O'CLOCK ON A SATURDAY AFTERNOON IN the *Sunset* test kitchen. Normally it would be empty, but today three men take it over. A battery of pans covers the cooktops, spices flank the workspaces, and knives fly as the men prepare their entries for the *Sunset* Salmon Cook-off. It'll be at least two hours before judges taste their dishes, but these specialties require precision preparation. Tom Cain slices purple-, red-, and yellow-skinned potatoes on the mandoline he brought from home. Roger McDorman plucks tiny thyme leaves from woody branches. Richard Kronick meticulously slices salmon to fashion "rays" for his Salmon Rising Sun.

The three female contestants chat leisurely outside—it's much too early to start. Says Leslie Tiano to Anna Jurgeleit, "Because we have children, we cook fast." Stephanie Zemler, who introduces herself (and has entered the contest) as Stephanie Z., says *easy and good* best describes her food.

By 3:15 all six cooks crowd the kitchen. "I was almost embarrassed to tell my friends I was a finalist. It was the first recipe I ever wrote," admits Cain. Tiano and McDorman also confess that these are their first recipes on paper. Conversations swirl around food. "A melon baller works great to seed chilies—just scoop down the center." "Food, music, and sports. What else is there in life?" asks Ms. Z., as she passes out the sched-

ule for her favorite soccer team. Glasses fill with more wine for the last creative surge as enticing smells infuse the kitchen. Smoke drifts from the back porch as salmon sears on the grill. Four o'clock arrives. Judging starts.

It's not an easy job. The contest started with almost 150 entries from 11 Western states and British Columbia. Entries featured salmon raw, smoked, broiled, baked, grilled, poached, and steamed—even cooked over an open fire in the traditional Makah way. And there was salmon sausage, salmon custard, salmon burgers, salmon-stuffed chile rellenos, salmon won tons, and salmon lasagna. These were winnowed by *Sunset*'s food

The Mustard-crusted Salmon captured

staff to 29 finalists (the staff aimed for 25, but there were ties). For five days, the testers cooked, tasted, and rated salmon nonstop, sampling all 29 recipes. *Sunset* invited the top six scorers to come and cook their entries for the judges.

Now finalists await the verdict of three food professionals, who rate their dishes for taste, use of salmon, and presentation. While judges mark ballots in the

It's a busy kitchen. Finalist Tom Cain, at front, works on fillet, Stephanie Z. juices lime, and Roger McDorman plucks thyme leaves for his thyme-encrusted salmon.

And the winners are...

"**H**OW CAN ANYONE GO WRONG WITH SALMON?" WRITES LESLIE TIANO, OF LA JOLLA, California, one of six finalists at the *Sunset* Salmon Cook-off held at *Sunset*'s Menlo Park headquarters. Indeed, the natural succulence of this fish makes it pretty forgiving. But the winners share a special talent: they know how to show off the naturally delicate, sweet nuttiness of this great Western fish.

Salmon Rising Sun

Prep and cook time: About 1 hour and 45 minutes

Notes: To fully re-create Richard Kronick's presentation, shop at a Japanese market for the exotic ingredients. Kronick makes the "sun's rays" from seared salmon that is raw inside. To minimize the health risk from eating raw fish, use commercially frozen fish or high-quality fish available at a

sushi bar. You may prefer to cook the fish, but it's more difficult to make neat slices.

Makes: 4 servings

- 1/3 cup *each* lemon juice and dark soy sauce
- 2 tablespoons rice vinegar
- 1 tablespoon plus 1 teaspoon mirin
- 2 garlic cloves, finely minced
- 1/2 teaspoon minced fresh ginger
- 4 small dried shiitake mushrooms

- 1 center-cut salmon fillet (1 1/2 lb.), skinned

  About 2 teaspoons Asian sesame oil

  Salt and pepper
- 1 1/2 cups chicken broth
- 1 teaspoon light soy sauce
- 3 large eggs
- 4 strips lemon peel, yellow part only (1/2 in. by 2 in.)
- 4 fresh shiso leaves
- 2 cups shredded daikon radish
- 1/2 cup red pickled ginger

  Asian red pepper sauce and cayenne

  Radish sprouts and chives in 2-inch lengths

  Finely diced lemon peel

third place for finalist Leslie Tiano. You can prepare it in 25 minutes.

studio, contestants taste the leftovers in the kitchen. Raves greet every dish. "Thumbs-up. This is good stuff. They're all so different—how are they going to choose?" Results are announced after a dinner on the *Sunset* patio.

"I share this prize with you guys. All your recipes were as good as mine," says Kronick as he receives the first-place award for a steamed Japanese seafood custard. Kronick's statement is close to fact. One judge, Jay Harlow, says, "It was real tight. All the dishes were very good. They showed an understanding of salmon, what its flavors and textures can do."

Sunset food and entertaining editor Jerry Anne Di Vecchio agrees. "It was not an easy contest—the diversity of the entries was a judging challenge. All of you here are winners."

1. Mix juice, dark soy, vinegar, 1 tablespoon mirin, garlic, and ginger. Cover and chill 3 tablespoons of mixture. Soak mushrooms in hot water until soft, 10 to 15 minutes.

2. With tweezers, pull out and discard any remaining bones in salmon. Rinse fillet; pat dry. Slice lengthwise into 4 equally wide strips. Cut each of the 2 outer strips (with thinner ends) into 4 equal-size chunks. Rub all salmon pieces with sesame oil; sprinkle lightly with salt and pepper. Coat salmon in remaining lemon-soy mixture; marinate in refrigerator 15 minutes.

3. Meanwhile, mix broth, light soy, and 1 teaspoon mirin. Lightly beat eggs. Stir broth mixture into eggs; pour through a fine wire strainer. Squeeze water out of mushrooms; trim and discard stems.

4. Lift fish from marinade (drain off excess); discard marinade. Reserve the 8 fish chunks. Set a 10- to 12-inch nonstick frying pan over medium-high heat. When hot, place the 2 fish strips in pan; cook to lightly brown both sides (center should be raw), 10 seconds a side. If you prefer fish fully cooked, cook until barely opaque in thickest part (cut to test), 1 1/2 to 2 minutes per side. Cover and chill browned strips.

5. In each of 4 decorative bowls, custard cups, or ramekins (about 1-cup size), place 2 of the raw salmon chunks, 1 mushroom, 1 lemon peel strip, and 1/4 of the egg mixture. Cover each bowl with foil.

6. To steam. Place bowls on a rack above 1 inch of boiling water in a deep pan, steamer, or wok. Cover pan; boil gently, adding more hot water as needed.

To bake. Place covered bowls in a deep baking pan. Place pan with bowls in a 325° oven; pour boiling water around bowls in pan until halfway up bowls.

7. Cook until custard jiggles only slightly when gently shaken, 15 to 20 minutes if steamed, 25 to 30 minutes if baked. Let custard stand 10 minutes before serving. (To serve custard cold, cool, cover, and chill up to the next day.)

8. Meanwhile, thinly slice chilled fish strips at an angle. (If fish is cooked, separate at natural divisions into thin slices, using hands.) Reserve scraps for another use. Place each custard in center of a dinner plate. Arrange shiso leaf, daikon, pickled ginger, and fish slices around custard. Drizzle red pepper sauce and sprinkle cayenne on custard and daikon. Garnish custard with radish sprouts and chives. Drizzle reserved lemon-soy mixture and finely diced lemon peel on fish slices and daikon. Serve custard hot or cold. (Custard may weep slightly when cut.)

Per serving: 467 cal., 35% (162 cal.) from fat; 42 g protein; 18 g fat (3.4 g sat.); 32 g carbo.; 1,608 mg sodium; 254 mg chol.

Thyme-encrusted King Salmon with Blackberry Gastrique

Prep and cook time: About 1 hour and 10 minutes

Notes: Roger McDorman prefers wild king salmon and wild blackberries for this elegant presentation, but any fresh salmon and cultivated blackberries will work well.

Makes: 4 servings

- 2 cups blackberries
- 1/4 cup sugar
- 1/4 cup red wine vinegar
- 1/2 tablespoon butter
- 1/4 cup minced shallot (1 1/4 oz.)
- 1/4 cup dry red wine
  Salt and pepper
- 4 salmon fillets (each about 1/2 lb.), skinned
- 3 tablespoons fresh thyme leaves, plus a few sprigs
- 1/4 teaspoon ground cloves
- 1 1/2 tablespoons salad oil

1. In a food processor or blender, purée 1 1/2 cups of the berries. Pour through a fine strainer into a bowl; discard seeds.

2. *To prepare gastrique.* In a 1- to 2-quart pan, mix sugar with 1/4 cup water; cook, uncovered, over medium-high heat until reduced to a thick caramel-colored syrup, 5 to 10 minutes. Remove from heat; carefully add vinegar. Return to low heat and stir until caramel is dissolved. Remove from pan and set aside. Rinse pan.

3. In the same pan, melt butter over medium-high heat; add shallot and cook, stirring often, until just golden, 2 to 3 minutes. Add wine and cook, uncovered, until most of the liquid evaporates (watch carefully), about 5 minutes. Add berry purée and cook, uncovered, until reduced by half, about 6 minutes. Add half the gastrique to pan. (Add more to taste, depending on sweetness of berries.) Add salt and pepper to taste; set aside.

4. With tweezers, pull out and discard any bones in salmon. Rinse fish; pat dry. Lightly sprinkle with salt and pepper. Mix thyme and cloves; spread on a large plate. Set fillets on thyme mixture; let stand a few minutes. Turn over; repeat to coat all sides.

5. Add oil to a 10- to 12-inch frying pan over high heat. When pan is hot, cook fish until lightly brown, 1 to 2 minutes per side; transfer to oven in same pan if handle is

Grilled salmon topped with a salsa of sweet pineapple, tart tomatillos, and hot chilies earns this award winner the name Sweet Heat Salmon.

ovenproof (or transfer fillets to a baking pan). Bake fish in a 375° oven until fish is barely opaque in thickest part (cut to test), 4 to 6 minutes.

6. While salmon cooks, add whole blackberries to sauce; over medium heat cook gently just until hot, about 3 minutes.

7. Spoon 1 to 2 tablespoons of sauce onto each of 4 heated plates; place a fillet on top. Place whole berries on top of and around fillet. Garnish with thyme sprigs.

Per serving: 478 cal., 40% (189 cal.) from fat; 46 g protein; 21 g fat (3.8 g sat.); 24 g carbo.; 117 mg sodium; 129 mg chol.

Mustard-crusted Salmon

Prep and cook time: About 25 minutes
Notes: Leslie Tiano serves a light pasta or rice with this delicious, quick entrée.
Makes: 4 or 5 servings

- 4 to 5 pieces (about 1/2 lb. each) salmon fillet
- 1/4 cup finely minced garlic
- 3 tablespoons butter or margarine
- 3/4 cup whole-grain Dijon mustard
- 1/2 cup dry white wine
  Lemon wedges

1. Rinse fish; pat dry. Place pieces, skin down, on an oiled broiler pan.

2. In 6- to 8-inch frying pan, stir garlic in butter over medium heat until soft, about 3 minutes. Spoon butter from garlic and drizzle over salmon fillets; reserve garlic in pan.

3. Broil salmon 2 to 3 inches from heat for 2 minutes. Meanwhile, mix mustard and wine with sautéed garlic.

4. Remove pan from oven. Spoon mustard mixture evenly over fillets. Return to oven; broil until crust is golden brown and fish is barely opaque in thickest part (cut to test), 4 to 6 minutes. Transfer to a serving platter. Serve with lemon wedges.

Per serving: 447 cal., 42% (189 cal.) from fat; 46 g protein; 21 g fat (6.5 g sat.); 2.8 g carbo.; 1,037 mg sodium; 143 mg chol.

Sweet Heat Salmon

Prep and cook time: About 45 minutes

Notes: Stephanie Z. varies this recipe by using either salmon fillets or steaks, and by broiling or barbecuing. She serves the salmon with jalapeño muffins and a salad of endive, hearts of palm, and grapefruit.

Makes: 6 servings

- 1 cup mesquite wood chips
- 1 1/4 pounds peeled and cored fresh pineapple
- 1/2 to 2 fresh jalapeño chilies (1/2 to 1 1/2 oz.)

5 fresh tomatillos (about 5 oz. total), husked and coarsely chopped

About ¼ cup freshly squeezed lime juice

¼ cup packed minced fresh cilantro

Salt

6 salmon steaks (each about ½ lb. and 1 in. thick)

About 1 tablespoon olive oil

Grated lime peel and lemon peel

1. Soak wood chips in water at least 15 minutes.

2. Coarsely chop pineapple to make about 3 cups. Stem, seed, and coarsely chop jalapeño.

3. In a blender or food processor, combine tomatillos, jalapeño, and ¼ cup lime juice. Purée until smooth. Pour mixture into a bowl; stir in pineapple and cilantro. Add more lime juice and salt to taste. (If making ahead, cover salsa and let sit at room temperature up to 1 hour.)

4. *If using a charcoal grill.* Prepare a solid single layer of hot coals (you can hold your hand at grill level only 2 to 3 seconds). Sprinkle drained wood chips over coals; set grill 4 to 6 inches above.

If using a gas grill, place drained wood chips in a small, shallow foil pan in a corner of the barbecue; set grill in place. Turn heat to high, close lid, and heat 10 to 15 minutes.

5. Brush both sides of salmon with oil. Lay fish on grill; cover barbecue. Cook, turning once, just until salmon is barely opaque in thickest part (cut to test), 6 to 8 minutes total. Transfer fish to serving platter. Spoon salsa over top. Garnish with lime peel and lemon peel.

Per serving: 398 cal., 38% (153 cal.) from fat; 46 g protein; 17 g fat (2.5 g sat.); 14 g carbo.; 101 mg sodium; 125 mg chol.

Oriental Fish and Chips

Prep and cook time: About 1 hour

Notes: For his striking presentation, Tom Cain encircles the potato-encrusted fish with a confetti of red and yellow bell peppers topped with steamed asparagus spears brushed with olive oil and browned under the broiler.

Makes: Serves 4

1 *each* red, purple, and Yukon gold thin-skinned potatoes (each about 3 oz. and 2 in. wide)

2 tablespoons butter or margarine

2 onions (about 6 oz. each), thinly sliced

½ teaspoon soy sauce

Salt and freshly ground pepper

1 salmon fillet (about 1¼ lb.), skinned

½ teaspoon ground coriander

2 tablespoons prepared horseradish

2 tablespoons coarsely chopped cilantro

2 tablespoons mayonnaise

½ teaspoon Asian sesame oil

4 teaspoons prepared wasabi

1 tablespoon toasted sesame seed

Fresh cilantro leaves

1. Slice potatoes on a vegetable slicer ⅛ to 1/16 inch thick. Fill a 10- to 12-inch frying pan with about 1 inch of water. Bring to a boil over high heat. Drop the potatoes in water; cook just until barely tender to bite, 5 to 6 minutes. Remove the potatoes from pan, and drain.

2. Rinse pan. Melt butter in pan over medium-high heat. Remove 1 tablespoon butter and reserve. Add onions and cook over medium-high heat, stirring often, until onions are tinged with brown, about 15 minutes. Stir in soy sauce. Add salt and pepper to taste.

3. With tweezers, pull out and discard any bones from salmon. Rinse fish; pat dry. Quarter fillet. Sprinkle the 4 pieces lightly with salt, pepper, and ¼ teaspoon of the coriander.

4. Mix horseradish, chopped cilantro, mayonnaise, sesame oil, and remaining ¼ teaspoon coriander. Spread 1 teaspoon wasabi on all sides of each fish piece, then liberally spread a quarter of the horseradish mixture over wasabi.

5. On a 10- by 15-inch baking sheet lined with baking parchment, overlap the different-colored potatoes in a pattern so that when a piece of fish is placed in the center, potatoes extend approximately ¾ inch beyond fish on all sides. With a sharp knife, cut potatoes (without cutting the paper) by tracing the outline of the piece of fish: gently press cutoff potato portions onto the sides of the fish. Place a layer of overlapping potatoes on top; brush tops with the reserved 1 tablespoon melted butter and lightly sprinkle with salt. Repeat with remaining fish pieces.

6. Bake, uncovered, in a 500° oven until fish is barely opaque in thickest part (cut to test) and potatoes start to brown around edges, 10 to 14 minutes.

7. With a spatula, carefully transfer each piece of fillet to a plate. Place ¼ of the cooked onions in a neat pile on top. Sprin-

kle with sesame seed and garnish with cilantro leaves.

Per serving: 409 cal., 48% (198 cal.) from fat; 31 g protein; 22 g fat (6 g sat.); 21 g carbo.; 223 mg sodium; 98 mg chol.

Salmon Wrapped in Filo with Cream Cheese and Pesto

Prep and cook time: About 40 minutes

Notes: Anna Jurgeleit serves this easy party entrée with basmati rice and a mixed green salad.

Makes: 6 servings

12 sheets (12- by 17-in.) filo dough (about half of a 1-lb. package), thawed, if frozen

About 6 tablespoons melted butter or margarine, or butter-flavored cooking oil spray

1 center-cut salmon fillet (about 1½ lb.; not wider than 5 in.), skinned

6 ounces cream cheese or neufchâtel (light cream) cheese, at room temperature

¼ cup prepared pesto with dried tomatoes, or plain pesto

Salt

Lemon wedges

1. Layer filo sheets on a baking sheet, brushing each filo sheet lightly with melted butter, or coating with butter-flavored cooking oil spray.

2. Lay the salmon fillet down length of dough 1 inch from a long edge.

3. Spread the cream cheese evenly over the salmon, then spread pesto evenly over cheese.

4. Fold the 1 inch of dough over the salmon and trim excess dough at the narrow ends of the fish with scissors. You may need to moisten filo with butter or cooking oil spray to make it stick to fish.

5. Fold the other half of the filo over the salmon and trim ends again to fit fish. Turn the filo-wrapped fish over; brush with butter or coat with cooking oil spray. Slice the filo-wrapped fish crosswise into 6 equal pieces; leave in place on pan.

6. Bake in a 400° oven until filo is golden and fish is barely opaque in thickest part (cut to test), about 20 minutes. Transfer the baked filo-wrapped fish to a serving plate. Add salt and lemon to taste.

Per serving: 526 cal., 62% (324 cal.) from fat; 28 g protein; 36 g fat (16 g sat.); 21 g carbo.; 507 mg sodium; 126 mg chol. ∎

Not just any eggplant

By Elaine Johnson

Photographs by Philip Salaverry

2. Globe

1. 'Rosa Bianca'

3. 'Lao Green Stripe'

4. 'Listada de Gandia'

At farmers' markets all over the West, it's peak season for specialty varieties. Now's the time to experiment

AT THE NAPA AND ST. HELENA farmers' markets in Northern California, Tom Nemcik sells some of the most striking eggplant you'll ever see. Eggplant in rich glossy solids, delicate to bold stripes, and soft blushes. "When people see these, their eyes pop out," he says. In fact, a few people buy eggplant simply for their beauty—to sketch, photograph, or use as centerpieces.

But most farmers' market customers buy the eggplant to eat. They've discovered that eggplant are as diverse in texture and flavor as they are in appearance. If your only previous experience has been with the standard globe type, you're in for a surprise.

Why all the new kinds of eggplant? Actually, most aren't new at all but are heirloom varieties recently introduced to the Western marketplace from around the world. Small-scale farmers like Nemcik are growing different kinds of eggplant for curious cooks, for ethnic populations that already appreciate them, and for those who just seek a little beauty.

EGGPLANT INTRODUCTIONS

The unique flavor, shape, texture, and cooking qualities of each type of eggplant will influence which kind you choose for a particular dish.

1. 'Rosa Bianca'. Italian farmers' market favorite. Nearly round, white skin with lavender streaks, white flesh. Sweet flavor; creamy yet firm texture; holds its shape cooked. Good all-purpose variety.

2. Globe. Generic name for large, oval-shaped eggplant; may be one of several commercial varieties, such as 'Black Beauty' and 'Black Bell'. Glossy black skin, cream to green flesh. Mild flavor with a hint of bitterness; soft texture, falls apart when cooked. Good as a backdrop in many dishes, such as dips and casseroles. Markets occasionally sell immature globes the size of chicken eggs.

3. 'Lao Green Stripe'. Also called 'Thai Green Stripe'. Hmong variety. Golf ball shape, pointy calyx "hat," and striped, somewhat tough skin. Seedy texture and assertive flavor (delicious to some). Good cut into chunks and simmered briefly (served crisp) in curries.

4. 'Listada de Gandia'. Italian. Stunning white and purple stripes, long oval shape, green thorny calyxes that curl like a '60s flip hairdo.

Mild white flesh and slightly bitter skin; meaty, creamy texture. Holds its shape cooked. Good all-purpose variety.

5. 'Pintong Long'. Taiwanese. A favorite for flavor. Long and slender, deep purple to lavender skin, green to purple-black calyxes, white flesh. Sweet, nutty flavor and buttery texture. Good for stir-frys.

6. 'White Egg'. Looks like a chicken or duck egg. Origin unknown, but the plant for which eggplant was named. Sweet, mild, and a little watery-tasting; fairly firm flesh; somewhat tough skin. Holds its shape when cooked; good for stuffing and grilling.

7. 'Thai Long Green'. Thai variety. Lime green skin, white flesh. Long, slender shape. Outstanding flavor: sweet, nutty, and reminiscent of green beans. Velvety flesh and skin. Most slices are seedless (seed cavity is at blossom end). Short shelf life. Good for stir-frys.

8. 'Rosita'. Puerto Rican. Bright lavender color. Long, oval shape, white flesh. Mild, sweet flavor; smooth, tender flesh and skin. Good all-purpose eggplant.

8. 'Rosita'

5. 'Pintong Long'

7. 'Thai Long Green'

6. 'White Egg'

Lebanese Baba Ghanoush

Prep and cook time: About 50 minutes
Notes: Khaled Alkotob of Fresno, California, shared this refreshing recipe from his native Lebanon.
Makes: 8 appetizer servings

- 2 pounds eggplant such as globe, 'Rosa Bianca', 'Rosita', or 'Listada de Gandia'
- 2 cloves garlic
- 2 tablespoons lemon juice
  Salt and freshly ground pepper

- ⅔ cup chopped soft-ripe tomatoes (yellow and red, if desired)
- 1 tablespoon extra-virgin olive oil
- 2 tablespoons minced fresh mint, plus mint sprigs
  About 10 ounces pocket bread, cut into triangles

1. Cook eggplant under the broiler or on a grill. To broil, place whole eggplant in a 12-by 15-inch pan. Broil 3 inches from heat until black all over and soft when pressed, 20 to 25 minutes; turn as needed for even cooking. To grill, place eggplant on a barbe-cue grill over a solid bed of medium-hot coals or over a gas grill on medium-high heat (you can hold your hand at grill level only 3 to 4 seconds); close lid on gas grill. Turn occasionally until black all over and soft when pressed, 20 to 25 minutes.

2. Let eggplant cool. Cut in half and scoop out pulp; discard skin. Use a mortar and pestle to crush garlic; add eggplant (a portion at a time if needed), and pound just until coarsely chopped (or coarsely chop foods with a knife). Add lemon juice, and season to taste with salt and pepper.

3. Mound eggplant on a platter. Scatter

tomatoes around it. Drizzle eggplant with oil and sprinkle with minced mint. Garnish with mint sprigs. Season to taste with additional salt and pepper. Spoon eggplant and tomatoes onto bread.

Per serving: 142 cal., 15% (21 cal.) from fat; 4.4 g protein; 2.3 g fat (0.3 g sat.); 27 g carbo.; 196 mg sodium; 0 mg chol.

Western Grilled Fish and Eggplant

Prep and cook time: About 30 minutes
Notes: John Borski, an eggplant grower in Kaysville, Utah, created this recipe.
Makes: 4 servings

3   tablespoons balsamic vinegar

1   teaspoon minced fresh thyme leaves, plus sprigs

1½   pounds eggplant (any variety except 'Lao Green Stripe')

1   pound sea bass or swordfish fillets (about 1 in. thick), cut into 4 pieces

2   tablespoons extra-virgin olive oil

    Salt and pepper

1   pound (about 6) firm-ripe Roma tomatoes

1. Combine vinegar and thyme; set aside.

2. Remove eggplant stems, then cut eggplant lengthwise into ½-inch slices. Lightly brush eggplant and fish all over with oil; sprinkle with salt and pepper.

3. Lightly oil a barbecue grill over a solid bed of medium-hot coals, or a gas grill on medium-high heat (you can hold your hand at grill level only 3 to 4 seconds). Lay eggplant, fish, and tomatoes on grill. Close lid on gas grill. Turn foods often until eggplant are soft when pressed, tomatoes are streaked black, and fish is no longer translucent in thickest part, 5 to 8 minutes; remove foods as cooked.

4. Arrange eggplant and fish on 4 plates. Coarsely chop tomatoes, add to vinegar mixture, and spoon over fish and eggplant. Garnish with thyme sprigs. Add salt and pepper to taste.

Per serving: 240 cal., 37% (88 cal.) from fat; 24 g protein; 9.8 g fat (1.7 g sat.); 16 g carbo.; 95 mg sodium; 47 mg chol.

Almost any kind of eggplant works in this grilled fish and eggplant entrée with tomato-balsamic vinaigrette.

Indian Stuffed Eggplant

Prep and cook time: About 50 minutes
Notes: Kusum Patel of West Sacramento, California, contributed this spicy and deliciously salty vegetarian entrée from her native north India. If 'White Egg' eggplant isn't available, look for egg-size globe, or use pieces of any slender eggplant.
Makes: 4 servings

⅔   cup finely chopped roasted, salted peanuts

    About ½ cup chopped fresh cilantro, plus sprigs

3   tablespoons salad oil

2   tablespoons plus 1 teaspoon minced fresh ginger

4   teaspoons sugar

    About 2 teaspoons salt

1   tablespoon ground coriander

1   tablespoon plus ½ teaspoon cumin seed

1   tablespoon hot chili flakes

1¾   teaspoons ground turmeric

1¾   pounds (8 to 12) 'White Egg' eggplant (each about 2 in. wide, 3 in. long); or use 8 to 12 pieces slender eggplant (each about 1½ to 2 in. wide, 3 in. long)

1½   cups basmati rice

¾   cup unflavored yogurt

1. In a bowl, combine peanuts, 6 tablespoons chopped cilantro, oil, 2 tablespoons ginger, sugar, 2 teaspoons salt, coriander, 1 tablespoon cumin seed, chili flakes, and 1½ teaspoons turmeric.

EGGPLANT INTELLIGENCE: *Here's help in buying and cooking eggplant.*

• **Finding specialty varieties.** Farmers' markets carry the widest selection. Asian markets may carry 'Thai Green Stripe' and 'Pintong Long', though they may not be labeled. You can also try our recipes with supermarket varieties.

• **Selection.** The best eggplant have fresh calyxes and smooth and unbruised skin with a good sheen, and they give slightly when pressed; very spongy eggplant have been on the shelf too long, while rock-hard eggplant have been left on the plant too long. Another sign of overmaturity is a color change: purple eggplant turn bronze, white and green eggplant turn yellow.

• **What about bitterness?** If you find some eggplant strong-flavored, selection and judicious trimming are more effective than salting. Eggplant with dark purple skin over green flesh, such as globe types, contain a slightly bitter-tasting pigment—anthocyanin—in the skin and just beneath it; for mildest flavor, trim these portions. Or choose milder white- or green-skinned eggplant (except for 'Lao Green Stripe', which is naturally assertive).

Any variety, if overripe, will acquire a strong taste as seeds enlarge and get bitter.

• **Storage.** Can be chilled a couple of days in paper bags.

• **What about oil?** Raw eggplant can soak up oil like a sponge, but it doesn't have to. For grilling, lightly brush eggplant with oil to keep slices moist. Before sautéing, steam eggplant to eliminate the need for lots of oil. Place eggplant slices or cubes in a wok or 12-inch frying pan with a little water (¼ cup for 1 pound of eggplant). Simmer, covered, until tender when pierced, about 5 minutes. To sauté, uncover, add 2 teaspoons oil per pound of eggplant, and turn often until browned, 8 to 10 minutes.

Small, cross-cut 'White Egg' eggplant are stuffed with a vibrant mixture of chopped peanuts and curry spices, which tints eggplant yellow.

2. Trim stems but not calyxes from eggplant. From bottom end, quarter each eggplant lengthwise ¾ of the way to stem end. (If using slender eggplant, trim 1 end of each piece to sit flat, then quarter each piece lengthwise from untrimmed end ¾ of the way to trimmed end.) Gently open cuts in eggplant and pack in cilantro filling. As filled, arrange eggplant upright in a 3- to 4-quart pan; they must fit snugly.

3. Add ⅔ cup water to pan. Cover, bring to a boil over high heat, then reduce heat and simmer until tender when pierced, 15 to 20 minutes (if overcooked they may fall apart).

4. Meanwhile, in a 3- to 4-quart pan over high heat, bring 3 cups water to a boil. Add ½ teaspoon salt (optional) and rice; reduce heat and simmer, covered, until liquid is absorbed, about 20 minutes.

5. While eggplant and rice cook, shake remaining ½ teaspoon cumin in a small pan over high heat until seeds darken, 1 to 2 minutes. Coarsely grind with a mortar and pestle or a clean coffee grinder, then combine with yogurt, ½ cup water, remaining 2 tablespoons chopped cilantro, 1 teaspoon ginger, and ¼ teaspoon turmeric. Season to taste with salt.

6. Gently spoon eggplant into a dish, taking care to keep pieces together. If desired, skim and discard fat from pan juices, then pour juices around eggplant. Serve eggplant over rice with yogurt sauce. If desired, garnish with additional chopped cilantro and cilantro sprigs.

Per serving: 558 cal., 37% (207 cal.) from fat; 18 g protein; 23 g fat (3.2 g sat.); 82 g carbo.; 1,373 mg sodium; 2.6 mg chol.

Italian Eggplant Gratin

Prep and cook time: About 1 hour
Notes: Deborah Madison of Santa Fe, the author of *The Savory Way* and *The Greens Cookbook,* created this delicious version of eggplant parmesan.
Makes: 4 servings

- 2 pounds soft-ripe tomatoes
- ¼ cup packed fresh basil leaves, plus 1 tablespoon chopped leaves, and sprigs
- 1 tablespoon lightly packed fresh marjoram leaves, plus 2 teaspoons minced leaves, and sprigs
- Salt and pepper
- 1½ pounds fleshy eggplant such as 'Rosa Bianca', 'Listada de Gandia', or globe
- 2 tablespoons olive oil
- 1¼ cups shredded mozzarella cheese
- ½ cup freshly grated parmesan cheese

1. Cut tomatoes into 2-inch chunks and place in a 2- to 3-quart pan with whole basil and marjoram leaves. Bring to a boil over high heat, then reduce heat and simmer rapidly, uncovered, until flesh turns to liquid, about 15 minutes; stir occasionally.

2. Push sauce through a strainer, extracting all liquid; discard skins and seasonings. Return sauce to pan and boil over medium-high heat, stirring often, until reduced to 1½ cups, 5 to 10 minutes. Stir in minced marjoram and all but 1 teaspoon chopped basil.

WHERE TO ORDER EGGPLANT SEED

The following catalogs sell seed for one or more of the eggplant varieties that are listed on page 171, along with other types of eggplant. The catalogs are free unless noted.

Seeds Blüm, H.C. 33 Idaho City Stage, Boise, ID 83706; (800) 528-3658 (catalog $3). Sells 'Rosa Bianca' and 'White Egg', as well as globe types such as 'Black Beauty'.

Seed Savers Exchange, 3076 N. Winn Rd., Decorah, IA 52101; (319) 382-5990. Preserves heirloom varieties and is an exchange for seed savers (members write directly to each other). Membership ($25) includes a list of more than 100 eggplant varieties, including all the ones mentioned on page 121.

Southern Exposure Seed Exchange, Box 170, Earlysville, VA 22936; (804) 973-4703 (catalog $3). Sells globe types, 'Listada de Gandia', and 'Thai Long Green'.

Stokes Seeds, Box 548, Buffalo, NY 14240; (716) 695-6980. Sells globe types and 'Rosita'.

Sunrise Enterprises, Box 1960, Chesterfield, VA 23832; (804) 796-5796 (catalog $2). Sells seeds and seedlings of 'Pintong Long' (listed as 'Extra Long Pintung').

—Lauren Bonar Swezey

Season to taste with salt and pepper.

3. Meanwhile, cut eggplant into ⅓-inch rounds. Brush both sides with oil and place on a 14- by 17-inch baking sheet. Broil 3 inches below heat until browned and soft to touch, about 12 minutes; turn halfway through cooking. Evenly sprinkle with salt and pepper.

4. Combine mozzarella and parmesan. Spread ½ cup sauce in a shallow 2-quart baking dish. Arrange half the eggplant rounds over the sauce, top with half the cheese and ½ cup more sauce. Layer with remaining eggplant, sauce, and cheese.

5. Bake in a 375° oven until bubbling throughout, 25 to 30 minutes. Sprinkle with remaining 1 teaspoon chopped basil; garnish with basil and marjoram sprigs.

Per serving: 314 cal., 54% (171 cal.) from fat; 16 g protein; 19 g fat (8 g sat.); 24 g carbo.; 388 mg sodium; 37 mg chol. ■

Sunset's Kitchen Cabinet

Readers' family favorites tested in our kitchens

**By Linda Lau Anusasananan
and Betsy Reynolds Bateson**

DICK COLE

Farmers' Market Salad

Mary Adams Kuyper, Sacramento

Mary Adams Kuyper enjoys shopping at her local farmers' market, where the produce she selects is usually picked the morning she buys it. She especially likes talking to the growers and exchanging cooking suggestions, and says, "That's half the fun." She created this salad after an inspiring visit.

Prep and cook time: About 45 minutes
Makes: 8 servings

- 4 ears corn on the cob (about 2½ lb. total), husks and silk removed
- ⅓ cup cider vinegar
- 2 tablespoons olive oil
- 1 tablespoon *each* Dijon mustard and honey
- 1 teaspoon *each* chili powder and ground cumin
- ¼ teaspoon pepper
- 1 cucumber (about ¾ lb.), peeled and cubed
- 1 red bell pepper (about 6 oz.), cored, seeded, and sliced
- 1 cup matchstick-size pieces peeled jicama
- ⅓ cup minced red onion
- ⅓ cup minced fresh cilantro
- 1½ to 2 pounds red leaf lettuce
- 3 firm-ripe tomatoes (about 1⅓ lb. total), cored and sliced
  Salt

1. In a 5- to 6-quart pan, bring about 3 quarts water to a boil; cook corn just until hot, about 4 minutes. Cool corn.

2. Mix vinegar, oil, mustard, honey, chili powder, cumin, and pepper in a large bowl. Cut corn kernels from cob. Add corn to dressing in bowl, along with cucumber, bell pepper, jicama, red onion, and cilantro; stir. Cover and chill at least 10 minutes or up to 4 hours.

3. Reserve 8 large lettuce leaves. Tear enough of remaining leaves to make 2 quarts. Line a large platter or 8 salad plates with whole lettuce leaves; top with torn lettuce. Along one side of platter or plates, arrange tomato slices over lettuce, then spoon corn mixture beside tomatoes. Add salt to taste.

Per serving: 133 cal., 31% (41 cal.) from fat; 3.8 g protein; 4.6 g fat (0.6 g sat.); 23 g carbo.; 140 mg sodium; 0 mg chol.

Umpqua Ribs

Wayne Misco, Roseville, California

When on vacation in Sunriver, Oregon, Wayne Misco and his two sons-in-law—each with a different cooking philosophy—worked together to bake and grill these sensational barbecued ribs.

Prep and cook time: About 1¾ hours
Makes: 6 to 8 servings

- ½ cup chopped green bell pepper
- ½ cup chopped onion
- ⅓ cup garlic cloves
- ¼ cup fresh basil leaves
- 2 jalapeño chilies, stemmed, seeded, and cut into chunks
- ¼ cup firmly packed brown sugar
- ¾ cup reduced-sodium soy sauce
- 1 can (12 oz.) beer
- 2 slabs (2 to 3 lb. total) back pork ribs
- 1 cup prepared spicy barbecue sauce
- ¼ cup maple syrup

1. In a food processor or blender, combine bell pepper, onion, garlic, basil, jalapeños, sugar, and soy. Whirl until puréed; pour into an 11- by 17-inch roasting pan and mix in beer. Set aside 1 cup of this marinade; cover and chill if held more than 1 hour.

2. Trim and discard excess fat from ribs. Add ribs to pan with soy mixture, turning to coat all sides. Cover and chill, turning occasionally, at least 30 minutes or up to next day.

3. Lift ribs from marinade and drain briefly; discard marinade. Arrange ribs in the roasting pan. Bake, uncovered, in a 350° oven for 50 minutes; turn over after 30 minutes.

4. Meanwhile, mix the 1 cup reserved marinade with spicy barbecue sauce and maple syrup; set aside.

5. Arrange ribs on a grill over a solid bed of medium-low coals or gas grill on medium-low (you can hold your hand at grill level only 5 to 6 seconds). Cover grill, and open vents. Cook, turning to brown evenly, about 15 minutes.

6. Baste ribs heavily on 1 side with marinade-barbecue sauce mixture; turn and baste remaining side. Continue to cook until sauce is sticky and sticks to ribs, about 6 minutes.

7. Transfer ribs to a large platter or carving board; keep warm. Heat remaining barbecue sauce until bubbly; pour into a serving bowl. Cut between ribs to make individual portions or individual ribs; accompany with sauce.

Per serving: 276 cal., 55% (153 cal.) from fat; 14 g protein; 17 g fat (6.1 g sat.); 15 g carbo.; 613 mg sodium; 64 mg chol.

Lemon Fusilli with Shrimp

Laurie Wilcox, Palm Desert, California

When the thermometer inched close to 120° last summer, the last thing Laurie Wilcox wanted to do was cook. But she searched her kitchen for ingredients, and put together this light pasta dish that refreshed her spirits. She enjoyed the leftovers as a cool salad the next day. Fusilli pasta comes long and short; Wilcox prefers the long curly noodles to the stubby corkscrews, but both work.

Prep and cook time: About 35 minutes
Makes: 4 servings

- ½ pound dried fusilli
- 1 package (9 oz.) frozen broccoli florets
- 1 zucchini (about 4 oz.), ends trimmed and thinly sliced
- 2 teaspoons grated lemon peel
- ¼ cup lemon juice
- 1 teaspoon chicken-flavor instant bouillon
- 1 or 2 cloves garlic, minced
- 1 tablespoon minced fresh dill or 1 teaspoon dried dill weed
- 2 tablespoons minced fresh ginger
- ¾ pound frozen cooked shelled and deveined shrimp (36 to 50 per lb.)

1. In a 4- to 5-quart pan over high heat, bring about 2 quarts water to a boil. Add fusilli and cook until barely tender to bite, about 10 minutes.

2. Meanwhile, place broccoli in colander. Rinse with hot water to loosen pieces and partially thaw. Add zucchini.

3. Combine peel, juice, ¼ cup water, bouillon, garlic, dill, and ginger.

4. When pasta is cooked, add shrimp, return to boil, and pour over vegetables in colander.

5. Place lemon mixture in pan used to cook pasta. Stir over high heat and bring to a boil; boil 1 minute. Reduce heat to low; add shrimp, broccoli, zucchini, and pasta. Stir to coat ingredients with sauce; serve.

Per serving: 327 cal., 5.8% (19 cal.) from fat; 28 g protein; 2.1 g fat (0.4 g sat.); 49 g carbo.; 474 mg sodium; 166 mg chol.

Pickled Vegetables

George Voynick, West Hollywood, California

George Voynick spends a good deal of time developing flavorful, nutritious foods that fit into his restricted low-sodium diet. Although Voynick loves pickles, most are off-limits because they contain a great deal of salt. His solution is this pickled vegetable recipe; the sweet-and-sour pickles have no added salt.

Prep and cook time: About 55 minutes, plus 1¼ hours to cool and 8 hours to chill
Makes: 6 cups

- ¾ cup cider vinegar
- ½ cup granulated sugar
- ⅓ cup firmly packed dark brown sugar
- 2 tablespoons *each* Dijon mustard and minced fresh ginger
- 1 teaspoon *each* celery seed and ground turmeric
- 3 pickling cucumbers (½ lb. total)
- 2 carrots (10 oz. total)
- 2 stalks celery (about ½ lb. total)
- 1 cup (about 5 oz.) green beans
- 1 onion (about 6 oz.), cut into ¼-inch-wide slivers
- 1 cup cauliflower pieces (about 1 in. wide)

1. In a 4- to 5-quart pan, combine 1½ cups water, vinegar, granulated and brown sugar, mustard, ginger, celery seed, and turmeric. Cover and bring to a boil over high heat; reduce heat to low and simmer 10 minutes.

2. Trim and discard ends from cucumbers, carrots, celery, and green beans. Cut cucumbers, carrots, and celery into ¼-inch-thick slices. Cut beans into 2-inch lengths.

3. Add onion to vinegar mixture and simmer, covered, over low heat until onion is translucent, about 5 minutes. Add cucumbers, carrots, celery, beans, and cauliflower pieces. Simmer, covered, 15 minutes. Remove pan from heat; let vegetables cool in seasonings.

4. When cool, pour mixture into a glass or plastic container. Serve, or cover and chill up to 1 week. Stir well before serving.

Per ½-cup serving: 134 cal., 2% (2.7 cal.) from fat; 3.8 g protein; 0.3 g fat (0 g sat.); 32 g carbo.; 97 mg sodium; 0 mg chol.

Chocolate Coffee Orange Mousse

David Stumpf, Tucson

David Stumpf loves chocolate mousse. Unfortunately, it's taboo on his low-cholesterol diet. But Stumpf, a vegetarian who uses tofu regularly, tried making his favorite dessert with tofu. The result is delicious. Cocoa, coffee-flavor liqueur, and orange peel provide great taste, and whipped topping adds a silky texture.

Prep and cook time: About 20 minutes, plus 2 hours for chilling
Makes: 12 servings

- 2 packages (about 14 oz. each) soft tofu
- ½ cup powdered sugar
- 6 tablespoons unsweetened cocoa
- 2 tablespoons coffee-flavor liqueur
- 1 tablespoon vanilla
- 2 teaspoons grated orange peel
- 1 package (8 oz.) reduced-fat frozen whipped topping, thawed
- 1 tablespoon miniature semisweet chocolate baking chips

1. Rinse and drain tofu, then gently press out liquid between thick layers of paper towels. Break each block into several pieces. In a blender or food processor, whirl tofu with sugar, cocoa, liqueur, vanilla, and orange peel until very smooth; scrape container sides as needed.

2. In a bowl, combine tofu mixture with whipped topping, folding to mix well.

3. Pour into a 6- to 7-cup serving bowl, sprinkle chocolate chips evenly over top, then cover and refrigerate until mousse is cold and jiggles only slightly when gently shaken, at least 2 hours or up to 1 day.

Per serving: 124 cal., 34% (42 cal.) from fat; 3.7 g protein; 4.7 g fat (2.7 g sat.); 15 g carbo.; 5.1 mg sodium; 0 mg chol.

Share a recipe you've created or adapted—a family favorite, travel discovery, or time-saver—including the story behind the recipe. You'll receive a "Great Cook" certificate and $50 for each recipe published. Send to *Sunset Magazine*, 80 Willow Rd., Menlo Park, CA 94025, or send e-mail (including full name, street address, and phone number) to recipes@sunsetpub.com.

FOOD Guide

BY JERRY ANNE DI VECCHIO

A layer of fresh figs covers fresh raspberries baked in this luscious tart.

TASTE OF THE WEST: Figs among friends

Fresh figs, ripe and ready to drop into your hand, hold great fascination for those who visit us in Provence each September. There are several fig trees on our French *petite ferme,* but the two biggest (one black, one green) arch over the steps that lead down to the driveway. Descending, you have access to choice fruit on upper limbs—and a forked stick

is kept handy below for pulling down those high, hard-to-reach branches.

On their first day, fig lovers invariably rush out to pick a basket of fruit. But by the next day, the ones in the basket look a bit tired and don't match the appeal of the plump, fresher bounty still on the trees. So those in the basket wither, and the urge to harvest in quantity

evaporates—until the next guests arrive.

One year, Mary Risley, a longtime friend who heads up San Francisco's Tante Marie's Cooking School, was in our neighborhood. She made her first stop up the road at Nyons to stay with a mutual friend, Lydie Marshall, who teaches cooking there. Lydie served a fig tart that Mary liked. Because of our fig trees, Mary shared the recipe with me, adding her own touches—then I added mine.

Fresh Fig and Raspberry Tart

Prep and cook time: About 1½ hours

Notes: If making ahead, let tart stand at room temperature up to 6 hours.

Makes: 8 or 9 servings

Crust

- 1 cup all-purpose flour
- 1 tablespoon sugar
- ½ cup (¼ lb.) butter or margarine, cut into chunks
- ½ teaspoon vanilla

1. Whirl flour, sugar, butter, 1 tablespoon water, and vanilla in a food processor (or beat with a mixer, slowly at first) until dough forms a ball.

2. Spreading and patting with floured fingers, press dough evenly over bottom and 1 inch up the sides of a 9-inch cake or tart pan with a removable rim. Bake in a 325° oven until pale golden brown, about 35 minutes. Pastry may puff, but don't pierce it. Use hot or cool.

Filling

- ⅓ cup blanched almonds
- ⅓ cup sugar
- 1 large egg
- 3 tablespoons butter or margarine
- 2 tablespoons fruit liqueur such as framboise (raspberry), kirsch (cherry), or Cointreau (orange)
- 1½ cups raspberries, rinsed and drained
  About 1 pound ripe figs, rinsed, stems trimmed
- ⅓ cup red currant jelly

1. In a food processor or blender, whirl the almonds until they are coarse crumbs. Add sugar, egg, butter, and liqueur and blend well.

2. Spread mixture evenly in baked crust. Top with raspberries. Bake in a 350° oven until filling is lightly browned around berries, 45 to 50 minutes. Remove from oven.

3. Thinly slice figs crosswise and arrange on tart. Melt jelly (in a pan over heat or in a microwave oven) and spoon evenly over fruit. Let cool, remove pan rim, and cut tart into wedges.

Per serving: 336 cal., 48% (162 cal.) from fat; 3.9 g protein; 18 g fat (9.2 g sat.); 41 g carbo.; 156 mg sodium; 62 mg chol.

ACEY HARPER

Why cook a duck when a prepared one is so reasonably priced?

COOK'S SECRET

The bargain bird— and how to eat it

The best way to avoid the mess of cooking duck is to buy it cooked. And the most masterfully cooked duck is found in Chinese meat markets and delicatessens, hanging unceremoniously by the neck. These barbecued (or roasted) ducks are usually no more expensive—and sometimes less—than a duck cooked at home.

A couple of pointers: When you buy a barbecued duck, indicate immediately whether you want it whole or cut with a cleaver into chunks. The purchase ordinarily includes a ladleful or two of the good cooking juices. Be sure to ask for them. If you don't serve these juices with the duck, save them for soups or sauces.

If you have to make a special buying trip, get several ducks. They freeze well. (Some Asian markets sell frozen barbecued ducks.) Thaw them for about 24 hours in the refrigerator in a pan to catch the juices.

I buy whole ducks, but you can have them cut into halves or quarters. A 2½- to 3-pound bird yields about 1 pound of meat and ½ pound of skin. Sometimes I serve the ducks whole. Other times, when I need meat and skin, I find it easier to pull both off the whole carcass. The duck meat goes into casseroles, crêpes, sauces, salads, and sandwiches. It also gets mixed with pasta or noodles. And I often add the duck juices to the seasoning mixtures in these dishes.

The skin gets used, too. I crisp it in the oven, then chop it. Or I sliver it and stir until crisp in a frying pan over medium to medium-high heat. These cracklings are certainly not for low-fat diets, but they make a fine topping for anything that contains the meat.

However, this is my favorite way to serve this bird:

Quack Beijing duck. Put a **barbecued duck** (2½ to 3 lb.) on a rack in a pan. Heat in a 350° oven until skin is crisp and meat is warm, 30 to 40 minutes. Accompany with warm **flour tortillas,** slivered **green onions, fresh cilantro leaves,** minced **fresh ginger,** and **prepared plum** or hoisin **sauce.**

If you like, stir some of the duck juices into the plum sauce. Eat the skin first, wrapping pieces with the accompaniments in tortillas. Then trim off the fat and slice the meat to eat the same way.

Makes 4 or 5 servings.

Tart red onions top a grilled turkey breast tenderloin that cooks in just minutes.

1 tablespoon butter or margarine

2 red onions (about ¾ lb. total), chopped

1 cup white distilled vinegar

1 cup chicken broth

About 1 tablespoon freshly ground pepper

6 turkey breast tenderloins (about ⅓ lb. each)

Olive oil

Salt

About 9 cups mixed baby salad greens, rinsed and drained

1. Melt butter in a 10- to 12-inch frying pan (not cast iron). Add onions and stir often over medium-high heat until limp, about 10 minutes. Add vinegar and broth. Turn heat to high and boil until mixture is reduced to about 2 cups, 6 to 8 minutes. Tasting, add up to 1 tablespoon pepper—seasoning should be bold. If making ahead, let cool, cover, and chill up to 1 day.

2. Rinse turkey tenderloins (boneless strips on underside of each turkey breast, also called fillets, tenders, or feathers); pat dry. Lay tenderloins 5 to 6 inches apart between sheets of plastic wrap. With a flat mallet, gently but firmly pound meat until about ¼ inch thick. If making ahead, wrap airtight and chill up to 1 day.

3. Unwrap turkey and rub lightly with olive oil, then lightly sprinkle with salt and additional pepper.

4. Lightly oil a barbecue grill over a solid bed of very hot coals or high heat on a gas grill (you can hold your hand at grill level only 1 to 2 seconds); close lid on gas grill. Quickly lay turkey slices on the grill and flip over as they turn white and brown slightly, 1½ to 2 minutes a side. When cooked, stack on a small platter and keep warm.

5. Stir onions over high heat just to warm. Drain turkey juices from platter into onions and add salt to taste.

6. Mound salad greens on 6 plates and place turkey on greens. Spoon onion mixture over the turkey.

Per serving: 249 cal., 18% (45 cal.) from fat; 40 g protein; 5 g fat (1.9 g sat.); 11 g carbo.; 125 mg sodium; 100 mg chol.

FOOD NEWS

Barbecued turkey steaks, in minutes

My first encounter with Susan Feniger was in the kitchen of a famous, now gone, Los Angeles restaurant. She came whirling in, grabbed a pot big enough for bathing, began to toss in vegetables for stock, then looked up, and we met. She radiated energy and enthusiasm, and her career, although relatively new at the time, was already taking an impressive path. Shortly thereafter, she teamed up with Mary Sue Milliken to open a little place on Melrose Avenue where the flavors were "ethnically influenced." Then they opened big and bold City Restaurant on La Brea Avenue, and later they migrated to Santa Monica, where they now serve Latin American food at the lively Border Grill—the source of this colorful but straightforward turkey dish.

Feniger and Milliken now have a Web site, host a radio show called *Good Food,* are stars of TV Food Network's *Too Hot Tamales,* and have written several cookbooks. Their most recent effort, out in September, is *Cantina: The Best of Casual Mexican Cooking* (128 pages, $19.95) from Sunset Books' Casual Cuisines of the World series.

Grilled Turkey Breast with Pink Onions and Black Pepper

Prep and cook time: 30 to 35 minutes

Notes: The onions get pinker if they stand at least 30 minutes.

Makes: 6 servings

GREAT TOOL

Dehydrating tomatoes

The oval, fleshy tomato we call Roma has a lot of other names, including Red Pear and San Marzano. Still other names come from their use or shape—paste, pear, and plum.

Raw, these tomatoes are rather insipid. Cooked, they are very good. But I think they are best dried. The tomato flavor becomes piquant, distinctive, and intense. The texture is meaty and chewy. As a snack food, dried Romas' only rival is dried apricots.

You can use the sun to dry your own Romas, but when I did this, bugs, fog, and wind made it a chore. So I took an easy out and bought a small dehydrator. Very simple but adequate models start at about $40. Hardware stores stock dehydrators, many cooking utensil catalogs offer them, and they're even sold on TV.

Although I got my dehydrator for

tomatoes, it's so easy to use that I make dried snacks with other fruits and vegetables—including regular tomato slices.

Does it pay to dry your own tomatoes? It takes at least a pound of fresh to get about an ounce of dried. This makes my dried tomatoes a better value than the ones at my market. You might want to check prices where you shop.

Dried Roma tomatoes. Start with 3 pounds ripe **Roma tomatoes** to get about 2½ ounces (about 1½ cups) dried tomatoes. Rinse tomatoes, cut in half lengthwise, and with a teaspoon scoop out seeds and juicy pulp. Also trim off any bruises or damaged spots. Sprinkle cut sides of tomatoes with a total of ½ teaspoon **salt.**

Set tomatoes cut side up and about an inch apart on dehydrator racks. Set dehydrator temperature at 125° (if there is no control, this is about the temperature of the dehydrator). Dry until tomatoes feel very dry and are rigid but not quite brittle, 16 to 18 hours.

As soon as the tomatoes are dry, they're ready to eat. To store, let them cool, then seal airtight in a plastic bag and keep at room temperature. Check the tomatoes the first 3 or 4 days, and if there's any hint of mold, trim it off and dry the tomatoes a little longer. Or just keep them in the freezer.

Per ½ ounce: 57 cal., 14% (8.1 cal.) from fat; 2.3 g protein; 0.9 g fat (0.1 g sat.); 13 g carbo.; 243 mg sodium; 0 mg chol.

Ricotta—beyond lasagna

I once took a poll, totally unscientific but telling nonetheless. My question was, What's ricotta for? Seven out of 10 said lasagna. While there's no question that ricotta does this job well, this role is as limiting as the character of Sherlock Holmes was for Basil Rathbone.

Ricotta folded into sweetened whipped cream with chunks of chocolate and grated orange peel is the classic cannoli filling. I also love ricotta slathered onto plain biscotti and sprinkled with sugar in which a few anise seeds have been crushed.

And ricotta is what makes these little pancakes so moist and tender. They're lovely for breakfast with maple syrup or honey, or for dessert with slightly crushed raspberries and powdered sugar.

Ricotta Pancakes

Prep and cook time: About 8 minutes, plus 4 to 6 minutes to cook each panful

Notes: Low-fat or regular ricotta can be used, too. If pancakes are turned before they're browned, they tend to break.

Makes: 12 to 14 pancakes about 3 inches wide

- 1 cup nonfat ricotta cheese
- 3 large eggs
- 1 tablespoon salad oil
- ¼ cup all-purpose flour
- 2 teaspoons sugar
- ¼ teaspoon salt

1. In a food processor or blender, whirl cheese, eggs, oil, flour, sugar, and salt until smooth; scrape container sides as needed.

2. Place a nonstick 10- to 12-inch frying pan or griddle over medium to medium-low heat. When hot, ladle 2 tablespoons of batter per pancake into pan, spacing pancakes slightly apart. Cook until tops are covered with bubbles, then turn with a wide spatula and cook until bottoms are brown, 4 to 6 minutes total.

3. Serve as cooked, or keep warm in a 150° oven in a single layer in a pan.

Per pancake: 49 cal., 39% (19 cal.) from fat; 3.8 g protein; 2.1 g fat (0.5 g sat.); 3 g carbo.; 72 mg sodium; 46 mg chol.

BOB THOMPSON ON WINE: ## When you're right to send it back

Murphy's Law—the one that says something will go wrong if it can—applies to wine, too. Not often, fortunately. But, alas, the rare occasion almost always happens in restaurants, where it costs the most in dollars, confusion, embarrassment, or all three.

There you are. You have just plunked down anywhere from $25 to $75, the waiter has poured the ritual trial sip, and your first thought is, "Gack!" Can you/should you send it back?

In three circumstances the answer is yes. Otherwise it is probably no. The three serious ailments of wine:

Corky. This is easy. Wines with bad corks smell very much like the old string mop your mother kept on the back porch through the wet of winter, and even more like books that have grown moldy in a dank basement. If you have to ask yourself, the wine is not corky enough to refuse. Corky wines are not the winery's or the restaurant's fault, but you are still entitled to ask for a different bottle of the same wine at no extra cost.

Vinegary. This is no harder to figure out than corky. Vinegar is vinegar. If you bought Cabernet and it smells like vinegar, the problem is the winery's, not yours. You will be smart not to ask for another bottle of the same wine. Look elsewhere on the list for something you know you like out of recent experience.

Maderized. Maderized is the fancy word for weary old wine. Sherry tastes this way, and is supposed to. Varietal white table wines should not remind you of sherry until they have earned the right by spending five or more years in bottle; figure eight or more in the case of reds. If you come across the flavor in a young wine, the most likely cause is overwarm storage conditions in the restaurant (or store) where you bought the wine.

Almost always, a browner color than expected is a dead giveaway in both reds and whites. Whites will also be much darker than normal.

If you get a maderized (oxidized) wine, try something different, younger if possible. In fact, ask what is the newest wine in the cellar and go with that because it will have had the least chance to be damaged by poor storage conditions.

Wine is subject to a few other problems, but they come rarely. If you get a dislikable bottle that does not taste moldy, vinegary, or worn out, the chances are it is simply a wine you do not like, in spite of what friends or critics have said about it. The correct social policy?

Make a note to yourself never to buy the wine again. Order a different bottle to make dinner a pleasure. Tell your companions it is the last time you will ever take advice from critic X. But don't blame anyone else, and don't send the bottle back. ■

Garlic
revival

*Give ordinary cloves a rest and start cooking with
rich, lively, vintage varieties*

Two dozen heads of roasted garlic and more than 50 raw cloves sit on the table. They represent nine varieties of garlic grown by Chester Aaron, a gardener and author widely known for his avid interest in this plant. None of these garlics is commercially significant. But most have an ancient lineage. Breathlessly, bravely, food professionals and farmers prepare to compare them.

Clove after clove, bite after bite, palates ride a wild roller coaster of intense sensations—rich and resonant, sharp and racy, piquant and hot, sweet and buttery—until they finally wither with garlic overload.

This gathering at Oakland's Oliveto Cafe and Restaurant is representative of many garlic tastings, including ones staged at *Sunset,* that have helped us pinpoint some of the most flavorful choices in this new garlic wave. Because even though Westerners have a measurable addiction to garlic, our options have been surprisingly limited. Of the 630 million pounds of garlic grown annually in California—most of the nation's

By Linda Lau Anusasananan and Lauren Bonar Swezey

You may not find ruby-skinned 'Creole Red' garlic at your supermarket. But you might come across it at a local farmers' market, along with other notable garlics that are savoring new popularity.

domestic supply—only two varieties, 'California Early' and 'California Late', make up the bulk of the crop, a quarter of which is consumed in-state.

It's this love that has stimulated richer garlic options. Garden hobbyists and specialized growers have rediscovered almost-forgotten varieties and expanded our resources for them. Many seed catalogs now offer dozens (one company has 400 varieties!). And garlic eaters are most likely to find these non-mainstream alternatives from late summer through late fall in farmers' markets, select produce markets, and natural food stores.

But with more garlic choices, the big questions are: which ones should you choose, and how do you know what you are getting?

GARLIC VARIETIES

The hundreds of varieties of garlic (*Allium sativum*) are divided into two subspecies, softneck (*A. s. sativum*) and hardneck (*A. s. ophioscorodon*). And neither should be confused with the massive elephant garlic (*Allium ampeloprasum*)—it's not a true garlic.

Most softneck garlics (including 'California Early' and 'California Late') are of the Artichoke group, which is named for the way the cloves form, not because of any kinship with artichokes. Each head consists of 12 to 20 cloves in overlapping layers. These are the most adaptable and easiest to grow.

The other softneck group, Silverskin, has heads that contain 12 to 40 cloves each—explaining, perhaps, why the late culinary bon vivant James Beard, along with the French, chose 40 cloves of garlic to go with a chicken. The skin colors of Artichoke and Silverskin range from white, creamy, or faintly pink to white with a brown blush. The peeled cloves of both groups are creamy to pale gold.

Hardneck garlics produce a woody flower stalk in late spring that grows 1 to 6 feet above the leaves and twists into a coil. As the garlic head forms, the stalk straightens. (Aboveground, the flower at the tip of the stalk develops many small bulblets, known as bulbils, which can be planted in the fall and used for garlic greens.) When the garlic head is mature, it is usually composed of a single circle of large cloves. The outer skin may be dull brown, red, or purple. The skin around the cloves is more intensely colored than the outer layers, but the cloves themselves are white. Of the three hardneck groups, Rocambole, with only 6 to 11 cloves per head, is the most acclaimed for flavor and ease of peeling.

DISHES THAT DEMAND GARLIC

Distinctive garlics bring individuality to dishes, and these recipes suggest ways to best use the five popular varieties described below.

But even supermarket garlics, with their fewer flavor nuances, work well. And if a recipe calls for garlic cloves by the cupful, purchase refrigerated peeled fresh cloves.

GARLICS THAT MEASURE UP

These five varieties of garlic are exceptional. But there are many more varieties to be discovered, each of which offers a range of flavor experiences.

PETER CHRISTIANSEN

'CELAYA PURPLE'
(hardneck, Rocambole). Raw, this garlic from Mexico is strong, with a lingering heat. Roasted, it's mild to strong and tastes a bit like an artichoke. The purple-streaked skin on the cloves is fairly easy to peel off, and the heads keep well for about three months. For best production, 'Celaya Purple' needs a cold winter and warm spring.

'CREOLE RED'
(softneck, Silverskin). This is one of the original red garlic varieties grown in America. Raw, it tastes slightly sweet at first, then follows with a lingering hot, peppery aftertaste. Cooked, it develops a rich, mild caramel quality with a touch of heat. The shiny pinkish red–skinned cloves are easy to peel. The heads keep well for three to four months. As a plant, 'Creole Red' performs best in mild-winter climates.

'INCHELIUM RED'
(softneck, Artichoke). This garlic was discovered on an Indian reservation. Says grower Chester Aaron, "Its mild, almost sweet flavor doesn't have a strong effect in cooking, but it's excellent raw on bruschetta." The skin on the cloves is white. The heads are large and store well for about six months. The plant grows almost anywhere.

'RED TOCH'
(softneck, Artichoke). The origin of this garlic is near Tochliavri in the Republic of Georgia. Some claim it has the perfect garlic flavor when raw. Roasted, it's mild and sweet. The skin on the cloves is streaked with red and pink. The large heads store well for about six months. This garlic grows readily in most places.

'SPANISH ROJA'
(hardneck, Rocambole). This garlic was introduced to the Portland area in the late 1800s. Raw, its flavor is mild to medium-hot with a piquant finish. Roasting emphasizes its robust side. Ron Engeland of Filaree Farm describes this variety as the one that epitomizes garlic flavor. The big, shiny reddish purple–skinned cloves are very easy to peel, and the heads keep well for about three months. The plant grows best in the Northwest and in Northern California.

Chicken with 24 cloves has moderate heat and is saturated with a mellow sweetness.

KEVIN CANDLAND

garlic heads, score outer skin, skirting the circumference. Pull off upper half of outer skin to expose cloves. Arrange heads, root ends down, in a close-fitting shallow casserole (6 to 8 in. wide). Drizzle with oil.

For half-heads. Cut garlic heads in half crosswise. Pour oil into a 9-inch-wide baking pan and set heads, cut sides down, in oil.

2. Bake garlic in a 350° oven until it is very soft when pressed and cut cloves are richly browned, 45 to 55 minutes.

3. Serve hot or at room temperature. Pull cloves from whole heads and squeeze garlic out. Pluck cut cloves from half heads. Add salt and pepper to taste.

Per serving: 38 cal., 32% (12 cal.) from fat; 1.2 g protein; 1.3 g fat (0.2 g sat.); 6.1 g carbo.; 3.1 mg sodium; 0 mg chol.

Chicken with 24 Cloves of Garlic

Prep and cook time: About 1 hour

Notes: Two heads of a large-clove Artichoke or Silverskin variety or two heads of a small-clove Rocambole variety will yield about the right amount of garlic. 'Creole Red', 'Spanish Roja', and 'Celaya Purple' work well.

Makes: 4 servings

> 1 tablespoon olive oil
>
> 4 whole chicken legs (about 2½ lb. total), skin removed if desired
>
> ½ cup chicken broth
>
> ½ cup dry white wine
>
> 24 large cloves garlic, peeled
>
> Parsley sprigs
>
> Salt and pepper

1. Coat a 10- to 12-inch frying pan (nonstick if chicken is skinned) with oil. Add chicken and cook, covered, over medium-high heat until browned, about 7 minutes. Turn pieces over, cover, and continue cooking until browned on the other side, 5 to 7 minutes longer. Uncover; pour off and discard fat.

2. Add broth, wine, and garlic. Cover the frying pan tightly and simmer for about 15 minutes. Turn chicken pieces over; continue to simmer, covered, until meat is no longer pink near bone, 10 to 15 minutes longer.

3. Transfer chicken and garlic to a platter. If necessary, boil juices, uncovered, over high heat until reduced to about ⅓ cup. Spoon juices over meat. Garnish with parsley sprigs. Add salt and pepper to taste.

Per serving: 388 cal., 51% (198 cal.) from fat; 38 g protein; 22 g fat (5.7 g sat.); 7 g carbo.; 133 mg sodium; 128 mg chol.

Green Garlic Soup

Prep and cook time: About 45 minutes

Notes: Paul Bertolli, chef at Oliveto Restaurant and Cafe in Oakland, California, uses immature garlic to give this silky soup exceptional subtlety. Look for garlic with green tops at farmers' markets, usually in spring. Or use ¾ cup peeled mature garlic cloves (do not chop) such as 'Celaya Purple' instead of immature heads.

Makes: 3 or 4 servings

> 6 to 12 immature (1 to 1½ in. wide) garlic heads
>
> 1 tablespoon butter or margarine
>
> About ¾ pound thin-skinned potatoes
>
> 3 cups chicken or vegetable broth
>
> 2 tablespoons whipping cream
>
> 1 teaspoon white wine vinegar
>
> Salt and fresh-ground pepper
>
> Crisp buttered croutons

1. Trim off garlic tops and root ends. If tops are tender, reserve for garnish. Rinse garlic, peel off any tough skin (do not peel off tender skin), and cut garlic into ½-inch chunks; you need ¾ cup.

2. In a 2- to 3-quart pan, combine garlic, butter, and ¼ cup water. Cover and simmer gently until garlic is very tender when pierced, about 15 minutes.

3. Meanwhile, peel potatoes and cut into 1-inch chunks. Add potatoes and broth to garlic and bring to a boil. Cover and simmer over low heat until potatoes are very tender when pierced, about 20 minutes.

4. With a slotted spoon, transfer potatoes and garlic to a blender or food processor. Smoothly purée, adding enough of the cooking liquid to blend well. If using immature garlic heads, rub puréed mixture and remaining broth through a fine strainer into a bowl; return mixture to pan.

5. Stir soup over medium heat until hot, then add cream, vinegar, and salt and pepper to taste. Ladle into bowls and garnish with croutons. Thinly slice reserved garlic tops and sprinkle onto soup.

Per serving: 208 cal., 29% (60 cal.) from fat; 6.7 g protein; 6.7 g fat (3.6 g sat.); 32 g carbo.; 86 mg sodium; 16 mg chol.

Roasted Garlic

Prep and cook time: 50 to 60 minutes

Notes: Whole heads taste mellow and mild; cut heads caramelize and get decidedly sweet as they brown. Serve with crusty bread and chèvre (goat) cheese for an appetizer. 'Spanish Roja' and 'Creole Red' are excellent roasted.

Makes: 12 appetizer servings

> 3 heads (3 to 4 oz. each) garlic
>
> 1 to 2 tablespoons extra-virgin olive oil
>
> Salt and pepper

1. *For whole heads.* About halfway down

Pickled Garlic

Prep and cook time: About 30 minutes

Notes: Use big cloves from 'Spanish Roja' or 'Creole Red' to make these mild pickles. Serve cloves whole as an appetizer, with grilled meats, or in sandwiches or salads.

Makes: 1 cup

 ¾ cup distilled white vinegar

 2 tablespoons sugar

Pickled, garlic loses its bite. Eat it fearlessly by the clove. It's surprisingly mild.

 ¼ teaspoon hot chili flakes

 ¼ teaspoon black peppercorns

 ¼ teaspoon cumin seed

 1 cup large garlic cloves, peeled

1. In a 1- to 1½-quart pan, combine vinegar, sugar, chili flakes, peppercorns, and cumin seed. Bring to a boil over high heat. Add garlic cloves and return to a boil; simmer, uncovered, for 2 minutes. Pour the mixture into a jar.

2. Cover, cool, and chill at least 24 hours or up to 1 month.

Per 2 tablespoons: 38 cal., 2.4% (0.9 cal.) from fat; 1 g protein; 0.1 g fat (0 g sat.); 9.4 g carbo.; 3 mg sodium; 0 mg chol.

TAMING GARLIC TO TASTE

Garlic's characteristic smell becomes pronounced when a compound in the garlic, alliin, meets the enzyme allinase, from which it has been separated by cellular membranes. When these membranes are broken—by chewing, pressing, or cutting—allinase comes into contact with alliin, forming the hot-tasting sulfur compound called allicin. The more thoroughly you crush the cells, as in a garlic press, the stronger and more pungent the results. The heat of cooking inactivates and eliminates the effects of allinase—mostly by driving away the volatile sulfur. Keep these techniques in mind to make garlic taste the way you want.

•**Hot and brash.** Use garlic raw, finely chopped or pressed. Use in salad dressings and aïoli.

•**Robust but not burning.** Chop garlic and cook briefly. (Take care not to scorch; this gives garlic an exceptionally bitter taste.) Use in cooked sauces and stir-fries.

•**Tame and mild.** Simmer whole cloves until soft and tender. Use cloves to pickle, eat plain, or add to dishes.

•**Sweet, nutty, and creamy.** Roast whole, unpeeled heads or slowly pan-brown whole, unpeeled cloves until garlic is very soft when pressed. Use when you want to eat quantities of garlic—as a spread for bread, for instance.

GROWING GARLIC AT HOME

•The best time to plant garlic in mild-winter climates is from mid-October through December: in Southern California, plant in November; in the Pacific Northwest, plant in October and November. In cold-winter climates, plant in late September.

•Choose a site that gets at least six hours of sun a day. Garlic—particularly Rocambole—prefers rich, well-drained soil full of organic matter. If your soil is clay-dense and poorly drained, grow garlic in raised beds. In heavy soils, the outer skin stains and the garlic may rot.

•To grow garlic in raised beds, fill beds with a good soil mix purchased from a garden supply company. In the beds or in the ground, mix in about a 2-inch layer of well-composted manure. Let the soil sit for about six weeks before planting, soaking it every four to five days.

•To plant, carefully separate the garlic cloves from the head, choosing cloves that are firm, unscarred, and unbroken. Keep in mind that large cloves produce large heads, small cloves produce small ones, and cloves from small heads also tend to produce small heads—especially in the hardneck varieties.

•Wet the soil thoroughly and plant cloves 6 inches apart in rows 6 to 8 inches apart, with scar (flat) end down. The tip of the clove should be 1 to 2 inches below the soil surface.

•Since different garlics mature at slightly different times, plant the same kinds of garlic together so that, at the end of the season, watering can be controlled.

•Fill the holes with soil, but don't tamp down. Soak the soil again. Cover the beds with a 6- to 8-inch-thick layer of mulch, such as straw, to help maintain the soil moisture and moderate soil temperatures.

•Garlic requires constantly moist soil. If rain isn't adequate, water when the soil several inches below the surface is almost dry. In mild climates, foliage growth starts in a couple of months.

•About March 1 (a week or two earlier in the south, later in the north), spray the foliage with a combination of fish emulsion and seaweed (kelp), and four weeks later, follow up with another application. Fertilizing after early May doesn't help heads grow.

•On Rocamboles, flower stalks appear in midspring. To get the largest head, cut off the stalk when it's 4 to 6 inches tall—either before or right at the time the first coil forms.

•To harvest garlic green, pull it in the spring when the heads are small and not distinctly formed. Plan to use immature garlic within several days; it's as perishable as green onions.

•Depending on the climate, garlic reaches maturity from late May to mid-July. Stop watering about two weeks before harvest—or when 25 to 30 percent of the leaves have turned brown. Harvest when 60 to 75 percent of the tops are brown.

•Get harvested garlic out of the sun immediately. Too much heat greatly impairs garlic's storage life. Brush the soil from roots (don't wash heads). Bundle stems together with string in groups of 5 to 10 heads.

•Hang garlic bundles for two to three weeks in a dry, shady, well-ventilated area that stays moderately cool (65° to 75°). Heads are cured when skins and stalks feel completely dry.

•It takes about two months for individual characteristics to fully develop. When garlics stand even longer, these differences grow more subtle, but Rocamboles may develop more of a bite.

•Store garlic at cool room temperature in a well-ventilated spot out of direct sun. ■

BUYING GARLIC TO GROW?

Filaree Farm, 182 Conconully Highway, Okanogan, WA 98840; (509) 422-6940. Sells more than 100 varieties; catalog $2.

The Montana Garlic Farm, 355 Sunny Dene Lane, Kalispell, MT 59901; (406) 752-3127. Maintains the world's largest collection of garlic—400 varieties; recommends 100 to grow.

Sweetwater Farms Garlic Division, 57707 Highway 204, Weston, OR 97886; (541) 566-2756. Offers about a dozen varieties.

ROBERT OLDING

Cooking at 500°

It's fast and easy, and it brings out the best in root vegetables

WHY COOK AT 500°? THE MOST obvious reason is speed. But that's not the only reason: The high temperature caramelizes the sugars in vegetables, producing naturally sweet flavors. And, a whole chicken cooked at 500° has a crisp, browned skin and succulent, juicy meat.

Since I learned about the technique some call "blasting," I rarely cook at lower temperatures. For one thing, it speeds up weeknight meals. And because the root vegetables and garlic potatoes need little attention—a stir every 10 minutes for even browning—I can sit down and talk with my family while dinner is cooking.

Roots at 500°

Cooking time: About 35 minutes
Prep time: About 10 minutes
Notes: Serve with barbecued steak, smoked pork chops, or chicken breasts.
Makes: 4 servings

- 1 Yukon gold or russet potato (about 1 lb.)
- 2 tablespoons olive oil
- ³/₄ cup (¹/₄ lb.) baby carrots
- 1 red onion (³/₄ lb.), coarsely chopped
- 1 yam (¹/₂ lb.)
- 1 beet (¹/₂ lb.)

  A few parsley sprigs or 2 tablespoons thinly sliced green onion

  Salt and pepper

1. Scrub potato and cut into ³/₄-inch cubes.
2. In a 500° oven, heat oil in a 10- by 15-inch roasting pan just until hot, about 1¹/₂ minutes. Add cubed potato, carrots, and red onion. Cook 15 minutes, stirring after 10 minutes.

Rich color and sweet flavor are the result when beets, carrots, onions, potatoes, and yams are "blasted" in your oven at 500°. Serve the vegetables with broiled fish, roast beef, or barbecued chicken.

3. Meanwhile, peel yam and beet; cut each into about ¹/₂-inch cubes. Add to pan after potato has cooked 15 minutes; cook about 20 minutes more, stirring every 10 minutes, until vegetables are golden brown.
4. Spoon vegetables onto a platter; garnish with parsley. Add salt and pepper to taste.

Per serving: 273 cal., 24% (66 cal.) from fat; 5.2 g protein; 7.3 g fat (0.9 g sat.); 49 g carbo.; 61 mg sodium; 0 mg chol.

Garlic Potatoes with Chicken

Cooking time: About 45 minutes
Prep time: About 10 minutes
Notes: A vertical poultry roaster leaves more room in your baking pan for potatoes and onion, but it's not essential.
Makes: 5 to 6 servings

- 2 pounds (about 18) thin-skinned red and/or white potatoes
- 1 tablespoon olive oil
- 1 onion (¹/₂ lb.), quartered
- 1 whole chicken (about 3¹/₂ lb.)
- 1 bulb garlic, cloves peeled
- 3 tablespoons minced, drained oil-packed dried tomatoes
- 2 teaspoons fresh rosemary leaves

  Fresh rosemary sprigs (optional)

  Salt and pepper

1. Scrub potatoes. In a 500° oven, heat oil in a 10- by 15-inch roasting pan until hot, about 1¹/₂ minutes. Add potatoes and onion; shake pan to coat vegetables with oil. Stand chicken upright on a vertical roaster at one end of pan. (Or place chicken on a V-shaped roasting rack and surround with potatoes and onion.)
2. Cook 15 minutes, then add garlic and cook 30 minutes more, stirring vegetables every 10 minutes.
3. Remove chicken to platter. Stir tomatoes and rosemary leaves into potato mixture; arrange alongside chicken. Garnish with rosemary sprigs; offer salt and pepper to taste.

Per serving: 603 cal., 51% (306 cal.) from fat; 38 g protein; 34 g fat (8.6 g sat.); 36 g carbo.; 144 mg sodium; 135 mg chol. ■

By Betsy Reynolds Bateson

Puréed mesquite-smoked tomatoes and broth form the base of a "grilled" soup topped with a sweet-tart relish of smoked corn and peppers, green onion, lime juice, and sage.

Succulent tomatoes, rich soups

Capture the season's best flavors in a bowl

By Christine Weber Hale • Photographs by Kevin Candland

A PLUMP, FULLY RIPE TOMATO JUST off the vine is a warm burst of earthy sweetness that is worlds apart from the anemic, rock-hard varieties that line supermarket bins during winter months.

Savor the incredible flavor now, before the season disappears. You don't need a lot of additional ingredients, as the fol-

lowing soups demonstrate so beautifully. It's easy to make extra batches of these recipes to enjoy throughout the winter. Just prepare the soup base and freeze, then add condiments shortly before serving.

If you find yourself with some slightly underripe tomatoes, don't refrigerate them: you'll stop the ripening process. Instead, keep the tomatoes in a single

layer at room temperature until they are fully ripe.

Charred Tomato Soup with Corn and Pepper Relish

Prep and cook time: About 40 minutes
Notes: The mesquite chips impart a bold smoky flavor—omit them if you want a more subtle grilled taste.
Makes: 4 servings

    1 cup mesquite smoking chips (optional)

To peel tomatoes:
Dip a few tomatoes at a time in boiling water for 1 minute. Remove and let stand until cool to touch. Use a small sharp knife to peel away the skin.

2 ears of corn (about 1¾ lb.), husks and silks removed

1 orange or red bell pepper, stemmed, seeded, and halved lengthwise

2½ pounds ripe Roma tomatoes, halved lengthwise

2 tablespoons olive oil

2 cups chicken broth

3 tablespoons thinly sliced green onion

1 tablespoon lime juice

1½ teaspoons minced fresh or ½ teaspoon crumbled dried sage leaves

Sage sprigs (optional)

Salt

1. If using mesquite chips, soak them in water to cover for at least 20 minutes or up to 1 hour.

2. Drain chips well. In a barbecue with a lid, scatter half the chips over a solid bed of very hot coals (you can hold your hand at grill level only 1 second). For gas grills, turn on high, let heat 10 minutes, then put half the chips in a foil pan and set directly on flame in a corner of the grill.

3. Place corn and pepper halves on a well-oiled grill 4 to 6 inches above coals. Close lid, open vents, and cook until vegetables are lightly charred, 8 to 10 minutes; turn occasionally during cooking. Remove from grill and set aside.

4. Scatter remaining chips over the coals (or place in the foil pan). Brush cut sides of tomatoes with olive oil. Place tomatoes cut sides down on the grill. Close lid and cook until tomatoes are slightly charred, about 7 minutes. With a spatula, carefully remove tomatoes from grill. Reserve 4 nice-looking tomato halves.

5. Place remaining tomatoes in a blender with the chicken broth. Whirl until smooth; blend in batches if necessary. Transfer tomato mixture to a 4- to 5-quart pan. Stir often over medium heat until steaming, 8 to 10 minutes.

6. While soup heats, cut corn from cobs and coarsely chop pepper. Mix together corn kernels, pepper, green onion, lime juice, and sage leaves.

7. Divide tomato soup equally among 4 bowls. Spoon equal amounts of corn relish into the center of the soup. Lay 1 reserved tomato half, cut side up, next to each pile of corn and garnish with a sage sprig. Add salt to taste.

Per serving: 203 cal., 41% (84 cal.) from fat; 6.4 g protein; 9.3 g fat (1.5 g sat.); 29 g carbo.; 91 mg sodium; 1.9 mg chol.

Tomato–Lemon Grass Bisque with Shrimp

Prep and cook time: About 25 minutes, plus at least 4 hours to chill

Makes: 4 servings

¼ pound lemon grass, tough ends trimmed, or 2 tablespoons grated lemon peel

1½ cups chicken broth

½ ounce fresh ginger, thinly sliced

2 teaspoons cornstarch smoothly mixed with 2 tablespoons water

2½ pounds very ripe red, yellow, or orange tomatoes, cored and coarsely chopped

½ pound cooked, peeled, and deveined shrimp

2 tablespoons minced chives

Low-fat sour cream and whole chives (optional)

1. Cut lemon grass into 2-inch pieces and crush stalks lightly with a mallet. Combine lemon grass with broth and ginger in a 2- to 3-quart pan. Bring to a boil over high heat, then cover tightly and simmer 15 minutes. With a slotted spoon, pick out and discard lemon grass and ginger. Briskly stir cornstarch mixture into broth until mixture boils again. Chill broth mixture until cold, at least 4 hours or up to 1 day.

2. In a blender or food processor, combine broth and tomatoes. Whirl until very smooth; blend in batches if necessary. If making ahead, chill airtight up to 4 hours.

3. Pour chilled mixture into soup bowls. Garnish with shrimp, minced chives, dollops of sour cream, and whole chives.

Per serving: 132 cal., 14% (18 cal.) from fat; 15 g protein; 2 g fat (0.6 g sat.); 15 g carbo.; 191 mg sodium; 112 mg chol.

Tomato-Bread Soup with Basil

Prep and cook time: About 45 minutes

Makes: 6 servings

⅓ pound sourdough bread, cut into ¾-inch-thick slices

3 tablespoons olive oil

2 onions (about 1 lb.), chopped

3 cloves garlic, minced

3 pounds ripe red or orange tomatoes, peeled, cored, and coarsely chopped

3 cups chicken broth

½ cup dry red wine

1 cup firmly packed basil leaves, slivered

Basil sprigs (optional)

1. Brush bread slices on both sides with half the oil. Spread in a single layer on a baking sheet. Bake in a 300° oven until lightly golden, about 10 minutes. If making ahead, cool completely, then store airtight up to 1 day.

2. In a 5- to 6-quart pan, combine remaining oil, onions, and garlic. Stir often over medium-high heat until onions are golden brown and taste sweet, about 15 minutes. Add tomatoes, broth, and red wine. Simmer until reduced to 8 cups, about 15 minutes. If making ahead, cool, cover, and chill up to 1 day. Reheat until simmering.

3. Stir slivered basil into soup. Divide toasted bread slices among 6 soup bowls. Top with soup and garnish with basil sprigs.

Per serving: 247 cal., 34% (84 cal.) from fat; 7.3 g protein; 9.3 g fat (1.6 g sat.); 34 carbo.; 229 mg sodium; 1.9 mg chol. ∎

Lemon grass and ginger delicately perfume a chilled tomato bisque garnished with shrimp, sour cream, and chives. Choose yellow or orange tomatoes to vary the color.

Chopped shrimp, mango, avocado, onion, and water chestnuts soak up a lime-ginger dressing to make new-wave poke.

Hawaii's favorite fish salad

Poke (po-key) is an Island treasure. Try it to start or as the heart of a light summer meal

POKE—JUST SAY *PO*-KEY—IS A survivor. Native to the Hawaiian Islands, it's a grand salad when ingredients are strictly local. But now poke is being more broadly interpreted by Hawaiians championing their own cuisine, by visiting cooks and migratory chefs, and even at a cooking contest.

Poke means *to slice* or *to cut*. What gets cut up is fish, mostly—usually raw tuna. Basic poke is tuna or other Island fish and crunchy seaweed seasoned with sea salt and the local kukui nut, which has been pounded to a paste. Nontraditional versions use shellfish and fish from distant waters. Some new-wave chefs even propose beef. And in the melting pot culture of Island kitchens, the seasonings of the Caribbean, China, Japan, Korea, Mexico, Southeast Asia, and the South Pacific are all making their marks on today's poke.

The most revealing diversity of poke is found at Sam Choy's Aloha Festivals Poke Recipe Contest. Last year's competition had more than 70 finalists from Hawaii and the Mainland. Some pokes were variations of the basic; others were wildly inventive and included cooked seafood, fruits, vegetables, noodles, lime juice, and chilies. The dishes' common denominator was taste: a good poke should be light, bright, and fresh.

Much of the contest fun is visual, ranging from high-style to off-the-wall presentations: poke encased in paper-thin *nori* (seaweed), poke fried as pseudo macadamia nut bonbons, or poke surfing on fried wonton skins. The 1996 contest is October 6 at the Hapuna Beach Prince Hotel, Kohala Coast, on the Big Island of Hawaii. The event is free for those with the Aloha Festivals ribbon ($5). The public is invited to taste at 11:30, after the judging is finished. For information contact Gloriann Akau, Aloha Festivals, Box 1921, Kamuela, HI 96743; (808) 885-8086.

Colorful shrimp poke, a synthesis of several sampled, has the proper Polynesian persona, but its ingredients are available to off-Islanders—*malihinis*. For traditional poke, try Sam Choy's Island Poke. If you expect to be eating poke in Hawaii, be sure to bone up on the lingo.

Malihini Shrimp Poke

Prep and cook time: 1½ to 2 hours, including chilling

Notes: To save about an hour, skip the raw shrimp and buy 1¾ pounds of shelled cooked tiny shrimp. Rinse before using.

Makes: 6 to 8 main-dish, 12 appetizer servings

- 2 pounds (about 35 per lb.) shrimp, shelled and deveined
- ¾ cup lime juice
- ¼ cup Asian fish sauce (*nuoc mam* or *nam pla*) or soy sauce
- 2 tablespoons minced fresh ginger
- 2 cloves garlic, pressed or minced
- ½ cup finely chopped Maui or other sweet onion
- 1 cup (or 1 can, 5 oz.) sliced water chestnuts, drained and chopped

1 1/2 to 2 tablespoons minced fresh red or green hot chili

1 firm-ripe avocado (about 10 oz.)

1 firm-ripe mango (about 1 1/4 lb.), peeled, pitted, and cut into 1/2-inch cubes

1/2 cup chopped watercress sprigs

Fresh ti leaves, thawed frozen banana leaves, or romaine lettuce leaves (optional)

Watercress sprigs, rinsed and crisped

1. In a 5- to 6-quart pan, bring 3 quarts water to a boil. Add raw shrimp, cover pan tightly, and remove from heat. Let stand until shrimp are white in thickest part (cut to test), about 3 minutes. Drain; immerse shrimp in cold water until cool, then drain again, rinse, and coarsely chop.

2. Mix shrimp with lime juice, fish sauce, ginger, garlic, onion, water chestnuts, and chili to taste. Cover poke mixture and chill at least 30 minutes or up to 2 hours; stir occasionally.

3. Peel and pit avocado. Cut 2 or 3 thin slices, coat with a little dressing from poke, and reserve for garnish. Cut remaining avocado into 1/2-inch chunks. Add avocado chunks, mango, and chopped watercress to poke; mix gently.

4. Line a large shallow bowl or rimmed platter with ti leaves. Spoon poke and dressing onto leaves, then garnish with reserved avocado slices and watercress sprigs.

Per main-dish serving: 207 cal., 29% (60 cal.) from fat; 21 g protein; 6.7 g fat (1.2 g sat.); 16 g carbo.; 445 mg sodium; 140 mg chol.

OLD-TIME POKE

For centuries, Hawaiian fishermen cut their catch of raw fish into cubes and seasoned it with ingredients at hand. Modern poke makes use of seasonings brought by recent Island immigrants, such as soy sauce, onions, tomatoes, and chilies. Mostly, the fish is used raw. But at Sam Choy's Restaurant in Kona, you get a choice. You can have poke raw (native-style) or briefly seared, then seasoned.

Sam Choy's Island Poke

Prep and cook time: 15 to 25 minutes; 20 minutes more if using frozen ogo

Notes: For raw poke, buy commercially frozen fish or freeze fish at 0° or colder at least 1 week to kill harmful parasites.

On the Mainland, the most likely sources for ogo (seaweed) are Japanese fish markets. Japanese grocery stores may have frozen ogo, which is salted. Let it thaw, rinse well, then soak in cold water, changing water frequently, until ogo no longer tastes heavily salted, about 20 minutes.

Makes: 4 main-dish, 8 appetizer servings

1 tablespoon sesame seed

1 pound ahi tuna, about 1 inch thick, rinsed and patted dry

1 teaspoon salad oil

1 cup fresh or soaked frozen ogo (see Notes), rinsed and coarsely chopped

1 firm-ripe tomato (about 6 oz.), cored and chopped

1/2 cup thinly sliced green onions

2 tablespoons soy sauce

1 teaspoon Asian sesame oil

1/2 teaspoon hot chili flakes

1. Stir sesame seed in a 10- to 12-inch non-stick frying pan over medium heat until golden, about 5 minutes; remove from pan and set aside.

2. If you want to serve the poke raw, cut tuna into 1/2-inch cubes. If you want to cook the fish first, place frying pan over high heat. When pan is very hot, add salad oil and swirl to coat pan bottom. Add the whole piece of fish and cook, turning once, just until lightly browned on outside but still red inside (cut to test), about 2 minutes total. Remove from pan and cut into 1/2-inch cubes.

3. Reserve 1/4 cup ogo for garnish. In a large bowl, mix tuna, remaining 3/4 cup ogo, tomato, green onions, soy sauce, sesame oil, and chili. Spoon into serving dish and garnish with reserved ogo and toasted sesame seed.

Per cooked main-dish serving: 179 cal., 23% (42 cal.) from fat; 30 g protein; 4.7 g fat (0.8 g sat.); 5.5 g carbo.; 595 mg sodium; 51 mg chol. ■

By Linda Lau Anusasananan

POKE LINGO

Here's how to interpret Hawaiian and Japanese descriptions of poke ingredients that you're apt to encounter on Island menus.

`Ahi.** Hawaiian name for yellowfin (also called bigeye) tuna. The fish is sold in two grades: Sashimi-grade has a deeper red color and is used for raw fish preparations such as poke and sashimi. Fry- or grill-grade is usually cooked but only until very rare. As the surface browns, the flesh beneath turns white, but the interior of the fish should remain red.

Aku. Hawaiian for bonito (also called skipjack tuna). The deep red flesh is bolder in flavor than ahi.

`Alaea.** Hawaiian coarse sea salt. The salt harvested on Kauai is red.

A`u. Hawaiian for swordfish.

`Inamona.** Roasted kukui nuts pounded to a paste with coarse salt. You can buy this mixture in Hawaii. Use sparingly as a relish or for seasoning; in large quantities it can act as a laxative.

Kukui nut. The nut of the kukui tree. Roasted, the nuts

taste a bit like toasted sesame seed and are used to make `inamona. Polished, walnut-size kukui nuts are exceptionally black and glistening, and are made into jewelry and ever-lasting *leis* (necklaces).

Limu. Hawaiian for any kind of seaweed. Locals consume more than 350,000 pounds annually.

Limu kohu. An edible small, red seaweed.

Mahimahi. Hawaiian for dolphinfish (also called dorado). The flavor of mahimahi is sweet and mild; the flesh is ivory or pink.

Ogo. Japanese name for the edible crisp red, green, or brown feathery seaweed traditionally used in poke. It is harvested wild and also farmed in the Islands.

Ono. Hawaiian for wahoo. This sweet and delicate mackerel, favored for poke and sashimi, has a firm texture and light color.

Pūpū. In Hawaii, this is the word for appetizers. Poke, originally in this category, is branching out.

Tako. Japanese for small squid.

A splash of olive oil makes the difference

ONE OF THE MOST CONFUSING principles in low-fat cooking relates to very low calorie foods like vegetables. If you add even a small amount of fat, such as olive oil, the percentage of calories from fat shoots up well over the 30 percent benchmark. But the dishes can still be considered low-fat. Here's why.

Compare the Cauliflower Piquant (recipe below) with an indulgent burrito. One serving of cauliflower has only 4.1 grams of fat and 76 calories, with 49 percent of these calories from fat. The burrito, on the other hand, has a whopping 42 grams of fat and 930 calories, but only 41 percent from fat. (For the percentage of calories from fat, multiply grams of fat by 9 calories per gram and divide by total calories.)

Because the burrito has a lower percentage of calories from fat, does it contain less fat? No—what you really need to focus on is the number of grams. The vegetables use up just a fraction of your allotted daily fat intake (65 grams for a typical woman, 80 grams for a man), the burrito much more. Can both foods be part of a healthy diet? Yes—though the cauliflower fits in on a daily basis, the burrito as an occasional treat.

Now, if a burrito sounds more appealing than cauliflower, be aware that a mere splash of good olive oil and a few simple Italian seasonings lift this cauliflower recipe—and the green beans as well— above the ordinary, making the motherly advice to eat your vegetables a pleasure, not a duty.

Cauliflower Piquant

Prep and cook time: About 20 minutes
Makes: 4 servings

- 5 cups cauliflower florets

- ½ cup 1-inch-square pieces roasted red peppers
- 1 tablespoon drained capers
- 4 canned anchovies, patted dry and chopped
- 2 tablespoons lemon juice
- 1 tablespoon extra-virgin olive oil
- Salt and freshly ground pepper

ROBERT OLDING

1. In a covered 2- to 3-quart pan over high heat, bring cauliflower and ½ cup water to a boil. Reduce heat and simmer until tender-crisp to bite, about 4 minutes. Drain.

2. Combine peppers, capers, anchovies, lemon juice, and oil. Mix with cauliflower; season to taste with salt and pepper.

Per serving: 76 cal., 49% (37 cal.) from fat; 3.7 g protein; 4.1 g fat (0.6 g sat.); 7.8 g carbo.; 258 mg sodium; 2.2 mg chol.

Green Beans Italian-style

Prep and cook time: About 25 minutes
Makes: 4 servings

- 1 pound slender green beans such as *haricots verts*, stems trimmed
- 1 cup chopped ripe tomatoes
- 2 tablespoons chopped fresh marjoram leaves, plus sprigs
- 1 tablespoon extra-virgin olive oil
- Salt and freshly ground pepper

In a 3- to 4-quart pan, combine beans, tomatoes, and chopped marjoram. Cover; bring to a boil over high heat. Reduce heat; simmer until beans are tender-crisp, 5 to 7 minutes. Stir in oil. Add salt and pepper to taste. Garnish with marjoram sprigs.

Per serving: 75 cal., 45% (34 cal.) from fat; 2.5 g protein; 3.8 g fat (0.6 g sat.); 10 g carbo.; 11 mg sodium; 0 mg chol. ∎

Refreshingly fresh fruit drinks

COOLING OFF, JAMAICAN-STYLE, IS an art form in a glass. And it's an idea that travels well. Just whirl a lush blend of fruit and juices into velvety frosted beverages, pour them into chilled tall glasses, then sit in the shade and sip.

Banana-Coconut Daiquiri

Prep time: About 5 minutes
Makes: About 4½ cups, 4 or 5 servings

- 2 ripe bananas (about 1 lb.), peeled and cut into chunks
- ¼ cup lime juice
- ¼ cup canned sweetened coconut cream
- About 3½ cups small ice cubes
- About ½ cup rum (optional)

In a blender, whirl bananas with lime juice, coconut cream, and ice until smooth; add rum to taste. Pour into glasses.

Per cup: 95 cal., 31% (29 cal.) from fat; 1.1 g protein; 3.2 g fat (2.7 g sat.); 18 g carbo.; 11 mg sodium; 0 mg chol.

Papaya Cooler

Prep time: 5 to 8 minutes
Makes: About 6 cups, 6 servings

- 1 ripe papaya (about 1 lb.), peeled and seeded
- 1 cup pineapple juice
- ¼ cup lime juice
- 1 can (12 oz.) or 1½ cups papaya nectar
- 2 cups sparkling water
- About ¾ cup rum (optional)
- Ice cubes

In a blender, whirl papaya with pineapple juice and lime juice until smooth. Mix with papaya nectar and sparkling water; add rum to taste. Pour into chilled glasses; add ice cubes.

Per cup: 67 cal., 1.3% (0.9 cal.) from fat; 0.5 g protein; 0.1 g fat (0 g sat.); 17 g carbo.; 5.2 mg sodium; 0 mg chol. ∎

By Christine Weber Hale

Sunset's Kitchen Cabinet

Readers' family favorites tested in our kitchens

By Linda Lau Anusasananan and Betsy Reynolds Bateson

NORMAN A. PLATE

Quick Ravioli Soup

Tammy Moore-Worthington, Artesia, New Mexico

Every summer Tammy Moore-Worthington buys three bushels of roasted mild New Mexico green chilies and freezes them to use throughout the year. She adds a couple of the chilies to this speedy soup (you can substitute canned green chilies). Leftover grilled chicken adds a smoky note.

Prep and cook time: About 30 minutes
Makes: About 7 cups, 4 servings

- 3   cans (14½ oz. each) reduced-sodium chicken broth
- ¾   cup *each* finely diced onion and carrot
- 1   can (4 oz.) diced green chilies
- 2   cloves garlic, minced

- 1½   tablespoons minced fresh or 1½ teaspoons dried basil leaves
- 1   package (9 oz.) fresh or frozen cheese ravioli
- 1   cup thin strips cooked chicken
- ¼   cup freshly shredded parmesan cheese

1. In a 4- to 5-quart pan over high heat, bring broth, onion, carrot, green chilies, garlic, and basil to a simmer. Cover, reduce heat to low, and simmer 15 minutes.

2. Turn heat to high and bring broth to a boil. Add ravioli and cook until just barely tender to bite, 4 to 6 minutes. Add chicken and cook until hot, about 2 minutes more.

3. Ladle soup into bowls, and sprinkle with parmesan cheese.

Per serving: 354 cal., 33% (117 cal.) from fat; 26 g protein; 13 g fat (6.4 g sat.); 30 g carbo.; 1,330 mg sodium; 92 mg chol.

Cheddar Pepper Puffs

Audrey Thibodeau, Mesa, Arizona

Prolific recipe creator Audrey Thibodeau adds cheddar cheese and jalapeño chili to a basic cream-puff paste, then bakes the puffs in a ring for a savory pull-apart bread. Thibodeau's tangy cheese-crusted puffs are especially nice served with soup or salad.

Prep and cook time: About 40 minutes
Makes: 12 puffs

- ¼   cup (⅛ lb.) butter or margarine
- ¼   teaspoon salt

- 1   teaspoon crushed dried jalapeño or hot chili flakes, or 1 tablespoon minced fresh chili
- 1   cup all-purpose flour
- 4   large eggs
- 1   cup shredded sharp cheddar cheese

1. In a 1½- to 2-quart pan, combine 1 cup water, butter, salt, and chili. Place over high heat and bring to a rapid boil.

2. Add flour all at once to boiling butter-chili mixture, then turn heat to low and stir vigorously until mixture forms a ball and pulls away from the sides of the pan.

3. Remove from heat and beat in eggs, 1 at a time, mixing each thoroughly into batter.

4. Set aside 2 tablespoons of the cheese. Stir remaining cheese into batter.

5. On a lightly oiled 12- by 17-inch baking sheet, spoon batter in 12 equal portions to form an 8- to 9-inch-wide ring. Sprinkle reserved cheese over ring.

6. Bake in a 425° oven until ring is well browned and feels very crisp, about 35 minutes. Serve hot or at room temperature.

Per puff: 140 cal., 60% (84 cal.) from fat; 5.6 g protein; 9.3 g fat (5 g sat.); 8.3 g carbo.; 166 mg sodium; 92 mg chol. ■

FOOD
Guide

BY JERRY ANNE DI VECCHIO

Bright orange persimmons sweetly back up pork and blue cheese in creamy risotto made with California-grown arborio rice.

KEVIN CANDLAND

A TASTE OF THE WEST: A risotto for two seasons

No longer do I have to wait until October to make one of my favorite dishes—Harolyn Thompson's pork risotto with Fuyu persimmons. Last spring (and the one before), Fuyus from Chile were in the market. Feeling a bit like a traitor, I slipped the risotto onto a May dinner menu. Once you've

tasted this simple main dish, you'll understand why I couldn't wait for fall.

Fuyus, like apples, are wonderfully compatible with pork. They are sweet, juicy, tender-crisp, and a vivid color.

As if these weren't reasons enough to try Harolyn's risotto, now there's another. In September, the second crop of

California-grown arborio rice was harvested. My cooking colleagues and I tasted both Italian arborio and arborio from the Lundberg Family Farms, near Sacramento, and could not discern any differences. You can find Lundberg's arborio on some supermarket shelves and in natural-food stores in bulk (about

$1.80 per lb.) and in 2-pound bags ($2.30 to $3.80). The rice comes white or brown.

Now that there are more arborio choices, plus persimmons spring and fall, I can think of only one more thing to improve. I could make this dish even more quickly if my butcher would slice the pork. Maybe I'll ask him—next time.

Pork and Persimmon Risotto

Prep and cook time: About 30 minutes

Makes: 3 or 4 main-dish servings

- ½ pound pork tenderloin, fat trimmed, sliced about ⅛ inch thick
- 1 tablespoon butter or olive oil
- 6 tablespoons minced shallots
- 1 cup white arborio rice or pearl rice
- ½ teaspoon ground allspice
- ¼ teaspoon pepper
  About 3 cups chicken broth
- 1¼ cups dry white wine
- 2 Fuyu persimmons (6 to 7 oz. each)
- ½ cup crumbled blue cheese
- 1 tablespoon minced parsley

1. In a 10- to 12-inch nonstick frying pan over high heat, stir pork until no longer pink, about 2 minutes. Remove from pan.

2. Add butter and shallots to pan. Stir over medium-high heat until shallots are limp, about 1 minute.

3. Add rice to pan and stir often until opaque, 2 to 3 minutes. Stir in allspice and pepper. Mix 3 cups broth and wine and add 1 cup of the mixture to rice. Stir frequently over medium-high heat until liquid is absorbed, about 3 minutes.

4. Add remaining broth mixture and stir often until rice is tender to bite and most of the liquid is absorbed, 12 to 15 minutes.

5. Meanwhile, cut stems from persimmons. Cut 1 fruit into matchstick-thin pieces, the other crosswise into thin slices.

6. Stir pork and any juices, ½ of the blue cheese, and matchstick persimmon pieces into rice. Stir in enough more broth to give risotto a creamy texture, then ladle into wide bowls. Garnish with persimmon slices, parsley, and remaining blue cheese.

Per serving: 525 cal., 19% (99 cal.) from fat; 22 g protein; 11 g fat (6.2 g sat.); 73 g carbo.; 379 mg sodium; 60 mg chol.

A clean sheet

In a bakery one day, I was amazed to see a panful of cooled oatmeal cookies slide free as the baker gave the pan a brisk shake. I'd always found it necessary to carefully remove cookies with a spatula while they were still hot. This baker's secret was a thin, flexible liner on the pan. It looked like tan parchment, felt very slick, didn't tear like paper, and was waterproof. Even before I could ask what it was, the baker had wiped it clean with a damp cloth and was busily covering it with more cookie dough.

The nonstick pan liner, I learned, is in many stores in many forms under different names. These liners are readily available, but as they don't have a pizzazzy presence, you may have to ask where to find them at a cookware, hardware, or department store.

The least expensive is as thin as fabric (which it looks like), and is sold by the sheet or roll and can be cut with scissors. I bought a 13- by 17-inch piece for about $6 and a roll that was 17 by 20 inches for a dollar more (later, I saw it on sale for $5).

Dupont offers a six-pack of nonstick sheets for about $20 (two 10 by 15 in., two 9-in. rounds, one 9 by 13 in., and one 12 by 16 in.) and several other choices.

The most costly are the sturdier silicone pads (Silpat, Exopat brands), which cost about $28 for a 16- by 24-inch piece, and about $20 for the 13- by 18-inch size. There is even a nonstick pad molded for muffins.

Regardless of thickness, the liners share the same pluses. You don't have to oil or butter them, and they rinse clean and drip-dry. Use slick side up if there's a choice. Some come with guidelines for maximum oven temperatures, but

Nonstick pan liner, washable and reusable, is so slick that even hard-to-handle lace cookies come off easily when cool.

others don't. And you can cut any of them to size.

The liners make the tricky job of handling fragile lace cookies a snap. Instead of trying to move these hot cookies before they get hard and stick to the pan, you can let them cool on the liner. I also liked one package's suggestion, which was to put the liner on a pan under fruit pies that are inclined to bubble over—no more charred drippings to clean up. Or put the liner in the pan under a roast— the dark drippings scrape free easily to make a sauce.

From the Andean plains

When I started writing at *Sunset Magazine*, there was a young woman on our copy desk who hailed from Colombia. Although her father was originally from Iowa, and she had gone to universities in Massachusetts and Paris, she was well acquainted with foods of the country where she was born and raised.

As an introduction to Colombian cooking, she showed me how to make *ajiaco*, a soup that's considered the national dish. Her favorite version takes its name from the capital city's full name, Santa Fé de Bogotá.

Not surprisingly, indigenous potatoes—three kinds—are the heart of the soup. One potato disintegrates and thickens the soup. One is small, white, and waxy. And one is tiny and golden. In Colombia, the last would be the bright yellow *papas criollas*, which I have tasted from California home gardens. But

Two Andean natives, potatoes and ají chilies—now available here—bring authenticity to Colombian ajiaco soup.

tiny Yukon Golds from the market are an acceptable alternative.

The *ají* part of the soup's name comes from the chili used in the simple sauce that is the final addition to ajiaco. Ají— which means *chili*—has a unique floral flavor and a fair amount of heat. You can find ají chilies in some Latino stores that specialize in Peruvian and Colombian foods. You can also order them by mail from Peruvian Chili Collection, Box 281525, San Francisco, CA 94128, or call (800) 442-5777. A ½-ounce bag with 4 or 5 whole ají chilies costs $1.50.

To make salsa de ají, discard stems, seeds, and veins from 1 or 2 **dried ají chilies** (varieties available are *escabeche, limo,* and *panca,* and all of them have a wide range of heat). Cover chilies with hot **water** and let stand at least 5 minutes to soften. Drain chilies (or use 2 tablespoons chopped fresh jalapeño chilies). Purée in a blender or food processor with 1 cup packed **fresh cilantro** and ½ cup **cider vinegar.** Serve, or cover and chill up to 4 hours. Makes about ¾ cup.

Per tablespoon: 2.6 cal., 0% (0 cal.) from fat; 0.1 g protein; 0 g fat; 0.8 g carbo.; 0.9 mg sodium; 0 mg chol.

Ajiaco Santafereño

Prep and cook time: About 45 minutes

Notes: Add salsa de ají to individual servings to taste. Cut large Yukon Gold potatoes into 1½-inch chunks if small ones aren't available. Big capers or caper berries (about ¼ in. wide) with stems look dramatic in this soup, but 4 to 6 tablespoons of smaller capers will do, too.

Makes: 6 to 8 servings

- 6 cups chicken broth
- 1 russet potato (½ lb.), peeled and thinly sliced
- 3 red-skinned potatoes (2 in. wide) scrubbed and cut in half
- 12 to 16 Yukon Gold potatoes (about 1 in. wide), scrubbed
- 1 package (10 oz.) frozen corn kernels

  About 1½ pounds boneless, skinless chicken breasts, cut into 1-inch strips

- 1 firm, ripe avocado (½ to ¾ lb.)
- 1 tablespoon lemon juice
- 6 tablespoons (a 3-oz. jar) drained prepared large capers
- 6 tablespoons whipping cream or crème fraîche
- 2 diced hard-cooked large eggs
- Salt
- Salsa de ají

1. In a 6- to 8-quart pan, combine broth and sliced, halved, and whole potatoes. Cover and bring to a boil over high heat. Simmer gently until potato slices are very soft and fall apart when pressed, and the other potatoes are very tender when pierced, about 25 minutes. Stir mixture occasionally.

2. Whack package of corn on a flat surface to separate kernels, then pour into soup. Add chicken, cover pan, and simmer very gently until meat is no longer pink in center (cut to test), 7 to 8 minutes.

3. Meanwhile, peel, pit, and dice avocado and mix with lemon juice.

4. Put avocado, capers, cream, and eggs in separate bowls.

5. Ladle soup into wide bowls and add equal portions of avocado, capers, cream, and eggs. Add salt and salsa de ají to taste.

Per serving : 353 cal., 28% (99 cal.) from fat; 34 g protein; 11 g fat (4 g sat.); 30 g carbo.; 349 mg sodium; 134 mg chol.

KEVIN CANDLAND

Tender ways with tough cuts

Beef shanks, short ribs, and cheeks don't have the same cachet that veal shanks do. Even so, these muscular, tough cuts of beef can achieve the same tenderness. And they have even more potential succulence, which comes from an abundance of connective tissue that melts to create a delectable illusion of richness.

These meats beg for a partner that's soft and creamy, like mashed potatoes or polenta, to cradle the good juices that develop.

If you don't think you have the time to prepare these meats, let me share how I make it work. Take five minutes to put the meat and some seasonings into a casserole, pop it into the oven for about a half-hour to brown, then add liquid, cover tightly, and let the baking continue. Devote the hours the meat needs to cook to other activities—weeding, needlepoint, Internet cruising. You can even make a fast supper to serve while the casserole is doing its own thing, then refrigerate it and serve later in the week for another quick meal.

Beef shanks and short ribs (not to be confused with beef back ribs) are available at any meat counter. Short ribs have a lot of fat, so be sure to trim well.

Boneless beef cheeks (*cachete de res*) are available mostly in Latino meat markets.

Oven-braised beef for 4. Choose 1 of the following: 3 pounds **beef shanks** with small bones or 4 pounds with big bones (cut into about 1½-in. sections), 4 pounds beef short ribs, or 1½ pounds beef cheeks. Trim and discard most of the fat (not the slightly transparent connective tissue). Rinse meat and arrange in a single layer in a close-fitting pan (meat should be at least ½ in. below the pan rim).

Dice 1 **onion** (½ lb.) and 1 **carrot** (¼ lb.), and scatter vegetables over the meat. Sprinkle meat with 1 teaspoon coarse-ground **pepper**, 1 teaspoon **dried marjoram** or oregano **leaves,** and ½ teaspoon **dried rosemary leaves.** Bake in a 450° oven until meat is browned, about 30 minutes.

Add ½ cup **beef** or chicken **broth,** ⅓ cup **dry wine** (red or white), and 2 tablespoons **madeira** or dry sherry to the pan. Cover tightly and bake in a 325° oven until meat is tender enough to tear apart with a fork, 2½ to 3 hours.

Check occasionally and maintain at least ½ inch liquid (add more broth or water) in the pan; reseal. When meat is tender, skim and discard fat from juices. Serve meat and juices with **salt** to taste.

Per serving: 339 cal., 24% (81 cal.) from fat; 52 g protein; 9 g fat (2.9 g sat.); 9.6 g carbo.; 177 mg sodium; 89 mg chol.

Hot for frozen peas

When I was growing up in Half Moon Bay, California, peas were an important local crop. A farmer-neighbor let me pick all I wanted, so getting really fresh peas was no problem.

But there were other issues.

It took a fair spell to shell enough peas for our dinner, especially since I snacked shamelessly as I worked. The tiny ones were tender and sweet just off the vine, but a goodly share of my peas were big and a little starchy.

And since I usually picked more than I felt like shelling at one sitting, the unshelled ones followed their natural inclination to get starchier and less sweet as the hours passed.

That said, I feel my endorsement for frozen tiny peas has merit. These peas are uniformly small and sweet, shelled with a speed I will never match, then blanched, chilled, and frozen in a whirl

that I once witnessed in a vegetable-freezing plant. I buy frozen petite peas in big plastic bags, pour them out as I need them, and return the rest to the freezer.

Peas with pasta—an Italian classic—is one of my favorite ways to use petite peas. Sizzle a few thin slivers of **prosciutto** (about ⅛ lb. is all you need) until lightly browned and crisp, and set them aside.

Then heat 1 to 2 cups **frozen petite peas** in enough **whipping cream** with **chicken broth** (1 part cream, 3 parts broth—2 to 3 cups total) to cover them, adding fresh-grated **nutmeg** to taste—don't be timid.

When the liquid is boiling, pour it over 3 to 4 cups hot, cooked **capellini pasta** (6 to 8 oz. dried); the mixture should be a little soupy. Add prosciutto and grated **parmesan cheese** to taste, a bit more grated nutmeg, if you like, and fresh-ground **pepper,** then mix and serve to 3 or 4.

Tackling the pucker factor

Jack Sprat and his wife may have disagreed about lean versus fat because they salivated differently. If so, they never would have chosen the same red wine, either.

The troublemakers here are tannins, the same natural compounds that make tea and spinach puckery.

New research shows that people who salivate freely notice tannins' drying effects immediately, then compensate in a trice. People who do not salivate much do not notice tannins right away. However, once they do, they do not unpucker for a good while. This puts a rub in the old red-wine-with-red-meat rule.

Tannins cut fat, refreshing an eater's palate for the next bite, so a tannic red fits well-marbled steak. But think how dry-tasting well-done roast beef can be on its own. Dry, grainy meat will feel drier yet with a tannic red.

Now it turns out that your individual response to tannins will exaggerate or minimize the reason for the rule. Some grape varieties play down tannins, others play them up.

Gamay and Pinot Noir hold the low end of the scale. In the middle come Merlot, Sangiovese, Syrah, and Zinfandel. Cabernet Sauvignon, Cabernet Franc, and Nebbiolo rank near the top. Bite-you-back Petite Sirah is in a class by itself.

Winery style matters. Region of origin can. Within any varietal category, a useful rule of thumb: the darker the wine, the more it is going to pucker. Here is a framework.

Pinot Noir: Estancia Monterey, Charles Krug Carneros, and Acacia Carneros are silky. Saintsbury Carneros holds the center. Sanford Central Coast is as tannic as Pinot Noir can be.

Merlot: Firestone Santa Ynez Valley is a smoothy. Columbia Winery Columbia Valley is middling. Beringer Napa Valley–Howell Mountain "Bancroft Vineyard" is gritty for the type.

Cabernet Sauvignon: Chimney Rock Napa Valley–Stags Leap District tames Cabernet tannins well. For a firm example, try Chateau Montelena Napa Valley "Montelena Estate."

Petite Sirah: Guenoc North Coast is as smooth as it gets. Parducci California typifies the middle. Stag's Leap Winery Napa Valley is as tannic as this variety gets. ■

We think the cream stout on the right makes a heavenly match with oysters. But you might prefer a dark lager, pilsner, or Oktoberfest—that's the fun of pairing beer and food.

Beer!

and the foods that love it

An eating and drinking guide for microbrew fans

Q: What do you call a deep brown (nearly black) ale with a malty aroma—one that's smooth and sweet on the palate and rich with complex hints of smoke, chocolate, and caramel?

A: Cream stout.

Q: What do you call a cream stout served with barbecued oysters?

A: Delicious!

The craft-brewing revolution has brought a cornucopia of beer styles to liquor stores and supermarkets. Today the spectrum of beer flavors runs from the crisp, slightly hoppy freshness of pale, European-style pilsners to the creamy-sweet maltiness of an English-style brown ale. Things have really changed in this universe since the days when just about the only beer you could find was character-free American lager.

The microbrewery boom is well

By Jeff Phillips
Recipes by Christine Weber Hale
Photographs by Rick Mariani

established, leaving open only one major question: What's best to eat with all the complex and flavorful brews so readily available around the West? As the variety of beer styles has mushroomed, so have the options for surprising and delicious pairings of beer with food. Chefs at Western brew pubs are expanding their menus beyond garlic fries and burgers. They're serving pilsner with caviar, stout with oysters, India pale ale with venison, porter with banana crêpes—and they've inspired us to experiment with combinations of our own.

This season, as tailgates swing open at football stadium parking lots and the last warm days of autumn beg for just one more barbecue, is a perfect time to plan your own Oktoberfest beer-and-food-tasting party. Our beer-tasting chart will help you identify the flavor components of some of the most widely brewed beer styles, examples of which can be paired with our menu for a meal you can serve indoors or out.

Don't worry if you can't find the specific beers located on the chart; each region of the West has its own microbreweries busily crafting examples of most of the beer styles we've identified (even though brewers don't always label their handiwork as clearly as consumers might wish). We've tried to suggest matchups of food and beer that work particularly well—but the rule here is that the only "correct" pairings are the ones that you and your guests, after dedicated and diligent slurping, decide you really like.

A Heads-Up Guide to Beer Styles

Don't know your pilsner from your porter? Use this chart to explore the universe of beer flavors

The proliferation of beer styles is potentially confusing to consumers. As one brewer admits, a beer's "style" is often defined as much by the demands of market positioning as by its flavor components.

We've tried to impose some order on this genial chaos by refining a prototype chart developed by Pete Slosberg, founder of Pete's Brewing Co. of Palo Alto, the maker of Pete's Wicked Ale. Our chart is designed to illustrate the broad spectrum of beer flavors and to show how the major beer-making styles generally fit within that spectrum. It doesn't purport to absolutely define the flavor universe, but it will help you distinguish between a wheat beer and a golden ale. If you decide to throw a beer-and-food-tasting party, consider making color copies of this chart for your guests to use.

Ales and lagers. For simplicity we've divided the beer universe into two families: ales and lagers. Ales are fermented at warmer temperatures and generally for a shorter time than lagers. Ales tend to have a fruity aroma; lagers tend to taste crisper and drier. The hops used for flavoring in both can make them bitter.

Color (and alcohol content). Both ales and lagers range in color from pale gold to black. In general, color indicates the intensity of flavor contributed by malted (just-sprouted) barley that has been roasted to a light tan for pale gold beers (grainy or bready flavors) up to a chocolate color for dark beers (smoky to

chocolaty and caramelly flavors).

Color is not an indicator of body (the thin or thick feeling of the beer in your mouth) or of potency. Alcohol level can range from 2.3 percent to 3.5 percent (by weight) for "light" beers to as much as 13 percent for barley wine.

Balancing sweet and bitter. This is where beer tasting gets both interesting and highly subjective. In general, the complex barley sugars contribute to a beer's sweetness, whereas hops, parts of a flowering plant added to beer as a natural preservative and for

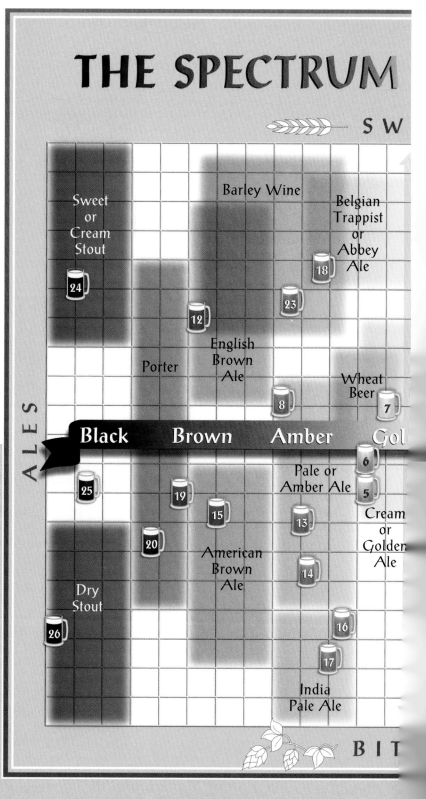

OF BEER FLAVOR

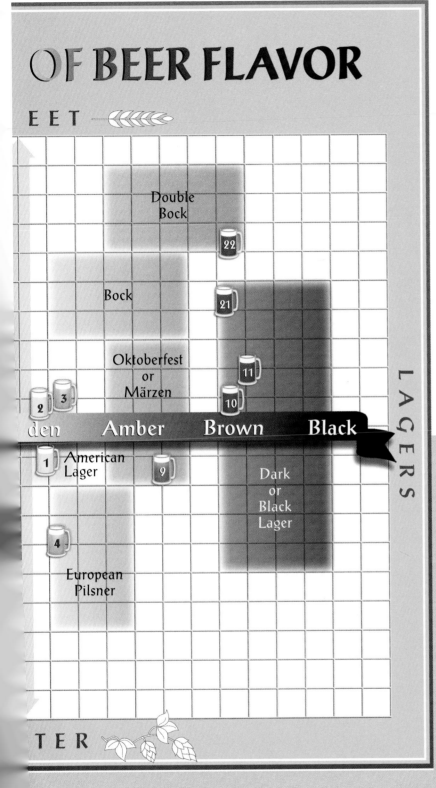

S**EET**

Double
Bock

Bock

Oktoberfest
or
Märzen

Amber   Brown   Black

den

American
Lager

European
Pilsner

L A G E R S

Dark
or
Black
Lager

BIT**TER**

This chart shows how beers we tasted—Western microbrews when possible—fell within generally accepted stylistic ranges. We tasted them in flights (from light to dark and sweet to bitter) in this order:

1. O'Doul's (nonalcoholic)
2. Budweiser (American lager)
3. Red Dog (American lager)
4. Hübsch Pilsner
5. Raincross Cream Ale
6. Pyramid Hefeweizen (wheat beer)
7. Oregon Honey Beer (golden ale)
8. Boont Amber Ale
9. Hübsch Märzen
10. Three Finger Jack Hefedunkel (dark lager)
11. Dixie Blackened Voodoo (dark lager)
12. Downtown Brown (English brown ale)
13. Anchor Steam Beer
14. Sierra Nevada Pale Ale
15. Pete's Wicked Ale (American brown ale)
16. Grant's India Pale Ale
17. Anchor Liberty Ale (India pale ale)
18. Hair of the Dog Golden Rose (Belgian-style)
19. Black Hook Porter
20. Black Jack Porter
21. Samuel Adams Double Bock
22. Celebrator Doppelbock (German import)
23. Old Foghorn Barleywine
24. Boulder Stout
25. Black Hawk Stout
26. Pike Street Stout

the refrigerator about half an hour before tasting. Ideally you'll pour each beer into a clean glass—connoisseurs distinguish among glasses for pilsner, wheat beer, Belgian, and other styles, but clear plastic tumblers work for a crowd. Assess the beer's color against a light source or white background. Swirl the liquid and sniff the aroma for hints of what is to come, then roll a big sip around in your mouth and swallow. Sweetness will register as its recognizable taste but also as a tingly sensation on the front of your tongue; bitterness will grab you at the back of your throat.

Buying bottled beer. Of the 37 brands we tasted, a fair number had oxidized or soured because of poor handling during shipping or aging too long on the shelf. That risk aside, the hardest part of buying beer is interpreting the label—since no consistent stylistic standards apply. Perhaps the most confusion occurs with generically named "amber" beers, any of which can be an ale or a lager made in any of several different styles.

No "right" answer. Our tasting panel included Pete Slosberg, Tom Young (brewmaster of Great Basin Brewing Co. in Sparks, Nevada), and Jeffrey Anderson (corporate executive chef of Gordon Biersch Brewing Company of San Jose). The experts didn't always agree on where a given beer should end up on the chart; in those cases, we struck an "average" rating that all panelists could live with.

And in fact, there are no "correct" answers for this kind of beer tasting. The goal should be to use such a tasting as an excuse to learn about the variety of flavorful craft beers now on the market and to explore how they match up with different types of foods.

flavor, contribute to bitterness. Not surprisingly, many good beers will have a pleasant balance of the two characteristics.

The dominant characteristic of a beer determined its placement on our chart. A sweet-starting beer with a lingering bitter aftertaste was put on the bitter side. Note that everybody has different thresholds for bitter and sweet; few people, including experienced brewers, will agree about the precise chart placement of any beer.

Tasting. Most beers have fuller flavor profiles if removed from

MENU FOR A CASUAL BEER-TASTING PARTY

We hope you've noticed by now that beer resists any efforts we might make to take it too seriously. Let's be frank: Even after it's been scientifically explained and dissected into different taste components, beer is 98 percent fun.

There are few hard-and-fast do's and don'ts for matching beer and food. But one thing we've discovered is that bitterness may be the most important flavor consideration to keep in mind. A bitter brew cooked down will become even more bitter (often unbearably so). Additionally, don't pair bitter beers with bitter foods. Instead, team an aggressively hopped beer with dishes that have other characteristics, such as sweetness, sourness, or saltiness. This rule actually applies to all beers, bitter or not. Match the beer you're drinking with foods that have complementary, not similar, characteristics.

These three recipes (with their suggested beer accompaniments) will help you create your own tasting party. Begin the meal with easy-to-fix appetizers, such as grilled oysters, grilled sausages with mustards, and a cheese board that includes sharp cheddar, creamy blue, gouda, and münster along with whole-grain breads and crackers. With the appetizers, offer a variety of beers for guests to sample.

For an even easier party, put together a collection of beers and a series of tasting stations. One of these might feature salsas and chips, another several kinds of grilled sausages with mustards, and a third grilled chicken and ribs dripping with thick, spicy-sweet barbecue sauce. Your guests can wander freely, making inventive matches with the beers. All you'll need to do is relax and enjoy the serendipitous pairings.

Fennel and Endive Salad with Wheat Beer Dressing

Prep and cook time: About 25 minutes
Notes: The dressing for this salad was inspired by a recipe in *Famous Chefs and Other Characters Cook with Beer*, by W. Scott Griffiths and Christopher Finch (Doubleday, New York, 1996; $25). Accompany this salad with additional wheat beer to drink.
Makes: 8 servings

1½ ounces very thinly sliced prosciutto

½ cup wheat beer such as Pyramid Hefeweizen

¼ cup lemon juice

2 tablespoons sugar

1 tablespoon Dijon or whole-grain mustard

1 tablespoon extra-virgin olive or salad oil

1 teaspoon finely grated lemon peel

2¼ pounds fennel heads (2 to 3), feathery greens still attached

1¼ pounds endive

   Salt and pepper

1. Cut prosciutto into very fine slivers. Place slivers in an 8- to 10-inch nonstick frying pan and stir often over medium-high heat until lightly browned and crisp, 3 to 4 minutes. Pour from pan; set aside.

2. In a blender or a small bowl, whirl or whisk together beer, lemon juice, sugar, mustard, oil, and lemon peel until smoothly blended.

3. Mince enough of the feathery fennel greens to make 2 tablespoons and set aside; discard remainder or reserve for another use. Trim off and discard tough fennel stems and root ends. Halve bulbs vertically. With a vegetable slicer or mandoline, cut fennel crosswise into paper-thin slices. Transfer to a large bowl and mix with about half the beer dressing.

4. Remove and reserve 24 whole endive leaves. Keep chilled until ready to use. Cut remaining endive crosswise into ¼- to ½-inch-thick slices. Add sliced endive and minced fennel greens to sliced fennel. Add remaining dressing and mix well.

5. Spoon mixture onto salad plates or a serving platter; tuck whole endive decoratively around salad. Sprinkle with prosciutto slivers and season to taste with salt and pepper.

Per serving: 75 cal., 32% (24 cal.) from fat; 3.4 g protein; 2.7 g fat (0.4 g sat.); 9 g carbo.; 252 mg sodium; 4.3 mg chol.

Grilled Pork Tenderloin with Golden Ale Gravy

Prep and cook time: About 2 hours, plus at least 2 hours for marinating

Notes: Serve with the same beer you use to make the gravy. You can start marinating the meat and cook the caramelized apples 1 day ahead.

Makes: 8 servings

1 bottle (12 oz.) golden ale such as Oregon Honey Beer

1 onion, finely chopped

1 carrot, peeled and finely chopped

¼ cup honey

2 tablespoons lemon juice

½ teaspoon pepper

3 pork tenderloins (¾ to 1 lb. each)

3 tablespoons butter

4 sweet-tart apples (about 2 lb. total), such as Pippin or McIntosh, peeled, cored, and each cut into 8 wedges

⅓ cup sugar

1 cup beef broth

1. In a large bowl or 2-gallon zip-lock plastic bag, mix together beer, onion, carrot, honey, lemon juice, and pepper. Trim off and discard excess fat and silvery membrane from pork. Add pork to beer mixture and turn to coat. Cover or seal and chill at least 2 hours or up to 1 day. Turn occasionally to keep meat evenly coated with marinade.

2. Melt half the butter in a 12- to 14-inch frying pan over medium-high heat. Add half the apple wedges and half the sugar. Stir often until sugar melts and butter mixture bubbles. Turn apple slices often until they are well browned and caramelized, about 10 minutes. Remove from pan and keep warm. Repeat to cook remaining apples, using remaining butter and sugar. (If you have 2 pans, divide apples, butter, and sugar between them and cook simultaneously.) Set aside and keep warm. (Or, if making ahead, cool, cover, and chill up to 1 day. To reheat, place apple slices on a baking pan, cover lightly with foil, and bake in a 350° oven until hot, about 10 minutes.)

3. Remove pork from the marinade; cover pork airtight and keep chilled. Pour the marinade and vegetables into a 4- to 5-quart pan. Cover and bring to a boil over high heat. Simmer until the carrot and onion

A pork tenderloin marinated in golden ale suggests that you pour nothing less as an accompaniment.

are very tender when pierced, about 45 minutes. Uncover, and if necessary boil until the mixture is reduced to 1½ cups. Whirl the mixture in a blender or food processor until it is very smooth, then pour through a strainer back into the pan. Add the beef broth, bring to a simmer, then cover and keep warm.

4. After vegetables have simmered 25 to 30 minutes in marinade in step 3, place pork on a lightly oiled barbecue grill above a solid bed of medium coals or a gas grill on medium (you can hold your hand at grill level only 4 to 5 seconds). Close lid on gas grill. Cook, turning often to brown evenly, until pork is no longer pink in thickest part (cut to test) or until a meat thermometer inserted into center of pork registers 155°, about 25 minutes.

5. To serve, cut pork into ½-inch-thick slices. Arrange pork on individual dinner plates or on a serving platter and garnish with apples. Serve with gravy to add to taste.

Per serving: 334 cal., 27% (89 cal.) from fat; 26 g protein; 9.9 g fat (4.6 g sat.); 36 g carbo.; 114 mg sodium; 89 mg chol.

Gingerbread Torte with Double Bock Caramel Syrup

Prep and cook time: About 55 minutes

Makes: 10 servings, to be enjoyed with the same double bock used to make the caramel syrup.

6 large eggs, separated

1¾ cups sugar

¼ cup molasses

1 teaspoon vanilla

¼ teaspoon cream of tartar

½ cup all-purpose flour

1 teaspoon *each* ground cinnamon and ground ginger

½ teaspoon baking soda

2 cups double bock such as Samuel Adams or Celebrator

Powdered sugar

Vanilla ice cream

1. In a large bowl, beat together the egg yolks, ¾ cup granulated sugar, molasses, and vanilla until thick and well mixed. In another bowl, with clean beaters, beat the egg whites with cream of tartar on high speed until stiff, moist peaks form. In a third bowl, mix together the flour, ground cinnamon, ground ginger, and baking soda. Alternately fold the egg whites and flour mixture into the egg yolk mixture, stirring just until evenly incorporated.

2. Pour batter into a greased and floured 9-inch springform pan. Tightly wrap a sheet of foil around the base and 2 inches up the sides of the pan. Place pan in a larger roasting or baking pan. Fill larger pan with 1 inch of very hot water. Bake the torte (still in the water-filled pan) in a 350° oven until top is browned and springs back when it is lightly

pressed, 35 to 40 minutes. Immediately remove cake from water, remove foil, and let torte cool on a rack. Use warm or cool.

3. While cake is baking and cooling, combine beer and remaining granulated sugar in a 5- to 6-quart pan. Bring to a boil over high heat. Let boil, stirring occasionally, until reduced to 1¼ cups, about 10 minutes. Keep warm.

4. To serve, arrange wedges of the torte on individual dessert plates. If desired, sprinkle the top with powdered sugar pressed through a sieve. Accompany with scoops of vanilla ice cream, and drizzle each portion equally with some of the warm double bock syrup.

Per serving: 242 cal., 13% (32 cal.) from fat; 4.6 g protein; 3.5 g fat (1 g sat.); 49 g carbo.; 106 mg sodium; 128 mg chol. ■

Southwest flavors come naturally in winter squash soup with sage, and turkey baked in squash.

An American original

The winter squash in today's market captures the spirit of native times.
For the most memorable dishes, here's what you need to know

J UST AS HIS HOHOKAM ANCESTORS did, Bob Stone plants squash in the Arizona desert. But the seeds he uses don't come in packets from the store—they are part of his family and his tribal history.

As a boy, Stone worked every day after school on his mother's 10-acre farm alongside the Gila River to help feed the family of 14. Seeds, handed down through generations from long before the Europeans came, were saved from

each crop for the next planting.

Squash probably originated in Mexico. Archaeologists have found evidence that it was cultivated there 7,000 to 10,000 years ago, and squash seeds were among the items traded from tribe to tribe along the ancient trails that wove through South, Central, and North America.

Hard-shelled, sweet-fleshed varieties that were grown in the summer kept well and provided food through the winter months. Despite their year-round availability in markets today, these descendants of the hard-shelled *Cucurbita maxima* are still commonly called winter squash. Other types of squash, such as pumpkins and small stuffing and long-necked squash (*C. moschata* and *C. pepo*), often get lumped into this category, too. Old standards flourish as Butternut, Hubbard, and Banana squash, as well as many variations, and they are grown around the world. New hybrids and varieties have joined them, providing even more choices, especially this time of year.

But not all squash are created equal. Some sport handsome shells that collapse into flat-tasting, watery masses when cooked. Others look plain and boring, but hide richly flavored, velvety-smooth flesh. Squash skin may be smooth or pebbly, and the skin color can be pure and intense, speckled or spotted, white, cream, yellow, golden, orange, or many shades of green. The flesh ranges from pale gold to burnt orange. And all squash store well.

Despite their diversity, squash that are best for cooking have in common a sweet to very sweet—and sometimes nutty—flavor and a smooth to creamy texture. We asked chefs, growers, and produce grocers which squash they prefer for cooking, and our chart on page 204 groups their top picks by variety, shape, and uses.

Nutritionally, winter squash provides at least twice as many carbohydrates and calories per pound as summer squash, and contains significantly more potassium and vitamin A.

American Indians often turned the hard squash into natural casseroles. Split, seeded, and filled with meat or fish, the squash was reassembled and cooked in ashes or stone pits. The oil-rich squash seeds were an important food and are still a popular snack. In Stone's tribe, and to others in the Southwest, squash is basic to many dishes, including soups and stews—or is simply enjoyed plain. These recipes take inspiration from this heritage.

Winter Squash Soup with Sage

Prep and cook time: About 1 hour

Notes: Deborah Madison, author of *The Greens Cookbook* and *The Savory Way,* prefers squash with deep orange, sweet flesh, such as Butternut, Kabocha, Red Kuri, or Buttercup, for this soup.

Makes: 6 servings

- 2 tablespoons olive oil
- 18 small fresh sage leaves
- 2½ to 3 pounds winter squash
- 2 unpeeled onions (about 6 oz. each), cut in half
- 6 cloves unpeeled garlic
- ¼ cup chopped fresh parsley
- 1 tablespoon chopped fresh sage leaves
- ¾ teaspoon fresh or ¼ teaspoon dried thyme leaves
- 4 cups water or vegetable broth Salt and pepper
- 3 ounces (½ cup) ½-inch cubes fontina cheese

1. Pour oil into a 6- to 8-inch frying pan and place over medium-high heat. When oil is hot, add whole sage leaves and stir until they turn a darker green, 45 seconds to 1 minute. With a slotted spoon, lift out leaves and drain on paper towels; set aside.

Reserve the oil.

2. Rinse squash; if not cut and seeded already, slice squash in half and scoop out seeds. Discard seeds (or save to roast). Brush cut surfaces of squash and onions with reserved oil. Place squash and onions, cut side down, in a 10- by 15-inch baking pan. Slip garlic under squash.

3. Bake in a 375° oven until all vegetables are soft when pressed, 45 to 60 minutes. Reserve pan juices. Scoop flesh from squash skins; discard skins. Peel garlic. Peel and chop onions.

4. In a 3- to 4-quart pan, combine squash, garlic, onions, parsley, chopped sage, and thyme. Mash squash mixture with a potato masher. Stir in reserved pan juices and the water. Bring mixture to a boil, then reduce heat to low and simmer, covered, to blend flavors, about 25 minutes. Season soup with salt and pepper to taste.

5. Stir any remaining sage cooking oil into soup. Distribute cheese equally among 6 bowls, and ladle soup into bowls. Top soup with fried sage leaves and fresh-ground pepper.

Per serving: 171 cal., 49% (84 cal.) from fat; 6.4 g protein; 9.3 g fat (3.4 g sat.); 18 g carbo.; 122 mg sodium; 16 mg chol.

FIVE BASIC WAYS TO COOK WINTER SQUASH

First, cut **winter squash** open to make halves, cut tops from small squash, or cut larger squash into slabs or chunks. For big, thick squash, use a heavy knife and, if needed, tap the top of the knife with a flat mallet to drive the knife through the squash.

Scoop out squash seeds and discard or save to roast.

Peel squash or not, depending on how it will be used. Use a vegetable peeler to pare skin from uncooked squash—or scoop cooked squash from the skin.

Rinse the squash and cook in one of the following ways, keeping in mind that the thickness of the squash walls, rather than the squash's overall dimensions, influences cooking time the most.

Season the cooked squash with **salt, pepper,** and, if desired, **butter** or **extra-virgin olive oil,** or use the plain flesh as an ingredient in other dishes.

Bake. Lay unpeeled **squash** halves or slabs cut side down, or small whole squash with tops in place, in a single layer in a nonstick (or lightly oiled) pan. Bake in a 375° oven until squash is very tender when pierced, 45 minutes to 1 hour.

Steam. Set unpeeled **squash** halves, slabs, or chunks or small unfilled squash with tops in place on a rack over boiling water. Cover and steam until squash is tender when pierced, 10 to 30 minutes for halves, slabs, or small whole squash, about 20 minutes for 2-inch chunks.

Butter-steam. In a 10- to 12-inch frying pan, melt 1 tablespoon **butter** or margarine over medium-high heat. Add 1 quart peeled **squash** cubes (about ¾ in.) and ⅔ cup **water.** Cover and stir occasionally, adding water if pan gets dry, until squash is tender when pierced, 6 to 8 minutes.

Boil. Drop unpeeled or peeled **squash** chunks (about 2 in.) into boiling water to cover. Boil gently until tender when pierced, 12 to 18 minutes. Drain.

Microwave. Put peeled **squash** chunks (about ¾ in.) and 2 tablespoons **water** in a shallow bowl. Cover and cook in a microwave oven on full power (100 percent) until tender when pierced, 8 to 10 minutes for 1 pound, stirring once.

Which squash to choose and how to use

CARNIVAL · ACORN · SUGAR PUMPKIN · CHINESE PUMPKIN · BUTTERCUP · HUBBARD · RED KURI · BANANA · SUGAR LOAF · SWEET DUMPLING · BABY HUBBARD · DELICATA · MINI PUMPKIN · KABOCHA · BUTTERNUT

NORMAN A. PLATE

Small enough for one or two servings (¼ to 3 lb. each), thin walls (⅜ to ¾ in.), generous seed cavities. Cooked skin is sometimes tender enough to eat. Flesh color ranges from pale yellow to orange. Flavor ranges from slightly tart to very sweet and nutty. Texture is slightly crisp to soft and smooth.

Seed squash and cook whole or in halves. Thin-walled squash are ideal to cook stuffed.

Small to medium-size (1 to 8 lb. each) with thick, dense, fleshy walls (¾ to 1 in.) and fairly large seed cavities. Smallest will serve two; others will serve more. Cooked skin is too coarse to eat. Flesh color ranges from medium orange to deep red-orange. Flavor spectrum is sweet, nutty, and honeylike. Texture is creamy.

Seed and cook whole, halved, or in chunks. Cook independently or with other ingredients, as in stews. Excellent mashed and puréed, and in soups, au gratins, and pies.

Medium to very large (2 to 70 lb. each) with dense, meaty walls (¾ to 4 in.; neck of Butternut is solid). Seed cavity is small in Butternut, large in Banana and Hubbard. Cooked skin is inedible. Flesh color ranges from yellow-orange to deep orange. Flavors are mellow and slightly buttery to very sweet. Texture ranges from soft and fibrous to creamy and smooth.

Cook in chunks or slabs. Cut or scrape cooked flesh from skin; mash, purée, or cut in pieces. Wonderful for soups and stews.

Turkey Baked in Squash

Prep and cook time: 1¼ to 1¾ hours

Notes: Use small squash with large cavities. Each small squash makes one main-dish serving. For first-course servings, use 6 even smaller squash such as Mini Pumpkins (about 6 oz. each); they are tender after about 30 minutes of steaming.

Makes: 3 main-dish servings

- 3 Acorn, Carnival, or Sweet Dumpling squash (about 1¼ lb. each), or Delicata or Sugar Loaf squash (about 10 oz. each)
- 3 collard green or Swiss chard leaves (leafy part 4 by 8 in.)
- ½ pound ground lean turkey
- 1 large egg white
- ½ cup finely chopped onion
- ¼ cup chicken broth
- 1 clove garlic, pressed or minced
- ½ teaspoon dried thyme leaves
- ¼ teaspoon hot chili flakes
- 3 tablespoons fine dried bread crumbs
- 2 tablespoons chopped dried cranberries

  Salt and pepper

1. Slice tops off round squash far enough down to make lids. For longer, narrower Delicata or Sugar Loaf squash, lay squash on its side and slice off enough of the tops to make lids. If needed, slice a little off the squash bases so they sit steady. Scoop out seeds and discard (or save to roast).

2. Trim and discard tough stem from center of collards (or chard). Line each squash cavity with a collard leaf, trimming the leaf so it extends about ½ inch above squash rim. Finely chop enough of the green leaf trimmings to make 2 to 4 tablespoons; save extra for another use.

3. Mix the 2 to 4 tablespoons chopped collards with turkey, egg white, onion, broth, garlic, thyme, chili, bread crumbs, cranberries, and ¼ teaspoon salt. Pack the turkey mixture into leaf-lined squash and set squash lids on top. Wrap each squash in a single layer of cheesecloth (or foil), tying knot on top (or twisting foil together) to make a handhold.

4. Set squash on a rack over about 1 inch of boiling water in a deep pan or wok. Cover and steam over high heat, adding hot water as water evaporates, until squash is tender when pierced and meat is white in the center, 45 minutes to 1¼ hours.

5. Carefully lift squash out, unwrap, and set on plates. Add salt and pepper to taste.

Per serving: 351 cal., 17% (61 cal.) from fat; 20 g protein; 6.8 g fat (1.7 g sat.); 59 g carbo.; 176 mg sodium; 56 mg chol.

Pueblo Lamb and Squash Stew

Prep and cook time: About 2 hours

Notes: Use meaty, thick-fleshed varieties such as Banana, Buttercup, Butternut, Hubbard, or Kabocha.

Makes: 6 to 8 servings

- 2½ pounds boned and fat-trimmed lamb (shoulder or neck), cut into 1 to 1½-inch chunks
- 1 onion (about 8 oz.), chopped
- 3 cloves garlic, pressed or minced
- 1 dried bay leaf
- 1 teaspoon cumin seed

2 or 3 dried small hot chilies

6 cups (about 2 lb.) 1½-inch chunks peeled winter squash

1 can (15 oz.) golden hominy, drained

Thinly sliced green onion

Salt and pepper

1. In a 5- to 6-quart pan, combine lamb, chopped onion, garlic, bay leaf, cumin, and ½ cup water. Bring to a boil over high heat. Cook, covered, over medium heat for 20 minutes. Uncover, return to high heat, and stir often until a brown film forms on pan bottom, about 10 minutes. Add another ½ cup water and stir to scrape browned bits free. Boil and stir until rich brown film forms on pan bottom again, about 3 minutes more.

2. Add 4 cups water and chilies. Cover and simmer over low heat until lamb is almost tender when pierced, 45 minutes to 1 hour. Skim off and discard fat. Add squash and hominy. Cover and simmer until squash and meat are very tender to bite, 25 to 30 minutes longer. Sprinkle with green onion. Add salt and pepper to taste.

Per serving: 300 cal., 30% (90 cal.) from fat; 31 g protein; 10 g fat (3.6 g sat.); 21 g carbo.; 217 mg sodium; 94 mg chol.

Roasted Squash Seeds

Prep and cook time: About 35 minutes

Notes: For even roasting, use similarly sized seeds in each batch.

Makes: 1⅔ to 2 cups

1⅔ to 2 cups (about ½ lb.) winter squash seeds

2 tablespoons salt

1. Place seeds, ¼ at a time, between 2 towels and rub to remove strings and flesh from seeds. In a colander, rinse seeds well and drain.

2. In a 1- to 2-quart pan, bring 1⅓ cups water and salt to a boil over high heat. Stir in seeds. Remove from heat and let stand until cool. Cover and chill 12 to 24 hours.

3. Drain seeds and spread evenly in a 10- by 15-inch baking pan. Bake in a 350° oven until seeds are dry and crisp throughout, 20 to 25 minutes for small seeds, 35 to 40 minutes for large seeds; stir often. Cool, stirring occasionally. Eat, or store airtight at room temperature up to 10 days.

Per serving: 71 cal., 39% (28 cal.) from fat; 3 g protein; 3.1 g fat (0.6 g sat.); 8.6 g carbo.; 92 mg sodium; 0 mg chol. ■

By Linda Lau Anusasananan

By Elaine Johnson

A secret ingredient for low-fat brownies

ED CAREY

GREAT BROWNIES—SO MOIST and chocolaty. They have an elusive flavor," said one taster at a low-fat brownie bake-off. "Prunes? You're kidding!"

If you're into low-fat baking, using puréed fruit such as prunes or applesauce to replace fat may not surprise you. But how do various purées measure up?

We tested seven purées in an old-fashioned brownie recipe we'd adjusted to a low-fat format (see how, below). Most contained prunes, which are naturally high in fiber (it traps air, as fat does) as well as sorbitol (a humectant to counteract dryness) and malic acid (a flavor enhancer).

The purées we tested included four all-prune types: Gerber prune baby food, WonderSlim (a fat substitute), Solo Prune Plum Lekvar Filling (a sweetened dessert filling and fat replacement), and a homemade purée (½ cup soft prunes whirled in a blender with 3 tablespoons hot water until smooth). Two fat replacements—Lighter Bake and Just Like Shortenin'—contained prunes and apples. Our seventh purée was unsweetened applesauce.

The results? Tasters were hard-pressed to tell the six prune brownies apart; all were judged moist and fudgelike (though the ones made with Solo filling and homemade purée were a tad heavy). The applesauce brownies differed dramatically from the others, with greater volume and a texture closer to devil's food cake's.

To create our low-fat brownies, we replaced fat with the same amount of applesauce or half as much prune purée. To counteract the purées' slight tendency toward gumminess, we kept a bit of but-ter and added a little leavening. Including one egg yolk (rather than all egg whites) also dramatically improved the texture.

Fudgy Low-fat Brownies

Prep and cook time: About 35 minutes, plus about 1 hour for cooling

Makes: 16 brownies

2 ounces unsweetened chocolate

1 tablespoon butter or margarine

1 cup sugar

1 large egg plus 1 egg white

6 tablespoons applesauce or 3 tablespoons prune purée (see choices at far left)

2 teaspoons vanilla

½ cup all-purpose flour

2 tablespoons unsweetened cocoa

¼ teaspoon salt

¼ teaspoon baking soda

1. In a 2- to 3-quart pan over low heat, stir chocolate and butter until melted. Remove from heat. Add sugar, whole egg and egg white, applesauce or purée, and vanilla; stir until smooth. Sift together flour, cocoa, salt, and soda into pan; stir to blend.

2. Evenly spread batter in a lightly oiled 8-inch square pan. Bake in a 350° oven until brownies pull from sides of pan, 22 to 24 minutes. If they do not pull from sides, bake no longer than 25 minutes. Cool on a rack. Cut with a serrated knife.

Per brownie: 101 cal., 31% (31 cal.) from fat; 1.5 g protein; 3.4 g fat (1.8 g sat.); 18 g carbo.; 69 mg sodium; 15 mg chol. ■

California's other wine country

*Central Coast vintners from Paso Robles
to Santa Barbara are producing wines
that Napa Valley vintners covet*

By David Lansing
Photographs by Gary Moss

Morning at Hope Farms Winery's Arbor Inn in Paso Robles: In the background are Merlot and Cabernet vines. Above left, Pinot Blanc grapes are harvested in Arroyo Grande's Maison Deutz, San Luis Obispo County's only producer of sparkling wines.

THE SILVER HORSE VINEYARDS tasting room sits in a converted pole barn. Outside, lazing in the sun, Tigger and R.D. (short for Ranch Dog) wait for the infrequent visitor to the 77-acre ranch tucked away in the rolling hills north of Paso Robles.

When R.D., a border collie–Australian shepherd mix, hears the distant hum of a car driving slowly up Pleasant Road, his ears snap to attention. If the car turns off the narrow, twisting country lane and onto the winery's gravel road, R.D. announces the arrival with a couple of short piercing yips.

The dog's barks alert Silver Horse owners Rich and Kristen Simons that they've got company. The Simonses are relative newcomers to the Central Coast wine scene, having bought their ranch in 1989 and produced their first wines in 1992. They fit right in. Pouring a barrel-fermented Chardonnay for a visitor, Rich notes that the wine is "unpretentious, but has lots of character." He might just as easily be referring to the dozens of wineries that, like Silver Horse, are hidden in the brown hills and oak-shaded valleys between Paso Robles and Santa Barbara, the heart and soul of the Central Coast

wine appellation's southern end.

Many of these wineries, including Silver Horse, produce fewer than 4,000 cases of wine a year, selling their accomplished vintages out of old barns, former living rooms, and—in at least one case— a trailer. Though the names of most Central Coast wineries are not exactly household words (few people have even heard of Norman, Qupé, and Talley), the wines

they produce are as fine as any being made in California.

Especially of late. "The '94 vintage was good, and a number of Central Coast wineries have been *very* good for quite a while," says David Russell, wine buyer for Santa Barbara's Wine Cask. "These are very impressive and very successful wines," he says. "And I think the best is yet to come."

With success, of course, has come change. The old barns and ranch houses are steadily giving way to million-dollar showpieces, such as the copper-roofed tasting room at Fess Parker Winery or Eberle Winery's underground caves (complete with a private dining room for special events).

Other changes go beyond cosmetics. Take the case of winemaker Byron "Ken"

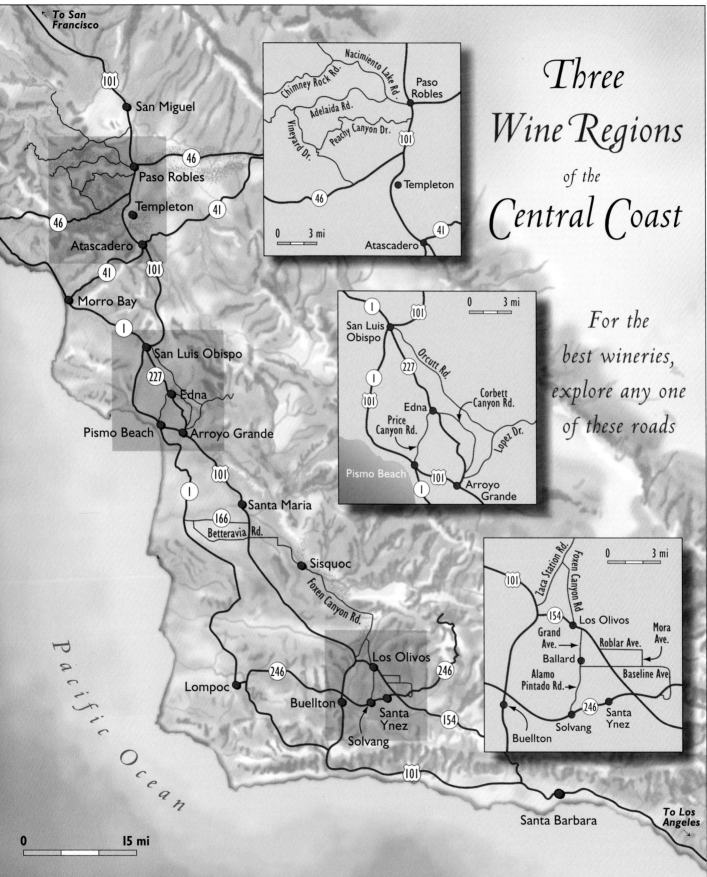

Three
Wine Regions
of the
Central Coast

For the best wineries, explore any one of these roads

To San Francisco

101
San Miguel

46
Paso Robles

Templeton
41

46
Atascadero

41
101

41
Morro Bay

1

San Luis Obispo

227
Edna

Pismo Beach
Arroyo Grande

101

1

Santa Maria
166
Betteravia Rd.

Sisquoc

Foxen Canyon Rd.

Los Olivos
246

246
Lompoc

Buellton
Santa Ynez
Solvang
154

101

Pacific Ocean

Santa Barbara

To Los Angeles

0   15 mi

Inset 1 (Paso Robles):

Chimney Rock Rd.
Nacimiento Lake Rd.
Paso Robles
Adelaida Rd.
101
Vineyard Dr.
Peachy Canyon Dr.
Templeton
46
41
Atascadero

0   3 mi

Inset 2 (San Luis Obispo):

1
101
San Luis Obispo
227
Orcutt Rd.
1
101
Corbett Canyon Rd.
Edna
Price Canyon Rd.
Lopez Dr.
Pismo Beach
101
Arroyo Grande
1

0   3 mi

Inset 3 (Los Olivos):

Zaca Station Rd.
Foxen Canyon Rd.
101
154
Los Olivos
Grand Ave.
Roblar Ave.
Mora Ave.
Ballard
Alamo Pintado Rd.
Baseline Ave.
246
Santa Ynez
Solvang
Buellton

0   3 mi

DEBRA LAMBERT

Oaks shrouded in late-afternoon fog along State Highway 46 east of Paso Robles.

Brown, who founded the Santa Maria Valley's Byron Vineyard & Winery in 1984 after five years of making award-winning wines for nearby Zaca Mesa. To grow and keep pace with the competition—and to avoid being marginalized as a mere "boutique" winery—Brown sold Byron in 1990 to the Robert Mondavi Winery. Brown, who has stayed on as general manager and winemaker of Byron Winery, believes that Mondavi's resources will allow Byron's line of Burgundy-style wines—Pinot Noir, Pinot Blanc, Chardonnay, and Pinot Gris—to compete with not only the best wines from Napa and Sonoma, but also those from France. "With Mondavi's backing, I sleep a lot better at night," he says.

Robert Mondavi's interest in the Central Coast is not limited to Byron. Recently, the winery acquired the nearby Tepusquet and Sierra Madre vineyards, as well as a 360-acre farm near Santa Maria that will soon be planted with Chardonnay and Pinot Noir grapes. All told, Robert Mondavi Winery owns about 1,700 acres of vineyards in Santa Maria Valley. And it has just built a state-of-the-art Byron winery, whose sleek, humidity-

and temperature-controlled facilities seem as distant from the Simonses' simple pole-barn tasting room as Byron's exquisite Pinot Gris is from unfermented grape juice.

Nor is Mondavi the only big-name

vintner moving into the neighborhood. Beringer Wine Estates owns the Paso Robles winery Meridian Vineyards, whose almost 3,000 acres of vines makes Beringer one of the area's largest owners. Beringer is also a partner with French

A friendly wave from Ron Benson, proprietor of Mattei's Tavern in Los Olivos, is typical of the greeting visitors will get at his Santa Barbara County landmark.

Guests at Mastantuono Winery's tasting room, surrounded by ribbons and trophies.

champagne maker Maison Deutz in Arroyo Grande, producing San Luis Obispo County's only sparkling wines.

Another French winemaker, Château de Beaucastel, has popped up down the road from John and Andrée Munch, who moved to Paso Robles from San Francisco in 1981 to found Adelaida Cellars. John Munch welcomes his new French-speaking neighbors, even as they eye the uncultivated hills around him. He plans to follow their lead and plant more of Adelaida's vineyards with Syrah and other Rhône varietals.

"The Central Coast is like Provence—not Nice or Napa," says Munch. "Everything is very down-to-earth. The appearances of what we do may be lowbrow, but the presentation is exquisite. The quality of our wine is very high. That's why the French have come here."

It would be simple, but inaccurate, to say that the Central Coast wine region is refreshingly un-Napa- like. Certainly there's a good dollop of "aw-shucks" in many of the region's vintners. Take Tobin James Shumrick of Tobin James Cellars. Like a lot of other winemakers in the area, Shumrick got his start working for Gary Eberle (who many consider the godfather of the region) at Eberle Winery. Shumrick's first crush came from a gondola of grapes that Eberle refused to take because he didn't have room for it. Shumrick talked Eberle into letting him take the grapes instead of spilling them. Thus were born Tobin James wines. Today, Shumrick mischievously slaps exotic nicknames, such as Huevos or Wild Child, onto the labels of his bold red wines.

Shumrick is definitely a character (rumor has it he's a distant relative of

Jesse James, a claim not made by Shumrick). John Munch is something of a character, too. How many winemakers can you name who used to play in a rock band with a late member of the Grateful Dead?

But more important than its characters is the Central Coast's isolation. Situated midway between San Francisco and Los Angeles, and bounded by the Santa Ynez Mountains to the south and the Coast Ranges to the north, much of the Central Coast's sleepy-eyed reputation comes from being "just far enough," as John Munch says, from the Big City.

Looking for hot spots? Pull into Paso Robles on a Friday night. One of the busiest places in town is the A&W drive-in on Spring Street, where, in a scene straight out of *American Graffiti,* carhops pick up your burger tray when you flash your headlights. A block away is the Paso Robles Vintners & Growers Association, housed in an old, green '40s-style California bungalow. It's right next to the Farm Credit office. At the opposite end of town, Takken's still sells Red Wings boots to young farmworkers, just as it's done for almost 60 years.

Sixty miles south lies Santa Maria, a town which has suffered from a growth spurt that has brought on miles of ticky-tacky strip malls. In Santa Maria, you can still get a great sandwich made of thin slices of seasoned tri-tip and fresh salsa from the portable barbecue stands that line Broadway most weekends.

Farther south is Los Olivos—gateway to the Foxen Canyon wineries of Santa Barbara County. The scene is tonier here, but an old stagecoach stop, Mattei's Tavern, continues to lure hungry travelers off the scenic San Marcos Pass, as it did years ago when Clark Gable used to dine here while on hunting trips in the Santa Ynez hills.

Ken Brown of Byron Vineyards appreciates these simple pleasures but wonders how much longer the area can stay at arm's length from its relentless suitor to the north, Napa, which, along with other Northern California wine regions, purchases 75 to 80 percent of all the grapes grown between Paso Robles and Santa Barbara. Central Coast wineries like Silver Horse and Adelaida may be on a road less traveled today, but they probably won't be for long. To paraphrase an old saying, if the grapes won't go to Napa, Napa, it seems, will go to the grapes. And when that happens, don't expect the Simonses' ranch dogs to greet you at the barn.

Central Coast essentials

Three vintner associations distribute free maps and guides to more than 70 Central Coast wineries: **Paso Robles Vintners & Growers** represents 32 wineries (805/239-8463), the **Edna Valley Arroyo Grande Valley Vintners Association** has 15 members (541-5868), and the **Santa Barbara County Vintners' Association** supports the efforts of 34 wineries (800/218-0881). The following area codes are 805 unless noted.

Many consider Ian McPhee's to be the best restaurant on the Central Coast.

• What to sip

Ask four Central Coast wine experts to name their favorite wines and you're likely to get four different answers.

David Russell is the wine buyer at the **Wine Cask** in Santa Barbara (813 Anacapa St.; 966-9463). "Two of my favorites, **Au Bon Climat** and **Qupé,** don't have their own tasting rooms, but you can sample their wines at the **Los Olivos Tasting Room and Wine Shop** [2905 Grand Ave.; 688-7406]." Russell likes Au Bon Climat's '94 Pinot Noir La Bauge Audessus and Qupé's '94 Syrah, Bien Nacido Vineyard. His other picks: **Byron Winery's** '93 Estate and '94 Reserve Chardonnays, **Justin Vineyards & Winery's** '93 Isosceles meritage blend, and **Foxen Vineyard's** '94 Chardonnay, Tinaquaic Vineyard.

Frank Ostini is the owner-chef of the **Hitching Post** in Buellton. "All the '94 wines from the Central Coast are outstanding, particularly the Pinot Noirs," he says. Ostini favors **Sanford Winery's** Sanford and Benedict Vineyard Barrel Select and **Foxen Vineyard's** Pinot, Bien Nacido Vineyard. For Merlot, try the '92s by **Sunstone Vineyards and Winery** or **Buttonwood Farm Winery,** says Ostini.

Ian McPhee is the owner-chef of **Ian McPhee's Grill** in Templeton. "There are so many great Central Coast wines coming out that my wine list has grown by 15 wines in

the last three months." Try **Norman Vineyards'** '94 Zinfandel, suggests McPhee, "a monster red with a big, rich taste." Or **Wild Horse Winery's** Malvasia Bianca, which McPhee recommends for those who usually drink a dry Chardonnay. Other picks: **Eberle Winery's** '95 Viognier and **Mastantuono Winery's** '94 Barbera.

Bill Hoppe is the owner-chef of **Hoppe's at 901** in Morro Bay. "The wines that really made this area are the Chardonnays from **Edna Valley Vineyard,**" says Hoppe. He also likes the dry, Alsatian-style Gewürztraminer from **Claiborne & Churchill, Alban Vineyards'** Viognier ("a world-class wine, really beautiful," he says), and **Eberle's** '93 Cabernet Sauvignon.

• Where to eat

If you're going to have only one meal, have it at **Ian McPhee's Grill** (416 Main St., Templeton; 434-3204). Sample the best of the Central Coast with the New York steak with a stuffed pasilla chili and wild rice pilaf.

Hoppe's at 901 (901 Embarcadero, Morro Bay; 772-9012) is known for its seasonally changing menu. If it's offered, try the roast duck with mango and tamarind sauce, or the wild mushroom and buckwheat griddle cakes with hazelnut and sweet corn coulis.

The Hitching Post (406 E. State Highway 246, Buellton; 688-0676) claims to have the world's best barbecued steaks. No argument here, but the Hitching Post also does a great job cooking quail, turkey, and even ostrich over an open oak pit fire. And don't pass up the grilled artichoke served with a smoked tomato-chili mayonnaise.

You *can* get a nice piece of grilled fresh fish at **Mat-**

tei's Tavern (corner of Grand Ave. and State 154, Los Olivos; 688-4820), but every time we go, we end up ordering a thick steak, medium-rare, accompanied by a bottle of Gainey Vineyard's Cabernet.

Cafe Chardonnay in the Ballard Inn (2436 Baseline Ave., Ballard; 800/638-2466) is well known for its Central Coast–heavy wine list as well as entrées like bowtie pasta with goat cheese, fresh mango slices, pesto, and prosciutto.

Remington's in the Los Olivos Grand Hotel (2860 Grand Ave., Los Olivos; 688-7788) has a new executive chef, Jose Ramirez, who has been the restaurant's sous-chef for five years. He presides over house specialties that include rolled veal stuffed with gorgonzola, mozzarella, and feta and topped with a tomato-basil cream sauce.

• Where to stay

The Arbor Inn (2130 Arbor Rd., Paso Robles; 227-4673), recently opened by Hope Farms Winery, is a stylish B & B whose eight rooms have names like Cabernet Suite; $115 to $225.

Paso Robles Inn (1103 Spring St., Paso Robles; 238-2660) is a great bargain. Its 70 rooms, some recently renovated, start at $75.

Black Oak Motor Lodge (1135 24th St., Paso Robles; 238-4740) is also a good deal at $56 to $105 a night.

The Apple Farm Inn (2015 Monterey St.; 544-2040), at the north end of San Luis Obispo, is roughly midway between Paso Robles and Arroyo Grande Valley. The Victorian motif is as heavy as the scent of the fresh apple pies baking in the adjacent restaurant. Room rates run $95 and up.

Also relatively economical is the **Santa Maria Inn** (801 S. Broadway, Santa Maria; 928-7777). The grounds are pleasant, rooms are tidy, Foxen Canyon wineries are just 15 minutes away, and doubles start at $119.

Things get pricier as you head south. A couple of good choices in the Santa Ynez area include the **Los Olivos Grand Hotel** (2860 Grand Ave., Los Olivos; 688-7788) and the **Ballard Inn** (2436 Baseline Ave., Ballard; 800/638-2466), both of which start at about $150 a night. ■

Stacked cases of wine give the tasting room at Edna Valley Vineyard its distinctive warehouse ambience.

Jerk spices and chilies give broiled bites of chicken a powerful punch in this version of a popular appetizer.

This chili chef blazes a flavor trail
Peppers and chilies go directly from the garden to a tasting party

BLAINE GRIFFITH LIKES HOT— specifically, food that's simmering to sizzling. And he knows his heat sources well. He grows about nine members of the capsicum family (peppers, including chilies) each year in his Oakdale, California, garden. While the sweet bells to hell-hot habaneros ripen, he plots their use, dreaming up new dishes for his annual pepper bash.

And then, at harvesttime, Griffith sails through two to three dozen dishes, inviting friends to dine upon his collection of fire-tinged creations.

Modest about this burst of invention, Griffith says, "It's really very simple. I don't use a lot of different spices … I vary taste by changing the chili." And he doesn't stop with fresh peppers and chilies. An extensive collection of hot sauces, plain old black pepper, and a miscellany of other fiery flavorings are some of his other inspirational resources.

Dessert for the dinner is his wife's domain. And Jane Griffith always gives traditional desserts a chili tweak, such as cheesecake with habaneros or chocolate mousse with jalapeños.

Last year, just as partygoers dug into the extensive buffet, the chili-pepper king whispered: "They'll be surprised. Most of these dishes aren't really hot, they're just spicy."

He was right—sort of. After the flames subsided from the first bite of Blaine's Hot Sticks, the remaining dishes were— or certainly seemed—much tamer.

This sampler of Blaine's dishes uses chilies and peppers readily available at the market, and takes you from brimstone to bliss in short order.

Hot Sticks

Prep and cook time: 30 to 40 minutes

Notes: The choice of chili seasoning— hot sauce—determines the heat of this dish. In lieu of a jerk spice blend, use this mixture: 2 teaspoons ground ginger, 2 teaspoons cayenne, 1 teaspoon sugar, and ½ teaspoon *each* ground allspice and ground nutmeg.

Makes: 24 to 30 skewers, 12 to 15 appetizer servings

24 to 30 thin wood skewers

4 boneless, skinless chicken breast halves (about 1½ lb. total)

4 teaspoons liquid chili seasoning

2 tablespoons olive oil

¼ cup soy sauce

2 tablespoons dried jerk spice blend

Salt

1. Soak wood skewers in water at least 10 minutes or up to 1 hour.

2. Cut chicken breasts into ½-inch-wide strips 3 to 4 inches long. Mix the chicken with chili seasoning, oil, soy sauce, and jerk spice. Cover and let stand 10 minutes or chill up to 4 hours.

3. Thread chicken strips onto skewers, dividing evenly. Lay skewers on a rack in a 10- by 15-inch pan. Broil 3 to 4 inches from heat, turning once, until chicken is lightly browned and no longer pink in the center of the thickest part (cut to test), 8 to 10 minutes. Add salt to taste. Serve warm or at room temperature.

Per serving: 71 cal., 31% (22 cal.) from fat; 11 g protein; 2.4 g fat (0.4 g sat.); 0.9 g carbo.; 347 mg sodium; 26 mg chol.

Devil's Dip

Prep and cook time: About 30 minutes

Notes: The heat of the jalapeños and the choice of salsa determine the degree of heat in this dish.

Makes: 10 to 12 appetizer servings

5 fresh jalapeño chilies (about 3½ oz. total)

1 onion (about ½ lb.), chopped

5 cloves garlic, chopped

2 tablespoons olive oil

1 pound ground lean beef

1 tablespoon coarsely ground pepper

1 tablespoon prepared habanero chili sauce

2 cups prepared medium to hot tomato salsa

1 can (16 oz.) nonfat refried beans

Salt

½ pound jack cheese, shredded

1 fresh Anaheim (California or New Mexico) chili (optional)

White or blue corn tortilla chips

1. Stem, seed, and chop jalapeño chilies.

2. In a 10- to 12-inch frying pan, combine jalapeños, onion, garlic, and olive oil. Stir often over medium-high heat until onion is limp, about 5 minutes. Add beef, pepper, and habanero chili sauce. Stir often until meat is browned and crumbly, about 10

minutes. Mix in salsa and beans. Stir occasionally over low heat until hot, about 5 minutes. Add salt to taste.

3. Pour bean mixture into a shallow 5- to 6-cup casserole and sprinkle with cheese. Cut Anaheim chili lengthwise into halves or quarters and lay on top of the cheese. Broil 4 inches from heat until cheese bubbles, 2 to 3 minutes. Serve hot; scoop onto chips.

Per serving without chips: 248 cal., 58% (144 cal.) from fat; 14 g protein; 16 g fat (6.8 g sat.); 12 g carbo.; 695 mg sodium; 48 mg chol.

Eggplant-Pepper Medley in Paper

Prep and cook time: 1 to 1¼ hours

Notes: The vegetables can be baked, covered, in a shallow 3-quart casserole instead of in individual portions.

Makes: 6 to 8 servings

4 slender eggplant (about ¾ lb. total)

3 red, green, or yellow bell peppers (about 1¼ lb. total)

3 fresh Anaheim (California or New Mexico) chilies (about ½ lb. total)

3 fresh jalapeño or serrano chilies (1½ to 2 oz. total)

1 onion (about ½ lb.)

4 Roma tomatoes (about ¾ lb. total)

2 tablespoons olive oil

1 tablespoon chopped fresh or 2 teaspoons dried basil leaves

1 tablespoon chopped fresh or 1 teaspoon dried oregano leaves

Salt and pepper

1. Cut and discard stems from eggplant, peppers, and chilies. Cut eggplant into ¾-inch chunks. Discard pepper seeds, and if you want less heat, discard chili seeds. Thinly slice peppers and chilies; cut long pieces into 1½-inch lengths. Cut onion into thin slivers. Core tomatoes and cut into ¾-inch chunks.

2. Mix eggplant, peppers, chilies, onion, tomatoes, oil, basil, and oregano. Place a quarter of the mixture in the center of a 16-inch square of cooking parchment. Bring opposite edges of paper together and fold over 2 or 3 times. Fold ends over several times and tuck underneath packet. Repeat to wrap remaining vegetables.

3. Set packets in a 10- by 15-inch pan. Bake in a 350° oven until vegetables are tender when pierced, 45 to 50 minutes. Open packets. Add salt and pepper to taste.

Per serving: 88 cal., 39% (34 cal.) from fat; 2.2 g protein; 3.8 g fat (0.5 g sat.); 14 g carbo.; 9.4 mg sodium; 0 mg chol. ■

By Linda Lau Anusasananan

Sealed in packets, pepper medley bakes sweet and mellow.

Sunset's Kitchen Cabinet

Readers' family favorites tested in our kitchens

By Linda Lau Anusasananan and Betsy Reynolds Bateson

NORMAN A. PLATE

Chicken and Rice Ensalada

Lora Lauer, Henderson, Nevada

When she worked in Chicago, Lora Lauer often ate a deli salad that she has never forgotten. Her version tastes so good that friends and family often beg her to bring it to picnics and potlucks. Lauer likes it best when it's made with grilled chicken. Serve it as a side dish (it's nice as a stuffing for crisp red peppers) or as a main course.

Cook and prep time: About 30 minutes
Makes: 8 side-dish or 4 main-dish servings

- 1 package (6 to 7 oz.) Mexican-seasoned rice
- 2 cups (about ½ lb.) shredded cooked chicken
- 1⅓ cups thinly sliced celery
- 1 can (2¼ oz.) sliced olives, drained
- 1 cup chopped green or red bell pepper (or ½ cup of each color)
- 1 tablespoon chopped fresh cilantro, plus a few sprigs
- 3 tablespoons cider vinegar
- 1 tablespoon liquid hot chili seasoning
- 1 teaspoon chili powder
  Lettuce leaves

1. Prepare rice according to package directions. Let cool.

2. Add chicken, celery, olives, bell pepper, and chopped cilantro.

3. Mix vinegar, hot chili seasoning, and chili powder. Stir into rice mixture. If rice seems a bit dry, mix in a few tablespoons water to taste. Line a serving bowl or platter with lettuce leaves, if desired. Spoon rice salad onto lettuce, and garnish with cilantro sprigs.

Per side-dish serving: 139 cal.; 22% (31 cal.) from fat; 10 g protein; 3.4 g fat (0.7 g sat.); 17 g carbo.; 578 mg sodium; 25 mg chol.

Mookies

Pam Afpinall, Sutter Creek, California

When Pam Afpinall first opened her coffeehouse, she began her quest to create the "best" oatmeal cookie. After many tests, her customers chose a big, chewy cookie that resembled a muffin. Thus came the word *mookie*.

Prep and cook time: About 40 minutes
Makes: 16 giant cookies

- 1 cup (½ lb.) butter or margarine, at room temperature
- 1½ cups firmly packed brown sugar
- 2 large eggs
- 1 teaspoon vanilla
- 3 cups regular rolled oats
- 1 cup all-purpose flour
- 1 teaspoon salt
- ½ teaspoon baking powder
- 1 cup chopped walnuts
- ½ cup *each* sweetened shredded dried coconut and raisins

1. Mix butter and brown sugar until thoroughly blended. Add eggs and vanilla; beat well. Combine oats, flour, salt, and baking powder. Blend oat mixture with butter mixture. Stir in walnuts, coconut, and raisins.

2. Pack cookie dough into an ice cream scoop (4-oz. size) or ½ cup measuring cup, scrape dough level with rim, and empty onto lightly oiled baking sheets, spacing dough about 3 inches apart.

3. Bake in a 350° oven until cookie edges are golden brown, about 20 minutes (if using one oven, switch pans halfway through baking). Cool cookies on a rack; serve, or store airtight up to 2 days.

Per cookie: 354 cal.; 48% (171 cal.) from fat; 5.4 g protein; 19 g fat (8.7 g sat.); 42 g carbo.; 294 mg sodium; 58 mg chol.

Spiced Wine-Poached Pears

Carmela M. Meely, Walnut Creek, California

When looking over a scant supply of fruit in the market last winter, Carmela Meely uncovered some beautiful pears. She poached the fruit in red wine and candied ginger, then coarsely mashed it to make a chunky sauce for roast pork. Since her first experiment, she often skips the mashing step and cooks the pears in slices. They are a pretty accompaniment to many meats and are also delicious spooned over vanilla ice cream for dessert.

Prep and cook time: About 20 minutes
Makes: About 2 cups

- 1/2 cup dry red wine
- 2 tablespoons chopped crystallized ginger
- 1 1/2 tablespoons sugar
- 1 cinnamon stick (3 in. long)
- 2 firm, ripe d'Anjou or Bosc pears (about 1 lb. total)

1. In a 10- to 12-inch frying pan, stir together wine, ginger, sugar, and cinnamon stick.

2. Peel and core pears. Cut lengthwise into about 1/2-inch-thick slices. Add pears to pan; turn to coat in wine mixture.

3. Cover and simmer over low heat, turning pears occasionally, until just tender when pierced, about 10 minutes. Serve warm or cool.

Per 1/2-cup serving: 129 cal.; 2.8% (3.6 cal.) from fat; 0.5 g protein; 0.4 g fat (0 g sat.); 28 g carbo.; 6.4 mg sodium; 0 mg chol.

Beef Ranchero Tijuana

Darwin A. Drake, Poway, California

More than 40 years ago, Darwin Drake met a group of five young farmworkers while strolling along a dusty trail through the Tijuana River bed. They invited him for a supper of beans and tortillas. He offered to buy them beef at a nearby market. A simple meal became a feast as they enthusiastically collaborated on cooking beef ranchero-style. Drake makes this Mexican stew with fond memories.

Prep and cook time: About 3 1/2 hours
Makes: 4 to 6 servings

- About 4 pounds bone-in beef chuck
- 1 onion (about 1/2 lb.), chopped
- 1 stalk celery (about 2 oz.), thinly sliced
- 2 teaspoons dried oregano leaves
- 1 teaspoon ground cumin
- 1/4 to 3/4 teaspoon hot chili flakes
- 1 can (8 oz.) tomato sauce
- 1 tablespoon Worcestershire
- 1 green bell pepper (about 1/2 lb.), stemmed, seeded, and diced
- 2 fresh jalapeño chilies (about 1 1/2 oz. total), stemmed, seeded, and diced
- 1/2 cup dry red wine
- 2 tablespoons tequila (optional)
- 1/2 ounce Mexican chocolate with cinnamon (or semisweet chocolate with 1/4 teaspoon ground cinnamon), finely chopped
  Salt
- 1/4 cup chopped fresh cilantro
  Hot corn tortillas

1. Trim and discard bones, fat, and gristle from beef; cut meat into pieces about 1 by 2 inches.

Put meat in a 4- to 5-quart pan and add 1 cup water, onion, celery, oregano, cumin, and 1/4 teaspoon chili flakes. Cover and bring to a boil over high heat; reduce heat to low and simmer 20 minutes.

2. Remove lid and boil over high heat, uncovered, until pan is dry and meat is sizzling and streaked with brown, stirring often, about 25 minutes. Add 1/2 cup water and stir often until pan is dry again, about 4 minutes.

3. Stir in tomato sauce, Worcestershire, bell pepper, jalapeños, and 2 cups water. Bring to a boil, cover, and simmer gently until meat is very tender when pierced, about 2 hours. Stir in wine, tequila, and chocolate. Season to taste with salt and remaining chili flakes, if desired. Spoon into bowls; sprinkle with cilantro, and accompany with hot corn tortillas.

Per serving: 340 cal.; 37% (126 cal.) from fat; 37 g protein; 14 g fat (5.5 g sat.); 12 g carbo.; 408 mg sodium; 118 mg chol.

Tabbouleh Vegetable Salad

Ann E. Aylesworth, Bishop, California

The traditional Middle Eastern wheat salad takes off in a new direction in Ann Aylesworth's hands. She omits the mint and adds lots of broccoli. Sometimes she varies the vegetables, adding diced zucchini or tomatoes. For a main dish, her family fills whole-wheat tortillas with the mixture to make a vegetarian burrito.

Prep and cook time: About 30 minutes
Makes: 8 salad or 4 main-dish servings

- 1 cup bulgur wheat
- 1 or 2 cloves garlic, minced
- 1 1/2 teaspoons pepper
- 3/4 cup lemon juice
- 1 cup chopped red onion
- 2 tablespoons olive oil
- 3/4 pound broccoli
- 3/4 cup chopped fresh parsley
- 1 can (15 1/2 oz.) garbanzos, rinsed and drained
- 1 carrot (1/4 lb.), peeled and shredded
  Salt

1. In a large bowl, combine bulgur, garlic, pepper, and 1 1/4 cups hot water. Let stand until cool, about 10 minutes. Add lemon juice, onion, and oil; let stand until bulgur is tender to bite, about 20 minutes.

2. Meanwhile, cut broccoli florets into about 3/4-inch pieces and coarsely chop the tender parts of the broccoli stems.

3. When bulgur is tender, stir in broccoli, parsley, garbanzos, and shredded carrot. Add salt to taste.

Per salad serving: 161 cal.; 26% (42 cal.) from fat; 6.1 g protein; 4.7 g fat (0.6 g sat.); 26 g carbo.; 89 mg sodium; 0 mg chol.

---

*S*hare a recipe you've created or adapted—a family favorite, travel discovery, or time-saver—including the story behind the recipe. You'll receive a "Great Cook" certificate and $50 for each recipe published. Send to *Sunset Magazine,* 80 Willow Rd., Menlo Park, CA 94025, or send e-mail (including full name, street address, and phone number) to recipes@sunsetpub.com.

FOOD
Guide

BY JERRY ANNE DI VECCHIO

A portabella cap with shrimp makes a dramatic first course.

A TASTE OF THE WEST: Start with portabella steaks

The first time I encountered portabella mushrooms, I was confused as to their identity. As it turns out, portabellas are just mature cultivated brown mushrooms (crimini).

And there is no question that the most appealing aspects of these mature mushrooms, beyond scale, are their meatiness and intense flavor. You can buy portabellas several ways—whole, caps only, or sliced. You can, of course, cut up portabellas and cook them any way you

would small, immature mushrooms. But it's their size—often 6 inches across—that gets attention on the plate.

Damon Brady, executive chef at Pasadena's Bistro 45, uses portabellas as a dramatic first course. I tried this dish in the dim light of dusk on the restaurant patio, and if I hadn't known I'd ordered mushrooms, I could easily have been persuaded I was eating very tender beef steak. This hearty, succulent dish fares best if followed by a light entrée of fish or pasta. When I use larger portabellas, I consider the dish quite sufficient as the main course for a light supper. Drop the shrimp and it's a vegetarian's dream.

Bistro 45 Portabellas

Prep and cook time: 40 to 45 minutes

Notes: It is easier to cook the spinach first, but then it needs to be reheated in the microwave oven just before you assemble the dish.

Makes: 4 first-course servings

- 4 portabella mushrooms (caps about 4 in. wide)
- 12 shrimp (about 1/2 lb. total, 24-per-lb. size)
- 1 pound spinach leaves
- 3 tablespoons olive oil
- 1 cup dry white wine
- 4 teaspoons minced shallots
- 1 teaspoon minced garlic
  About 4 tablespoons (1/8 lb.) butter
- 3/4 teaspoon curry powder
- 1/2 teaspoon ground cumin
- 1/4 cup finely diced seeded tomato
- 8 whole chives
  Salt and pepper

1. Trim mushroom stems flush with caps; save stems for other uses. Quickly rinse the mushroom caps and drain on towels, smooth side up.

2. Peel shrimp, leaving on tail section. Devein shrimp and rinse.

3. Rinse and drain spinach leaves.

4. Rub mushroom caps lightly all over with olive oil. Broil in a pan on a rack about 4 inches from heat, gills down, for 5 minutes, then turn over and broil until juice in caps bubbles, 6 to 7 minutes more. Keep warm.

5. Meanwhile, cook spinach in a 6- to 8-quart pan over high heat, stirring often, until leaves wilt, about 4 minutes. Drain spinach in a colander.

6. In an 8- to 10-inch frying pan, boil white wine, 3 teaspoons shallots, and 1/2 teaspoon garlic over high heat until reduced to 1/3 cup, about 5 minutes. Pour into mea-

suring cup. Add to pan about 1/2 teaspoon butter, curry powder, and cumin. Stir over medium heat until spices are more aromatic, about 30 seconds, then return wine mixture to pan and set aside.

7. In another 8- to 10-inch frying pan over medium-high heat, combine remaining shallots and garlic with 1 tablespoon butter. When butter is melted, add shrimp and turn often until pink, 2 to 3 minutes. Take off heat.

8. Mound spinach equally in the centers of 4 plates and top each mound with a hot mushroom, gills up; keep warm. Return

shrimp to high heat until butter is sizzling, about 30 seconds. Lift out shrimp and put 3 on each plate; keep warm.

9. Scrape shrimp drippings into wine mixture and bring to a boil. Add 3 tablespoons butter, in several lumps, and stir rapidly until it melts. Immediately, rub sauce through a fine strainer back into the measuring cup, then pour over food on plates. Garnish with tomato and chives. Season to taste with salt and pepper.

Per serving: 297 cal., 70% (207 cal.) from fat; 15 g protein; 23 g fat (8.8 g sat.); 11 g carbo.; 284 mg sodium; 102 mg chol.

TOOL TIP

The turn of the screw

In a cleaning fit the other day, I finally took the plunge and threw out several wine openers that we avoided using because the screw that entered the cork really was a screw (a grooved solid shank). Sometimes it worked, but bits of cork almost always tore free and dropped into the wine. In the worst of times, the screw pulled out only the center of the cork.

A proper corkscrew looks more like one of Shirley Temple's youthful, bouncy curls. The screw is actually a coil, and when it enters the cork, it weaves its way through and gets a tight hold.

The difference between these two screws is easy to see—and equally easy to overlook, as I've done, regretfully, when in a hurry to get dinner ready.

Curiously, the price of a basic corkscrew isn't apt to alert you to the nature of the screw—good and bad cost about the same in comparable-looking tools. So save yourself some grief and take a good look before buying that corkscrew.

Wine cork facts: Coil, left, gets a good grip. Screw, right, bores a hole.

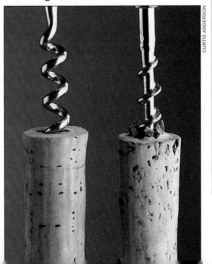

CURTIS ANDERSON

BACK TO BASICS

The pudding that loves beef

With holidays and big roasts in the offing, it's time to dig out the recipe for Yorkshire pudding. But did you know that the same recipe makes popovers, too?

The difference is shape. Both puff as they bake, but Yorkshire pudding does it as a single piece, while popovers are baked individually, like muffins, and swell to impressive heights. (In more indulgent times, Yorkshire pudding batter literally floated in sizzling roast drippings as it baked. Some cooks even put the roast on a rack and let drippings fall onto the batter as it cooked.)

Despite rumors to the contrary, Yorkshire pudding and popovers are among the easiest breads to make and are far less temperamental than terrorist culinarians would have you believe. However, popovers are slightly vulnerable to drafts if you open the oven—frequently—just as they swell above the rim of the baking cup. The only vital detail is to bake the breads enough to hold their shape but not so long they are overly crusty. Underbaked, they get limp and sink.

Both breads are excellent simply buttered, go very well with a roast and its juices, and accommodate all manner of toppings, from eggs in cream sauce to a tomato-meat sauce.

Yorkshire Pudding or Popovers

Prep and cook time: About 50 minutes

Notes: The batter can be made several hours ahead and chilled; stir before using. Be sure no oven rack is close to the top of the popovers.

A crusty popover is an ideal accompaniment for savory roast beef.

Makes: 6 servings

3 large eggs

   About 1 cup all-purpose flour

1 cup milk

¼ teaspoon fresh-ground pepper

¼ teaspoon salt

   About 1 tablespoon melted butter or roast beef drippings

1. Combine eggs, 1 cup flour, milk, pepper, salt, and 1 tablespoon butter. Whisk or whirl (in a blender or food processor) until smooth.

2. *For Yorkshire pudding,* generously coat a 9- by 13-inch pan with butter and dust with flour (or butter a nonstick pan). Pour egg mixture into pan.

3. *For popovers,* generously coat 6 custard cups, popover pan cups, or individual soufflé dishes (5- to 6-oz. size) with butter and dust with flour. Divide batter equally among cups. Set cups well apart on a baking sheet.

4. Bake pudding or popovers in a 375° oven until puffed and browned, about 45 minutes. Remove from oven. Ease a wide spatula under pudding to loosen, then cut into 6 pieces. To release popovers, hold each cup with a hot pad and slide a thin-bladed knife between bread and cup.

5. Serve the bread hot, or let the pudding cool in the pan, popovers on a rack. Wrap airtight and keep up to 1 day. Reheat, uncovered (popovers on a baking sheet), in a 375° oven until hot and crisp, about 5 minutes.

Per serving: 172 cal., 41% (71 cal.) from fat; 6.6 g protein; 7.9 g fat (4 g sat.); 18 g carbo.; 181 mg sodium; 122 mg chol.

GREAT INGREDIENT

Chinese black vinegar

Even on my grandfather's farm—way, way back—there were always two vinegars in the kitchen, cider and distilled white. My own cupboard is a bit more crowded. The two "basics" are stuck behind a veritable vinegar wardrobe: rice, balsamic, sherry, wine (red and white—one or two with herbs), and at least raspberry, if not several other fruit flavors. And then there is Chinese black vinegar, with a personality all its own.

Chinese black vinegars, in general, are salty and sour with a faintly bitter, almost medicinal edge. In his book *Asian Ingredients,* noted Chinese cooking authority Bruce Cost recommends

Gold Plum's Chinkiang vinegar, from Zhejiang on China's coast, for its aged, smoky, complex, and faint but pleasantly bitter flavor. I agree.

Many brands of black vinegar are found in Chinese food markets and any ethnically diverse Asian supermarket. You need to look carefully to be sure you get plain black vinegar. It can be made from glutinous rice, sorghum, wheat, and/or millet, along with salt and various other elements. The liquid is dark, and the label may say merely vinegar, or Chinkiang vinegar or black vinegar. Sweetened vinegar and sweetened black vinegar are not the same as each other or black vinegar.

I find that Chinese black vinegar works better for seasoning than salad dressings. And my favorite use is in a

speedy, sophisticated sweet-sour dip for cooked sausage chunks, cooked and cut-up pork spareribs or beef short ribs from the deli, boiled shrimp, or even plain roasted chicken wings.

Black Vinegar Sweet-Sour Dip

Combine ½ cup *each* **Chinese black vinegar** and **sugar** in a 1½- to 2-quart pan. Stir often and boil over high heat until reduced to about ½ cup, 4 to 6 minutes. Use hot or cool. The sauce thickens as it cools, and if you want it thinner, stir in **water,** 1 to 2 teaspoons at a time. Makes ½ cup.

Per tablespoon: 50 cal., 0% (0 cal.) from fat; 0 g protein; 0 g fat; 13 g carbo.; 0.3 mg sodium; 0 mg chol.

Fragile filo dough is now sold in a smaller pack and a more useful size, eliminating the potential for waste.

FOOD NEWS

Sizing up filo

Two years ago in this column, I complained about filo dough. I was disgruntled because all the filo I'd ever been able to buy came in 1-pound packages of very large sheets that had to be cut or folded to fit any pan I owned. And unless I was making baklava for 30, I had to plan carefully before opening the package in order to preserve the quality of the unused dough for future use—especially if the dough had been frozen.

Well, the folks at the Fillo Factory (yes, there are a lot of ways to spell filo) have come up with a ridiculously simple solution: they now package filo in ½-pound boxes that contain about 22 sheets of dough in a very usable 9- by 13-inch size. You can always overlap the sheets if you want bigger pieces. As I write, supermarket distribution is in the works. But all you have to do to get fresh filo is pick up the phone and order for next-day delivery. The toll-free number is (800) 653-4556; ½ pound of filo costs $1.49, plus shipping. Your favorite pastries with crisp crusts are now easier than ever, and I'm happy.

GREAT ALTERNATIVE

Quick-cooking quail

Turkey dominates November menu plans, but there are other meals and other birds to consider. For a small dinner party, I often make use of quail because it cooks fast, has all dark meat, and looks fancier than it really is. Many supermarkets stock fresh quail regularly, or you can order them (usually with only a day or two's notice). And they aren't terribly expensive, typically $2.50 each.

With these chili-mustard-glazed birds, I like to serve cornbread sticks, mashed yams, and stir-fried broccoli rabe. If your Thanksgiving table is set for three or four, this menu is fitting.

Chili-Mustard Quail

Prep and cook time: 40 to 45 minutes

Notes: A red or pale green jelly gives the sauce the most appealing color. To make ahead, complete through step 4, cover, and chill up to 1 day. Bake, uncovered, for about 20 minutes.

Makes: 3 or 4 servings

  8 or 9 quail (4 to 5 oz. each)
  1 tablespoon *each* olive oil and butter
  ½ cup hot jalapeño jelly
  1½ tablespoons Dijon mustard
  2 tablespoons vinegar
     Salt
     Fresh-ground black pepper

1. Rinse quail and pat dry.

2. In a 10- to 12-inch ovenproof frying pan, combine oil and butter over medium-high heat. When fat is hot, add quail, without crowding, and turn as needed to brown the birds evenly, 6 to 7 minutes each. As each quail is browned, set aside to make room for more.

3. When all the quail are browned, discard fat, saving any browned drippings. To empty pan add the jelly, mustard, and vinegar and stir until jelly melts, then bring to a rolling boil over high heat.

4. Drain any accumulated juices from quail into pan and stir to mix. Remove from heat, add birds, and coat each well with the jelly mixture. Arrange quail, breasts up, together in pan.

5. Bake in a 450° oven, basting several times with jelly mixture, until birds are browned a little more, about 15 minutes. Breasts may still be pink at breastbone (cut to test).

6. Season with salt and pepper and serve with pan juices.

Per serving: 549 cal., 51% (279 cal.) from fat; 40 g protein; 31 g fat (9.1 g sat.); 24 g carbo.; 281 mg sodium; 7.8 mg chol.

BOB THOMPSON ON WINE

For festive occasions, the smart host sticks with the tried-and-true

When the time comes to plan holiday feasts, a lot of people think they need to do something extraordinary about wine.

Quite the contrary. Holiday feasts are the time to retreat as deep into your comfort zone as possible, whether that means Sutter Home White Zinfandel or a Château Latour from a good year, such as '55.

What is the point in having palpitations about an unknown wine in the midst of a complicated dinner, especially when a crowd is coming?

Staying comfortable with wine (and a lot of other things) comes down to a line long attributed to Herman Wente, who said, "We like best what we know best."

So, for all but the relentlessly experimental among us, the most satisfying choice will be an all-time favorite wine to go with a menu that qualifies as a tradition.

To be even more comfortable in the wine department, trot out two or three all-time favorites for a crowd, to make sure everybody at the table will find something to like. If your roster of favorites runs to only one, you might ask your guests to cart along something they would love to drink with the meal.

My short list? The meal is going to be turkey and all the fixings, which means some red, some white.

Pinot Noir leads the list of reds because its soft tannins don't make the white meat any drier than it already is. Among Pinot Noirs, first-round choices include Lane Tanner Santa Barbara, Byron Santa Barbara, Saintsbury Carneros, De Loach Russian River Valley, Dehlinger Russian River Valley, and Erath Willamette Valley. And we always put out a bottle of Beringer North Coast Gamay Beaujolais for my cousin.

Chardonnay tops the list of whites because it has enough oomph to stand up to the fixings. Foremost among them are Buena Vista Carneros, Cuvaison Carneros, Freemark Abbey Napa Valley, Trefethen Napa Valley, and De Loach Russian River Valley. And we always put out a special bottle of Hogue Cellars or Hoodsport Washington Semillon for me.

Not a one of these wines has ever let me down. ■

A Treasury *of* Western
NUTS

SAVOR THE TASTES AND TEXTURES OF SEVEN REGIONAL NATURALS

by JERRY ANNE DI VECCHIO

Like love, the nature of nuts runs the gamut from sacred to profane, coarse to classic. As part of the language, each defines many shades of emotion, modifies countless things.

And the taste of nuts can be as memorable, as indulgent, as a romantic moment.

A case in point: a dream meal I once experienced on a shady lanai on a Hawaiian macadamia plantation. It began with trays of mai tais and large monkeypod bowls mounded with roasted, salted whole macadamia nuts. The tender salad leaves cradled chunks of macadamias. The sautéed fish entrée had a crust of macadamias. The dessert was a creamy macadamia nut pie. In each dish, the nut crunched with subtle, tantalizing differences. And in each presentation, its flavor stood out, albeit harmonically, much like Cecilia Bartoli backed up by a chorus of angels.

But macadamias don't have an exclusive on luxurious flavor. Another moment, many years ago: when I was young, poor, and headed home from France, a traumatic ticket mix-up landed me a first-class seat. Drained and exhausted, I fell into it. In an instant, the flight attendant handed me a glass of elegant champagne with the tiniest of bubbles on the rise, and a dish of warm, roasted, skinned hazelnuts. Wow! That's what I felt then. I still feel it when I replicate this combination.

Even the most prosaic nuts conceal surprises. Take workhorse walnuts. Plentiful, practical, eaten in all manner of ways—what more can they offer? A great cook and friend, restaurateur Cecilia Chiang, showed me. She skins walnuts. With all those nooks and crannies, this sounds absurdly extravagant. But the skins can make walnuts bitter. Blanching loosens the papery brown exteriors so that they pull off easily. Ivory pale, toasted just enough to crisp, these walnuts make very dainty fare.

However, the good cook never lets the poetry of nuts interfere with their inestimable value in the kitchen. They offer many pleasures, whether savory or sweet, plain or gussied. And we're fortunate because so many of the tastiest varieties grow in profusion throughout the West.

From the high, dry deserts of Arizona to the cool, green forests of Oregon, from California's sun-filled Central Valley to Hawaii's plantations, nuts are a delicious dividend of where we live.

In a nutshell

by **CHRISTINE WEBER HALE**

Hazelnuts
• In the United States, these buttery-tasting nuts (also called filberts) are grown primarily in Oregon's Willamette Valley. Oregon's first hazelnut tree was planted in 1858; today that state produces almost 99 percent of the domestic crop.

• To remove hazelnuts' papery skins, just wrap the warm nuts in a clean cloth towel after roasting and rub them; most of the skins will slip off.

• Roasted hazelnuts have such rich flavor, you don't need to fuss over them. Serve them warm and lightly salted with drinks, or in an elegant salad (a wonderful example is hazelnuts, sliced pears, and arugula, with a simple vinaigrette). Of course, one of the best combinations around is hazelnuts and chocolate—sprinkle the nuts over a hot fudge sundae, add them to brownies or chocolate mousse, or use them in chocolate cakes and candies.

• *The rich-tasting hazelnut is at the high end of the fat and calorie scale for nuts, with 188 calories and 19 grams fat per ounce—91 percent of calories from fat.*

Almonds
• It's no accident that the almond is a significant player in many world cuisines. Because it stores well, the almond often traveled with nomads in their search for new lands. Although the nut was first cultivated in the Nile Valley, California now produces two-thirds of the world's supply.

• A versatile nut, the almond enhances foods' flavors without overpowering them. Roasted and chopped, these nuts are delicious stirred into cooked rice, couscous, other cereals, and yogurt, or sprinkled over cooked fruit, vegetables, and salads. And, of course, they're great for baking.

• *Almonds are a little leaner than most nuts, with 167 calories and 15 grams fat per ounce—81 percent of calories from fat.*

Pine Nuts
• The tiny pine nut, or piñon, has been a significant part of the diet of the Hopi, Navajo, and other Native American tribes for thousands of years. In the 1930s, the nut was an important source of income for the Navajo, who sold them to traders who in turn introduced them to the New York market. Other pine nut varieties are revered around the world, especially in the Mediterranean region where they feature prominently in Italian and Greek cuisine.

• Toasted pine nuts have a wonderfully nutty aroma and flavor. Sprinkle them over steamed asparagus, broccoli, or other vegetables, stir them into a rice or barley pilaf, and try them in place of other nuts in your holiday baking.

• *Pine nuts have 161 calories and 17 grams fat per ounce—95 percent of calories from fat.*

Macadamias
• Macadamias are one of Hawaii's signature crops, but California grows plenty of them, too. In fact, the Australian native has been cultivated in California for as long as it has in Hawaii: the first trees were planted in both places in 1888. Today, three of the original California trees are still living.

• Nothing matches the lush flavor and texture of a macadamia, especially when roasted, chopped, and sprinkled over a tropical salad of mangoes, guavas, red bananas, and star fruit. Chop them fine for a luxurious substitute for bread crumbs to use to coat fillets of sole or thinly pounded chicken breasts. And they're delicious in baked goods.

• *Macadamias top the scales at 199 calories and 21 grams fat per ounce—95 percent of calories from fat.*

Pecans

• Southerners may lay claim to pecan pralines and pies, but these delicious nuts thrive in the sandy soils of New Mexico and Arizona. Just south of Mesilla, New Mexico, the world's second largest pecan orchard sprawls over 3,600 acres. If you're traveling on State Highway 28, you'll pass under a 3-mile canopy of pecan tree branches as you cut through the orchard.

• Pecans are wonderful in waffles and pancakes, stirred into turkey dressings just before serving, and in all manner of baked goods.

• *Pecans contain 187 calories and 18 grams fat per ounce—87 percent of calories from fat.*

Pistachios

• Originally from the Middle East, pistachios were considered such a delicacy by the Queen of Sheba that she hoarded the entire Assyrian supply for herself and her court. The nuts were imported by American traders in the 1880s and soon became popular. California didn't produce its first commercial crop of pistachios until 1976, but within 10 years the state had become the second largest pistachio producer in the world.

• Remember when pistachios were red? The color was an attempt to hide stains on the shells of imported nuts caused by the hulls being left on too long after picking. Today, Western growers hull pistachios almost immediately after harvesting, producing nuts with beautiful ivory shells. (A few processors still dye them, but only because some consumers prefer the red color.)

• Roasted, chopped pistachios are delicious tossed into a pasta salad, mixed into a tomato-based pasta sauce, scattered over glazed carrots or sweet potatoes, or sprinkled on top of vanilla ice cream drizzled with honey.

• *Pistachios are among the leanest nuts, with 172 calories and 15 grams fat per ounce—78 percent of calories from fat.*

Walnuts

• Believed to be the oldest tree food known to man, walnuts date back to about 7000 B.C., in Persia. The Franciscan missionaries brought walnuts to the West from Spain or Mexico, but the first commercial planting was in California in 1867. Today, walnuts are grown throughout the Central Valley from Redding to Bakersfield. California produces 98 percent of the total U.S. crop and a third of the world's commercial crop.

• Walnuts are prized for their versatility. Sprinkle them over pasta with gorgonzola sauce, toss warm roasted walnuts into a spinach salad, or use the nuts in a wide variety of baked goods.

• *Walnuts have 182 calories and 18 grams fat per ounce—89 percent of calories from fat.*

NUTRITION

A nut is simply a large seed, encased in a shell, that contains all the necessary ingredients to start a new plant. It therefore follows that nuts are nutritional powerhouses for people, too. While specific nutrients differ by nut variety, almost all nuts are great sources of fiber and vitamin E, as well as of several essential amino and fatty acids.

Admittedly, nuts aren't the leanest foods around. But while they are high in fat and calories, the fat that is present in nuts is largely monounsaturated or polyunsaturated, which may actually lower the risk of heart disease and stroke.

photographs by **KEVIN CANDLAND**

Nuts have three parts: the outer husk, the shell, and the nut (which itself may be encased in a papery sheath). They need to be husked and, usually, dried before you can eat them. Buying dried, unshelled nuts in bulk is an economical way to stock up, but you'll need to shell them, and it's best to roast them to bring out their flavor.

Shelling. A skillfully used hammer or a nutcracker is the chief tool for successful shelling—along with some patience. Practice definitely makes perfect: it takes a few mistakes with a hammer to learn how to apply just the right amount of pressure to crack the shell without smashing the nutmeat. Almonds and pine nuts have soft shells and need only a tap; other kinds need a firmer whack. For very hard-shelled nuts such as macadamias, you might want to invest in a gizmo called the MacCrak. This device, resembling a miniature guillotine, easily cracks the hardest shells while leaving the nutmeat intact. The MacCrak is available from Cooper's Nut House for $12 plus $3 shipping; send a check to 1378 Willow Glen Rd., Fallbrook, CA 92028.

Another good nutcracker is made by Monopol, a German company. The sturdy utensil retails for $19.95 and is available from Williams Cutlery Co., stores in Palo Alto, San Jose, and Sunnyvale, California. For mail order, call (800) 405-6433.

To store shelled nuts on a long-term basis, package them airtight in plastic bags.

A thick layer of toffee-glazed nuts crowns a moist, tender ground-nut torte.

Double Nut Torte

Prep and cook time: About 1 hour and 20 minutes, plus 10 minutes for cooling

Notes: If using almonds, blanch the nuts before roasting them. For a festive touch, serve wedges of the nut torte with whipped cream or your favorite warm chocolate sauce.

Makes: 10 to 12 servings

- 4 cups nuts, 1 kind or an assortment
- 1½ cups sugar
- ¾ cup (⅜ lb.) butter or margarine
- 5 large eggs, separated
- 1½ tablespoons lemon juice
- 1 tablespoon grated lemon peel
- ⅓ cup all-purpose flour

1. Roast 1½ cups nuts as directed on facing page (and skin hazelnuts; see directions on page 222). Whirl in a food processor or blender until finely ground.

2. In a bowl, beat ½ cup of the sugar and ¼ cup of the butter until blended. Add the egg yolks, 1 at a time, beating well after each addition. Mix in the ground nuts, the lemon juice, lemon peel, and all but 2 tablespoons of the flour.

3. In a deep bowl, beat egg whites with a mixer on high speed until soft peaks form. Gradually beat in ¼ cup sugar until the whites hold stiff, shiny peaks. Gently fold the whites into the yolk mixture.

4. Spoon the batter into a buttered and floured 9-inch cheesecake pan with removable rim. Bake in a 350° oven until the torte is very lightly browned and the center feels barely firm when gently pressed, 20 to 25 minutes.

5. Toffee topping. As torte comes out of oven, melt remaining ½ cup butter in a 2- to 3-quart pan over medium heat. Add remaining sugar, flour, and nuts; stir until bubbling.

6. Immediately spoon toffee topping evenly over hot torte, pushing nuts with spoon to arrange decoratively. Return to oven and bake until nuts and topping are slightly browner, 15 to 20 minutes longer.

7. Cool torte in the pan for 10 minutes, then run a knife inside the pan rim to release. Remove pan rim. Serve the torte warm or cool.

Per serving: 510 cal., 71% (360 cal.) from fat; 8.2 g protein; 40 g fat (11 g sat.); 36 g carbo.; 151 mg sodium; 121 mg chol.

Chipotle-Honey Glazed Nuts

Prep and cook time: About 40 minutes, plus 30 minutes for cooling

Notes: If using hazelnuts, roast and skin them (see roasting advice at far right, how to remove skins on page 222) before mixing with honey and chilies.

Makes: 3 cups, about 12 servings

- 2 dried chipotle chilies
- 1/4 cup honey
- 2 tablespoons sugar
- 2 tablespoons salad oil
- 3/4 teaspoon salt
- 1/4 to 1/2 teaspoon cayenne
- 3 cups nuts, 1 kind or an assortment

1. Remove and discard chili stems. Whirl chilies with seeds in a blender or food processor until finely ground.

2. In a bowl, mix ground chilies, honey, sugar, oil, salt, and cayenne. Add nuts and stir until coated with seasonings.

3. Pour nuts onto oiled 10- by 15-inch pan and shake into 1 layer. Bake in 300° oven, stirring often, until nuts are golden brown (under skins, if not blanched) and honey mixture has hardened, 25 to 30 minutes.

4. If necessary, push nuts apart; let cool in pan. Serve or store up to 3 days.

Per 1/4-cup serving: 247 cal., 77% (189 cal.) from fat; 3.5 g protein; 21 g fat (2 g sat.); 14 g carbo.; 140 mg sodium; 0 mg chol.

Cinnamon Nut Brittle

Prep and cook time: About 15 minutes, plus 15 minutes for roasting, and 30 minutes to cool and firm

Notes: Roast nuts as directed at right (and skin hazelnuts; see page 222). Watch carefully as sugar melts; it scorches easily. Work fast when you stir in the nuts because brittle hardens rapidly.

Makes: 1 1/4 pounds, about 20 servings

- 2 cups sugar
- 1/4 teaspoon ground cinnamon
- 1 1/2 cups roasted nuts, 1 kind or an assortment

1. Line a 10- by 15-inch pan with foil; lightly butter foil.

2. Mix sugar and cinnamon in a 10- to 12-inch frying pan. Shake pan often over medium-high heat until most of the sugar melts, about 10 minutes. Reduce heat to medium, and tilt pan to mix melted and dry sugar until combined and amber colored, 2 to 5 minutes longer.

3. Quickly stir nuts into melted sugar, then immediately pour into foil-lined pan. Working fast, use a spoon to spread nut mixture into as thin a layer as possible. Let cool until firm, at least 30 minutes.

4. Peel cooled brittle from foil, and break candy into pieces. Serve, or package airtight up to 3 days.

Per 1-ounce serving: 137 cal., 35% (48 cal.) from fat; 1.9 g protein; 5.3 g fat (0.6 g sat.); 22 g carbo.; 3.2 mg sodium; 0.5 mg chol. ■

or containers and freeze them. There's no need to thaw them before using.

Roasting. This process brings out the rich, buttery taste of nuts and eliminates the bitter or slightly grassy taste that some kinds have when raw. All of these nuts taste best when roasted. (Salting and/or blanching, if desired, should be done first.)

To roast. Spread shelled nuts (except macadamias) in a single layer on a baking pan. Bake in a 350° oven, stirring often, until golden. Allow 5 to 7 minutes for pine nuts; 8 to 10 minutes for pecans, pistachios, and walnuts; about 15 minutes for almonds and hazelnuts. Macadamias need lower heat because they scorch very easily; roast them at 300° about 20 minutes. Watch nuts carefully since they brown quickly. For more toasted flavor, bake nuts to a darker color.

Salting. Place nuts in a bowl, cover with water, then drain. Place wet nuts on a baking pan, sprinkle with salt to taste, then roast according to directions above.

Blanching almonds and walnuts. To remove the skins of unroasted walnuts or almonds, immerse nuts in rapidly boiling water until the skins shrivel and loosen, 15 to 20 seconds. Drain nuts, then let them stand until cool enough to handle. The skins should slip off easily when the nut is squeezed or pressed between your fingers. Pat blanched nuts dry with paper towels, then roast (see instructions above) or use as desired.

The kick in these honey-glazed nuts comes from spicy chipotle chilies.

ROBERT OLDING

Save that turkey carcass

WITH BROTH LIKE THIS, who needs gravy?" said a friend as he spooned some over mashed potatoes. Good broth transforms the simplest recipe into something grand—with little fat. I make a big batch, then freeze it for risottos, sauces, and soups.

There are two secrets to making exceptional broth. Brown the bones, and simmer the works for at least eight hours. (Start the broth in the morning, strain it around suppertime, cool briefly, then chill. The next day, ladle it into containers.)

For the soup shown above, bring 6 cups broth to a boil with 2 cups *each* diced potatoes and thinly sliced, slender leeks. Simmer 5 minutes, then add ⅓ cup alphabet pasta and 1 cup matchstick-size carrot pieces; simmer 4 minutes. Before serving, add 1 cup paper-thin slices fennel bulb and ¾ cup frozen peas. Serves 6.

Roasted-Turkey Broth

Prep and cook time: 9 to 13 hours, plus at least 1 hour for cooling

Makes: 4 to 5 quarts

> Carcass from a 12- to 18-pound cooked turkey (and roasting pan it was cooked in, if available)

4 unpeeled onions (2 lb. total)

1 head fennel (3¾ in. wide, 1 lb.)

2 carrots (½ lb. total)

3 outer stalks celery

1 teaspoon black peppercorns

2 dried bay leaves

1. If using roasting pan from turkey, pour drippings into a 1-quart glass measuring cup, and set aside. With hands and sturdy scissors, break and cut carcass into chunks to fit in a 12- to 16-quart pan. Place chunks in a single layer in turkey roasting pan or in a clean 11- by 17-inch roasting pan. Roast in a 500° oven until well browned, 35 to 40 minutes. Meanwhile, bring a large teakettle of water to a boil.

2. With tongs, lift turkey pieces to the 12- to 16-quart pan. Pour pan drippings into cup with other drippings. Place roasting pan across 2 burners over high heat. Add 2 cups water and stir to loosen browned bits, about 3 minutes. Pour liquid and scrape loosened bits into pan with turkey pieces. Discard fat from drippings, then add drippings to pan.

3. Quarter onions. Cut fennel tops into 3-inch lengths; quarter head. Cut carrots and celery into 3-inch lengths. Add vegetables, peppercorns, and bay leaves to pan with bones. Add boiling water from teakettle plus enough water (5 to 5½ qt. total) to cover bones and seasonings by 2 inches. Cover pan; bring to a boil over high heat. Reduce heat and simmer 8 to 12 hours.

4. Set a large colander over a 6- to 8-quart pan. With tongs and a ladle, lift most of the bones and seasonings into colander. Let drain, then discard contents of colander. Set pan with colander in sink. Protecting hands with mitts, pour broth through colander. Lift colander to drain; discard seasonings. Let broth cool 1 to 2 hours, stirring occasionally.

5. Skim and discard fat from broth, or place pan on a thick towel and chill, uncovered, until cold, then skim fat. Use broth, chill airtight up to 4 days, or freeze up to 6 months.

Per cup: 21 cal., 13% (2.7 cal.) from fat; 2.8 g protein; 0.3 g fat (0.1 g sat.); 1.9 g carbo.; 98 mg sodium; 3.4 mg chol. ∎

WE'D LIKE TO HEAR FROM YOU

Do you have tips or recipes for low-fat cooking? Write to Everyday Low-fat Cooking, Sunset Magazine, 80 Willow Rd., Menlo Park, CA 94025, or send e-mail (including your full name and street address) to lowfat@sunsetpub.com.

A burnished turkey stars in a sumptuous dinner. It's smoked over wine-infused chips for richer flavor.

The lightest, *richest*
Thanksgiving

Two memorable menus for two kinds of Thanksgiving cooks

Let's face it. There are two views of Thanksgiving. Either it's the high point of the culinary year—a chance to show off some artistry in the kitchen, forget about calories, and splurge on rich-tasting dishes. Or it's a day for laid-back, strain-free entertaining. Sure, the meal has to be great, but not at the expense of sanity and 10 extra pounds.

If you're the first kind of cook, try our extravagant wine-smoked turkey dinner. But if you prefer a more pragmatic approach, turn to our menu that's streamlined for time and fat. Both menus include a detailed countdown and make-ahead steps to help pace preparation so everything arrives at the table hot.

An orange-glazed turkey breast with couscous dressing, apricot-ginger sauce, and trimmings is as good for you as it is good-tasting.

BY LINDA LAU ANUSASANANAN • BETSY REYNOLDS BATESON
CHRISTINE WEBER HALE • ELAINE JOHNSON

A Wine-smoked Turkey Dinner

- *Blue Cheese Puffs*

- *Wine-smoked Turkey* • *Zinfandel Gravy*

- *Bread Dressing with Pancetta and Greens*

- *Arugula Salad with Preserved Lemon Dressing*

- *Brandied Potato Gratin*

- *Corn-Chipotle Pudding in Miniature Pumpkins*

- *Grapevine Bread*

- *Marbled Pumpkin Cheesecake*

A wine-smoked turkey dinner

Every detail—from the Zinfandel gravy
to the pumpkin cheesecake—delivers
a sumptuous experience

We invite our favorite guests, we bring out the good wines and best linens, yet sometimes Thanksgiving dinner seems much too reminiscent of years past: same turkey, same stuffing, same potatoes, same pie.

Ready for a dramatic change? Here it is.

Our menu includes a luscious wine-smoked turkey, a grape cluster–shaped bread, corn pudding–filled pumpkins, and a stuffing even a dyed-in-the wool traditionalist will savor.

And this lavish dinner is easier to produce than you might imagine. The secret lies in cooking ahead and following our step-by-step countdown on page 237. Come Thanksgiving Day, much of your work will be done, and you can enjoy the dinner as much as your friends and family will.

Wines to match your feast

With the Blue Cheese Puffs appetizer *serve a California blanc de noirs sparkling wine (Domaine Chandon, Gloria Ferrer, or Mumm Cuvée Napa).*
For dinner *serve J. Pedroncelli Dry Creek Valley Zinfandel Rosé and Seghesio Sonoma County Zinfandel, Nalle Dry Creek Valley Zinfandel, Hogue Cellars Columbia Valley Merlot, or Columbia Winery Columbia Valley Merlot. If you'd like a white, try Byron Santa Barbara Chardonnay.*
—Bob Thompson

Rich blue cheese puffs can be baked and frozen ahead, then reheated.

Wine-smoked Turkey

Prep and cook time: About 3 hours
Makes: 10 to 12 servings, with leftovers

- 4 to 6 cups wine-infused wood chips or shavings, lightly packed
- 3 tablespoons olive oil
- 2 tablespoons minced fresh sage or 2 teaspoons dried rubbed sage
- 1 tablespoon minced parsley
- 2 teaspoons minced fresh marjoram or ½ teaspoon dried marjoram
- ½ teaspoon pepper
- 1 turkey, 16 to 18 pounds
- 1 Golden Delicious apple (about 8 oz.)
- 1 onion (about 6 oz.)
  Sprigs of fresh sage and marjoram

1. Soak wine-infused chips or shavings in water at least 20 minutes; set aside. (For purchasing information, see facing page. If you are unable to find them, soak mesquite or apple wood chips in equal parts red wine and water instead.)

2. Mix oil with minced sage, parsley, marjoram, and pepper; set aside.

3. To prepare turkey, remove and discard leg truss. Pull off and discard lumps of fat and remove giblets. Rinse bird inside and out; pat dry. Rinse giblets, drain, and reserve for gravy (recipe follows). Insert a meat thermometer straight down through the thickest part of the breast to the bone (if using an instant-read thermometer, insert later). Brush turkey all over with 2 tablespoons oil mixture. Cut apple and onion into 1-inch chunks, and mix with remaining oil mixture; place mixture in turkey cavity.

4. *On a large charcoal barbecue with a lid.* Mound and ignite 40 charcoal briquets on firegrate. When coals are spotted with gray ash, in about 20 minutes, push equal portions to opposite sides of firegrate. Place a metal drip pan between coals. To each mound of coals, add 5 briquets and ½ cup soaked wood chips or shavings now and every 30 minutes while cooking. Set grill 4 to 6 inches above coals. Set turkey, breast side up, on grill over drip pan.

On a gas barbecue. Turn gas heat to high. Place 1 cup wood chips in the barbecue's metal smoking box or in a small, shallow foil pan set directly on heat in a corner. Close lid until barbecue is hot, about 10 minutes. Adjust gas for indirect cooking (no heat

Blue Cheese Puffs

Prep and cook time: About 55 minutes, including 15 minutes for standing
Makes: 24 puffs, about 8 servings

- ¼ cup (⅛ lb.) butter or margarine
- ¾ cup all-purpose flour
- 3 large eggs
- ⅔ cup crumbled blue-veined cheese such as Roquefort, Stilton, or Maytag Blue

1. In a 2- to 3-quart pan over high heat, bring ¾ cup water and butter to a full rolling boil. Remove from heat, add flour all at once, and stir until mixture is a smooth, thick paste with no lumps. Add eggs 1 at a time, stirring vigorously after each addition until dough is no longer slippery. Stir in cheese, then let stand for 15 minutes.

2. Evenly space 24 equal mounds of dough (about 1 rounded tablespoon each) on a buttered 12- by 15-inch baking sheet. Bake in a 400° oven until puffs are dry and richly browned, about 30 minutes.

3. Loosen puffs from pan. (If making ahead, let puffs cool on a rack, then wrap airtight up to 1 day or freeze up to 2 weeks. Reheat thawed puffs on baking sheet at 350° until warm, about 3 minutes.)

Per serving: 165 cal., 60% (99 cal.) from fat; 6 g protein; 11 g fat (6.5 g sat.); 9.4 g carbo.; 289 mg sodium; 106 mg chol.

down center) and set a metal drip pan in center. Add another 1 cup wood chips or shavings, if they have burned away. Set grill in place. Set turkey, breast side up, on grill over drip pan. When chips have burned up, add another cup of chips (sprinkle through grill spaces, or lift grill to add shavings) to pan, about every hour.

5. Cover barbecue (open vents for charcoal) and cook turkey until thermometer registers 160°, 2½ to 3 hours. Because temperature, heat control, and size and shape of the bird all can vary, start checking doneness after 2 hours. If parts of the turkey begin to get dark before the bird is done, drape those areas with foil.

6. Drain juices, apple, and onion from turkey cavity; reserve for gravy. Transfer turkey to a large platter; let rest 15 to 30 minutes. Remove drip pan from barbecue; skim and discard fat from juices. Reserve pan juices for gravy; if burned, discard. Garnish platter with sprigs of sage and marjoram.

Per ¼ pound boneless cooked turkey, based on percentages of white and dark meat found in average turkey (including skin): 243 cal., 41% (99 cal.) from fat; 32 g protein; 11 g fat (3.1 g sat.); 1.3 g carbo.; 82 mg sodium; 94 mg chol.

Zinfandel Gravy

Prep and cook time: About 2 hours
Makes: About 4½ cups

> Giblets and neck from a 16- to 18-pound turkey
> 2 onions (about ¾ lb. total), quartered
> 2 carrots (about ½ lb. total), cut into chunks
> ¾ cup sliced celery
> 3½ cups chicken broth
> 2 cups Zinfandel
> 2 strips (each 3 in.) orange peel (orange part only)
> ½ teaspoon pepper
> ⅓ cup cornstarch
> Salt

1. Rinse giblets and neck. Reserve liver for another use. In a 5- to 6-quart pan combine giblets, neck, onions, carrots, celery, and ½ cup broth. Cook, covered, over medium-high heat 20 minutes. Uncover; cook over high heat, stirring often as liquid evaporates, until giblets and vegetables are browned and browned bits stick to pan, about 5 minutes. Add another ½ cup broth; stir to loosen browned bits. Repeat cooking and browning, uncovered, as directed.

Wine-infused chips or shavings
Enjoy wine's smoky aroma in foods from the barbecue

NORMAN A. PLATE

Wine-infused wood chips or shavings release fruity oak aromas in flavorful smoke when placed over hot coals on a barbecue. Look for the chips and shavings in hardware stores, cookware stores, and wine shops, or buy them from the sources below.

You can order Wine Barrel Emberosia—chips from old wine barrels—from Cakebread Cellars, Box 216, Rutherford, CA 94573; (707) 963-5221. Or purchase the chips at the tasting rooms at 8300 St. Helena Highway, Rutherford. Cost is $12.50 for a 2-pound box, plus shipping.

Barrel Select Oak Shavings can be purchased by mail from Fetzer Vineyards, Box 611, Hopland, CA 95449; (800) 846-8637. Or buy them at the tasting rooms at 13601 East Side Rd., Hopland, or 45070 Main St., Mendocino, California. Cost is $6.95 for about a 4-ounce bag, plus $3 for shipping.

A grilling kit of vintage barrel chips (two bags, each 1½ pounds, plus recipe cards) can be ordered from Woodbridge Vintage Chips, 12424 Research Parkway, Suite 275, Orlando, FL 32826; call (888) 982-2447, 5:30 A.M.-2:30 P.M. PST Mon-Fri. Cost is $16.95, including shipping.

Charcoal Companion sells oak chips soaked in wine. To locate the store nearest you that sells its Cabernet Oak Smoking Chips (distributed nationwide), call (800) 521-0505. Cost is about $5 for a 2-pound bag.

Barbeques Galore sells Woodbridge and Charcoal Companion chips at its 19 stores in California, Nevada, and Arizona. Call (800) 474-5587 for locations.

2. Add remaining broth, 1½ cups Zinfandel, peel, and pepper to pan. Cover; simmer gently over low heat 1 to 1½ hours. (If making ahead, cool, cover, and chill up to 1 day. Reheat to simmering.) Add reserved turkey pan juices (if juices are burned, omit) and apple mixture from cavity; bring to a boil. Simmer, covered, 3 to 5 minutes.

3. Pour broth mixture through a fine strainer into a bowl; reserve giblets for another use and discard remaining contents of strainer. Measure broth; if needed, add water to make 4 cups. In pan, mix cornstarch with ¼ cup water until smooth. Stir in remaining ½ cup wine and broth mixture. Stir over high heat until boiling, about 5 minutes. Season to taste with salt.

Per ½ cup serving: 80 cal., 9% (7.2 cal.) from fat; 2.3 g protein; 0.8 g fat (0.4 g sat.); 7.4 g carbo.; 52 mg sodium; 5.9 mg chol.

A robust bread dressing is flavored with pancetta, greens, and roasted red peppers.

RICK MARIANI

Bread Dressing with Pancetta and Greens

Prep and cook time: About 1¾ hours

Notes: Pancetta is available seasoned "hot" or "mild"; if you use "hot" you may want to delete the pepper.

Makes: 12 servings

About 1½ pounds sweet French bread, cut into ½- to ¾-inch cubes (6 quarts total)

½ pound thinly sliced pancetta or bacon, chopped

2 onions (about 1 lb.), chopped

2 tablespoons minced garlic (about 6 cloves)

¾ to 1 pound *each* kale and curly endive (chicory), rinsed and drained

1 jar (about 16 oz.) roasted red peppers, rinsed, drained, and chopped

½ cup dry white wine

1 tablespoon poultry seasoning

1 teaspoon summer savory

½ teaspoon pepper

2 large eggs, beaten

2½ cups chicken broth

1 cup milk

1. Spread bread cubes in a single layer on 10- by 15-inch baking pans (use 3 pans, or toast in sequence). Toast in a 350° oven until very crisp and golden brown, about 20 minutes; stir cubes after 15 minutes and switch pan positions. (If making ahead, cool cubes and store airtight up to 2 days.)

2. To a 6- to 8-quart pan over medium-high heat, add pancetta, and cook, stirring often, until golden, about 15 minutes (if using bacon, discard all but 1 tablespoon fat). Add onions and garlic; cook until tinged golden, stirring occasionally, about 15 minutes more. Meanwhile, cut off and discard tough stems on kale and endive. With a large knife, thinly slice leaves; you should have about 20 cups.

3. Add kale and endive to pan with pancetta, a quarter at a time, to allow greens to cook down slightly. Then add roasted red peppers and wine. Cook, stirring often, until all

greens are soft and most of their moisture has evaporated, about 10 minutes. Scrape any browned bits from pan bottom.

4. In a large bowl, mix cooked vegetables with toasted bread cubes, poultry seasoning, summer savory, and pepper. Whisk together eggs, broth, and milk, and pour over vegetable-bread mixture; stir until ingredients are well coated.

5. Spoon dressing into a shallow 4- to 4½-quart baking dish. (If making ahead, cover and chill up to the next day.) Bake dressing, covered, in a 375° oven until warm in center, 35 to 45 minutes (50 minutes if made ahead). Uncover, and bake until browned and crisp, about 15 minutes longer.

Or use to stuff a 16- to 20-pound turkey, and roast turkey according to chart instructions on page xxx, adding 30 to 50 minutes roasting time because bird is stuffed. Bake any remaining dressing in a 1½- to 2-quart baking dish alongside turkey during the last 45 minutes of roasting time.

Per serving: 276 cal., 24% (66 cal.) from fat; 11 g protein; 7.3 g fat (2.4 g sat.); 41 g carbo.; 578 mg sodium; 44 mg chol.

Arugula Salad with Preserved Lemon Dressing

Prep time: About 25 minutes

Notes: Preserve the lemons a week before using them. Or you can purchase preserved lemons (they are expensive) in some specialty and gourmet food stores.

Makes: 8 to 12 servings

- 1 head (about 1¼ lb.) fennel
- About 3⅓ quarts (½ lb.) arugula leaves, rinsed and crisped, tough stems removed, leaves torn in half if exceptionally large
- ½ pound small radishes, rinsed, trimmed, and sliced, if desired
- ¼ cup minced Italian parsley
- 3 tablespoons extra-virgin olive or salad oil
- 3 tablespoons cider vinegar
- Preserved lemons (recipe above right)
- Salt and pepper

1. Trim root end of fennel; cut off and discard leaves and stems, reserving a few of the feathery sprigs for garnish. Halve bulb vertically. Very thinly slice crosswise into strips about ⅛ inch by 3 inches (you should have about 2½ cups).

2. Mix fennel with arugula, radishes, and parsley; set aside.

3. Combine oil and vinegar. Remove pulp from 4 to 6 preserved lemon quarters (1 to 1½ lemons); discard pulp. Finely chop lemon rind and stir into oil-vinegar mixture; pour over vegetables. Gently fold together. Add salt and pepper as desired, and garnish with reserved fennel sprigs. Serve salad immediately.

Per serving: 43 cal., 77% (33 cal.) from fat; 1 g protein; 3.7 g fat (0.5 g sat.); 2.4 g carbo.; 173 mg sodium; 0 mg chol.

Preserved Lemons

Prep time: About 2 minutes, plus 8 hours for freezing and 6 days for storing

Makes: 8 preserved lemon quarters

- 2 lemons (4 to 5 oz. each)
- 2 tablespoons kosher or sea salt

1. Quarter lemons lengthwise and place in an airtight, noncorrodible container (about 8 by 5 by 2 inches). Freeze for 8 hours.

2. Add salt. Store airtight at room temperature for 6 days, rotating lemon quarters occasionally.

3. Use as suggested in salad recipe at left. To store lemons, refrigerate up to 6 months (color darkens).

An arugula salad with fennel and radishes reaches new flavor dimensions with a tangy preserved lemon dressing.

ROBERT OLDING

Miniature pumpkins hold a spicy corn and sage pudding; spoon additional corn mixture over the pudding before serving.

ROBERT OLDING

Brandied Potato Gratin

Prep and cook time: About 1¾ hours
Makes: 8 to 10 servings

2 pounds Russet potatoes

2 pounds yams or sweet potatoes

Fresh-ground pepper

¾ cup chicken or beef broth, heated

⅓ cup brandy (or additional broth)

⅓ pound teleme or jack cheese, thinly sliced (or in small chunks if teleme is too soft to slice)

¼ cup grated parmesan cheese

Salt

1. Peel potatoes and yams. With a food processor or vegetable slicer, cut them into very thin (about ⅛-inch-thick) slices.

2. Line the bottom of a buttered 2½- to 3-quart shallow casserole dish with an overlapping layer of alternating potato and yam slices. Sprinkle lightly with pepper. Repeat layers to use all potatoes and yams.

3. Mix hot broth with brandy; pour over potatoes. Bake, covered, in a 375° oven until tender when pierced, about 1¼ hours. Uncover, and top evenly with teleme and parmesan. Continue baking until cheese topping melts and is browned, about 15 minutes. Add salt to taste.

Per serving: 214 cal., 19% (41 cal.) from fat; 6.4 g protein; 4.5 g fat (0.7 g sat.); 37 g carbo.; 142 mg sodium; 5.6 mg chol.

Corn-Chipotle Pudding in Miniature Pumpkins

Prep and cook time: About 1 hour

Notes: You can steam and scoop out the pumpkins 1 day ahead.

Makes: 8 servings

8 miniature pumpkins (6 to 8 oz. each)

1 dried chipotle chili

1 onion (½ lb.), chopped

1 package (10 oz.) frozen corn kernels, thawed

2 tablespoons butter or margarine

1 tablespoon minced fresh sage leaves or 1 teaspoon crumbled dried sage

Salad oil

1 cup milk

3 large eggs

Fresh sage sprigs

Salt

1. Rinse pumpkins; set on a rack over 1 inch boiling water in a 5- to 6-quart pan or wok (use 2 pans or steam in batches if necessary). Cover; steam until tender when pierced, about 20 minutes. Lift from rack; let stand until cool enough to handle. Slice off top quarter of each pumpkin; reserve. With a small spoon, gently scoop out and discard seeds, taking care not to break shell. If necessary, gently scrape out some flesh so shell is no more than ½ inch thick. (If making ahead, cover and chill pumpkins and tops airtight up to 1 day.)

2. Combine chipotle and 1 cup water in a small pan. Bring to a boil over high heat, simmer 5 minutes, then drain. Cut off and discard stem. Finely mince chili.

3. In a 10- to 12-inch frying pan, mix onion, corn, butter, and minced sage. Stir often over medium-high heat until lightly browned, about 10 minutes. Stir in chili.

4. Lightly rub each pumpkin and its top with oil. Place the pumpkins, with their tops alongside (stems up), in 2 oiled 10- by 15-inch baking pans.

5. In a bowl, beat together milk and eggs. Stir in all but 1/2 cup of the corn mixture; then spoon into hollowed-out pumpkins.

6. Bake filled pumpkins and tops in a 350° oven until center is barely firm when lightly pressed, about 25 minutes. Remove from oven. Briefly reheat remaining corn mixture; spoon over puddings. Garnish with sage sprigs and pumpkin tops. Add salt to taste.

Per serving: 161 cal., 44% (71 cal.) from fat; 6 g protein; 7.9 g fat (3.3 g sat.); 19 g carbo.; 71 mg sodium; 92 mg chol.

The following recipe comes from Walter Goetzeler, owner of the **Freeport Bakery** at 2966 Freeport Boulevard in Sacramento; (916) 442-4256.

Grapevine Bread

Prep and cook time: About 3 1/4 hours, including 1 hour and 40 minutes for rising

Notes: If you're short on time, use 1 package of three 1-pound loaves of thawed frozen bread dough instead of the following bread dough. Just before baking, combine 1 whole egg and 1 teaspoon water and generously brush over assembled grape cluster–shaped dough.

Makes: A 3-pound grapevine loaf

About 6 1/4 cups bread flour

1 3/4 cups milk, heated to about 110°

1/4 cup sugar

2 packages active dry yeast

4 large eggs

5 tablespoons butter or margarine, melted

1/2 teaspoon salt

1/2 teaspoon *each* vanilla, almond extract, and lemon extract

1. To a large bowl, add 6 cups flour (only 3 cups if you'll mix and knead by hand rather than with a dough hook). Make a hole in center of flour. Add milk, sugar, and yeast. Mix with a small amount of the flour to make a very soft dough; let rest about 10 minutes. Add 3 eggs, butter, salt, vanilla, and almond and lemon extracts.

2. *If using a dough hook,* mix at low speed until ingredients are mixed. Then beat at high speed until dough pulls cleanly from sides of bowl, about 10 minutes. If dough is sticky, add flour, 1 tablespoon at a time, until it releases from the bowl.

To mix and knead by hand, stir ingredients until moistened; beat with heavy spoon until dough is stretchy, about 5 minutes. Stir in 3 cups more flour; scrape onto a lightly floured board; knead until very smooth and elastic, adding as little flour as possible to prevent sticking, about 10 minutes. Return to bowl.

3. Cover with plastic wrap; let stand in a warm, draft-free place until doubled, about 1 hour. If using frozen dough, thaw three 1-pound loaves at room temperature; let rise until nearly doubled, about 2 hours.

4. Knead with dough hook, or on a lightly floured board, to expel air bubbles. Divide dough into 24 equal pieces.

5. Roll 20 pieces into smooth balls. On a lightly oiled 12- by 15-inch baking sheet, place 12 balls (1/2 inch apart to allow room to rise) in triangle form (see top diagram at right). Then top the 12 balls with 8 more balls, forming a second, smaller triangle on top. Using one of remaining pieces, form a 1/2- by 3-inch stem and place on the largest end of grape cluster. Roll out 2 other pieces 1/4 inch thick and cut each into a leaf the size of your palm. (Draw veins on leaves with back of knife.) Place leaves next to stem and over balls. From leaf scraps and the last piece, roll 3 ropes about 1/2 inch wide and 12 inches long, then lay and twist over grapes to look like tendrils.

6. Cover loaf with plastic wrap; let rise until small dent remains when touched, about 40 minutes (30 minutes for thawed frozen dough).

7. Combine 1 egg and 1 teaspoon water; generous-ly brush loaf with egg mixture. Bake in a 350° oven until golden brown, about 35 minutes. Let cool slightly; serve warm. Or cool, wrap airtight, and store at room temperature up to next day or freeze. Thaw to serve. Reheat, lightly covered, in a 350° oven until warm, about 30 minutes.

Per 1-oz. serving: 94 cal., 23% (22 cal.) from fat; 3.1 g protein; 2.4 g fat (1.1 g sat.); 15 g carbo.; 45 mg sodium; 22 mg chol.

Follow the instructions at left and the illustrated steps below to make a fantastic, grape cluster–shaped loaf.

a. Bread base triangle
12 balls

b. Second layer and stem
8 balls, 1 piece

c. Leaves and vines (tendrils)
3 pieces, including scraps

DEBRA LAMBERT

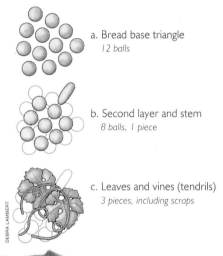

An elegant marbled cheesecake has the familiar flavor of pumpkin pie.

ROBERT OLDING

Marbled Pumpkin Cheesecake

Prep and cook time: About 1 hour and 20 minutes

Notes: Serve with sweetened softly whipped cream flavored with a little Chinese five-spice powder or candied ginger.

Makes: 8 to 10 servings

- 8 ounces gingersnap cookies
- 2 tablespoons granulated sugar
- 3 tablespoons melted butter or margarine
- 2 large packages (8 oz. each) neufchâtel cheese (light cream cheese) or regular cream cheese
- ¾ cup firmly packed brown sugar
- 2 large eggs
- 1½ teaspoons Chinese five-spice powder or pumpkin pie spice
- 1 can (1 lb.) pumpkin

1. Place about a third of the gingersnap cookies in a zip-lock plastic bag, seal, and roll with a rolling pin until cookies are finely crushed; repeat to crush remaining cookies (you need 1¾ cups). In a 9-inch cheesecake pan with removable bottom, mix cookie crumbs, granulated sugar, and butter. Press crumb mixture over bottom and about 1 inch up sides of the pan. Bake crust in a 325° oven until lightly browned, about 15 minutes.

2. With an electric mixer, beat together the cheese and the brown sugar until they are blended. Add the eggs, one at a time, beating well after each addition. Remove ½ cup of the cheese mixture and set it aside. Stir the five-spice powder and the pumpkin into the remaining mixture until they are well blended.

3. Pour pumpkin mixture into crust-lined pan. Drop rounded tablespoons of the reserved cheese mixture randomly over the pumpkin mixture. With a knife or metal spatula, draw blade through the white and orange mixtures to marble.

4. Bake in a 325° oven until the center barely jiggles when cake is gently shaken, about 50 minutes. Cool on a rack. Cover and chill until cold, at least 2½ hours or up to 1 day. Run a knife around edge of cake and remove pan sides.

Per serving: 346 cal., 44% (153 cal.) from fat; 7.6 g protein; 17 g fat (9.6 g sat.); 41 g carbo.; 386 mg sodium; 86 mg chol.

Wine-smoked turkey dinner countdown

This step-by-step schedule assumes that only one person is doing the cooking, although serving the appetizer and getting dinner to the table is easier with a little help. The Thanks-giving countdown also assumes that you have just one oven. If you have two ovens, follow the instructions at the end of the countdown.

AT LEAST I WEEK AHEAD
• *Make* preserved lemons for salad.

UP TO I WEEK AHEAD
• *Bake* cheese puffs and grapevine bread and freeze.

AT LEAST 3 DAYS AHEAD
• *Purchase* a frozen turkey; thaw the turkey in the refrigerator for 3 full days (72 hours).

UP TO 3 DAYS AHEAD
• *Shop* for all remaining ingredients except a fresh turkey.

UP TO 2 DAYS AHEAD
• *Purchase* a fresh turkey.
• *Toast* bread for stuffing.

UP TO I DAY AHEAD
• *Make* cheesecake; chill.
• *Make* bread dressing; chill.
• *Steam* pumpkins; hollow and chill.
• *Rinse* and crisp salad greens.

THANKSGIVING DAY: 3 ½ HOURS BEFORE SERVING
• *Remove* bread and cheese puffs from freezer.
• *Soak* wood chips and prepare turkey for charcoal barbecue.
• *Ignite* charcoal briquets if using a charcoal barbecue.

3 ¼ HOURS AHEAD
• *Preheat* gas barbecue, adding wood chips to metal box as needed.

3 HOURS AHEAD
• *Add* wood chips to briquets if using a charcoal barbecue; set turkey on grill of charcoal or gas barbecue.
• *Preheat* oven to 375°.
• *Assemble* potato gratin.

2 ½ HOURS AHEAD
• *Add* more wood chips and briquets to charcoal barbecue.
• *Place* potato gratin in oven.
• *Cook* corn mixture and rub pumpkins with oil.

2 ¼ HOURS AHEAD
• *Place* bread dressing in oven.

2 HOURS AHEAD
• *Add* more wood chips and briquets to charcoal barbecue, wood chips to gas barbecue.
• *Cook* giblets and neck with vegetables for gravy.
• *Cut* fennel, parsley, and lemons; clean radishes and make dressing for salad. Cover and chill.

I ½ HOURS AHEAD
• *Add* more wood chips and briquets to charcoal barbecue.
• *Add* broth and wine to giblet mixture and simmer.
• *Add* eggs and milk to corn mixture and fill pumpkins.

I ¼ HOURS AHEAD
• *Remove* potato gratin and bread dressing from oven; keep warm.
• *Reduce* oven temperature to 350°.
• *Place* filled pumpkins in oven.

I HOUR AHEAD
• *Add* more wood chips and briquets to charcoal barbecue, wood chips to gas barbecue. Start checking turkey for doneness.

45 MINUTES AHEAD
• *Place* bread in oven to reheat.

30 MINUTES AHEAD
• *Check* turkey for doneness. If done, transfer to platter, keep warm, and let rest.
• *Remove* pumpkins from oven; keep warm.
• *Reheat* cheese puffs.
• *Pour* turkey pan juices and apples into giblet broth; simmer.

25 MINUTES AHEAD
• *Remove* cheese puffs; serve warm.
• *Return* potato gratin, covered, to oven.
• *Strain* broth for gravy; cover broth to keep warm.

I5 MINUTES AHEAD
• *Remove* bread from oven.
• *Increase* oven temperature to 375°.
• *Uncover* potato gratin, add cheese, and continue baking.
• *Uncover* bread dressing; return to oven.
• *Reheat* remaining corn mixture; spoon mixture into pumpkins; transfer to serving dishes.

5 MINUTES AHEAD
• *Thicken* broth for gravy and pour into serving container.
• *Garnish* turkey.

IMMEDIATELY BEFORE SERVING
• *Add* fennel, parsley, and radishes to salad greens; mix with dressing; garnish with fennel sprigs.
• *Remove* potato gratin and bread dressing from oven.

AT DESSERT TIME
• *Remove* pan sides from cheesecake; garnish with whipped cream.

If you have two ovens, set one at 375° and bake the potatoes and bread dressing completely, without standing time. Start baking the potatoes 1½ hours before serving, the dressing 1¼ hours before.

Set the second oven at 350°. Place pumpkins in oven 45 minutes—and bread 30 minutes—before dinner; reheat cheese puffs 3 to 5 minutes before serving.
—*L. L. A.* ∎

Turkey basics: *Barbecued* or *Oven-roasted Turkey*

TURKEY WEIGHT with giblets:	OVEN TEMP.:	INTERNAL TEMP.:**	COOKING TIME***
10 to 13 lb.	350°	160°	1½ to 2¼ hr.
14 to 23 lb.	325°	160°	2 to 3 hr.
24 to 27 lb.	325°	160°	3 to 3¾ hr.
28 to 30 lb.	325°	160°	3½ to 4½ hr.

* See *Wine-smoked Turkey, page 230,* for heat control for charcoal or gas grill.
** *Insert thermometer through thickest part of breast to bone.*
*** *Add 30 to 50 minutes to cooking time for an oven-roasted stuffed turkey.*

The Lightest Feast

- *Grilled Oysters and Shrimp with Chili-Cranberry Mignonette*

- *Orange-glazed Turkey Breast with Apricot-Ginger Sauce*

- *Spiced Couscous Dressing*

- *Mashed Garnet Yam Puff*

- *Fennel with Mushrooms and Prosciutto*

- *Merlot-poached Pears with Salad Greens*

- *Cranberry Sorbet with Vodka Splash*

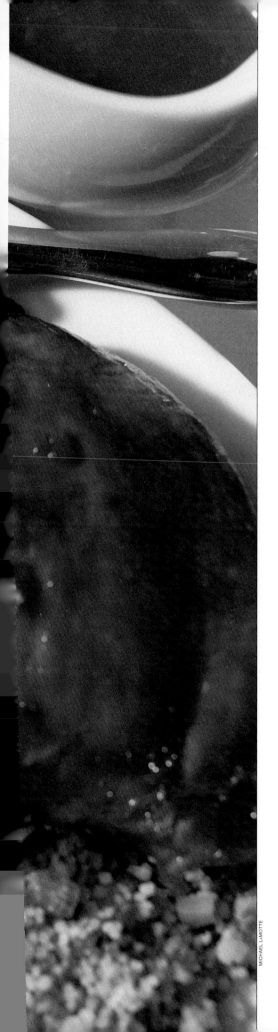

The lightest feast

It only tastes extravagant. Less than 6 percent of this dinner's calories come from fat. And making it won't keep you in the kitchen all day

Great-tasting, easy on the waistline, and ready in about two hours after some make-ahead steps: if that describes your ideal Thanksgiving dinner, here's the menu for you.

We've included the traditional components of the meal but mixed them up a little, leaving out most of the fat, keeping all the flavor, and choosing quicker-cooking options.

Instead of a big bird, roast a turkey breast. A simple fruit-based sauce serves as glaze and gravy. Fast couscous dressing stands in for traditional stuffing (but if you're a traditionalist, try the low-fat stuffing recipe on page 232). Vegetables and salad, made a day ahead, get lots of flavor from citrus, spices, and wine. Cranberries show up at both ends of the meal, in a dunk sauce for seafood appetizers off the grill, and in sorbet drizzled with icy vodka.

So go ahead—relax about the cooking and enjoy the meal, knowing these dishes are as good for you as they are good-tasting.

Wines to match your feast

With the oysters and shrimp appetizer *serve a California brut sparkling wine such as Mumm Cuvée Napa, Domaine Carneros, or Maison Deutz.*
With dinner *serve Preston Vineyards Dry Creek Valley Viognier, Navarro Anderson Valley White Riesling, or Jekel Arroyo Seco Johannisberg Riesling.*
—Bob Thompson

Spoon cranberry-chipotle sauce onto grilled shrimp and oysters for a lively appetizer with almost no fat.

Grilled Oysters and Shrimp with Chili-Cranberry Mignonette

Prep and cook time: About 40 minutes

Notes: At the store, oysters should have tightly closed shells, feel heavy for their size, and smell fresh. Don't store oysters in plastic bags, as they need a little air; chill covered with damp towels. Grilling warms oysters only enough to pop shells open (or at least make them easier to open). They should still be raw. One person can start shucking oysters while another grills shrimp.

Makes: 8 servings

- 1/3 **cup garlic-flavor red wine vinegar**
- 1 1/2 **tablespoons minced shallot**
- 1 **tablespoon minced cranberries**
- 1/2 **teaspoon minced canned chipotle chili in adobado sauce**
- 16 **oysters in the shell**
- 16 **raw shrimp in shells (14 to 16 per lb.)**

1. For mignonette sauce, combine vinegar, shallot, cranberries, and chili in a bowl. Set aside and chill.

2. Scrub oysters with a stiff brush under cold running water. Devein shrimp (but do not peel). To devein, poke a toothpick about 1/8 inch deep on outer curve between shell sections; pull up vein (if present).

3. Place oysters cupped sides down, touching to support each other, on an oiled char- coal grill over a solid bed of medium-hot coals or medium-high heat on a gas grill (you can hold your hand at grill level only 3 to 4 seconds). Close cover on gas grill. Grill oysters (do not turn) until liquid escapes (some may open slightly), 2 to 5 minutes (you do not want to cook them). As liquid escapes, remove from grill. Place shrimp on grill; close cover on gas grill. Cook shrimp, turning once, until no longer translucent in center (cut to test), 3 to 4 minutes.

4. Place any unopened oyster cupped side down on a heavy towel, grip curved end with a gloved hand (an oven mitt works well), and hold oyster level. Firmly push an oyster knife into hinge between top and bottom shells; twist to open. On all oysters, slide oyster knife along underside of top shell to muscle, then cut muscle to free oyster. Remove top shell. Cut oyster free from muscle on bottom shell.

5. Arrange oysters, resting in shells, on one side of a serving platter (if unsteady, place on a crumpled cloth napkin on platter); arrange shrimp alongside. Pour chilled sauce into a small bowl and place on platter.

6. Direct guests to peel shrimp. Spoon mignonette over seafood.

Per serving: 72 cal., 19% (14 cal.) from fat; 11 g protein; 1.5 g fat (0.3 g sat.); 2.3 g carbo.; 103 mg sodium; 85 mg chol.

Orange-glazed Turkey Breast with Apricot-Ginger Sauce

Prep and cook time: About 1 hour and 40 minutes, including 10 to 20 minutes for standing

Notes: Order the turkey breast half a few days ahead to get the right size.

Makes: 8 to 10 servings

    1   boneless, skinless turkey
        breast half (3 to 3 1/2 lb.), fresh
        or frozen
    1/3 cup orange marmalade
    2   tablespoons soy sauce
    2   tablespoons lemon juice
    1   teaspoon ground ginger
    3 1/2 cups chicken broth
    1/4 cup cornstarch
    1/2 cup apricot nectar
        Salt and pepper

1. If turkey is frozen, thaw in refrigerator at least 48 hours. Rinse breast and pat dry. Set on a rack in a foil-lined 10- by 15-inch roasting pan. Bake in a 375° oven until a thermometer inserted in center of thickest part reaches 120°, 45 to 50 minutes.

2. Meanwhile, in a 1 1/2- to 2-quart pan melt marmalade over medium-low heat. Stir in 1 tablespoon soy sauce, 1 tablespoon lemon juice, and the ginger.

3. When turkey reaches 120°, brush some of the marmalade mixture over breast; continue roasting, basting twice more with marmalade mixture, until a thermometer inserted in center of thickest part reads 155° to 160°, about 30 minutes longer. Transfer turkey to a platter and keep warm; let rest 10 to 20 minutes.

4. To the remaining marmalade mixture in the pan, add remaining soy sauce and lemon juice, and the broth. Smoothly mix cornstarch with apricot nectar. Add to broth mixture and stir over high heat until it boils, about 4 minutes. Pour any accumulated juices from turkey platter into broth mixture, add salt and pepper to taste, and serve with turkey.

Per serving: 210 cal., 6.2% (13 cal.) from fat; 35 g protein; 1.4 g fat (0.5 g sat.); 13 g carbo.; 316 mg sodium; 86 mg chol.

Spiced Couscous Dressing

Prep and cook time: About 30 minutes
Makes: About 8 servings

    1   onion (1/2 lb.), chopped
    1   cup chopped carrot
    1   teaspoon salad oil
    1   teaspoon ground coriander
    1/2 teaspoon ground cumin
    1/2 teaspoon ground ginger
    1/4 teaspoon ground cinnamon
    3 1/3 cups chicken broth
    2   cups couscous
    1/2 cup chopped dried apricots
    1/2 cup golden raisins
        Salt and pepper
    1/3 cup chopped fresh cilantro

1. In a 5- to 6-quart pan stir onion, carrot, and oil over medium-high heat until onion is soft, about 8 minutes. Stir in coriander, cumin, ginger, and cinnamon.

2. Add broth; bring to a boil over high heat. Stir in couscous, apricots, and raisins. Cover pan and remove from heat; let stand until couscous absorbs broth, 2 to 5 minutes. Add salt and pepper to taste. Stir in cilantro. Serve with turkey.

Per serving: 255 cal., 5.5% (14 cal.) from fat; 8.2 g protein; 1.6 g fat (0.4 g sat.); 52 g carbo.; 56 mg sodium; 1.6 mg chol.

Mashed Garnet Yam Puff

Prep and cook time: About 55 minutes
Notes: You can steam the yams and assemble the casserole 1 day ahead.
Makes: 8 servings

    3 1/4 to 3 1/2 pounds garnet or
        jewel yams
    3/4 cup nonfat or low-fat sour cream
        About 2 tablespoons grated
        lemon peel
    1/4 teaspoon ground nutmeg

1. Peel yams and cut into 1/2-inch pieces; steam until tender when pierced with a fork, about 15 minutes. Place yams in a large bowl. Add sour cream, 2 tablespoons lemon peel, and nutmeg to bowl; beat with an electric mixer on medium speed until very smooth, about 3 minutes. Spoon into a buttered 1 1/2- to 2-quart casserole. (If making ahead, cover and chill up to 1 day.)

2. Place covered casserole in a 375° oven until yams are hot, about 20 minutes (30 minutes if yams have been chilled). Garnish with additional lemon peel, if desired.

Per serving: 204 cal., 1.3% (2.7 cal.) from fat; 3.9 g protein; 0.3 g fat (0.1 g sat.); 46 g carbo.; 29 mg sodium; 0 mg chol.

A delicate garnet yam puff with lemon peel and nutmeg has less than 1 gram of fat per serving.

Sautéed mushrooms and crisp prosciutto pieces peek out from tender wine-poached fennel bulbs.

MICHAEL LAMOTTE

Fennel with Mushrooms and Prosciutto

Prep and cook time: About 1 hour and 20 minutes (1 hour and 30 minutes if prepared ahead and chilled)

Notes: You can steam the fennel, make the mushroom filling, and stuff the bulbs 1 day ahead.

Makes: 8 servings

8 heads fennel (each 3 inches wide at base), about 6½ lb. total

1¼ cups chicken broth

¾ cup slightly sweet white wine, such as Johannisberg Riesling

1 pound mushrooms, sliced

2 ounces thinly sliced prosciutto, minced

1. Trim off fennel stalks and feathery greens. Reserve feathery greens, mincing enough of them to make ¼ cup. (If making ahead, chill 2 tablespoons of the minced greens, as well as the remaining feathery sprigs to use to garnish platter when served.) Reserve fennel stalks for use in soups or stocks. Trim any brown spots from bulbs; arrange in a single layer in a 5- to 6-quart pan. Pour broth and wine over them; cover and bring to a boil over high heat, then simmer until fennel is very tender when pierced, 35 to 45 minutes. Set aside until cool enough to handle; reserve cooking liquid.

2. While fennel cooks, combine mushrooms, prosciutto, and 2 tablespoons of the minced fennel greens in an 8- to 10-inch nonstick frying pan. Cover and cook over medium-high heat until mushrooms exude juice, about 7 minutes. Uncover and cook, stirring often, until liquid evaporates and mushrooms are browned, about 15 minutes; set aside.

3. With a small knife and a sharp-edged spoon, carefully scoop out inner part of fennel bulbs so that you have a ¼-inch-thick intact shell. (Reserve scooped-out fennel for soups or other uses, if desired.) Spoon the mushroom mixture equally into the bulbs. Arrange bulbs in a baking dish large enough to hold them in a single layer. Spoon the reserved cooking liquid over them. (If making ahead, cover and chill up to 1 day.)

4. Bake stuffed fennel bulbs, covered, in a 375° oven for 15 minutes; uncover and continue baking until hot, about 10 more minutes (20 minutes if made ahead and chilled). Transfer bulbs to a serving platter; sprinkle lightly with remaining minced fennel greens, and garnish platter with fresh fennel sprigs.

Per serving: 67 cal., 21% (14 cal.) from fat; 4.9 g protein; 1.6 g fat (0.4 g sat.); 6 g carbo.; 253 mg sodium; 6.3 mg chol.

Merlot-poached Pears with Salad Greens

Prep and cook time: About 50 minutes
Makes: 8 servings

- **4** Red d'Anjou, Green d'Anjou, Bosc, or Comice pears, or about 12 Seckel pears (1½ to 2 lb. total)
- **3** cups dry red wine, such as Merlot
- **½** cup packed brown sugar
- **¼** cup *each* balsamic vinegar, orange juice, and lemon juice
- **2** teaspoons grated lemon peel
- **½** teaspoon black peppercorns

Poach winter pears in a Merlot sauce. Then reduce the flavorful sauce to dress a luscious salad of pears, mixed greens, and crunchy jicama.

1   cinnamon stick (3 in.)

12 cups (about 12 oz.) mixed salad greens, rinsed and crisped

1½ cups matchstick-size jicama pieces

1. Cut the pears vertically into halves; core and stem.

2. In a 3- to 4-quart pan, bring wine, brown sugar, vinegar, orange and lemon juices, lemon peel, peppercorns, and cinnamon stick to a simmer over medium-high heat. Add pears, reduce heat, and simmer, covered, until pears are tender when pierced with a fork, about 15 minutes. With a slotted spoon, lift pears from wine mixture; set in a 9- by 13-inch baking dish to cool. Return heat to high; boil until dressing is reduced to 1 cup, about 20 minutes. Discard cinnamon and peppercorns; cool slightly. (If making ahead, cover and chill pears and dressing separately up to 1 day, and rinse and crisp salad greens.)

3. In a large bowl, gently mix salad greens with ⅔ cup of the dressing. Evenly distribute dressed greens on 8 salad plates. Place a pear half (or 3 halves if using Seckel pears) in the center of each plate and scatter jicama pieces around pears on greens. Spoon the remaining dressing equally over pears and greens.

Per serving: 133 cal., 2.7% (3.6 cal.) from fat; 1.3 g protein; 0.4 g fat (0 g sat.); 32 g carbo.; 23 mg sodium; 0 mg chol.

Prime time for pears

Winter pear varieties, clockwise from upper left, include Forelle, Green d'Anjou, Bosc, Seckel, and Red d'Anjou.

CURTIS ANDERSON

W inter pears are now in peak season. For this Thanksgiving menu, Red d'Anjou pears are poached in a Merlot wine sauce that then dresses a salad of the pears and mixed greens. But the pears are also delicious baked, canned, or eaten out of hand.

If you find pears a bit on the hard side when you shop, don't despair. They'll actually ripen better on your counter than in the store or on the tree. Just remember to select them a couple of days before you want to eat or cook them. If a pear yields to gentle pressure near the base of the stem, it's ripe.

Cranberry Sorbet with Vodka Splash

Prep time: About 10 minutes, plus 6 hours for freezing

Notes: Place a bottle of vodka in the freezer, then offer it to pour over the sorbet for a brisk topping. Chill glasses before filling with sorbet.

Makes: 8 servings

- 2 cans (12 oz. each) frozen cranberry juice cocktail concentrate, thawed
- 1/4 cup lemon juice

  Fresh or frozen cranberries, thin lemon slices, and fresh mint sprigs

About 1 1/2 cups cold vodka (optional)

1. Mix cranberry juice cocktail concentrate, 2 3/4 cups water, and lemon juice in a 9- by 13-inch pan or dish. Freeze until solid, at least 6 hours or up to 1 week. Cover if freezing for more than 1 day.

2. Break into small chunks and whirl in a food processor until a smooth slush forms. Spoon into chilled glasses; return to freezer for at least 20 minutes or up to 3 days (cover if storing more than 1 day).

3. Garnish with whole cranberries, lemon slices, and mint. Drizzle with vodka to taste.

Per serving: 218 cal., 1.7% (3.6 cal.) from fat; 0 g protein; 0.4 g fat (0 g sat.); 55 g carbo.; 9.2 mg sodium; 0 mg chol.

Splash icy vodka on cranberry sorbet for an indulgent but refreshing finish to your Thanksgiving meal.

MICHAEL LAMOTTE

The lightest feast Thanksgiving countdown

For easiest preparation, make the sorbet, yams, fennel, and pears for the salad ahead as noted, or prepare them Thanksgiving morning; allow about two hours. This countdown assumes that only one person is cooking, though an extra pair of hands is especially helpful shucking oysters and serving the appetizer, then getting dinner to the table.

UP TO 1 WEEK AHEAD
- *Freeze* sorbet (step 1).
- *Order* turkey breast half.

2 TO 3 DAYS AHEAD
- *Shop* for all ingredients except oysters and shrimp. Buy a fresh turkey breast half 1 to 2 days ahead, or a frozen turkey breast half at least 2 days (a full 48 hours) ahead and begin thawing in refrigerator.
- *Beat* sorbet into a slush; freeze in glasses (step 2).

1 DAY AHEAD
- *Buy* oysters and shrimp.
- *Cook* yams, spoon mixture into a 1 1/2- to 2-quart casserole, and chill (step 1).
- *Cook* and fill fennel (through step 3).
- For salad, *poach* pears and *reduce* syrup; *rinse* greens and *chill* to crisp (through step 2).

THANKSGIVING DAY: 2 HOURS BEFORE SERVING
- *Prepare* barbecue grill.
- *Make* sauce for seafood; chill.

1 3/4 HOURS AHEAD
- *Preheat* oven for turkey.
- *Assemble* and chop ingredients for dressing.

1 1/2 HOURS AHEAD
- *Place* turkey breast in roasting pan, insert meat thermometer, and begin roasting.
- *Scrub* the oysters and devein the shrimp.

1 1/4 HOURS AHEAD
- *Grill* the oysters and shrimp, and shuck the oysters.

50 MINUTES AHEAD
- *Serve* seafood appetizer with chili-cranberry mignonette.

45 MINUTES AHEAD
- *Make* sauce for turkey; brush some on bird when the temperature reaches 120°.

40 MINUTES AHEAD
- *Begin* baking fennel.
- *Begin* baking yam casserole.

30 MINUTES AHEAD
- *Make* couscous dressing: cook vegetables, add liquid and seasonings, bring to a boil, and add couscous, apricots, and raisins. Let stand.

25 MINUTES AHEAD
- *Uncover* fennel.

15 TO 20 MINUTES AHEAD
- *Remove* turkey from oven when thermometer reaches 155° to 160°; place turkey on platter, and keep warm.
- *Finish* apricot-ginger sauce for the turkey, pour sauce into a gravy boat, and keep warm.

10 MINUTES AHEAD
- *Arrange* salad: dress, distribute on plates, top with pears and jicama, and add more dressing.

5 MINUTES AHEAD
- *Remove* yam puff from oven; garnish with lemon peel.
- *Transfer* fennel to a serving platter; keep warm.

IMMEDIATELY BEFORE SERVING
- *Stir* cilantro into couscous; spoon next to turkey.
- *Garnish* turkey platter as desired. Sprinkle fennel lightly with minced fennel greens, and garnish platter with fennel sprigs.

AT DESSERT TIME
- *Decorate* sorbet with cranberries, lemon slices, and mint, and drizzle with vodka. —E. J. ∎

KEVIN CANDLAND

Orange Yogurt Scones
Ann Holmberg, Coeur d'Alene, Idaho

As owner of the Country Ranch Bed and Breakfast, Ann Holmberg continually searches for breakfast breads for her health-conscious guests. She modernized this "handed-down" recipe with citrus-flavor yogurt, and uses fresh orange juice and grated peel to emphasize the fruit flavor.

Prep and cook time: About 35 minutes
Makes: 8 servings

    2   cups all-purpose flour
    ⅓   cup plus 2 teaspoons sugar
    2   tablespoons baking powder
    ¼   teaspoon *each* baking soda and salt
    3   tablespoons cold butter or margarine

    1   carton (6 oz., about ⅔ cup) orange- or lemon-flavor yogurt
    2   teaspoons grated orange peel
    ¼   cup orange juice

1. In a bowl or food processor, mix or whirl together flour, ⅓ cup sugar, baking powder, baking soda, and salt. Cut in or whirl butter until mixture forms fine crumbs. Mix yogurt, orange peel, and juice; add to flour mixture and stir just until evenly moistened.

2. Mound dough on an oiled 12- by 15-inch baking sheet. With well-floured hands, pat mound into an even 9-inch round. With a floured knife, cut through dough to make 8 wedges; leave in place on pan. Sprinkle with remaining sugar.

3. Bake in a 375° oven until scones are golden brown, about 25 minutes. Serve hot, or slide onto a rack and let cool until warm. Cut into wedges.

Per serving: 221 cal., 22% (49 cal.) from fat; 4.2 g protein; 5.4 g fat (2.9 g sat.); 39 g carbo.; 529 mg sodium; 12 mg chol.

Cranberry Citrus Relish
Midge du Bray,
Redwood City, California

Last year, Midge du Bray strayed from a basic cranberry relish recipe. She added ingredients she had on hand for the holidays—a tangerine, dried apricots, molasses, raspberry vinegar, and pumpkin pie spice. The result was a relish with lively tartness and full flavor. She serves it with turkey or pork, and uses it in muffins.

Prep and cook time: About 25 minutes
Makes: 3¾ cups

    1   bag (12 oz., 3 cups) fresh or
        frozen cranberries

    1   tangerine (about 6 oz.)
    ½   cup dried apricots, coarsely
        chopped
    ½   cup firmly packed brown sugar
    ¼   cup granulated sugar
    ¼   cup light molasses
    ¾   cup raspberry vinegar
    1   teaspoon pumpkin pie spice
    ½   teaspoon vanilla

1. Sort and remove debris from cranberries; rinse and drain. Place cranberries in a 2- to 3-quart pan.

2. Cut tangerine into 1-inch chunks; remove and discard seeds. Using a food processor or a knife, finely chop tangerine, including peel.

3. Add chopped tangerine, apricots, brown sugar, granulated sugar, molasses, raspberry vinegar, pumpkin pie spice, and vanilla to pan. Stir to mix.

4. Cook, uncovered, over medium heat, stirring occasionally, until berries are soft and begin to pop, 12 to 15 minutes. Let cool. (If making ahead, cover and chill up to 1 month.)

Per ¼-cup serving: 83 cal., 1.1% (0.9 cal.) from fat; 0.3 g protein; 0.1 g fat (0 g sat.); 21 g carbo.; 5.7 mg sodium; 0 mg chol.

Sauerbraten Short Ribs

Chuck Allen, Dana Point, California

For 16 years, Chuck Allen ran a diner in Laguna Beach called Chuck and Matt's. One of his customers' favorites was the short ribs, which were braised in a thick, slightly sweet sauce. Now Allen is retired and makes this hearty dish at home for his grandchildren.

Prep and cook time: About 2 hours
Makes: 6 servings

- 3 pounds beef short ribs, cut into 2-inch lengths
- 1 cup catsup
- 1 tablespoon *each* white wine vinegar, Worcestershire, and prepared cream-style horseradish
- 1 tablespoon sugar
- 1 teaspoon dry mustard
- 2 onions (1 lb. total), thinly sliced
- 1 dried bay leaf
- Salt

1. Trim excess fat off ribs. Place the ribs and ⅓ cup water in a 5- to 6-quart pan. Bring to a boil, cover, and cook ribs over medium heat for 20 minutes. Uncover and cook over high heat, turning meat occasionally, until the liquid evaporates, about 10 minutes. Turn meat in pan to brown all sides.

2. Add 1 cup water, catsup, vinegar, Worcestershire, horseradish, sugar, mustard, onions, and bay leaf. Cover and simmer over low heat until meat is very tender when pierced, about 1½ hours.

KEVIN CANDLAND

3. Skim off and discard fat. Add salt to taste. Serve meat and juices with noodles or potatoes.

Per serving: 245 cal., 36% (89 cal.) from fat; 19 g protein; 9.9 g fat (4.1 g sat.); 21 g carbo.; 567 mg sodium; 55 mg chol.

Golden Root Soup

Kathryn Altus, Seattle

A friend of Kathryn Altus's made savory root pies for a restaurant. Altus loved the sweet, earthy taste of the pies and wanted to create something with the same vegetables—parsnips, rutabagas, and yellow-fleshed potatoes. Her experimentation ended with this smooth soup, which has a warm, pale golden hue. When the soup is made with carrots, its color deepens.

Prep and cook time: About 45 minutes
Makes: 4 servings

- 1 tablespoon butter or margarine
- 1 onion (about ½ lb.), chopped
- 4 parsnips or carrots (about ¾ lb. total)
- 2 Yellow Finn or Yukon Gold potatoes (about 10 oz. total)
- 1 rutabaga (about ½ lb.)
- 3½ cups chicken or vegetable broth
- About 1 teaspoon finely shredded orange peel
- 2 tablespoons dry sherry (optional)
- 1 tablespoon chopped fresh cilantro
- Salt and white pepper
- Plain nonfat yogurt

1. In a 2- to 3-quart pan, melt butter over medium-high heat. Add onion; cook, stirring often, until golden, about 10 minutes.

2. Meanwhile, peel parsnips, potatoes, and rutabaga. Thinly slice parsnips. Cut potatoes and rutabaga into ½-inch cubes.

3. Add broth, parsnips, potatoes, rutabaga, and 1 teaspoon orange peel to onion. Bring to a boil, cover, and simmer over low heat until vegetables are tender when pierced, 20 to 25 minutes.

4. Purée mixture in a blender or food processor, a portion at a time. (If making ahead, cool, cover, and chill up to 1 day.) Return soup to pan and reheat over medium heat until hot. Stir in sherry and cilantro. Add salt and pepper to taste. Pour into bowls or a tureen. If desired, garnish with a dollop of yogurt and a few shreds of orange peel.

Per serving: 197 cal., 21% (42 cal.) from fat; 6 g protein; 4.7 g fat (2.5 g sat.); 35 g carbo.; 145 mg sodium; 11 mg chol.

Thanksgiving Burgers

David Vásquez, West Hollywood, California

When David Vásquez added cranberry sauce to these turkey burgers, they reminded him of Thanksgiving, so he added sage. Then he spread mustard on the buns to balance the sweetness of the sauce. It's a quick, lean meal that fits perfectly into his schedule.

Prep and cook time: About 15 minutes
Makes: 4 servings

- 1 pound ground turkey
- ½ cup minced onion
- 1 teaspoon dried sage, crushed
- ¼ teaspoon white pepper
- 4 hamburger buns, toasted
- 4 teaspoons Dijon mustard
- 4 butter lettuce leaves
- Salt
- ½ cup whole-berry cranberry sauce

1. Mix turkey with onion, sage, and pepper. Shape into 4 equal patties about ½ inch thick.

2. Set a 10- to 12-inch nonstick frying pan over medium-high heat. When pan is hot, place patties in pan and cook, turning once, until meat is white in center (cut to test), 8 to 10 minutes.

3. Spread buns with mustard. Lay lettuce leaf and turkey patty on bottom half of each bun.

Add salt to taste, and spoon cranberry sauce onto patty. Place upper half of bun on top.

Per serving: 380 cal., 33% (126 cal.) from fat; 24 g protein; 14 g fat (3.6 g sat.); 37 g carbo.; 441 mg sodium; 57 mg chol.

*S*hare a recipe you've created or adapted—a family favorite, travel discovery, or time-saver—including the story behind the recipe. You'll receive a "Great Cook" certificate and $50 for each recipe published. Send to *Sunset Magazine,* 80 Willow Rd., Menlo Park, CA 94025, or send e-mail (including full name, street address, and phone number) to recipes@sunsetpub.com.

F O O D
Guide

BY JERRY ANNE DI VECCHIO

Trim your Yule log with mint leaves and sugar-coated cranberries (dip berries in egg white first).

RICHARD JUNG

A TASTE OF THE WEST: A Yule log to remember

The standing order for Christmas dessert at our house is my version of Bûche de Noël. It's quite handsome and perfectly delicious. It's also sinfully rich because there are no adequate substitutes for its components. Imagine but-

ter cream without butter, whipped cream without real cream, chocolate without real chocolate, roasted hazelnuts without the nuts. Why bother? And, frankly, once in a while it's a joy to give way to total indulgence.

Best of all, my Bûche de Noël looks complicated, but it's not. Even though it takes a couple of hours to make, it's really not much more than a gussied-up jelly roll.

At one time, this dessert barely accommodated our table of 12. But now we are wiser, cut slices thinner, and sleep better.

Bûche de Noël

Prep and cook time: About 2 hours, plus about 50 minutes to chill

Notes: Many of the steps overlap when this dessert is made all at once. Or separate steps this way:
• up to 3 days ahead, make butter creams (about 1 hour); cover and chill
• up to 2 days ahead, make cake (about 40 minutes); let cool, wrap airtight, and hold at room temperature
• up to 1 day ahead, shape dessert (about 30 minutes); cover and chill.

Makes: 18 to 20 servings

- 1½ cups hazelnuts
- 5 large egg yolks
- 1⅓ cups granulated sugar
- About 1 cup (½ lb.) cold butter, cut into chunks
- 4 ounces semisweet chocolate
- 6 tablespoons hazelnut-flavor liqueur
- 5 large eggs
- About ¼ cup all-purpose flour
- 1½ teaspoons vanilla
- 1 cup whipping cream
- 2 tablespoons powdered sugar

Two butter creams
1. Spread hazelnuts in a single layer in a 10- by 15-inch pan. Bake in a 350° oven until nuts are golden under skin, 15 to 20 minutes; let stand until cool enough to handle. Rub nuts in a clean towel to remove loose skins. Lift nuts from towel and discard skins.

2. With a mixer, beat egg yolks at high speed until thick, about 5 minutes. Meanwhile, boil ¾ cup granulated sugar with ¼ cup water, stirring until sugar dissolves, then boil until syrup reaches 232°, about 5 minutes. Still beating yolks on high speed, slowly add syrup, taking care not to pour it into beaters. Beat until bowl is cool to touch, about 3 minutes.

3. Whip 1 cup butter, a few chunks at a time, into the egg yolk mixture; chunks should be smoothly incorporated before more are added. Put 1⅔ cups of this mixture in a separate bowl. Set aside bowl with remaining mixture.

4. Melt chocolate (in a pan over very low heat or in a microwave oven) and let stand.

5. In a food processor or blender, whirl ½ cup hazelnuts with 2 tablespoons hazelnut liqueur until they form a smooth paste,

scraping container sides. (If using a blender, you may need to add a spoonful or so of butter cream—from the 1⅔-cup-portion—to help paste form.)

6. Stir chocolate into the 1⅔ cups butter cream, then stir in the ground nut mixture. Cover and keep at room temperature.

7. Melt ⅓ cup granulated sugar in a 10- to 12-inch nonstick frying pan over high heat, tilting pan until all the sugar is melted and amber-colored, about 3 minutes. Pour caramelized sugar at once onto a sheet of foil. Let cool. Put caramel in a heavy plastic food bag and coarsely crush with a rolling pin. Coarsely chop remaining toasted hazelnuts. Add caramel and nuts to remaining ⅔ cup butter cream. Cover and keep at room temperature.

The cake
8. Butter a 10- by 15-inch rimmed pan. Line with waxed paper cut to fit, then butter again and dust with flour.

9. Separate the 5 whole eggs. With mixer at high speed, whip yolks, gradually adding ¼ cup granulated sugar. Mix in ¼ cup flour and beat to blend well. Stir in 1 teaspoon vanilla.

10. With clean beaters, whip whites until they hold soft, distinct peaks; fold thoroughly into yolks.

11. Pour batter into flour-dusted pan. Spread evenly with a spatula. Bake in a 350° oven until cake is browned and center springs back when lightly pressed, about 15 minutes. Let stand 3 to 4 min-

utes, run a thin knife between cake and pan rim, then turn cake out onto a clean towel. Gently remove paper and trim cake edges to make a neat rectangle. Lift towel and cake onto a rack to cool completely. Spoon 4 tablespoons liqueur evenly over cake. Slide cake and towel off rack onto a flat counter.

Making the log
12. Whip cream until it holds soft peaks, then stir in ½ teaspoon vanilla and powdered sugar.

13. Dot cake evenly with spoonfuls of caramel-hazelnut butter cream, then spread butter cream gently—don't tear cake. Swirl whipped cream over butter cream to cake edge. Lift towel on a long side of cake and let cake roll into a smooth, compact log. Lifting carefully, set cake onto a large flat platter. With a very sharp knife, cut through cake diagonally about 3 inches from an end. Fit diagonal end of short piece of cake against the cake roll to form a forked log.

14. Carefully spread chocolate butter cream over cake (not the ends). Using the tines of a fork, swirl butter cream to create "bark" and "knots." Chill, uncovered, just until frosting begins to firm, about 50 minutes. Serve, or cover lightly—but airtight—with plastic wrap and chill up to 2 days. To serve, unwrap, and slice cake into rounds.

Per serving: 304 cal., 68% (207 cal.) from fat; 4.2 g protein; 23 g fat (10 g sat.); 22 g carbo.; 118 mg sodium; 145 mg chol.

BACK TO BASICS

Crisp potatoes

When Ken Frank was a teenager living with his family in France, he became so hooked on that country's

food that he made it his profession. And one of the dishes that he credits for putting him on the path to chefdom and fame is pan-browned potato cakes. You certainly can't call rosti—the name this dish goes by in Switzerland—fancy, but the version Frank serves at his West

The perfect holiday appetizer: caviar-topped potato wedges.

Hollywood restaurant, Fenix at the Argyle, most certainly is. He blankets the rosti rounds with crème fraîche, then blackens the cream with a dense layer of fresh caviar.

For the holidays, I borrowed his idea, but instead of pan-browning rosti cakes one at a time, I make a single big round one—starting it on the stove, finishing it in the oven—then cut it into wedges. Another liberty I take is to top the crème fraîche or sour cream with red salmon caviar and green chives.

Oven Rosti

Prep and cook time: 45 to 50 minutes

Notes: For fresh salmon caviar, buy *ikura* in Japanese fish or food markets.

Makes: 6 to 8 servings

3   russet potatoes (about
    1 1/2 lb. total)

2   tablespoons lemon juice

    Salt

2   tablespoons butter or margarine

6   tablespoons salmon caviar

    About 1/2 cup sour cream or
    crème fraîche

3   tablespoons snipped chives

1. Peel potatoes, then shred them and quickly mix with lemon juice (to reduce darkening) and 1/4 teaspoon salt.

2. Melt butter in a nonstick, ovenproof frying pan that measures 9 1/2 to 10 inches across the flat bottom. Pour in the potato mixture, and gently spread evenly. Cook on medium heat just until edges begin to lightly brown, 4 to 5 minutes (do not disturb base of potatoes).

3. Set pan in the upper half of a 450° oven and bake until potatoes are brown and

crisp on the bottom (lift an edge to check, disturbing potatoes as little as possible), 35 to 40 minutes. The top will be only partially browned.

4. Meanwhile, put salmon caviar in a fine strainer and rinse with cold running water to reduce saltiness. Drain well, then cover and chill.

5. Remove potato rosti from oven. (If making ahead, let cool in pan, then cover and let stand up to 4 hours. Reheat, uncovered, in a 350° oven until crisp and hot, about 5 minutes.)

6. Invert hot rosti onto a flat plate and cut into wedges.

7. Put wedges on individual plates and top equally with sour cream, caviar, and chives. Add salt to taste.

Per serving: 149 cal., 50% (74 cal.) from fat; 4.9 g protein; 8.2 g fat (sat. fat not available); 15 g carbo.; 224 mg sodium; 85 mg chol.

India in a box

As an easy introduction to the exotic dishes of India, seasoning kits produced by three San Francisco Bay Area companies make ideal gifts for curious cooks, like me, who haven't mastered the use of *asafetida* and *amchoor*.

Culinary Alchemy's Indian Spice Kitchen is an exceptionally handsome package containing 25 items, including tiny pots and big tins of spices that look as though they belong on a dressing table. A small cookbook not only contains recipes but also explains much about Indian cookery itself and gives directions for blending spices. Produced by Kathleen O'Rourke, the kit costs about $50 and can be purchased at many cooking and fancy food stores. You can also order it by calling (800) 424-0005.

Ranjan Dey of New World Spices takes a different approach. His spice blends are available in individual tins for about $4 each, or in a variety of gift packs. The Complete Indian Meal Planner, which costs about $22, contains all six of the spice blends plus a menu planning book with Indian food lore, recipes, and some everyday ways—like stir-fry and barbecue—to use the spices. Smaller kits contain two spice blends ($7) or three ($11). These spice blends are also available in cooking and fancy food stores, or you can order them by calling (800) 347-7795.

Sukhi Singh's Quick-N-Ezee Indian Foods come in three kits with 4 to 12 items apiece; kits are priced from $17 to $45. Recipes on the packages give directions for typical Indian curries, soups, and rice dishes, as well as more mainstream dishes. For example, the tandoori marinade mixed with yogurt gives broiled or barbecued chicken a refreshing lift. Retail distribution of the kits is limited, but you can order them by calling (510) 633-1144; or write to 1933 Davis St., Suite 284, San Leandro, CA 94577.

For the real food lover, give an introduction to Indian cooking.

RICHARD JUNG

A quick dinner

Fontina cheese is the essence of Italian fonduta—a cross between fondue and cheese sauce, only better. Fonduta is usually topped with white truffles, which have an extraordinary affinity for fontina, and served on pasta or risotto.

But it's tricky and can be expensive—unless you try my one-pan pasta version. Serve it with a green salad, good bread, and a light, smooth red wine, then follow with some Chilean Bing cherries and an Italian Moscato d'Asti, and pat yourself on the back.

Does my fonduta include truffles? Depends on the company. A ¾-ounce can costs about $30, though prices vary. One tiny fresh truffle (in season now) may be a little less. The easy out is a drizzle of fragrant white (not black) truffle oil. It's available in fancy food stores, and a 1-ounce bottle will set you back about $8. But a little goes a long way.

Fettuccine Fonduta

Prep and cook time: About 20 minutes

Notes: If using white truffles, finely shave them onto each serving (if canned, pour the juice into the pasta when adding cheese). Or drizzle ½ to 1 teaspoon white truffle oil onto each serving.

Makes: 3 to 4 servings

3 cups chicken broth
8 ounces dried fettuccine
1 tablespoon cornstarch
1 cup milk
4 large eggs
½ pound shredded fontina cheese
Fresh-ground pepper
Fresh-grated nutmeg
Salt

1. In an 11- to 12-inch frying pan on high heat, bring broth to a boil. Break fettuccine strands in half and add to broth. Boil gently (uncovered, and stirring often to prevent sticking) until pasta is just tender to bite, 8 to 9 minutes.

2. Meanwhile, smoothly blend cornstarch and milk. Mix into pasta and stir frequently until boiling.

3. At the same time, beat eggs to blend, then ladle a couple of spoonfuls of the hot liquid from pan into the eggs.

4. Turn heat to lowest setting and pour egg mixture into pan. Stirring with a wide spatula, cook just until a little of the egg thickens on the bottom of the pan. Remove from heat. Sprinkle with cheese; stir until melted. Mixture should be very creamy.

5. Ladle pasta into wide bowls and sprinkle generously with pepper and nutmeg. Add salt to taste.

Per serving: 579 cal., 44% (252 cal.) from fat; 33 g protein; 28 g fat (15 g sat.); 48 g carbo.; 638 mg sodium; 344 mg chol.

The right times for roasts

Last year, several very disappointed friends and a couple of readers called with the same problem. They had decided to go all out, and had purchased whole beef rib roasts, envisioning rosy, rare slabs of meat for dinner. But the roasts were gray and overdone—not good when you've invested upwards of $100.

They had based cooking time on minutes-per-pound, an outdated method that many butchers and cookbooks still recommend. And I'm sad to report that none of the cooks used meat thermometers, which start at about $4.

This year, along with using a meat thermometer, follow these new time guidelines from Marlys Bielunski, director of the test kitchens at the National Cattlemen's Beef Association. They are calculated for medium-rare beef, which is cooked to 135°. If you want rare meat, cook beef to 125°, but start checking the thermometer at least 45 minutes before the minimum cooking time.

ROASTING BEEF

Meat: At refrigerator temperature
Oven temperature: 350°
Cook: Times given are for medium-rare (temperature is 135° in center of thickest part).
Time: Start checking at least 20 minutes before minimum time.
Rest: Let meat stand at least 15 minutes before carving. Expect up to a 10° temperature increase.

BEEF ROAST	WEIGHT	TIME
Ribeye, small end	4 to 6 lb.	1¾ to 2 hr.
	6 to 8 lb.	2 to 2¼ hr.
Ribeye, large end	4 to 6 lb.	2 to 2½ hr.
	6 to 8 lb.	2¼ to 2½ hr.
Rib roast	6 to 8 lb.	2¼ to 2½ hr.
	8 to 10 lb.	2½ to 3 hr.

Good buys for great gifts

The question was put this way: If you were to recommend good-value wines for Christmas giving, which ones would they be? Taking my interlocutor to mean *this* Christmas, and allowing potential gift-givers broad leeway about price, here you are:

Less than $15: Collio Sauvignon 1995, Marco Felluga; Buena Vista Carneros Chardonnay 1994; Navarro Anderson Valley Gewürztraminer 1994.

$15 to $20: Domaine Chandon Napa Valley Brut Reserve, nonvintage; Chianti Classico 1991 "Petrignano" from Dievole; Louis M. Martini Napa Valley Cabernet Sauvignon 1991 Reserve.

$20 to $25: Chablis Premier Cru 1990 "Beauroy" from La Chablisienne; Chianti Classico Riserva 1991 Castello della Paneretta; Chianti Classico Riserva 1991 Castello di Verrazzano; Clos du Val Napa Valley–Stags Leap District Cabernet Sauvignon 1991; Columbia Winery Yakima Valley Cabernet Sauvignon 1992 "Red Willow."

$25 to $35: Champagne Brut Premier nonvintage, Louis Roederer; Chablis Premier Cru 1991 (or 1995) "Vaillons," Moreau et Fils; Chablis Premier Cru 1995 "Vaudevey," Domaine Laroche; Freemark Abbey Napa Valley Cabernet Sauvignon 1991 "Sycamore Vineyard"; Chianti Classico Riserva 1991 or, better yet, 1990 "Tenute Marchese," Antinori (open it when there are no more than two at table—this is the only wine in the list I treasure that much); St.-Julien 1988, 1989, or 1990, Château Gruaud–Larose; Schramsberg Napa Valley Blanc de Noirs 1990; Roederer Estate Anderson Valley L'Ermitage Brut 1991.

Sky's the limit: Champagne Cristal 1988 from Louis Roederer; Gary Farrell Russian River Valley Pinot Noir 1994 "Allen Vineyard"; St.-Julien 1988, 1989, or 1990, Château Ducru-Beaucaillou; Pessac-Léognan 1988, 1989, or 1990, Château Haut-Brion; Tignanello 1991 from Antinori.

An eclectic list, beyond doubt. What is behind it? Two simple rules:

1. The most important gift a wine can give is to make dinner taste better. So, a gift wine ought to do that. These have.

2. Wines given as gifts tend to wait a long time for just the right occasion. So gift wines ought to age well. These should do that, too. ■

Carlo Middione hosts a luxurious Christmas Eve dinner that includes a spectacular entrée of boned, roasted capon with stuffing and marsala sauce (at right).

Christmas Eve
at Carlo's

*For a memorable holiday feast, celebrate with
chef Carlo Middione's family recipes*

Glasses are raised, and Carlo Middione proposes a toast. Like his father before him, he savors any opportunity to preside over a table of southern Italian specialties. For Middione, a first-generation Sicilian American, these dishes bring back nostalgic memories of earlier gatherings.

In the old days, his father presided at the head of the table—periodically scanning for breaches of manners among his offspring—while Middione's diminutive mother, Guiseppina, orchestrated the ebb and flow of the multiple-course repast. "We had these huge meals at the holidays," recalls Middione, "easily 20 people for Christmas—and don't forget the priests. They particularly liked eating at our house."

Understandably so. Middione's parents possessed exceptional culinary talent. His father, a chef and baker, was a partner in a bread bakery in Buffalo, New York, during Middione's earliest years. And Middione, the youngest of 13 children, was recruited for kitchen work at an early age.

"Between the ages of 8 and 9, I became a true apprentice in every sense of the word. That's when I started serious cook-ing—enforced cooking," he laughs. "I helped my father. First I poured the water—he'd tell me when to stop. After I learned to weigh out the flour, I cut the yeast. By the time I was 9 years old, I was making a 70-loaf batch of bread, kneading by hand."

That year, Middione's family moved to Glendale, California, where they converted an enormous house surrounded by extensive property into a restaurant, which his father called simply *da Middione*—in English, Middione's.

His father was the chef of the restaurant (he was spectacularly good at desserts, recalls Middione), but his mother also cooked in the restaurant. And she was definitely the queen of both their home and restaurant kitchens. At home she preferred doing all of the cooking herself, even for Christmas Eve; it was not uncommon for her to prepare more than a dozen dishes for the celebratory evening, which usually started at 7 and ended at midnight.

Middione's mother acquired her culinary skills in her own mother's trattoria in Termini Imerese, a small town outside Palermo, Italy. Says Middione, "The number of dishes put out from that tiny kitchen was amazing."

"I'm very proud of my palate," he says, "and I think that

BY BETSY REYNOLDS BATESON • PHOTOGRAPHS BY GARY MOSS

I have it because of my mother. My mother was a natural cook. She was so serene. She worked very steadily, with focus—not fast or frenzied."

With his culinary inheritance, it's not surprising that Middione has a natural passion for food and an innate understanding of ingredients and flavors—or that he is regarded as an authority on southern Italian cuisine. The executive chef of Vivande Ristorante in San Francisco, Middione is also chef and co-owner with his wife, Lisa, of Vivande Porta Via, where in 1981 he introduced the European concept of prepared take-out food to San Francisco.

His book *The Food of Southern Italy,* the first American cookbook devoted to the cuisine of that area, won a Tastemaker Award when it was published in 1987 (William Morrow & Co., New York; $29.95). An earlier book, *Pasta, Cooking It, Loving It,* was updated and reissued this year in softcover as *Carlo Middione's Traditional Pasta* (Ten Speed Press, Berkeley; $15.95). His latest book, *La Vera Cucina* (Simon and Schuster, New York; $35), is a tribute to the dishes of the Italian home table.

What does Middione enjoy most about cooking? "It's the inner peace," he explains. "All of my cooking has a memory. The memories have lots of tradition, and the tradition represents who I am." He is particularly fond of *pignolata* balls (fried honey cookies), for instance, because he has been eating them his whole life—for more than six decades.

Asked if he has any advice for readers who prepare this holiday menu, he suggests reading the recipes before starting to cook. "Think about them," he says, "and get a vision in your mind about how everything is going to go together—and don't be too rigid. Of course, a glass of wine before you start is always a good idea."

The outstanding flavor combinations of these dishes reveal Middione's talent. We've assembled nine of the dozen or more dishes he would include in a holiday menu; some have been adapted from his books. Other foods Middione would be likely to serve on Christmas Eve are homemade pickled eggplant (his sister Caroline always does this, says Middione), risotto balls made with saffron and filled with provolone cheese, snails cooked in a chunky tomato sauce, grilled mackerel, and lemon granita.

Carlo's Christmas Eve Menu

ANTIPASTI
Garbanzos with Garlic and Olive Oil
(*Ceci all' Olio*)

"Fixed" Green Olives
(*Ulivi Cunzati*)

Fennel with Prosciutto and Parmesan
(*Finocchio al Prosciutto
e Parmigiano Reggiano*)

PRIMO PIATTO
Baked Pasta with Tomato Sauce and Meat
(*Pasta al Forno*)

SECONDO PIATTO
Roasted Capon
with Spinach-Walnut Stuffing
(*Cappone Ripieno*)

CONTORNI
Orange and Lemon Salad
(*Insalata di Arancia e Limone*)

PANE
Sicilian Sesame Bread
(*Pane Siciliano al Giuggiulena*)

DOLCI
Almond-stuffed Figs
(*Ficchi Imbottiti Arrostiti al Forno*)

Honey Cookies
(*Pignolata*)

VINI
Antipasti
1993 Corvo Bianco,
Duca di Salaparuta

1992 Chardonnay,
Sylvio Jermann

Primo Piatto
1985 Aglianico, Sasso

Secondo Piatto
1987 Corvo "Duca Enrico,"
Duca di Salaparuta

Dolci
1990 Marsala Superiore Oro
"Vigna la Miccia,"
da Marco de Bartoli

1989 Vin Santo,
Marchese Antinori

Garbanzos with Garlic and Olive Oil

Prep and cook time: 30 minutes

Makes: 4 cups, 8 servings

- 3 cups finely chopped onions (about 14 oz. total)
- 2 or 3 cloves garlic, minced
- About 3 tablespoons extra-virgin olive oil
- 2 cans (about 1 lb. each) chickpeas (garbanzos), rinsed and drained
- 1 cup chicken broth
- Salt and fresh-ground pepper
- 1 tablespoon minced parsley

1. In a 10- to 12-inch frying pan over medium-high heat, cook the onions and garlic in 2 tablespoons of oil, stirring often, until onions are golden, about 7 minutes.

2. Add chickpeas and broth. Cook 10 minutes more to blend flavors. Stir to release any browned bits from pan. (If making ahead, cool, then chill in airtight container up to 4 days. Reheat over medium heat until hot, about 10 minutes.)

3. Pour into a serving bowl, add salt and pepper to taste, drizzle with remaining oil, and sprinkle with parsley; serve hot.

Per ½-cup serving: 146 cal., 45% (66 cal.) from fat; 5 g protein; 7.3 g fat (0.9 g sat.); 16 g carbo.; 140 mg sodium; 0.5 mg chol.

A wonderfully flavored baked pasta dish follows three deliciously simple antipasti (at left): garbanzos with onions and garlic, cracked cured green olives with celery, red onions, and oregano, and prosciutto-wrapped fennel.

Fennel with Prosciutto and Parmesan

Prep time: About 20 minutes

Notes: Use a vegetable peeler to shave parmesan.

Makes: 12 servings, about 36 pieces

- 1 head (about 1 lb.) fennel
- ¼ pound thinly sliced prosciutto
- 2 ounces (about ¾ cup) thinly shaved parmesan

    About 1 tablespoon extra-virgin olive oil

    Fresh-ground pepper

1. Rinse fennel; remove ¼ inch at bottom and cut off top stalks, reserving featherlike greens. Cut bulb in half vertically; lay halves cut side down and cut into ¼-inch slices.

2. Wrap each fennel piece with a 1½- by 4-inch piece of prosciutto. Place on a serving platter. Sprinkle prosciutto-wrapped fennel with parmesan shavings and drizzle all with oil. Grind pepper over top. Serve, or hold at room temperature up to 1 hour.

Per serving: 55 cal., 60% (33 cal.) from fat; 4.7 g protein; 3.7 g fat (1.3 g sat.); 1 g carbo.; 281 mg sodium; 11 mg chol.

Baked Pasta with Tomato Sauce and Meat

Prep and cook time: About 5 hours

Notes: You can prepare the sauce and meat (through step 3) up to 2 days before assembling and baking this dish.

Makes: 12 to 16 servings

- 2 pounds pork butt roast or beef rump roast
- 2 tablespoons olive oil
- 1½ cups finely chopped onion
- 3 cloves garlic, minced
- 2 cans (1 lb. 12 oz. each) tomatoes with juice
- 1 cup dry red wine
- ¼ cup tomato paste
- 1 teaspoon dried oregano
- 1 pound dried penne pasta
- ⅓ cup plain dried bread crumbs
- 4 hard-cooked large eggs, peeled and sliced
- 2 cups (10-oz. box) frozen peas, thawed

    About 2 cups (½ lb.) shredded pecorino cheese

"Fixed" Green Olives

Prep time: About 10 minutes, plus at least 30 minutes for standing

Notes: You can buy cracked cured green olives by the ounce at delis or bottled at specialty food shops.

Makes: 4 cups, 12 servings

- ¾ pound cracked cured green olives
- 1½ cups diced celery (¼-in. dice)
- ½ cup finely chopped red onion
- ¾ teaspoon dried oregano

    Fresh-ground pepper

- 4 to 5 teaspoons extra-virgin olive oil

In a noncorrodible bowl, combine olives, celery, onion, oregano, pepper, and olive oil; stir to mix well. Let stand at least 30 minutes or up to 4 hours. For longer storage, cover and chill up to 1 week; bring to room temperature before serving.

Per ⅓-cup serving: 52 cal., 90% (47 cal.) from fat; 0.6 g protein; 5.2 g fat (0.6 g sat.); 1.6 g carbo.; 695 mg sodium; 0 mg chol.

1. In a 5- to 6-quart pan over medium-high heat, brown roast in oil, turning until all sides are browned, about 10 minutes.

2. Add onion and garlic; cook, stirring, until just golden, about 4 minutes. Reserving juice from cans, cut whole tomatoes into quarters. Add tomatoes, reserved juice, wine, 1 cup water, tomato paste, and oregano to pan. Bring mixture to a boil, reduce heat, and simmer, covered, until meat is fork-tender and pulls apart easily, about 3 hours; turn roast every hour.

3. Remove roast from sauce; let stand until cool enough to handle. Using a fork, pull meat into shreds, discarding any fat; spoon off and discard any fat from sauce. (If making ahead, chill meat and sauce separately in airtight containers up to 2 days.)

4. In a 6- to 8-quart pan over high heat, bring about 4 quarts water to a boil. Add pasta and cook just until tender to bite, about 10 minutes. Drain and toss with 1 cup of the sauce; set aside.

5. To a buttered shallow 4½- to 5½-quart ovenproof casserole (about 12 by 16 in.), add bread crumbs; twist and turn casserole until sides and bottom are evenly coated. Reserve excess crumbs to top casserole.

6. To assemble casserole, layer a third of the pasta (about 2½ cups) in dish, then half the meat, half the eggs, half the peas, ¾ cup of the shredded cheese, and 2 cups of the sauce. Repeat layers, finishing with a layer of pasta. Top pasta with remaining sauce, shredded cheese, and reserved bread crumbs.

7. Bake, uncovered, in a 350° oven until top and sides are golden brown, about 1 hour. Let cool at least 20 minutes before serving. (If making ahead, cool, cover, and chill up to 2 days. To serve, cover with foil and reheat in a 350° oven until hot, about 1 hour; let cool at least 20 minutes before serving.)

Per serving: 310 cal., 32% (99 cal.) from fat; 18 g protein; 11 g fat (4.7 g sat.); 32 g carbo.; 536 mg sodium; 93 mg chol.

Roasted Capon with Spinach-Walnut Stuffing

Prep and cook time: About 2 hours

Notes: Request a capon or large roasting chicken ahead. Have the butcher bone it, including the legs and wings (as for a galantine); remember to ask for the bones (to simmer with the reserved mushroom liquid and marsala for a flavorful sauce).

Makes: 8 servings

- 1 ounce (¾ cup) dried porcini mushrooms
- 1½ cups finely chopped onion
- 2 cloves garlic, minced
- 1 tablespoon olive oil
- About 1 pound fresh spinach
- 1 capon or roasting chicken (about 7 lb.), boned
- ½ teaspoon *each* salt and pepper
- ¾ cup walnuts, chopped
- 2 tablespoons raisins, chopped
- 2 tablespoons chopped fresh rosemary leaves
- 3 tablespoons butter
- About ½ cup dry marsala
- About 1 tablespoon brandy
- Reserved capon or chicken bones

1. Place mushrooms in a bowl; cover with 2½ cups hot water and soak at least 20 minutes. Scoop mushrooms from water and squeeze dry, then coarsely chop. Strain soaking water through a coffee filter or paper towel to remove any grit; reserve.

2. In a 10- to 12-inch nonstick frying pan over medium-high heat, cook mushrooms, onion, and garlic in oil, stirring often, until just golden, about 6 minutes; set aside.

3. Wash spinach leaves and discard tough stems (you need 8 cups lightly packed leaves). In a 4- to 5-quart pan, bring about 2 quarts water to a boil over high heat. Add spinach and blanch 30 seconds; drain in colander and press to remove as much water as possible.

4. Lay boned bird flat, cavity up. Pull split-open legs together to form a square. Fold inner breast (breast fillets) toward legs to cover skin. Sprinkle meat with half the salt and pepper. Cover interior of bird with spinach leaves. Then evenly spread mushroom mixture over spinach and top evenly with walnuts, raisins, and rosemary; sprinkle remaining salt and pepper over all (see photo below).

Spinach, porcini mushrooms, walnuts, and raisins compose the stuffing for a rolled boneless capon that's roasted in cooking parchment, then carved into slices.

5. Starting from the leg edge, roll up bird so leg meat will be in the center and white meat on the outside (photo below).

6. Using cotton string, tie roll every 1½ to 2 inches to contain filling and to form a cylindrical roast about 16 inches long. Rub butter all over bird; sprinkle with about 2 tablespoons marsala and 1 tablespoon brandy (photo below).

7. Wrap in cooking parchment; fold paper edges shut (as you would with butcher wrap). Set parchment-wrapped roast in an 11- by 17-inch baking pan (photo below).

8. Bake wrapped bird in a 375° oven until internal temperature is 160° (stick an instant-read thermometer through parchment), 45 to 50 minutes.

9. Meanwhile, to a 3- to 4-quart pan over medium heat, add reserved porcini soaking water, bones, and remaining marsala and bring to a boil. Reduce heat, cover, and simmer 30 minutes. Strain cooking liquid and discard bones and other particles; spoon off fat and discard. Return strained liquid to pan. Over high heat, boil juices until reduced to ½ cup, about 15 minutes; set aside.

10. Let bird rest 15 minutes before slicing. (If making ahead, leave unsliced bird in parchment, cool, then refrigerate up to 1 day; chill sauce separately. Reheat wrapped bird in a 350° oven until hot, 30 to 40 minutes.) Unwrap and lift to serving platter;

Blood oranges and lemons combine with red onion and mint in a refreshing salad.

remove strings. Add any cooking juices from paper pouch to reduced sauce and reheat until hot. Cut bird into 16 to 20 slices about ¾ inch thick. Serve bird with the sauce to add as desired.

Per serving: 609 cal., 52% (315 cal.) from fat; 59 g protein; 35 g fat (9.7 g sat.); 12 g carbo.; 324 mg sodium; 175 mg chol.

Orange and Lemon Salad

Prep time: About 25 minutes, plus at least 30 minutes for standing

Notes: If you can't find blood oranges, you can use navel oranges. Do not substitute dried herbs for the fresh mint or basil in this recipe.

Makes: 8 to 10 servings

- 6 to 8 blood oranges (about 2½ lb. total) or navel oranges
- 2 ripe lemons (about 10 oz. total)
- ½ cup thinly sliced red onion
- 8 fresh mint or basil leaves, finely slivered
- 1 to 2 tablespoons extra-virgin olive oil

  Fresh-ground pepper

1. Over a bowl (to catch juice), use a sharp knife to cut off peel and white membrane from fruit; discard peel. Cut oranges crosswise into ¼-inch slices, lemons into ⅛-inch slices, cutting right through seeds.

2. On a platter, overlap orange slices in a circular pattern, then top in center with overlapping lemon slices. Pour any reserved juice from peeling and slicing over the fruit. Scatter onion evenly all over citrus, then top with mint. Drizzle oil over salad; top with fresh-ground pepper to taste. Let salad stand at least 30 minutes or up to 2 hours at room temperature; serve.

Per serving: 55 cal., 25% (14 cal.) from fat; 1.2 g protein; 1.5 g fat (0.2 g sat.); 12 g carbo.; 2.3 mg sodium; 0 mg chol.

A traditional Sicilian loaf, braided and topped with sesame seeds, accompanies the Christmas Eve dishes.

Sicilian Sesame Bread

Prep and cook time: About 1¼ hours, plus 4¼ hours for rising

Notes: Look for "fancy durum flour" (semolina that is milled as fine as regular all-purpose flour) in the bulk section at specialty stores or natural-food stores.

Makes: 2 loaves, about 1¼ pounds each

- 1 package active dry yeast
- 2 tablespoons extra-virgin olive oil
- 2 teaspoons salt
- 3½ to 3¾ cups all-purpose flour
- 2 cups fancy durum flour (see notes above)
- ½ cup sesame seeds

1. To a large bowl, add 2 cups warm (98°) water (if you don't have a thermometer, dribble some on the inside of your wrist; if you can't feel it, it's the right temperature). Sprinkle yeast over water and let stand until dissolved, 4 to 5 minutes. Stir in oil and salt, then gradually mix in 3 cups all-purpose flour and the durum flour. Beat with a spoon until stretchy, about 5 minutes. Add ½ cup more all-purpose flour and stir until dough pulls away from sides of bowl.

2. *If kneading by hand,* scrape dough onto a lightly floured board. With fingertips, lift the side of dough farthest from you and fold dough toward you, overlapping itself. Push away with heels of hands to seal fold. Turn dough a quarter turn; repeat process, kneading about 8 minutes. Dough should look and feel as if it needs more flour, but do not add unless necessary to prevent sticking.

3. *If kneading with a mixer,* using a flat beater, mix dough on low speed. When dough begins to pull together, switch to a dough hook and increase speed. Let dough knead about 4 minutes. The surface will have the texture of orange peel and pull away from the sides of the bowl.

4. Shape dough into a ball. Sprinkle a little flour into the bowl and set ball on top. Cover bowl with plastic wrap and a couple of kitchen towels; let rise in a warm (75° to 85°), draft-free place until dough is at least doubled or tripled, about 2 hours. Punch dough down in bowl and reshape into a ball. Repeat process and let rise again, about 1½ hours. Knead on a lightly floured board to expel air, about 10 turns.

5. Divide dough in half. Then cut each half into thirds. Roll each third into a long rope, about 1 inch in diameter and 14 inches long. Attach the ends of three ropes, then braid ropes. To finish loaf, pinch ends together and tuck under loaf. Repeat with remaining ropes to form a second loaf.

6. On counter or in a baking pan, scatter half the sesame seeds in a strip about 3 inches wide and a foot long. Brush the loaves lightly with water. Pick up a braid and turn it face down onto the seeds; rock the braid back and forth to completely cover the top and sides of the loaf. Turn braid over and press more seeds onto any spots that were missed. Then lay the braid on a lightly floured 12- by 15-inch baking sheet. Repeat the process with the second braid on another baking sheet.

7. Cover braids with lightly floured cotton towels or plastic wrap. Let rise in a warm place until the loaves are doubled and dough holds a faint impression when lightly pressed, about 1 hour.

8. Bake the loaves in a 425° oven for 20 minutes; reduce the oven heat to 350°, switch rack positions, and continue to bake the loaves until they are deep golden, about 20 minutes longer. To test doneness, lift a loaf with a towel and thump the bottom; it should sound hollow. Place the loaves on a rack to cool.

Per 1-ounce serving: 83 cal., 19% (16 cal.) from fat; 2.4 g protein; 1.8 g fat (0.2 g sat.); 14 g carbo.; 111 mg sodium; 0 mg chol.

Almond-stuffed Figs

Prep and cook time: About 2½ hours

Notes: Middione likes the figs plain, but you can roll them in cocoa for a fancy presentation if you prefer.

Makes: 24 stuffed figs

- 24 almonds
- ½ teaspoon ground cloves
- 24 dried large Calimyrna figs (about 1 lb. total)
- ½ cup sweet marsala
- 2 tablespoons granulated sugar
- ¼ cup unsweetened cocoa (optional)
- 1 tablespoon powdered sugar (optional)

1. Place almonds in an 8- or 9-inch square pan and toast in a 350° oven until golden in center (break open to check), about 15 minutes; shake pan occasionally. Sprinkle cloves over hot almonds and mix well; let cool.

2. Cut off fig stems, then make a small slit in the side of each fig. Gently press a clove-dusted almond into each fig, then press fig closed. Place figs in same square pan, pour marsala over all, and let stand about

15 minutes, stirring occasionally.

3. Sprinkle figs with granulated sugar. Cover the pan with foil and bake in a 300° oven until most of the liquid has been absorbed, about 2 hours; after 1½ hours, check the figs every 10 minutes to make sure they are not burning.

4. Cool completely. Store in an airtight jar up to 2 weeks or chill up to 3 months. Serve at room temperature. Roll figs in cocoa and dust with powdered sugar before serving.

Per stuffed fig: 61 cal., 10% (6.3 cal.) from fat; 0.8 g protein; 0.7 g fat (0.1 g sat.); 14 g carbo.; 2.8 mg sodium; 0 mg chol.

The simplicity of preparation belies the flavor complexity of these delicious figs.

Tiny puffs of deep-fried dough are coated with honey, then dusted with candy sprinkles.

Honey Cookies

Prep and cook time: About 2 hours and 20 minutes

Notes: It's easiest to make these cookies when you have a couple of helpers to roll the dough pieces into ropes.

Makes: About 2½ dozen cookies

1½ cups all-purpose flour

2 large eggs

1½ tablespoons brandy

⅛ teaspoon salt

1 quart vegetable oil

¾ cup honey

½ cup sugar

2 teaspoons grated orange peel

1 teaspoon grated lemon peel

About 2 tablespoons multicolored candy sprinkles

1. In a mixer bowl, combine flour, eggs, brandy, and salt. On low speed, mix ingredients until a firm dough is formed, 8 to 9 minutes. Cover dough with plastic wrap; let rest about 30 minutes.

2. Pinch off a knob of dough the size of a walnut and roll into a long, thin rope until it is unable to stretch farther. Let rest 5 to 10 minutes; then continue to roll until rope is the diameter of a pencil or a bit larger. To help with rolling, keep a damp cloth nearby and pat your hands on cloth between ropes. Cut rope into ¼-inch pieces. Continue to pinch off, roll, and cut remaining dough.

3. In a 5- to 6-quart pan, heat oil on medi-um-high heat until it reaches 300° on a candy thermometer. Add a fourth of the small dough pieces; gently stir with a slotted spoon. Cook until golden and puffed, 5 to 6 minutes. Check thermometer and adjust heat as needed to maintain temperature, watching carefully to avoid boilovers. Using slotted spoon, lift puffed pieces from oil; drain on paper towels. Repeat process until all pieces are cooked.

4. To a 2- to 3-quart pan, add honey, sugar, and peels. Over medium heat, bring to a simmer and cook 1 minute.

5. Heat a large metal bowl in a 250° oven until warm to touch, about 4 minutes. Add fried pieces to the bowl; pour hot honey mixture over all. Carefully stir to evenly coat all pieces.

6. While still warm, use 2 tablespoons to mound about 2 tablespoons of pieces together to form a cone shape on buttered cooking parchment or foil. Repeat with remaining pieces. Sprinkle cones with candies and let cool; serve. Store leftover cones in a single layer in an airtight container up to 2 days (you may need to reshape the sticky cookies into more precise cone shapes).

Per cookie: 87 cal., 23% (20 cal.) from fat; 1.1 g protein; 2.2 g fat (0.3 g sat.); 16 g carbo.; 14 mg sodium; 14 mg chol. ■

For a memorable, manageable New Year's Eve supper, serve hot foie gras salad.

For pure indulgence on a special occasion, try fresh foie gras

It's less costly and easier to buy than you might expect

FOIE GRAS. FIRST IT WAS FRENCH and expensive. Now it's scattered among first courses and main dishes on every upscale menu and even a few that aren't so grand. What's behind this luxurious explosion?

Availability. Until recent years, foie gras—fatted liver from specially fed ducks and geese—was imported. But now there are two well-established domestic producers, one in New York and the other in Sonoma, California, where Guillermo and Junny Gonzalez set up operations in 1986. The Gonzalezes produce 500 duck foies gras a week, doubling that figure during December.

Foie gras bears little resemblance to what most of us think of as liver. Its color ranges from cream to a pale café au lait. When sautéed quickly, the meltingly silky foie gras becomes delicately crisp on the surface. Its flavor is subtle to some, sublime to others, and always delicate.

A whole foie gras, composed of two lobes, weighs from 1 to 2 pounds and costs $29 to $38.50 per pound. It will make as many as 12 generous appetizer portions. Grade—A (the best), B, or C—

determines the price and is based on the appearance and texture of the livers. If making a classic foie gras terrine, in which imperfections such as blood spots will show, use grade A. But if slices are to be browned, a lesser grade is quite acceptable.

High prices and high fat content will undoubtedly keep foie gras in the special-occasion category. Even so, there is an economical side: few restaurants offer servings for less than $10, so home-cooked is almost a bargain.

You can order fresh foie gras from the Gonzalezes; call (800) 427-4559.

HANDLING AND COOKING— LESS IS BEST

Keep foie gras chilled until you're ready to use it—as long as a week if it's sealed in its wrapper. Foie gras gets soft and difficult to handle when warm.

To sauté, you need a hot pan and good ventilation, because the rendered fat spatters and smokes. Foie gras melts and shrinks dramatically when cooked. Pour off the fat as it accumulates and use oven mitts to protect your hands.

Seared Foie Gras with Caramelized Apples

Prep and cook time: About 50 minutes

Notes: As early as the day before, caramelize the apples, let cool, cover, and chill. Reheat apple wedges in a single layer in a shallow pan in a 350° oven until hot, about 10 minutes. Toast bread and organize salad before cooking the foie gras.

Makes: 6 to 8 main-dish servings

- 1 duck foie gras (1 to 1⅓ lb.)
- ¼ cup (⅛ lb.) butter or margarine
- ½ cup sugar
- 6 Newtown Pippin or Granny Smith apples (2½ to 2¾ lb. total), peeled, cored, and each cut into 6 wedges
- 6 slices coarse-texture bread (sourdough, dark rye), toasted
- ½ cup chicken broth
- ¼ cup balsamic or red wine vinegar
- ½ pound butter lettuce or mixed salad leaves, rinsed, crisped, and torn into bite-size pieces
  Salt

1. Rinse foie gras, pat dry, and gently pull or cut apart the 2 lobes. Discard any tough membrane. Cut foie gras pieces crosswise into ¾-inch-thick slices; cover and chill.

2. Divide butter between 2 nonstick frying pans, 12 to 14 inches wide. Melt butter over medium-high heat. Stir ¼ cup sugar into each pan. Lay apple wedges equally in pans. Cook apples until wedges are browned and soft but still hold their shape, 15 to 20 minutes; turn as needed with a wide spatula.

3. Set a slice of toast on each of 6 dinner plates; arrange apples equally beside toast, and place in a 150° oven.

4. Quickly rinse and dry frying pans. Place pans over high heat, and when hot, fill with a single layer of foie gras; pieces can touch, but do not crowd them. Brown foie gras on 1 side, about 30 seconds, then turn slices over and brown other side, about 30 seconds more. As foie gras is browned, quickly put slices on toast and keep warm.

5. Pour all but 3 tablespoons of the foie gras drippings from 1 pan; reserve all the fat for other uses. Add chicken broth and balsamic vinegar to drippings in frying pan and bring to a boil on high heat. Pour hot dressing over salad greens, mix, and mound beside apples and toast. Serve at once, adding salt to taste.

Nutritional information is not available, but foie gras is very high in fat. ■

By Christine Weber Hale

A delicious new approach to a Hanukkah tradition

Giant latkes are easier to cook and serve.
For an inspired pairing, top wedges with Persian chicken stew

EVERY HANUKKAH, FOOD WRITER and cooking teacher Louise Fiszer noticed a small problem with making latkes. Like most pancakes, latkes taste best hot from the pan, but by the time Fiszer finished cooking them and could sit down to eat, they were cold and soggy.

Her solution? Make one or two large latkes and cut them into wedges. It's easier—and everyone, including the cook, can enjoy them while they're crisp and hot. Fiszer tops the latke wedges with Persian chicken stew for an entrée that blends two major Jewish cuisines: the latkes are from the Eastern European Ashkenazi tradition, while the chicken stew has its roots in the Sephardic cuisine of the Middle East.

Fiszer is the coauthor (with Jeannette Ferrary) of five cookbooks, including two 1995 releases, *Jewish Holiday Feasts* ($9.95) and *A Good Day for Soup* ($16.95), both published by Chronicle Books. If you surf the Internet, you'll find Fiszer's food columns at Sally's Place (www.bpe.com) and Virtual Vineyards (www.virtualvin.com).

Potato Latke Wedges

Prep and cook time: About 45 minutes

Notes: If you use one pan, cook the latkes one at a time. Keep the first latke warm by transferring it to a lightly oiled baking sheet, covering it loosely with foil, and placing it in a 300° oven until the second latke is ready.

Makes: 8 servings

- 4 russet potatoes (about 2½ lb. total)
- 2 onions (about 1 lb. total)
- 3 large eggs
- 4 tablespoons all-purpose flour or matzo meal
- 2 teaspoons salt
- ½ teaspoon fresh-ground pepper
- ½ cup peanut or vegetable oil for frying

1. Peel potatoes, then grate them using a food processor or the large holes on a hand grater. Place potatoes in a large strainer; press out as much liquid as possible. While potatoes drain, grate onions in the same manner and drain if necessary. In a large bowl, beat eggs to blend; mix in potatoes, onions, flour, salt, and pepper. Let mixture stand 10 minutes.

2. Add ¼ cup oil to each of two 12-inch nonstick frying pans. Heat oil on medium heat. When oil is hot, add half the potato mixture to each pan. With a spatula, spread mixture out to pan sides; smooth tops.

3. Cook over medium heat, pressing tops down with a spatula occasionally, until undersides are brown and crispy, about 8 minutes. Quickly slide each latke onto a large plate, then invert back into pan and cook to brown other side, about 8 minutes longer.

4. Slide latkes out of the pans onto plates again. Cut each into 4 wedges, top with chicken-apple stew (recipe follows), and serve immediately.

Per serving: 212 cal., 31% (66 cal.) from fat; 5.9 g protein; 7.3 g fat (1.5 g sat.); 31 g carbo.; 585 mg sodium; 80 mg chol.

Persian Chicken-Apple Stew

Prep and cook time: About 45 minutes

Notes: You can make the stew a day ahead, chill it, then gently reheat it on the stove before serving.

Makes: 8 servings

- 1 cup dried apple rings, coarsely chopped
- ½ cup dried cranberries or cherries
- 1½ pounds boneless, skinless chicken breast halves
  - About ¾ cup all-purpose flour
- ¼ cup peanut or vegetable oil
- 1 onion (about ½ lb.), chopped
- 1 cup *each* chopped chives and parsley
- ¼ cup chopped fresh mint leaves
- ½ teaspoon turmeric (optional)
- About 1½ cups chicken broth
- Salt and pepper

1. In a bowl, combine chopped dried apples, dried cranberries, and 1 cup hot water. Let stand until very soft, about 20 minutes, or up to 1 hour.

2. While fruit is soaking, pound chicken with a mallet to flatten slightly. Cut into 1-inch pieces. Place flour in a large plastic bag; add chicken. Shake to coat all pieces equally. Discard excess flour.

3. In a 5- to 6-quart pan, heat 2 tablespoons oil over medium-high heat. Add as much of the chicken as will fit in a single layer. Cook, stirring often, just until pieces are golden, 13 to 14 minutes. Remove with a slotted spoon; set aside. Repeat, using 1 tablespoon more oil, to cook remaining chicken; set all aside.

4. To pan, add remaining oil and the onion; cook until onion is translucent, about 5 minutes. Add chives, parsley, mint, and turmeric. Cook, stirring constantly, until mixture is fragrant, about 2 minutes. Add 1½ cups broth, apples, cranberries, and their soaking water. Bring to a boil, then simmer gently 5 minutes. Return chicken pieces to pan; simmer 10 more minutes. (If making ahead, cool, cover, and chill up to 1 day. Reheat over medium-high heat, about 15 minutes, stirring often. If stew seems dry, add a little chicken broth until desired consistency.) Spoon over latke wedges (recipe precedes). Serve immediately. Add salt and pepper to taste.

Per serving: 265 cal., 29% (76 cal.) from fat; 22 g protein; 8.4 g fat (1.6 g sat.); 25 g carbo.; 89 mg sodium; 50 mg chol. ∎

By Christine Weber Hale

Perfect timing
If you don't make the stew ahead, follow this plan of action to get the latkes and stew on the table at the same time: start soaking fruit for stew, then grate potatoes and onions and let them drain while you brown the chicken; add the eggs, flour, and salt to the potatoes and brown the latkes while the stew simmers.

Apricot Liqueur

gifts *in* glass

Homemade vinegars, oils, liqueurs, and honeys make quick and beautiful presents for friends who love good food

You see them in shops everywhere: wonderfully tempting bottles and jars filled with rich ingredients cooks love to have in the kitchen or on the dinner table. And, often, these culinary goodies have price tags that are just as rich, which is a problem if your gift list is even longer than your last credit card statement. It's enough to drive even the most reluctant cookie baker back to the kitchen. • Well, go to the kitchen, but don't pull out the baking sheet. Instead, make flavored vinegars, oils, liqueurs, and honeys. They're easy—many recipes take less than half an hour—and the results are simply beautiful. The finishing touches—tags with serving suggestions—can be as minimalist or as grand as you like. • As for the containers themselves, airtight lids and your imagination are the only limits.

by LINDA LAU ANUSASANANAN,
CHRISTINE WEBER HALE, AND ELAINE JOHNSON
photographs by ED CAREY

People who love to cook usually have a kitchen full of vinegars—red wine, raspberry, tarragon, balsamic. But they're unlikely to have the three listed below—and you can make them. Just a few fresh herbs, citrus peel, and a little spice can turn plain vinegars into gourmet gifts. Let them mellow for at least a week before giving.

GREAT WAYS WITH SEASONED VINEGARS
• Splash Provençal Vinegar over grilled fish.
• Sweeten Orange-Spice Vinegar with orange juice; drizzle over sliced oranges and red onions.
• Mix Asian Vinegar with a little sesame oil and sugar and use as a dressing for sliced cucumbers, cooked asparagus spears, or shredded carrots. Or mix the vinegar with soy sauce for a dip for potstickers.
• Add a little sugar and water to create low-fat dressings for vegetables and fruit.

Orange-Spice Vinegar

Prep time: About 10 minutes, plus at least 1 week for standing
Notes: Use a vegetable peeler to cut a thin spiral strip of peel from an orange.
Makes: 1 bottle (12 to 16 oz.)

    1 spiral strip orange peel, 8 to 10 inches long
    1 feathery sprig fresh fennel (about 4 in.), rinsed, or ½ teaspoon fennel seed
   10 cardamom pods, crushed
    2 teaspoons coriander seed
   1½ to 2 cups rice vinegar

With a chopstick or skewer, gently push the orange peel strip and fresh fennel sprig into a clean 12- to 16-ounce bottle. Remove hulls from cardamom pods; drop cardamom seeds into bottle. Also add coriander seed, and fennel seed if used. Pour vinegar through a funnel into the bottle. Seal and store in a cool, dark place at room temperature at least 1 week or up to 4 months.

Per tablespoon: 2.8 cal., 0% (0 cal.) from fat ; 0 g protein; 0 g fat; 0.6 g carbo.; 0.1 mg sodium; 0 mg chol.

Asian Vinegar

Prep time: About 10 minutes, plus at least 1 week for standing
Makes: 1 bottle (12 to 16 oz.)

    2 tablespoons slivered peeled fresh ginger
    2 cloves garlic, slivered
    5 dried small hot red chilies
    5 sprigs (each about 4 in.) fresh cilantro, rinsed
   1½ to 2 cups rice vinegar

With a chopstick or skewer, gently push the ginger, slivered garlic, chilies, and cilantro sprigs into a clean 12- to 16-ounce bottle. Pour vinegar through a funnel into the bottle to fill. Seal and store in a cool, dark place at room temperature at least 1 week or up to 4 months.

Per tablespoon: 3.4 cal., 0% (0 cal.) from fat; 0 g protein; 0 g fat; 0.8 g carbo.; 0.2 mg sodium; 0 mg chol.

Provençal Vinegar

Prep time: About 10 minutes, plus at least 1 week for standing
Makes: 1 bottle (12 to 16 oz.)

    1 sprig (5 in.) fresh rosemary, rinsed
    1 or 2 sprigs (each 3 in.) fresh sage, rinsed
    2 or 3 sprigs (each 4 in.) fresh thyme, rinsed
   1½ to 2 cups white wine vinegar

With a chopstick or skewer, push rosemary, sage, and thyme into a clean 12- to 16-ounce bottle. Pour vinegar through a funnel into bottle to fill. Seal and store in a cool, dark place at room temperature at least 1 week or up to 4 months.

Per tablespoon: 2.3 cal., 0% (0 cal.) from fat; 0 g protein; 0 g fat; 0.5 g carbo.; 0 mg sodium; 0 mg chol.

Infused (flavored) oils are a quick way to add flavor to marinades, salad dressings, and grilled foods, but purchasing these oils as gifts can be prohibitively expensive.

Fortunately, infused oils are surprisingly easy and economical to make. All you need to do is whirl the oil with seasonings in a blender. You can double or triple the recipes if you'd like. The flavored oils are ready to use the same day they're made and will last up to a month if you store them airtight in the refrigerator.

Although making these oils is exceptionally easy, there are a few rules you shouldn't break. First, start with fresh, high-quality oil—the flavor of an old or low-quality oil can't be masked by seasonings. Second, make sure flavoring additions are completely dry. Any excess water in the oil speeds rancidity. Finally, always store the oils in the refrigerator.

HOW TO USE INFUSED OILS
• Substitute for plain oil in marinades and salad dressings.
• Use as a "dip" for crusty breads and focaccia.
• Drizzle lightly over grilled fish or shellfish.
• Use to sauté vegetables to give them extra flavor.

Smoked Chili Oil

Prep and cook time: About 20 minutes
Notes: Leave the chili pieces in the oil for a rustic look, or strain the oil before bottling.
Makes: 2 cups

    4 dried chipotle chilies (about ½ oz. total)
    2 cups extra-virgin olive oil with light olive flavor or canola oil

1. Combine chilies with 1 cup water in a small pan. Bring to a boil over high heat; cover tightly, remove from heat, and let chilies stand until soft, about 10 minutes. Drain chilies; blot completely dry with paper towels. Stem and seed chilies, then coarsely chop.

2. Combine chilies and oil in a blender. Whirl until chilies are puréed or very finely chopped, about 2 minutes.

3. If desired, strain oil; discard residue. Pour into decorative bottles; store airtight in refrigerator up to 1 month.

Per tablespoon: 121 cal., 100% (121 cal.) from fat; 0.1 g protein; 13.4 g fat (2 g sat.); 0.3 g carbo.; 0.1 mg sodium; 0 mg chol.

Provençal Vinegar

Orange-Spice Vinegar

Smoked Chili Oil

Lemon-Orange Oil

Cherry Liqueur

Raspberry-Mint Honey

Glass for Gifts

Packaging counts. Show off your honeys, oils, vinegars, and liqueurs in clear glass bottles or jars with airtight lids. If you choose a cruet with a loose top, tape it down when in transit. For honeys, choose 4- to 12-ounce jars; for oils, vinegars, and liqueurs, 8- to 16-ounce bottles. Many cookware stores sell a good selection of attractive, reasonably priced containers. The following are good resources.

Cost Plus World Market, 201 Clay St., Oakland, CA 94607; (510) 893-7300. Call or write for store locations. No catalog, but stores will mail-order specified items.

Crate and Barrel, Box 9059, Wheeling, IL 60090; (800) 323-5461. 46 stores nationwide; mail order.

Pier 1 Imports, Customer Service, Box 961020, Fort Worth, TX 76161; (800) 245-4595. 690 stores nationwide; no mail order.

Sur La Table, Catalog Division, 410 Terry Ave. N., Seattle, WA 98109; (800) 243-0852. Retail stores in Seattle and Kirkland, Washington, and in Berkeley, California.

Williams-Sonoma, Mail Order Department, Box 7456, San Francisco, CA 94120; (800) 541-2233. 250 stores; catalog available.

Lemon-Orange Oil

Prep time: About 15 minutes
Notes: Leave the peel in for extra flavor and color, or strain it out.
Makes: 2 cups

¼ cup shredded lemon peel (yellow part only)

¼ cup shredded orange peel (orange part only)

2 cups canola oil or extra-virgin olive oil with light olive flavor

1. Combine peels and oil in a blender. Whirl until peels are thoroughly puréed, about 2 minutes.

2. If desired, strain through 2 layers of cheesecloth or a very fine strainer. Pour into decorative bottles; store airtight in the refrigerator up to 1 month.

Per tablespoon: 122 cal., 100% (122 cal.) from fat; 0 g protein; 13.6 g fat (1 g sat.); 0.3 g carbo.; 0.1 mg sodium; 0 mg chol.

Friends on your list will conclude their meals on a sweet, spirited note as they sip a liqueur made from dried apricots or sour cherries. These liqueurs have such rich, sweet-tart flavors that few will guess they take only 15 minutes to prepare. Use the leftover soused fruit to make luscious, chocolate-covered candy (recipe on page 276).

SERVING IDEAS FOR FRUIT LIQUEURS
• Drizzle over ice cream for an instant but elegant dessert.
• Add a little to mixed fresh fruit; spoon over pound cake.
• Splash into sparkling wine for a festive aperitif.
• Flavor holiday fruit cakes with liqueur instead of rum.

Apricot or Cherry Liqueur

Prep time: About 15 minutes, plus at least 2 weeks for mellowing
Notes: Slab apricots are the sweetest dried apricots; they're picked extra-ripe and soft, and are slightly misshapen. Inexpensive vodka works fine.
Makes: About 8 cups apricot liqueur or 7⅓ cups cherry liqueur

2 pounds dried apricots or dried pitted sour cherries

1 bottle (1.75 liter) vodka

4 cups sugar

1. Place apricots or cherries, vodka, and sugar in a glass jar (at least 3-quart size). Stir until sugar is mostly dissolved. Cover tightly and let stand at least 2 weeks or up to 2 months; after a few days, shake jar until sugar completely dissolves. Cherry liqueur may form a slightly cloudy, harmless residue at top of jar.

2. Pour liqueur and fruit, a portion at a time, through a fine strainer into a pitcher, letting fruit drain completely. Save fruit for other uses (see recipe on page 276). Line strainer with four layers of damp cheesecloth, set over a spouted container, and pour liqueur through it. Or for maximum clarity, strain liqueur through a coffee filter, changing filter often (takes several hours).

3. Pour liqueur into small airtight bottles. Serve liqueur, or store airtight up to 6 months. (If storing in containers with rubber stoppers, place a couple of layers of plastic wrap between rubber and bottle top to prevent alcohol from softening rubber.)

Per ounce (2 tablespoons) apricot liqueur: 91 cal., 0% (0 cal.) from fat; 0.1 g protein; 0 g fat; 10 g carbo.; 0.5 mg sodium; 0 mg chol.

Per ounce (2 tablespoons) cherry liqueur: 91 cal., 0% (0 cal.) from fat; 0 g protein; 0 g fat; 11 g carbo.; 0.4 mg sodium; 0 mg chol.

It's 10 P.M. on December 23. As you finish your Christmas wrapping, you suddenly remember those remaining holiday parties—and the gifts you should bring. Relax. A quick trip to the supermarket will solve your problem.

With just a jar or two of honey, two or three other ingredients, and the simple instructions that follow, you can create gifts in a matter of minutes. If you have them, use pretty jars or bottles to package the flavored honeys (see facing page). Or dress up leftover jars you have around the house.

GREAT IDEAS FOR FLAVORED HONEYS
• Drizzle over warm biscuits, scones, banana bread—or add to a peanut butter sandwich.
• Stir into marinades and barbecue sauces for pork or chicken.
• Mix a tablespoon or two with cider vinegar, extra-virgin olive oil, and a little Dijon mustard for a flavorful vinaigrette.
• Enjoy a teaspoonful in a cup of tea.

Flavored honeys

Prep and cook time: About 25 minutes, plus cooling
Notes: Recipe can be doubled or tripled. Use a large enough pan, as the honey expands dramatically while simmering.
Makes: About 4 cups

4 cups mildly flavored honey (such as clover or orange blossom)

Flavoring options (choices follow)

In a 3- to 4-quart pan, combine honey and flavoring options over medium-high heat. Stir occasionally until honey simmers, about 5 minutes. Simmer 10 minutes; remove from heat and let stand until completely cool. Pour into clean decorative jars. Store at room temperature up to 1 month.

Lemon grass and ginger. Cut off leafy top and peel tough outer layer from ½ pound fresh lemon grass. Trim off and discard discolored or dry parts of root ends. Cut trimmed, woody sections into 2-inch lengths; crush lightly with a mallet. Add to honey with 1 cup finely chopped crystallized ginger. Simmer as directed. When cooled slightly, pick out and discard lemon grass. Cool and package as directed.

Per tablespoon: 62 cal., 0% (0 cal.) from fat; 0.1 g protein; 0 g fat; 17 g carbo.; 2.6 mg sodium; 0 mg chol.

Grapefruit "marmalade." To honey, add finely chopped peel (colored part only) of 3 to 4 grapefruit (Ruby and Texas Flame are nice). Simmer, cool, and package as directed.

Per tablespoon: 58 cal., 0% (0 cal.) from fat; 0.1 g protein; 0 g fat; 16 g carbo.; 0.8 mg sodium; 0 mg chol.

Raspberry-mint. To honey, add 2 cups frozen raspberries and ¼ pound (4 oz.) fresh mint leaves. Simmer 10 minutes longer than directed. Pour through a fine strainer; discard pulp and mint leaves. Cool and package as directed.

Per tablespoon: 67 cal., 0% (0 cal.) from fat; 0.1 g protein; 0 g fat; 18 g carbo.; 0.8 mg sodium; 0 mg chol. ■

Slash and stencil breads

Try these easy decorating techniques to make two fabulous roasted garlic–cheese loaves

By Elaine Johnson

L OOK IN THE DISPLAY CASE AT CRAIG Ponsford's bakery and you might not think it's possible to duplicate his elegant loaves.

But Ponsford's decorative breads offer gorgeous results that anyone can achieve. He simply stencils designs in flour onto bread dough, then applies a few attractive slashes to give an especially polished look to loaves.

Ponsford uses these techniques at Artisan Bakers, the bakery his family owns in Sonoma, California. He also incorporated the ideas in a first-ever win for the American team at baking's equivalent to the Olympic Games, the Coupe du Monde, held in France last February.

Simple designs—such as spirals—and more intricate patterns all work well as stencils. If you're artistically inclined, you can create your own stencils; if not, it's easy to enlarge Ponsford's design, shown at right, on a photocopier.

To make slashes in the dough, Ponsford uses a device called a *lame,* basically a curved, very sharp razor on a stick (see sources on page 272). We found the lame worked better than a knife. The angle and placement of slashes, shown on page 272, are also important for getting the best results.

As the base for the design, we've used Ponsford's recipe for one of Artisan Bakers' most popular breads—one that combines the rich flavors of roasted garlic with tangy dry jack cheese. The dough has a pre-ferment step called a poolish, which gives it an extra depth of flavor.

The team at Artisan Bakers prides itself on its no-shortcuts approach to baking. But for home bakers who are a little more pressed for time, we've created an easy option: simply knead the garlic and cheese into thawed frozen bread dough.

Handsome star-patterned breads begin with dough made from scratch or with frozen bread dough. Roasted garlic and aged jack cheese add rich flavor.

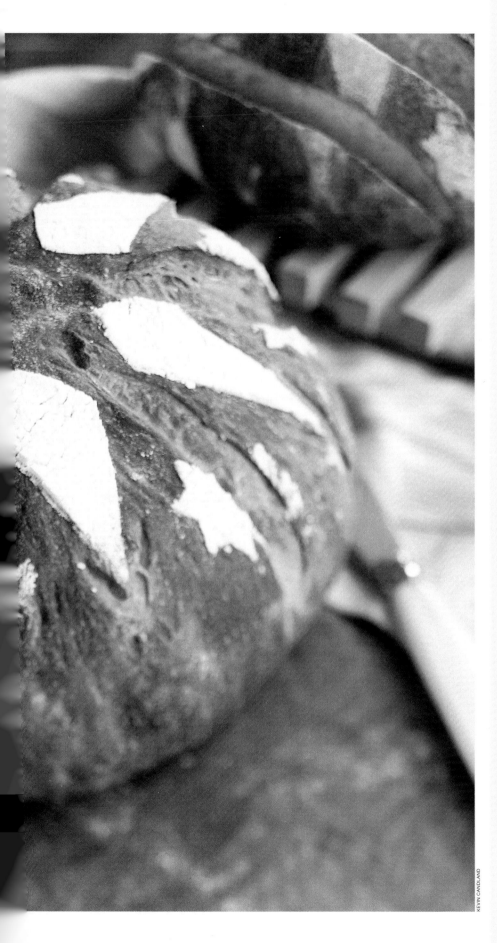

How to stencil and slash dough

Make stencil. Use the design above by enlarging it 200 percent on a photocopier, then 155 percent, to get a 7- to 8-inch circle. (Or draw your own 7- by 8-inch design.) Cut out enlarged white portions with a craft knife and discard; trace onto a manila folder, and cut out again. (Stencil needs to be a little stiff, so don't use the photocopy.)

Dust bottom of stencil with flour and lay on dough on baking sheet. Lightly mist cutout areas with water.

Sift about 1 tablespoon flour over stencil, evenly covering cutouts. Lift off stencil, being careful not to spill flour on dough. Repeat on second loaf.

KEVIN CANDLAND (2)

To slash dough, use a lame (see ordering information below) or a small, thin, extremely sharp knife. Make six evenly spaced ¼- to ½-inch-deep slashes in the dough as shown, holding the blade at a 45° angle. The angle and spacing of the slashes will direct rising.

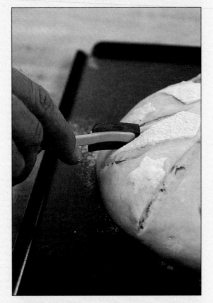

Make small cuts around tips of the large star. Hold the blade at a 90° angle to dough; cut slashes about ⅛ inch deep. Repeat slashing on second loaf. Cuts made at this angle and depth will produce decorative marks.

To order a lame: Sur La Table sells a disposable lame for $6.95 (800/243-0852); King Arthur Flour's "Baker's Catalogue" sells a non-refillable lame for $9.25 or a refillable lame with 10 blades for $30.50 (800/827-6836).

Slash and Stencil Roasted Garlic–Dry Jack Breads

Prep and cook time: About 1½ hours, plus about 5½ hours for rising (if using frozen dough, 1 hour and 50 minutes, plus 1¼ hours for rising)

Notes: Have stencils, cutting tool, mister, and sifter ready at baking time.

Frozen dough version. Substitute 4 pounds completely thawed frozen bread dough for yeast, water, flour, and salt in recipe. On a floured board, knead in roasted garlic and cheese until evenly incorporated and no longer sticky, adding flour (about ¼ cup) as required to prevent sticking. Place dough in oiled bowl, turn over, and proceed with second rising (takes 60 to 80 minutes), in step 6.

Makes: 2 loaves, each about 2 pounds

- 2 cakes (0.6 oz. each) fresh compressed yeast or 2 packages active dry yeast
- 8 to 8½ cups all-purpose flour
- ½ pound (2 to 3 heads) garlic
- 5 teaspoons salt
- 1⅓ cups (6 oz.) grated dry jack or parmesan cheese

1. Poolish. In a 1-quart glass measure, crumble ½ cake fresh yeast or sprinkle 1 teaspoon dry yeast over 1 cup cool (70°) water. Let stand until yeast is dissolved, about 5 minutes. Stir in 1½ cups flour until fairly smooth. Let stand in a warm place (80°) until batter is very bubbly and has doubled, 2 to 2½ hours.

2. Roast garlic. Meanwhile, place garlic in a small pan and bake in a 350° oven until very soft when squeezed, about 45 minutes. Let cool, then cut in half horizontally and squeeze out cloves; set aside.

3. Mix dough. In a bowl, crumble or sprinkle remaining yeast over 1½ cups cool (70°) water. Let stand until yeast is dissolved, about 5 minutes. Stir in salt, poolish, garlic, and cheese, then 3 cups flour. Beat dough with a spoon until stretchy and shiny, about 5 minutes. Then stir in 2 cups more flour.

4. Knead. Scrape dough onto a lightly floured board. Knead until dough is smooth, elastic, and no longer sticky, 15 to 20 minutes; add flour as required to prevent sticking.

5. First rise. Place dough in an oiled bowl. Turn over, cover airtight; let dough rise in a warm place (80°) until doubled (dough should hold an impression that doesn't spring back when a floured finger is poked into it), 1½ to 2 hours.

6. Second rise. Punch a floured fist into dough and knead a few times in bowl to work out most of the air; turn so a smooth side is up. Cover and let rise until almost doubled (dough just holds an impression when touched with a fingertip), 45 to 60 minutes; do not punch down.

7. Shaping. Gently scrape dough onto a lightly floured board; cut dough in half. To shape, pull up sides of each piece of dough toward center until underside is smooth, and pinch together at top; turn dough over and pat into a 7-inch round. Diagonally space the loaves on an oiled 15- by 17-inch baking sheet. (Or if you have 2 ovens, put each loaf on a 12- by 15-inch baking sheet and bake in separate ovens.) If dough has deflated slightly, cover loaves lightly and let rise in a warm place until almost doubled, 5 to 10 minutes.

8. Stencil and slash loaves as directed, starting on page 270.

9. Bake. Place baking sheet on rack in a 400° oven. Vigorously mist each side wall of oven (avoid oven lightbulb and breads) with water about 10 times and quickly close door. Bake 5 minutes, then remist oven walls. Bake until breads are deep brown and sound hollow on the bottom when tapped, 35 to 40 more minutes. Lift to racks to cool.

Per 1-ounce portion: 74 cal., 12% (9 cal.) from fat; 2.9 g protein; 1 g fat (0.5 g sat.); 13 g carbo.; 222 mg sodium; 2.1 mg chol. ∎

TERRENCE McCARTHY

Craig Ponsford of Artisan Bakers in Sonoma, California, displays a sampling of his bakery's slash and stencil breads in a variety of designs.

A warm tortilla wraps up creamy potatoes and eggplant with carrots and onion.

The fajita reconsidered

Mexican seasonings beef up no-fat roasted-vegetable filling

TINA WILLIAMS OF PASADENA HAS moved fajitas into a contemporary mode by tackling head-on two of today's hottest food angsts: fat and red meat.

Her remarkably good-tasting fajita filling is made with vegetables and no fat. Even better—it's easy. You just stick the mixture into the oven to roast, with only an occasional stir.

Vegetable Hash Fajitas

Prep and cook time: About 1½ hours

Makes: 4 to 6 servings

- 4 russet potatoes (about 3 lb. total), peeled
- 1 eggplant (about 1¼ lb.), stem trimmed
- 1 pound carrots, peeled
- 1 red bell pepper (about ½ lb.), stemmed and seeded
- 1 onion (about ½ lb.), chopped
- ¼ cup lime juice
- 3 cloves garlic, minced or pressed
- 2 tablespoons chili powder
- 1 tablespoon minced fresh or 1 teaspoon crumbled dried oregano leaves
- 2 teaspoons pepper
- 1 teaspoon sugar
- ½ cup vegetable or chicken broth
- 8 to 12 warm flour tortillas (about 10-in. size)
  Lime wedges
  Fresh cilantro sprigs
  Nonfat, reduced-fat, or regular sour cream
  Salt

1. Cut potatoes and eggplant into ½-inch cubes. Cut carrots and bell pepper into thin slices. In a 12- by 17-inch roasting pan, combine potatoes, eggplant, carrots, bell pepper, onion, lime juice, garlic, chili powder, oregano, pepper, and sugar. Cover pan tightly with foil.

2. Bake in a 450° oven until vegetables exude juice, about 25 minutes. Uncover pan and bake, stirring occasionally, until liquid evaporates and vegetables are browned and stick to pan, about 30 minutes. Add broth; stir to scrape browned bits free. Bake until liquid evaporates again. (If making ahead, let cool, cover, and chill up to 1 day. Mix in ¼ cup water and bake, uncovered, in a 450° oven until hot, about 15 minutes.)

3. Transfer vegetable fajita mixture to a bowl. Spoon into warm tortillas and add juice from lime wedges, cilantro, sour cream, and salt to taste; fold or roll tortillas around filling and hold to eat.

Per serving: 618 cal., 13% (82 cal.) from fat; 16 g protein; 9.1 g fat (1.3 g sat.); 120 g carbo.; 683 mg sodium; 0 mg chol. ■

By Christine Weber Hale

Chocolate-Peppermint Shortbread Bars

Prep and cook time: About 1 hour

Notes: Either scatter cookies with candy or stencil a diagonal line of candy on top. (Make a 1- by 2-inch cardboard stencil with a diagonal slit ¼ in. wide. Place gently over a bar, then sprinkle candy onto it with a small spoon so candy won't stick to your fingers.)

Makes: 5 dozen bars

- 1⅔ cups all-purpose flour
- ½ cup unsweetened cocoa
- 2½ cups powdered sugar
- ¼ cup firmly packed brown sugar
- ¼ teaspoon salt
- 1 cup (½ lb.) plus 2 tablespoons unsalted butter, softened
- 2 ounces unsweetened chocolate, melted
- 2 tablespoons finely crushed peppermint candy

1. In a food processor or bowl, whirl or stir flour, cocoa, ½ cup powdered sugar, brown sugar, and salt to blend. Cut 1 cup butter into 1-inch slices, add to mixture, and whirl or stir until smoothly blended.

2. Scatter pieces of dough in a 10- by 15-inch rimmed pan. With palm, pat dough to evenly cover pan bottom. Bake in a 300° oven until dough feels slightly firm and dry, 30 to 35 minutes. Let cool on a rack.

3. In a bowl, beat melted chocolate, remaining 2 tablespoons butter, remaining 2 cups powdered sugar, and 3 tablespoons hot water until smooth. Spread evenly over shortbread.

RICHARD JUNG

Holiday miniatures

Buttery cookies by expert Flo Braker prove smaller is better

THE GREAT THING ABOUT bite-size cookies is they're all yours—you don't have to share them with anyone else!" laughs Flo Braker, a San Francisco baking columnist and author of *The Simple Art of Perfect Baking* (Chapters Publishing, 1992). Braker's signature small cookies have another advantage: their size encourages sampling a whole assortment.

When Braker puts together a holiday cookie tray or gift package, she definite-ly keeps sampling in mind, opting for a diversity of shapes, textures, and flavors (citrus, spices, chocolate, and nuts are among her favorites).

She prefers variety in preparation as well, choosing some cookies to make quickly in large quantities (such as the Chocolate-Peppermint Shortbread Bars), others to make in stages, and often a batch of dazzling cookies, like the 10-point, double-glazed stars, to show off her artistry.

4. While frosting is soft, cut shortbread into 1- by 2-inch bars; decorate with candy as explained in Notes. Serve bars, store airtight up to 2 days, or freeze.

Per cookie: 75 cal., 49% (37 cal.) from fat; 0.6 g protein; 4.1 g fat (2.5 g sat.); 9.6 g carbo.; 11 mg sodium; 9.4 mg chol.

White Chocolate Spice Cookies

Prep and cook time: About 1 1/4 hours, plus about 1 hour for chilling

Makes: About 7 dozen cookies

- 2 cups all-purpose flour
- 2/3 cup firmly packed brown sugar
- 1 teaspoon ground ginger
- 3/4 teaspoon fresh-ground pepper
- 1/2 teaspoon *each* baking soda and unsweetened cocoa
- 1/4 teaspoon ground cinnamon
- 1/8 teaspoon *each* salt and ground allspice
- 1 cup (1/2 lb.) unsalted butter, softened and cut into 1/2-inch slices
- 1 teaspoon *each* vanilla and grated lemon peel
- 6 ounces high-quality white chocolate, finely chopped
- 3 tablespoons vegetable shortening

1. In a food processor or bowl, whirl or stir flour, sugar, ginger, pepper, soda, cocoa, cinnamon, salt, and allspice to blend. Add butter; pulse or cut in with a pastry blender until mixture has the consistency of cornmeal.

2. In a cup, stir vanilla, lemon peel, and 1 tablespoon water. Add to food processor or bowl; whirl or stir until dough forms a ball.

3. Divide dough in half. Following tip 3 on page 276, roll out each half 1/4 inch thick. Then stack and chill (see tip 4) until firm, about 45 minutes (or freeze about 25 minutes).

4. Following tip 4, cut out circles using a

1 1/2-inch round cutter. Space 1/2 inch apart on 12- by 15-inch baking sheets lined with cooking parchment.

5. Bake cookies in a 325° oven until they are pale brown, about 15 minutes. Lift to racks to cool.

6. Fill bottom of a double boiler with 1/2 inch of water. In top pan, combine chocolate and shortening. Over high heat, bring water just to simmering; remove from heat. Stir chocolate occasionally until smooth.

7. Dunk each cookie halfway into chocolate, then place on baking sheet lined with waxed paper or plastic wrap. With a fork dipped in chocolate mixture, flick streaks over cookies. Chill just until glaze sets, about 15 minutes. Serve cookies, store airtight up to 2 days, or freeze.

Per cookie: 53 cal., 58% (31 cal.) from fat; 0.5 g protein; 3.4 g fat (1.9 g sat.); 5.1 g carbo.; 14 mg sodium; 5.9 mg chol.

Twin Crimson Stars

Prep and cook time: About 3 1/2 hours, plus about 1 1/2 hours for chilling and setting

Notes: If time is short, bake cookies one day, glaze them the next.

Makes: About 5 1/2 dozen double cookies

- 1 batch dough from Lemon Fruit Swirls (recipe at right), made without apricots, citron, cherries, or walnuts
- 3/4 cup strawberry jam
- 1 cup plus 2 teaspoons sifted powdered sugar
- 2 teaspoons lightly beaten egg white

1. Divide dough into thirds. Following tip 3 on page 276, roll each portion into a circle 1/8 inch thick. Then stack and freeze (see tip 4) until firm, about 30 minutes (or chill for about 2 hours).

2. Following tip 4, cut out dough shapes with a 2-inch, 5-point star cutter (a sharp-pointed metal cutter works best). Space 1/2 inch apart on 12- by 15-inch baking sheets lined with cooking parchment.

3. Bake cookies in a 325° oven until pale golden at tips, 8 to 10 minutes. Lift to racks to cool. Reduce oven heat to 150°.

4. In a 1-quart pan over medium heat, stir jam until melted. Push through a fine strainer, discard fruit, and return liquid to pan. Bring to a simmer and cook for 2 minutes to thicken, stirring occasionally. Let cool just until warm to touch, 7 to 8 minutes. Meanwhile, in a bowl, stir 1/2 cup plus 2 teaspoons sugar and 4 teaspoons water until smooth.

5. Brush cookies with jam, then place slightly apart on 12- by 15-inch baking sheets. With a clean pastry brush, paint a thin film of sugar glaze over each cookie to completely cover jam, beginning with the cookies coated earliest with jam.

6. Bake cookies until glaze is set and dry, 15 to 18 minutes. Lift to racks to cool.

7. For icing cement, stir remaining 1/2 cup sugar and egg white until smooth. To assemble cookies, spoon a dot (1/8 teaspoon) of cement in center of one cookie, then gently press another cookie on top with star points offset.

8. Let cookies stand until cement is set, about 1 hour. Serve, store airtight up to 2 days, or freeze.

Per double cookie: 71 cal., 37% (26 cal.) from fat; 0.6 g protein; 2.9 g fat (1.8 g sat.); 11 g carbo.; 11 mg sodium; 11 mg chol.

Lemon Fruit Swirls

Prep and cook time: About 1 1/4 hours, plus about 2 1/2 hours for chilling

Notes: King Arthur Flour's "Baker's Catalogue" sells high-quality candied citron ($2.25 per 1/2 lb., plus shipping) and lemon peel ($1.75 per 1/2 lb., plus shipping); call (800) 827-6836. For easy handling, roll dough between sheets of cooking parchment (not waxed paper).

Makes: About 5 1/2 dozen cookies

2½ cups all-purpose flour

1 cup sugar

¼ teaspoon salt

1 cup (½ lb.) unsalted butter, softened and cut into ½-inch slices

1 large egg

1 teaspoon vanilla

1 teaspoon lemon juice

4 teaspoons finely grated lemon peel

½ cup *each* finely chopped dried apricots, candied citron or lemon peel, glacé cherries, and walnuts

1. In a food processor or bowl, whirl or stir flour, sugar, and salt to blend. Add butter; whirl or cut in with a pastry blender until dough has the consistency of cornmeal.

2. In a bowl, whisk egg, vanilla, and lemon juice and peel to blend. Add to food processor or bowl; whirl or stir until dough forms a ball.

3. Divide dough in half. To 1 half, stir in apricots, citron, cherries, and walnuts. Follow-

ing tip 3 at right, roll each half into an even 8- by 16-inch rectangle, then stack and chill (see tip 4) until firm, about 2 hours.

4. Peel off top sheet of cooking parchment from each dough half. Very lightly brush plain dough with water. Place fruit dough face down on plain dough. Lightly press to seal. Remove top sheet of parchment. Trim edges even. If necessary, let dough stand (to warm) just until pliable. Beginning with a long side, roll into a cylinder. Discard parchment. Cut in half crosswise. Wrap each half in plastic wrap; freeze until firm, about 30 minutes, or up to 2 weeks.

5. Working with half of dough at a time, unwrap; with a thin, sharp knife, cut unwrapped dough into ⅛-inch rounds. Place ½ inch apart on 12- by 15-inch baking sheets lined with parchment. Bake in a 350° oven until pale golden, 12 to 14 minutes. Lift to racks to cool. Serve cookies, store airtight up to 2 days, or freeze.

Per cookie: 73 cal., 44% (32 cal.) from fat; 0.7 g protein; 3.5 g fat (1.8 g sat.); 10 g carbo.; 15 mg sodium; 11 mg chol. ∎

By Elaine Johnson

HOLIDAY COOKIE TIPS

1. For flavor, Braker prefers butter to margarine. She uses unsalted butter so she has more control over the cookies' saltiness and because it doesn't mute other flavors. If you prefer margarine, she suggests buying an unsalted brand.

2. You can chill the unbaked doughs for all of these cookies (except the shortbread) up to three days, or freeze up to two weeks. (Prepare as in tip 3, wrap airtight, and chill as in tip 4.)

3. To keep roll-out cookies tender, don't roll on a floured board. Roll unchilled, flattened portions of dough between sheets of cooking parchment or waxed paper. (Look for cooking parchment near the plastic wrap in supermarkets.)

4. To keep roll-out cookies from sticking during cutting, stack rolled-out dough (still in parchment—see tip 3) on a baking sheet; chill or freeze until firm. Remove one layer at a time. Peel off top sheet of parchment, loosely replace, and turn package over. Peel off second sheet. Cut cookies. If dough begins to soften, freeze briefly. Gather scraps; roll and chill as before.

5. For no-stick cooking and easy cleanup, line baking sheets with cooking parchment. Parchment can be reused several times on a baking day.

6. Bake a single sheet of cookies in the center of the oven, or evenly space two sheets, switching them halfway through baking.

7. Store soft cookies in rigid containers up to two days at room temperature, or freeze up to two months. Keep chocolate cookies separate from others.

Chocolate-dipped fruit from liqueur

WHEN THE APRICOT OR CHERRY liqueur on page 269 finishes aging, you'll have a generous amount of flavorful fruit with a kick. Dunk the fruit in melted chocolate for a second set of extravagant treats.

Chocolate-Covered Fruit

Prep and cook time: About 40 minutes
Makes: About 200 chocolate-coated apricots (3 lb.) or 175 chocolate-coated cherry clusters (4¼ lb.)

Drained apricots or cherries from liqueur (page 269)

2½ cups (15 oz.) semisweet chocolate chips or 5 cups (30 oz.) finely chopped high-quality white chocolate

2 or 6 tablespoons vegetable shortening

1. Pat fruit completely dry. *For apricots,* place chocolate chips and 2 tablespoons shortening in top of a double boiler; set aside. *For cherries,* place 2½ cups white chocolate and 3 tablespoons shortening in top of a double boiler; set aside. Fill bottom pan with 1 inch water. Over medium heat, bring water to steaming (120°). Remove from heat, place pan with chocolate chips or white chocolate over water, and stir often until melted, about 5 minutes.

2. *For apricots,* dunk into chocolate to coat halfway, letting excess drip off; then place pitted side down on baking sheets lined with plastic wrap. Chill until chocolate firms, about 15 minutes. *For cherries,* stir half of fruit (4 cups) into white chocolate. Drop rounded teaspoons of mixture onto lined pans; chill to firm. Repeat with remaining white chocolate, 3 tablespoons shortening, and cherries. Serve fruit, chill airtight up to 2 weeks, or freeze up to 1 month.

Per chocolate-dipped apricot: 27 cal., 23% (6.3 cal.) from fat; 0.2 g protein; 0.7 g fat (0.4 g sat.); 4.8 g carbo.; 0.5 mg sodium; 0 mg chol.

Per chocolate-dipped cherry cluster: 49 cal., 35% (17 cal.) from fat; 0.3 g protein; 1.9 g fat (1 g sat.); 7.4 g carbo.; 4.5 mg sodium; 0 mg chol. ∎

By Elaine Johnson

SUNSET'S KITCHEN CABINET

Readers' family favorites tested in our kitchens

By Linda Lau Anusasananan

NORMAN A. PLATE

30-Minute Cioppino

Edward Mairani, Atherton, California

Most people make a big deal about cioppino. Not Edward Mairani. He jump-starts the stew with a package of spaghetti sauce mix. After making the sauce and seasoning it to taste, he poaches seafood in the tomato base. We find it's even faster to use a jar of marinara sauce and canned diced tomatoes.

Prep and cook time: About 30 minutes
Makes: 4 to 6 servings

      1   tablespoon olive oil
      1   onion (about 8 oz.), chopped
      3   cloves garlic, minced
      1   jar (about 27 oz.) marinara sauce
      1   can (14½ oz.) diced tomatoes, including juice
      ¾   cup dry red wine
      1   dried bay leaf
      ¾   teaspoon dried tarragon

      ½   teaspoon pepper
      2   cooked crabs (about 3½ lb. total), rinsed and cracked
     16   hard-shelled clams suitable for steaming, scrubbed
      1   pound calamari steak, cut into ½- by 2-inch strips
     16   shrimp (26 to 31 per lb.), shelled and deveined
     16   mussels, scrubbed
          Chopped parsley and lemon wedges

1. In 6- to 8-quart pan, mix oil, onion, and garlic; stir over high heat until tinged brown, 8 to 10 minutes. Add 1 cup water, marinara, tomatoes, wine, bay leaf, tarragon, and pepper. Bring to a simmer over high heat.

2. Stir in crabs; return to a simmer. Lay clams on top. Cover and cook 5 minutes over medium-high heat. Add calamari and shrimp to sauce, leaving clams on top; lay mussels alongside clams. Cover and cook until clams and mussels open and shrimp and calamari are barely opaque in thickest part (cut to test), 10 to 15 minutes. With a slotted spoon, lift out seafood as done; continue cooking remainder. Discard clams or mussels that don't open. Ladle into bowls; garnish with parsley and lemon.

Per serving: 392 cal., 23% (90 cal.) from fat; 46 g protein; 10 g fat (1.6 g sat.); 26 g carbo.; 1,360 mg sodium; 299 mg chol.

Sweet Onion Wheels

Deborah A. Daily, Santa Ynez, California

Onions cooked in red wine. Grilled onions in puff pastry. Deborah Daily merges these into an intriguing appetizer. She sautés onions in wine, but adds sugar and raisins. Then she rolls the candied mixture in puff pastry and slices the roll to make pinwheels. Baked, they're golden and flaky.

Prep and cook time: About 1¼ hours
Makes: About 36

      4   onions (½ lb. each), sliced thin
      1   cup dry red wine
      1   cup firmly packed brown sugar
     1½   cups golden raisins
      1   package (17¼ oz.) frozen puff pastry sheets

1. Place onions in a 5- to 6-quart nonstick frying pan. Add wine, sugar, and raisins; bring to a boil. Cook over medium-high heat, uncovered, until all liquid evaporates and onions begin to brown, 30 to 40 minutes; stir often. Cool; cover and chill at least 30 minutes.

2. Thaw pastry sheets at room temperature

just until pliable, 20 to 30 minutes. Unfold; spread half the onion mixture evenly over each sheet. Starting from narrow end, gently roll each sheet into a tight roll and cut into ½-inch slices; lay slightly apart on nonstick baking sheets. (If making ahead, freeze, covered, up to 1 week.)

3. Bake freshly made or frozen pinwheels in a 350° oven until golden brown, 25 to 30 minutes; watch to prevent scorching near end of baking. While warm, transfer to platter and serve.

Per onion wheel: 126 cal., 37% (47 cal.) from fat; 1.5 g protein; 5.2 g fat (0.7 g sat.); 19 g carbo.; 38 mg sodium; 0 mg chol.

Asian-Flavors Salad

Judy Burk, Oakland, California

Judy Burk uses ingredients from her Chinese heritage to add pleasant contrasts of textures and tastes to this unique salad. Chili oil and rice vinegar lightly dress the salad, which makes a beautiful opener for a holiday dinner.

Prep and cook time: About 45 minutes
Makes: 6 to 8 servings

NORMAN A. PLATE

- ¼ pound fresh water chestnuts or 1 can (6 oz.) sliced water chestnuts, drained
- 3 tangerines or mandarin oranges (about 6 oz. each) or 8 kumquats (about 3 oz. total)
- 1 Asian pear (about ½ lb.), peeled
- 3 quarts (about 1 lb.) bite-size pieces romaine lettuce, rinsed and crisped
- 1 cup *each* fresh cilantro leaves, mint leaves, and thinly sliced green onions
- ¼ cup *each* rice vinegar and lime juice
- 2 tablespoons sugar
- 1 to 2 teaspoons chili oil
  Salt

1. If using fresh water chestnuts, peel and thinly slice. Cut tangerines deep enough to remove peel and white membrane; over a bowl to catch juice, cut between membranes to remove segments. If using kumquats, rinse and cut into thin crosswise slices. Remove and discard any seeds from citrus fruit. Thinly slice pear.

2. In a large bowl, combine romaine, cilantro, mint, onions, water chestnuts, citrus fruit, and pear. In the bowl used to catch juice, mix collected tangerine juice, vinegar, lime juice, sugar, chili oil, and salt to taste. Pour over salad and mix.

Per serving: 82 cal., 9.9% (8.1 cal.) from fat; 1.8 g protein; 0.9 g fat (0.1 g sat.); 18 g carbo.; 10 mg sodium; 0 mg chol.

Spiced Vegetable Stew

Heide Gohlert, Cheney, Washington

Vegetarian Heide Gohlert finds this aromatic spiced vegetable stew delicious over grains. One of her favorite grain combinations contains equal portions of basmati rice and millet. She also serves the stew with couscous or plain rice.

Prep and cook time: About 50 minutes
Makes: 4 to 6 servings

- 1 tablespoon olive oil
- 2 onions (1 lb. total), chopped
- 4 cloves garlic, chopped
- 2 teaspoons ground cumin
- 1 teaspoon ground coriander
- ¼ teaspoon *each* cayenne and pepper
- 1 can (14½ oz.) diced tomatoes
- 1 carrot (¼ lb.), sliced ¼ inch thick
- 1 eggplant (1¼ lb.), cut into ½-inch cubes
- 1 red bell pepper (½ lb.), stemmed, seeded, and cut into ½-inch pieces
- 1 zucchini (¼ lb.), sliced ½ inch thick
- 1 can (15½ oz.) garbanzos, rinsed and drained
- ¼ cup raisins
  Salt
  Cooked basmati rice, millet, or couscous

1. In a 4- to 5-quart pan, combine oil and onions, and cook, stirring, over medium-high heat until onions are limp, about 8 minutes. Add garlic, cumin, coriander, cayenne, and pepper; stir until garlic is soft, about 2 minutes.

2. Add tomatoes with their juice, and carrot. Bring to a boil, cover, and simmer over low heat for 5 minutes. Add eggplant, bell pepper, and zucchini; continue simmering until carrot is tender when pierced, 25 to 35 minutes. Add garbanzos and raisins; cover and simmer until hot, about 3 minutes. Add salt to taste. Transfer to serving dish. Serve with rice.

Per serving without rice: 175 cal., 20% (35 cal.) from fat; 6 g protein; 3.9 g fat (0.4 g sat.); 32 g carbo.; 197 mg sodium; 0 mg chol.

Nut and Orange Biscotti

Jennifer A. Kirkgaard, Burbank, California

Dunking homemade biscotti into coffee is now an afternoon ritual for Jennifer Kirkgaard. In her first attempt at making the Italian cookies, a Christmas gift for her stepmother, she used Meyer lemons and fennel. Then she tried a favorite combination—orange, chocolate, and nuts.

Prep and cook time: About 1¼ hours
Makes: About 30

- ¾ cup whole almonds
- 2 teaspoons salad oil
- 3 large eggs
- ¾ cup sugar
- 2 tablespoons almond-flavor liqueur
- 1 tablespoon vanilla
- 1 tablespoon grated orange peel
- 1 teaspoon almond extract
- 2⅓ cups all-purpose flour
- 2 teaspoons baking powder
- ⅓ cup chopped semisweet chocolate

1. Place almonds on a 12- by 15-inch baking sheet. Bake in a 325° oven until golden under skin, about 15 minutes. Place oil and ¼ cup of the hot almonds in a blender; whirl until a buttery paste forms. Chop remaining nuts.

2. In a large mixing bowl, beat together eggs, ground almond paste, and sugar until blended. Add liqueur, vanilla, orange peel, and almond extract. Mix flour and baking powder. Gradually stir flour mixture into egg mixture until well blended; stir in chopped almonds and chocolate.

3. Spoon batter down length of a greased or cooking parchment–lined 14- by 17-inch baking sheet. With floured hands, pat into a flat log about ¾ inch thick and 3¼ inches wide.

Bake in 325° oven until golden, about 25 minutes. Remove from oven; let cool 5 minutes.

4. Lower oven temperature to 225°. Cut log crosswise into ½-inch slices. Lay slices flat on pan and return pan to oven. Continue baking until golden all over, 45 to 55 minutes. Cool on rack. Store airtight up to 1 week.

Per cookie: 99 cal., 30% (30 cal.) from fat; 2.4 g protein; 3.3 g fat (0.7 g sat.); 15 g carbo.; 40 mg sodium; 21 mg chol.

---

*S*hare a recipe you've created or adapted—a family favorite, travel discovery, or time-saver—including the story behind the recipe. You'll receive a "Great Cook" certificate and $50 for each recipe published. Send to *Sunset,* 80 Willow Rd., Menlo Park, CA 94025, or send e-mail (include name, address, and phone number) to recipes@sunsetpub.com.

Articles Index

Index of Recipe Titles

Bob's blue cornmeal blueberry pancakes, 78

Braised oxtails from Little Saigon, 40

Brandied potato gratin, 234

Bread dressing with pancetta and greens, 232

Broccoli, onion, and bacon salad, 21

Brown rice and apple meat loaf, 81

Bûche de Nöel, 249

Butterflied poussins with bourbon-molasses sauce, 155

Caesar potato salad, 139

Cantaloupe-orange margaritas, 147

Caponata fettuccine, 122

Caramelized miniature-banana sundaes, 98

Cauliflower piquant, 190

Ceviche salad, 133

Charred tomato soup with corn and pepper relish, 186

Cheddar pepper puffs, 191

Cherry-glazed pork, 18

Chicken and rice ensalada, 214

Chicken–bok choy stir-fry, 17

Chicken chutney burgers, 16

Chicken curry soup with low-fat coconut milk, 8

Chicken–goat cheese burritos, 94

Chicken halves with New Mexico chili sauce, 154

Chicken with corn relish, 16

Chicken with 24 cloves of garlic, 183

Chili beef salad, 159

Chili-mustard quail, 219

Chinese five-spice oatmeal cookies, 59

Chinese green onion cakes, 84

Chinese shrimp salad, 101

Chinois beef, 124

Chipotle and red pepper salsa, 54

Chipotle corn soup, 54

Chipotle-honey glazed nuts, 225

Chocolate-coffee frozen pie, 148

Chocolate coffee orange mousse, 175

Chocolate-covered fruit, 276

Chocolate-peppermint shortbread bars, 274

Chocolate sauce, 41

Cilantro pesto, 133

Cinnamon nut brittle, 225

Clams in tomato-fennel broth, 14

Classic baked ham, 69

Classic salsa fresca, 93

Cookie crust, 149

Corn-chipotle pudding in miniature pumpkins, 234

Corn-jalapeño relish, 139

Cranberry citrus relish, 246

Cranberry sorbet with vodka splash, 245

Creamy corn polenta, 12

Devil's dip, 213

Double nut torte, 224

Dried Roma tomatoes, 179

Dried tomato–basil bread, 38

Dried tomato dip, 77

Edinburgh eggs Florentine, 159

Eggplant-pepper medley in paper, 213

Emu medallions with gin sauce, 20

Everybody's chili, 59

Fajita sandwiches, 143

Family hoagie, 132

Farmers' market salad, 174

Fast fajitas, 22

Fennel and endive salad with wheat beer dressing, 200

Fennel with mushrooms and prosciutto, 242

Fennel with prosciutto and parmesan, 255

Feta and basil biga bread, 103

Fettuccine and smoked salmon, 11

Fettuccine fonduta, 251

Fiesta beef salad, 100

"Fixed" green olives, 255

Flavored honeys, 269

Fresh fig and raspberry tart, 177

Fresh ginger ale, 146

Fresh pear cake, 158

Fudgy low-fat brownies, 205

Garbanzos with garlic and olive oil, 254

Garlic bread salad with black beans and salsa, 131

Garlic potatoes with chicken, 185

Gingerbread torte with double bock caramel syrup, 201

Gingersnap granola, 99

Golden California slaw, 80

Golden root soup, 247

Grandma Reynolds's peach ice cream, 117

Grapefruit and avocado salad, 23

Grapevine bread, 235

Great Western crab cakes, 32

Greek Easter bread, 72

Greek tabbouleh salad, 100

Green bean and curried potato salad, 162

Green beans Italian-style, 190

Green-chili stew, 47

Green curry with chicken, 133

Green garlic soup, 183

Green goddess dressing, 77

Grilled chicken salad with raspberries, 152

Grilled-fish tacos with green salsa, 144

Grilled lamb with garlic and rosemary, 72

Grilled lime-chili pork, 81

Grilled onion quesadillas, 13

Grilled oysters and shrimp with chili-cranberry mignonette, 240

Grilled pork tenderloin with golden ale gravy, 200

Grilled shrimp with mango salad, 134

Grilled turkey breast with pink onions and black pepper, 178

Grilled whole chicken with plum sauce glaze, 152

Guacamole, 93

Halibut with horseradish mashed potatoes and chard, 15

Ham-stuffed manicotti, 45

Hawaii 5-0, 121

Herb cheese artichokes, 68

Hoisin-honey lamb tacos, 161

Hoisin lamb in pita pockets, 18

Honey cookies, 260

Honey-nut cake, 73

Hot sticks, 212

House burger, 161

Iced green tea, 146

Indian stuffed eggplant, 172

Italian biga bread, 103

Italian cornmeal cake, 126

Italian eggplant gratin, 173

Italian fusilli, 123

Lebanese baba ghanoush, 171

Lemon cheesecake soufflé, 59

Lemon fruit swirls, 275

Lemon fusilli with shrimp, 175

Lemon grass flank steak, 142

Lemon-orange oil, 269

Lemony apple honey smoothie, 121

Lentil and kale soup, 44

Lime-chipotle sauce, 48

Linguine with chicken breasts in orange sauce, 158

Low-fat garlic mashed potatoes, 23

Main squeeze, 121

Malihini shrimp poke, 188

Malted date deluxe, 121

Mango mimosas, 85

Mango-peach smoothie, 121

Mango, pear, and avocado with feta cheese, 141

Marbled pumpkin cheesecake, 236

Mary Etta's tomato sformata, 129

Mashed garnet yam puff, 241

Mediterranean potato salad, 139

Meringue cream, 107

Merlot-poached pears with salad greens, 243

Mookies, 214

Moroccan vegetable stew, 12

Mushroom soup your mother never made, 33

Mushrooms vinaigrette, 52

Mushroom torte, 53

Mussels with wine and cream, 61

Mustard-crusted salmon, 168

Mustard roast chicken, 82

New chocolate decadence, 107

New classic potato salad, 140

New Mexican red chile breakfast burritos, 93

Nut and orange biscotti, 278

One-hour lasagne, 34

Orange ambrosia, 42

Orange and lemon salad, 257

Orange butter cookies, 42

Orange-glazed turkey breast with apricot-ginger sauce, 241

Orange roly-poly, 42

Orange-spice vinegar, 266

Orange yogurt scones, 246

Oriental fish and chips, 169

Orzo with mint and tomatoes, 72

Orzo with shrimp, feta, and artichoke hearts, 11

Oven-braised beef for 4, 195

Oven-fried meatballs, 62

Oven-roasted green beans with pasta, 80

Oven rosti, 250

Panna cotta, 136

Papaya cooler, 190

Papaya, orange, and berry salad with lime-chili dressing, 141

Party polenta, 159

Pasta with salmon, 135

Patty's killer noodle salad, 109

Peach cobbler, 117

Peas with pasta, 195

Penne with sausage, roasted peppers, and greens, 11

Persian chicken-apple stew, 263

Pesto, 101

Pickled garlic, 184

Pickled vegetables, 175

Pineapple-melon salad with mint and basil, 142

Plum dessert bars, 132

Polenta lasagne, 37

Porcini tomato sauce, 36

Pork and persimmon risotto, 193

Postrio granola, 99

Potato latke wedges, 263

Preserved lemons, 233

Pressed-rice triangles, 125

Presto paella, 14

Primo lasagne, 36

Low-fat Recipes

(30 percent or less calories from fat)

General Index